P9-ELR-276

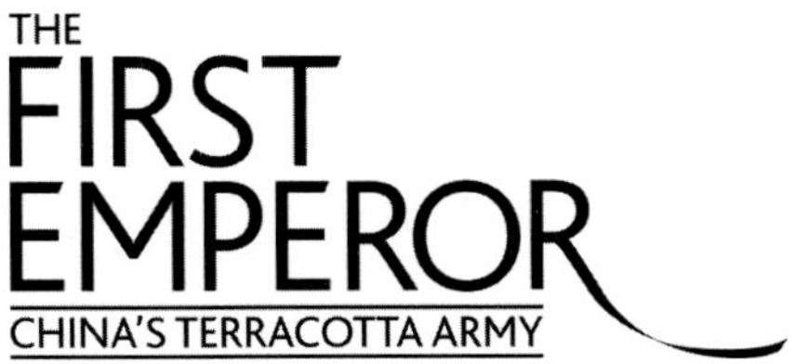
THE
FIRST
EMPEROR
CHINA'S TERRACOTTA ARMY

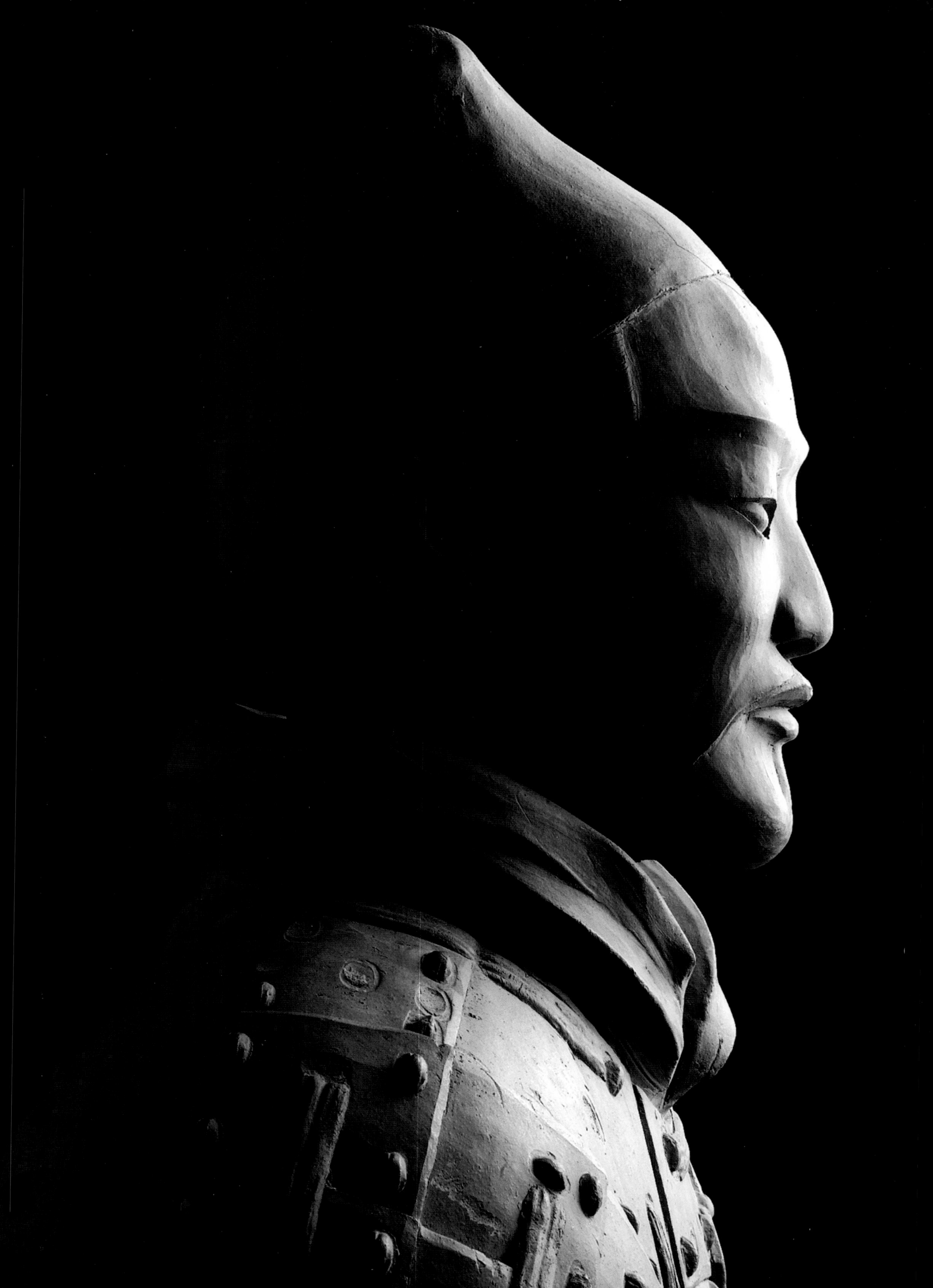

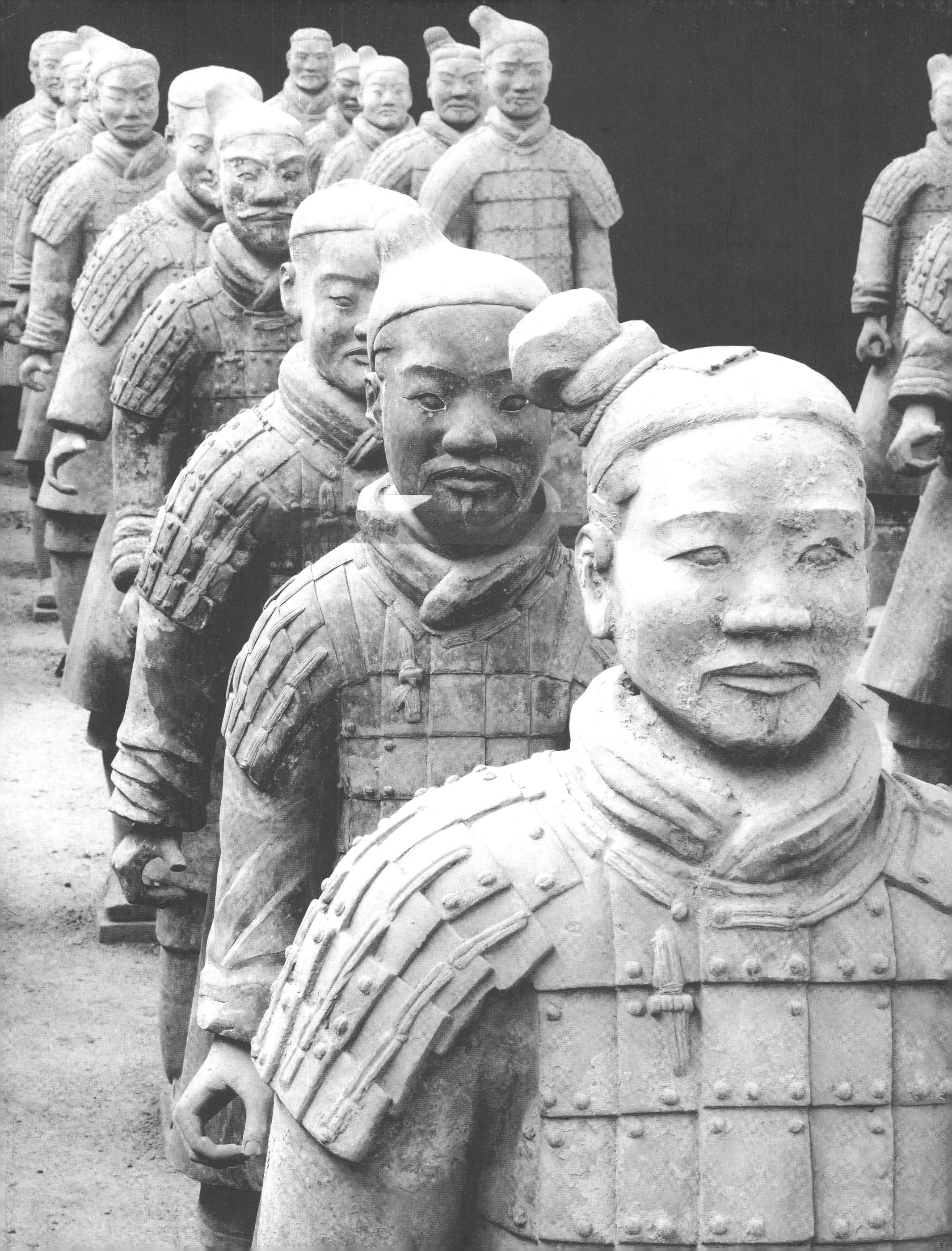

THE FIRST EMPEROR

CHINA'S TERRACOTTA ARMY

EDITED BY JANE PORTAL
WITH THE ASSISTANCE OF HIROMI KINOSHITA

HARVARD UNIVERSITY PRESS
Cambridge, Massachusetts

Library of Congress Cataloging-in-Publication Data

The first emperor : China's Terracotta Army / edited by Jane Portal with the assistance of Hiromi Kinoshita.
p. cm.
First published in 2007 by The British Museum Press
A division of The British Museum Company Ltd
This book is published to accompany the exhibition at the British Museum from 13 September 2007 to 6 April 2008.
Includes bibliographical references and index.
ISBN-13: 978-0-674-02697-1 (alk. paper)
ISBN-10: 0-674-02697-7 (alk. paper)
1. Qin shi huang, Emperor of China, 259-210 B.C.—Tomb—Exhibitions. 2. Terra-cotta sculpture, Chinese—Qin-Han dynasties, 221 B.C.-220 A.D.—Exhibitions. 3.Shaanxi Sheng (China)—Antiquities—Exhibitions. 4. Excavations (Archaeology)—China—Shaanxi Sheng—Exhibitions. I. Portal, Jane. II. Kinoshita, Hiromi. III. Title: China's Terracotta Army.
DS747.9.Q254F57 2007
931'.04—dc22

2007015527

Designed by Price Watkins
Copyedited by Colin Grant
Index by Ann Barrett
Printed in Spain by Grafos, SA, Barcelona

Frontispiece: Armoured infantryman from Pit 1 (cat. no. 113)
Opposite: Unarmoured general from Pit 1 (cat. no. 35)

The Editor and Contributors

Jane Portal is Curator of the Chinese and Korean collections at the British Museum.

Duan Qingbo is a Research Fellow at the Shaanxi Institute of Archaeology.

Martin Kern is Professor of Chinese Literature in the East Asian Studies Department at Princeton University.

Hiromi Kinoshita is Exhibition Assistant in the Department of Asia at the British Museum.

James Lin is Assistant Keeper of Applied Arts at the Fitzwilliam Museum, Cambridge.

Michael Loewe was University Lecturer in Chinese Studies at Cambridge University from 1963 to 1990 and is now an Emeritus Fellow of Clare Hall.

Carol Michaelson is Curator of Chinese jade and early Chinese material at the British Museum.

Lukas Nickel is Lecturer in Chinese Archaeology at the School of Oriental and African Studies (SOAS) and University College, London.

Jessica Rawson is Warden of Merton College, Oxford and was Keeper of Oriental Antiquities at the British Museum from 1987 to 1994.

Helen Wang is Curator of East Asian money at the British Museum.

Wu Yongqi is Director of the Museum of the Terracotta Army.

Robin Yates is Professor of History and East Asian Studies at McGill University and Chair of the Society for the Study of Early China.

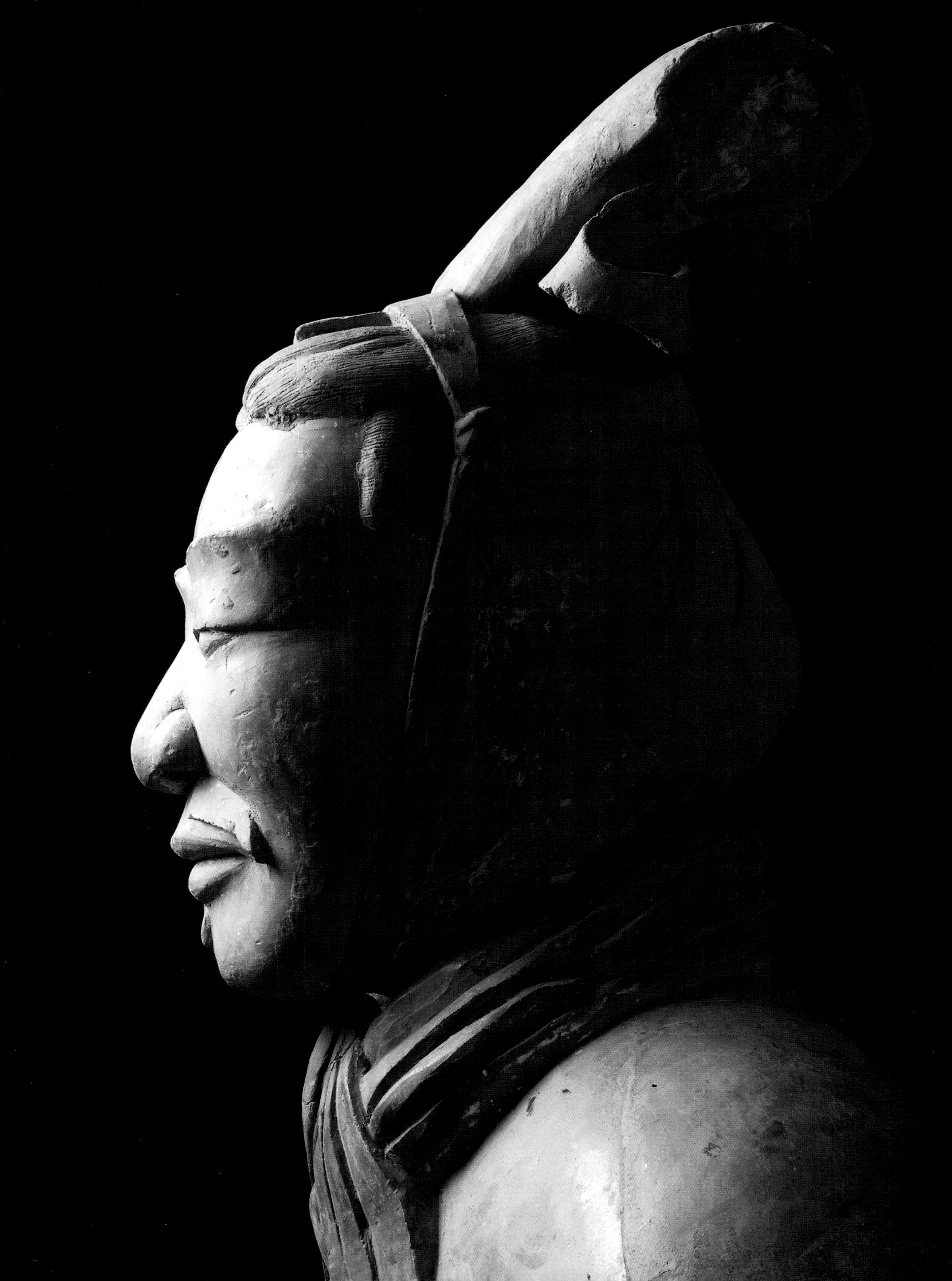

CONTENTS

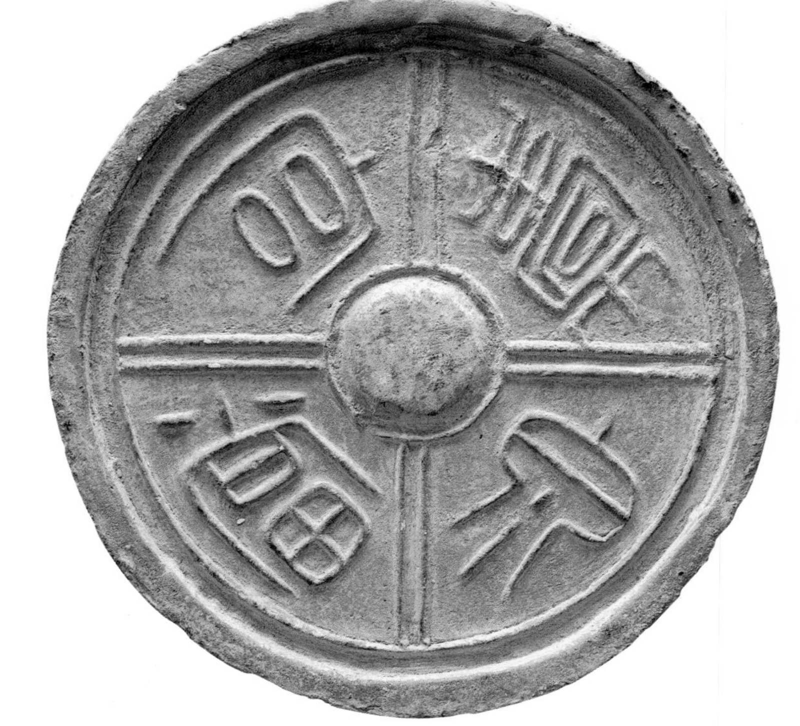

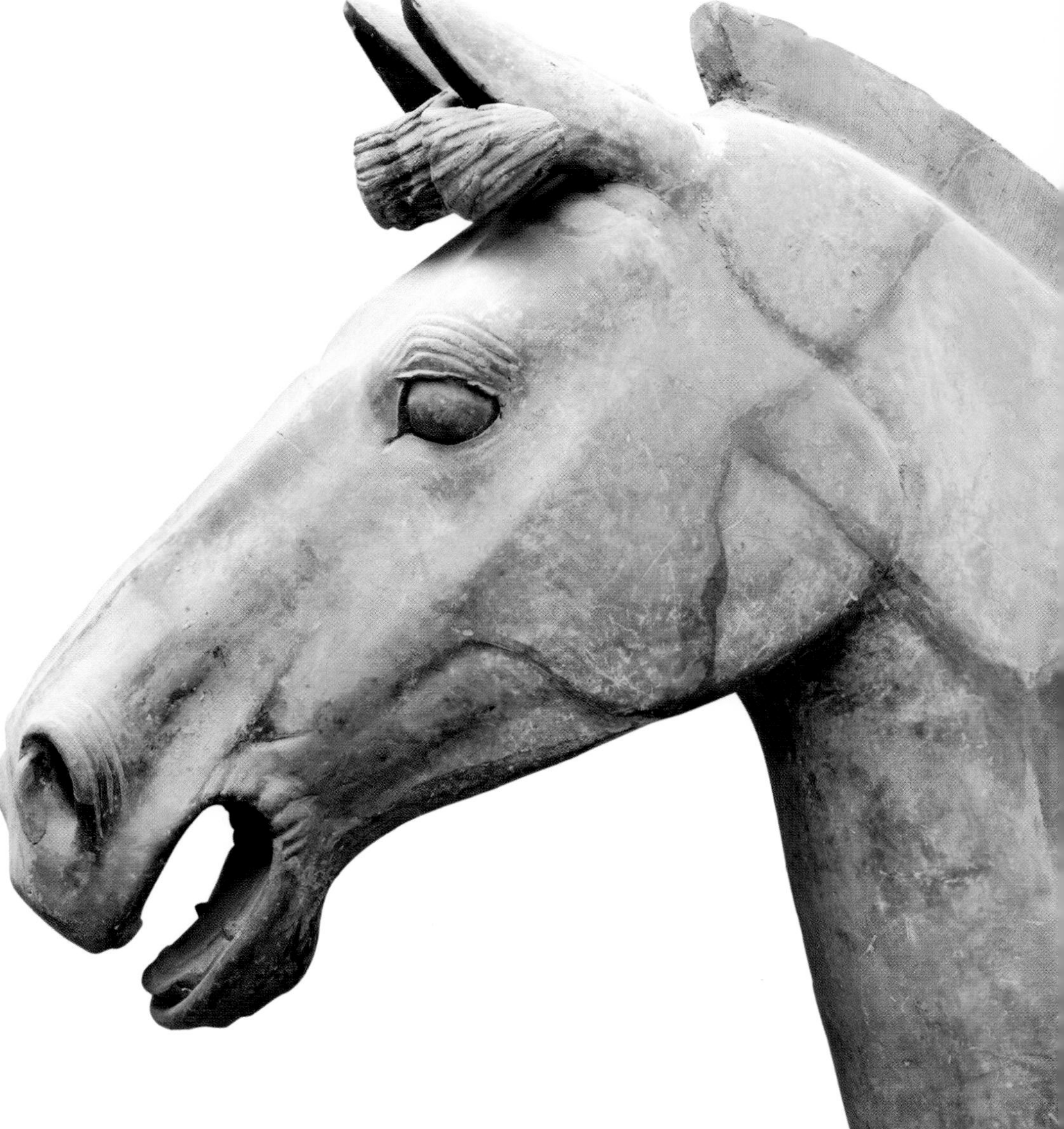

SPONSOR'S FOREWORD

Morgan Stanley is delighted to support this unique exhibition and give visitors to the British Museum an opportunity to see these iconic objects from one of the most important archaeological discoveries of the twentieth century.

The exhibition is of tremendous significance to our Firm: Morgan Stanley was the first to offer international investment banking services in China and since then we have been working with our clients for many years to increase our presence and grow our franchise in the country. We believe that the importance of China's rapidly growing participation in the global economy cannot be overestimated, and we therefore continue to invest heavily in our business in China. We also believe that an understanding of the past is a very useful tool in understanding both the present and the future, and we are therefore very proud to help bring to London this rare insight into China's past.

The First Emperor of China was a truly remarkable figure whose legacy is still visible in many aspects of present day China, and we are confident that this exhibition will be equally as remarkable. We hope that you enjoy visiting the exhibition as much as we have enjoyed being part of its genesis.

Jonathan Chenevix-Trench
Chairman, Morgan Stanley International Ltd

Morgan Stanley

DIRECTOR'S FOREWORD

Qin Shihuangdi, China's First Emperor and ruler of the Qin dynasty between 221 and 210 BC, was profoundly ambitious and a dazzlingly successful leader. With exceptional military prowess, he gained control over a large, disunited territory to create a unified China, making it the world's oldest continuous political entity. It is hardly an exaggeration to say that he invented the idea of China. He is perhaps best known in modern times for the wonder of his tomb complex featuring life-size terracotta warriors, but the First Emperor's lifetime achievements were also of supreme importance. He imposed standardization on the written language, currency and measurements and harnessed the skills of talented officials in an early meritocracy to create a highly centralized government more efficient than any previously known. The First Emperor also entertained a grand, new conceptualization of the universe that mapped a vision of the cosmos onto the landmass. He designated some mountains as sacred and inscribed them to proclaim his accomplishments. His vision of his supreme authority extended to the afterlife, prompting him to build a tomb site of unheralded complexity. In much of what he did the First Emperor established major paradigms followed by subsequent dynasties.

The accidental unearthing in 1974 of a terracotta warrior opened the way for decades of archaeology in China devoted to the unimaginably extensive and comprehensive burial site of the First Emperor. This book and exhibition present new historical, art historical and archaeological interpretations of the excavated material, casting light on the life, death, and times of the First Emperor. The British Museum is most grateful for the co-operation of the Chinese Cultural Ministry, the Bureau of Cultural Relics, and especially for the friendship and support of the Shaanxi Provincial Cultural Relics Bureau in making it possible to carry out this project. The Chinese Embassy in London also offered much appreciated assistance.

Special mention is owed to Professor Dame Jessica Rawson of Merton College, Oxford University, who has helped guide every stage of the project, including the selection of objects and catalogue authors, and defining exhibition themes, as well as writing a key chapter in this book. The rigour of the project is founded on Professor Rawson's insights. Jane Portal of the British Museum has commanded and contributed to every facet of the project with great intellect and administrative finesse. The exhibition could not have been realized without the tremendous support of Morgan Stanley.

The book and exhibition, *The First Emperor: China's Terracotta Army*, exemplifies the growing exchanges and collaborations between China and the British Museum. Three major exhibitions of British Museum artefacts have toured Chinese museums during the last two years and many more are planned in both directions to foster better mutual appreciation of the wealth and depth of each nation's cultural history. Through studying the past, it is possible better to understand the present and to prepare for the future. By focusing on the rich archaeological finds associated with China's First Emperor, the British Museum is pleased to show the achievements of China's early imperial age and to foster ever wider public interest in this great world civilization.

Neil MacGregor

Neil MacGregor
Director, The British Museum

ACKNOWLEDGEMENTS

JANE PORTAL

I would like to express my gratitude to all the authors of this book, who are named individually in the contents list. I would, however, especially like to thank Jessica Rawson, a constant source of good advice in her role as Academic Advisor to the project. Other academics who have provided specialist advice include Chris Cullen, Duan Qingbo, Robert Harrist, Lothar von Falkenhausen and Jeffrey Riegel. My excellent assistant, Hiromi Kinoshita, has worked ceaselessly and with calm commitment, for which I am deeply grateful.

This book is written to accompany the exhibition *The First Emperor: China's Terracotta Army* at the British Museum, but also to stand alone. Both the book and the exhibition have involved many people working together, both in China and in London. First I would like to thank Shaanxi Province Cultural Relics Bureau for lending the largest number of grade-one pieces relating to Qin Shihuangdi ever sent abroad. Zhao Rong, Liu Yunhui, Wu Yongqi, Jin Xianyong, Duan Qingbo, Zhang Zheng, Li Tongxian, Li Xiuzhen, Han Zhao and Zhang Tong have all played an invaluable part in this co-operation. In Beijing the project has been facilitated by Li Dongwen and Cai Lian in the Ministry of Culture and Zhang Jianxin in the National Cultural Heritage Bureau. Ambassador Sir William Erhman, Michael O'Sullivan and Neil Webb have also been extremely helpful, while their counterparts in London, Ambassadors Zha Peixin and Fu Ying and Cultural Counsellor Ke Yasha and Ma Xiaoru, have provided invaluable support and advice.

At the British Museum there are too many people involved in such a large project to be able to name them all. However, Andrew Burnett and Zoe Hancock, who led and co-ordinated the project-delivery group, must take credit for its success. Co-operation over the exhibition between the Exhibitions Department, led by Carolyn Marsden-Smith, and Metaphor, led by Stephen Greenberg, has been a thoroughly enjoyable and rewarding experience. Simon Neale and David Meink masterminded the transformation of the Reading Room and Catherine Cooper and Susan Dymond the Interpretation, while Emma Kelly and Catherine Sidwell managed the project; Caroline Ingham co-ordinated the design process and accompanied me to Xi'an. I am also grateful for the support of all my colleagues in the Department of Asia, particularly Jan Stuart, Carol Michaelson, Jessica Harrison-Hall and Mary Ginsberg.

At the British Museum Press Coralie Hepburn and Melanie Hall have overseen the catalogue editing and production admirably and Ray Watkins the book design. Many of the wonderful photographs in the book, including the cover picture, were taken in Xi'an by John Williams and Saul Peckham. Jim Rossiter helped with photographic scanning, Paul Goodhead produced many of the maps and Ann Searight a number of line drawings. Translations are by Shu-chi Huang-Souillard, Judy Xu and Celine Lai, who also helped compile the initial loan list. Meixin Wang, a volunteer in the Department of Asia, has provided ongoing help over translations of all sorts and Zhang Chunchun compiled and summarized the scientific appendix with the help of Kenneth Kar. Sally McMullen helped with German translations and Keith Southwell and J.D. Hill with the timeline.

Other people who have assisted me in different ways include Wenzel Jacob, Henriette Pleiger, Bettina Zorn, Mario De Simoni, Alexandra Andresen, Manfred Koob, Catherina Blaensdorf, Felix Horn and Graham Hutt. I am grateful to all those mentioned above and many others not mentioned, who have worked far beyond the call of duty to ensure the successful completion of this exciting project.

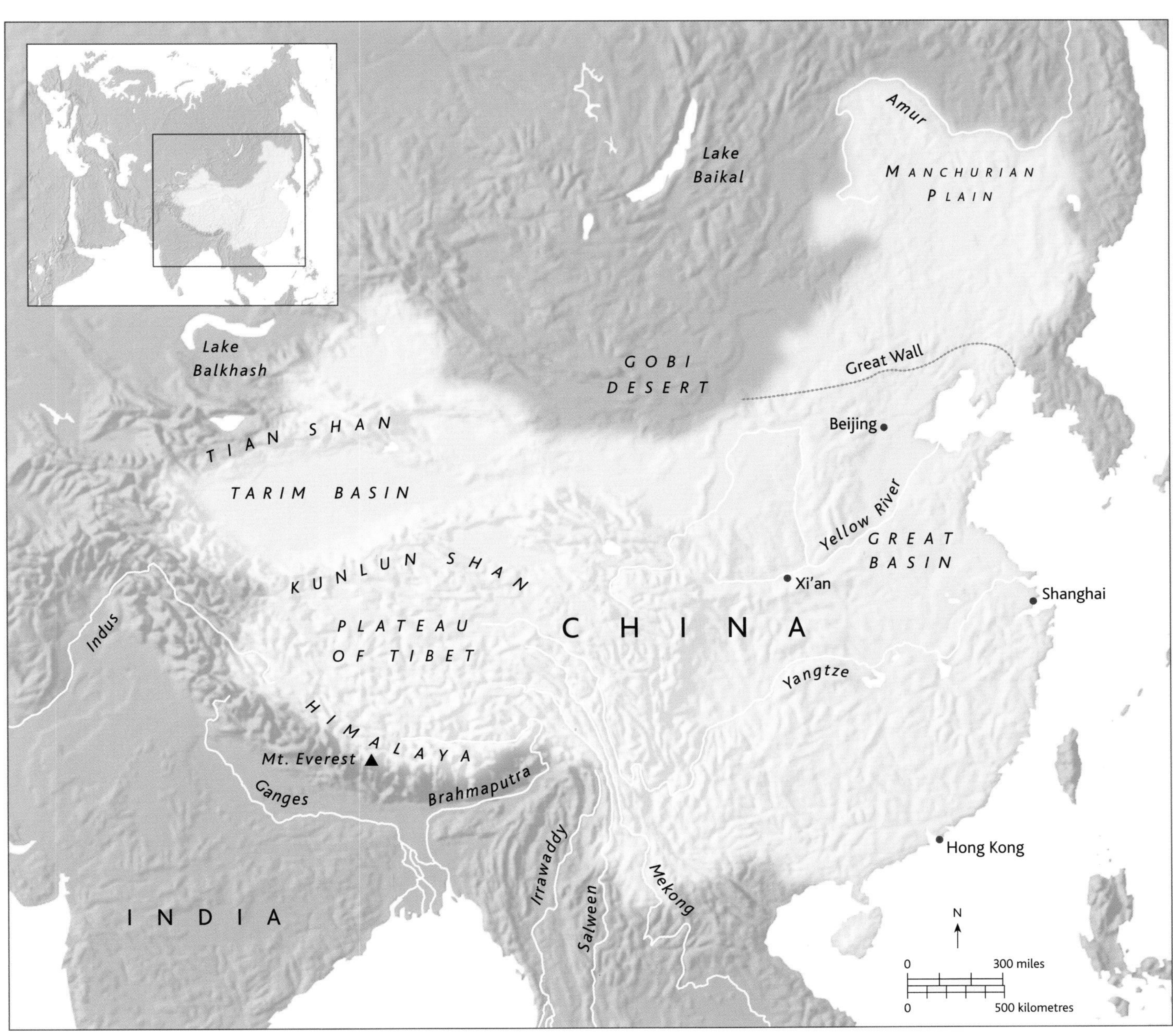

China in the world, 2007.

CHRONOLOGY

		CHINA	REST OF THE WORLD
3000 BC		*c.*3500 BC Hongshan-culture jades	
2500 BC		2697 BC Mythological reign of Huangdi, legendary Yellow Emperor	
2000 BC		*c.*2500 BC Jade *cong* and *bi* produced in large numbers by Liangzhu culture *c.*2000 BC Bronze casting technology developed *c.*2000 BC Putative start of Xia dynasty/emergence of Erlitou culture	*c.*2400–2100 BC Stonehenge built
1900 BC			2030–1640 BC Middle Egyptian Kingdom
1800 BC			
1700 BC		1766 BC Traditional date of beginning of Shang dynasty (now considered to be *c.*1600 BC) *c.*1700 BC Earliest-known bronze ritual vessels	1800 BC Earliest-known version of Epic of Gilgamesh – early Sumerian heroic tale; events thought to date to 3000–2000 BC
1600 BC			1792–1600 BC Height of Babylonian empire; Code of Hammurabi – 'first known legal document'
1500 BC	SHANG DYNASTY 1600–1050 BC	*c.*1500 BC First glazes used on ceramics	
1400 BC			*c.*1450 BC Mycenaean forces conquer Knossos on Crete *c.*1400 BC Linear B – first-known Greek writing – in general use
1300 BC		*c.*1350 BC Earliest-surviving Chinese writing, on oracle bones	*c.*1340 BC Tutankhamun buried
1200 BC		*c.*1200 BC Sanxingdui culture in Sichuan – large bronze figures	
1100 BC			*c.*1190 BC estimated date of Trojan War
1000 BC		1050 BC Beginning of Western Zhou dynasty	
900 BC	W. ZHOU DYNASTY 1050–770 BC		*c.*1000 BC Israelite kingdom established by King David
800 BC			814 BC Carthage founded
700 BC	E. ZHOU DYNASTY 770–221 BC	770 BC Beginning of Eastern Zhou dynasty (Spring and Autumn period)	*c.*800–700 BC Homer traditionally considered to have composed *Iliad* and *Odyssey* 776 BC First Olympic Games
600 BC		697–678 BC Duke Wu of Qin 604 BC Birth of Laozi (founder of Daoism)	753 BC Traditional date of founding of Rome by Romulus 605–562 BC Nebuchadnezzar ruled Babylon
500 BC		551 BC Birth of Confucius (Kongzi) (*c.*551–479 BC)	509 BC Roman Republic founded

		CHINA	REST OF THE WORLD
500 BC 400 BC 300 BC	EASTERN ZHOU DYNASTY 770–221 BC	475 BC Beginning of Warring States period of Eastern Zhou dynasty *c.*433 BC Death of Marquis Yi of Zeng 409 BC Duke Jian of Qin active 387 BC Duke Hui of Qin active 384–362 BC Duke Xian of Qin reigned 372 BC Birth of Mencius (Mengzi) 361–338 BC Duke Xiao of Qin reigned 356 BC Shang Yang takes charge of military and political affairs. His Legalist reforms lead to Qin's increasing dominance 325 BC King Huiwen of Qin adopts the title 'King' 316 BC Qin state conquers Shu state	520–322 BC Lifetime of Pythagoras, Sophocles, Socrates, Plato and Aristotle 500 BC Approximate lifetime of historical Buddha in India 323 BC Death of Alexander the Great
		286 BC Qin state conquers Song state 259 BC Ying Zheng born (will become Qin Shihuangdi) 256 BC Qin state conquers Zhou state 246 BC Ying Zheng becomes King of Qin 235 BC Lü Buwei commits suicide after exile 230–225 BC Qin conquers states of Han, Zhao and Wei 227 BC First unsuccessful assassination attempt on Ying Zheng, by Jing Ke 223 BC Qin state conquers Chu state	c.250 BC–AD 68 Dead Sea Scrolls
200 BC	QIN DYNASTY 221–206 BC	221 BC Second unsuccessful assassination attempt 221 BC Qin army conquers Qi. Beginning of Qin dynasty 218 BC Third unsuccessful assassination attempt	
100 BC 0	WESTERN HAN DYNASTY 206 BC–AD 9	215 BC Beginning of construction of Great Wall by Meng Tian 210 BC Qin Shihuangdi dies of illness on a tour; 'terracotta army' buried 1.5 km east of his tomb; Son Ershi becomes Emperor 209 BC Qin Ershi (Second Emperor) makes eastern tour 207 BC Qin Ershi compelled to commit suicide 206 BC Qin dynasty ends; Western Han dynasty establishes power *c.*168 BC Death of Lady Dai *c.*150 BC Invention of paper 122 BC King of Nanyue dies – tomb famous for its contents 89 BC Sima Qian completed his *Records of the Historian (Shiji)*	196 BC Carving of Rosetta stone, Egypt 101–44 BC Lifetime of Julius Caesar 30 BC Death of Cleopatra 4 BC–AD 30 Lifetime of Jesus Christ
	INTERREGNUM	AD 9 Beginning of Xin dynasty; brief rule of Wang Mang	
AD 100 AD 200	EASTERN HAN DYNASTY AD 25–220	AD 25 Eastern Han dynasty restored, ruling from Luoyang AD 220 Han dynasty ends, weakened by corruption and rebellion	AD 79 Pompeii destroyed by eruption of Vesuvius AD 81 Completion of Colosseum, Rome AD 122 Hadrian's Wall started

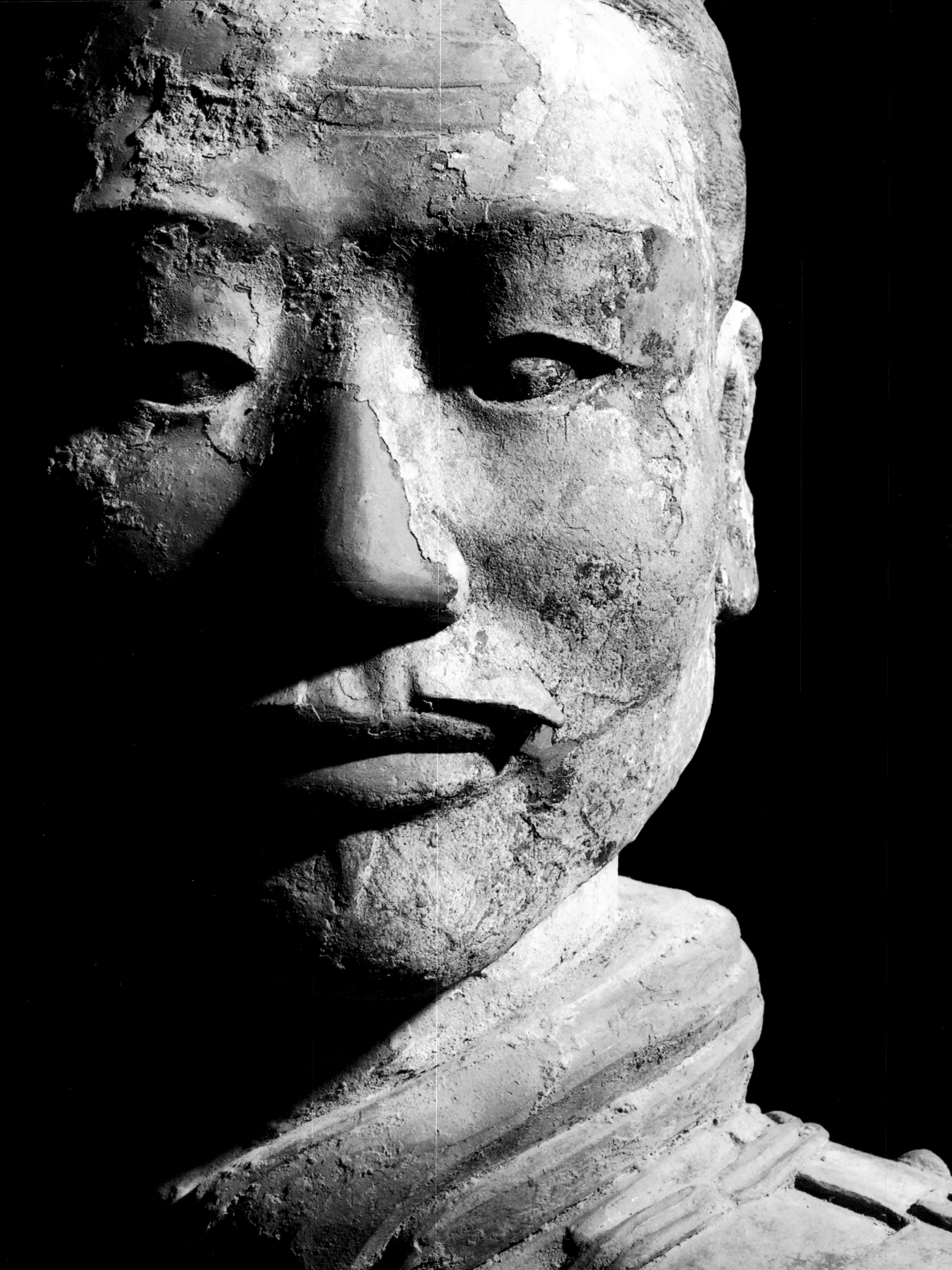

THE FIRST EMPEROR
THE MAKING OF CHINA

JANE PORTAL

FIG. 1
(left) **Detail of face of a kneeling archer showing original pigment.**
Cat. no. 1

FIG. 2
(following pages) **The First Emperor's terracotta army lined up in military formation in Pit 1, which is estimated to hold about 6,000 warriors. About 1,000 have been excavated so far.**

The chance discovery in 1974 of the life-size terracotta army of the First Emperor of China astounded the world. Since then the tomb of the First Emperor (r.221–210 BC), which the warriors protect, has become arguably the most famous archaeological site on earth, and the most important ongoing excavation in China. Archaeologists predict that it will keep them busy for generations, as new discoveries are made year by year and new techniques of conservation and scientific research are introduced and perfected. In fact, it will doubtless take longer to excavate the First Emperor's tomb complex than the approximately thirty-six years it took to build it. It might have taken much longer to construct, had not the emperor died suddenly and had to be buried with the magnificent monument unfinished. We infer this because one of the four underground army pits was discovered empty of warriors.[1] The tomb site on the outskirts of present day Xi'an had been known for over two thousand years from a description by Sima Qian, official historian of the Han dynasty (206 BC–AD 220) which overthrew the Qin, as the First Emperor's dynasty was named. Sima wrote about a hundred years after the death of the First Emperor. The tomb mound, in the shape of a square, flattened pyramid, had long been visible above ground, but the terracotta army came as a complete surprise to all, because there had been no record of it. The interior of the tomb itself was described in some detail by Sima Qian, but he did not mention an underground army.[2] The pits containing the terracotta army were discovered over 1 km away from the mound itself, drawing attention to the fact that the underground tomb complex was on a much larger scale than had been anticipated, in fact around 56 sq. km. The four terracotta

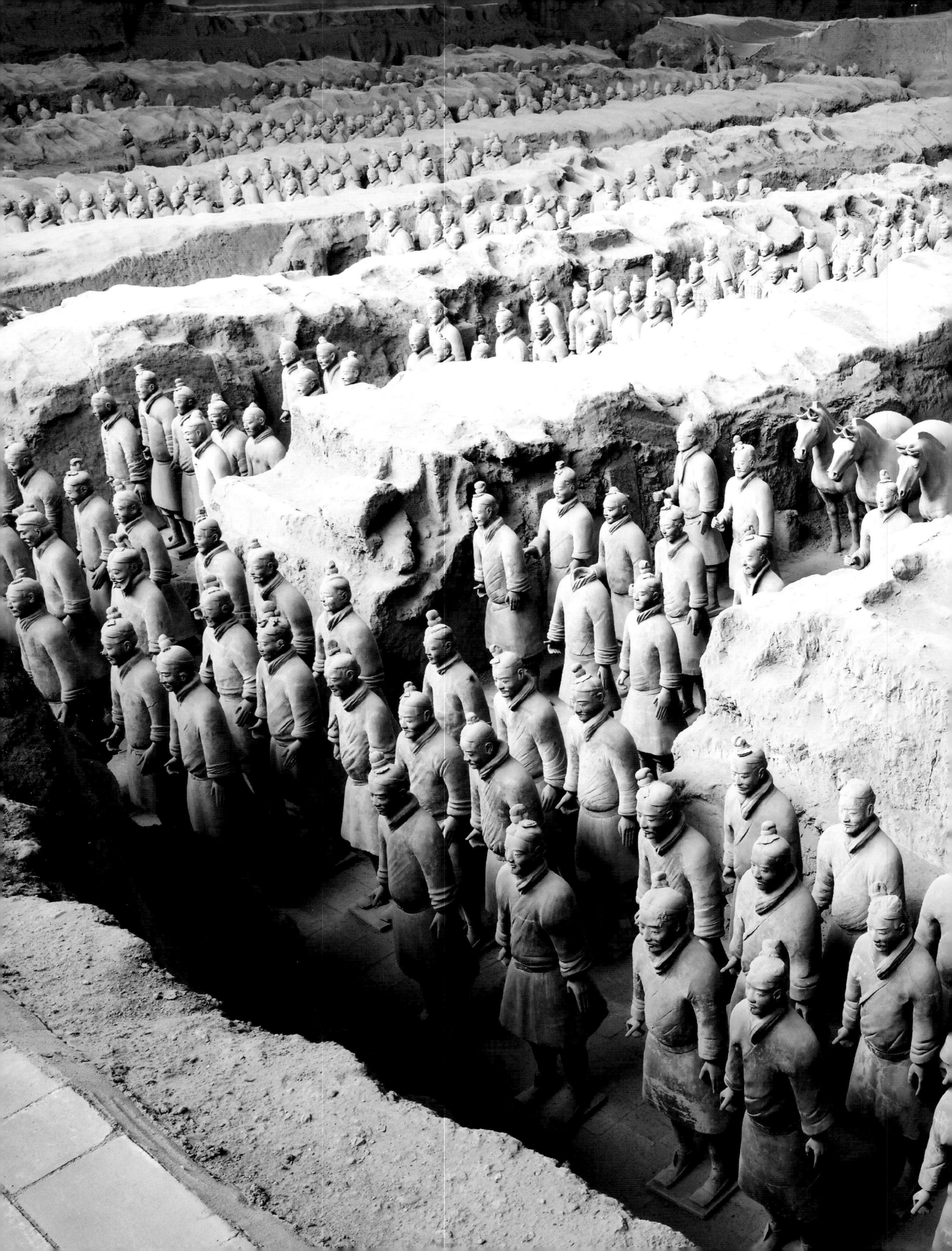

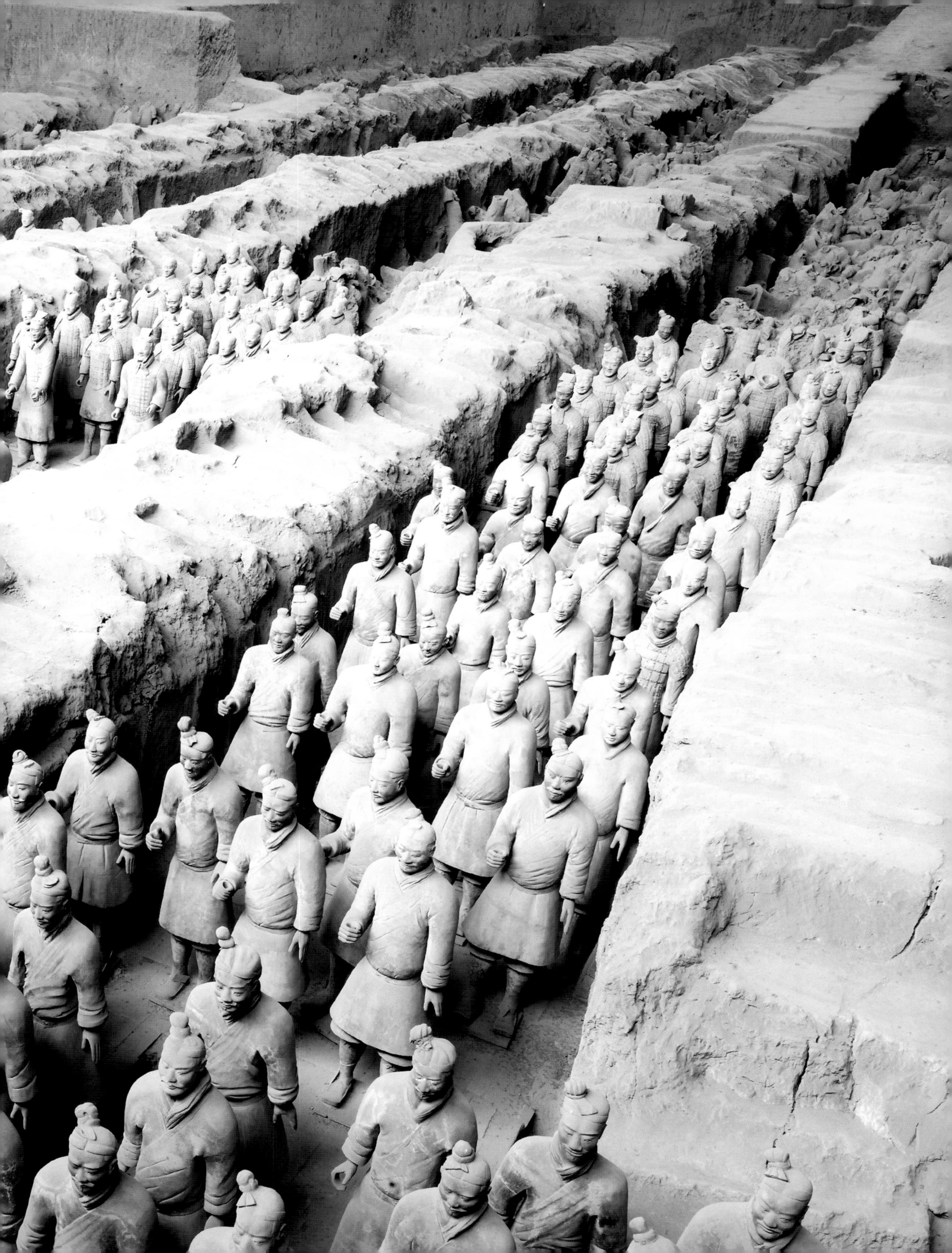

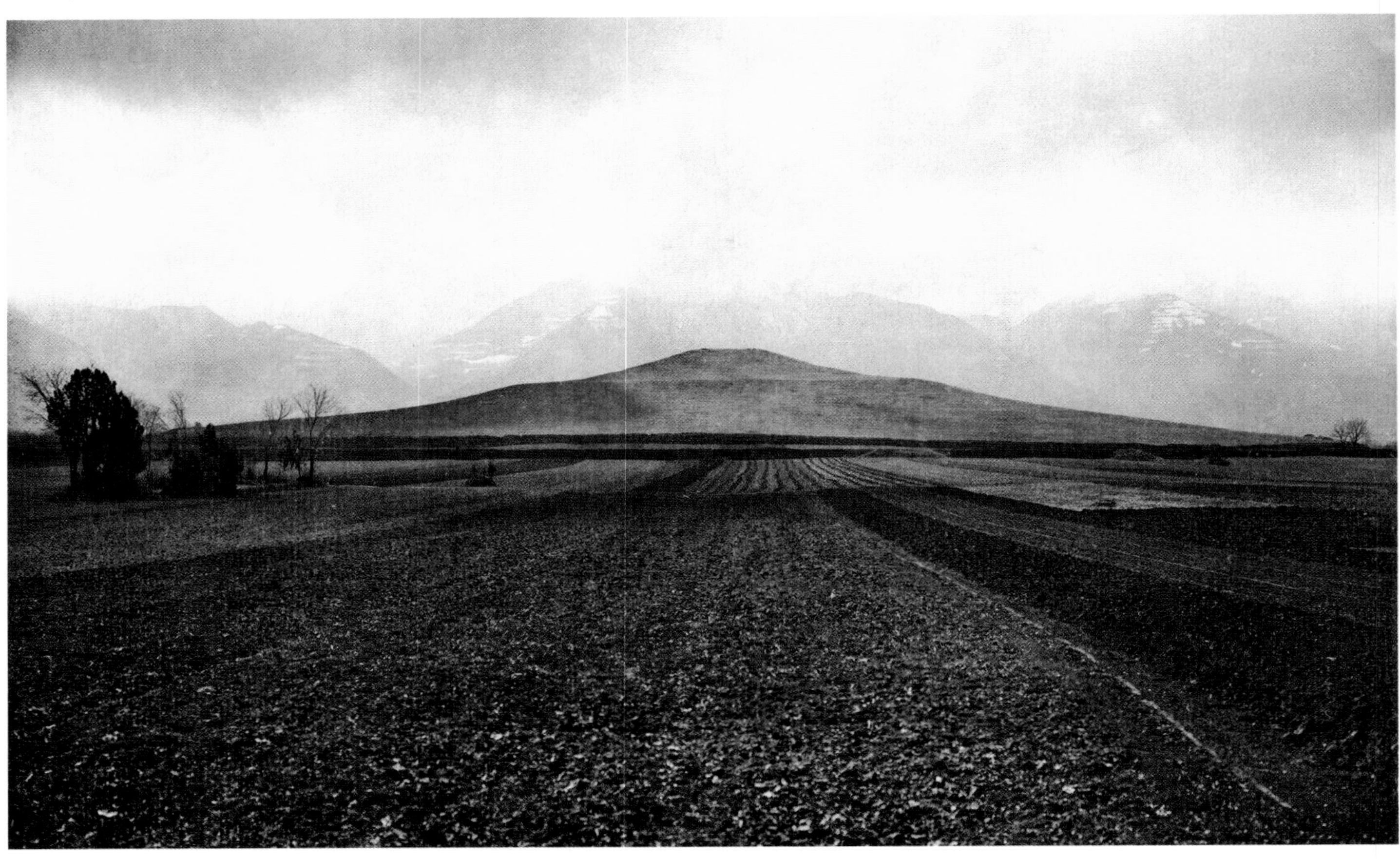

FIG. 3
The First Emperor's tomb mound, photographed by the French explorer Victor Segalen in 1914.

warrior pits alone cover a total area of over 25,000 sq. metres, while the mound itself is about 400 sq. metres.[3] The grandeur of the First Emperor's tomb and his underground army of clay poses many questions about the man who conceived it and what he achieved. It is these questions that this book aims to explore.

Themes covered in this book

Before the First Emperor's time China had for hundreds of years been divided into different states or kingdoms, many of which were at war with one another at different times. This period, known as the Warring States period of the Eastern Zhou dynasty (475–221 BC), was also a time of itinerant philosophers who would travel from state to state advising the rulers. Confucius (Kongzi) and Mencius (Mengzi), Laozi and Zhuangzi are perhaps the best known of these philosophers, founders of what later came to be known as Confucianism and Daoism.

Building on his own state's martial prowess, the First Emperor became one of the greatest military leaders of all time. His was a massive feat of organization and military strategy, culminating with the unification of all of the states under the Qin empire. It is thought that the western name 'China' probably derived from Qin, the First Emperor's home state, which became the name of the entire country during his rule.[4] Defence against the nomads to the north was also greatly improved through the unification of a number of walls on the northern borders into an early form of the defensive structure we know today as the Great Wall. A new road system facilitated communication across a vast territory. The Qin achievements and developments in weapons technology and production, military strategy and communications are further described and explained in Chapter 1.

Following on from the military success came civilian and cultural achievements, including the establishment of a unified law code, coinage, script and system of weights and measures. Architectural projects on a grand scale, such as the building of gigantic palaces in the new capital of Xianyang, were initiated, as well as replicas of the palaces of conquered states and enormous bronze sculptures commemorating the emperor's conquests. The question of whether the military and civil achievements were driven personally by the First Emperor or by his advisors, such as the chancellor Li Si, is explored in Chapter 2. Also explained are the underlying ideas that influenced the emperor and the origins and development of the Legalist philosophy he favoured, as well as the new system of government.[5]

Perhaps the best illustration of the First Emperor's immense ambitions and grand view of himself is seen in the series of tours he went on around his newly unified empire, making sacrifices to spirits of the different regions. By making these progresses and by installing inscriptions on mountains along the eastern seaboard, the emperor expressed his vision of his rulership as continuing the achievements

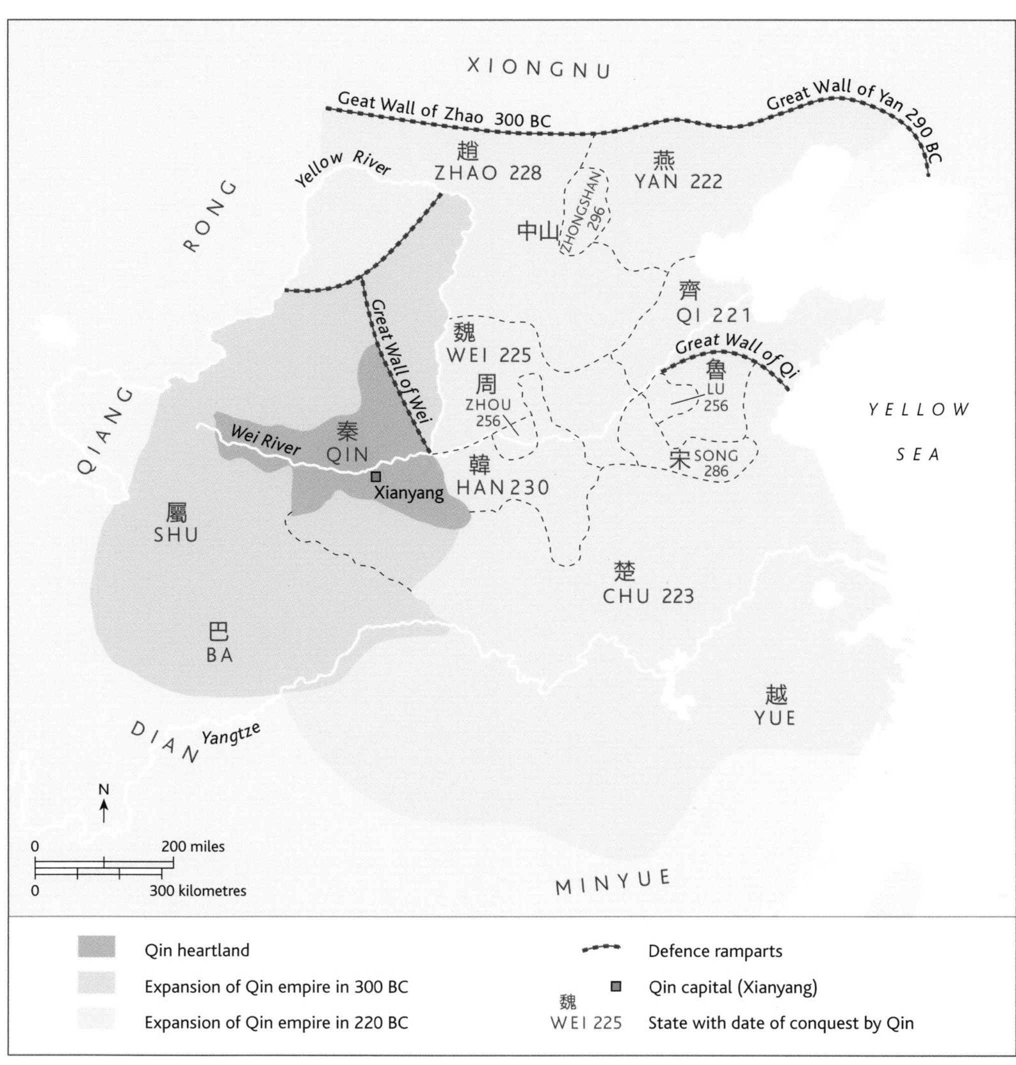

FIG. 4
Map showing the Warring States and the Qin state.

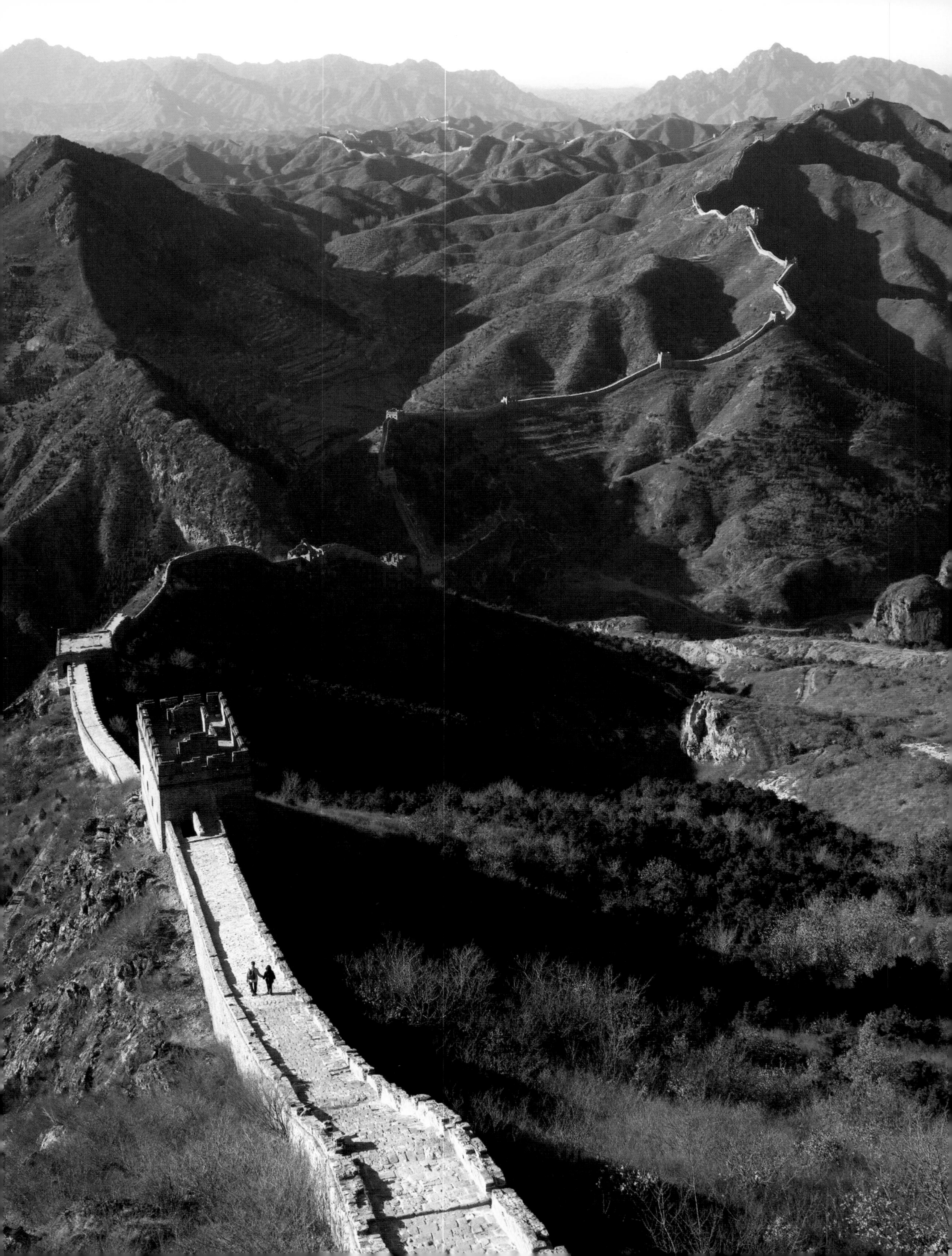

FIG. 5
(left) The Great Wall we see today was made of brick in the Ming dynasty (1368–1644). The Qin Great Wall was made of pounded earth and stones. Some parts still remain.

FIG. 6
(below) This inscribed weight is an example of those standardized under the First Emperor. The sides are engraved with two 'standardized' imperial edicts, one by the First Emperor and the other by the Second Emperor.
Cat. no. 2

of the ancient 'sage kings'. He also established his presence and made his mark on the sacred geography of China. This theme is developed in Chapter 3.

The First Emperor wanted to live for ever and go on ruling eternally. Following several assassination attempts on his life, he tried to achieve physical immortality with the help of alchemists who prescribed pills and potions featuring large amounts of mercury. He also sent groups of envoys to the mythical isles of the immortals off the east coast to seek elixirs of immortality. He is recorded as having dreamt of fighting a sea divinity in human form and having shot a huge fish with a crossbow shortly before he died suddenly on a tour in the east in 210 BC.[6]

In parallel with his attempts to avoid death, the emperor also undertook the traditional preparations for a great tomb. These he started when he became King of the state of Qin and greatly expanded in scale after his investiture as First August Great Qin Emperor (or 'Thearch') in 221 BC. His ideas about life after death and those of his time are reflected in the way he carefully designed his tomb as a great underground palace complex under a mountain-shaped tomb mound, in contrast to the tombs of earlier Chinese kings, which were predominantly large shafts in which the grave goods were concentrated. These included ritual items, such as sets of bronze vessels and bells, which varied in size and scale according to the status of the incumbent. The emperor's tomb was far more complex, with additional underground buildings around the main tomb. The range of objects the First Emperor planned to have buried with him and the materials of which they were made reflected his control of his entire world. His intention was nothing less than never-ending rule over the universe. His ideas about the afterlife are explored in Chapter 4, as is the significance of the change in tomb design and burial practice brought about by the Qin.

Chapter 5 concentrates on the tomb layout and the ongoing excavations around the actual tomb mound, which have revealed more and more of the grand size and scale of the entire complex, designed to reproduce the First Emperor's empire underground for eternity. The process of manufacture of the terracotta army and the control of the workforce is explored. It is perhaps the enormous scale of the terracotta army as well as the quality of the representation and manufacture of its members that continue to move visitors so greatly. These perfectly executed, life-size sculptures, some over 190 cm in height, seemed to have appeared out of nowhere, as there had been no tradition of such large or such realistic ceramic sculptures in the centuries preceding the Qin. Existing traditions of figurative sculptures had been found in isolated regions, such as the bronze figures at Sanxingdui in west China, dating to *c.*1200–1000 BC and the third-century-BC wooden figures of the Chu state in southern China (*figs* 8, 9). Although the terracotta warriors have been described by some as individual portraits in clay of actual soldiers, in fact it has now been shown that the manufacture of the army was an early feat of mass production: a small and quite limited repertoire of body parts were joined together in a multitude of combinations, with details worked by hand afterwards. Then the whole figures were painted. Endless variety, for example of costumes, hairstyles, hand

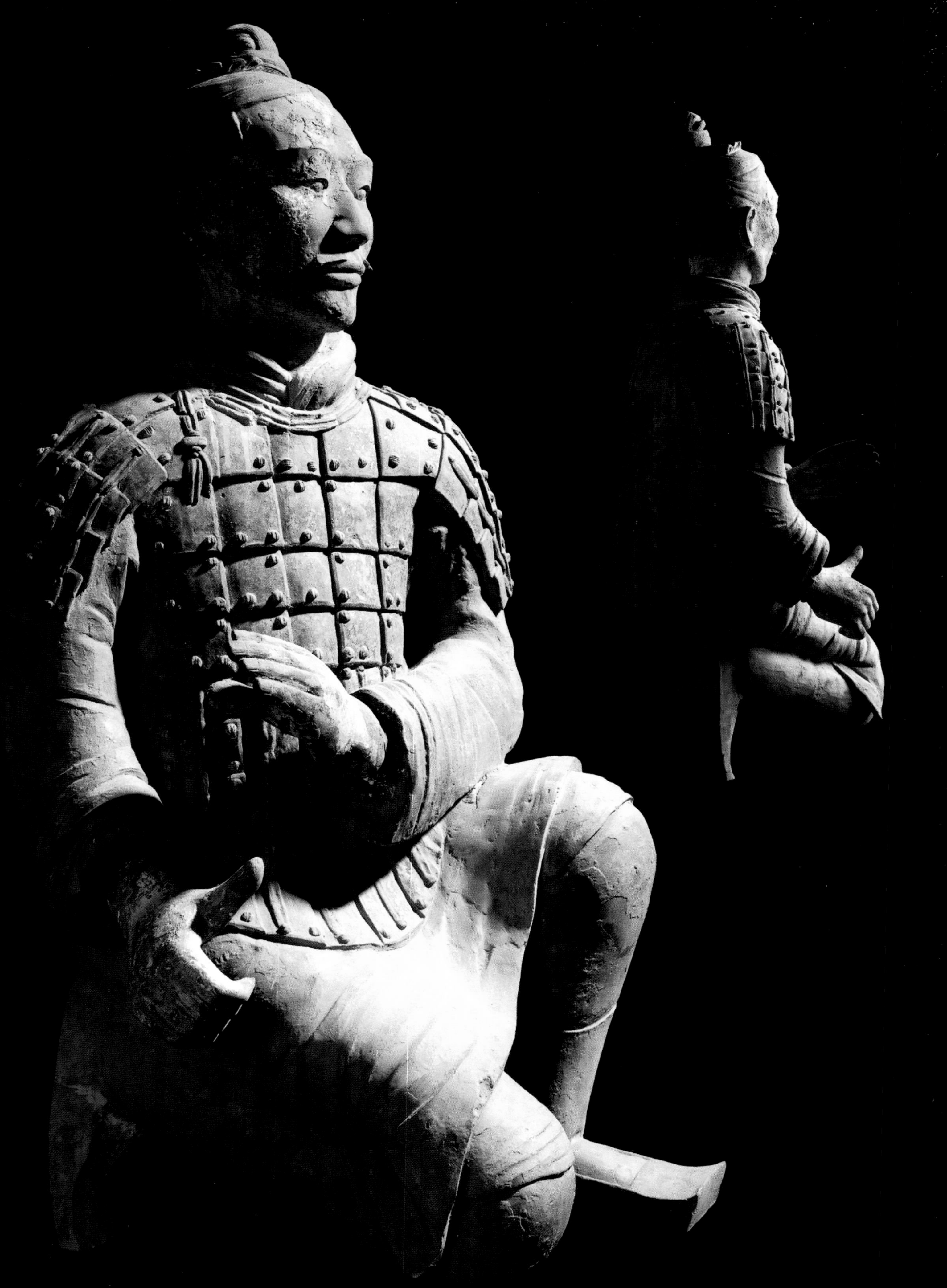

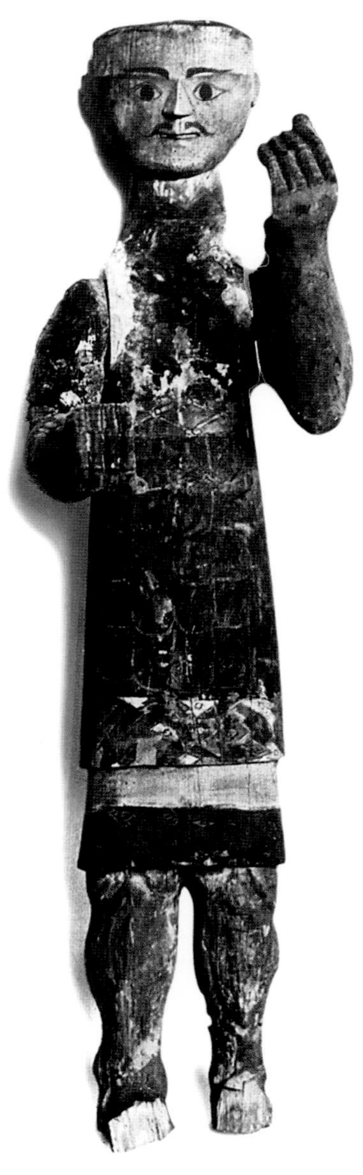

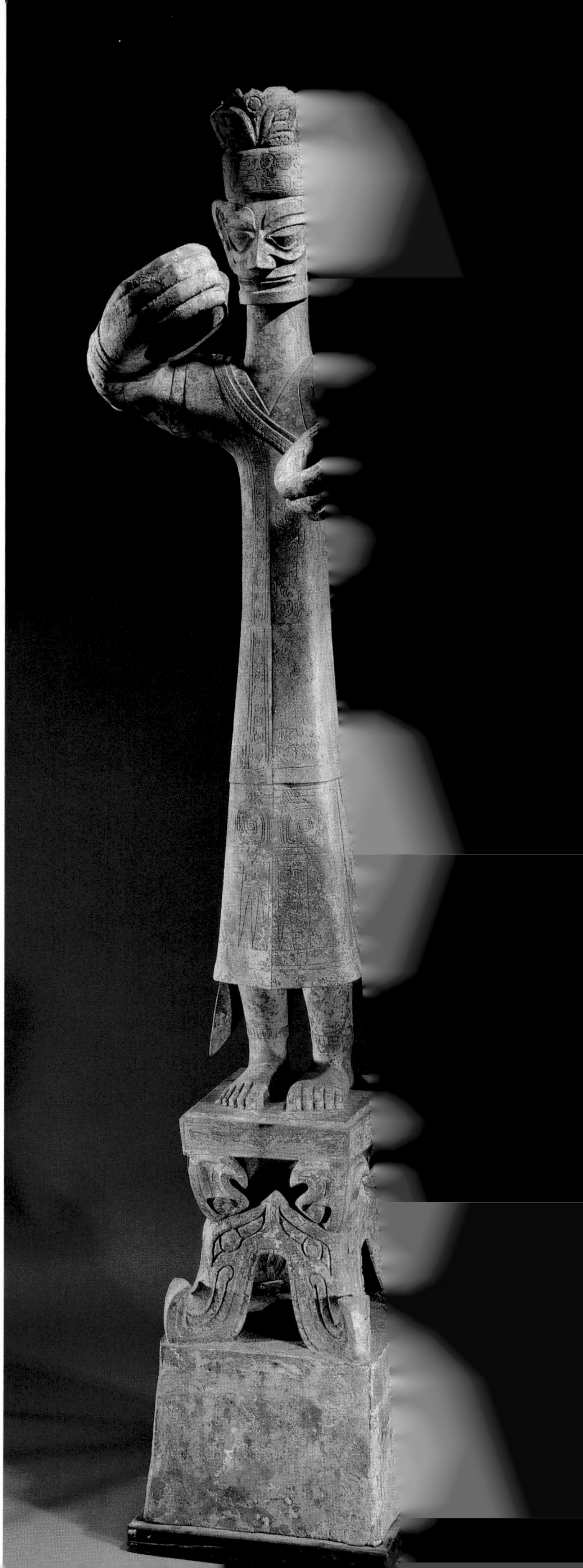

FIG. 7
(left) **Kneeling archer found in Pit 2. Pit 2 is thought to represent a military guard.**
Cat. no. 1

FIG. 8
(above) **Third-century-BC wooden figure excavated from a tomb in the Chu state. Although Chu was more culturally developed than Qin during the Warring States period, it never produced sculptures to match the Qin terracotta army.**

FIG. 9
(right) **Bronze figure from Sanxingdui, Guanghan, Sichuan province, dating to c. 1200–1000 BC.**

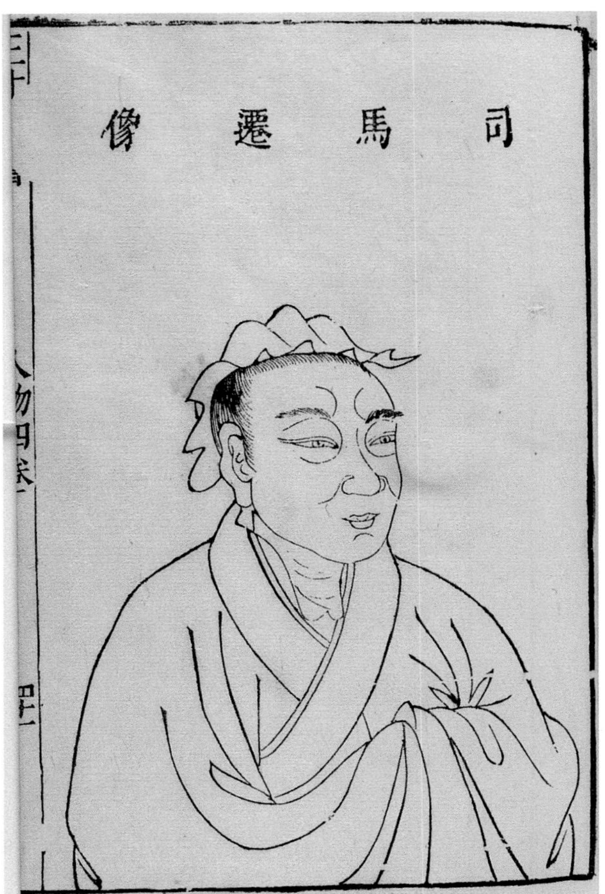

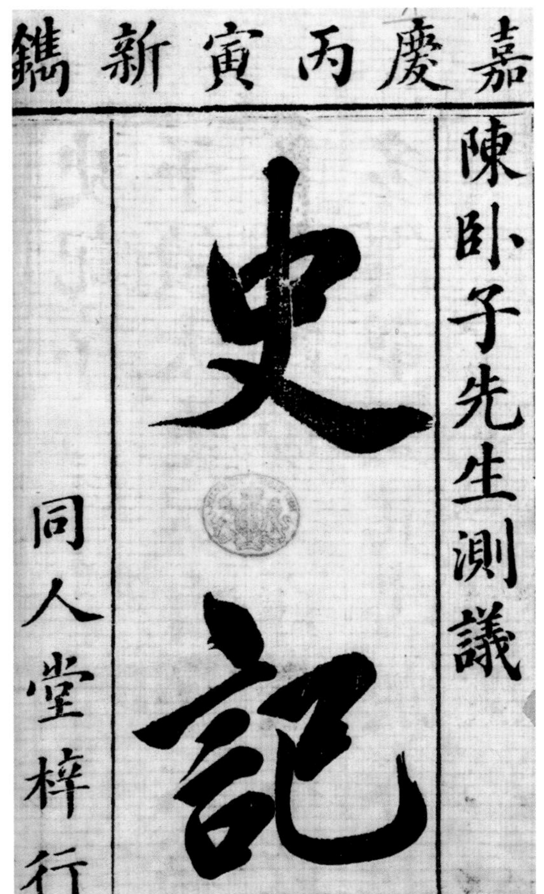

FIG. 10
(above left) **Woodcut portrait of the Confucian historian Sima Qian (*c.*145–87 BC), author of the *Records of the Historian* (*Shiji*), from the Chinese encyclopaedia *Sancai tuhui*, dated 1609.**

FIG. 11
(above right) **Title page of a nineteenth-century edition of the *Records of the Historian* (*Shiji*) by Sima Qian, written about a hundred years after the First Emperor died. The First Emperor was portrayed in the *Shiji* as ruthless and cruel, a result of Sima Qian's personal agenda, which may have been influenced by his own animosity towards the emperor under whom he lived, Han Wudi.**

FIG. 12
(opposite) **Kneeling terracotta figure of a musician, excavated in 2001 from the bronze bird pit (K0007) in the tomb complex of the First Emperor, thought to be designed to entertain the emperor in the afterlife by playing for dancing bronze birds. The musical instrument he was playing was perhaps a percussion instrument such as a bell or drum.**
Cat. no. 3

positions or facial features, was therefore possible, but in no way were they individual portraits. The clay warriors were stamped with the name and unit of the foreman of a group of workmen, as part of an elaborate system of quality control.[7]

However, the emperor needed not only an army to defend his empire but also a bureaucracy to help him carry out administration: further discoveries following that of the terracotta warriors include pits containing terracotta civil officials. Entertainment was also provided by terracotta acrobats and strongmen and terracotta musicians playing to life-size bronze water birds beside an underground river. These are described and interpreted in Chapter 5 while the significance of the recently discovered suits of armour made of stone is discussed, as well as the question of whether they are prototypes of the famous jade burial suits of the following Han dynasty.

Later reputation of the First Emperor

The question of how the First Emperor has been viewed throughout China's long history is to some extent coloured by the fact that his story was written by the official historian of the Han dynasty, Sima Qian, who had his own agenda. Some parts of this record have been used in later times to emphasize the cruelty of the First Emperor. However, it is highly likely that the most controversial parts were actually later additions to the record, judging from the language used in them. The later additions include the description of the First Emperor burning the books of Confucianism

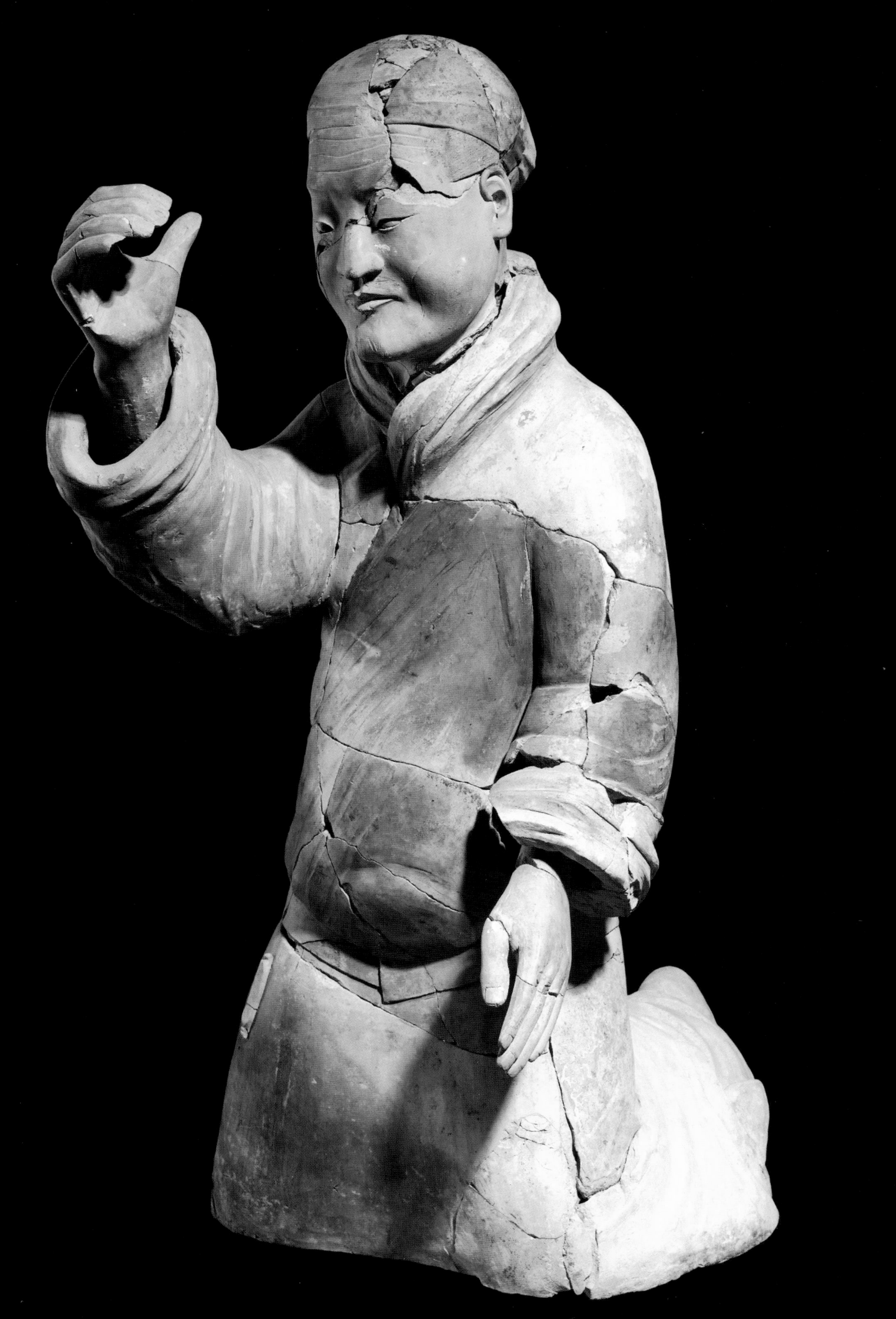

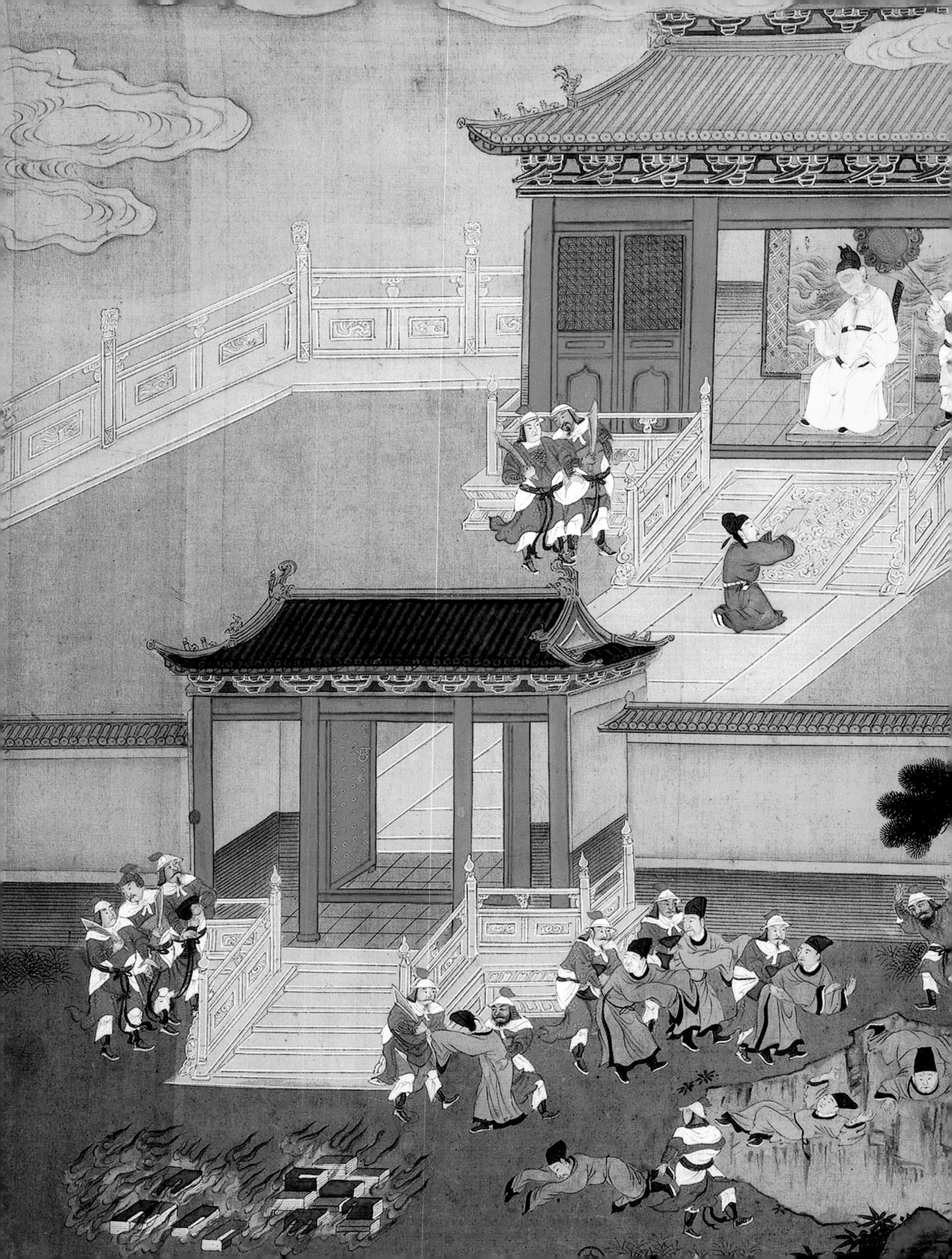

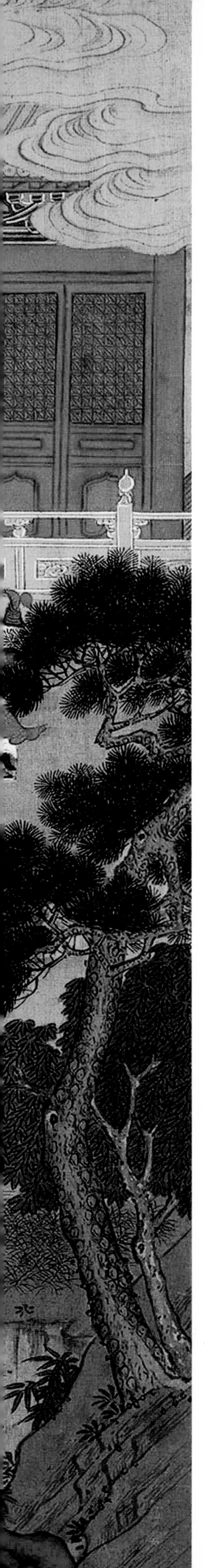

FIG. 13
(left) **In this eighteenth-century album, the First Emperor is seen ordering Confucian scholars to be buried alive and Confucian books to be burned. This is a later depiction of a story told in the *Records of the Historian* (*Shiji*) which may not have been true or may have been exaggerated. It has, however, influenced many peoples' opinions about the First Emperor.**

and burying scholars alive in 212 BC, as well as the fall of a meteor in 211 BC inscribed with the words: 'The First Emperor will die and his land will be divided.' Scholars also doubt the description of the First Emperor ordering three thousand convicts to denude a mountain of trees and paint it red to punish the mountain god for causing a storm that stopped one of his journeys.[8]

Another later addition to the record was an essay by a Han-dynasty poet and statesman called Jia Yi, entitled 'How Qin Went Too Far'. This greatly affected the general view of later Chinese dynasties and became the standard Confucian view on the reasons for Qin's collapse. Jia Yi said that the people had no choice but to overthrow the First Emperor as he was a ruthless tyrant who had no moral right to rule. Sima Qian had been slightly more even-handed, saying that 'Qin conquered the world through much violence, but the world changed, its accomplishments were great'. During the Tang dynasty the famous writer Liu Zongyuan (AD 773–819) in his 'Essay on Feudalism' praised the First Emperor for establishing the imperial system, while blaming his 'inhuman policies' for Qin's downfall. The two essays by Jia and Liu were frequently quoted throughout later dynasties when evaluating the First Emperor.[9]

In the twentieth century, there was a gradual re-evaluation of China's past and the First Emperor came to be used in political debate, particularly during the Cultural Revolution (1966–76), when Mao Zedong identified himself with the First Emperor.[10] In 1938 a leading historian, Hsiao I-shan, compared the First Emperor to Alexander the Great, Cromwell and Napoleon, in terms of his greatness and impact on world history. A biography of the First Emperor published in 1941 subtly compared him with Chiang Kaishek and praised both men. In 1943 Guo Moruo, who was a leading left-wing scholar, described the First Emperor in overwhelmingly negative terms, but by 1958 it seems that Mao Zedong had decided to take a positive view of him. Among other references he made to the First Emperor, Mao said: 'Qin Shihuang was an authority in emphasizing the present while slighting the past.' Mao's praise of the First Emperor was followed by a huge surge in positive publications epitomized by Hong Shidi's '*Qin Shihuang*', published in 1972. By the time of the sixth printing of the second edition in December 1973, the total number of copies of Hong's popular biography had reached 1.85 million.[11] There are still differing opinions within China on the assessment of the First Emperor and he remains a controversial figure. However, he continues to be invoked in popular culture as the star of films and operas produced by Chinese, such as Zhang Yimou's film *Hero* (2002) and Tan Dun's opera *The First Emperor* (2006).

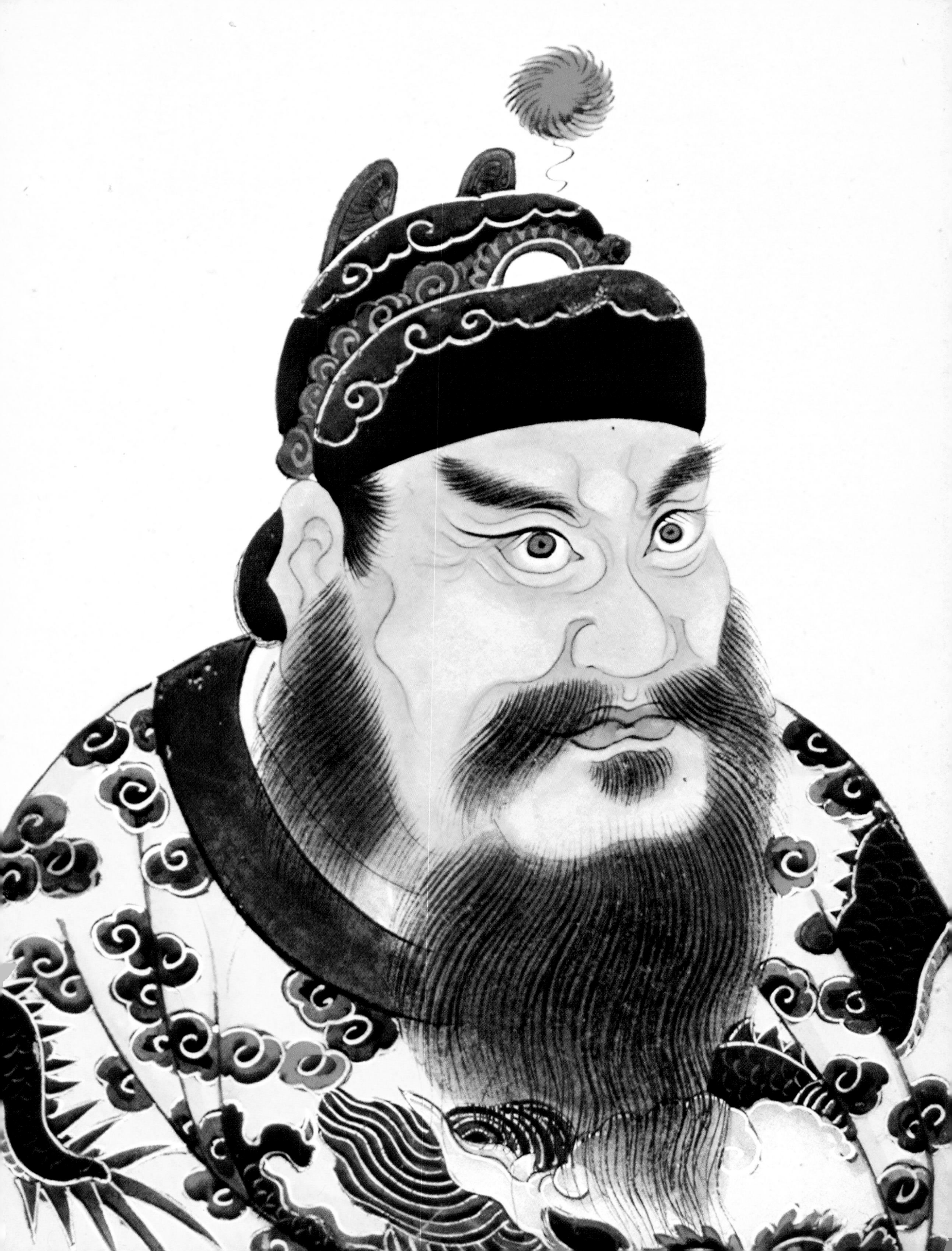

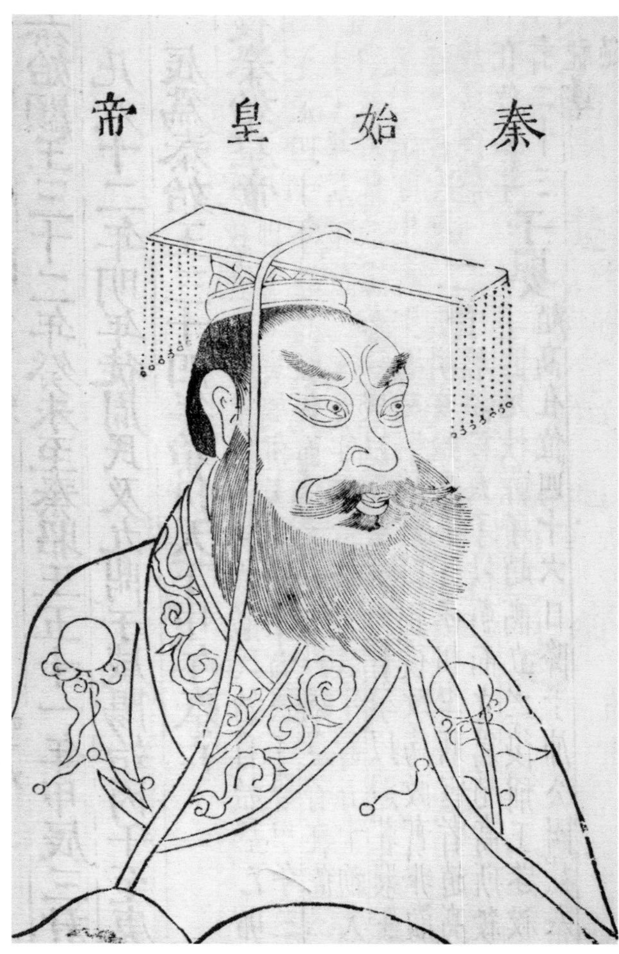

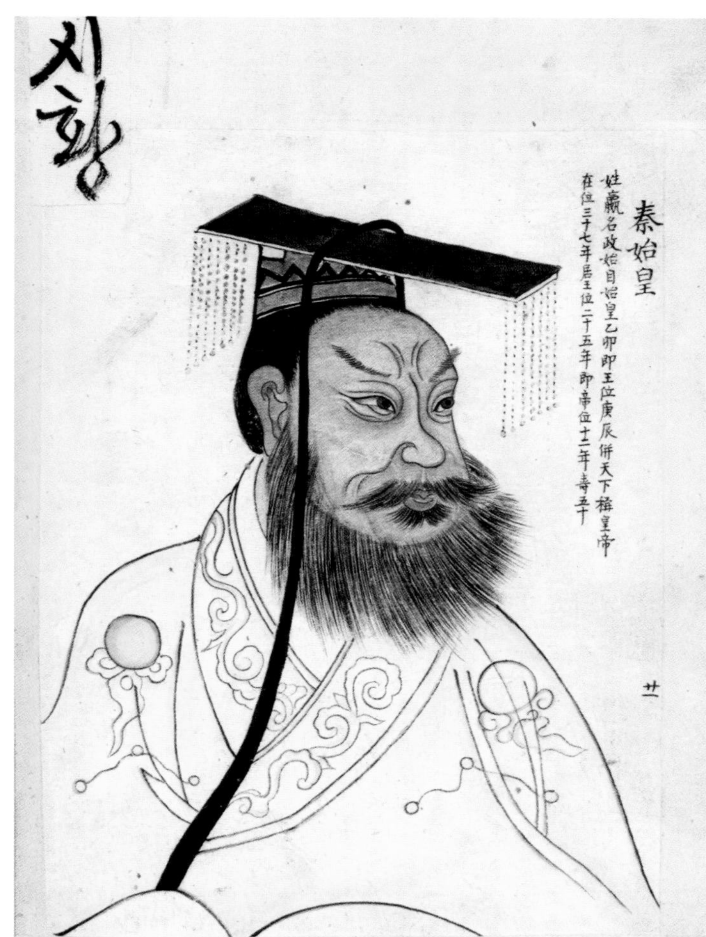

FIG. 14
(left) Eighteenth-century imaginary portrait of the First Emperor from an album of portraits of eighty-six emperors of China, *Lidai diwang xiang*.

FIG. 15
(above left) Imaginary woodcut portrait of the First Emperor from the Chinese encyclopaedia *Sancai tuhui*, dated 1609. There are no images of him surviving from the Qin dynasty.

FIG. 16
(above right) Nineteenth-century portrait, with Korean colophons, of the First Emperor from an album portraying famous historical figures, clearly copied from the earlier Chinese woodcut in the *Sancai tuhui*.

Legacy of the First Emperor

In the light of Mao's comments about the First Emperor, it is interesting to note that in 1986 a major Western scholar of the Qin, the late Derk Bodde, concluded: 'whether one admires the Qin achievement or not, it must be recognised for what it was: a transformation of the face of China so great ... that it deserves the name "revolution".... Indeed it was China's only real revolution until the present century.'[12] There is no doubt that the achievements and the legacy of the First Emperor are enormous. Not only did he create a unified territory that we now call China, but he also introduced a centralized bureaucracy and a culture in which writing and merit played an important part. His concept of the role of the tomb in the afterlife was also entirely new, reflecting his vision of himself as a ruler on a cosmic scale.

It is precisely because of the limitations of the historical sources for the First Emperor that the archaeological evidence presented here from his tomb is so important. The historical record may be prejudiced, may have been altered later and can be interpreted to suit, but the artefacts that have been unearthed were actually made for, and may have been seen and used by, the First Emperor. They had been lying undisturbed under the ground for over two thousand years until their recent excavation. They are tangible evidence of the First Emperor's existence, his great achievements and his vision. In fact, they ensure that he lives for ever, although perhaps not quite as he planned.

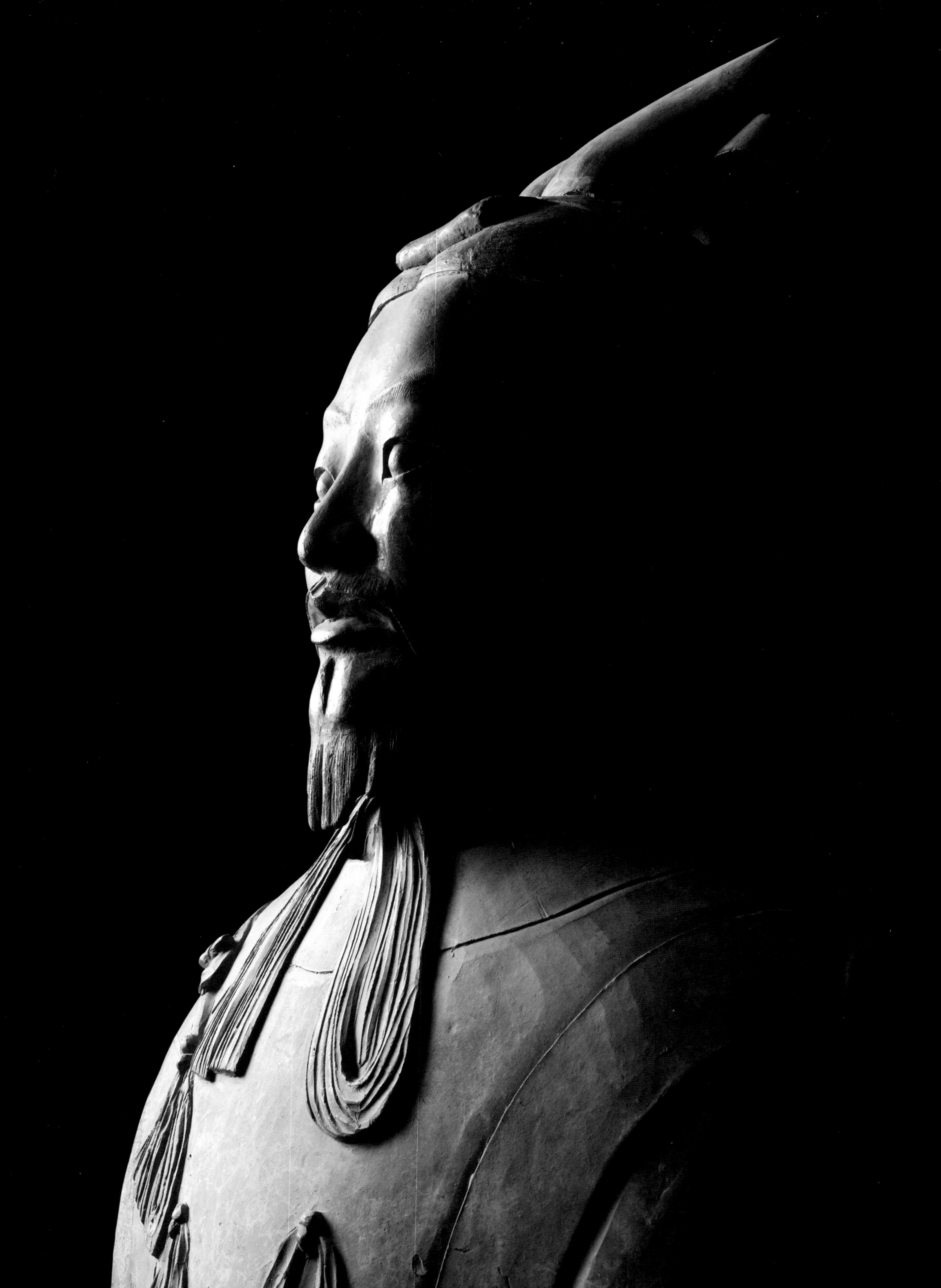

THE RISE OF QIN AND THE MILITARY CONQUEST OF THE WARRING STATES

ROBIN D.S. YATES

FIG. 17
(opposite) Detail of a bearded general, showing his 'pheasant-tail' cap tied under the chin.
Cat. no. 112

Introduction

By the time that Ying Zheng, surnamed Ying, came to the throne of the state of Qin as a young teenager in 246 BC, Qin was already more than 600 years old. It had been officially recognized by the Zhou king as a minor subordinate state on the northwestern borders of the civilized world, modern Gansu province, responsible for breeding and raising horses for the Zhou. Within twenty-five years of becoming king, Ying Zheng was able to eliminate all the rival powers in the country, declare himself 'First Emperor' in 221 and extend the Qin administrative and political system to the rest of the east Asian subcontinent, establishing the 'Chinese Empire', which lasted down to the beginning of the twentieth century. His was a spectacular achievement and he can justly claim to be one of the most significant and influential individuals in the course of world history.

Yet, within a few years of Ying Zheng's death in 210, his dynasty, which he had hoped would last through ten thousand generations, collapsed in bloody civil war, and the inheritance that he had planned to bequeath to his descendants vanished into thin air. His history seems to be one of hubris ending in deserved tragedy not just for himself but for his immediate family and leading ministers, and all the millions of nameless officials and peasants who had supported his rise. The rulers of the Han dynasty (206 BC–AD 220), their apologists and later Chinese historians distorted the memory of those fateful years and portrayed him as a ruthless, vainglorious, superstitious tyrant who stopped at nothing to achieve his goals.

What is the truth behind the story of the founding of the Chinese empire? It is only in the last forty years or so that a series of amazing archaeological excavations of both material remains and texts from the years prior to and during the Qin dynasty has given us insights into the long- and short-term historical processes that shaped the creation of the Chinese empire, processes that were not obvious to the participants themselves. This chapter will focus on the military dimensions of Qin history, especially in its later stages. But, before we turn to discuss military matters, a few words should be said about the early history of the Qin.

There are two modern views about the origins of the Qin ruling house of Ying. One claims that it derived from indigenous peoples of east China, the other, that they were descendants of the Rong, a so-called western barbarian people.[1] Sima Qian, the Grand Historian or Scribe of China, who completed his *Records of the Historian (Shiji)* in about 89 BC relying on Qin state archival materials, claimed that the dynasty was descended from Emperor Zhuanxu, the (mythical) second of the Five Emperors who supposedly reigned in China's most ancient past.[2] It is unlikely that this issue will be resolved even with future archaeological discoveries. However, recent archaeological excavations have revealed much about early Qin cultural and ritual practices. They show conclusively that there is no reality to Sima Qian's description of the Qin as being outside the Zhou culture sphere and basically a marginal 'barbarian' state that only learnt proper 'central states' customs from roughly the middle of the fourth century BC as a result of innovations brought in from the east by a series of inspired immigrant statesmen and generals.

In 770 BC the Western Zhou kings were forced from their homeland in the lower Wei River valley, Shaanxi province, and moved to Luoyang, Henan province, in the central Yellow River Plains. The Qin were left to guard the western frontier and they gradually moved eastward, occupying the original Zhou domains (*fig. 18*). In the Spring and Autumn period (eighth to fifth centuries BC) Qin, with its capital

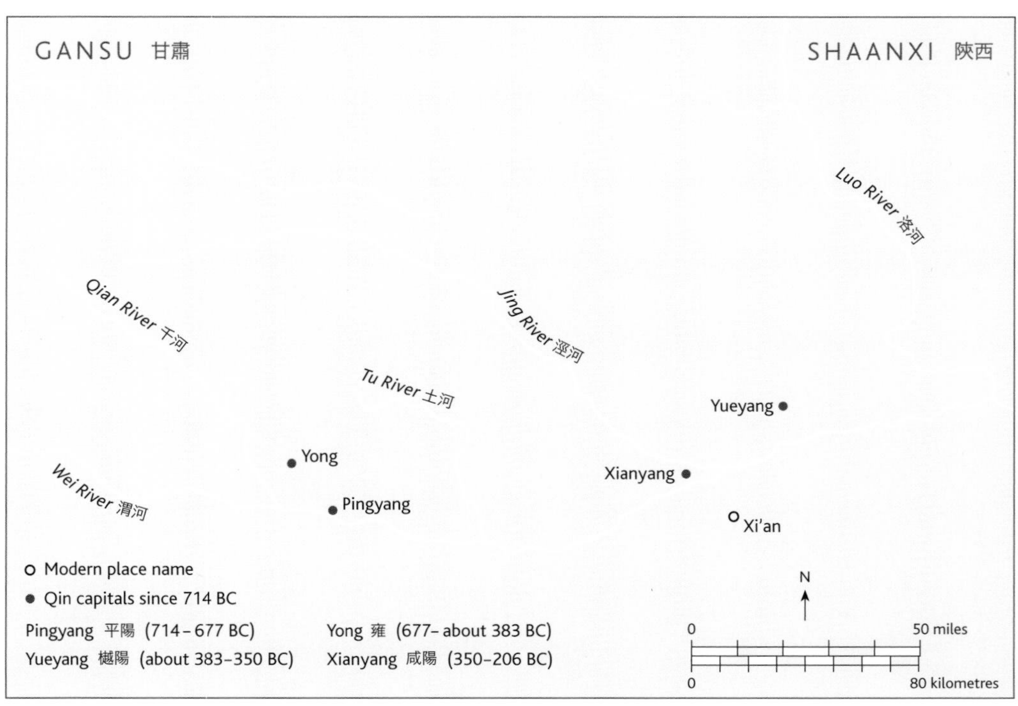

FIG. 18
Map showing the various Qin capitals since 714 BC and their gradual move to the east.

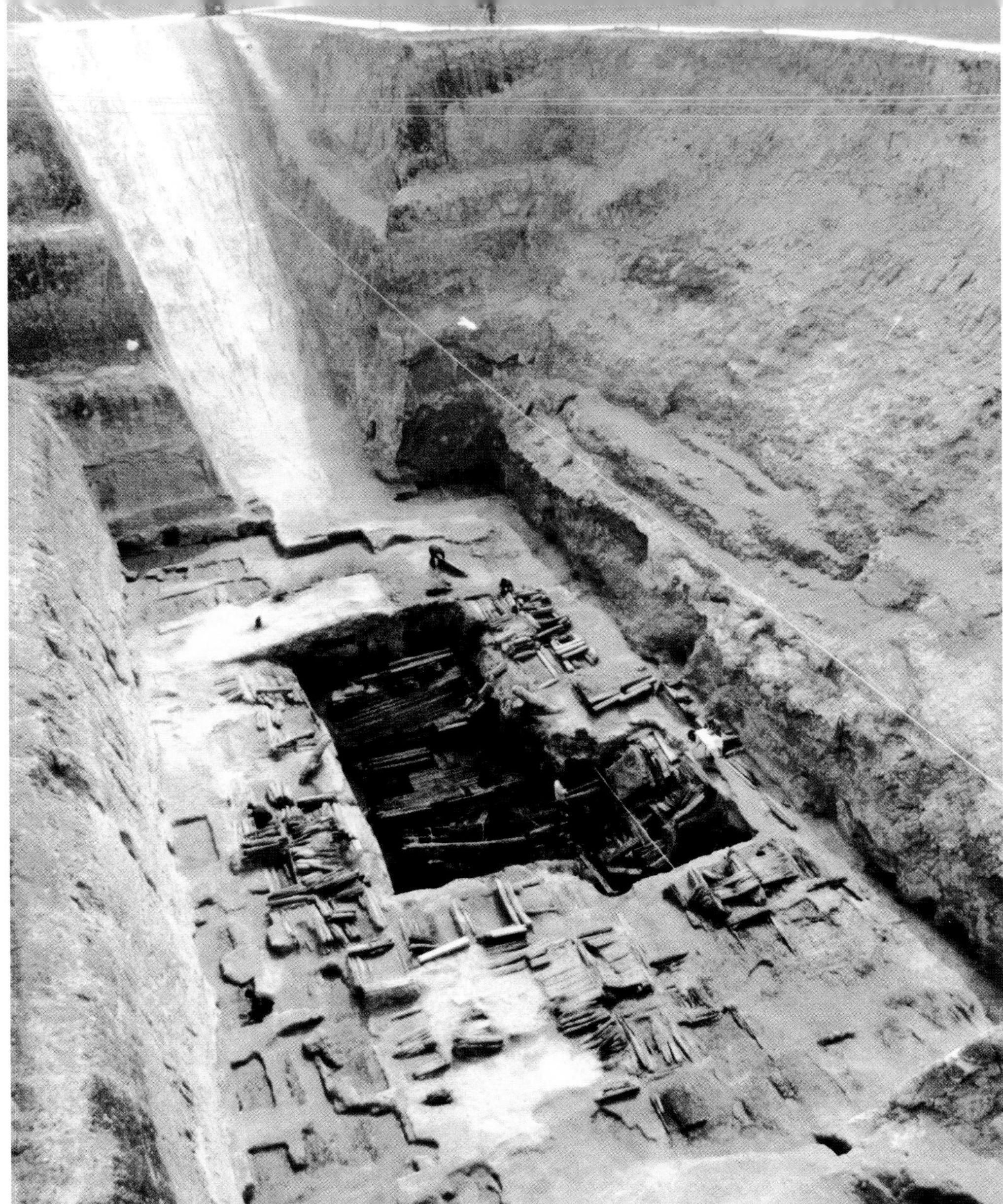

FIG. 19
The tomb of Duke Jing (r. 576–537 BC) was found in a burial site along with nineteen other tombs belonging to previous Qin dukes. Measuring 300 metres long by 24 metres deep, it is the largest pre-Qin dynasty burial. Chariots as well as human sacrifices accompanied the duke in death. The tomb had been robbed many times in antiquity, yet 3,000 objects including gold, jade and lacquer pieces were found, indicating that the original burial must have contained an extraordinary number of items.

city Yong located in modern Fengxiang, Shaanxi province, was closely allied to the Zhou and had marriage relations with the Zhou ruling lineage.[3] Qin followed the Zhou system of ancestor worship in temples where ritual offerings were presented in bronze vessels,[4] and preserved rather conservative burial customs handed down from antiquity, even though they showed local characteristics. These practices included burying the dead in walled enclosures and with the heads sometimes facing in an east–west direction, not in a north–south direction as was more common in the central states to the east.[5] Nevertheless, according to recently discovered inscriptions on bronze bells, the Qin rulers claimed to have inherited the Mandate of Heaven, a prerogative of the Zhou king, the only Son of Heaven, and, in the case of rulers such as Duke Jing of Qin, vastly exceeded the tomb size and the offerings placed to accompany the coffin that were permitted by Zhou ritual sumptuary regulations: 166 individuals accompanied Duke Jing to the grave, some willingly, some evidently unwillingly (*fig.* 19).[6] As Falkenhausen points out, the Qin rulers and elite were perfectly familiar with Zhou standards, and they may have been very consciously competing with their rivals to the east, manipulating their practices to demonstrate not only that they were their cultural equals but materially richer, too. He and Teng

Mingyu also note that Qin aristocrats and commoners seem to have pioneered burial customs such as placing replicas of vessels and objects in tombs that came to be disseminated throughout China in later Qin and Han times.

In the late fifth century BC Qin's leading aristocrats played havoc with the succession to the Qin throne, yet it was a time when Qin began a long process of changing its legal, political, military and social institutions, a process that would culminate in its victory in uniting all the other rival states into a single polity under King Zheng, the First Emperor. In 409 BC Duke Jian ordered all his officials to wear swords, signifying the emphasis that was now going to be placed on military skill and values, and in 387 Duke Hui launched an attack to the south into the territory of the Shu peoples of modern Sichuan province. The pace of reform picked up under Duke Xian (r. 384–362 BC), who moved the capital from Yong east to Yueyang, and especially under his son Duke Xiao (r. 361–338 BC). The latter monarch called for suggestions as to how to reform Qin's institutions to make it competitive with the powerful states to its east and south-east. A minor prince by the name of Gongsun Yang or Wei Yang, better known as Shang Yang (c.385–338 BC), answered the call (see pp.64–5). Despite opposition from native aristocrats, Shang Yang was permitted to institute two sets of reforms, which laid the foundation for Qin's rise to dominance in the next century.

FIG. 20
This bronze finial (*dun*), possibly for the end of a dagger-axe, was excavated from a Qin tomb in Xianyang. The fourteen-character inscription translates as 'Shang Yang supervised the making of this *dun* in 343 BC'.
Cat. no. 4

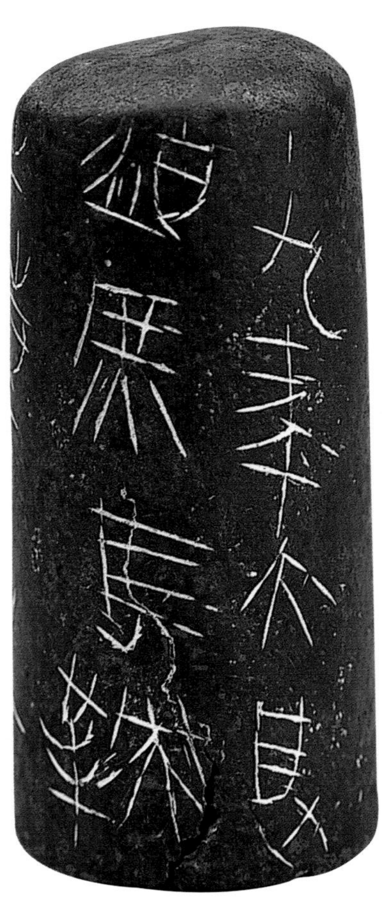

Shang Yang is said to have brought with him a *Canon of Laws* in six fascicles, which he used as the basis of his reform, but this is surely a later fabrication. In addition, in the light of recent discoveries of Qin legal texts, we can be sure that not all of Shang Yang's policy recommendations as they are laid out in the still extant *Shang jun shu (Book of Lord Shang)* were actually adopted. Nevertheless, we can surmise that in roughly 356 BC the following regulations were promulgated. First, families were organized into groups of five and members were held legally accountable for each other's actions: they were obliged to report crimes and, if they did not, they were held guilty of the same crime the perpetrator had committed. One male was taken from each household to form a squad of five, the basic unit in the army, and these soldiers were also held responsible for each other's safety. If they lost one man, it was their duty to capture the head of an enemy in exchange. It is probably from this time that the Qin established its conscript army.

Second, the Qin created a system of ranks or grades for all male members of the population where previously only aristocrats had such ranks. This system linked together all members of the population, aristocrats and commoners alike, up to the ruler at the top with cosmic powers, which must have encouraged social solidarity and a common sense of purpose and identity. Probably there were initially seventeen ranks, with commoners being allowed to rise no higher than rank 8 (*gongcheng*). Rank 9, known as *wu daifu*, was the rank of a number of the commanding generals who led the campaigns against Qin's enemies in the wars of unification in the late third century BC. Rank was awarded for success in battle, manifested by cutting off a head and reporting it to the army headquarters; one head was awarded with one degree or rank, two heads with two ranks; and officers were given ranks depending on the number of heads their subordinates cut off. Since their responsibility was to manage the troops under their command, they were not supposed to cut off heads themselves, which explains why the officers in the First Emperor's terracotta army are represented without weapons. This rank gave an individual social prestige and legal and economic benefits.[7]

Third, to increase the number of families capable of sending men into the army, elder and younger brothers, who would normally reside together, were told to divide their households and live separately. Fourth, the state encouraged the development of agriculture and disparaged commerce. This measure was designed to ensure the production of enough grain to supply the army and the increasingly complex administration. By the First Emperor's time the state had developed a highly sophisticated system of granaries and granary management, as well as procedures for the reception and disbursal of grain, and had laid down in minute detail the regulations that were supposed to be used in agricultural production.[8] Finally, the state prevented feuds, rewarded denunciations of treason and punished cases of suspected treason.

A second set of laws and policies, promulgated between 344 and 341 BC, prevented married brothers from living together; organized the system of local government (see pp. 73–4); standardized and unified weights and measures; established a new land tenure system that Shang Yang evidently adopted from the neighbouring state of Zhao, whereby the size of the Qin 'acre' was increased from 100 to 240 square 'paces';[9] and required the collection of military taxes on the basis of the size of the population. Shang Yang also recommended that the capital be moved again from Yueyang back further west to Xianyang, on the north bank of the Wei River, probably to be less exposed to attack from Qin's eastern enemies.

In the decades following Shang Yang's and Duke Xiao's deaths in 338 BC, a series of rulers built on their legacy and expanded Qin territory to the east, south and north, incorporating peoples and territories that had very different cultural and social customs. Sichuan was conquered: convicts, settlers and officials were sent south-west to occupy the land and exploit its extensive natural and mineral resources.[10] By the middle of the third century Qin was, by any comparative measure, an empire, although it had not yet claimed exclusive right to rule the 'All under Heaven'. How did it achieve this success and was its ultimate triumph inevitable? Since the historical records do not provide details of campaigns and of battles, we still cannot be sure of the tactics that it used and there were occasions when the outcome was anything but certain. But generally speaking, its strategy in the third century was to ally itself with distant states and strike at those closest, using its armies to either physically attack and annihilate its enemy's soldiers or threaten them into yielding cities and territory, or using shrewd diplomatic manoeuvres, spies and other forms of intimidation to achieve the same goal. What perhaps distinguished it from its rivals was its willingness to throw all its human and material resources into campaigns in an all-or-nothing effort to gain victory.

Military organization: chariots, infantry and cavalry

In the early Bronze Age warfare was primarily an activity engaged in by members of the male aristocratic elite mounted in chariots and accompanied by foot soldiers. It was closely related to sacrifice: warriors demonstrated their expertise in ritual decorum, and gained social prestige, by the way they performed in combat,

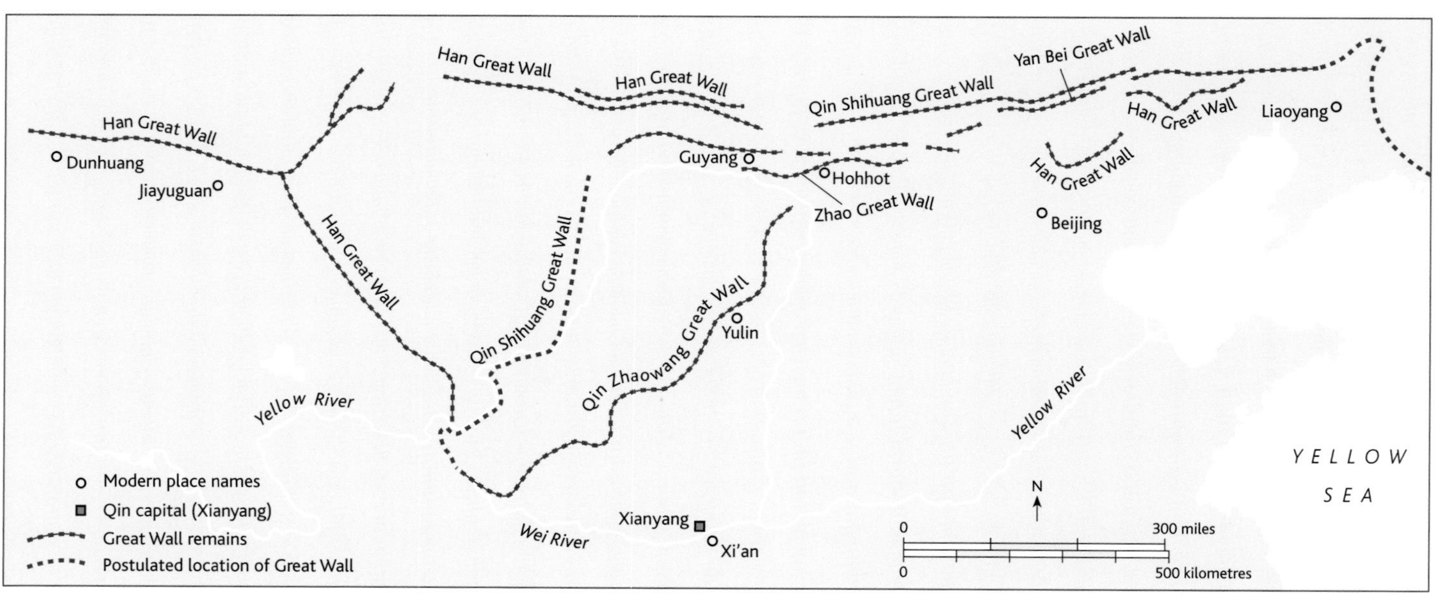

FIG. 21
(above) **Map showing Qin- and Han-period walls.**

FIG. 22
(below) **The introduction of the crossbow in the Warring States period revolutionized military warfare. It required less skill and strength to use than a composite bow and was said to be able to fire arrows for distances of over 800 metres. The bronze trigger mechanism was made in three separate pieces and had to be precisely cast in order to function effectively.**
Cat. no. 5

chariot driving and archery competitions. By the middle of the fourth century BC, however, the nature of warfare had changed. Aristocratic society and values were in steep decline. Although ritual still played an important role, the final outcome, victory or defeat, was much more important, and war was, as Sunzi said, a vital matter of state that could not be neglected by any ruler. Wars lasted much longer and were fought by larger armies composed primarily of conscripted peasants who provided the bulk of the infantry forces. Chariots were still important, but a new element had been adopted from the steppe nomads, cavalry. Thus a field army was composed of four parts: chariots, infantry, cavalry and the baggage train loaded with supplies.[11] As urbanization expanded, towns and cities became targets of attack, and siege warfare reached new levels of sophistication. Even women were expected to take part in defence, and they operated complex machinery such as revolving bridges fired by trigger mechanisms, while the males shot lever-drawn catapults and

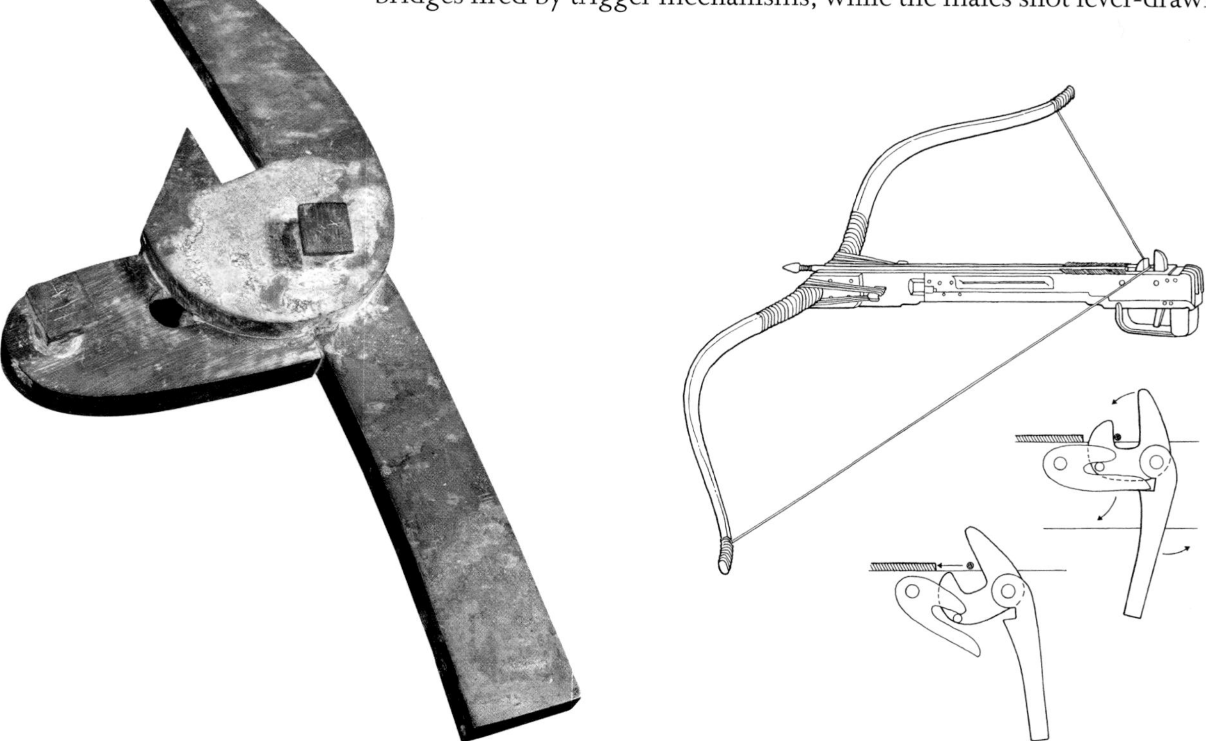

multiple-bolt *arcuballistae* (huge crossbows firing volleys of 3-metre-long arrows), and engaged in underground gas warfare.[12] Over time, military theorists, such as Sunzi's reputed grandson, Sun Bin, whose works were rediscovered in an early Han tomb only in 1972, developed new formations for fighting in the field on different types of terrain depending on the relative strength of the opposing sides: the square, round, sparse, dense, awl, wild goose, hooked, dark wings, fire and water formations.[13] Qin forces and Lian Po, a Zhao general, even engaged in a kind of static months-long fortification and trench warfare at the Battle of Changping in 260 BC until the Qin spread rumours and paid bribes, encouraging Zhao to replace the wily Lian with the incompetent Zhao Kuo. Qin thereupon appointed its great general Bai Qi, who scored a crushing victory through a classic manoeuvre. The Qin pretended to flee and then ambushed the pursuing Zhao forces, cutting them off from their lines with 5,000 cavalry so that the Zhao army was split in two and ran out of provisions after forty-six days. Bai then massacred the 450,000 Zhao men who surrendered (probably an exaggerated figure), allowing only the youngest 240 to flee back to the Zhao capital, Handan, to report what had happened.[14]

What did Qin chariots, infantry and cavalry look like? The discovery of the terracotta horse and warrior figurines in the pits to the east of the First Emperor's mausoleum provides some of the answers (see also pp. 158–79).

FIG. **23**
(below) In 1980 two half life-sized chariots, each drawn by four horses, were excavated from one section of a larger pit located 20 metres west of the First Emperor's tomb. Both chariots and their horses are cast from bronze and the details painted and embellished in gold and silver. Chariot no. 1, pictured here, is 225 cm long and 152 cm high and is the battle or inspection chariot.

FIG. **24**
(following pages) The fully enclosed carriage of Chariot no. 2 is accessed through a door at the rear. Small windows on the sides provide ventilation. Painted lozenge and cloud motifs reminiscent of textile patterning decorate the exterior and interior walls.
Cat. no. 6

Chariots

First, there were obviously a wide variety of chariots. Two extraordinarily detailed bronze miniature models of chariots, possibly intended for the use of the dead emperor's spirit to travel abroad after his death, provide two examples. Chariot no. 1 (*fig.* 23) was a light chariot, driven by a standing charioteer wearing a long tunic and armed with

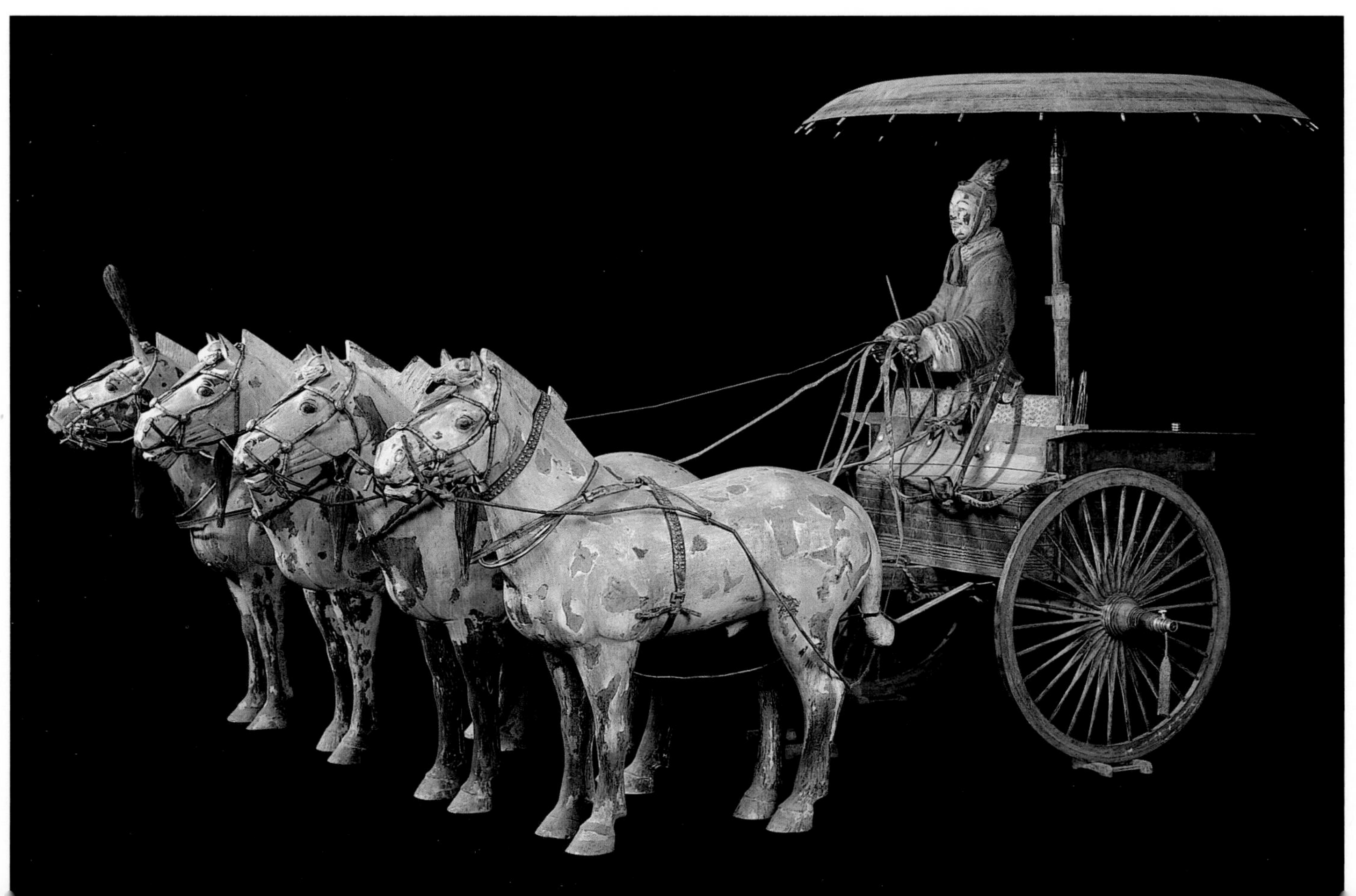

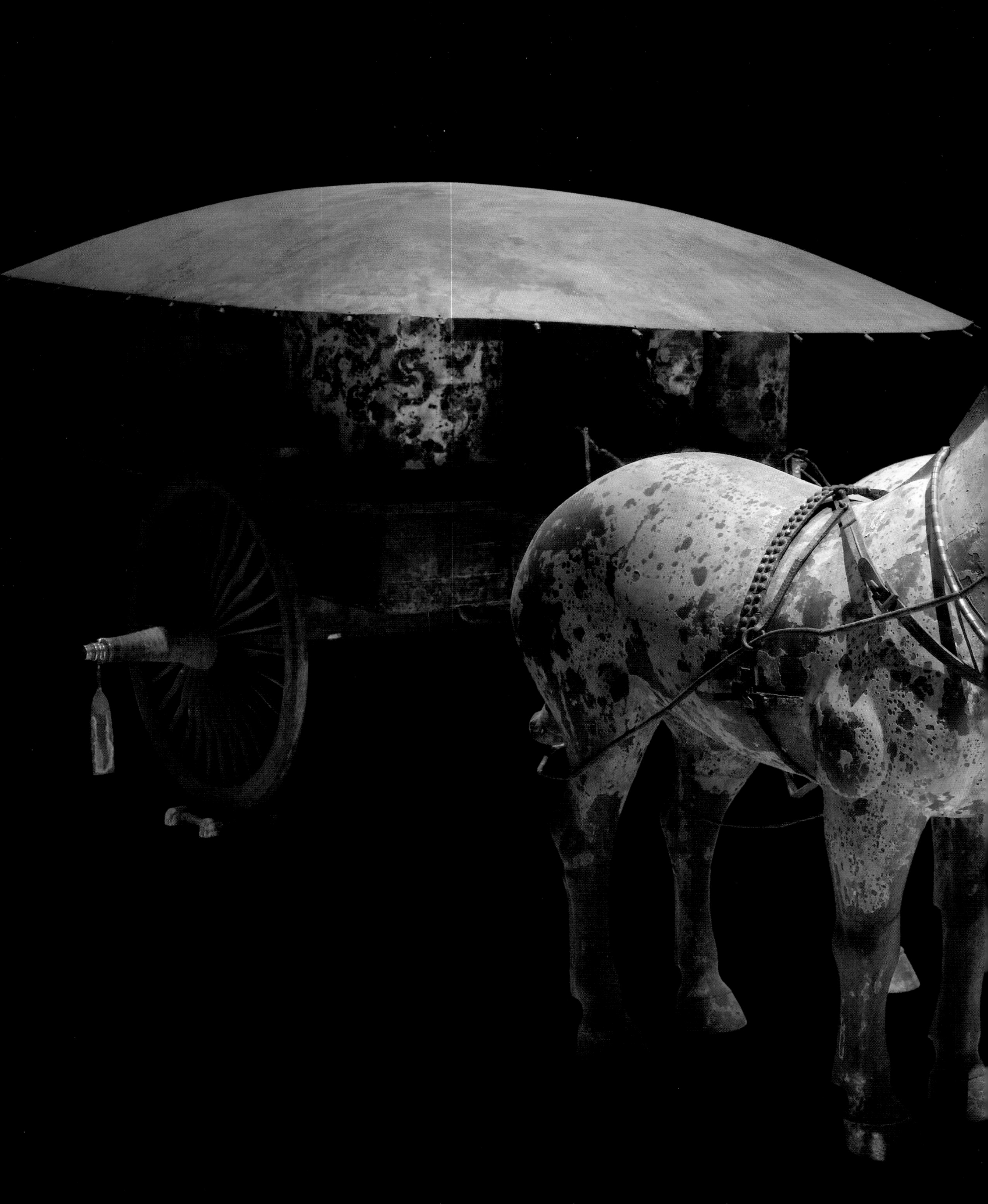

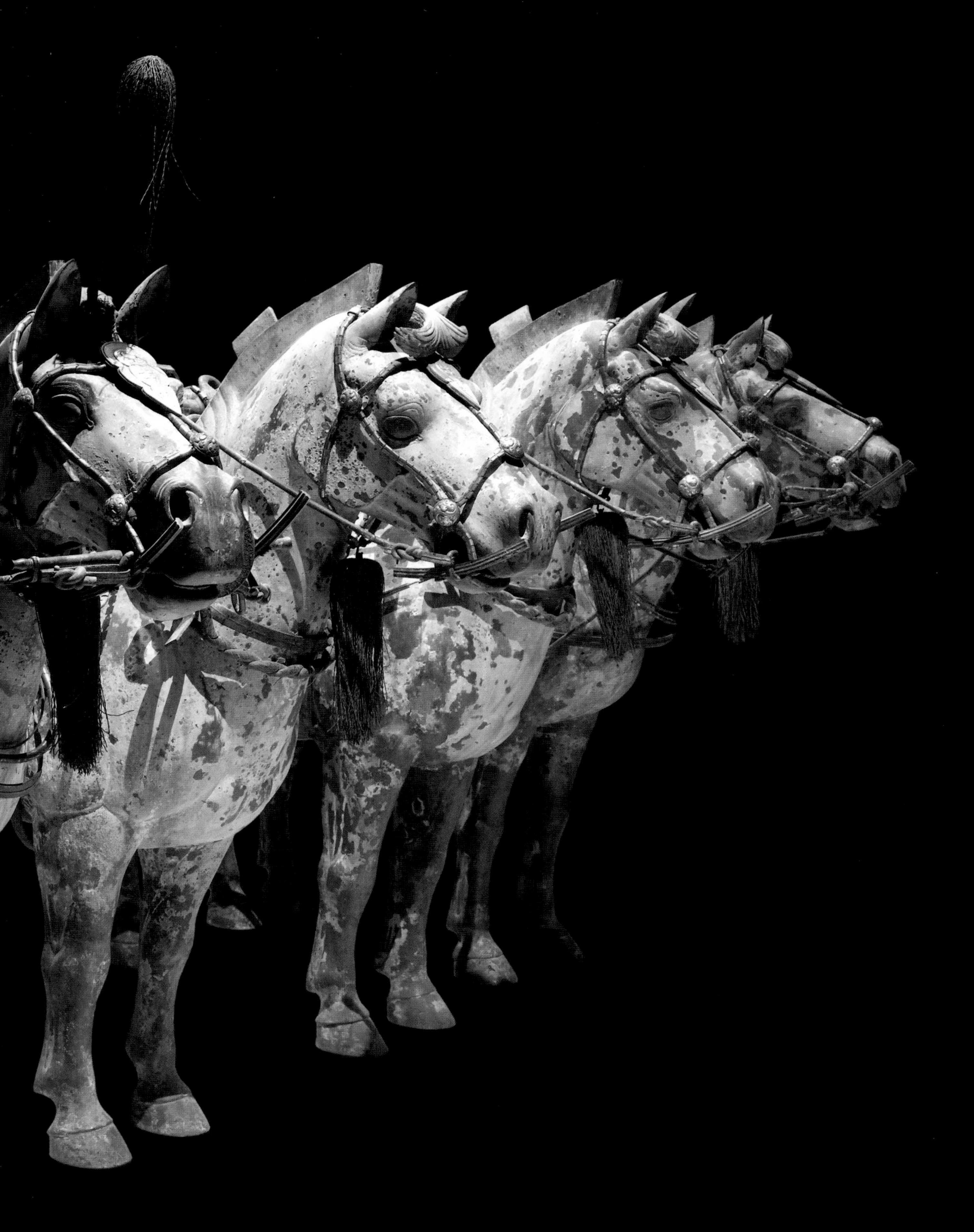

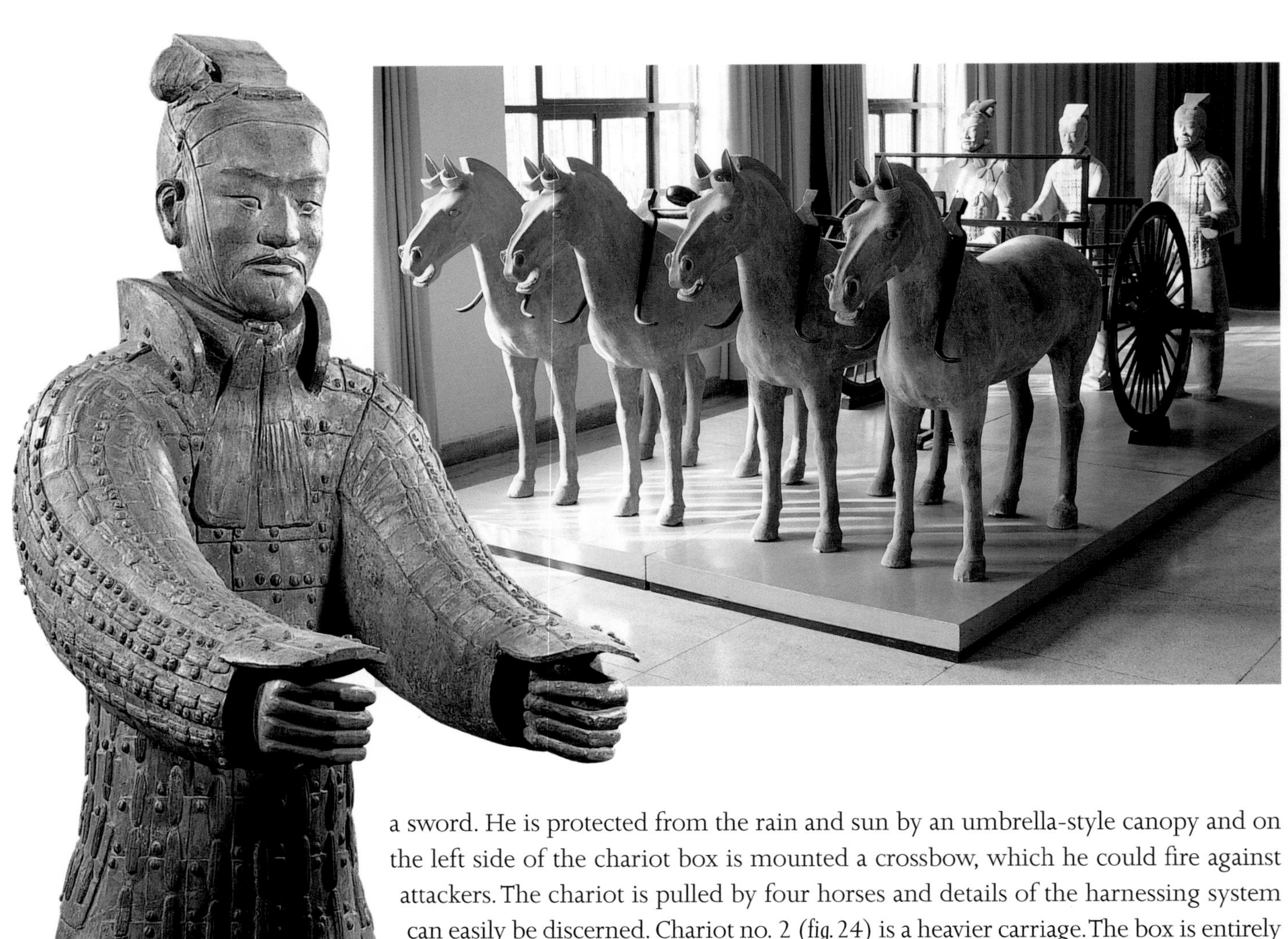

a sword. He is protected from the rain and sun by an umbrella-style canopy and on the left side of the chariot box is mounted a crossbow, which he could fire against attackers. The chariot is pulled by four horses and details of the harnessing system can easily be discerned. Chariot no. 2 (fig. 24) is a heavier carriage. The box is entirely enclosed, although there are windows that can be opened on either side. The driver in this chariot kneels and he is armed with a shorter sword that is tucked into his belt at his back. This chariot was large enough to sleep in and to carry passengers, and may represent the chariot in which the First Emperor toured the country after his final victory, the same chariot that carried his corpse back to Xianyang for his funeral.[15] We can see that, in comparison with earlier chariots, the Qin had improved chariot technology by reducing the size of the wheels and increasing the number of spokes, up to thirty, thus increasing the stability and durability of the vehicle.

About 130 war chariots have so far been excavated in the pits of the pottery army and they can be divided into four basic types, all of them originally constructed of wood with bronze fittings and a door at the back for mounting and dismounting. The first type is the command chariot, in which the middle and lower military officers rode. The officer usually stood at the left side of the carriage box with the driver in the middle and an assistant on the right, who wielded a long dagger-axe or halberd.[16] These chariots carried bells, drums and flags for directing the infantry under the officer's command and were drawn by four horses. The second type was a light chariot, found exclusively in Pit 2, where sixty-four examples were drawn up in tight formation. Here the driver stood in the middle with his arms and hands protected by armour, flanked by two charioteers on either side equipped with long

FIGS 25 & 26
(left) **This chariot driver's flat head-dress with a central divide identifies him as a middle-ranking officer. The size of the armour plates also indicated status: the larger the number of plates (or the smaller the size of each plate), the higher the rank. Wooden war chariots such as the example opposite would have been driven by an armoured charioteer.**
Cat. nos 7 & 8

dagger-axes or halberds. Their shoulders are protected with armour but their forearms are bare, allowing them to wield their weapons against enemy infantry or other chariots. The third type, also found exclusively in Pit 2, was a heavy chariot, and was intermingled with cavalry and infantry. Its purpose seems to have been to reinforce the strength of the other two units, and thus can be viewed as a 'reserve' chariot. The fourth type, again only retrieved from Pit 2, was a smaller, lighter chariot, with only two men on board, the driver and an armed charioteer. Placed in front of the cavalry, these 'rapid response' chariots probably coordinated their movements with the cavalry.[17] Although the historical texts state that a fixed number of infantry, usually seventy-five, accompanied a chariot, the numbers of infantry in Pit 1 under the command of the chariot-mounted officers vary; but it would appear that all of them adopted a 'two-chariot' formation when attacking enemy lines.[18]

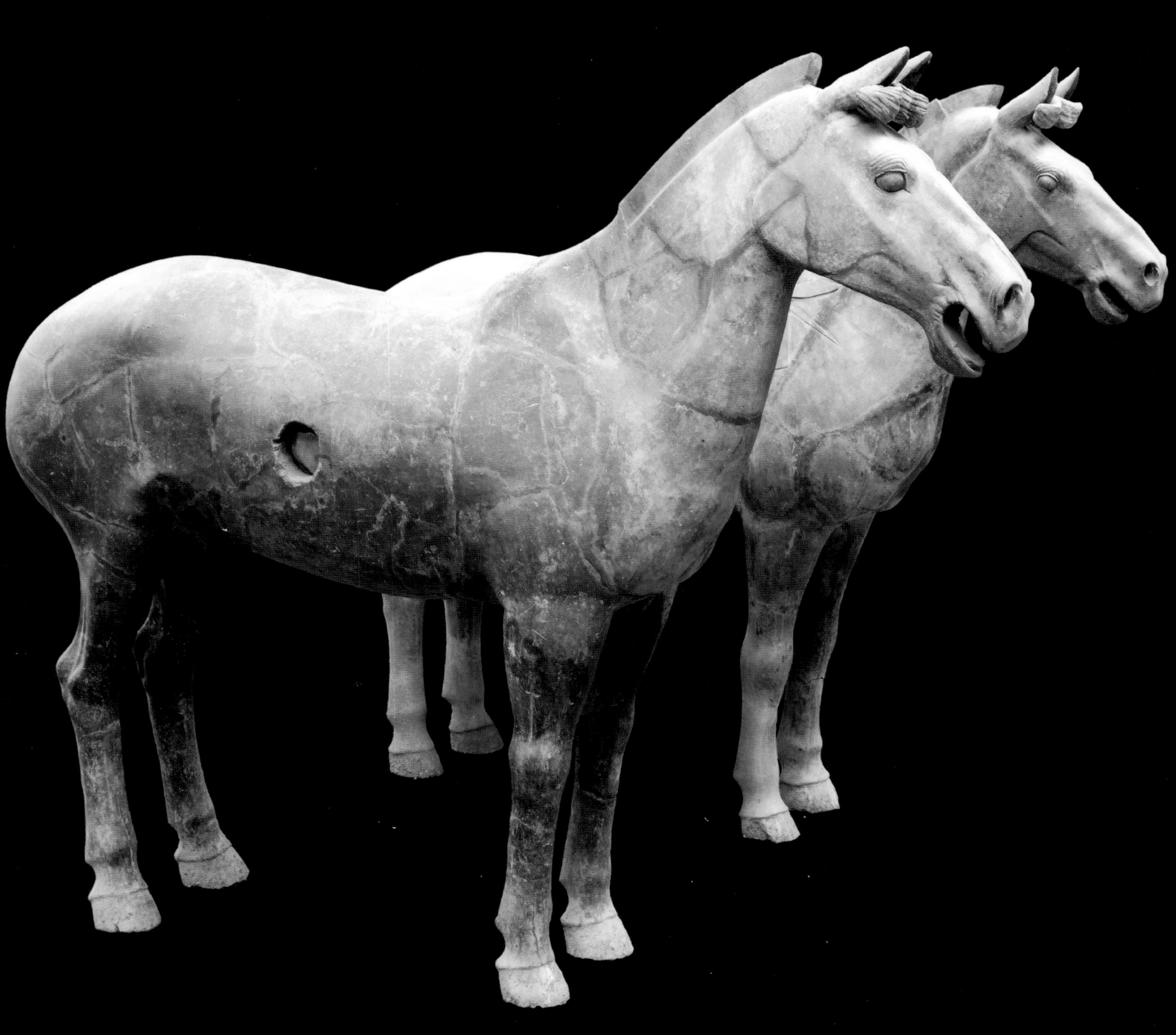

FIG. 27
(below) **Chariot horses were made with a hole in their side to prevent their hollow body cracking during the firing process.**
Cat. no. 9

FIG. 28
(below) **Standing archer excavated from Pit 2.**
Cat. no. 10

FIG. 29
(below right) **Reconstructed crossbow.**
Cat. no. 11

FIG. 30
(bottom) **This dagger-axe blade was hafted onto a wooden pole. The inscription on the blade, 'Made in the 26th year [of Ying Zheng]', shows that the manufacturing of weapons was strictly controlled and accounted for during the period when Lü Buwei was Chancellor of the Qin state from 249 to 246 BC.**
Cat. no. 12

Infantry

Qin foot soldiers specialized in a variety of weapons and were basically divided into two types, heavy and light infantry. Some of these were subordinate to the chariots, while others acted independently, in their own formations. The former generally wore heavy armour made of small plates of leather stiffened with lacquer and stitched together with coloured strings, while the latter could be similarly protected or wear long robes that allowed them to move quickly in advance or retreat.[19] These light infantry were either equipped with long weapons, such as spears (*mao*), dagger-axes (*ge*), halberds (*ji*) or lances (*pi*), or could be archers with long bows, or crossbowmen. The length of the shafts of the long weapons depended on the position of the men in the formation and on their function. Generally speaking, the charioteers would have wielded the longest-shafted weapons; those guarding the formation on the outside, the next longest; and those placed in the middle of the formation, the shortest, although there could be some variations.

The regular long-robed, light archers would have given the Qin formation speed and mobility, and the crossbows would have permitted them to fire heavier

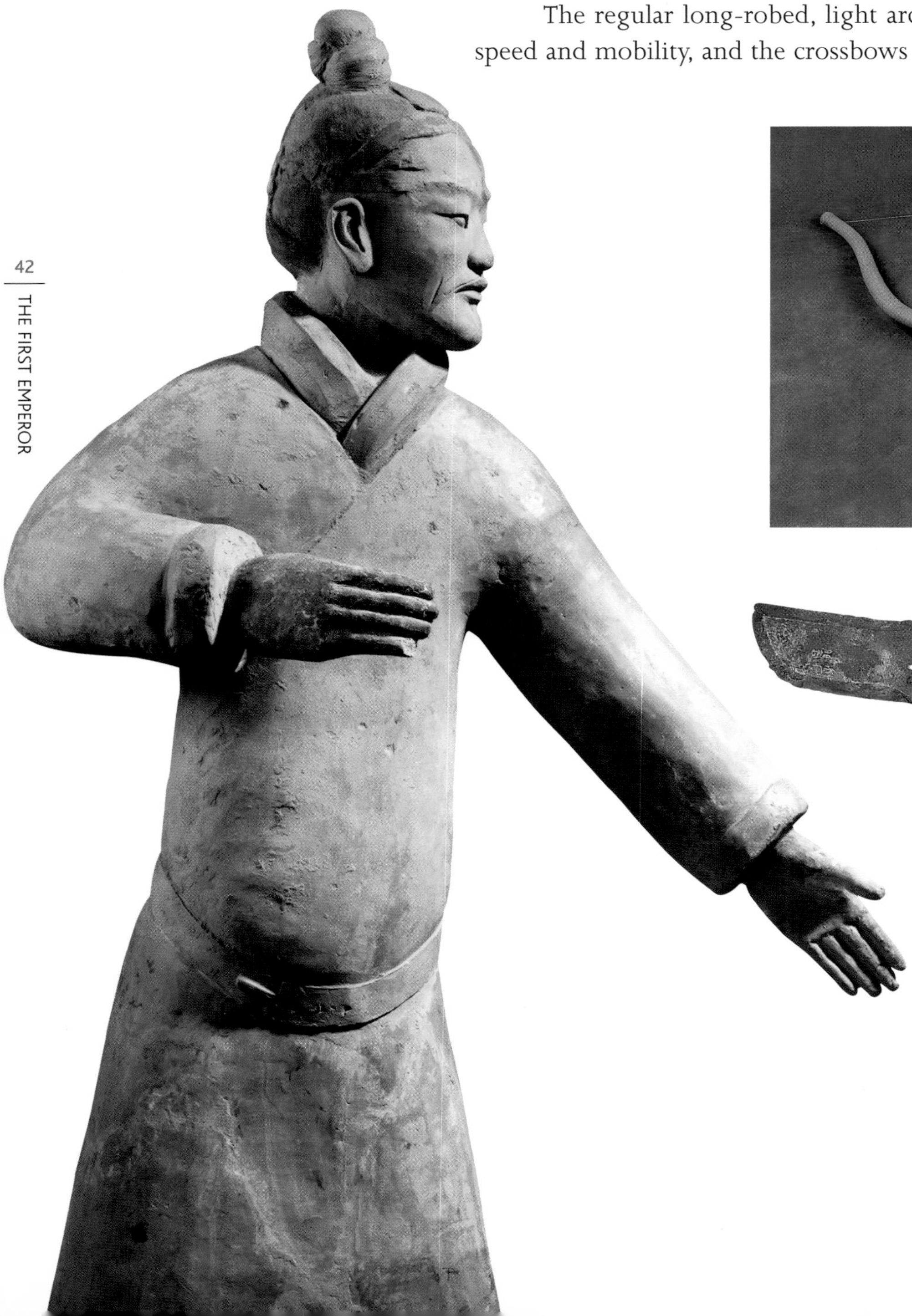

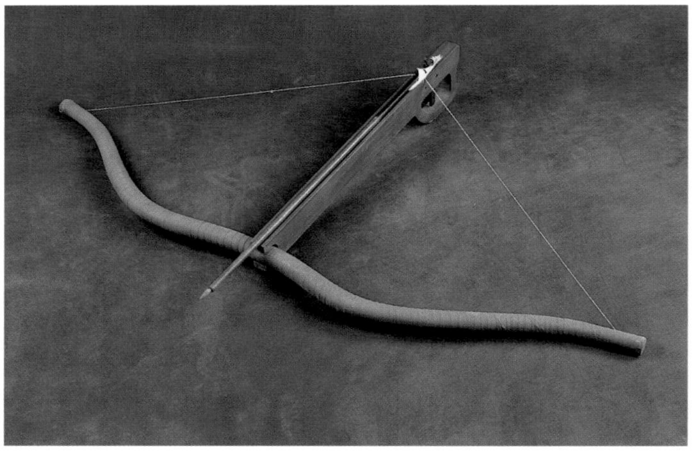

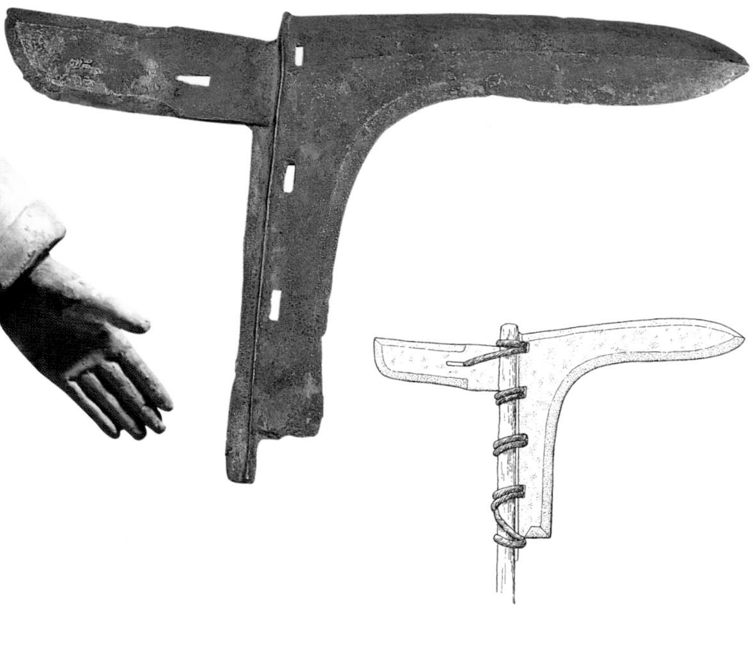

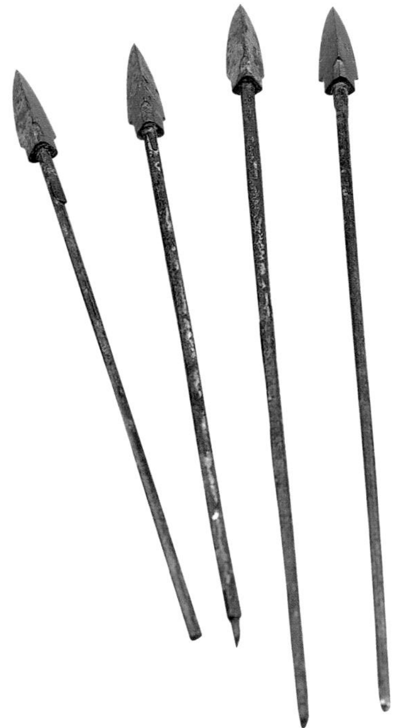

FIG. 31
(above) **More than 40,000 arrowheads have been excavated from among the terracotta army in Pit 1. Each of the arrowheads' long tapering circular stems was inserted into a wooden or bamboo shaft, exposing just the tripartite tip. They were fired from crossbows in batches and carried on the back in quivers made of woven hemp.**
Cat. no. 13

bolts, or quarrels, more accurately, with greater force and penetrating power, and longer distances. The disadvantage of crossbows was that they were much slower to load. However, training the crossbowmen to act in unison could have compensated for this. While the front line was firing together, the line behind would be arming their weapons. Once the front line had fired, the second line would move forward to replace them. This kind of manoeuvre seems to be what is represented in Pit 2. Qin crossbows appear to have been armed by hand and therefore cannot have been as powerful as they became in Han and later times.

The bronze spear was an ancient weapon dating back more than a thousand years and was one of the two weapons – the other being the dagger-axe – that had been traditionally issued to charioteers in the early Bronze Age. In the period just before the unification of China, the Qin seem to have changed the shape of their spears, making them shorter and broader, with the blade only 15 cm long. This alteration seems to have been undertaken so that they could also be attached to the tops of the curved dagger-axes to create the six-bladed halberd. They also improved the hafting of their dagger-axes, increasing the number of rectangular holes in the vertical blade to four. Through these holes leather strings were passed to bind the bronze head more tightly to the wooden shaft.[20] The lances discovered in the warrior pits range in length from 3.82 to 3.59 metres with the wooden or bamboo shaft and double-edged, flat, sharp-pointed, bronze blades measuring 34–5 cm. The blades are inscribed with the names of the artisans who made them and date from the fifteenth to the nineteenth years of the First Emperor's reign (i.e. 232–228 BC). The shafts are inserted into the blades, making the attachment very strong.

Swords

One theory that was proposed to account for Qin's success in defeating its rivals was that Qin must have developed the capacity to manufacture large quantities of wrought-iron swords: how else could its armies have executed the 450,000 soldiers of the state of Zhao said to have surrendered at the Battle of Changping? The discovery of the terracotta army effectively destroyed this idea because out of the more than ten thousand weapons so far discovered in the pits, only one is made of iron. Qin

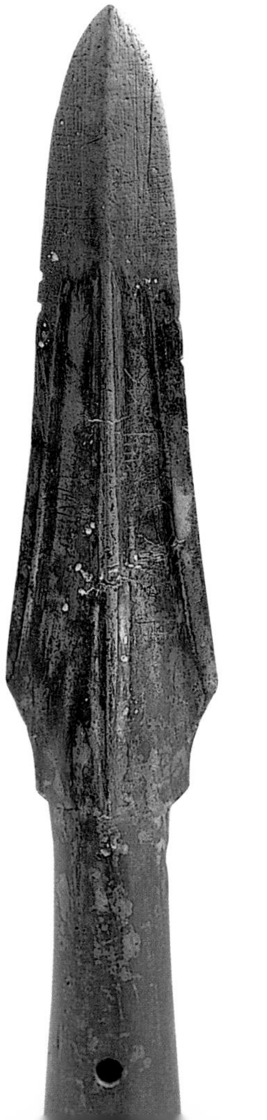

FIG. 32
(left) **This spearhead has four sharp blades and was originally fixed to a long wooden pole.**
Cat. no. 14

FIG. 33
(below right) **Sword excavated from Pit 1.**
Cat. no. 15

FIG. 34
(below left) **This bronze lance head (*pi*) is inscribed on its blade with an eight-character inscription identifying it as made in 232 BC by the Government Workshops, supervised by master Bang and made by worker Mu.**
Cat. no. 16

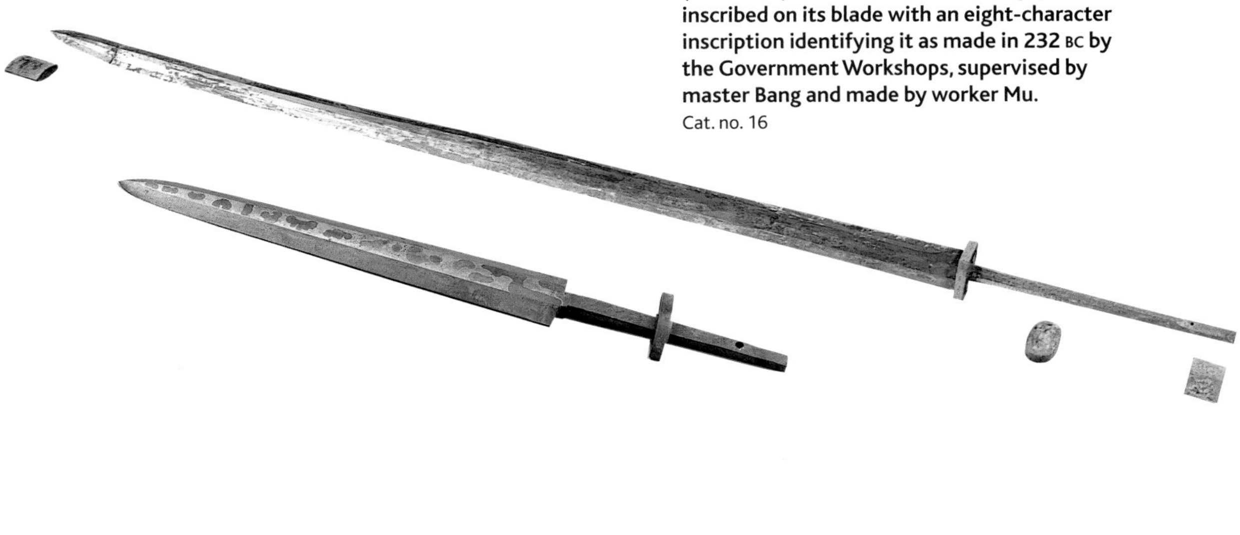

certainly had the capacity to make iron weapons, but its rivals, such as Chu, Yan and Zhao, were more advanced in iron and steel technology. Rather, Qin seems to have equipped its soldiers with extremely sharp bronze weapons and most of their armour was probably made of leather reinforced with lacquer, not of iron as Yan's was.

For defence and fighting at close quarters there were two types of double-edged straight-bladed swords, one short about 45–50 cm long and similar to the swords of the other states of the Eastern Zhou period, and the other slightly under a metre long. The former seems to have developed from shorter, dagger-like weapons, usually not more than 30 cm long, that had been developed by mounted steppe nomads, and Qin's early swords are similar in shape to those found along China's northern borders.[21] The latter, found in the pits, seem to have been treated with oxidized chrome, preserving their sharpness and lustre undiminished despite having been buried for two thousand years (*fig.* 33). They may well have been copied from the long sword that had been invented in Austria in the eighth and seventh centuries BC and made its way across central Asia.[22] Such long swords are generally associated with warriors mounted on horseback, but Qin cavalry do not seem to have been equipped with them. Since Qin men were generally shorter in stature, it would have been difficult for them to draw such a long sword from its scabbard, and that is why the charioteer driving the miniature bronze Chariot no. 1 carries his sword on his back.[23]

Cavalry

The riding of horses was first developed in east Asia by steppe dwellers in the north-eastern regions of modern China by Eastern Zhou times,[24] but cavalry only seems to have been adopted by the Chinese in the mid-fourth century BC.[25] Cavalry clearly played crucial roles in campaigns in the mid-third century leading up to the wars of unification under the First Emperor, yet judging by the numbers of cavalry horses and men in the warrior pits, cavalry still seems to have had a tertiary function in battle, supplementing the main fighting force of infantry and chariots. Noticeable in the figure of the Qin cavalry horse is the lack of any stirrups that would have helped the rider mount and given him stability in the saddle, and the forms of saddle and the saddle pad are very similar to ones discovered by Russian archaeologists in the frozen Siberian graves in Pazyryk.[26] No weapons have been discovered associated with the Qin cavalry figurines, but they may have been equipped with bows and arrows, light crossbows or some other weapons. Perhaps these weapons were all stolen by the rebels when they sacked the pits (see p. 143), or perhaps this omission by the artisans was intentional. The short tunic, light armour and well-fitting trousers were clearly intended to enhance the rider's mobility and reduce his weight.

Military texts reveal the kind of actions these early cavalry would

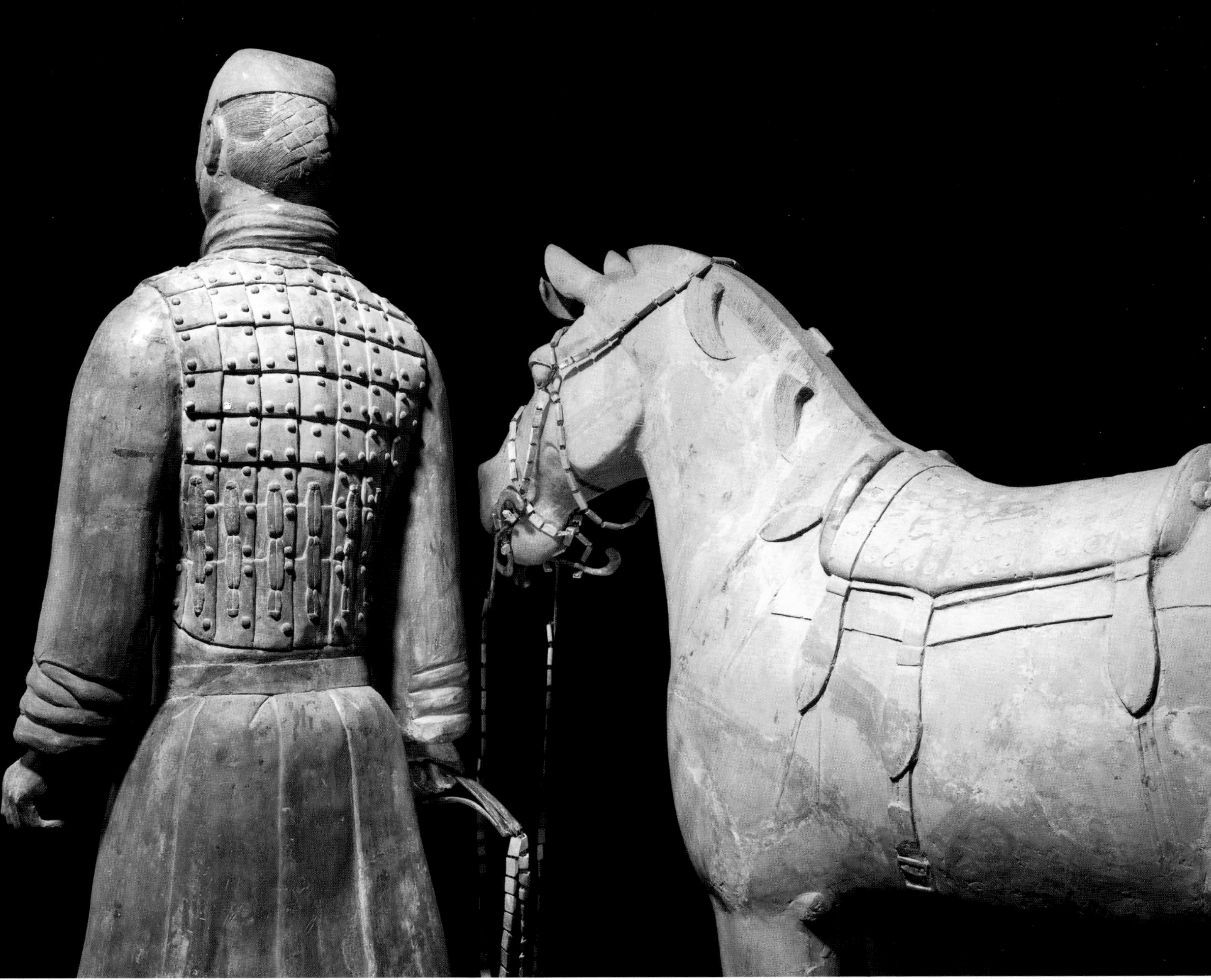

FIG. 35
(opposite) **Cavalrymen wore protective armour over short pleated robes to allow for maximum movement on horseback, and a soft cap tied under the chin. In the northern area of Pit 2, behind ranks of kneeling and standing archers, 108 standing cavalrymen were found holding the reins of their horses.**
Cat. no. 17

FIG. 36
(above) **Back of cavalryman and horse. Note the lack of stirrups on the saddle. The earliest archaeological evidence for the use of stirrups is from a pottery model of a saddled horse found in a fourth-century tomb in south China, and there is only one stirrup.**

have engaged in. They would have acted as scouts or raiders who could devastate an enemy's crops, destroy his ferries or boundary gates, cut off and burn his supply train and lines of communication, harry his stragglers or vanguard before the general was ready to deploy his forces in good order, and make sudden strikes at unexpected places, either during a pitched battle or when the opposing armies were on the march. Sun Bin recommended that a general should split his units of cavalry and chariots into three detachments, one on either flank and one at the rear. He suggested that on flat and easy ground the general should deploy more chariots, but on rugged terrain he should commit more cavalry, and in really precipitous terrain he should use his crossbow men.[27]

Thus by the time of the First Emperor, military specialists had analysed the strengths and weaknesses of the different types of units that composed an army, and the correct deployment of forces in the field of battle depended on the experience and competence of highly skilled generals.

FIG. 38
(opposite) This bronze, tripod cooking vessel (*ding*) was found in a pit containing eleven terracotta figures of acrobats (K9901) located in the south-eastern corner between the inner and outer wall of the First Emperor's tomb (see fig. 161 and p. 140). Its distinctive interlaced decoration is representative of bronzes cast at the Eastern Zhou bronze foundry in Xintian (present-day Houma in Shanxi province). The area was controlled by the Jin kingdom during the Eastern Zhou dynasty and was later conquered by the Qin.
Cat. no. 19

Training

In the society of the Spring and Autumn period aristocrats were trained from a young age in six arts appropriate to their station. Those relevant for war were chariot driving and archery. Under Shang Yang's new social and military system, this educational system was vastly expanded. Both adult males and females were expected to provide corvée labour duty to the state, during which they engaged in construction projects, such as building walls and digging ditches, and all males were expected to perform military service as part of their tax obligation; women seem only to have been required to participate in war if the cities or town in which they lived came under attack. Individuals were registered as adults when they reached the height of 4 feet 11 inches (1.5 metres), normally between the ages of sixteen and seventeen, and from that time on until they retired at fifty-six or sixty years or age, depending on whether they had gained rank or not, they were expected to serve if the state so ordered. In the first two years after reaching adulthood, it seems that males were required to receive military training for one year in their home county or prefecture and then spent one year at the capital or standing guard at the frontiers; then they returned home to work the fields. After that, in each of the four seasons, a time was specified for military training and every three years there was a general review. Thus, although the Qin did not maintain a professional army, its policy of continually refreshing the skills of its conscripts must have ensured that all who served, whether officers or men, were ready and able to perform the duties the state required of them. However, it was not legal for the prefectural overseer, commandant (*wei*) or sergeant major to call up two men from the same household at the same time. If they did, they were heavily fined: this was probably to ensure that each household was capable of producing enough grain to survive.

Exactly how the Qin trained their soldiers is not revealed by the extant sources. Contemporary military manuals suggest, however, that training started with the five-man unit, and when that unit was ready, it was incorporated into the next highest, the ten-man squad, further trained, and so on up to the entire army. They would have been taught how to respond to commands (see below) and to wield weapons in unison or fire bows and crossbows. They may also have received strength and fitness training, since weight-lifting seems to have been a popular pastime: figurines of half-naked muscle-bound entertainers have been found in the First Emperor's tomb complex (see *fig.* 153).

It is likely that Qin selected the tallest and strongest men for service as charioteers and cavalrymen and that they would have received the special training necessary for their tasks: under law, if a recruit failed to learn how to drive adequately after four years of training, his coach was fined and he was obliged to make up four years of statute labour and military service. So undoubtedly there were bad drivers, even in Qin! An overseer of crossbowmen who himself failed to hit the target was fined and dismissed, and his superior officer, the county prefect, was held responsible and punished for his failure.[28] Wang Xueli suggests that the

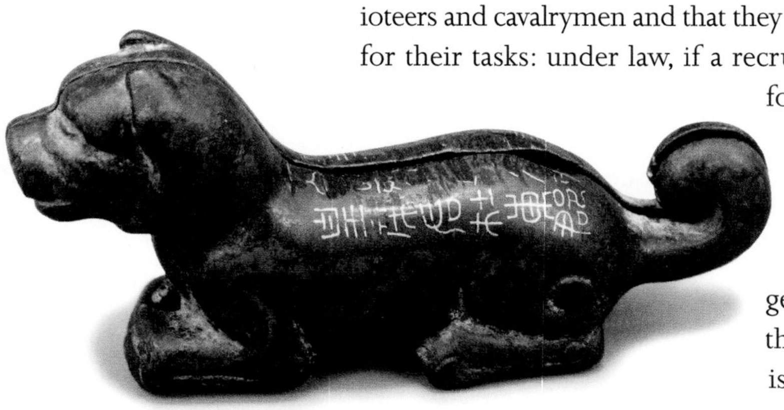

FIG. 37
This bronze tiger-shaped tally has a twelve-character inscription inlaid in gold. It describes it as a tally for the armoured forces. The left half of the tally was kept by the emperor and the right half with the commander in the east (today's Puyang, Henan province).
Cat. no. 18

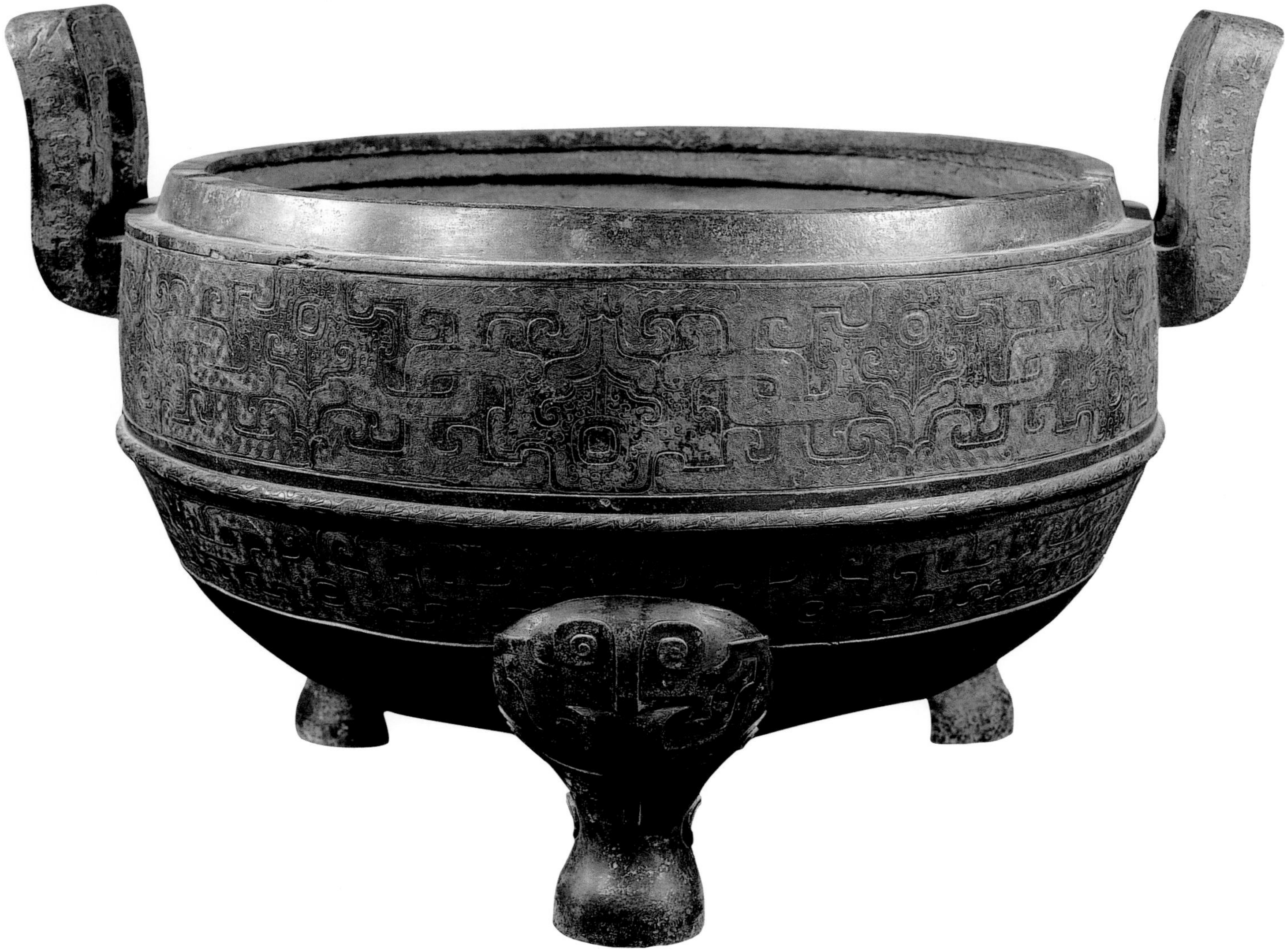

332 figurines in the north-eastern corner of Pit 2 of the First Emperor's mausoleum represent men in a training camp. Eight rows of 160 armoured crossbowmen are kneeling; in front of them are two rows of men, the first in tunics, the second in armour; on either side there stand 96 figurines in tunics, and at the rear are 16 armoured men divided into four groups, of which two comprise officers. According to Wang Xueli, these last depict the overseers of crossbowmen mentioned in the laws.[29]

Military ritual and law

Texts reveal that before any campaign the ruler would have presented an axe to the commanding general in a formal ritual as a symbol of his legal authority to kill the enemy and to execute any officer or man who disobeyed his orders. In fact, it would appear that, until the general returned the axe, even the ruler could not countermand his orders in the field and the ruler's representatives were subject to the general's orders. Quite possibly, cavalry horses attending this ceremony and the formal departure of the army for war would have been clothed with the type of armour found fashioned from stone in the model armoury Pit K9801 (see pp. 181–9).

FIG. 39
(below) **Ritual mace heads (*shu*) were found in Pit 3 of the terracotta army among guards arranged facing each other.**
Cat. no. 20

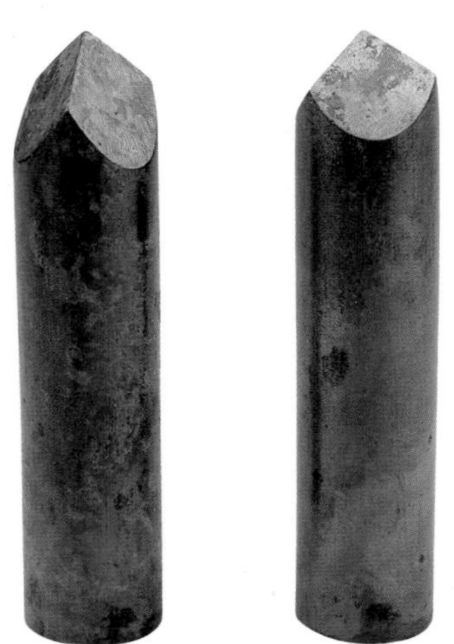

FIG. 40
This percussion instrument (*chunyu*) was sounded, along with bells and drums, during warfare to indicate whether troops should advance or retreat.
Cat. no. 21

In order to ensure that the officers would not abuse their delegated authority, the Qin and its rivals developed a system of tallies that conferred the right to raise forces. These were cast in metal, usually bronze, and often in the shape of a tiger, symbolizing war, and came in two identical parts that were inlaid with inscriptions specifying the number of soldiers the officer could raise (*fig.* 37). On receiving his posting, an officer would be given one half of the tally and the ruler would keep the other half. Only when the central authorities sent out the second half and the officer could 'match' the two halves together, could he legitimately raise the forces listed in the inscription.

Probably before any serious engagement, the general would perform a sacrifice and divine the outcome of the battle in a ceremony attended by ritual specialists and his senior officers. This seems to be what is represented in Pit 3 where the remains of an animal sacrifice were discovered. The cooking of the meats in these sacrifices would normally have been accomplished in bronze vessels, such as the huge bronze *ding*-tripod, probably captured from the ancestral temple of one of Qin's enemies (*fig.* 38). An honour guard of men standing to attention in two rows and holding maces (*shu*) fitted into long wooden poles (*fig.* 39) protects the officiants of the ceremony. These rituals were designed to bring the unseen spiritual forces to aid the combatants, but of course late Warring States armies also used practical means to control their forces on the battlefield.

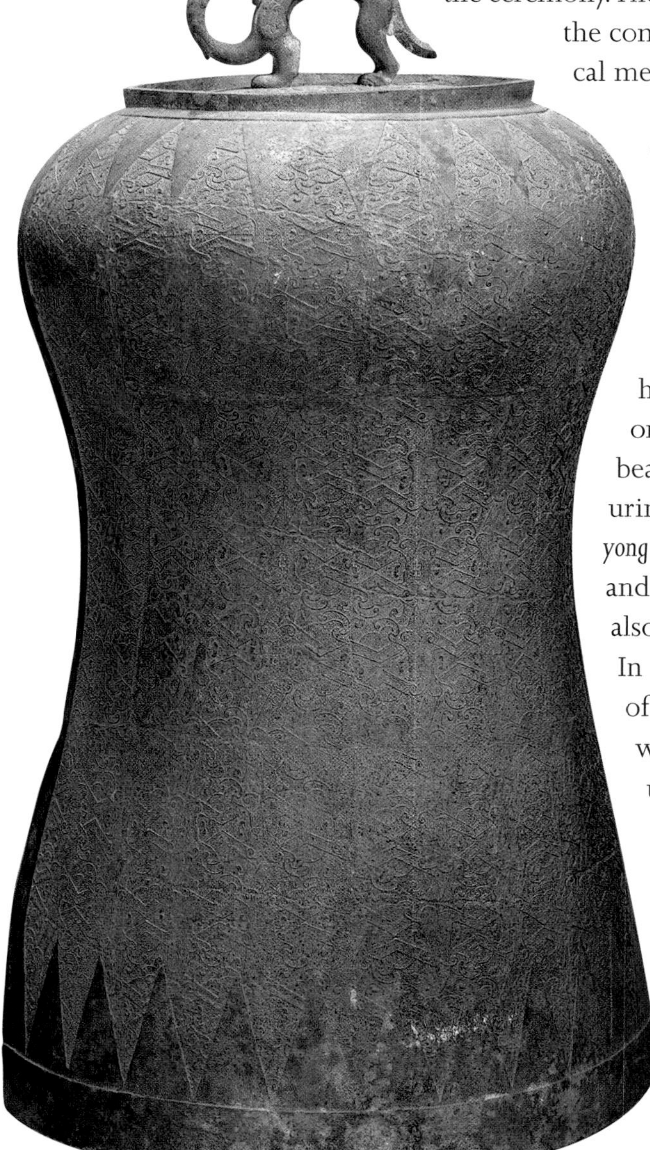

Control of forces on the battlefield

Flags had been invented in the Shang dynasty as a means of attracting the attention of the gods and ancestors and encouraging them to descend to help their living descendants. By the Qin period all stores were marked by flags bearing different designs, all officers had their special flag, and long weapons and chariots were also decorated with long banners and streamers. Various types of drums were beaten to signal advance; large *chunyu* bells, often decorated with figurines of animals in the shape of a bridge at the top (*fig.* 40), and small *yong* hand-bells (*fig.* 41) were rung to signal retreat or redeployment; and flags and banners, carried by the officers in their chariots, were also waved to signal movements to the troops under their command. In addition, it is likely that some armies distinguished the positions of their constituent units by different coloured uniforms,[30] and there would have been badges indicating the placing of men within their unit. However, a letter from a couple of young Qin soldiers, recently discovered in a tomb, reveals that soldiers were expected to buy their own clothing on the open market (they would have been issued their armour), and the colouring on the Qin pottery warriors does not suggest any particular organizational structure.

There is no description of an actual Qin battle, so we do not know exactly how the drums and bells were sounded and the flags and banners waved, but we do know that military forces and their behaviour in the field were governed by a stringent set of written laws, a few of which have recently been discovered: there was a 'Law on Abandoning Positions and Fleeing' and a 'Law on Battlefield Executions', which must have specified the circumstances and manner by which officers could administer punishment to their men. Given the size of the Qin armies by late Warring States times and the necessity for enforcing discipline in what was a conscript army composed mostly of peasants, this is hardly surprising.

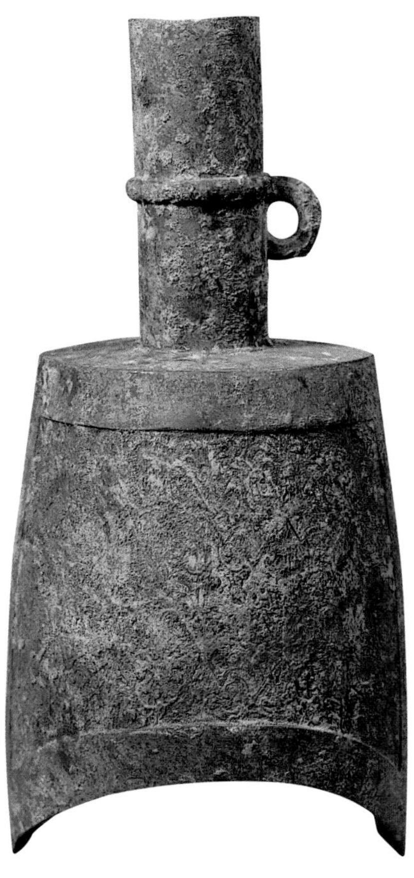

FIG. 41
This *yong* bell was found in Pit 1 near the command chariots. A loop around its handle indicates that it was suspended, and as it lacks a clapper, it would have been struck on its side.
Cat. no. 22

Armouries and storage facilities

Judging from recent archaeological discoveries of legal and administrative texts, the Qin were obsessed with managing the production, manufacture, distribution and circulation, from raw materials to finished goods, of every sort of object, and they tried to control who had access to and authority over materials, equipment and weapons that could be used in warfare. Their development of a sophisticated accounting and management system may have been one of their principal achievements and one of the main factors that enabled them to supply their field armies and support them with the entire state economy. Government factories produced bronze vessels and utensils, textiles made from silk cloth, lacquerware and probably various types of pottery, and sold them on the open market, while ordinary citizens produced and sold all sorts of grains, beans, hemp and other agricultural products; horses, oxen, sheep, goats, pigs, ducks and chickens, together with their flesh, skin, horns, fat and bones; and objects made of stone and jade, various types of wood and bamboo, pottery, bronze and iron, textiles and articles of daily life.[31] Qin officials taxed market transactions and a statutory regulation specified that all goods sold in the market had to have a price tag if they were offered for sale at one 'cash' or more.[32] So, despite the fact that the 'Legalist' chancellor Shang Yang had emphasized that the state should pay attention only to agriculture and warfare, and had despised mercantile activities, later Qin bureaucrats and rulers obviously ignored his narrow-minded advice and chose to develop and exploit all the resources of the state and all means of production for their long-term policy objective, the conquest of all the rival Warring States. Weapons, however, were another matter and a state monopoly in Qin, not being allowed to circulate on the open market.

So far archaeologists have not discovered any of the Qin armouries that were probably largely responsible for the manufacture and storage of weapons and armour used in battle. No building has been found within the site of Xianyang city comparable to the enormous Han armoury found in the southern section of their capital, Chang'an.[33] Protected by rammed-earth walls 710 metres long east to west and 322 metres north to south, the Han armoury consisted of seven separate buildings divided into individual rooms that probably contained different types of equipment: over 40,000 iron armour plates alone were discovered in one section. An inventory dating from the middle of the Han dynasty, recently discovered in a tomb in eastern China, probably records the vast holdings of this storehouse. Since the armoury was built at the very beginning of the Han, it may have been modelled on Qin precedent; and it is most likely that Pit K9801 at the First Emperor's mausoleum, where enormous quantities of stone armour, helmets and bardings (horse armour) were uncovered, was meant to be a replica of an above-ground armoury.[34]

Excavated in the 1999 season, this is the largest accessory pit to the south of the tomb, covering more than 13,000 sq. metres, but the armour for both men and horses deposited there was probably not meant for actual combat. If it was ever used in real life, it is more likely to have been worn on ritual occasions, during special ceremonies.

Other states in competition with Qin, like Qi in the north-east, also built armouries within the walls of their capital cities and in other metropolitan areas, and even in county towns, where they manufactured and stored weapons.[35] Qi apparently issued rules on armouries, too, which specified the responsibilities of the various officials in charge and laid down regulations for annual inspections and control of the heat and humidity inside, as well as the precise measurements of the different types of weapons to be produced.[36] That walled towns contained such important facilities is perhaps why they became such tempting targets in the warfare of late Warring States times.

Quality control mechanisms

So far no Qin legal statutes or other regulations on armouries have been discovered, but other related laws have. Every single item stored or owned by the state had to have its identifying mark stamped on it, including animals like horses and oxen, and the officials had to keep registers of the material under their control. Every item leaving or entering a depository had to be accounted for and checks were made regularly to ensure that the total number of items corresponded with what was recorded in the register. This was especially true when an official left his post, whether to be transferred, promoted or demoted. The officials responsible had to make up any deficiencies out of their own salaries. Artisans working in government workshops that produced poor quality goods were fined and three years of continuous poor quality were punished even more heavily. To ensure that responsibility was shared, all members of the unit were punished together, those in supervisory positions being obliged to pay the heavier penalty.

Furthermore, most weapons were inscribed with the name of the artisans and officials responsible for their manufacture, all the way up to the chancellor, as well as the date of manufacture. This allowed the authorities to check the quality of the workmanship and assign responsibility should any defect appear. Similar inscriptions are found on the weapons of other states. What particularly marks Qin arms in the period of King Zheng's reign is the standardization of weapons and their component parts. The shafts of all arrows were manufactured to be precisely 70 cm long and painted in three colours, with a triangular-prism head of exactly the same dimensions, so that if a shaft broke, another head could be attached without any effect on the arrow's aim or penetrating power. If part of a crossbow trigger mechanism broke, it could be replaced with a spare without any impairment of function.

Medical treatment of wounds

No army can stay in the field for long, fight offensive engagements or defend successfully against determined aggressors without carefully ministering to the injuries suffered by its soldiers. With the growing size of battle groups in late Warring States times, the increasing length of campaigns and modifications in the types of forces put into the field, it is likely that the armies of Qin and its enemies suffered a variety of injuries from weapons such as swords, dagger-axes, halberds, spears, arrows and crossbow bolts, as well as from falling off horses and infectious diseases, the result of gathering large numbers of men in densely crowded camps and formations. The same is true of the animals, especially horses and oxen that accompanied the troops on campaign, the cavalry and chariot horses and the beasts of burden pulling the grain supplies. By the third century BC, when Qin was battling for supremacy, all armies were accompanied by doctors and veterinarians.

FIG. **42**
Cavalry horse from Pit 2. Horses were initially used to draw chariots. It was not until the Warring States period that mounted cavalry first appeared. Pit 2 of the terracotta army, thought to represent the Left Army, was the only pit that contained mounted cavalry. Cavalry horses appear to have been modelled slightly taller, but shorter in length, than chariot horses. Like the terracotta army figures, the horses are all slightly different even though they were made in moulds.
Cat. no. 23

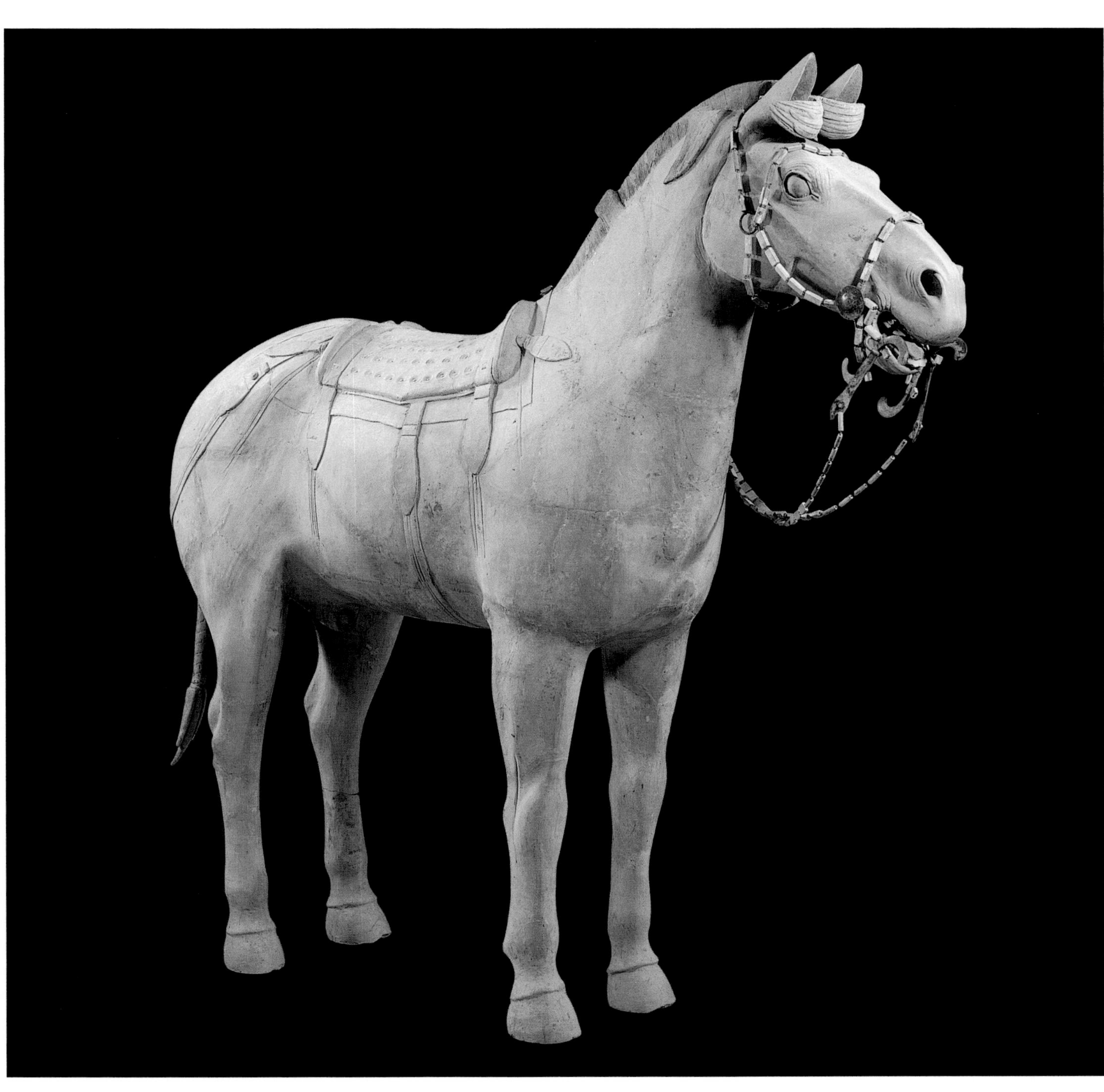

The earliest mention of a treatment for a military injury, sores suffered by soldiers and navy personnel in the winter, is found in a fourth-to-third-century BC Daoist philosophical text. The story records that the man bought the recipe for a song from a family of silk-workers who had invented a salve to treat chapped hands. He marketed the recipe to the contending armies of the south-eastern states of Wu and Yue and made a fortune. Not the last person to benefit financially from warfare.

Much more information about early treatment of wounds from weapons is found in the recently discovered medical text 'Recipes for Fifty-Two Ailments', which was buried in 168 BC during the early Han dynasty and probably represents medical traditions handed down from Qin and Warring States times. The range of ingredients and of methods of treatment is quite large. In some cases there is a strong element of magic and ritual performance. For example, some recipes recommend the incineration of scalp hair and pressing the remains in the wound to stop bleeding, where hair is used to magically 'bind' the wound, while another advises the chanting of the incantation 'Man, staunch! Woman, vinegar!' and then drawing five lines on the ground while the victim is still losing blood.[37] None of the other recipes recommend vinegar to stop bleeding; rather, wounds are swabbed with a variety of salves made out of pig lard, pig faeces and human snot or semen, which were used to prevent the formation of a scar. From a strictly scientific point of view, the last two ingredients would be likely to encourage, rather than limit, infection, and their application can be attributed to a belief in the ritual power of bodily excreta. Semen and snot were also thought to be refined *qi*, the primordial energy out of which the cosmos was believed to be made, and semen was also considered, in the newly emerging medicine of systematic correspondence, as quintessentially *yang* and thus a generator of life. The word for faeces, on the other hand, was the same as that for 'arrow' (*shi*), and arrows were fired to exorcise evil spirits. Thus, in the third-century-BC Qin-dynasty almanac texts from Shuihudi, Hubei province, buried in 217 BC, dog faeces were used to drive ghosts from people's houses.[38] As a consequence, the chant may not necessarily be just a description of an act but may be making use of the sound of the words to drive off evil spirits and be calling on the symbolic role of man and woman as joint procreators to effect a cure and ensure continued life.

Other recipes in the Mawangdui corpus called for the drinking of mixtures of drugs made out herbal and animal (such as moles) ingredients and consuming them with wine. In one instance, the taking of the medicine to eliminate pain from a metal wound has to be accompanied by abstention from eating 'fish, pork, horseflesh, turtles, snakes, odorous foods and *mazhu* greens' and avoiding sexual intercourse in the 'inner chamber', while no other temporal taboos are necessary.[39] This last injunction suggests that in treating wounds there were rules derived from popular religious and ritual beliefs and practices that specified on what days or at what times of the day therapy could be applied. Thus, by Qin times the basic patterns of treatment of wounds had been established: the Chinese primarily used herbal remedies accompanied by various ritual procedures, while surgery for broken bones sustained in falls was not normal until the arrival of the Mongols in the thirteenth century.

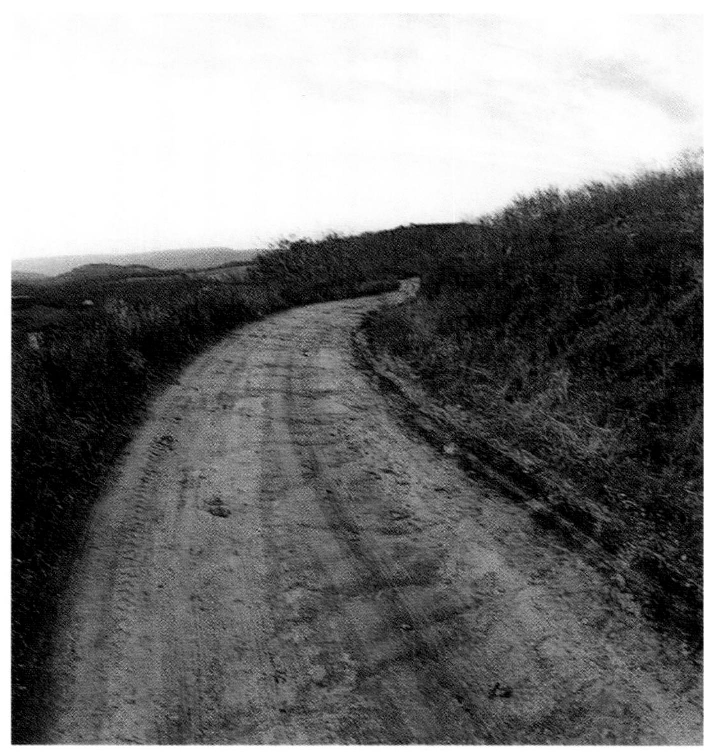
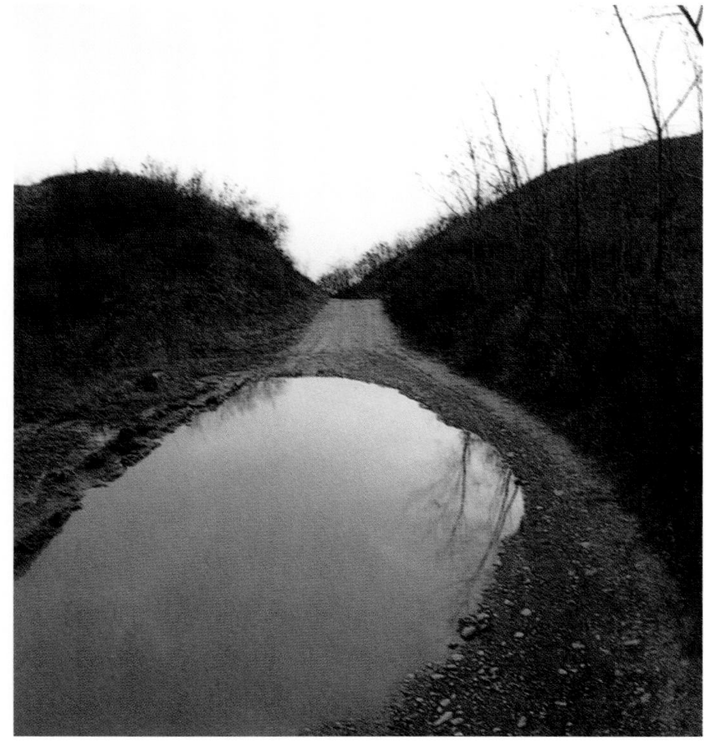

FIIG. 43
Two views of the Qin Straight Road. The First Emperor built a network of highways radiating out from Xianyang and a Straight Road north to the Great Wall and the northern frontier.

FIG. 44
(following pages) **Aerial view of the Qin wall at Guyang, Inner Mongolia.**

Long walls in the Warring States and the Qin Great Wall

In 215 BC the First Emperor ordered General Meng Tian to march north into the steppe with 300,000 soldiers to attack the Xiongnu nomads, drive them out of their pastureland south of the bend of the Yellow River and construct what is now known as the Great Wall. This massive military and engineering effort was a culmination of several hundred years of wall building by the rival states. These earlier walls, sometimes made of stones and rubble, and sometimes of tamped earth, were built for multiple functions. First, they symbolically marked the boundaries of a state's territories, indicating to both its enemies and the population that it claimed legal and religious jurisdiction of what lay inside. Second, they were of military and economic importance. The walls made it that much more difficult for raiding enemy mounted on either chariots or cavalry horses to roam at will inside and gather information or booty. As the walls were penetrated by roads traversing through gates and passes at strategic points, enemy forces were naturally forced to approach those well-defended locations and merchants and travellers were also obliged to enter or leave a state by the same roads. This allowed a state to tax the trade passing through the border and verify the credentials of travellers – the Chinese had invented passports to monitor travellers by about 500 BC. Third, they could be used as part of a signalling system. Men patrolling the walls and gates could report back to their superiors the movement of enemy forces outside the walls. The Great Wall continued to function in these ways: it was not manned along the entirety of its length, but only intermittently, at strategic points.

In fact, General Meng's wall was not the first to be built along the northern border: both the Yan and Zhao states had pushed into the territory of the nomads,

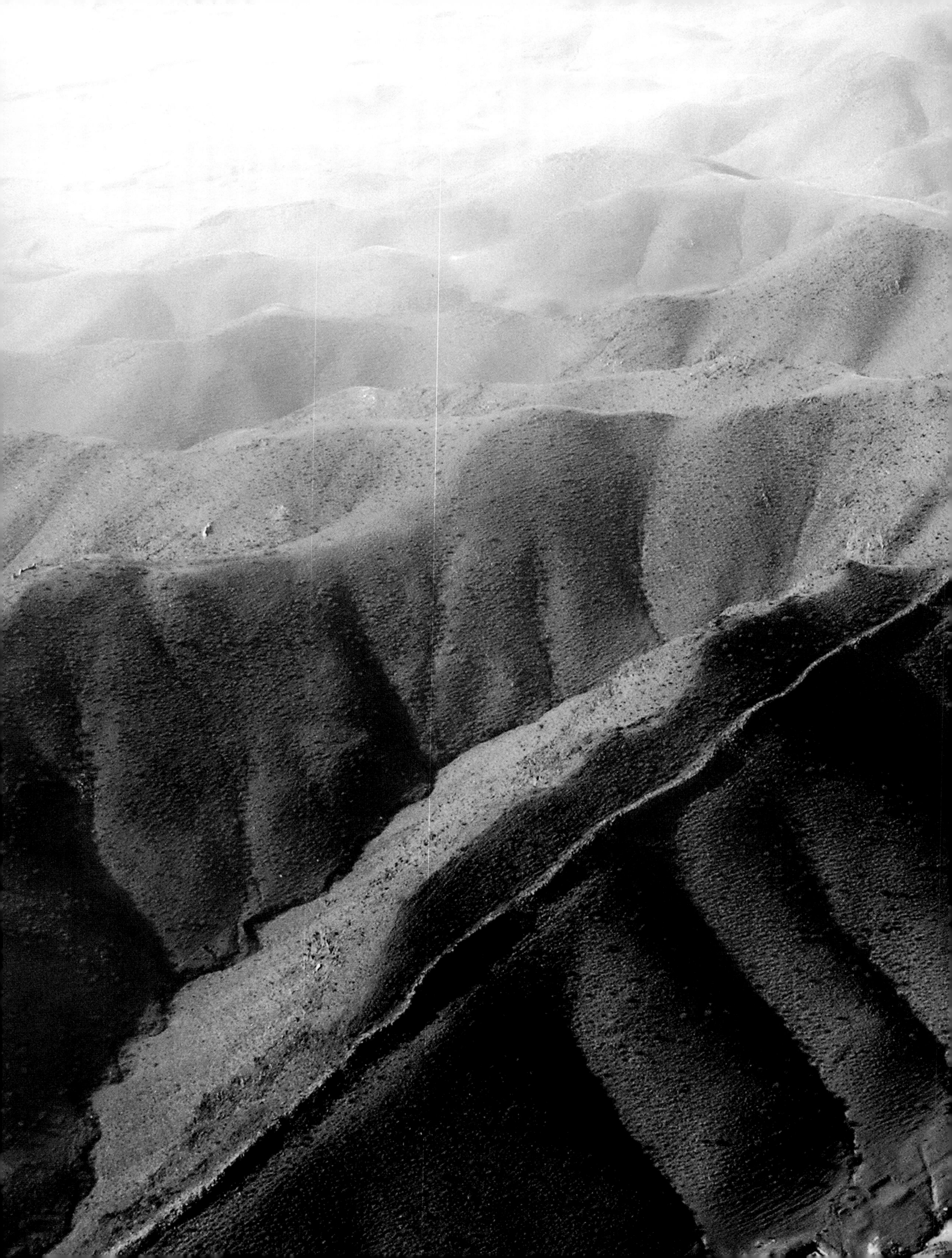

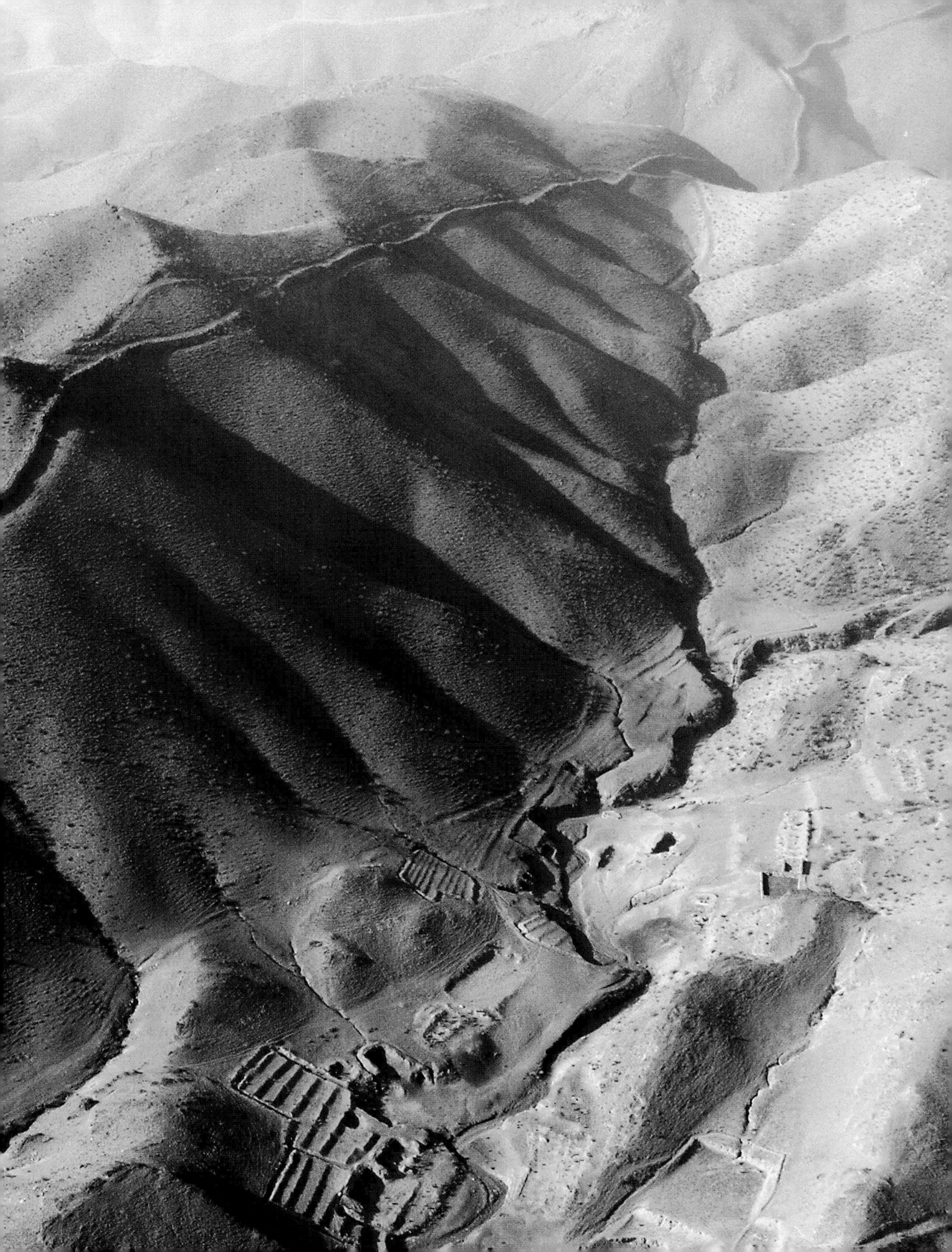

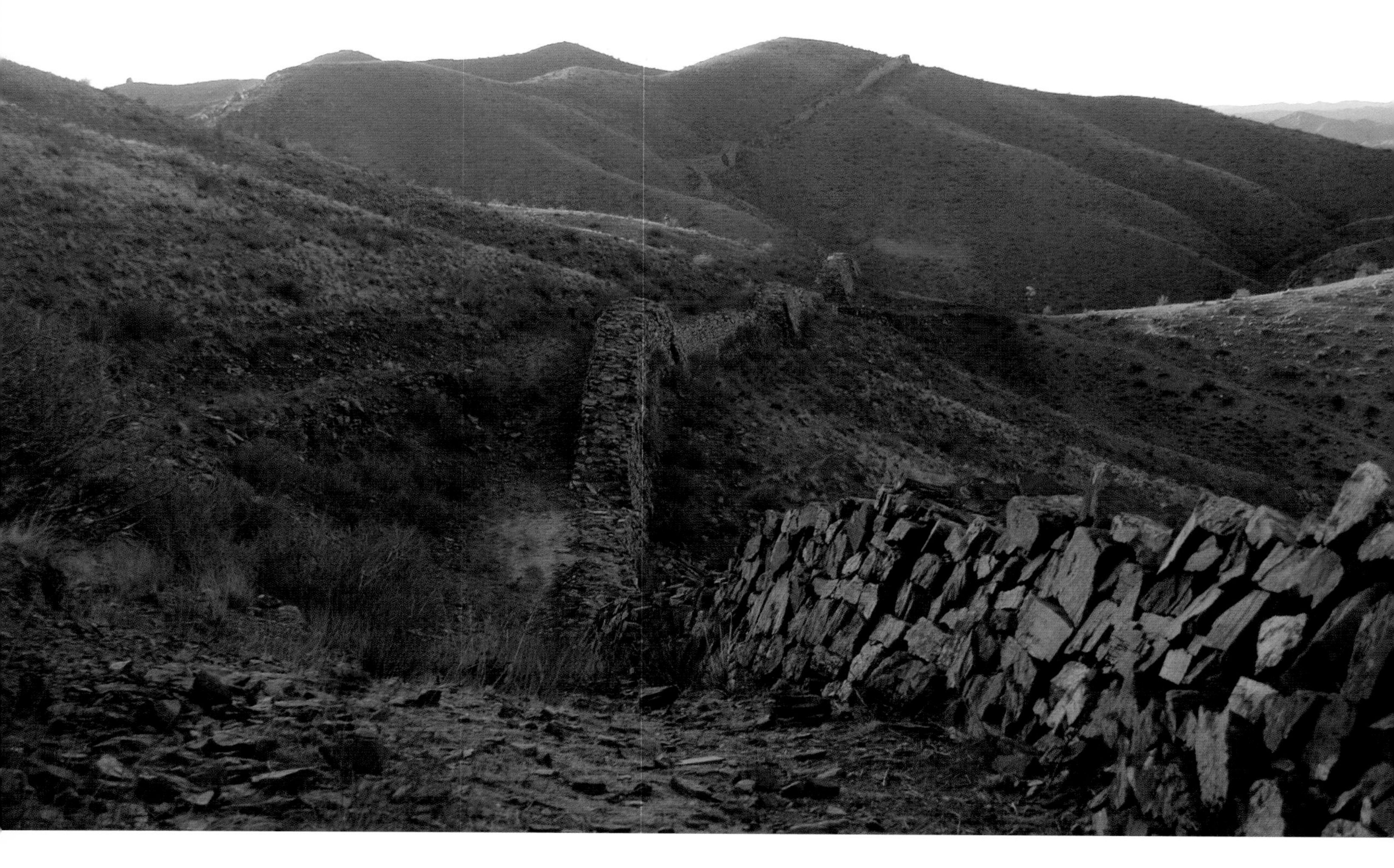

FIG. 45
Section of wall built during the Qin dynasty at Guyang, Inner Mongolia.

as had the First Emperor's grandfather, King Zhaoxiang. The latter had built a wall diagonally across the territory to the north into the Ordos south of the Yellow River, one of the prime grazing areas of the Xiongnu nomads. Archaeologists have recently been tracing the lines of the Qin and later Han Great Wall, as well as the Qin Straight Road that was built to link the capital region with the northern borders (*fig.* 21),[40] and have found that the Qin Great Wall was composed of three main sections. The first was built to the west of King Zhaoxiang's wall along the western edge of the Yellow River. The second to the north generally ran outside the earlier Zhao walls. The easternmost section ran parallel to the Yan walls and further south into modern Korea. Thus the Qin claimed much more territory from the steppe nomads than Chinese polities had ever done before.[41] General Meng's advance caused a crisis in the leadership of the Xiongnu. Shortly after the First Emperor's death in 210 and the coup d'état that led to the forced suicide of the heir apparent, Fu Su, and Meng's execution, the Xiongnu reorganized their military and political institutions and founded a steppe empire that challenged the Chinese for several centuries.[42] The Great Wall, in reality a series of multiple walls, thus became a source of great contention between the steppe nomads and the sedentary Chinese and could never be occupied or controlled for any length of time by either side until the Manchu Qing conquered central Asia and destroyed the power of the Mongols in the eighteenth century. It was never a static line of defence that was able to hold the nomads at bay outside Chinese territory.

Conclusion

In the light of the evidence outlined above, can we isolate any particular factors that enabled the Qin under the leadership of King Zheng to conquer his enemies and unify China in 221 BC? Was it the sophistication of their military technology, and their ability to motivate their officers and soldiers with their system of rewards and punishments and with their religious beliefs? Was it their long-term strategy maintained through successive rulers after the deaths of Duke Xiao and Yang Shang? Was it their tactics and their ability to integrate, coordinate and exploit the advantages of chariots, infantry and cavalry on the battlefield, or the brilliance of their generals, like Bai Qi and Meng Tian? Was it their organization of weapons production and their logistical systems, or the failures of their enemies, who themselves had access to the same or even more advanced technology and to the same techniques of control and exploitation of human and natural resources? Or was it a combination of these and other factors? Perhaps we shall never know. But at least with the ongoing excavations and analysis of the First Emperor's terracotta army and associated burials, and the continuing discoveries of texts and government archives of Qin and early Han date, we are closer to understanding the long- and short-term historical processes that were involved in the creation of the world's longest-lasting empire by one of history's most influential figures, the First Emperor, King Zheng.

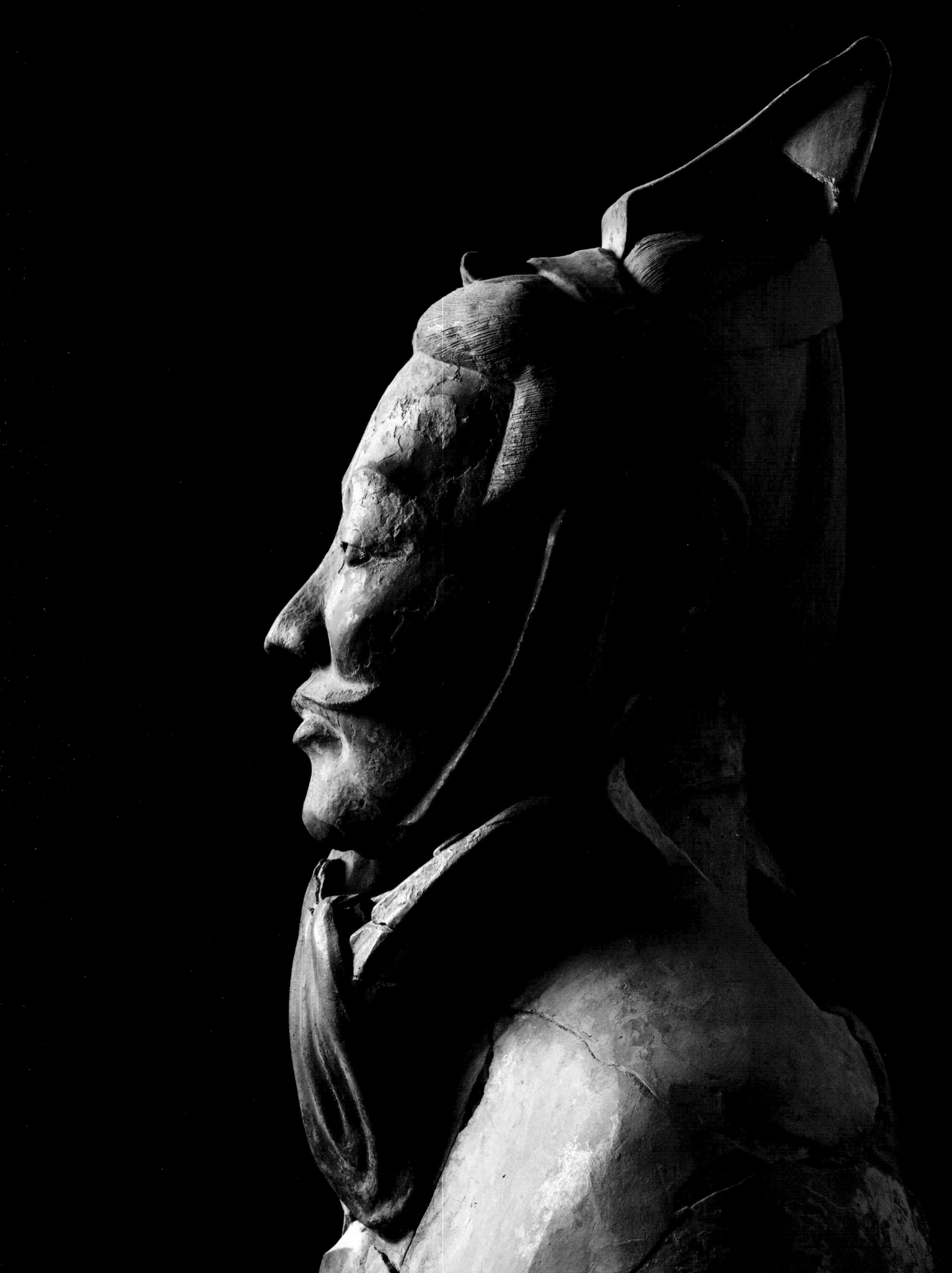

CHAPTER 2

THE FIRST EMPEROR AND THE QIN EMPIRE

MICHAEL LOEWE

Ying Zheng, who ruled as the First Emperor of the Qin dynasty from 221 to 210 BC, bequeathed a legacy to China that long affected the rise and fall of dynasties, shaped the form of government and established firm, authoritarian ways of governing the land and its peoples. This heritage developed from the practices of the separate kingdoms that had preceded his formation of the one and only empire, the radical innovations that he introduced and the ruthless measures by which his authority was maintained. The forms of his imperial administration remained largely unchanged for some 800 years until major modifications, which suited new social and economic conditions, took place under the Sui (AD 589–618) and Tang (AD 618–907) dynasties. Nevertheless, much of what he had established, such as territorial divisions between small units of territories known as 'counties', was unaffected. Many of these would survive until the end of the imperial era (1911) and can even be recognized today after the adoption of political and other systems from the Western world.

Like some other Chinese dynasties, Qin was short-lived and its achievements were seen to their full extent only during the rule of its immediate successor, the Western Han dynasty, which lasted for 200 years (206 BC–AD 9). Western Han was able to exploit the radical successes of Qin to build up even greater power and influence and enjoy material prosperity on a new scale. Similar examples, in which a long-lasting dynasty drew strength from a short-lived predecessor's example, are seen in the cases of the Xin (AD 9–23), the Sui (AD 589–618) and perhaps the Yuan (1271–1368) dynasties. However, as the histories of these brief regimes were

FIG. 46
(left) **Detail of a terracotta official showing his official hat with ribbon tied under the chin. These officials show the First Emperor's government for the afterlife, modelled on that in real life.**
Cat. no. 24

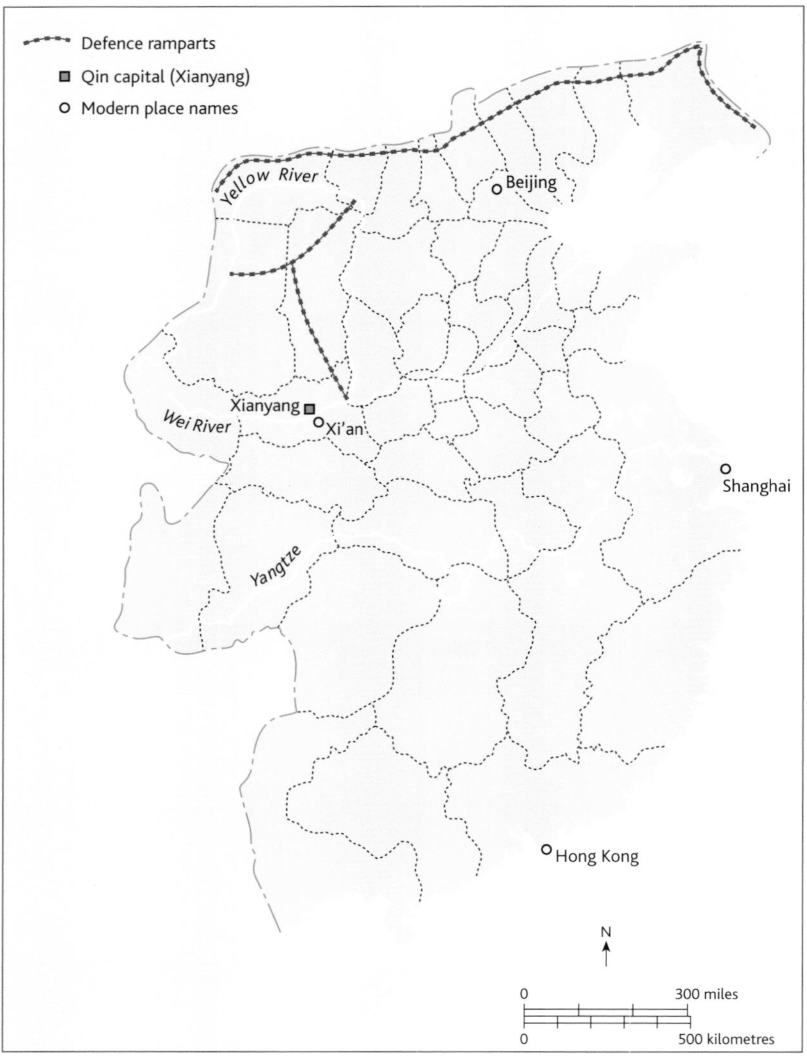

FIG. 47
Map of the Qin empire showing the thirty-six commanderies or administrative divisions.

written by officials who were obliged to paint their rulers as ruthless tyrants and to vilify their memories, a harsh reputation has attached to the First Qin Emperor and Wang Mang, sole emperor of Xin. Occasionally in later centuries, when a dynasty was losing its power and the country its social cohesion, a few brave men would ignore the virulent criticism that had become traditional and call for a restoration of some of the ways of the Qin dynasty.

Early rulers in China and the emergence of Qin

Although Ying Zheng is correctly described as China's first emperor, the term 'emperor' often appears somewhat loosely and incorrectly in accounts of the centuries and millennia that preceded him. China's mythology includes stories of 'emperors' of antiquity, either human beings who acted as leaders of a populace, or human or divine culture heroes who taught mankind rudimentary skills such as those of agriculture or metallurgy. There were also rulers, such as the 'Yellow Emperor', who were endowed with nothing but fine and noble qualities that they devoted to the welfare of the people. None of these, however, could be said to have been 'emperors' in the same way as Ying Zheng and his successors of later dynasties.

In more strictly practical and realistic terms archaeology tells of various types of human habitation in China during different neolithic periods (from 5,000 to 3,000 BC). In historical times the earliest examples of writing record the activities of leaders who were acknowledged as kings under the term *wang* and ruled a kingdom known as Shang or Yin (*c.*1500–1050 BC). China was now in the Bronze Age, as the ritual and sacrificial vessels buried with those kings, and bearing inscriptions, testify. From perhaps the twelfth century BC information became more profuse. Inscriptions, cast on the enduring medium of a bronze vessel, and some existing documents, which were framed perhaps *c.*800 BC, bear witness to the practice of kingship in Western Zhou (1050–771 BC). Records of the following centuries, known as the Spring and Autumn period (*Chunqiu*, 770–475 BC),[1] include much that is anecdotal, much that stems from rhetoric rather than statements of attested fact. Such documents may tell of ritual acts, alliances and fighting that took place between leaders who emerged from the eighth century onwards almost independently of the kings of Zhou. Fuller accounts chronicle the actions and words of the leaders in the next few centuries during a phase known as the Warring States (*Zhanguo*, 475–221 BC), but these again cannot be accepted as a reliable historical record.

One of these eighth-century leaders bore the title of Duke of Qin (Qin Gong, from 777 BC), which was transmitted to his descendants on a hereditary basis; and it was to this line that the First Emperor of Qin was to trace his descent and claim his authority. Twenty-four dukes followed the founder of the line until 325 BC when one of them assumed the more glorious and senior title of King of Qin, to be known as Huiwen Wang. Five kings followed, the last being named Zheng Wang, who took the further step of adopting the title of emperor (*huangdi*), thereby claiming and demonstrating his superiority over two parties: his kingly predecessors in Qin and the self-styled kings of the other Warring States whom he had conquered.

Qin had arisen in the west (present-day Shaanxi province or further west) and in subsequent years came to be scorned as deriving from a hinterland, distant from those areas where it was boasted that a civilized way of life had been developed. As early as 645 BC Qin had gained territory west of the Yellow River at the expense of Jin, and a few years later it acquired more by taking over lands in which some of the non-assimilated peoples of the north (the Rong) operated. But with the failure to take these expansionist moves further, Qin remained outside the central area that was now witnessing the major growth of Chinese culture.

By the later part of the fifth century BC or perhaps earlier new political forms were appearing. Many of the leaders during the Spring and Autumn period had succumbed to the ambitions of their neighbours and their lands had been amalgamated into larger units ruled by one of these newly proclaimed kings. Like their predecessors, they too engaged in fighting their contemporaries in order to strengthen their power; and they were now able to do so with greatly superior organs of government and material means. By the fourth century a leader of a state could call on more individuals who had mastered the art of writing and could perform the duties of government officials; documents that were being written in the new form of strips of wood carried some of the facts and figures upon which an effective control of a population must depend; and refinements in metallurgical skills were producing more and better weapons of war, defensive armour and agricultural tools.

In this period, the latter part of the Warring States, the kingdom of Qin rose

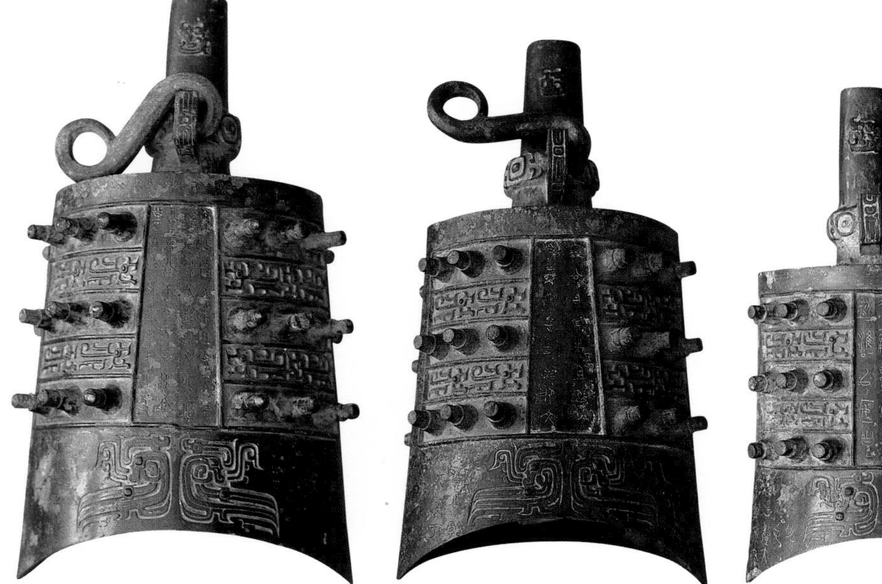

FIG. **48**
Three *zhong* bells, part of a set of five *zhong* bells and three *bo* bells probably belonging to Duke Wu of Qin (r. 697–678 BC), one of the First Emperor's ancestors. Excavated from Pingyang, the Qin capital from 714 to 677 BC, their inscriptions are important as they show that the Qin believed that they had inherited the heavenly mandate to rule, which had previously belonged to the Zhou. The language used is also in the same style as that of the First Emperor's mountain inscriptions (see pp. 108–11). These types of ritual bells were buried in sets in the period before the Qin unification.
Cat. no. 25

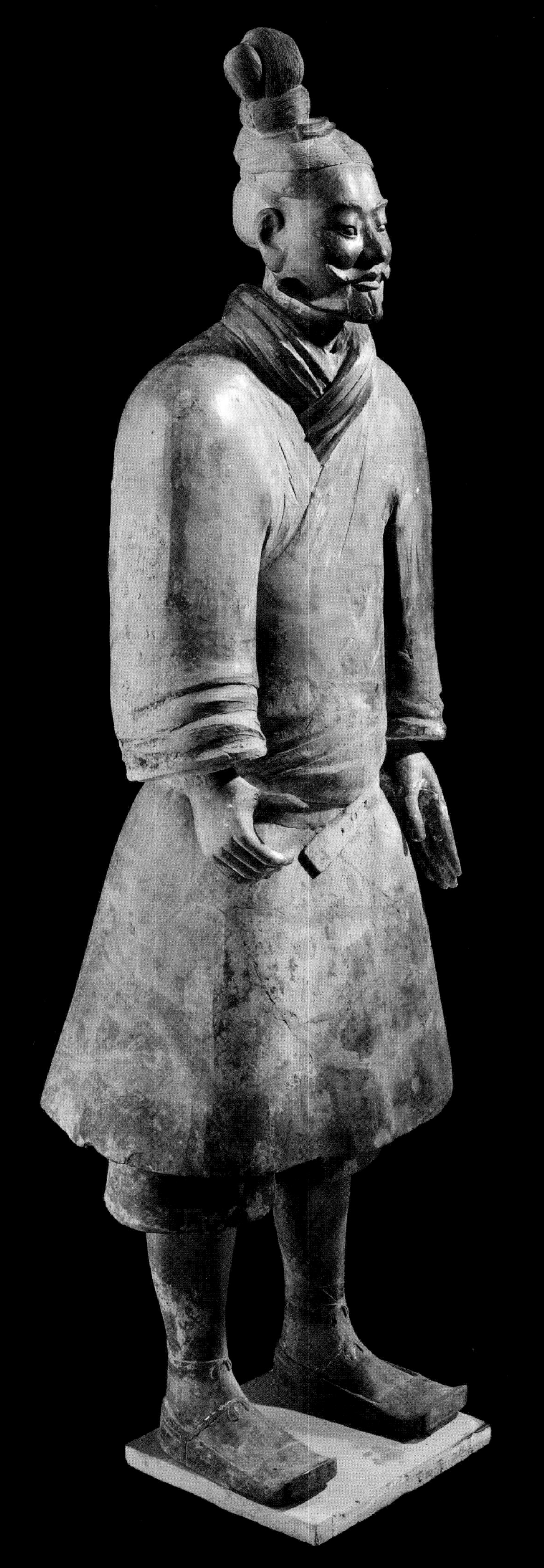

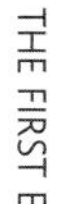

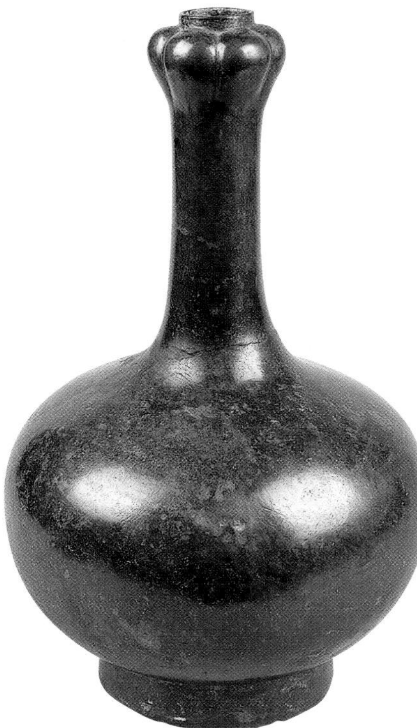

to a dominant position, conquering contemporary kingdoms on the field of battle or forcing their leaders to cede territory and then to surrender their lands and their authority completely. At times Qin was defeated by its adversaries, as when it lost territory to the neighbouring kingdom of Wei in 385 BC. But a major change occurred when Shang Yang started to build up Qin's military strength. Acquisition of the rich lands of Shu and Ba to the south-west, corresponding to the present-day province of Sichuan, marked a major growth of territory and an increase of material resources (started 441 and completed 316 BC). Aware that Qin's ambitions now posed a dangerous threat, a few men of eloquence and standing in other states persuaded some of the kingdoms to forge an alliance whereby they would take joint action to prevent such an advance; in response, others persuaded some of the kings that resistance to Qin's power would be impossible and that their safety lay in acting together to appease the newly arisen conqueror. Neither party's efforts saved a kingdom from elimination.

In the course of its advances, which lasted for some seventy years, Qin took over the territory of Song (286 BC), which had been associated with the earlier regime of Shang, and the remnant of Western Zhou (256 BC). The three much larger territories of Han, Zhao and Wei followed (between 230 and 225 BC), as did Chu in the Yangtze River valley (223); Yan in the north-east (222), and Qi in the Shandong peninsula (221). Lu, a small enclave there that had become renowned in literary and scholarly circles for its association with Kongzi (Confucius, 551–479 BC), had already been taken by Chu and was thus now within Qin.

A single authority could for the first time claim to govern the greater part of the area that we now call China. There is, however, no reliable account of the diplomatic steps or military campaigns whereby other kingdoms were brought to heel, and much remains to be learnt about how exactly this was achieved. Nor can we necessarily assume that those who effected Qin's successes had complete knowledge of the territorial extent of the lands whose names they knew or a concept of a single realm that corresponded to what we now call China. In addition, effective as Qin's elimination of the other kingdoms was, their names survived in China's history, to be adopted as dynastic titles some five centuries or more after Qin itself had disappeared.[2]

FIG. **49**
(left) **Light infantryman, found in Pit 1.**
Cat. no. 26

FIG. **50**
(above) **This garlic-headed vessel (*hu*) is an example of a bronze made in the Qin state (5th–3rd century BC).**
Cat. no. 27

FIG. **51**
(below) **This bronze vessel (*gui*) is inscribed with its capacity and date, 222 BC. It was found in a hoard in the vicinity of Xi'an. Warring States period, Qin state.**
Cat. no. 28

FIG. **52**
(right) **This bronze vessel (*zhong*) has an inscription showing that it was made in the state of Wei. It was probably captured during the process of unification and was excavated in Xianyang, the Qin capital. Warring States period, Wei state.**
Cat. no. 29

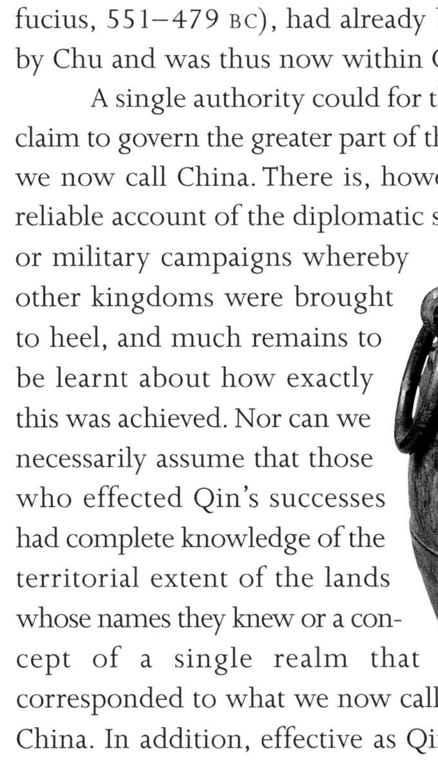

Developing principles of government

Several advisers are named as men who gave guidance to the rulers of Qin from the fourth century BC onwards, enabling them to increase their power and assert their strength. Slender and somewhat questionable as our sources of information are for this time, they are reasonably reliable in their accounts of Shang Yang and Shen Buhai in this connection, and for Han Fei in the century to follow.

Shang Yang (c.385–338 BC), also known as Gongsun Yang, was a native of a small community or state named Wey (to be distinguished from the much larger contemporary kingdom of Wei), whence he moved to Qin (see pp. 34–5). There he acted as the senior official of government, termed chancellor, from 359 to 350 BC. Adopting and implementing the suggestions made by his predecessors, and complementing those with ideas of his own, he transformed Qin's government in radically significant ways; he was to leave a characteristic stamp on the administration of the First Emperor.

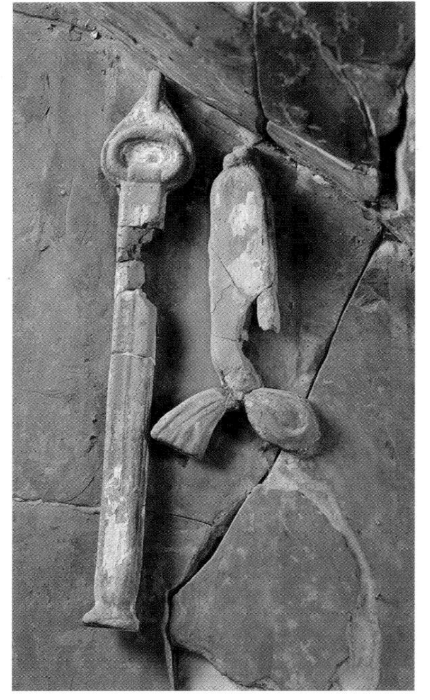

In the earlier days of Zhou and its successor kingdoms a hereditary title brought with it the possession of land, social and political prestige, and material and legal privileges. Such distinctions, sometimes seen as those of an aristocracy or as part of a so-called 'feudal system', survived in different forms and in different degrees throughout China's dynastic history until 1911. But, thanks in the first instance to Shang Yang and his teachers, a further highly significant principle was introduced that characterized much public service thereafter: it was recognized that individual merit could be of as great or greater value to the ruler of a kingdom than descent from a distinguished ancestor, that it could be exploited for the benefit of the government and that it deserved rewards of the highest order. Qin introduced this principle in Shang Yang's time by setting up a series of seventeen ranks or grades or orders (*jue*), which were conferred in direct response to services rendered to the kingdom. At the lowest level such services were valued according to the number of enemy soldiers whom a man had killed in battle; at the highest level, where the rewards might include investiture with land, the gift of an order followed successful advice that a minister presented to his sovereign.

FIGS **53, 54 & 55**
(opposite) **Terracotta official, found in Pit K0006, to the south-west of the First Emperor's tomb mound. Some of these officials had knives hanging from their belts. The bronze knives** (below) **were used for scraping off the mistakes made when writing on wood slips, while the grindstone** (below, right) **was for sharpening the knives. These examples were found in Fengxiang, site of one of the earlier Qin capitals (Yong) before it moved to Xianyang.**
Cat. nos 24, 30 & 31

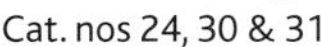

While these rewards were instituted to encourage service, the complementary arrangements for deterring and punishing crime were receiving greater strength. The terms of such punishments were made clearly known to the public and included

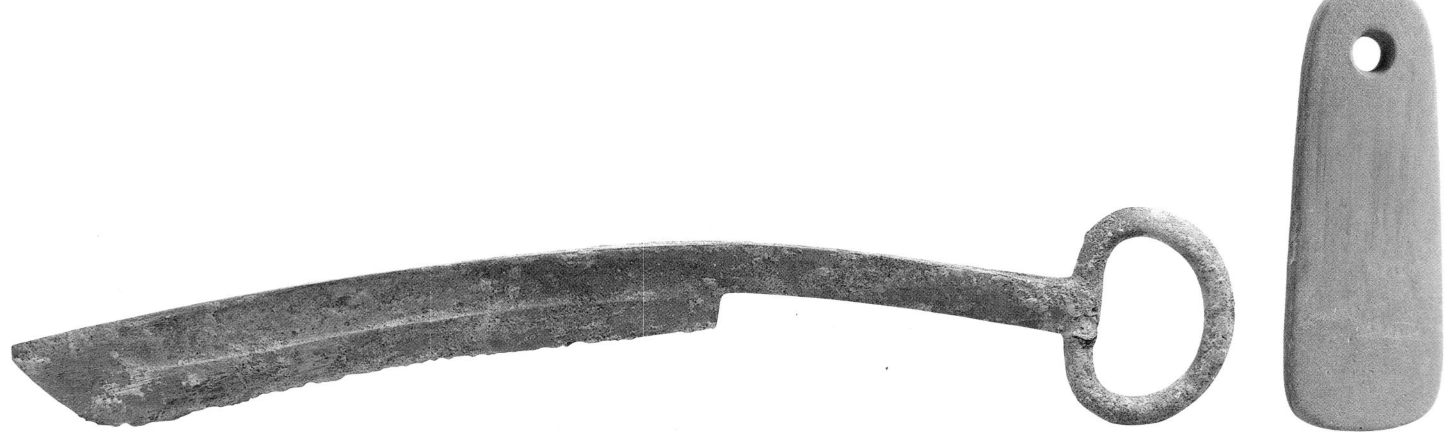

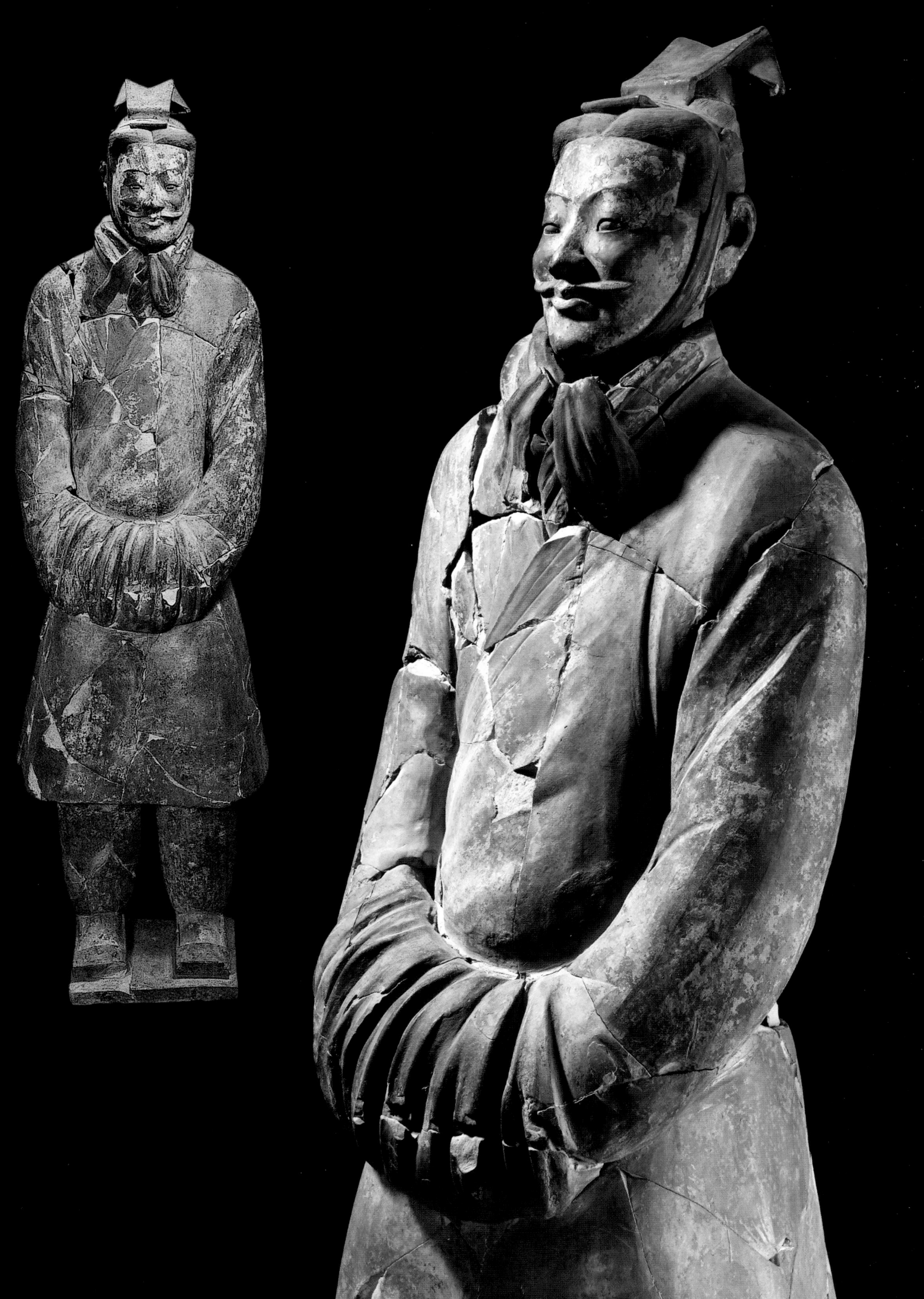

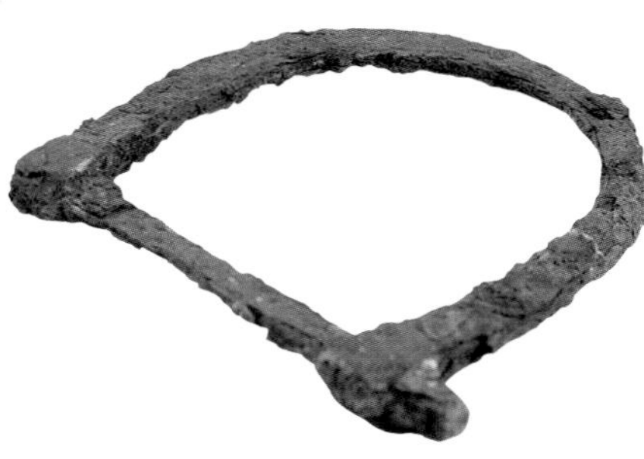

FIG. 56
Restraining iron, possibly for the leg, excavated from the First Emperor's tomb complex. This shows the use of prisoners or convicts in the construction process.
Cat. no. 32

a new feature: they were to apply to all inhabitants of the land alike, whatever a person's social level, whatever the degree of nobility to which his or her family might lay claim. No exceptions would be made so as to favour the high and mighty; even the teachers of the heir apparent would be liable to punishment of the most demeaning kind, such as permanent disfigurement by mutilation or tattooing of the face. But at the same time officials were enjoined to refrain from ordering severe punishments simply to assuage their own anger against an individual.

This stress on the implementation of the laws of the kingdom and their punishments led to a general description of Shang Yang and his successors as 'Legalists'. As such they have been distinguished, somewhat loosely, from other thinkers and advisers of monarchs who are described as *ru*; these were traditionalists and specialists in old writings and their lessons, and they have often been incorrectly termed 'Confucianists'. The writings of the times also refer to other terms such as *geng fa* or *bian fa*, meaning new versions of administrative or other models. This suggests that Shang Yang himself may well have seen his ideas and consequent actions as a radical innovation that changed the system of government to the point of destroying some of its existing features. Particular measures led to tighter social discipline and an increase in agricultural production and therefore of revenue. The population was organized in small groups, perhaps of five or ten persons, who formed 'responsibility groups' (*wu*), each member being responsible for reporting crimes committed by his colleagues. Households, the recognized unit of taxation and duly registered as such, were to include no more than one able-bodied male, others being sent to earn a livelihood in newly opened land, where they would set up their own households. Official rules determined how plots of land were to be measured and distinguished with clear pathways marking their boundaries.

Much is known about Shang Yang thanks to the collection of essays named after him called *Shang jun shu* (*Book of Lord Shang*), some parts of which he may have written. Unfortunately, no more than fragments survive of writings attributed to Shen Buhai, another thinker of the times whose views influenced some of the men who built up Qin's power and took leading parts in achieving the unification. Shen Buhai (*c.*400–337 BC) had himself experienced some of the problems of governing a kingdom and ensuring its safety from rivals, but he did not serve in an official capacity in the kingdom of Qin. The views held by both Shang Yang and Shen Buhai were restated in a piece of writing that was much longer than the *Shang jun shu* and had a major influence in Qin. This was *Hanfeizi*, a book ascribed to Han Fei (*c.*280–*c.*233 BC), a member of the royal house of Han who had put his services at the disposal of Qin but was put to death there, thanks perhaps to the machinations of a rival named Li Si.

FIG. 57
Bronze dagger-axe (*ge*) made in the eighth year of Ying Zheng (238 BC), KIng of Qin (First Emperor from 221 BC) on the order of the Chancellor Lü Buwei. Lü Buwei, originally a merchant, became chancellor in 249 BC. He was the lover of the First Emperor's mother and was dismissed in 237 BC. He was succeeded by Li Si.
Cat. no. 33

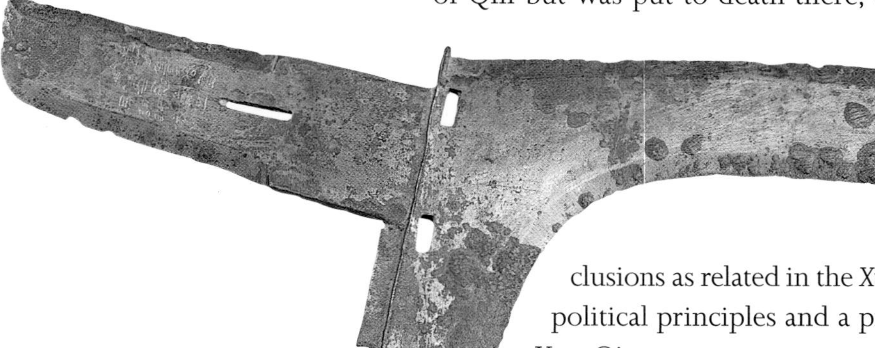

Han Fei and Li Si had been fellow students of Xun Qing (335–238 BC), one of the most acute thinkers to emerge in China at this time. His views and conclusions as related in the *Xunzi* show an exceptional depth in understanding political principles and a presentation of arguments in a systematic form. Xun Qing was more concerned with intellectual problems than immediate matters of administering a country, seeing even in these early times how conflicts could arise between an individual's quest for moral integrity and the demands of an ordered society. By no means can all his views be found in Han Fei's writings or reflected in the decisions taken by Li Si as a minister of state, but it is perhaps likely that both of these men, whose views and advice influenced the Qin kingdom and empire so profoundly, had benefited from a training imparted by Xun Qing.

Han Fei can only have been too well aware of the political events of the fourth and third centuries BC, marked as they were by the rivalries and warfare in which the kingdoms were engaging. His essays show how successful government of a kingdom depends on three principles: *fa*, a model or pattern of government with which practical measures such as the laws should be consonant; *shu*, the means and expedients whereby the aims of organized government are achieved; and *shi*, the possession and display of authority by the acknowledged ruler.

The First and Second Emperors

Such were some of the intellectual influences under which Ying Zheng, born in 259 BC, grew up at the court of the kingdom of Qin. He was to be the fifth king in succession to Huiwen Wang, who had adopted that title in 325 BC. Later allegations that it was not the fourth king who had sired Ying Zheng may probably be discounted as arising from malice. At the age of thirteen he acceded to the throne of the Qin kingdom (246 BC); then, following the conquest of the last of the other kingdoms in 221, he coined the term *huangdi*, usually rendered as 'emperor', as his title.

Historical writing customarily refers to Ying Zheng as *Qin Shihuangdi*, 'First Emperor of Qin'. In this expression *shi* signifies the 'start' or 'starter', and it follows from a proud proclamation in which he boasted that he was the first of a whole line of emperors that would number as many as ten thousand. No record remains of the name of his empress or secondary consorts; as will be seen below, he fathered at

FIG. 58
Detail of a stone rubbing showing the most famous of the three assassination attempts on the First Emperor's life. This attempt, by Jing Ke, involved hiding a knife in a scroll. It took place in 227 BC when Ying Zheng was still only king of the Qin state and was unsuccessful as the knife hit a pillar. This incident is the focus of the film *Hero* (2002) by Zhang Yimou. Wu Family Shrine, Chamber 2, South Wall, second century AD. Ink rubbing on paper, late nineteenth to early twentieth century.

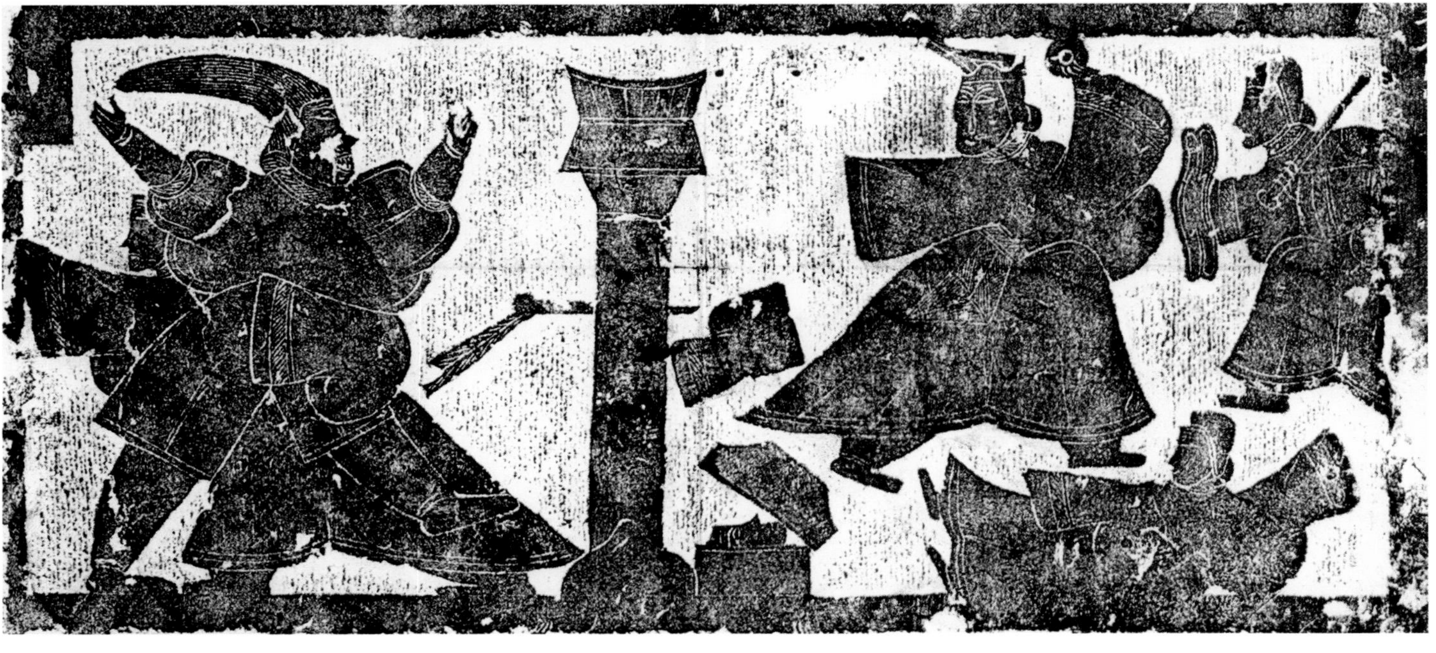

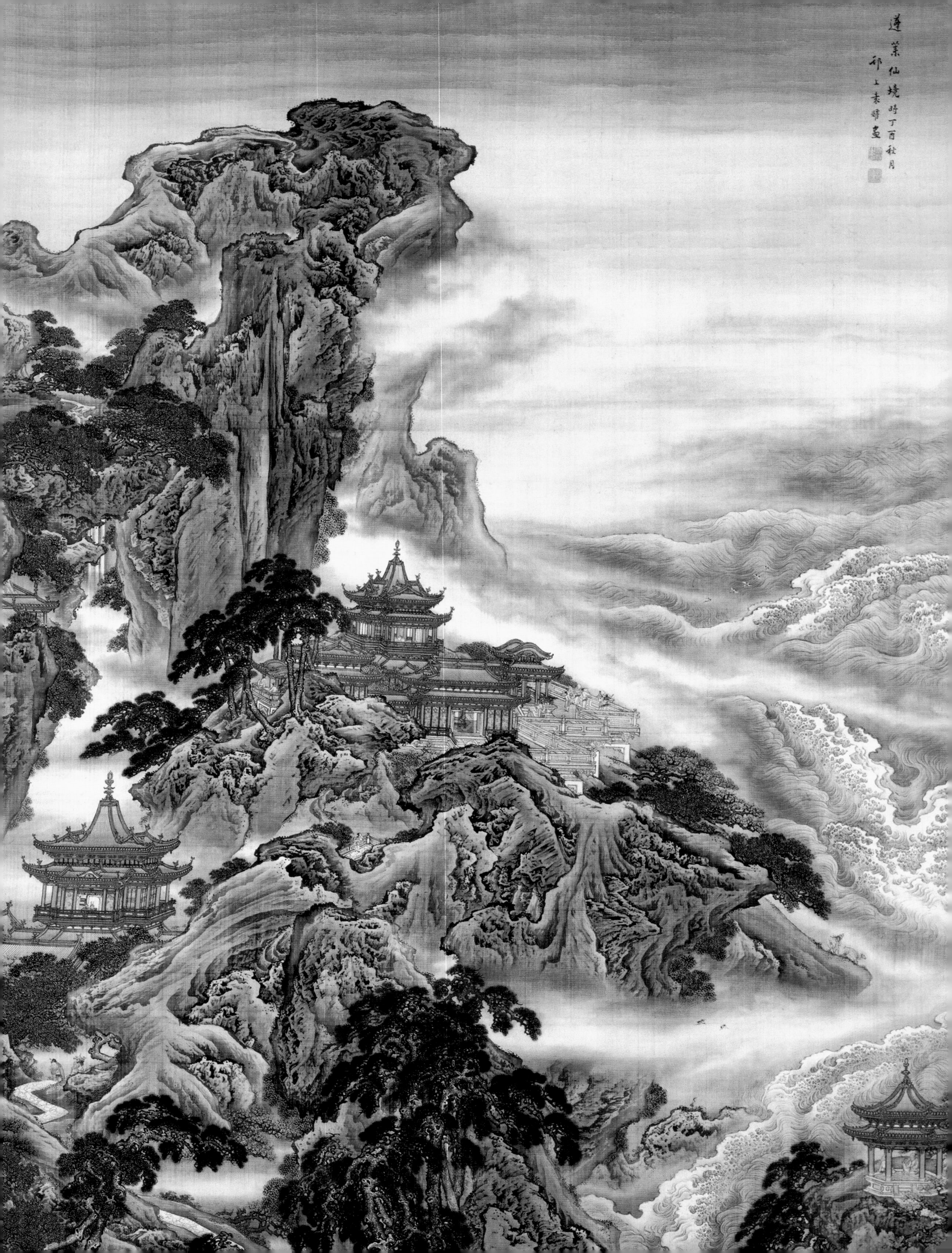
蓬萊仙境 時丁酉秋月
邗上袁耀畫

FIG. 59
(left) *Penglai* (detail) by Yuan Yao, hanging scroll, ink and colours on silk, Qing dynasty, eighteenth century AD. Paintings depicting the mythical isles of the immortals were produced throughout Chinese history.

least two sons. On at least three occasions (227, 221 and 218 BC) an attempt was made on his life, the incidents being recollected by artists of later times who depicted them on the decorated bricks or sculptured stones that took their place in tombs of the Han dynasty (*fig.* 58).

The First Emperor is usually assumed to have been ruthless in implementing his decisions but few precise actions testify to this, other than one. This was the punishment that he ordered for some persons in the kingdom of Zhao after its defeat, which is said to have been due to the enmity that they had showed towards his mother. He is reported to have sought means of prolonging his life indefinitely and despatched a mission to Penglai, the Isles of the Blest in the Eastern Ocean, in order to acquire the means of immortality from some of its white-clad immortal inhabitants (*fig.* 59).

Qin Shihuangdi made several imperial progresses throughout his domains, thereby displaying his presence and authority, and ordered the commemoration of these visits on a series of stone stelae that recounted his successful exploits (see pp. 104–13). On one such journey (219 BC) he is said to have undertaken the arduous ascent of Mt. Tai in present-day Shandong to perform certain religious rites. On the last of these progresses, again to the east, the emperor fell ill and died in 210 BC. Those who accompanied him concealed the news of his death, perhaps in the interests of security or to ensure that the succession to the throne would pass according to their own wishes. The manner in which this issue was resolved is discussed below.

Orders had already been given in his lifetime to construct a tomb fit for an emperor. The historians who recorded these events described the precautions taken to ensure its safety from marauders and the measures designed to put the emperor to rest in a manner that would provide him with an auspicious and suitable position in the scheme of the cosmos. Controlled excavation of the tomb has yet to show evidence that confirms the account of the historians.

The surviving written accounts of the reign derive in the first instance from Sima Tan (died 110 BC) and his son Sima Qian (c.145–c.87 BC), two officials who served in the succeeding Han dynasty as directors of archives (*taishi ling*). In the prevailing dynastic circumstances in which they were writing, praise of the Qin dynasty would not have endeared either of them to their emperor or his officials, for they had to display the Qin as being worthy of destruction and replacement by Han. For these reasons we can only expect to encounter bias in their writings, as may be seen especially in their record of the way in which the throne passed to one of the First Emperor's sons. Throughout the recorded history of the Qin dynasty, there is no reference to troubles that arose owing to the excessive power of one of the imperial consorts and her family. As historians of later dynasties would have relished a chance of denigrating Qin on this score, the absence of any mention of such incidents is telling.

Our histories leave the impression that the Qin empire was cohesive but short-lived: cohesive, in so far as the First Emperor exercised firm control over his peoples and lands, but short-lived and perhaps hollow in view of its abrupt end due to the influence of one man, Zhao Gao, and the weakness of the Second Emperor. Zhao Gao is said to have been a eunuch, but there is no certainty that this was so, nor indeed is there any firm evidence that eunuchs were engaged to serve the kings or emperors, queens or empresses of Qin. Before the foundation of the empire Zhao Gao had been condemned to death for an unknown crime and pardoned only at the intervention of Ying Zheng, the king. Ying Zheng was evidently impressed by his abilities or his personality and perhaps by his skill at judiciary matters. Advanced in the First Emperor's court, he accompanied him on his last progress and may have been able to take command of the situation at his death.

Ying Fusu, eldest son of the First Emperor, might well have had a strong claim to succeed him, but he had once incurred his father's anger and been sent away from the capital city. Nevertheless, the emperor had given orders that included the implication that he should become his successor. However, Zhao Gao circumvented these by bringing about the accession of Ying Huhai, a younger son of the emperor with whom he had become friendly. To achieve this result, Zhao Gao had overcome Ying Huhai's own misgivings and persuaded Li Si, on whose advice and counsel imperial policies had been taken, to condone his plan. Ying Fusu took his own life; Zhao Gao also contrived the death of Meng Tian, known for his military abilities and for the construction of the Great Wall, and the very man who in days gone by had had Zhao Gao accused of crime. No records show whether, once enthroned as Second Emperor, the young Ying Huhai was able to take any personal part in governing the empire and he seems to have remained gullible and under the influence of Zhao Gao. It may well have been Zhao Gao who in the end forced him to commit suicide.

If a note of triumph marked the beginning of the Qin dynasty, it was brought to end in a state of weakness and a prevailing lack of purpose. Some twenty-one years old at the time of his accession, the Second Emperor seems to have been manipulated by those who stood around him and tried to profit from the situation. Zhao Gao is said to have introduced a greater degree of severity into the rule of the land; in response, several insurgent leaders arose independently of each other. Some regional governors met their deaths in the ensuing fighting. After the suicide of the Second Emperor Zhao Gao placed his own nominee on the throne, only to lose his own life quite soon. Two protagonists, Xiang Yu and Liu Bang, now arose on the scene to determine China's destiny. Xiang Yu attempted to restore a pre-imperial system of nineteen co-existent kingdoms over which he would himself act as overlord. After some ten years of civil warfare Liu Bang emerged as the victor, to assume the title of emperor in 202 BC in an empire named Han.

Imperial administration

Effective as the changes wrought to the fabric of China during the reign of the First Qin Emperor were, we have no reliable means of estimating how far these were due to his own personal initiative or to the force of his character. He may have been personally responsible for steps that would enhance the dignity of his regime, such as the adoption of formulae that emphasized his superiority over all others, and he may have ordered the provision of a splendid palace in the capital city of Xianyang (see pp. 83–93).

Drawing on the precedents of Qin's own kingdom and the practices of some of the kingdoms that Qin had overcome, the institutions of the newly formed empire created a new order of government. They ensured a more purposeful type of admin-

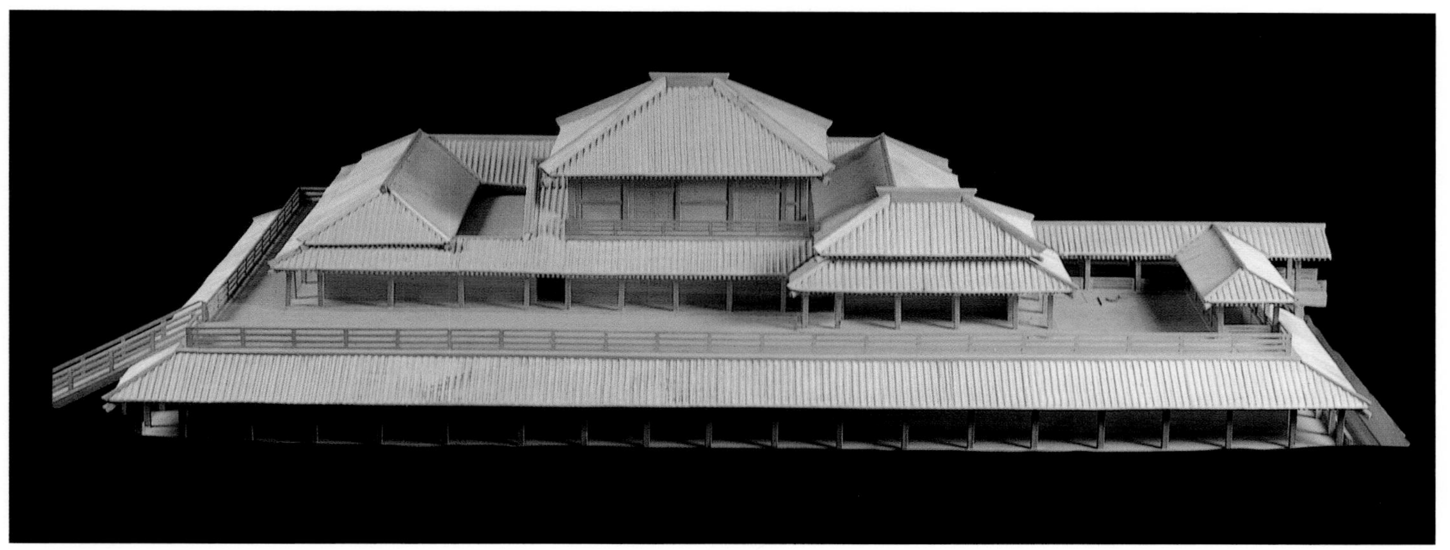

FIG. 60
Model of Qin Palace No. 1 at Xianyang. The palace's brick floor, which remains, measures 60 by 45 metres.
Cat. no. 34

istration and control of the land and its inhabitants; and they would act as a model for imperial governments of subsequent dynasties without any major changes until shortly before AD 600. Imperial government depended on a disciplined obedience to orders, an acceptance of social hierarchies and a clear devolution of authority. It did not call on a general or popular agreement to support activities in public life; while ministers of state and officials might rely on the arts of persuasion to impress their ruler, there was no opportunity or call for an orator whose skills would command the support of the multitude.

In constitutional terms, and in theory, final authority to govern rested with the emperor, who devolved responsibilities to his ministers and officials and whose decisions could not be gainsaid. It was by his word that men were named for appointment to senior positions in the government; it was by decrees issued in his name that decisions were taken. In practice, during both Qin and the later dynasties it was by no means certain that the emperor would possess the right qualities and characteristics for these functions. As has been seen, historians tend to credit the First Emperor with taking a personal part in affairs of state, but scornfully show up his successor as being a weakling utterly unfit for the position that he had inherited.

As in later dynasties, and indeed as in other cultures, so in Qin the tasks of government lay in raising revenue, suppressing crime and maintaining security against external threats. Officials, graded in a series of ranks and paid accordingly, were appointed or dismissed on the basis of their merits and achievements; they did not inherit titles and responsibilities from their fathers in hereditary fashion. They proffered counsel, advised on major decisions and implemented the emperor's orders, bringing his will to bear on his subjects. A sense of hierarchy prevailed in all these aspects of government and informed its conduct. The scope of an official's authority was prescribed, and he was obliged to work to his immediate superior; reference or appeal to a more senior authority could perhaps be punishable.

In the central government the chancellor and the imperial counsellor, who had direct access to the emperor, stood at the head of the scale. At a lower grade there were nine ministers of state who controlled specialist departments of government

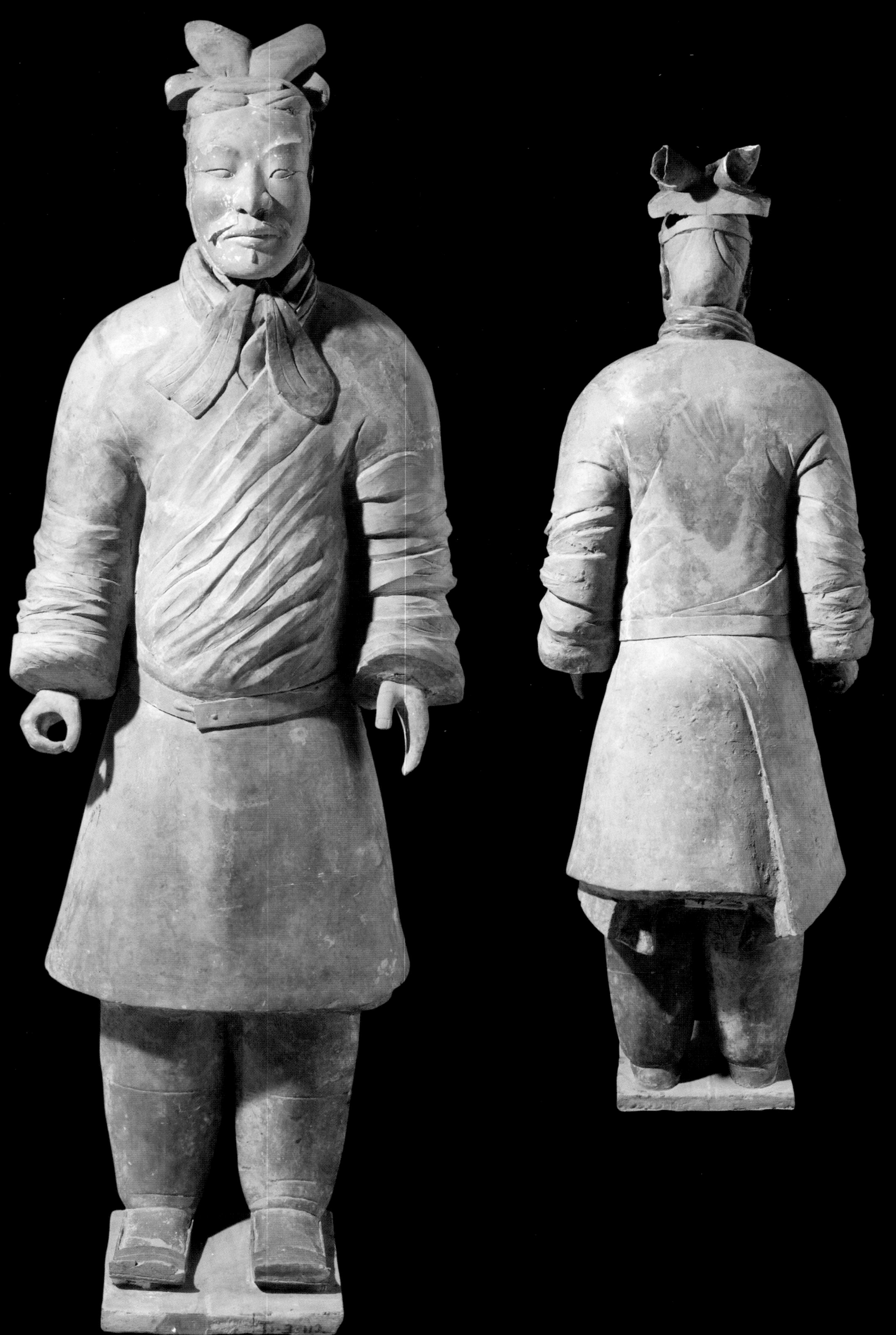

FIG. 61
(left) **Terracotta unarmoured general from Pit 1, wearing his 'pheasant-tail' cap.**
Cat. no. 35

FIG. 62
(below) **Pottery model of a granary, excavated from a tomb at the Qin early capital (Yong).**
Cat. no. 36

that looked after matters such as finance, criminal trials, security of the palace, command of the guards, horses and carriages required by the emperor, affairs of the imperial family and relations with leaders of peoples who were unassimilated to a Chinese way of life. These officials were concerned first and foremost with mundane matters of daily life that might call for attention. A ninth minister cared for services and sacrifices to divine powers; his title, 'Respecter of that which is constant' (*fengchang*), suggests that, realistic and practical as most of these arrangements were, in this particular case government might have in mind the existence of powers that lay beyond its own control.

Xianyang, the capital city, lay within a large territorial unit that was administered by a metropolitan superintendent. Territories that the kings of Qin had acquired or annexed in the course of defeating their neighbouring rivals were organized in units known as commanderies (*jun*) and counties (*xian*), and when the process of unification was complete, the whole empire was made up of at least thirty-six commanderies, each of which comprised a number of constituent counties. A commandery came under the administration of a governor, and a county under that of a magistrate, supported in all cases by subordinate staff and able to call on labour gangs (see below) to carry out their duties of patrolling, policing, collecting tax and maintaining lines of communications. In pre-imperial times armed servicemen were commanded by leaders who were sometimes self-appointed and sometimes commissioned by one of the kingdoms to achieve a specified aim. The kings and then the emperors of Qin nominated men to serve them in this way; imperial government may have included a formal provision for a complement of such 'generals', with assigned ranks and salary.

Senior officials could address their views directly to the emperor in a written report, or 'memorial', as these documents were termed; they would do so to draw his attention to a problem and suggest a solution, or to initiate a plan of action for civil or military purposes. The emperor would respond to such overtures or he might himself instigate activities by issuing orders in the form of a decree, to be circulated as widely as was necessary. Alternatively, a decree that was of limited relevance would be addressed to a few persons or perhaps to the one person who was required to respond. It was by fabricating such imperial orders that Zhao Gao had brought about the deaths of Ying Fusu and Meng Tian.

Taxation and laws

It is probable that imperial Qin controlled the inhabitants of the land, encouraged their production of staple goods and raised revenue by a combination of three devices or institutions. There were precedents for the kingdom of Qin and they were developed in an intensive way by Qin's successor. First, as seen above, in the fourth century or perhaps earlier kings had rewarded and encouraged services by the grant of a grade in a series of orders of honour (*jue*). Such an award brought the recipient mitigation of punishment for crime and possibly entitlement to a plot of land, where he could establish a household consisting of his own immediate kin. Secondly, officials drew up registers of the households, and on the basis of these units the principal forms of taxation were collected, either in kind (grain; or perhaps hemp for textiles, or perhaps rare products such as choice fruits

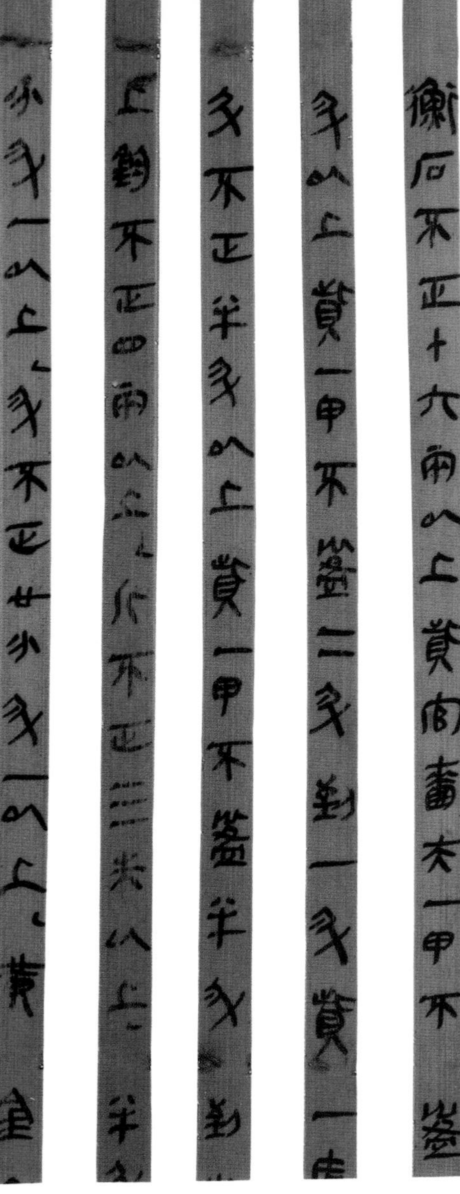

FIG. 63
Qin laws are known through the discovery of 1100 bamboo strips like these found in the tomb of a local magistrate at Shuihudi near Wuhan, dating to 217 BC. On these strips are written guides for the magistrate in his decisions over criminal and civil law. The death penalty was exacted in various cruel ways. However, forced labour was a much more common punishment, applied for a variety of crimes.

of the south, or even pearls) or in cash. The third institution was that of the 'responsibility group', as noted above; members of the group were obliged to spy on one another and report their crimes, which could include evasion of registration of a household, its members and its land. Whether or not these three devices had come into being as parts of a corporate scheme is not known, but they would seem to have evolved independently.

By means of these three institutions and with the unremitting work of its officials, the imperial government of Qin raised the revenue that it needed. No complete information is available to show how this was achieved, but in all probability the types of tax were the same as those levied by the same means in the succeeding Han dynasty. After the collapse of the Qin empire it was claimed by its successors that the rate of tax imposed on the land had been exorbitant.

In the same way writers of subsequent dynasties alleged that Qin had imposed exceptionally high demands in a third form of taxation, which called for able-bodied males to render service annually. This included service as conscript labourers, called up probably for at least one month in each year. Able-bodied males were also obliged to join the armed forces for specified periods of a year or longer, perhaps as members of a force sent to fight a campaign, or perhaps to form the static garrisons of the north. Convicts sentenced to a period of hard labour were put to the same sort of work as conscripts who served in the labour gangs organized by officials of the commanderies and counties. They humped grain from the field to the granary where taxes were stored; they raised water to irrigate the fields; they repaired bridges, waterways or roads; they were engaged in building an imperial palace or mausoleum; and they built some of the defensive lines set up in the north to thwart enemy attacks on Chinese farms, fields and cities.

Officials implemented and the population obeyed two series of regular written orders, the statutes and ordinances, which are sometimes named 'laws' but are better understood as expedient arrangements for the administration of the empire. Copies of both these orders were circulated as was necessary, each statute and ordinance bearing its own title or number. The fortunate discovery of a set of these documents dated 217 BC shows that they could concern a whole variety of subjects, including agriculture, stabling and storage of crops; accountancy, to check on government property and stores, and for commercial transactions; standards of work for artisans; the use of conscript labour and restrictions on convicted criminals; the terms and conditions of service of officials; and the delivery of official documents. Some of the provisions are concerned with minute details, such as reports on damage to government property and the removal of marks of ownership incised or branded on discarded items; rations for sentenced criminals or for horses used in the official courier service; storage, registration, measurement and security of grain; storage of cash; issue of clothing; checks on weights and measures; the use of lubricants for carts. In its turn the Han imperial government inherited and applied many of these provisions.

No standing body or authority existed to determine the principles or to frame

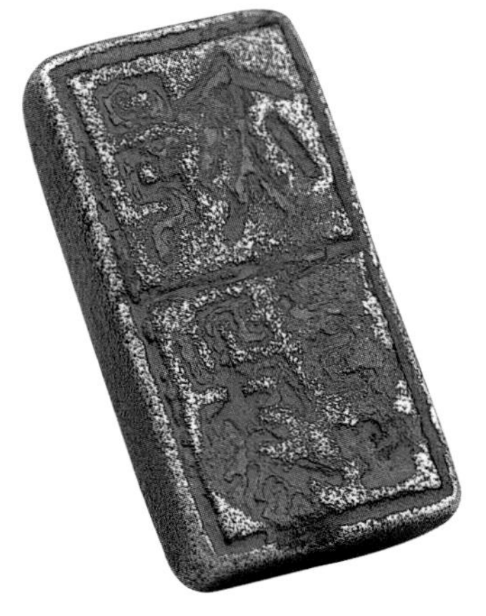

FIG. **64**
Qin-dynasty bronze seal. The standardization of the script was necessary for efficient administration.
Cat. no. 37

FIG. **65**
Bronze weight cast in relief with an inscription detailing that it was made in 244 BC in Gaonu (present-day Yanchuan, north-east Shaanxi); the manager of production was Xi of Qiyuan, the supervisor was Qu and the worker was Ping. The other side is inscribed with two edicts, one by the First Emperor (dated 221) which decrees that all weights be standardized, and another by the Second Emperor (dated 210) which calls for the compliance of the system of weights and measures introduced under the first Emperor.
Cat. no. 38

concepts of rights, privileges and duties upon which these rules depended. Statutes and ordinances seem to have been issued as and when occasion arose, with the result that over the years inconsistencies and discrepancies could arise. Along with the circulation of the laws, other types of document were framed, such as collections of cases where the application of a statute was in doubt and an official required guidance. Legal niceties might involve a father's right to punish a son; investigation of the corpse of a suicide; the circumstances of a robbery carried out by tunnelling into a house; or the disputed ownership of a cow. Or else officials might ask for the precise meaning of an expression in one of these documents and a written answer was duly supplied. With decades and then centuries of imperial government, the volume of legal documentation grew to be cumbersome and immense enough to defy easy consultation.

Many of the statutes and ordinances laid down an obligation or correct mode of procedure, or they named prohibited activities; and they specified the punishment for failure to comply or for disobedience. Punishments ran from banishment, fines, flogging, mutilation or tattooing to five years' hard labour and the death penalty, executed perhaps in a gruesome manner. In some cases punishment could involve not only a criminal but also his or her closest kin, who could be forcibly taken into custody and then service as ordered by an official. Redemption from some forms of punishment was possible, but only at a very high price of money. Criminal cases were judged at the different levels of provincial and central government, with some extreme cases perhaps being referred to the emperor for a decision. Possibly men or women who were charged could appeal for a review of a sentence, but at the risk of increased severity of punishment if their pleas failed.

Technical innovations and achievements

The earliest imperial decree to be mentioned, in 221 BC, set out the formal conditions of the newly founded empire, carefully laying down the formulae to be used in state documents and in communications with the emperor. Perhaps at the same time, or possibly earlier, the system of writing was adjusted so that it would meet the growing demands of an enlarged administration and could be used by the increased number of officials and their clerks, some of whom had had no more than a short training. The earliest examples of Chinese writing seen in inscriptions on shells and bone of perhaps 1700 BC were complex and by no means consistent; the forms used in inscriptions on bronze vessels, of 1000 BC and later, are in some ways more complex and difficult to master; but documents on silk or wooden strips of the fourth century BC or so show how some characters were being modified and how a degree of regularity was being introduced. One of the reasons for these changes lay in the employment of different materials for writing, as the brush came into use for literary, historical or official documents, some of which were to be copied

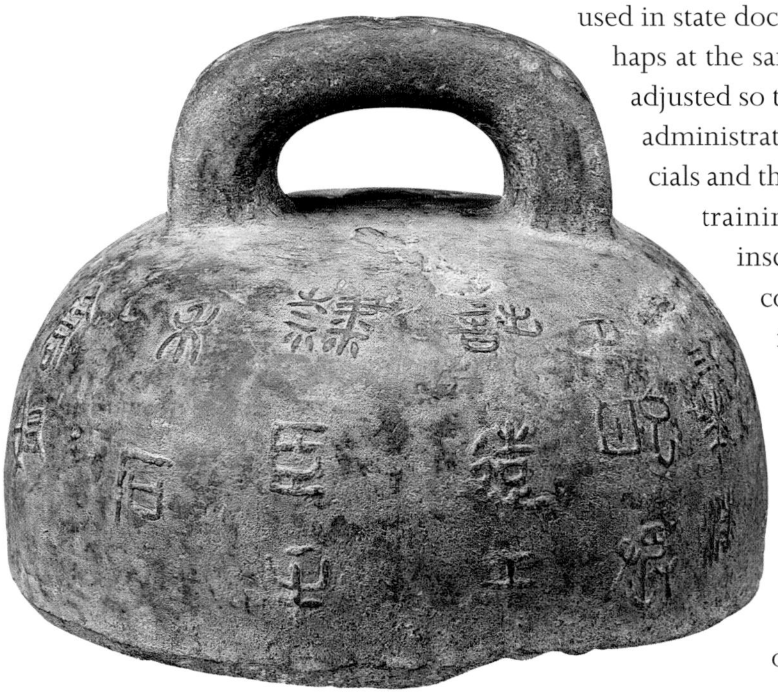

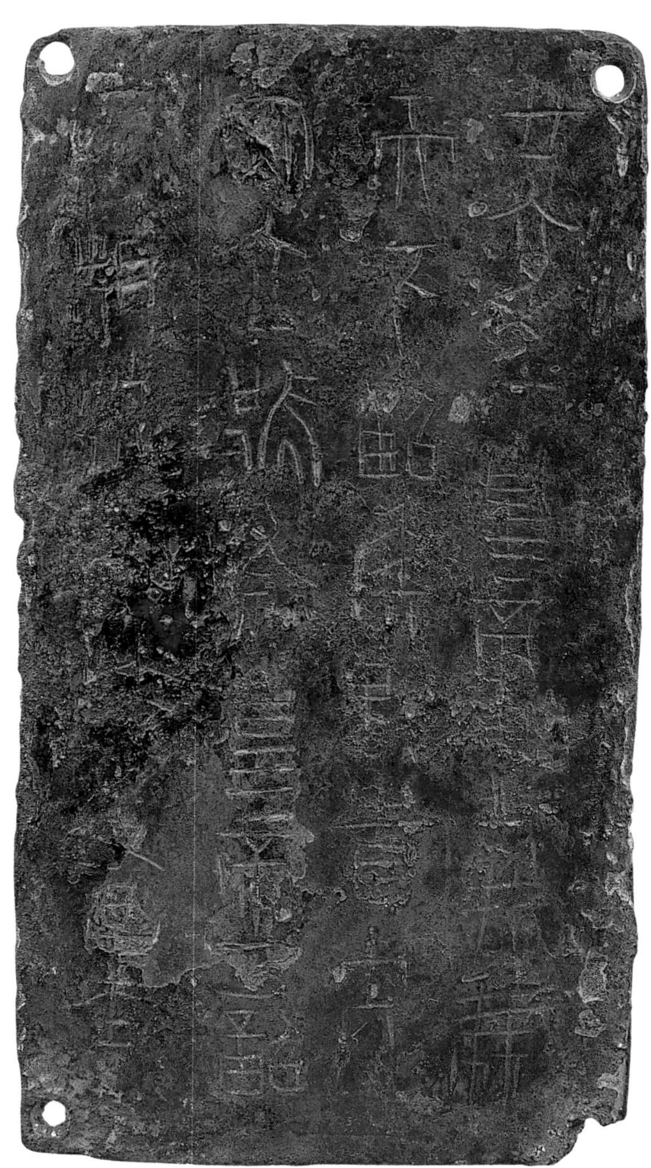

FIG. 66
Bronze plaque cast with an inscription, dated 221 BC, calling for compliance with the standardized weights and measures introduced under the First Emperor.
Cat. no. 39

frequently. With the foundation of the empire it became necessary to ensure that official documents were produced in a standard form of writing, irrespective of variations that might have grown up in some of the kingdoms. Surviving documents of 217 BC show how a simpler form of writing, as compared with earlier types, had come into use for at least some official records.

Positive steps to unify the script are credited to Li Si, who was perhaps responsible more than any other person for introducing the new order of government successfully. After service in a junior capacity in the large kingdom of Chu that bestrode the Yangtze River, he moved to Qin, still in the days of the kingdom, in the hope that he would find greater opportunity for putting his ideas into practice. On his advice some of the moves to eliminate the other kingdoms were taken, and it is alleged that in the course of these negotiations he had Han Fei, not a native of Qin, put to death. Li Si served as superintendent of trials in the kingdom of Qin and became chancellor once the empire had been created. He advocated the provincial system that was adopted, with its dependence on merit rather than on hereditary receipt of a title and appointment to high responsibility. He advised against entering into expensive and dangerous ventures against the Xiongnu, the potential enemy in the north; and he encouraged both the First and the Second Emperor to uphold and display the power that fell to their charge.

Zhao Gao appears to have enjoyed paramount powers in the short reign of the Second Emperor, thus arousing protests from Li Si, whom he had executed as a criminal in 208 BC. In a statement in his own defence Li Si claimed credit for a number of measures, including that of unifying the script. He also claimed to have started projects in road building and to have had the severity of some legal punishments reduced in an attempt to make imperial government more popular. During the reign of the First Emperor, when Li Si's influence was strong, Qin introduced several practical measures that would bring uniformity to matters of everyday life, such as the use of coins and the reliance on weights and measures.

Centuries earlier, cowry shells, themselves of a rarity value, had been employed as the earliest medium of exchange for goods. With the increasing use of bronze the kingdoms of the pre-imperial age cast articles of exchange that simulated the shapes of tools such as shovels or knives; or else they simply took the upper part of the knives as their model and produced a coinage of bronze rings or circular discs. Exceptionally, ingots of gold were used for these purposes. The single bronze coin universally introduced in the Qin empire was of just such a shape, with a square hole in the centre; a cord threaded through this hole could tie together one hundred 'cash', as the coins were termed, to form a string (see pp. 80–2).

The government of imperial Qin introduced a unified set of weights and measures in place of the different series of units that had been in use hitherto. In order to do so, standard weights and measures of capacity were circulated, some of them inscribed with the text of a decree of 221 or 209 BC issued by the First or Second Emperor (fig. 65). These weights were made in various sizes, ranging from 8 to 24 *jin*, where the *jin* was probably 250 grams. By contrast with texts of the statutes that survive, inscriptions found on some vessels were rendered in a more formal or decorative script, as befitted the text of an imperial decree (fig. 67). The vessels were mostly of copper or bronze, with some iron. A further measure of uniformity specified the gauge of certain types of carriage or cart.

Over the years Chinese historians have exaggerated the effect of a more controversial measure, of 213 BC, which was again due to Li Si. Interpreted by some as amounting to a wholesale destruction of literature, it was limited to certain writings that

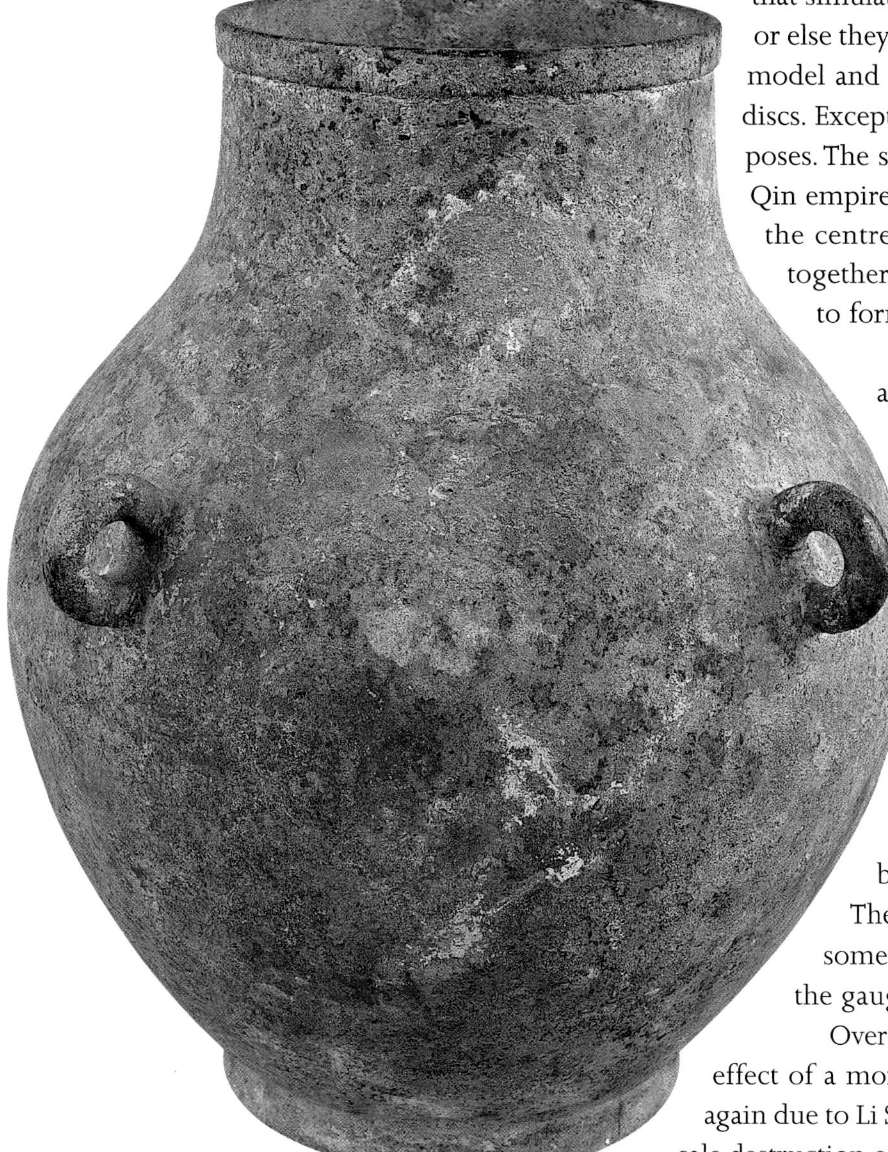

FIG. 67
Bronze vessel (*zhong*) excavated from the First Emperor's tomb complex. Inscribed with its capacity and weight. Qin dynasty, 221–210 BC.
Cat. no. 40

evoked the models of the past and that might support criticism of Qin as having deliberately abandoned the ways of the earlier kings. Suppression was in fact limited to private possession of such texts, which became subject to severe punishment. In his recommendation Li Si specifically urged that texts that concerned technical matters, such as medicine or agriculture, should not be destroyed. Much significance was attached in later generations to the further charge that in 212 no less than 460 men of letters were put to death with a view to eliminating the influences that their traditional views might bring to bear. This tale cannot, however, be substantiated.

The government of the Qin empire built roads to facilitate communications between the capital city and the provinces. At the same time it very probably took precautions to control the free passage of travellers, possibly to prevent the escape of criminals or deserters who were anxious to evade their terms of duty. Such precautions may have included the establishment of official posts at key points on mountain passes and at river crossings, where passage may have depended on presentation of wooden documents or passports. The movement of horses may have been subject to control.

Perhaps the best-known achievement of the Qin empire was the construction of a systematic set of defences in the north, usually termed the Great Wall. This project, the first of several of this type that were put in hand in dynastic times, was started in 215 BC, under the supervision of Meng Tian and took perhaps ten years to complete (see pp. 53–6).

The Qin legacy

Short-lived as it was, Qin bequeathed a heritage that has informed every type of government in China thereafter, be it imperial, republican, Maoist or post-Maoist. This is seen in the acknowledged principle that authority throughout the realm stems eventually from a single source of power and that in this way the peoples and lands governed by that power form a unity. The emperor stood possessed of an unquestioned right to issue commands and laws, with no suggestion that these should have received the consent of any other person, let alone that of an assembly.

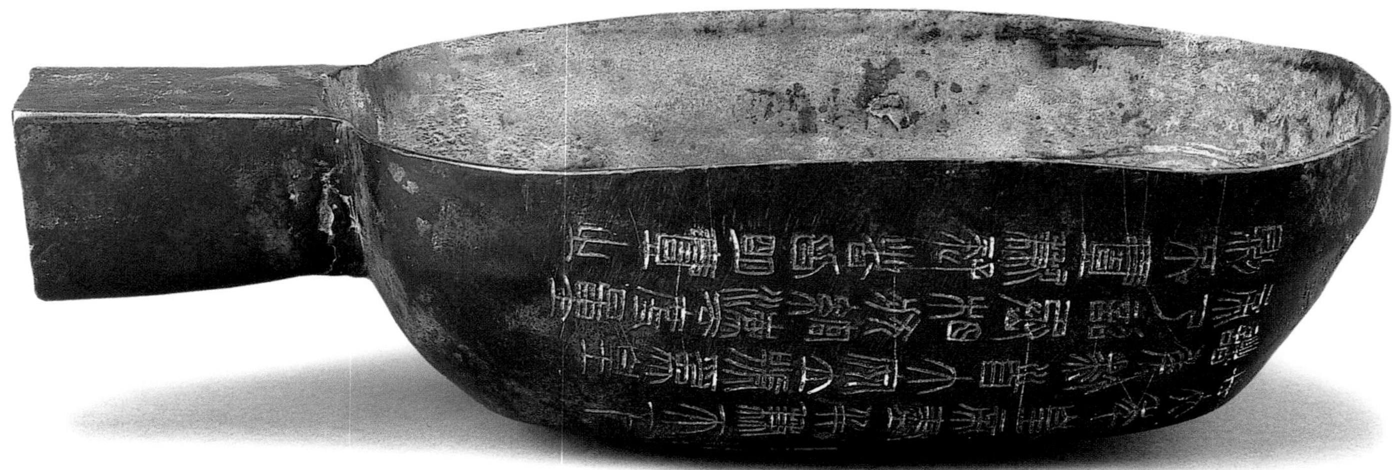

FIG. 68
Bronze measure for half a *dou* (1 litre) from the Qin imperial palace. Its sides are inscribed with the First Emperor's edict of 221 BC decreeing the standardization of all weights and measures. Its base is inscribed with the Second Emperor's edict of 210 BC which calls for compliance of the First Emperor's orders.
Cat. no. 41

Such was the ideal seen as a norm throughout the succeeding centuries, but it was by no means always achieved.

The Qin empire was able to put this into practice for a short time and other dynasties, such as Han, Tang, Song, Ming and Qing were to do so at much greater length. But all too often a dynasty ruled in name but could not control its population effectively; independent movements robbed an emperor of his claim to universal obedience; and there were times when two or three claimants to exercise such power existed independently. That each one of these would style himself 'emperor' demonstrates that he saw himself as the sole ruler of the land, in the same terms as those of the First Emperor of Qin.

Qin also left its successors a new acceptance of official rule and a system of government by duly prescribed commands or laws. Critics of later dynasties castigated Qin for the severity with which it had applied those laws and its ruthless execution of its punishments. That the Han dynasty had inherited and adopted those laws and probably applied them with comparable rigour did not deter Han writers, such as Sima Qian, author of *Records of the Historian* (*Shiji*) completed *c*.89 BC, from expressing such criticism. It was claimed that, in contrast to their own Han ways of thought, which have sometimes loosely been termed Confucian, the regime of Qin drew from diametrically opposed opinion described as Legalist. Such claims have served the needs of dynastic propagandists, but the distinction that is drawn, as between an oppressive and unjust Qin and a more humane Han or Tang, is by no means as clear cut as they would wish. Many of Qin's ways of thought survived to find a following, if only tacit, in later dynasties.

Criticism of Qin started from the early days of the successor dynasty of Han. In an essay entitled 'How Qin Went Too Far', a brilliant and somewhat disappointed young official named Jia Yi (201–169 BC) recounted how that empire had been formed in triumph after long years of travail and how a single rebel leader had brought it to an ignominious end. Jia Yi probably intended his tract to be a word of warning to the current dynasty that he served, which had adopted nearly all of Qin's institutions and way of government. Dangers lurked in the system and it was essential to avoid its excesses; and he perhaps hoped that Han would not suffer a similar fate. Before long criticism of Qin moved into a direct expression of the evil nature of its ways, and this moral tone marked nearly all references to Qin in later writings. Exceptionally, at times when the authority of emperor and officials had waned and a dynasty had lost its hold on the people and the land, a far-seeing statesman would point to the value of the kind of discipline that Qin had imposed. But it is perhaps ironic that the First Qin Emperor should be one of two leaders singled out in China's historical writing for their moral shortcomings, abandonment of tradition and merited end, with scant appreciation of the enduring mark that they left on the conduct of imperial government.

COINS

HELEN WANG

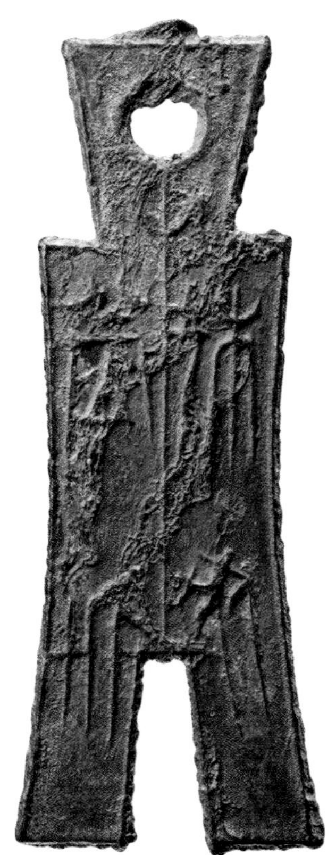

Introduction

In *Records of the Historian* (*Shiji*) Sima Qian (*c.*145–*c.*87 BC) wrote that the Qin state issued coins in 336 BC and listed the standardization of coinage among the achievements of the First Emperor after 221 BC. Archaeological discoveries – of coins and contemporary written documents – show that coins were already in circulation in the Qin state before that date, and suggest that 336 BC must refer to the issue of a new coin, a reform of the existing coinage or the state monopolization of coinage. As the Qin state expanded, so the distribution of the Qin coin, the *banliang*, spread. Standardization of the coinage throughout the new Qin empire after 221 BC was not merely for economic convenience, it was essential for the effective running of the state administration. The dominance of the *banliang* was also politically symbolic.

Coinage in the Warring States before unification

A variety of different forms of money were used in pre-Qin China, including gold, silver, textiles, tortoise shells and cowries. During the fourth century BC cast bronze money became widespread in all the Warring States, though in different forms: spade money (modelled on farming tools), knife money (modelled on hunting or fishing tools) and 'ant-nose' money (a compact inscription on a small piece of bronze, modelled on cowrie shells). These different forms were initially issued in different states: spade money in the central states, knife money in the northern and eastern states, and 'ant-nose' money in the south-east. The form of the round coin with the hole was probably derived from the *bi*, a round jade disc with a round hole in the middle, which was an early symbol of wealth. It was adopted by the Qin state, and as Qin power spread, this form also came to be known in all the larger states.

FIG. 69
(above and below) **Spade money of the states of (a) Chu, (b, c) Zhao, (d) Wei, (e) Han and (f) (Zhao).**
Cat. nos 42–7

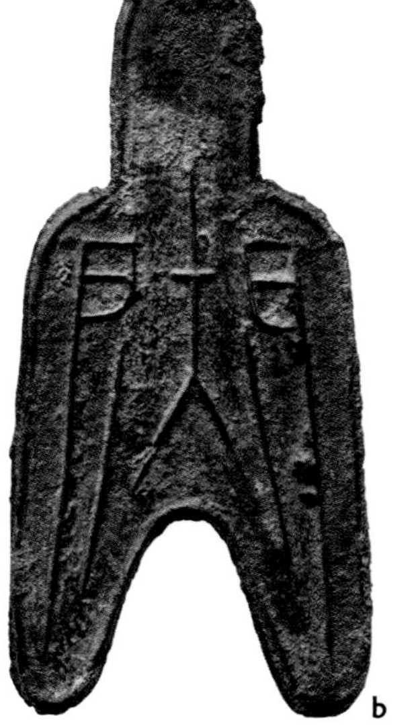

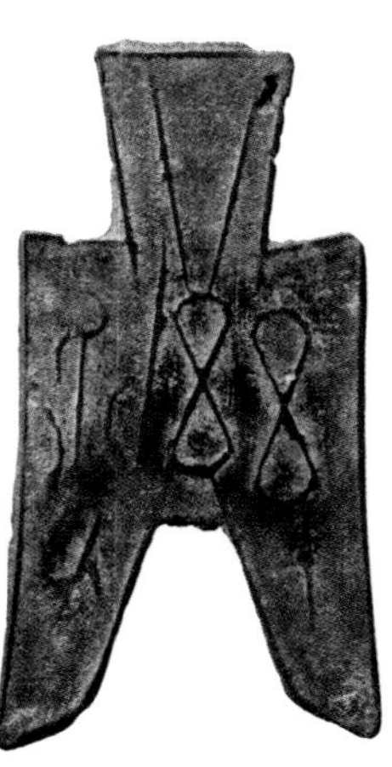

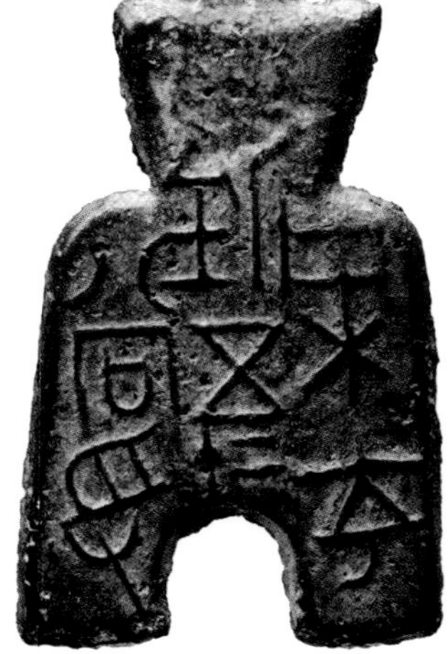

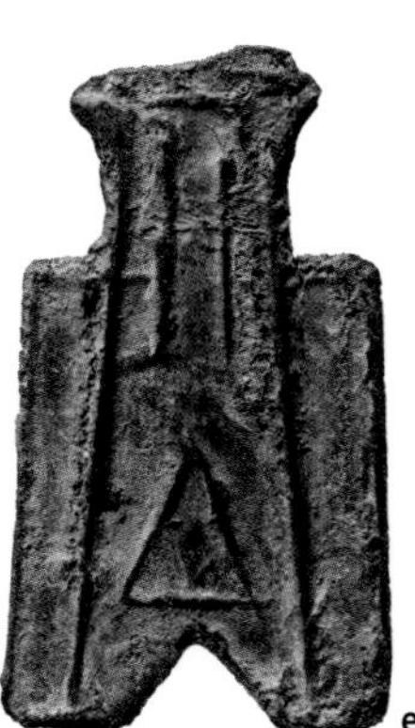

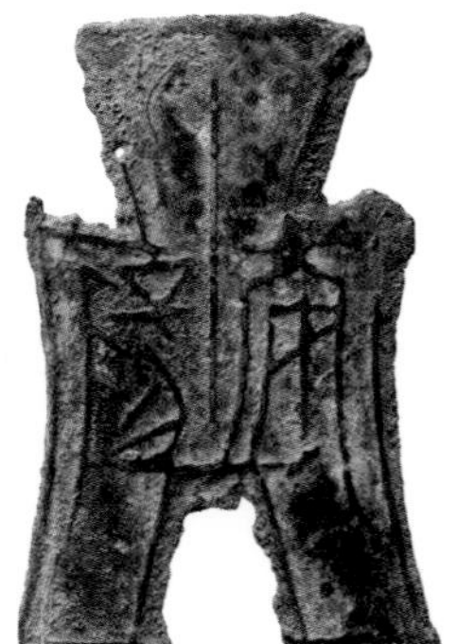

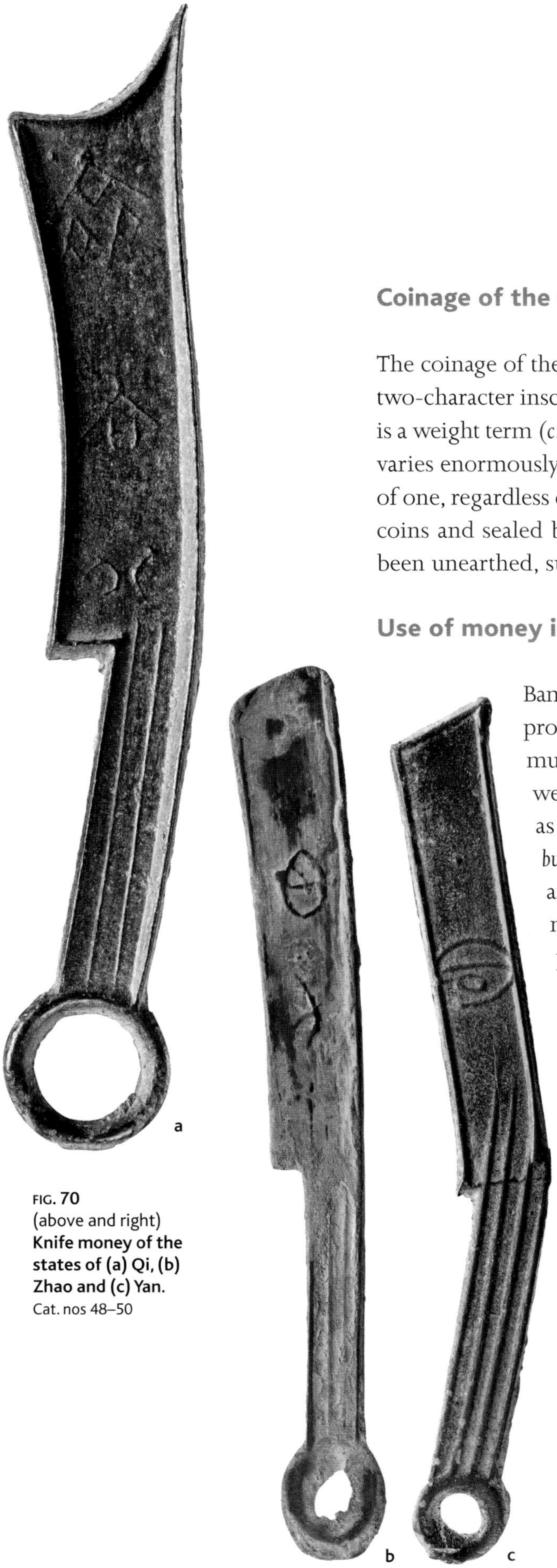

Coinage of the Qin state

The coinage of the Qin state was round with a square hole in the middle, and had a two-character inscription, *banliang*. The inscription translates as 'half-*liang*', where *liang* is a weight term (*c*.16 grams). While some *banliang* coins do weigh 8 grams, the weight varies enormously. The excavated documents tell us that each coin (*qian*) had a value of one, regardless of its size or weight. Special coin containers (*ben*) containing 1,000 coins and sealed by officials are mentioned in the documents, and examples have been unearthed, suggesting that the *ben* (or 1,000 *qian*) was also a unit of account.

Use of money in the Qin state

Bamboo slips discovered in Tomb 11 at Shuihudi, near Yunmeng (Hubei province), in 1975 record Qin laws of the third century BC and tell us much about money in the Qin state. From these we know that coins were the most important form of money, but that textiles also served as money. Textile money was reckoned in standard units known as *bu*, with one *bu* measuring 8 *chi* x 2 *chi* 5 *cun* (1.85 x 0.51 metres) and equivalent in value to 11 *qian* (coins). This would explain why multiples of 11 *qian* are frequently seen in the documents: for example, 110, 220, 660, 1100 and 2200 *qian*. Gold was used for rewards with the usual amount being 2 *jin* (500 grams) of gold. However, all quantities of money were reckoned in *qian*. All items with a value of 1 *qian* or more for sale in the market had to be labelled. A day's labour was reckoned as 8 *qian*, or 6 *qian* if food was provided. Hemp was about 3 *qian* per jin (*c*.250 grams), with three sizes of hemp jackets costing 36 *qian*, 46 *qian* and 60 *qian*, respec-

FIG. 70
(above and right)
Knife money of the states of (a) Qi, (b) Zhao and (c) Yan.
Cat. nos 48–50

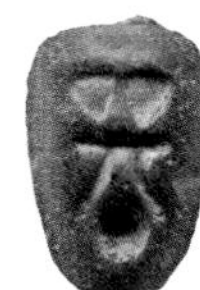

FIG. 71
(above) **Ant-nose money of the state of Chu.**
Cat. no. 51

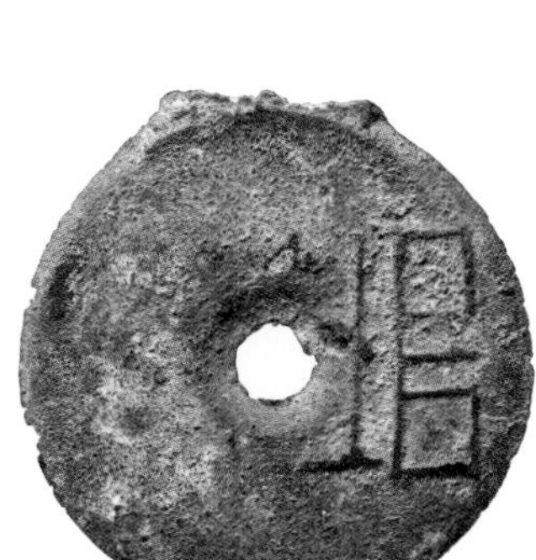

FIG. 72
(left) **Round coin with a round hole of the state of Wei.**
Cat. no. 52

tively. Fines were often stated in terms of shields, but were payable in *qian*, at the rate of 5000 *qian* per shield. These are just a few examples showing that there can be no doubt that coins were the normal form of money in the Qin state.

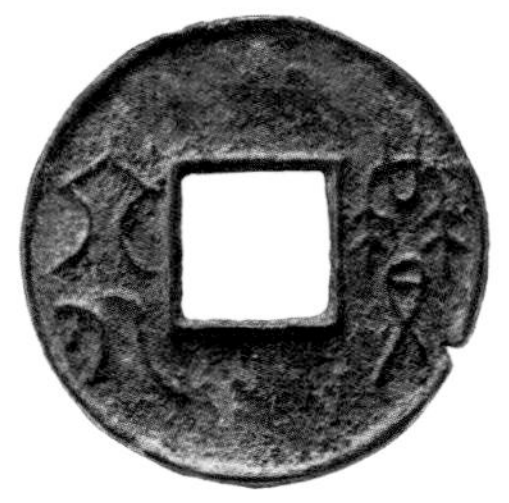

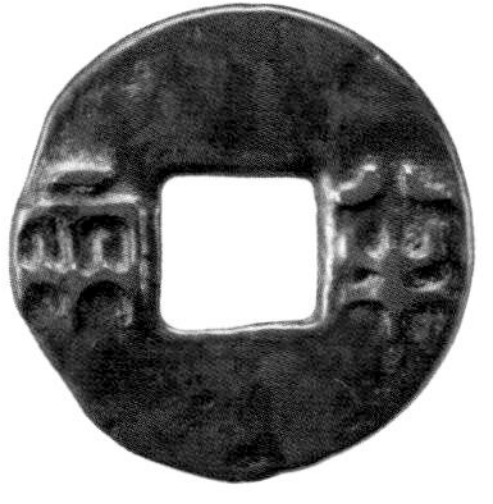

FIG. 73
(top) **Round coin with a square hole of the state of Qi.**
Cat. no. 53

FIG. 74
(above) ***Banliang* coin of the state of Qin.**
Cat. no. 54

FIG. 75
(below) **Mould for making *banliang* coins.**
Cat. no. 55

Standardizing the coinage of the Qin empire

There is nothing explicit in the written records about how the standardization of coinage was achieved, and we must assume that it was through the strict enforcement of Qin laws. As the power of the Qin state had expanded, so had the use of round coins with square holes, to the extent that this form of money was already in use in most of the states on the eve of the establishment of the Qin empire. This situation, combined with the Qin law that all coins regardless of size and weight had a value of 1 *qian*, must have facilitated the standardization of the coinage. The *Records of the Historian* reports that all other forms of money were rendered obsolete. The other metal types were probably collected in and melted down to make new *banliang* coins.

Symbolic importance of standardizing the coinage

Coins are man-made and usually have just one function: to serve as money. The act of issuing coins is an assertion of political authority and the right to rule. Coins are always symbolic and coin design is very important. While the First Emperor did not design the *banliang* coin, he approved it as the coin of his empire. The designer of this coin form must have been aware of its similarity with the *bi* and *cong* jades, which were ancient symbols of cosmological power, linking heaven and earth. The *bi* is a flat round disc of jade with a round hole in the middle; the *cong* is a square tube with a central circular hole. In early Chinese cosmology the earth was square and the heavens were domed. In this way the *banliang* can be seen as a powerful symbol of both heaven and earth, issued through the agency of the state. Even after the demise of the Qin dynasty, the form of the *banliang* – round with a square hole in the middle – remained the model for all Chinese coins until the late nineteenth century.

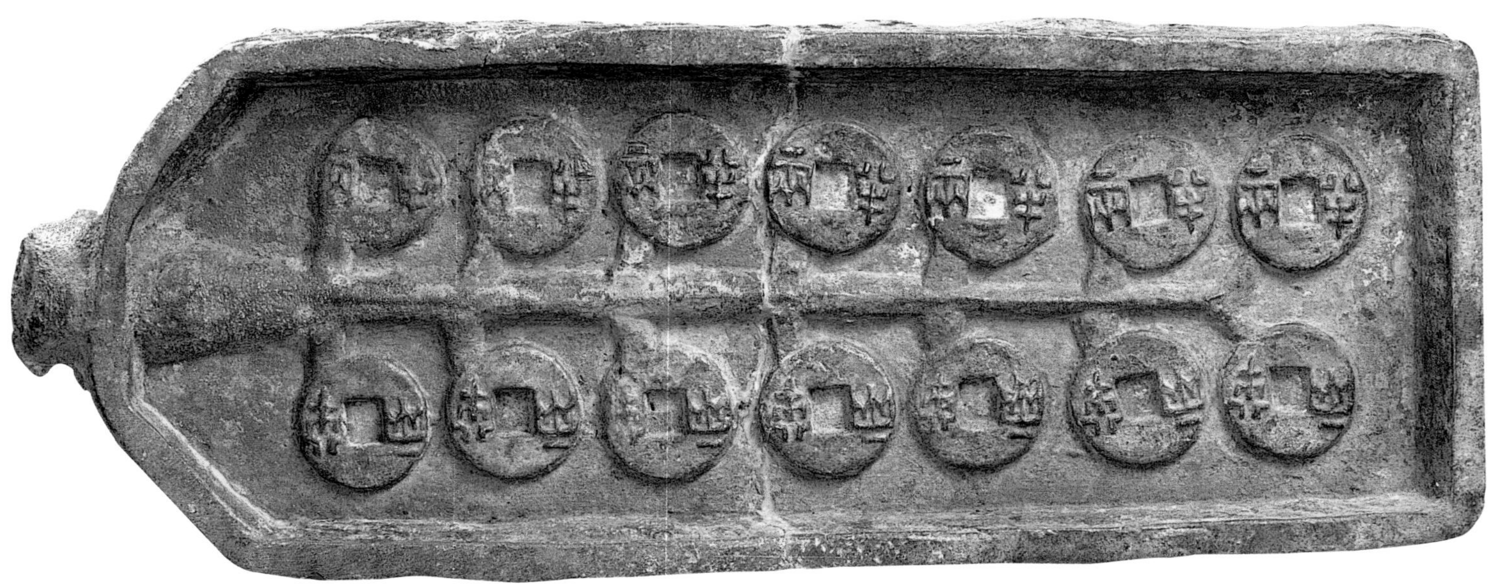

QIN PALACES AND ARCHITECTURE

HIROMI KINOSHITA

When King Zheng of Qin declared himself emperor in 221 BC, having conquered the last of the Warring States, his grand scheme to unify his territories also included a number of large and ambitious building projects. From his capital in Xianyang he established a central government and commissioned grandiose palaces and gardens.

In stark contrast to modern-day Rome, where ancient buildings still remain from the days when the city was the centre of the Roman empire, there is little visible evidence of Qin or pre-Qin architecture today in Xianyang. As with all ancient Chinese architectural structures, buildings were made of wood and tamped earth, materials that do not survive well. Through archaeological evidence and literary record, however, we are able to gain a sense of the buildings of the time, even though the lines between fact and fantasy are blurred.

In *Records of the Historian* (*Shiji*) Sima Qian, the historian of the succeeding Han dynasty, writes that the First Emperor aligned his rule on earth with the order of the heavens, erecting temples and palaces in parallel with the stars and other cosmic

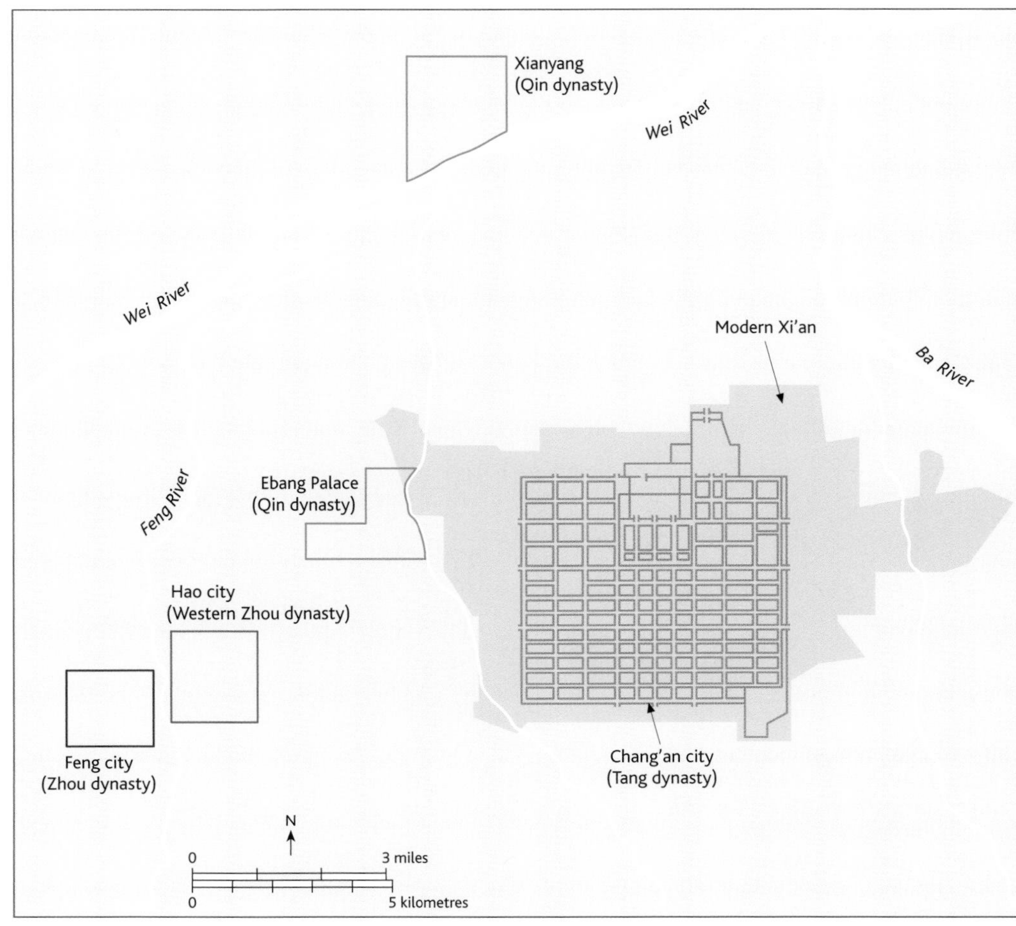

FIG. 76
Map of the Xi'an area, Shaanxi province. Xianyang, located on the northern banks of the Wei River, was the Qin capital from 350 to 206 BC.

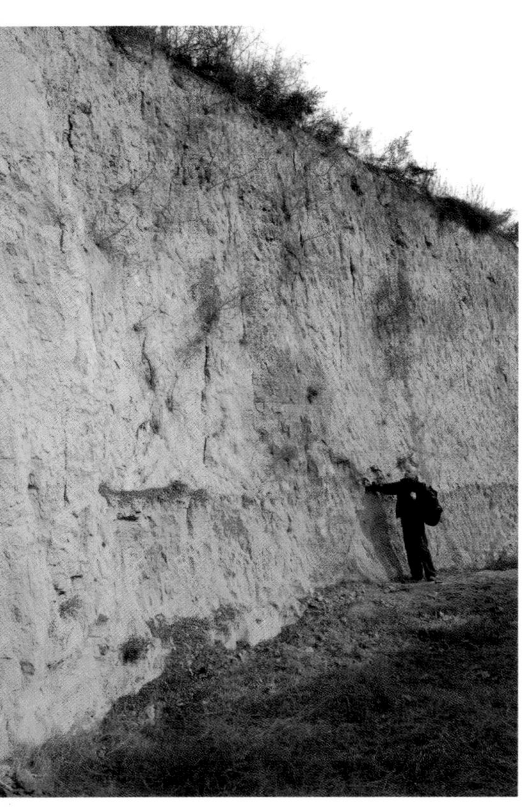

FIG. 77
Tamped earth foundations of the Qin palace at Xianyang.

bodies (see p. 119).[3] His palaces in Xianyang were considered to be the earthly equivalent of the Royal Chamber star and the Heavenly Apex star, while the Wei River was the Milky Way.[4] Symbolically, it was as if he commanded the entire universe.

Xianyang, the capital city of the Qin state since 350 BC had developed and grown to a considerable size under the rule of five previous Qin kings before the First Emperor. Excavations have revealed that it was located 15 km east of present-day Xianyang city and covered an area roughly 7,200 metres east to west and 6,700 metres north to south (fig. 76). The city boasted a thriving industry with bronze and iron foundries, pottery workshops and a palace district with government and private workshops.[5] During the rule of the First Emperor the layout of the city changed. More than 270 palaces were said to have been built around the city. In a deliberate display of power, each time one of the feudal states was conquered, the First Emperor ordered a palace modelled on that of the conquered state to be built on the hills north of Xianyang. They were filled with beautiful women, bells and drums appropriated from the different states.[6]

The royal palace at Xianyang

The royal palace where previous Qin kings and the First Emperor resided and administered state affairs was located in the north-central part of the city. Originally built in the time of the Warring States,[7] it was enlarged during the First Emperor's reign. Within the entire complex three palace foundations have so far been excavated all built on raised platforms and connected to each other (fig. 77). Palace 1, measuring 60 metres by 45 metres north to south, was raised on a 6-metre rammed-earth platform and is thought to have been a galleried building with many halls joined by stairways, corridors and a large open balcony facing south with views overlooking

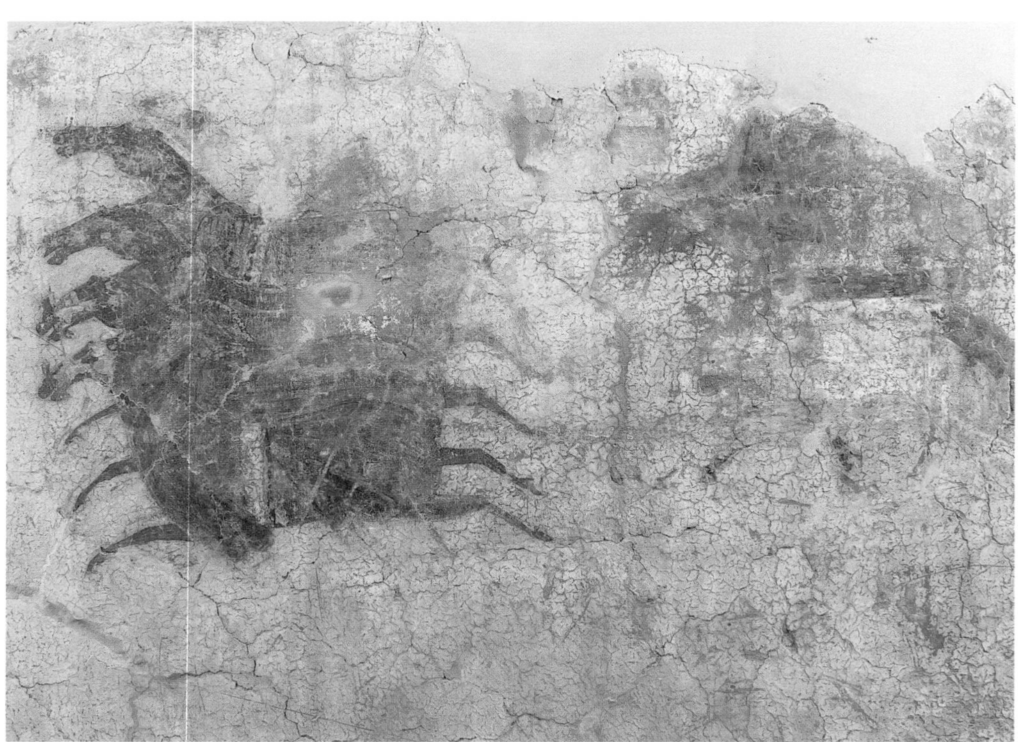

FIG. 78
This mural fragment of four horses drawing a carriage decorated one of the corridor walls in Palace 3 at Xianyang. Other mural fragments discovered at the same site depict figures in an interior setting, animals, birds and flora within lozenge-design borders.

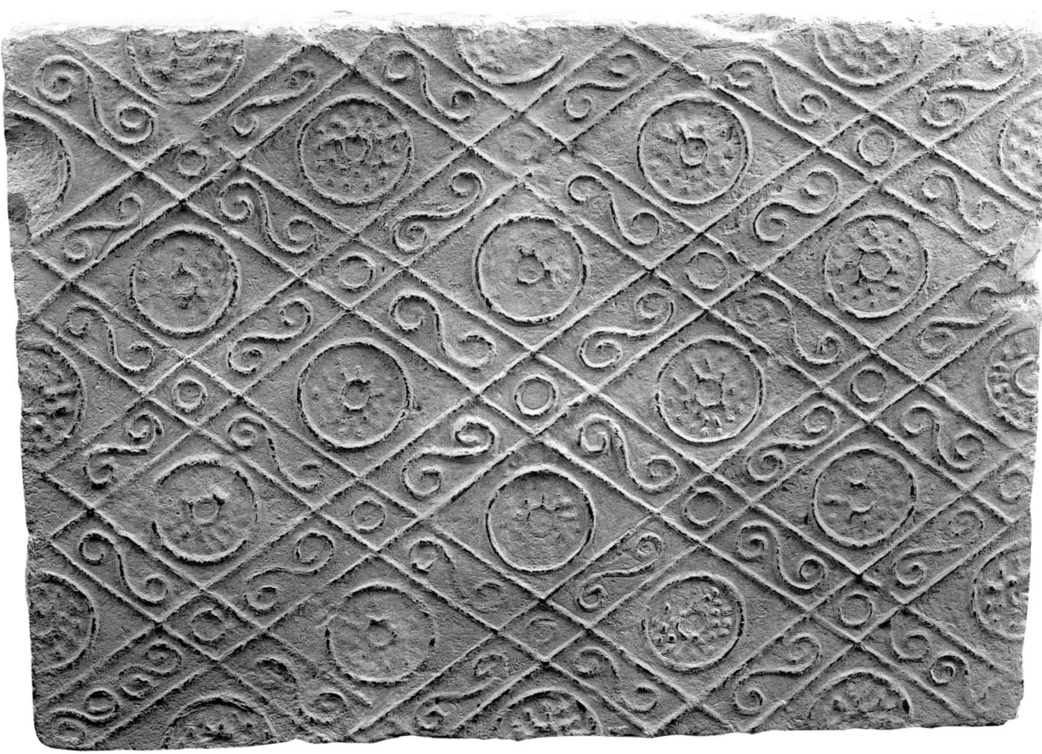

FIG. 79
(left) **Decorative pottery tiles paved the floors of Qin palaces. The designs, often geometric, were moulded or stamped on square and rectangular tiles before firing.**
Cat. no. 56

FIG. 80
(below) **Steps of the palaces were paved with hollow bricks decorated with zoomorphic and geometric designs. The bricks were placed on the floor with the designs pictured here facing upwards.**
Cat. nos 57 & 58

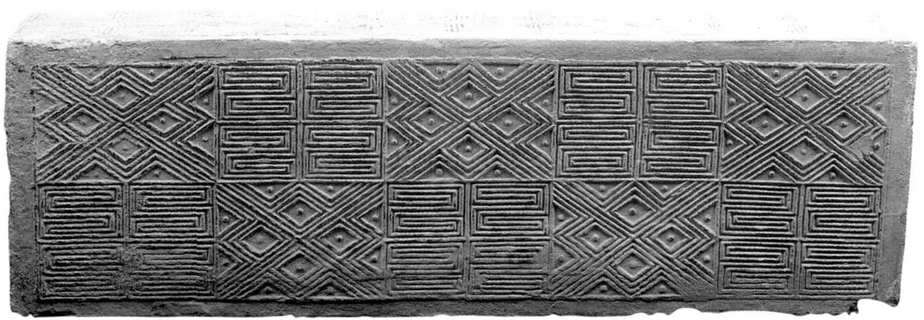

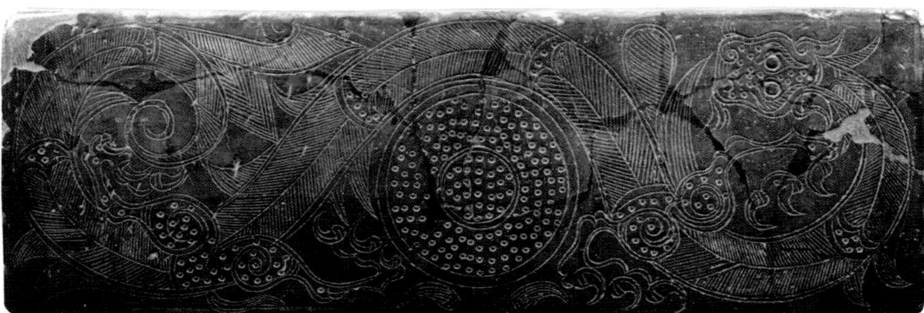

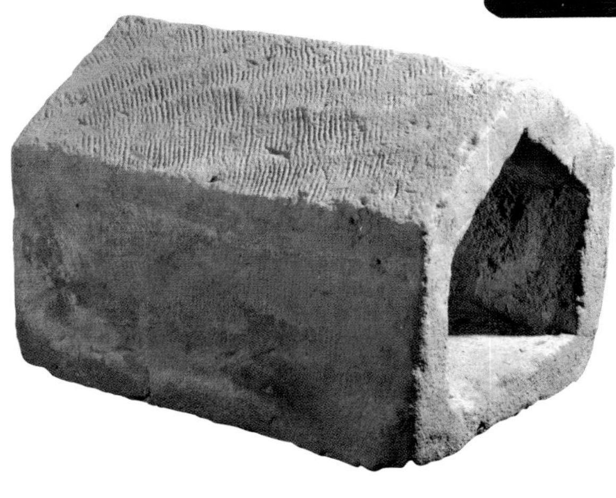

FIG. 81
(left) **Pentagonal pipes were used in complex drainage systems in both the palaces at Xianyang and the First Emperor's tomb complex. Made of a mixture of clay and sand, they were mass-produced in moulds.**
Cat. no. 59

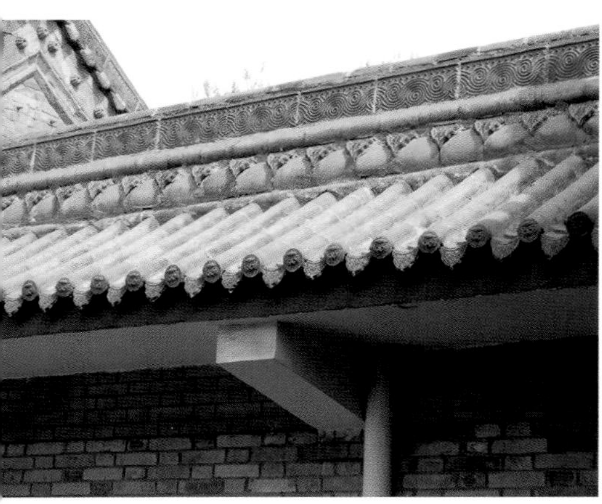

FIG. 82
Roof of the Xianyang Municipal Museum, Xi'an.

the city and the Wei River (*fig.* 60). The floors were paved with plain, square, clay bricks or bricks impressed with geometric patterning (*fig.* 79), while large, rectangular, hollow clay bricks decorated with zoomorphic and geometric designs (*fig.* 80) were used as steps.[8] Part of a wall painting depicting a carriage drawn by a team of four horses (*fig.* 78) was found in Palace 3, and more than 440 other painted fragments have been excavated from the palace complex indicating that the interiors were once decorated with brilliantly coloured murals painted in plaster.[9] Pottery pipes (*fig.* 81) preserved in the foundations of the buildings show that the palaces were equipped with an efficient drainage and sewage system. Stoves have been found in some rooms and a number of well-like pits are thought to have served as food coolers.[10]

Seventh-century-BC architectural remains show that Qin architecture followed the urban and palatial architectural tradition of the previous Zhou dynasty.[11] Excavations in the south part of Yongcheng, the capital of the Qin during the Spring and Autumn to Warring States periods (677–*c*.388 BC), reveal foundations of numerous large palace complexes and an ancestral temple. The beauty of the palaces at Yong is documented in the annals of the Qin. Bronze fittings (*fig.* 83) excavated in the palace area were used to decorate structural wood beams and reinforce the joins between beams and columns. Roofs were lined with differently shaped overlapping tiles (*fig.* 84), some decorated with circular ends embellished with the name of the palace (*fig.* 87) or with a variety of bird and animal designs (*fig.* 88). A recent discovery in 2006 of five kilns and over 2,000 pottery bricks, wall and roof tile ornaments, as well as crafting tools and moulds (*fig.* 86), suggests that there was a separate workshop area within the city for producing architectural elements.[12]

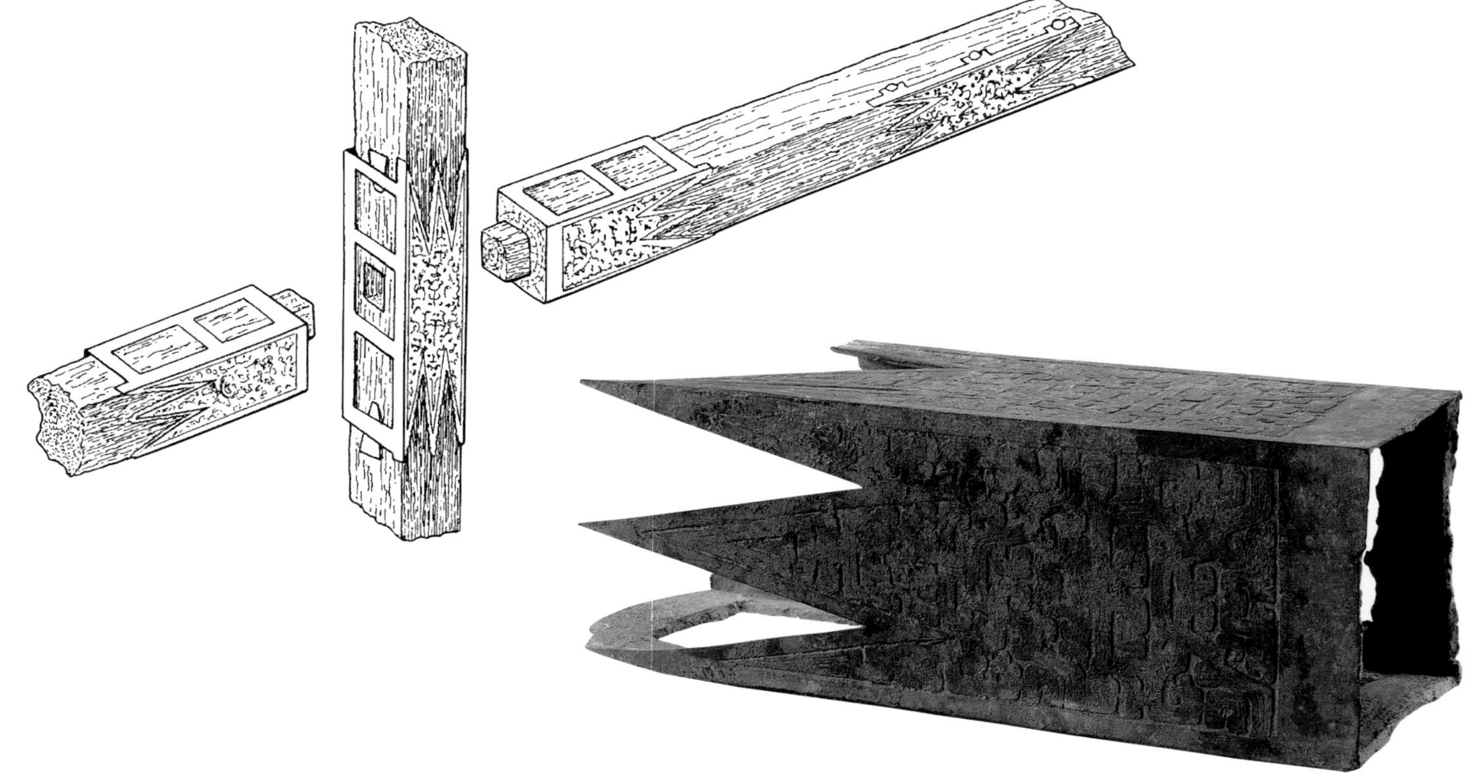

FIG. 83
These bronze structural fittings served both a decorative and a functional purpose. They would have ornamented the ends and middle sections of wooden beams and acted as reinforcements between beams and columns (see line drawing). These were found in a storage area of one of the palaces at Yong (today's Fengxiang, Shaanxi), the old capital of the Qin.
Cat. no. 60

With an established workshop tradition, large amounts of human and material resources as well as an excellent administration at his disposal, the First Emperor was able to commission vast numbers of building projects. Seal impressions found on architectural elements as well as on terracotta warriors (see pp. 132–4) indicate that craftsmen from local and state factories all over the country as well as smaller local centres worked together to create architectural parts for the First Emperor's building projects above ground as well as below ground.[13] The process of making a pipe or hollow brick is thought to have been relatively simple. Clay was coiled around an inner mould made of wood – circular in form for a drainpipe, rectangular if making a hollow paving tile (*fig.* 80) or step – which was lined with material to prevent the clay from sticking to the mould. The coiled clay would then be beaten down with a paddle or smoothed over with the hand to create an even surface. After drying, the hardened clay could be cut to various sizes, then fired.[14] This technique could produce a variety of different architectural elements: pipes, paving slabs, roof tiles, even stoves and cooling pits, as described above. The loess earth landscape meant that there was a plentiful supply of clay available, and the very long Chinese pottery tradition facilitated the establishment of an efficient system of mass production. Manpower was not a problem. Sima Qian records that more than 700,000 convicted men were assigned to work on the Ebang Palace and the First Emperor's tomb at Mt. Li (see p. 93), 30,000 households were transported to the town at Mt. Li and 50,000 households moved to Yunyang, the site of the Qin summer palace, Palace of Sweet Springs (*Ganquan gong*).[15]

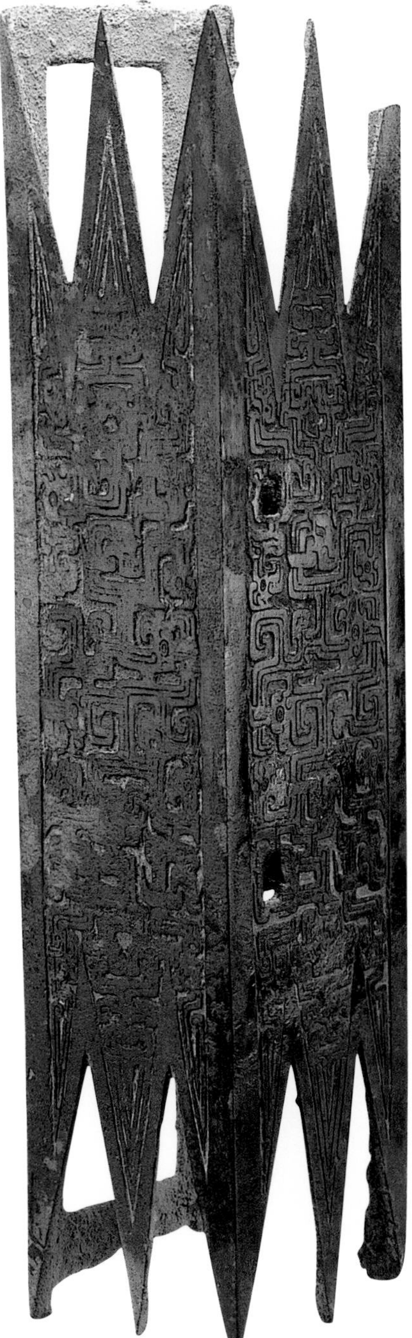

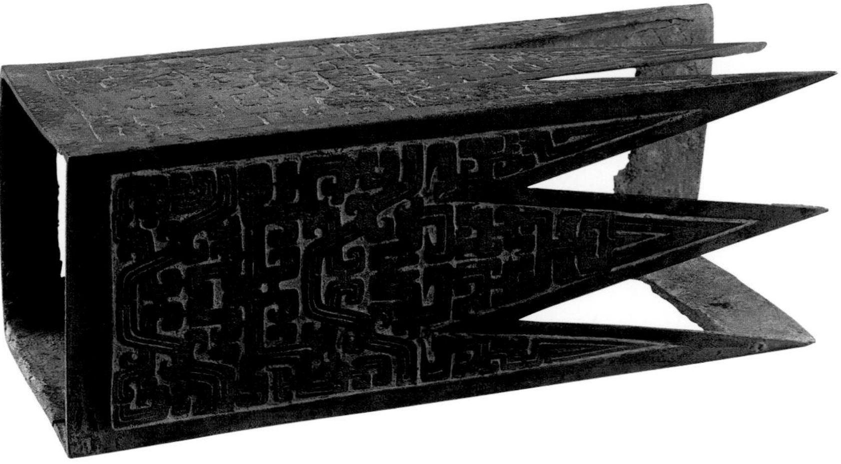

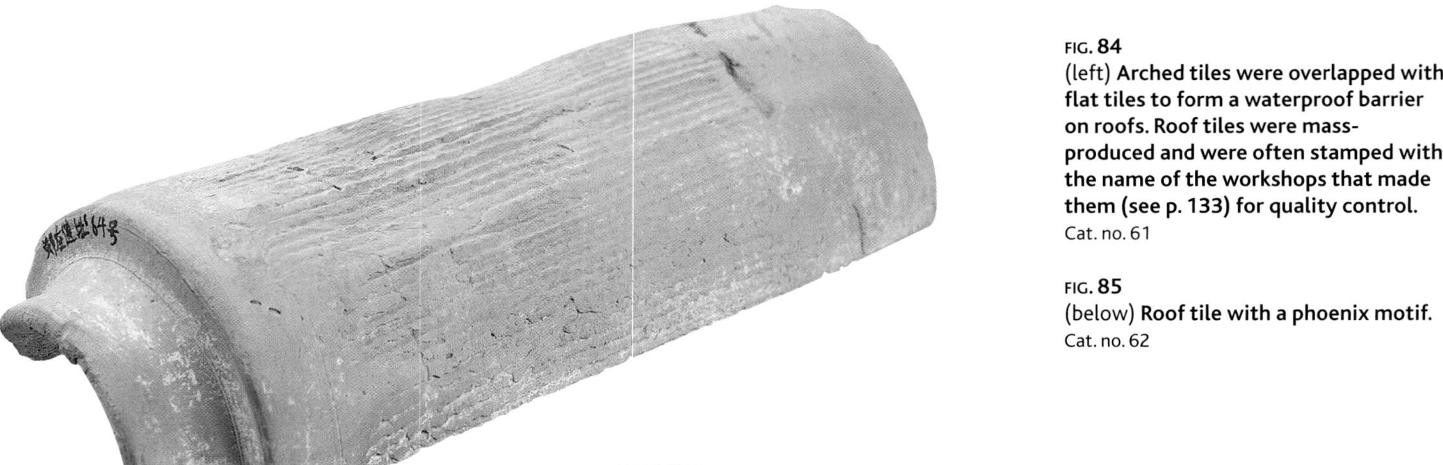

FIG. 84
(left) **Arched tiles were overlapped with flat tiles to form a waterproof barrier on roofs. Roof tiles were mass-produced and were often stamped with the name of the workshops that made them (see p. 133) for quality control.**
Cat. no. 61

FIG. 85
(below) **Roof tile with a phoenix motif.**
Cat. no. 62

FIG. 86
(opposite page and below) **These pottery architectural pieces were excavated in 2006 from Doufu village, Fengxiang, which was part of the old Qin capital of Yong. The site covers an area of 330,000 sq. metres and is thought to date to around the early to middle period of the Warring States. The similarities in design between tile ends found around Yong and those from this site suggest that the Doufu village site was a workshop area that specially produced tiles and bricks for the city.**
Cat. nos 63–8

Moulds with the design carved out in intaglio (below; and opposite page, centre and lower left) were used to produce a design in relief on the tile end (opposite page, top right) or wall ornament (opposite page, lower right). The bird (below right) has a hole in its base and is thought to be a roof ornament.

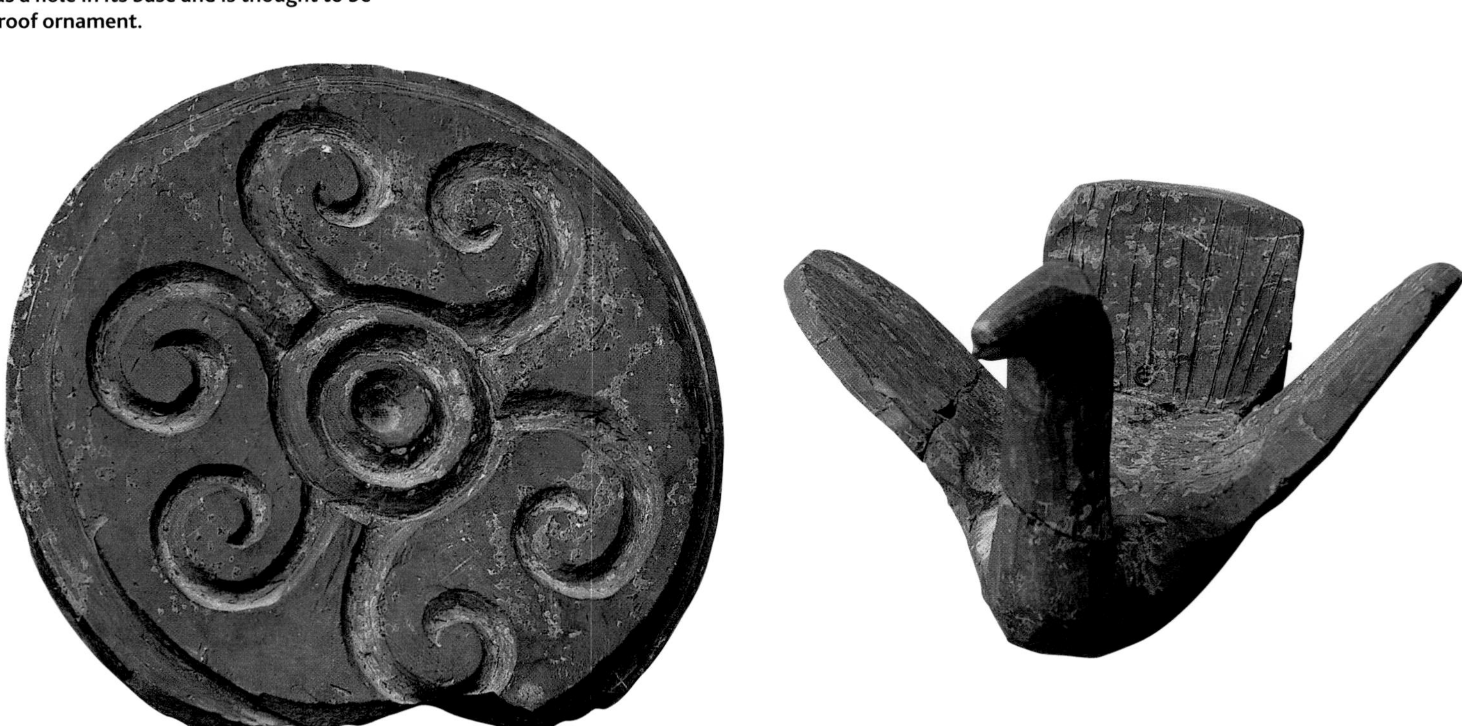

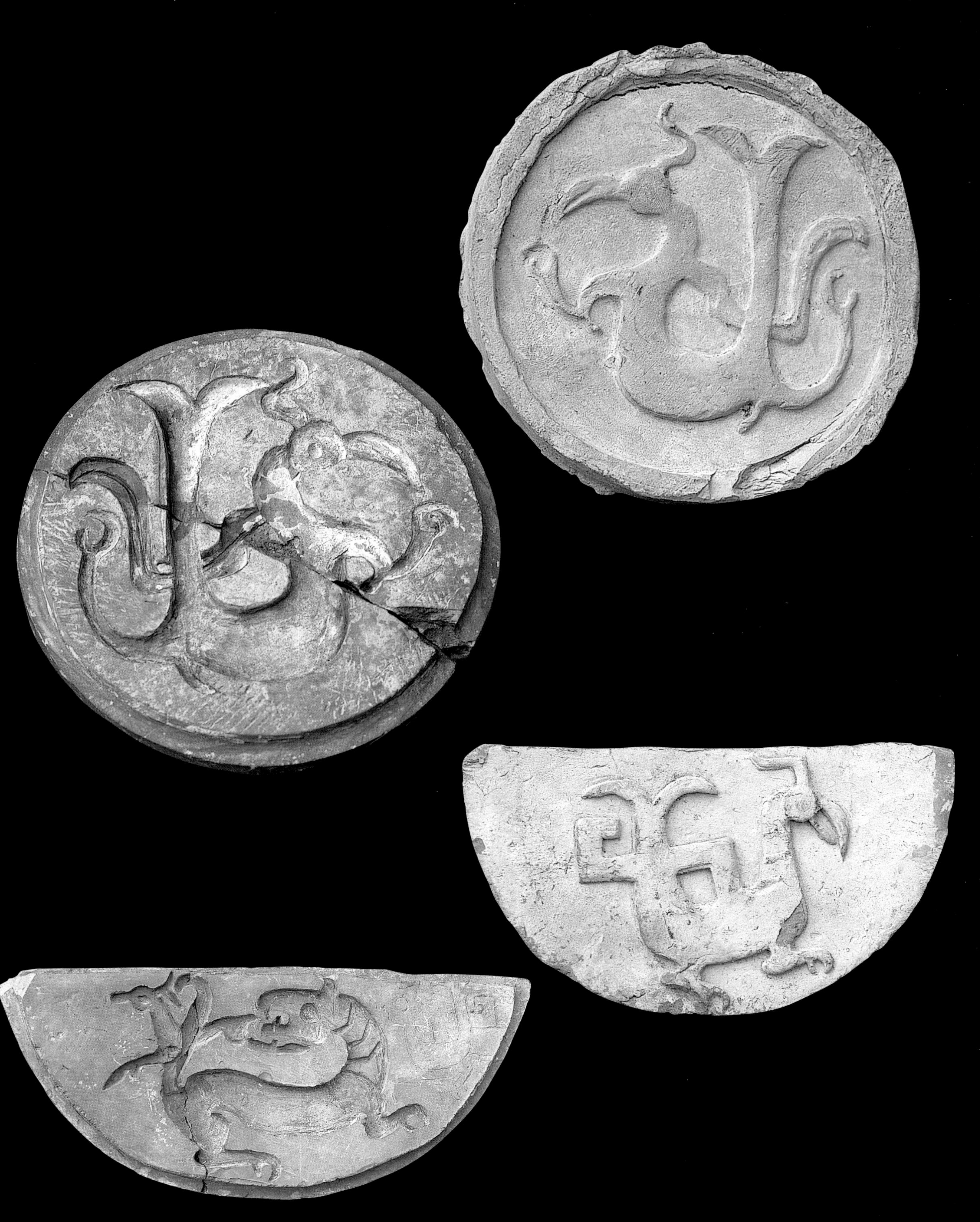

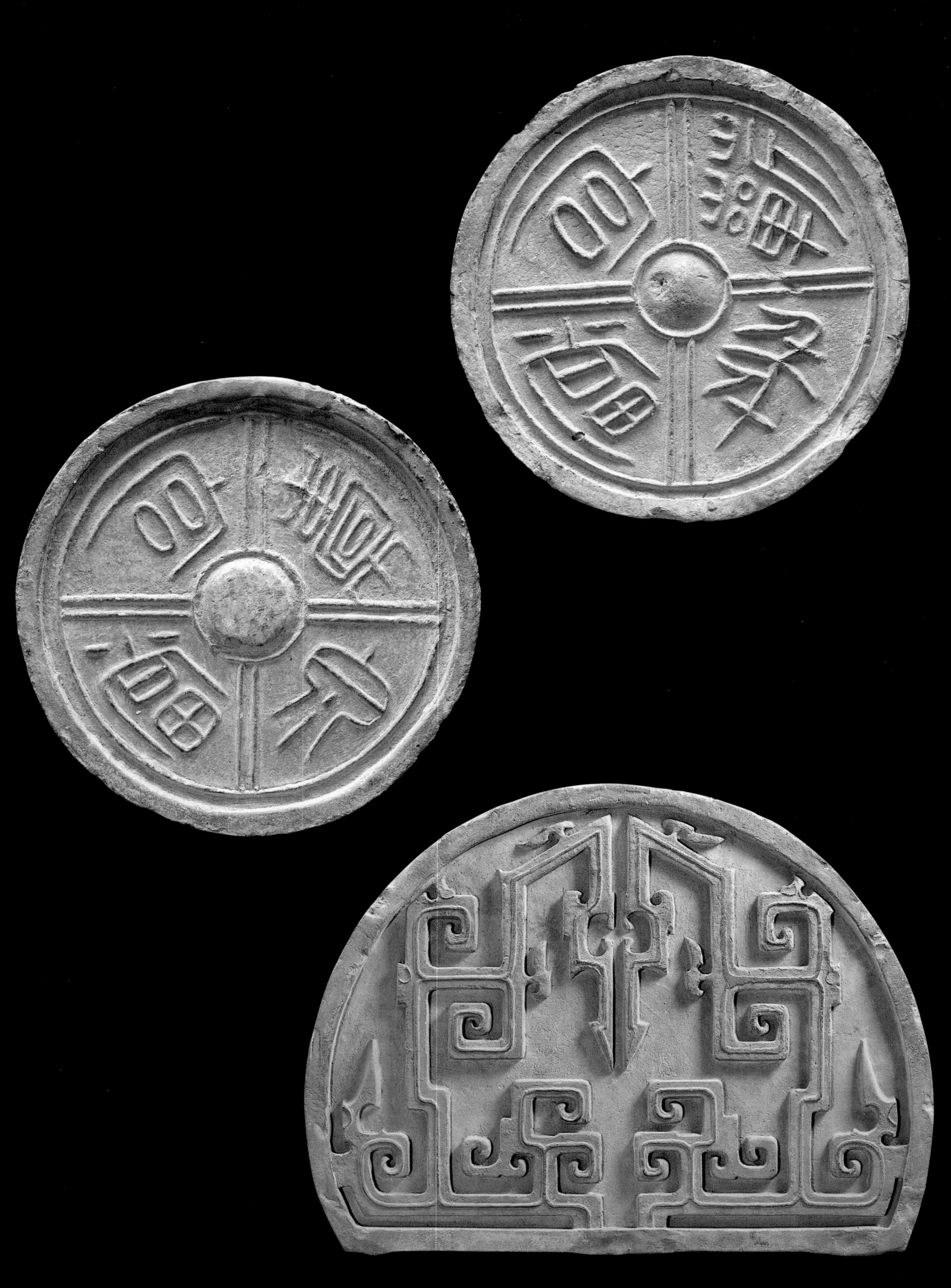

FIG. 87
(left) **The two tile ends, each decorated with four characters in relief, read (top right) 'Tile end of the Qinian Palace' and (far left) 'Tile end of the Tuoquan Palace'. Qinian palace was commissioned by Duke Hui (r. 399–387 BC) and along with Tuoquan Palace was one of the many large palaces at Yong, the old Qin capital. The very large tile end (bottom), with distinctive *kui* design, was excavated from Huangshan Palace at Xingping, Xianyang. Examples have been found at other Qin-palace sites: from the Jieshi Palace in Shibeidi, Liaoning province, a palace used by the emperor whilst on tour; and within the southern inner wall of the First Emperor's tomb complex at Lintong.**
Cat. nos 70–2

FIG. 88
(top right, right, below) **Roof tile ends decorated with deer, frog and dragon motifs. The first two were found at Fengxiang, where Yong, the Qin capital from 677 to *c.*383 BC, was located. Tile ends with similar dragon motif to the one below have also been found at Fengxiang; this example was excavated from the First Empeor's tomb complex.**
Cat. nos 73–5

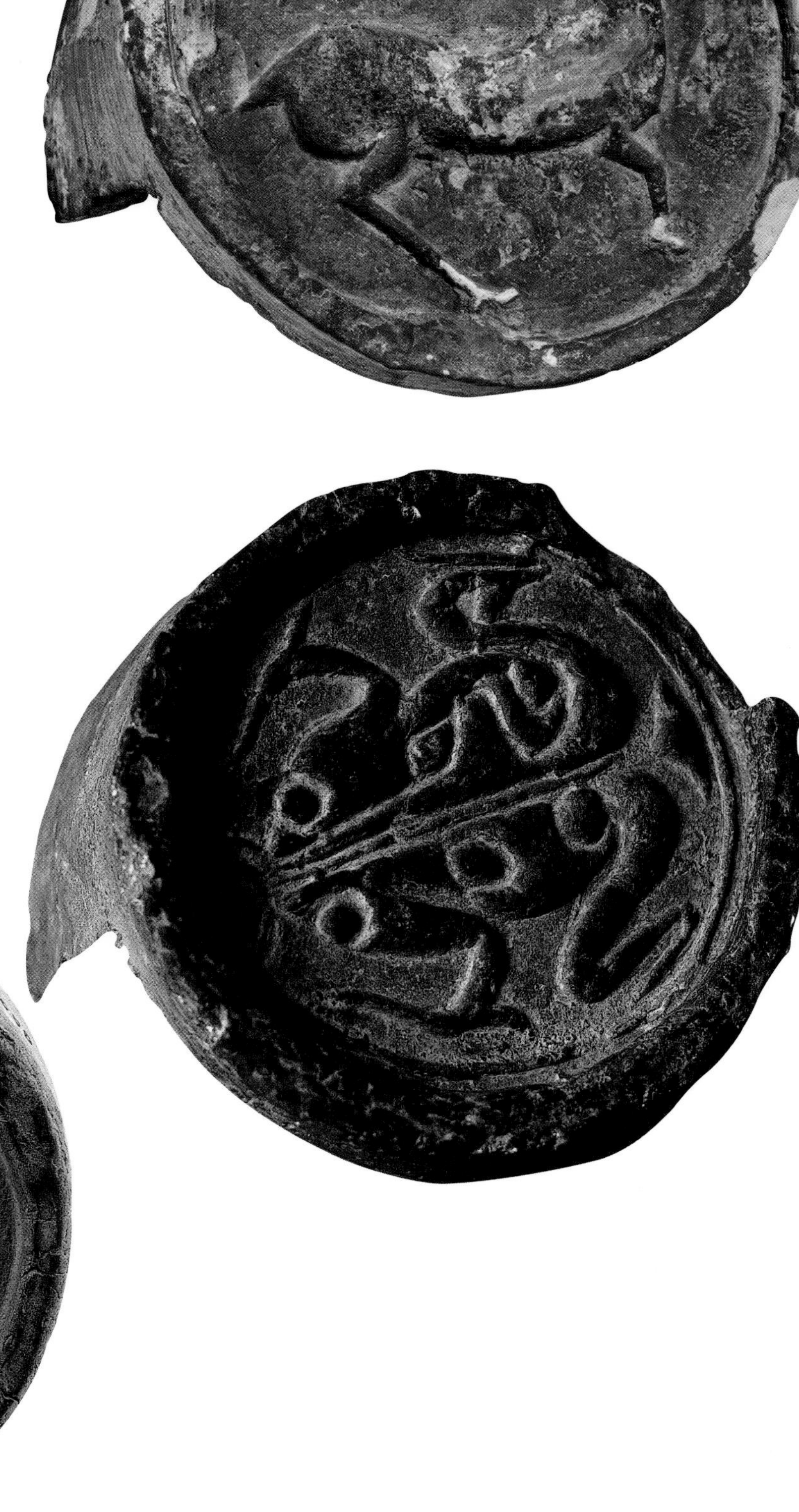

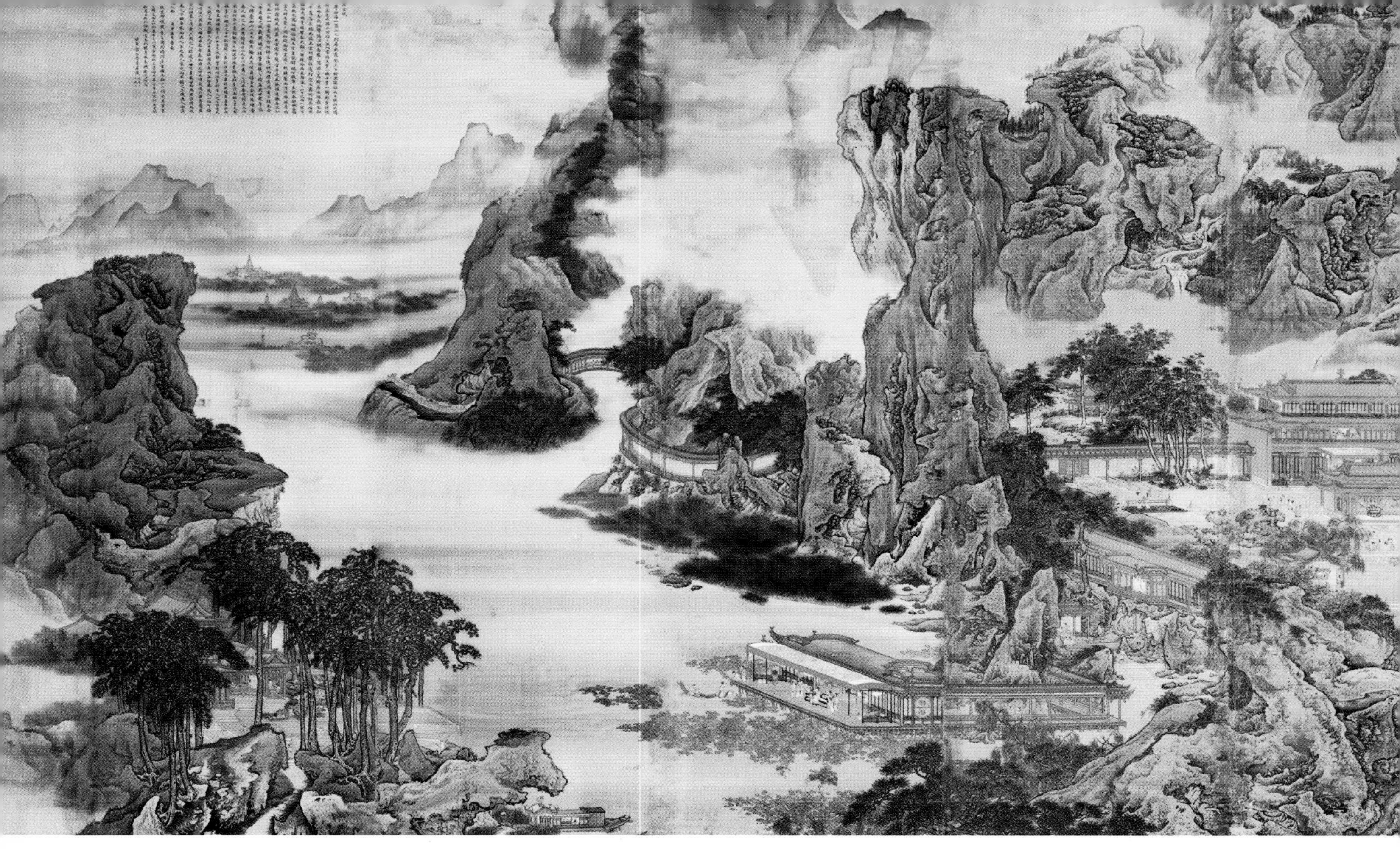

FIG. 89
Ebang Palace **by Yuan Jiang (active c.1690–c.1746), painter of the Manchu court during the Qing dynasty (1644–1911). Yuan Jiang was a successful professional artist from Yangzhou in southern China. He is known for his paintings of intricate Qing-style palatial architecture set within fantastic monumental landscapes in the style of the Tang and Song dynasties. Yuan produced large hanging scroll paintings and multi-panel screen paintings like** ***Ebang Palace*** **to decorate the mansions of Yangzhou's rich merchant elite.**

Ebang Palace

Armed with a massive workforce, the First Emperor could start construction on what has been thought of as the most magnificent palace ever built. Ebang Palace[16] in Shanglin Park, a hunting park south of the Wei River, was located on hallowed ground in an area between the ancient capitals of Feng and Hao established by previous Zhou kings.[17] The throne room is said to have measured 500 paces (*bu*) from east to west and fifty *zhang* from north to south, a staggering 690 by 115 metres.[18] The upper part could seat 10,000 persons and in the lower part flag poles five *zhang* (over 11 metres) high could be erected. It was surrounded by covered walks that led from the hall directly south to the Southern Mountains. The summit of the Southern Mountains was designated to be the gate of the palace. An elevated walk extended from Ebang north across the Wei River to connect the palace with Xianyang, in imitation of the way in which in the heavens a corridor leads from the Heavenly Apex star across the Milky Way to the Royal Chamber star.

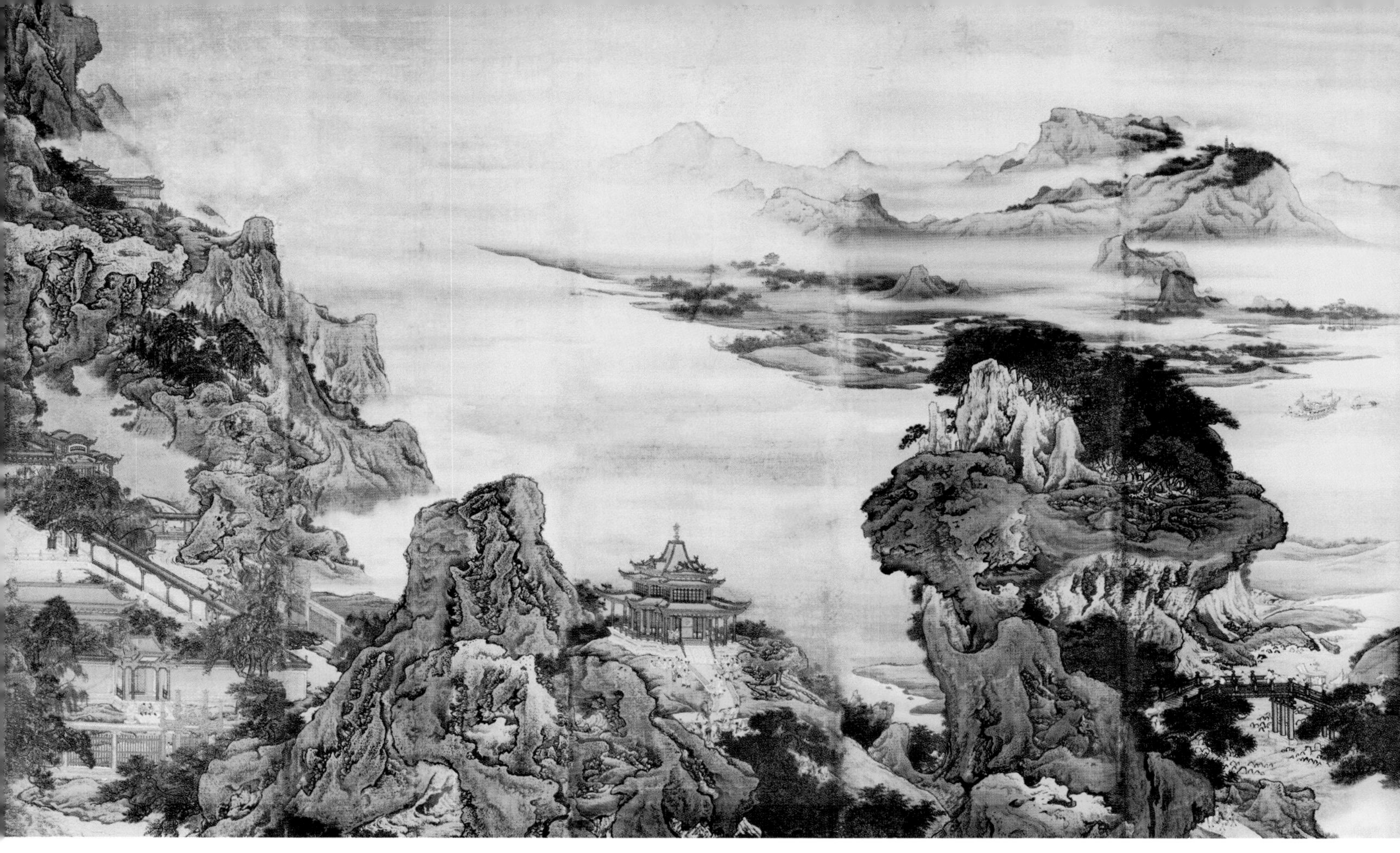

Sima Qian records that during uprisings led by Xiang Yu (232–202 BC), the peasant leader who overthrew the Qin dynasty, Xianyang was captured and its palaces razed to the ground. Fires burned for three continuous months. Although traces of burnt soil and ashes have been excavated from Xianyang Palace, archaeological evidence shows that Ebang seems to have been left untouched, although it was destroyed at the end of the Qin period.[19] Believed to be the largest and most luxurious palace in history, Ebang Palace captured the imagination of later artists and poets. In literature the grandeur of the palace is kept alive in *Ode to Ebang Palace* (*Ebang gong fu*) by the Tang poet Du Mu (AD 803–53), while a visual record of the building expressing the imagination of the eighteenth-century architectural painter to the Manchu court, Yuan Jiang, is preserved in an impressive screen painting on silk (*fig.* 89). The First Emperor built architectural monuments to show his consolidation of political and cultural unity and to glorify his achievements, and in this poem and painting, whether intrinsically accurate or not, a part of the First Emperor's vision is still very much present with us today.

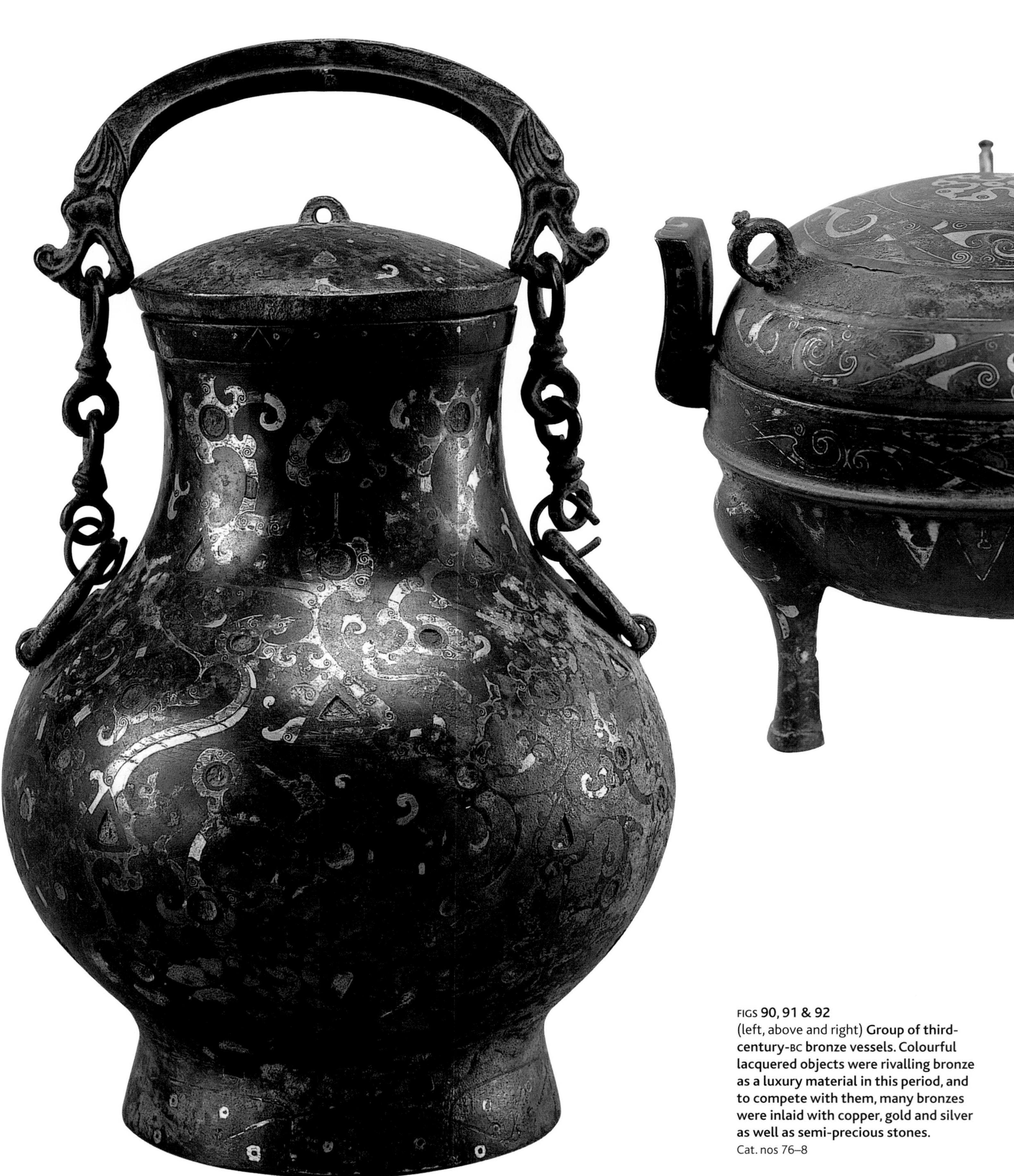

FIGS **90, 91 & 92**
(left, above and right) **Group of third-century-BC bronze vessels. Colourful lacquered objects were rivalling bronze as a luxury material in this period, and to compete with them, many bronzes were inlaid with copper, gold and silver as well as semi-precious stones.**
Cat. nos 76–8

QIN GOLD AND JADE

CAROL MICHAELSON

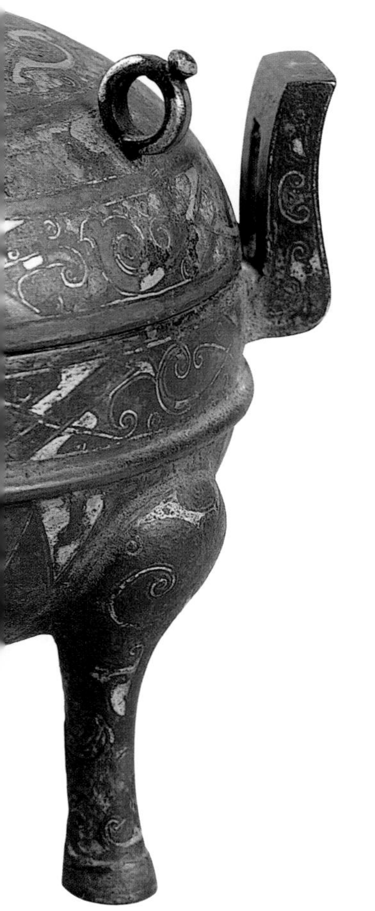

During the Warring States period, 475–221 BC, the Qin and other states within what is today China were competing with each other not only for hegemony but also in levels of ostentation at the various courts. The wealthy and successful were fully equipped in death to continue the courtly existence that had been so essential to their power in life. The great luxuries at this time included not only the long revered jades and bronzes that had been so much a part of Chinese tradition for millennia but also beautifully crafted lacquers, textiles and a new interest in objects of gold.

At a time when bronze was being used extensively for the many wars that were being fought between the states, a small state, such as Zeng, could bury one of its rulers, the Marquis Yi, who died in 433 BC, with 10 tonnes of bronze vessels and other luxuries of lacquer, textile and jade. He also had a solid gold ritual vessel and ladle buried with him, shaped like one of the contemporary bronzes and made in the cast-mould method, which therefore needed much more gold than if it had been hammered.[20]

Jade and bronze were the materials most prized by the ancient Chinese and were used by them for their most precious ritual vessels and ornaments.[21] The Chinese were working jade from about 5000 BC and bronzes, cast in ceramic moulds, from about 2000 BC. However, during the Warring States period the Bronze Age was gradually coming to an end and lacquer vied with it in popularity. To compete with the more colourful lacquers, therefore, the bronze manufacturers began inlaying bronze with gold, silver and copper and there are many bronzes remaining with such form of decoration today.

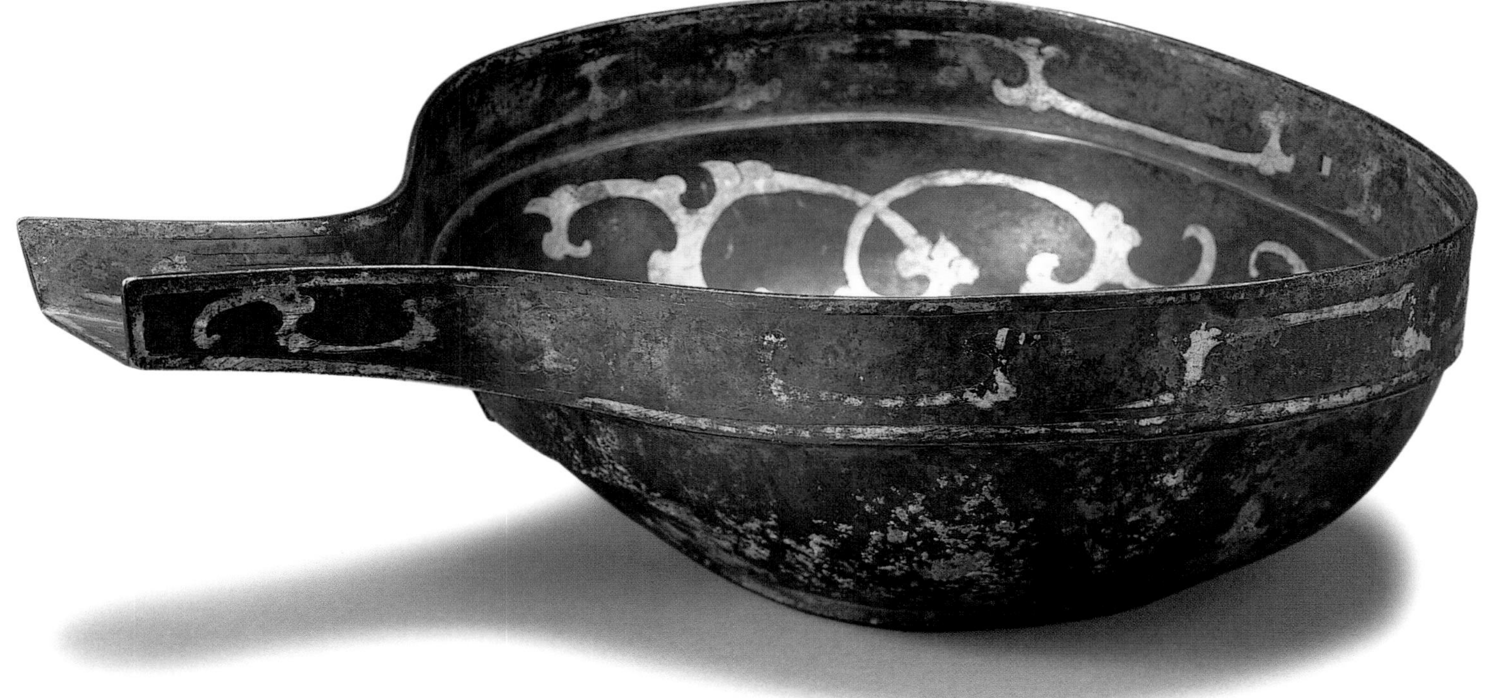

FIGS 93 & 94
(right and below) **Gold tiger fitting (Warring States period) and gold washer (middle–late Spring and Autumn period). These two gold items are cast, the same method used by the Chinese for making their bronzes. The washer is the heaviest item of gold that has so far been found in the Qin state. However, as it is quite a bit smaller than its bronze prototypes, it is possible that it was made specifically for burial.**
Cat. nos 79 & 80

Qin gold

Gold had played very little part in luxury objects until the peoples living on the western periphery of what is today China came into contact with the nomadic peoples of the Steppe.[22] A defining characteristic of the Western and Eastern Zhou dynasties (c.1050–221 BC) is this growing influence of gold and its impact on the luxury objects of the period.[23]

The nomadic peoples of the Steppe had always valued gold in a way that the Chinese had not; they had worked the metal with hammer and anvil, particularly for shaping vessels, from at the least the second millennium BC. Gold, especially when compared to jade, is a very malleable metal well suited to intricate design, and the peoples of the Steppe made ornaments in gold, including forms such as belt plaques. Such gold artefacts were often placed in, for example, Scythian tombs; the common motif of animals in combat on these gold ornaments reflects the taste of nomadic culture. Over time, as the Chinese became more expert in working gold, their imports of horses, cattle and other typical northern products, such as furs, mentioned in texts like the *Zhanguoce*,[24] may have been paid for with gold and silver objects, which they fashioned in a style attractive to the nomads.

The Qin state, situated in part of what is today Shaanxi province and on the far west of the Zhou state, had plenty of opportunities to come into contact with these nomadic peoples and was influenced by their interest in gold. From the Spring and Autumn period (770–475 BC) to the beginning of the following Warring States period gold was cast into ornaments and weapon accessories, such as the gold hilt from Yimen, Baoji, an earlier example of the type represented by the well-known dagger hilt in the British Museum.[25] Gold vessels seem to have been extremely rare in the Spring and Autumn period, although a gold xi, or washer, was buried in Shaanxi province (*fig.* 80).

Daoist priests had worked assiduously to try and produce an elixir of immortality using the ingredients of mercury and gold. Such experiments led indirectly to the invention of the mercury gilding technique on bronze vessels. By the end of the Eastern Zhou and during the Qin and Han dynasties, the technique of gilding was used more and more extensively as it was realized that this was a less expensive way of achieving a golden surface than by making a solid item or by inlaying with metal.[26]

Another important Chinese appropriation from its nomadic neighbours was the practice of horseback riding and mounted warfare. This refers not only to the introduction of riding astride but also to the clothing and horse equipment that made this practical. A comparison between the saddles and bridles shown on the cavalry horses of the First Emperor's terracotta army and those found at the southern Siberian site at Pazyryk (fifth century BC) indicates the Chinese debt to the mounted tribes of the Eurasian Steppe.[27] The Chinese were not natural riders; China was an agrarian country, entirely dissimilar to the pastoral culture practised by its neighbours. Oxen were seen as more economical to feed and keep for draught work on a farm and China's chronic horse shortages meant that the use of horses was

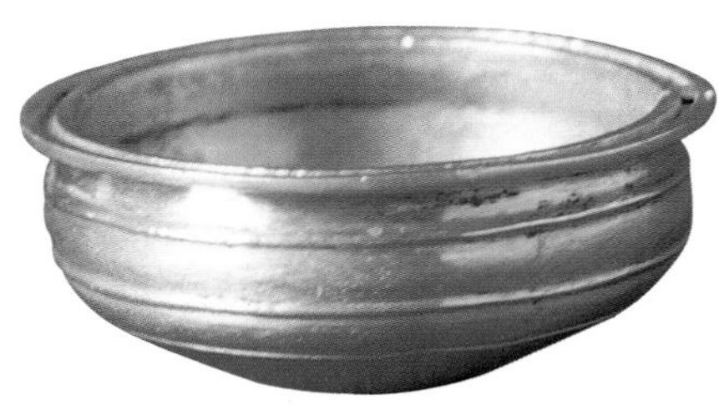

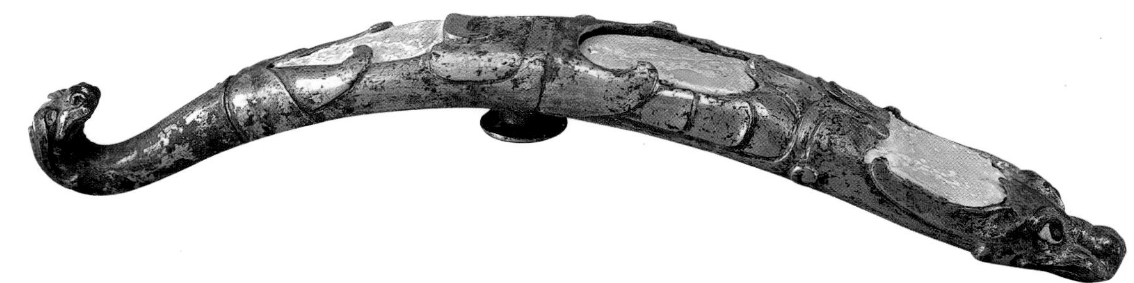

FIG. 95
(right) **Gilt-bronze belt hook, Warring States period, which has been inlaid with shell. Many such materials were considered very precious and broken pieces of shell and jade were often reused as inlays on belt hooks and other decorative items.**
Cat. 81

FIG. 96
(below) **Gold belt hook with dragons, Qin state, late Spring and Autumn period. This hook is comprised of convoluted, writhing dragons and is a very good example of the fine workmanship achieved by the Qin craftsmen of the Spring and Autumn period of the Zhou dynasty. The body is formed by four dragons and their scale-like bodies are clearly delineated in the gold material.**
Cat. no. 82

restricted to government and court officials and the military. The long robes traditionally worn by the Chinese also presented a serious barrier to riding astride.

The Chinese adoption of cavalry warfare is generally dated to the Warring States period. There is a much quoted reference to King Wuling (r. 325–299 BC) of the Zhao state (located in modern Shanxi and western Hebei provinces). Because of the frequent incursions by foreign tribes from the north, Wuling realized the value of developing a mobile cavalry to fight these nomads. Despite the resistance of his people, in 307 BC the king decreed that his troops should adopt the more practical nomadic costume, including trousers,[28] which needed a belt and hooks to keep them up (*figs* 95–7).

The earliest reference to a garment hook in a Chinese text is in the *Jinyu* section of the *Guoyu* (*Conversations from the States*) generally dated to about the third century BC. Some belt hooks are extraordinarily large and long, which suggests that not all of them were used for tying belts but were designed as a sword sling or to act as an attachment to a belt. Some other small metal hooks may also have been worn vertically on a belt to support small knives, pouches or related personal paraphernalia, as the Chinese had no pockets in their gowns.[29] Some of the belt hooks of this period from Shaanxi province also have a pattern of dots, emulating the effect of granulation, a Western technique exploited in gold and silver.

The use of gold and silver for luxuries, including such objects as the reins and horse decorations found on the chariots made for the First Emperor, Qin Shihuangdi, is testimony to the very high standards of technology and organization that Qin artisans achieved.

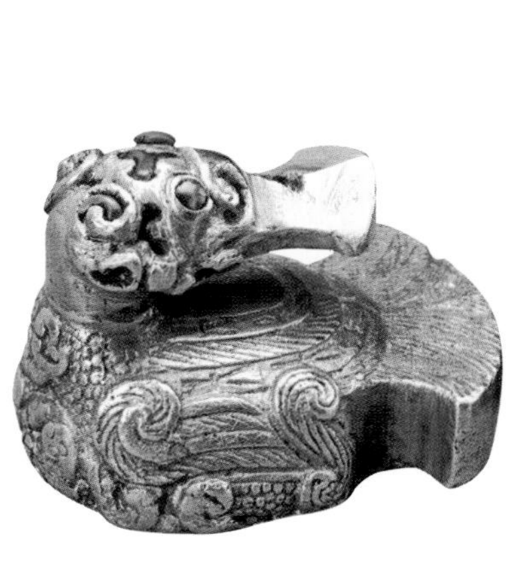

FIG. 97
(left) **Gold duck-shaped belt hook, Spring and Autumn period, Qin state (770–475 BC). This belt hook is in the shape of a duck, with its head facing backwards and the beak acting as the hook. Engraved lines and dots on the surface represent the wings and feathers. On the body are several holes that have been filled with turquoise, though some are now missing.**
Cat. no. 83

Qin jade

Despite the popularity of gold as a new material for luxury objects, jade was still the material most highly prized by the Chinese of all materials. Jade is deeply embedded in Chinese culture and had come to represent abstract qualities of purity and excellence. Gold never reached such high esteem in the hierarchy of valued materials, but during the Warring States period it was occasionally paired with jade as, for example, on a handle (*fig. 101*).[30] The combination of jade and gold here is interesting: jade is the traditional Chinese material and gold the newer foreign one, but in this instance the gold bears the familiar *taotie* mask, a popular motif often found on early bronzes. The juxtaposition of the traditional and the exotic perhaps conferred some special value to this object. Such mask designs may well have been inspired by ceramic pattern-block motifs used on bronzes and found in large numbers in Houma, the capital of the state of Jin.

Jade was worked at least 7,000 years ago and some of the earliest finds have been unearthed from the Chahai sites in Liaoning province. Apart from the excavations in north-east China, Neolithic jades have also been found in Shandong, the river basins of the Yellow and the Yangtze rivers, and in south-east and south-west China, demonstrating the wide spread of jade working. From the end of the Neolithic period jade was sourced from the far western reaches of what is today Xinjiang province. Quite unlike gold, jade is very hard to work and cannot be carved but rather has to be abraded with tools and abrasive materials. This is very labour-intensive and time-consuming work. During the Shang dynasty (*c.*1570–1050 BC) bronze rivalled the importance of jade, but the political and economic stability in late Shang brought about a revival of the jade industry. The advent of iron tools, from about 650 BC, further improved the crispness and fluidity of jade workmanship, and there evolved distinct regional decorative styles, among which the ornate curl or spiral motif of the Chu state (*fig. 100*)[31] and the very geometric and angular incised forms of the Qin state are particularly notable (*figs 98–9, 102–4*).[32]

FIGS **98 & 99**
(below) **Jade *xi* and *heng* pendants, late Spring and Autumn period. Tombs of high ranking nobles from the late Western and early Eastern Zhou periods have revealed long sets of ornaments that covered the body from the neck to the knees. This practice might have been linked to a belief in jade's ability to provide symbolic and physical protection for the body against decay. Such sets were composed of arc-shaped jades, plaques, tubular jades, and turquoise and faience beads strung together. These pendants are decorated with dragon heads in the typical Qin geometric style.**
Cat. nos 84 & 85

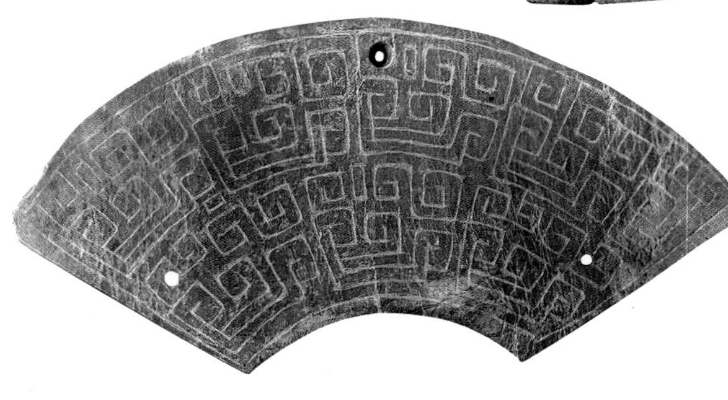

Aesthetically and technically, the jades of the Warring States period are among the finest that have ever been produced in China. A whole range of relief decoration evolved on the surfaces of jades and bronzes that complemented and echoed gold work. Gold could be very easily formed into openwork with intricate surface decoration, effects that were very difficult to create in jade, yet Eastern Zhou jade carving managed to emulate so many of the decorative effects of the gold objects. Openwork, too, was exploited on jade pendants and later on elaborate discs. It could be said that the ways in which jade reflected the light were greatly increased through openwork, thereby mimicking the light-reflecting capacities of gold.

Several times in Chinese history ancient jade forms were rediscovered and to some extent reused. During the Liangzhu Neolithic culture, *c.*3000 BC, of Zhejiang and Jiangsu provinces the quintessential jades were the *bi* (a flat disc with a central round hole) and the *cong* (a square tube with a central circular hole). After the Liangzhu period completely undecorated

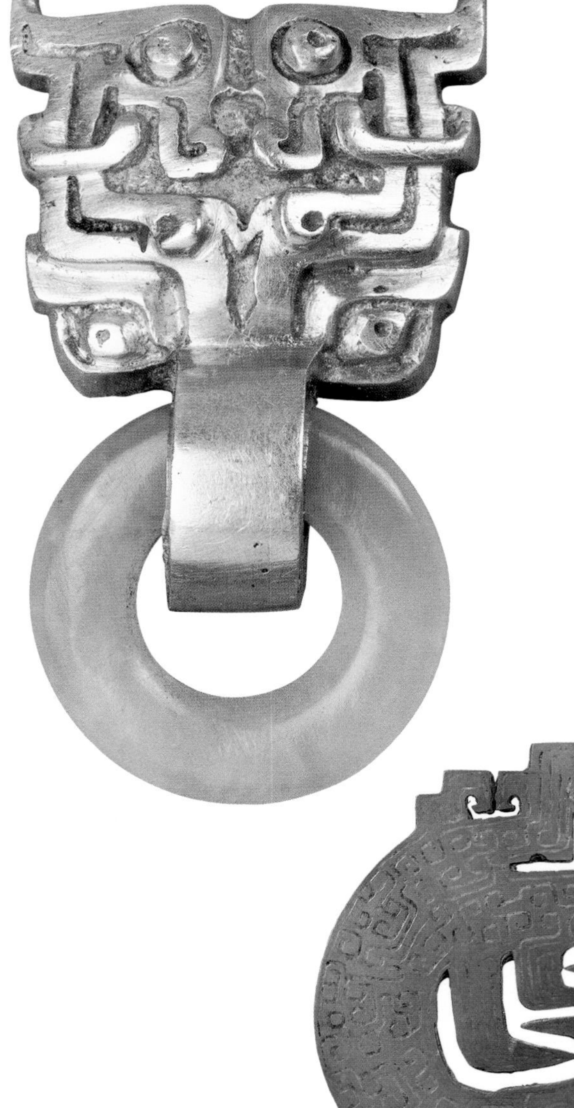

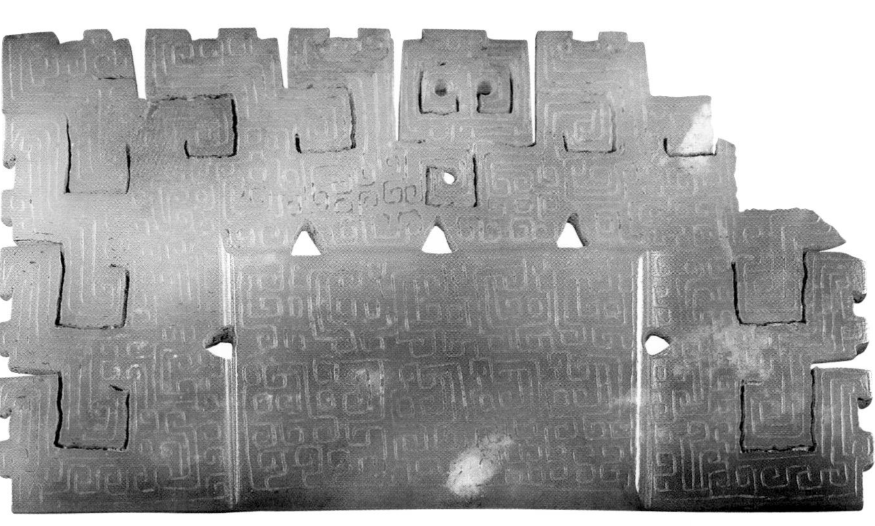

FIG. 100
(far left) **Jade *pei*, late Spring and Autumn period. This *pei* is decorated with a distorted coiled serpent design, which is very similar to that found on jades from a Chu state tomb of the late Spring and Autumn period, sixth century BC, in Xiasi, Sichuan district, Henan province.**
Cat. no. 86

FIG. 101
(left) **Gold *taotie* monster mask with a jade ring, Qin state, Warring States period. One of the most valued treasures of the period, this miniature gold and jade handle is very unusual as generally they were made of bronze or iron. Its small size might indicate that it was specifically made for burial. The gold is worked into two monster masks, one above the other, showing teeth and horns, and the lower monster has a tongue or nose extended to hold the jade ring. At the back is an iron bar for attachment.**
Cat. no. 87

FIGS 102 & 103
(left and below) **Jade circular *pei* and pendant with Qin-style angular carved relief decoration, late Spring and Autumn period. Both these jades have holes in them by which they could have been strung together with other ornaments. The angular incised scroll decoration is inspired by contemporary work in gold. The inner plaque within the rectangular pendant has fifteen square-shaped intertwined dragon-head patterns and on both pendant pieces there are remains of cinnabar, often found on ancient jades.**
Cat. nos 88 & 89

cong continued to be used in the north-west in the late Neolithic period and perhaps into historical times.[33] The Qin state, which occupied the north-west, probably inherited and perhaps copied the undecorated *cong* from that area,[34] particularly those of the Qijia culture, located in today's Gansu province, close to the area where Qin state originally emerged (*fig.* 105). It has also been suggested that Qin reworked some undecorated older Qijia jades.[35] Examples of *cong* found in western Shaanxi, such as at Shangquan, Chang'an county and at Fengxiang county, typically have a glossy polish and are undecorated. *Bi* almost disappeared in the Shang and the Western Zhou periods, but discs and some rings of that kind started to reappear in some numbers from the fifth century BC (*fig.* 104). At this date they carried various forms of relief scrolls, and the high polish on these rings betrays the influence of the gold decorative forms on the jade with which it was competing.

Many jades during the Western and Eastern Zhou periods were parts of pendant sets, usually strung with beads, to make ornaments that hung from the waist or shoulders. These pendant sets have been found in many burials of the period, such as those of the Qin state at Yimen, Baoji, as well as other Warring States tombs of Jin, Zhou, Wei and Chu.[36] Zhou and Han replica figures in lacquered wood, bronze and jade, which were buried in graves to act as servants in the afterworld, depicted such pendants and give us some clue as to how they were worn, perhaps in life as well as in death. The profuse pendants that covered the face and the body in death would appear to have been intended to protect the dead against malign forces; they cannot have been simply for display (see also, pp. 188–9). Pendant sets are also mentioned in texts, often associated with the sound of tinkling, as such harmonious sounds, produced by officials wearing these jades at official audiences, were supposed to prevent evil thoughts entering the mind.

There are frequent references to jade libation cups in poetry of the Zhou and Han periods, but jade vessels were almost unknown before the third century BC and their rather sudden appearance seems to be linked to the use of vessels in other luxurious materials such as bronze, lacquer, glass and silver, of which the jade versions are rare copies. From the end of the Warring States period there was a popular belief that to eat and drink from utensils made of gold or jade could prolong peoples' lives; the Chinese seem gradually to have believed that gold and jade could prevent bodily decay because these two kinds of material were highly resistant to corrosion.

There are only six known jade cups dating from the late Warring States to Han periods and it is thought that the beaker shape (*figs* 106–8) has its origins in a Western glass vessel from Begram in Afghanistan dating to the third to first century BC.[37] The shape is also found in rock crystal in a Warring States vessel as well as in lacquer of the same period. There is a similar beaker in the slightly later,

FIG. **104**
Jade ritual disc (*bi*) with angular Qin-style angular carved-relief decoration, late Spring and Autumn period. In the Liangzhu Neolithic period the best-quality *bi* were placed on the chest and stomach of the deceased and lesser-quality *bi* were often piled up at the foot. We can only speculate as to the early significance of these objects in Neolithic times, but later generations prized the best-quality *bi* and they were used as bribes and gifts between the different states of the Zhou dynasty, as well as being buried with the deceased. This *bi* is covered with Qin-style dragon patterns arranged in circles, with a total of ninety-eight dragons on both sides. The decoration of such discs may well have begun in Shaanxi in the area of the Qin state and have been based on the fine incised lines on gold ornaments that were popular here before spreading to the rest of China.
Cat. no. 90

Han-dynasty King of Nanyue's tomb in Guangzhou, dating to about 122 BC, mounted in a bronze basin stand. It has been suggested that such beakers may have been intended to collect the dew left by the immortals. The king was also buried with a jade rhyton, another Western shape, which again was probably introduced to the Chinese from the West in a metallic form and copied by them in jade.[38] A jade vessel with an eagle's head, in the Freer Gallery, Washington, DC, can be compared to two others, one in gilt bronze and one in lacquer, found in the Chu state period tombs at Baoshan. The use of eagles' heads and the gilding on the bronze suggest that the model for these pieces came from central Asia. As jade was the most precious Chinese material, it would seem appropriate to copy such foreign, exotic vessels in this most revered mineral.

During the Warring States period the Qin and other states expended much time, money and effort on fighting, but it was also a time when luxuries were produced in astonishing quantities. This reflects both the great wealth and the technical skills of the artisans of the period, a time when gold made an impact as a material in its own right as well as influencing contemporary jades.

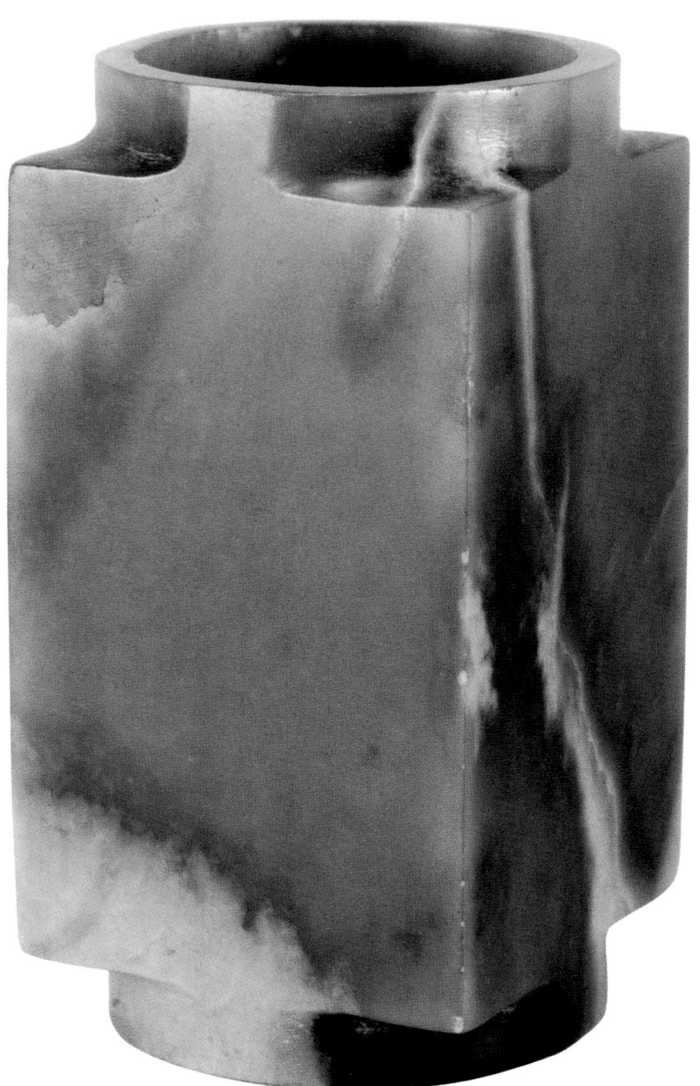

FIG. 105
Jade ritual object (*cong*), late Neolithic to early Dynastic period. *Cong*, many decorated with monster masks, were found aligning the body in the graves of the Liangzhu Neolithic culture of south-east China (*c*.3000–2000 BC). The undecorated form of this example, with its fine polished surface, is a later version of the older *cong* and is found in western China, in Shaanxi province, dating to the Longshan Neolithic period, and in the Qijia culture in Gansu province, dating from the late Neolithic period into the Shang and Zhou periods. We can only speculate as to the significance of these enigmatic objects, as any writings about them were written thousands of years after they were first made.
Cat. no. 91

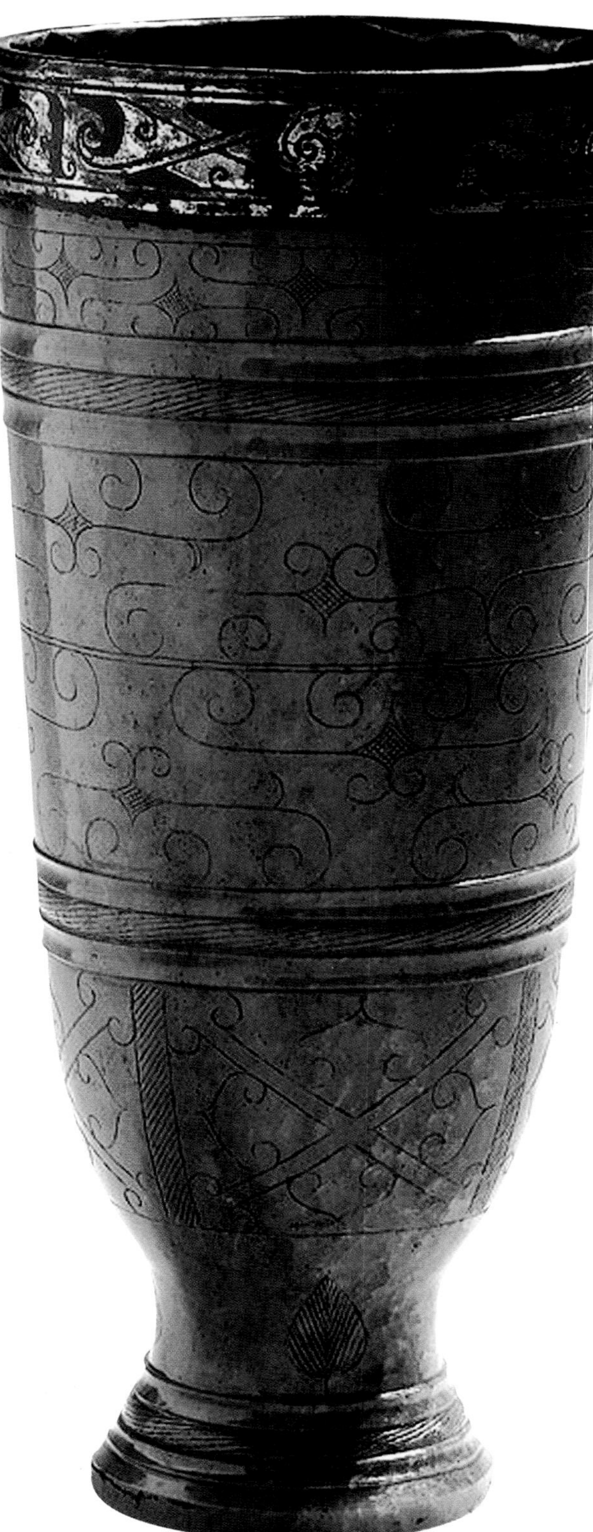

FIGS 106–8
Jade beakers and lacquer beaker, Warring States to Han period. This jade beaker (right), found at the site of the Qin-dynasty Ebang Palace, has decoration similar to one found in the tomb of the King of Nanyue in Guangzhou, who died *c.* 122 BC. The decoration is worked in low relief, and has small interlocking scrolls with borders of scrolling decoration reminiscent of contemporary lacquer. Like the Nanyue beaker, this one has a hole in the base so that it might have been fixed onto a stand, as does the other example in jade (left), which has a metal liner, probably added in the Tang dynasty (AD 618–906). The lacquer beaker (below) is one of a pair and is decorated in a painterly style typical of southern lacquer ware of the period. It is inlaid with gold and silver and has bronze mounts on the rim and foot.
Cat. no. 92 (right)

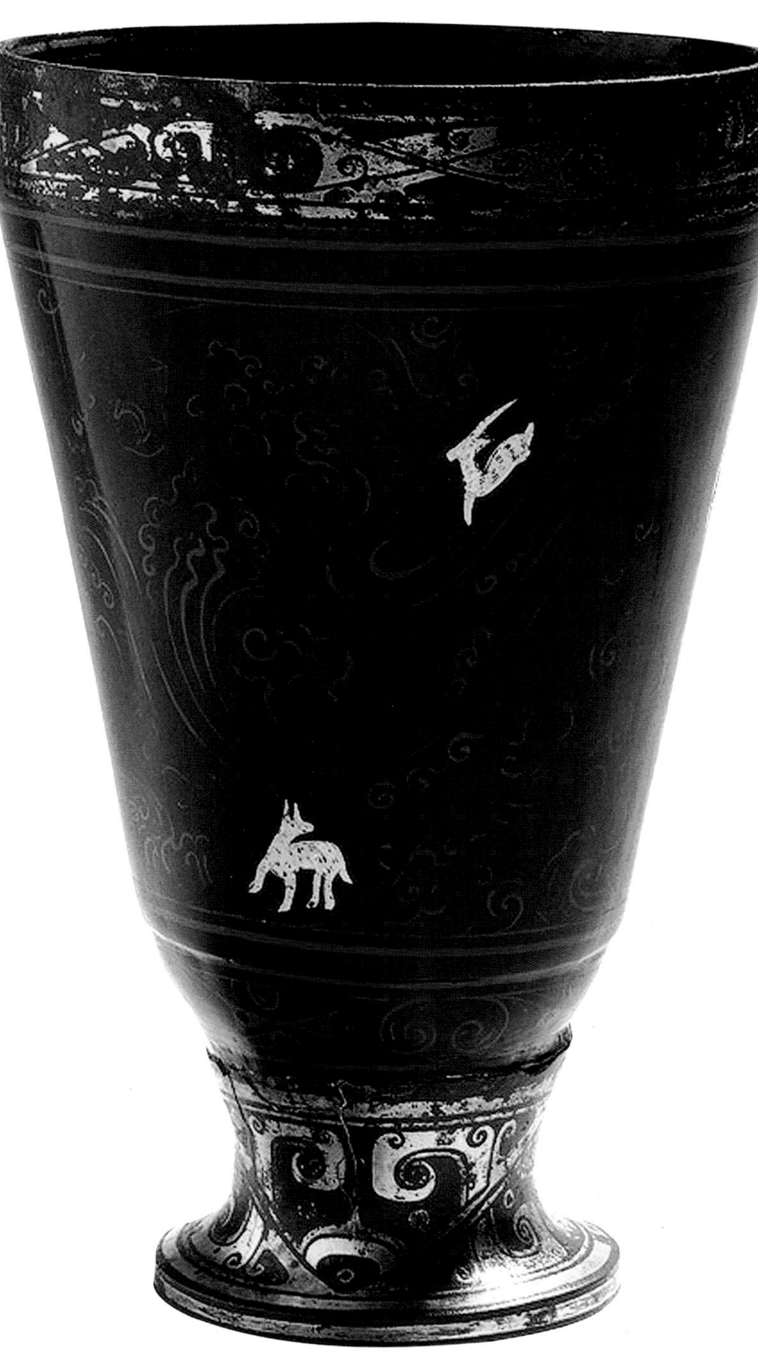

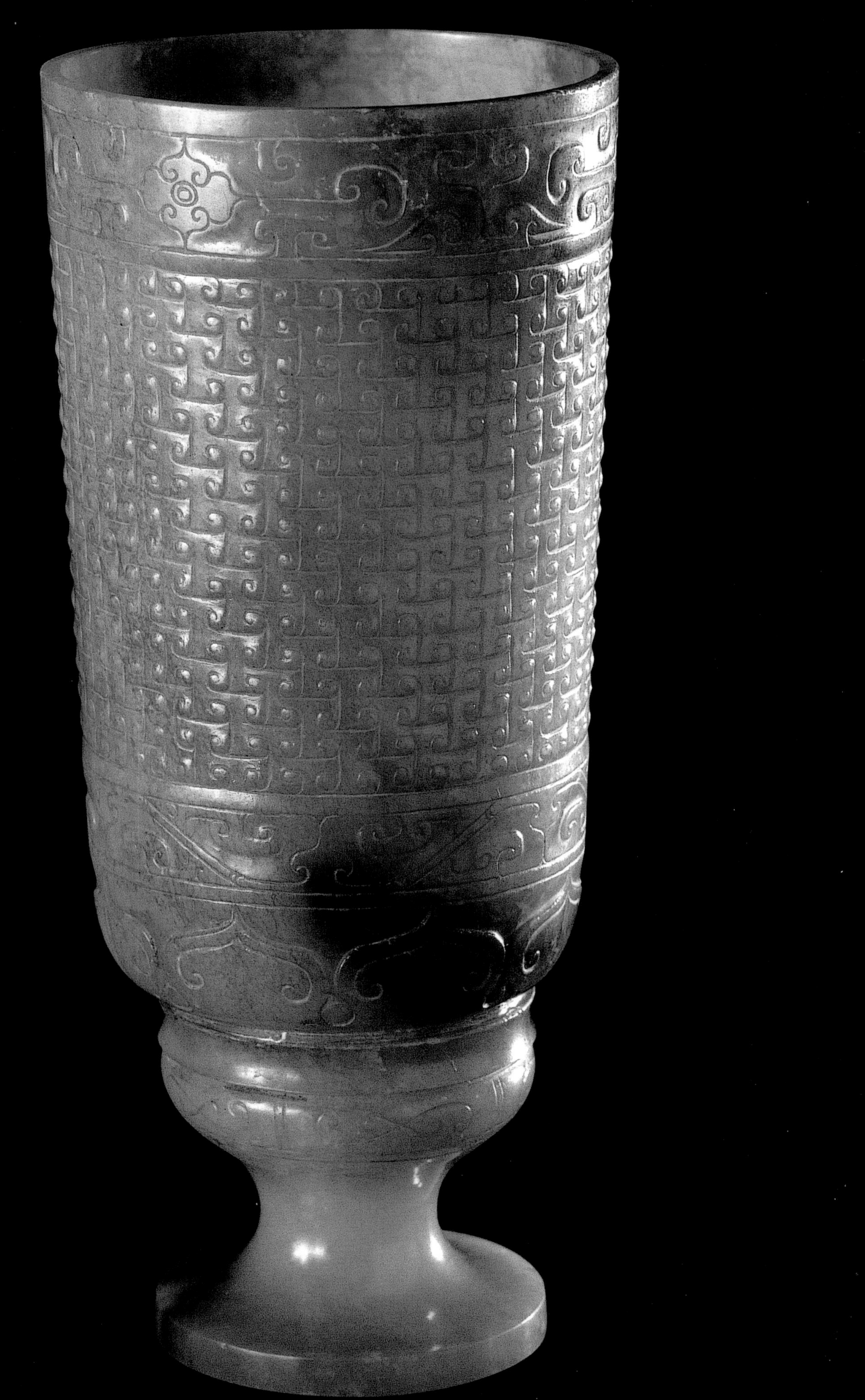

IMPERIAL TOURS AND MOUNTAIN INSCRIPTIONS

MARTIN KERN

In 221 BC King Zheng of Qin completed his conquests of the eastern states of the former Zhou realm and established the unified empire. He thereupon adopted the religious title 'First August Thearch' (*Shihuangdi*), usually just called 'First Emperor', to position himself as the progenitor of a new universal rule. Placing his new dynasty into the cosmological sequence of the Five Powers (*wu de*), he chose to govern under the Power of Water (*shuide*) to mark his victory over the preceding Zhou dynasty era of Fire. He changed the calendar, and arranged all official regalia according to the number Six associated with the Power of Water. He divided the empire into thirty-six commanderies, changed the designation for the common folk to 'the black-haired ones' (*qianshou*), confiscated and melted down the weapons from throughout the realm, unified the weights and measures together with the writing system, and moved the powerful and wealthy families to the capital area, uprooting them from their place of origin. In the following year the emperor went on a tour of inspection through the old heartland of Qin. From the capital Xianyang he travelled to the border commanderies of Longxi in the west and Beidi in the north. South of the Wei River, facing the capital on the northern bank, he built a new palace, which he named 'Polar Temple' (*Jimiao*) to represent the celestial pole, the cosmic counterpart to his own position on earth. From Xianyang to the sacrificial site at Ganquan, some 80 km northwards, he constructed a walled road sheltered from the gaze of the ordinary folk. He granted his officials a raise of one rank and began to build a system of speedways, with a privileged centre lane for the emperor.

In these activities, all compressed into a two-year period, the First Emperor

FIG. 109
(left) Detail of a rubbing of a later carving (AD 993) of the inscription that the First Emperor erected on Mt. Yi in 219 BC. The original inscribed stones are all lost but the text of all but one is recorded in Sima Qian's *Records of the Historian (Shiji)*. While the inscriptions have sometimes been dismissed as boastful propaganda, in fact the text of them is a valuable source of information about Qin literature and ritual.
Cat. no. 134

displayed his ambitions to transform the territory of his realm – a vast area saturated with the cultural and political memory of eight centuries under the nominal rule of the Zhou royal house – into a radically new political entity. This polity, and its projection over a future of 'ten thousand generations', was an empire defined by cosmological measures of space and time. While pre-imperial rulers had claimed their legitimacy from the inherited merits of their ancestors, the Qin First Emperor grounded his universal sovereignty in the alignment of political and cosmological order. Looking back on some seven centuries of Qin rulers, he dutifully endowed his late father with the new title of 'Great Supreme August' (*taishanghuang*), observed the sacrificial services to his forebears and maintained the traditional tropes of political rhetoric. Yet at the same time he shifted the religious base of his rule from the ancestral temple to the cosmic forces, that is, from the spirits of the past to the powers concurrent with, and immediately responsive to, his own actions.[1]

The tours

The two complementary aspects of old and new were fully on display in the series of tours of inspection that the emperor conducted through his newly conquered territories between 219 and 210 BC (*fig. 110*). On these tours, extending over thousands of kilometres, he ascended prominent mountains and other religiously charged sites of the former eastern states, performed sacrifices to the cosmic spirits, and erected a series of seven stele inscriptions proclaiming his new rule. In terms simultaneously political and religious, he measured out the limits of his realm, addressing at once his new subjects below and the cosmic forces above. Speaking from the peaks of famous mountains, he physically occupied the liminal sphere between heaven and earth and inscribed the natural cosmos with his record of accomplishments.

The source that provides all the information above is *Records of the Historian* (*Shiji*) by Sima Qian (*c.*145–87 BC), a work that oscillates between admiration for the First Emperor's accomplishments and dismay at his purported megalomania and excessive pursuit of personal immortality. Some of the emperor's most notorious acts of violence and lunacy that have since captured the historical imagination are recorded in chapter six of the *Records*, the 'Basic Annals of the Qin First August [Thearch]' (*Qin Shihuang benji*), where they are juxtaposed with the solemn texts of the imperial inscriptions. Apparently, Sima sought to undermine the First Emperor's own rhetoric; in addition, his portrait of the emperor as a deluded megalomaniac may have served as veiled criticism of his own ruler, Emperor Wu of Han (r. 141–87 BC), who from the *Records* emerges

FIG. 110
Map of the mountains visited by the First Emperor on his tours.

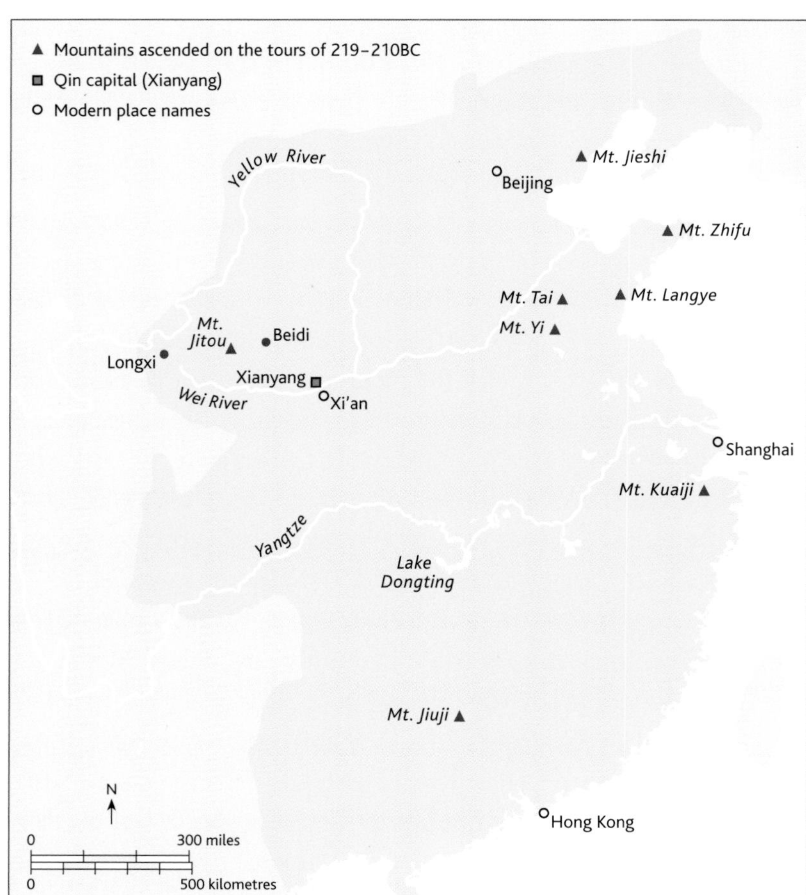

FIG. 111
(right) Mt. Tai, in Shandong province, one of the mountains the First Emperor visited in 219 BC. Before he inscribed the stone on Mt. Tai, he carried out sacrifices to the cosmic powers.

FIG. 112
(below) Remains of the Jieshi Palace built by the First Emperor on the north-east coast. He visited Jieshi in 215 BC, marking the north-east border of his empire.

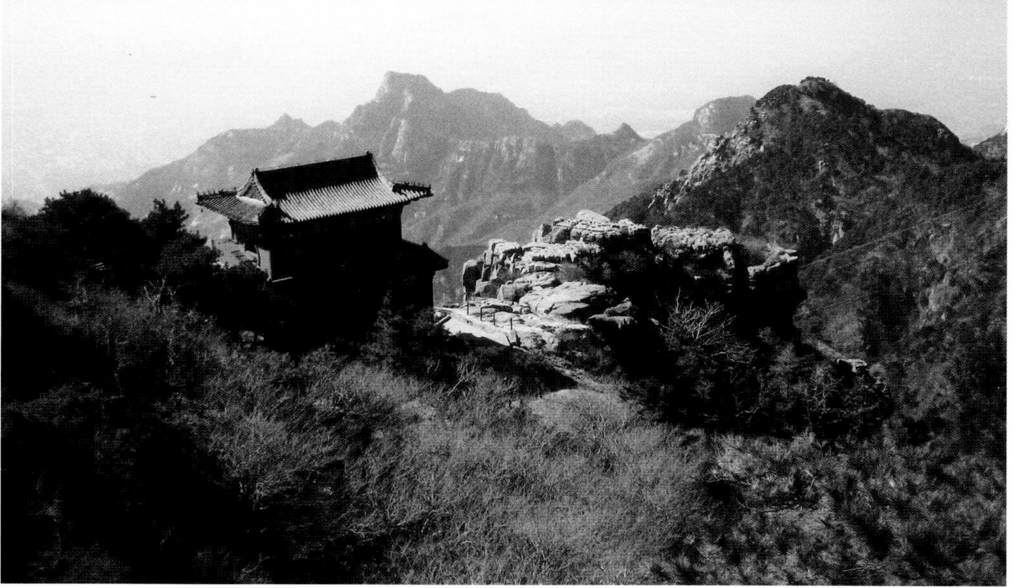

as a mirror image of the First Emperor.[2] In short, our source for the Qin imperial tours and inscriptions is a deeply complicated and problematic text, but it remains the only one available.

According to the 'Basic Annals', the emperor toured the eastern, new territories of the Qin empire between 219 and 210 BC and erected a series of seven inscribed stelae: in 219 BC on Mt. Yi (*fig. 113*), Mt. Tai (*fig. 115*) and Mt. Langye (fig. *116*); in 218 BC on Mt. Zhifu and, in addition, on its 'eastern vista' (Zhifu *dongguan*); in 215 BC at the 'gate' of Jieshi (Jieshi *men*); and in December 211 or January 210 BC on Mt. Kuaiji.[3] These sites – all of them mountains except for Jieshi – were each between 800 and 1,200 km away from the capital. In visiting them, the First Emperor marked the eastern border of the Qin empire, just as he had surveyed the north-western limits in 220 BC; in addition, on his way to Mt. Kuaiji in 211 BC he went to the southern frontier of his realm, probably no further than the area of Lake Dongting. At Yunmeng, north of Lake Dongting, he gazed southwards and offered a *wang* ('viewing from the distance') sacrifice to the legendary ruler of high antiquity, Shun, who was now venerated as a mountain spirit residing (after his burial there) at Mt. Jiuyi.[4] At Mt. Kuaiji, site of the capital of the old state of Yue at the south-eastern edge of Chinese civilization, he sacrificed to Yu, the mythic hero who had first measured and transformed the Chinese realm into a cultural geography and who in his own final tour of inspection had passed away at Mt. Kuaiji.[5]

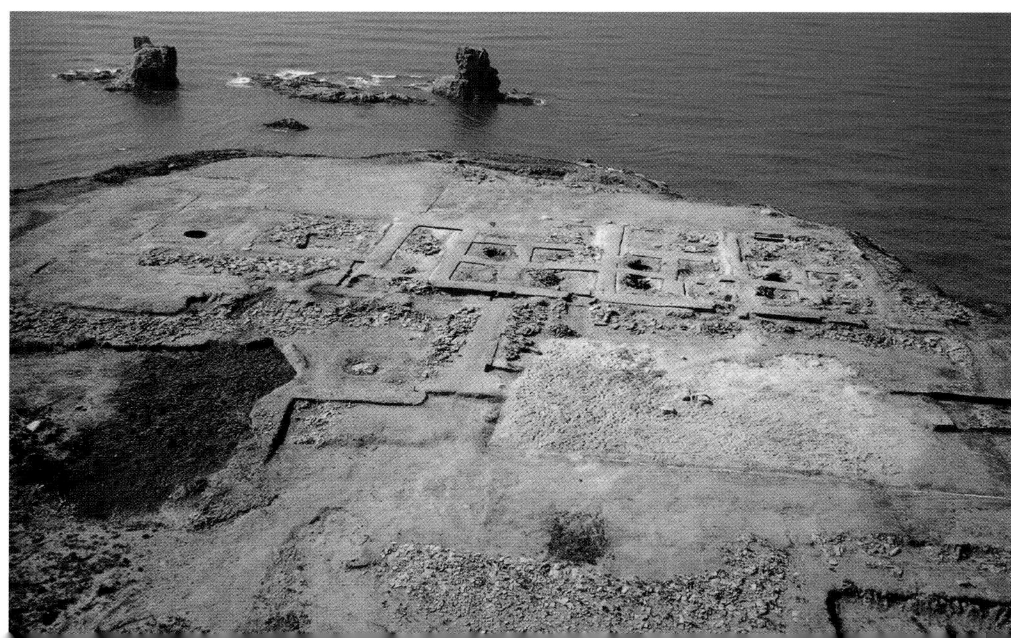

The inscription texts

The texts of six of the seven inscriptions are preserved in chapter six of the *Records*. While the inscription from Mt. Yi is only found in later sources, its use of rhyme (and overall coherence with the other inscriptions) still suggests its authenticity.[6] The *Records* further note that the First Emperor's son Ershi (r. 210–207 BC), the 'Second Generation (Emperor)', later toured all the sites again in order to complement the stelae with additional inscriptions glorifying the First Emperor's earlier visit.[7] The original stones are lost except for some fragments of the Mt. Langye and Mt.

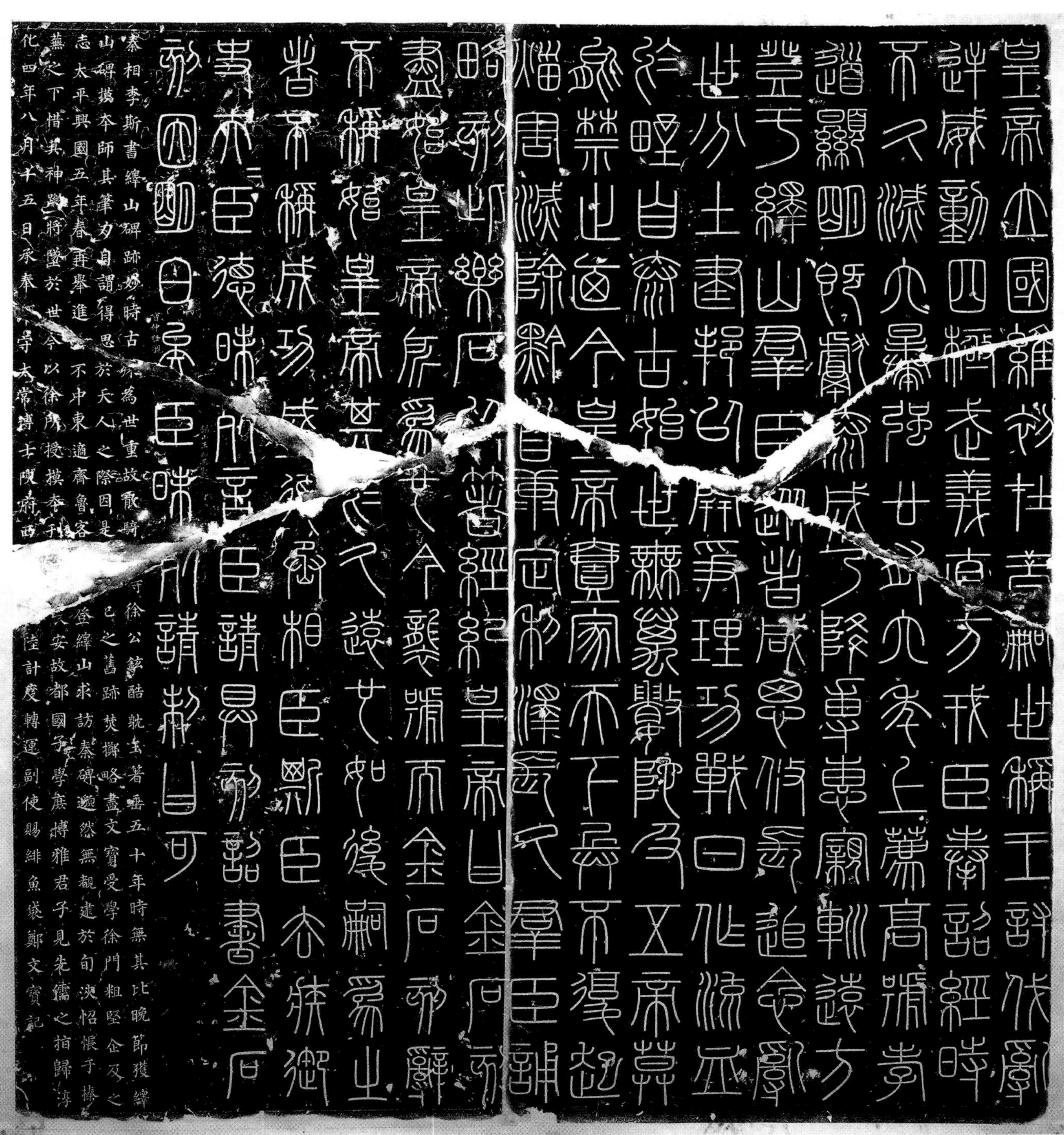

FIG. 113
Text of the original Mt. Yi inscription, preserved on a stone stele in the Forest of Stelae Museum in Xi'an. The beautiful calligraphy is in the small seal script style favoured by the First Emperor. In later imperial times, rubbings made of ancient texts inscribed on stone stelae such as this enabled them to be circulated.

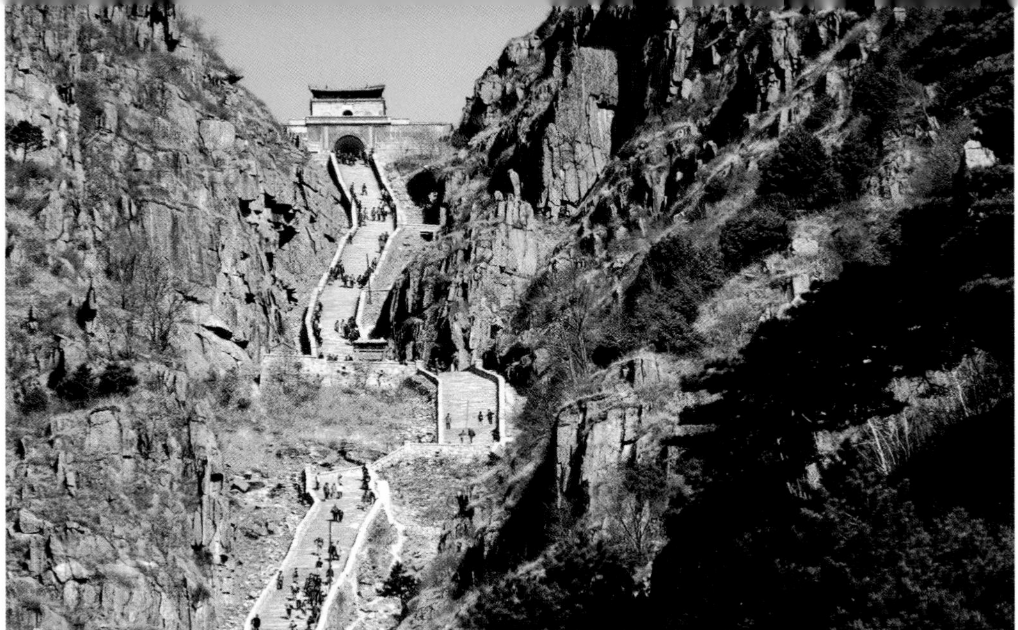

FIG. 114
(right) **Stairway leading to the top of Mt. Tai and the Gateway to Heaven Temple. Mt. Tai is still a holy mountain today and a site of pilgrimage. There are many later inscriptions on it, following in the tradition of the First Emperor.**

FIG. 115
(below) **The Mt. Tai inscription fragment, which may not be authentic, but is preserved in the Mt. Tai Temple in Tai'an, Shandong province.**

Tai stelae. These fragments – in the case of the Mt. Tai stone of questionable authenticity – only include passages from the Second Emperor's additional inscriptions.[8] Traditional collections of stone rubbings, dating from Song times (AD 960–1279) onwards, contain rubbings of all seven inscriptions, albeit of unknown origins. In some cases, rubbings of the same inscription show noticeable differences and may come from separate recarvings.

For the First Emperor's initial tour to Mt. Yi the *Records* note that his entourage included court classicists from Lu – home state of Confucius and purportedly the area where the ancient rituals of Zhou were still preserved – who deliberated and recited the texts and then carved them into stone to 'eulogize the virtuous power of Qin'.[9] Likewise, when the emperor proceeded to Mt. Tai, he was reportedly accompanied by seventy classicists and court-appointed erudites (*boshi*) from the former

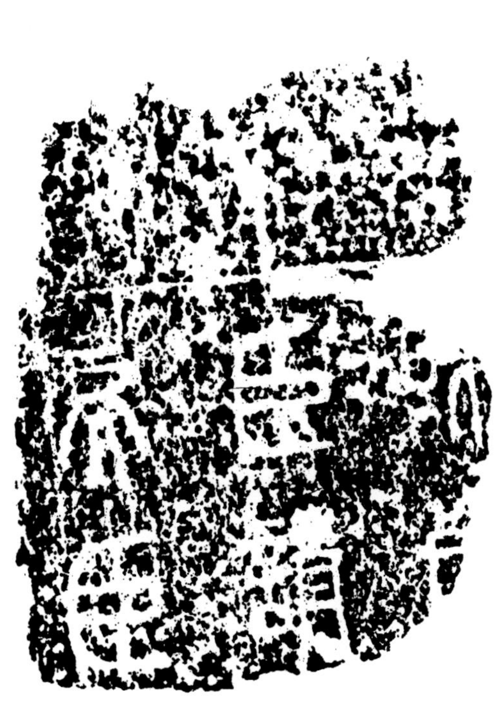

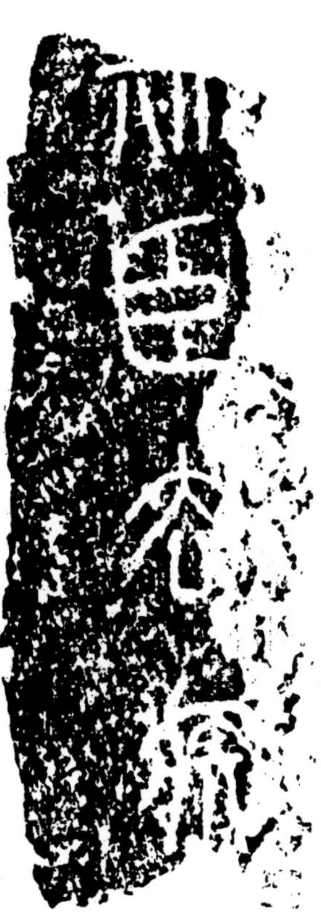

north-eastern states of Qi and Lu.[10] In both locations the act of inscribing the stones was preceded by sacrifices to the cosmic powers. While the *Records* briefly contextualize each inscription by providing the location and year, the inscriptions themselves, in a self-referential gesture, also relate the historical occasions on which they were recited and inscribed. The Mt. Zhifu inscription illustrates the diction of the entire series, which are written in four-character phrases:[11]

Now, in His twenty-ninth year,
According to the season of mid-spring,
The mildness of *yang* has just arisen.
The August Thearch travels to the east,
On His tour He ascends [Mt.] Zhifu,
Looks down on and illuminates [the lands by] the sea.
The attending officials gaze in admiration,
Recollect the origins of [His] excellence and brilliant feats,
Recall and recite the fundamental beginning:
The Great Sage created His rule,
Established and fixed the rules and measures,
Made manifest and visible the line and net [of order].
Abroad He instructed the feudal lords;
Brilliantly He spread culture and grace,
Enlightening them through rightness and principle.
The six kingdoms had been restive and perverse,
Greedy and criminal, insatiable –
Atrociously slaughtering without end.
The August Emperor felt pity for the multitudes,
And consequently sent out His punitive troops,
Vehemently displaying His martial power.
Just was He in punishment, trustworthy was He in acting,
His awesome influence radiated to all directions,
And there was none who was not respectful and submissive.
He boiled alive and exterminated the violent and cruel,
Succored and saved the black-haired people,
And all around consolidated the [land within the] four poles.
He universally promulgated the shining laws,
Gave warp and woof to all under heaven –
Forever to serve as ritual norm and guideline.
Great, indeed, is [...]!
Within the universe and realm
One follows receptively His sage intent.
The multitude of officials recite His merits,
Ask to carve [the present text] into stone,
To express and transmit the constant model.

The seven inscriptions eulogize the unified rule in contrast to the preceding ages of warfare and chaos. Their rigid formal features, like rhyme and tetrasyllabic metre,[12]

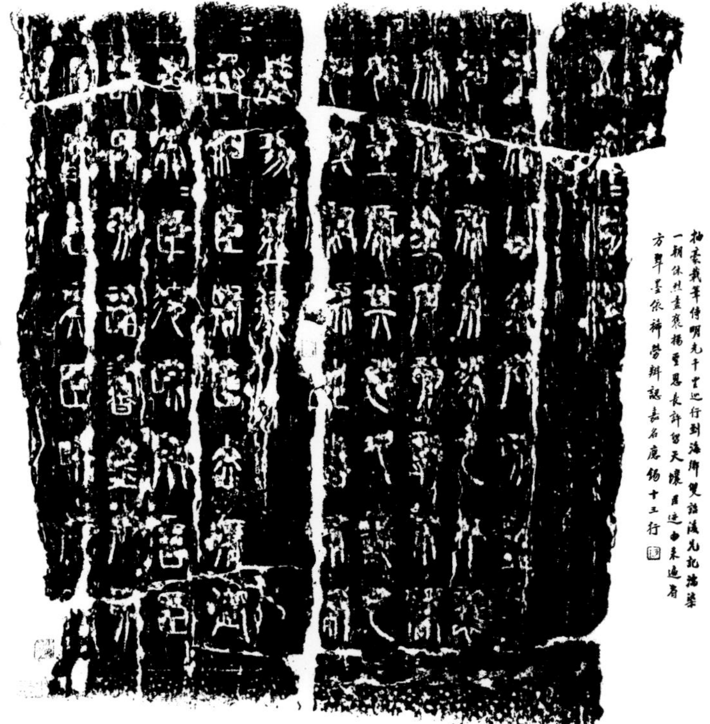

FIG. 116
The Mt. Langye inscription fragment. The Mt. Langye stele survived until 1900 when it fell into the sea during a storm. Fragments have been preserved in the National Museum of China, Beijing.

as well as their adherence to the restricted diction of traditional political rhetoric and normative ritual language – in particular of the *Classic of Poetry* (*Shi*) and the *Classic of Documents* (*Shu*) – show them as products of ritual and textual scholarship at the Qin imperial court.[13] Their tight linguistic uniformity over nearly a decade and across vast geographic distances suggests an underlying blueprint of highly ritualized speech. This blueprint, manifested in seven variations, was now imposed on the natural landscape of Qin's former enemies. While the inscriptions recognized each location in its own right, they integrated the formerly unrelated religious sites of different polities into the universal space of the unified empire. Furthermore, as monuments of a now unified political memory, they absorbed the histories of the former states into a teleological vision of universal Qin rule, replacing the multiple identities of the pre-imperial world with the single and central one of the cosmic sovereign. What the chancellor Li Si (d. 208 BC) proposed in administrative terms – to burn all historical records except those of Qin, and to proscribe the private ownership of classical texts in order to wipe out all competing memory[14] – the imperial inscriptions displayed on the level of political and religious ritual.

Precedents and ritual revivals

Despite their emphasis on the new political order, the inscriptions were phrased in the language of pre-imperial bronze inscriptions that for centuries had been used in the ancestral sacrifice, the central institution of early Chinese cultural memory and religious custom. Moreover, their context of a 'tour of inspection' by which a ruler asserted the sovereignty over his land, was a political ritual that by the third century BC was imagined as an ancient practice of political representation.[15] Its most important source can be found in several cosmological *Documents* chapters that may

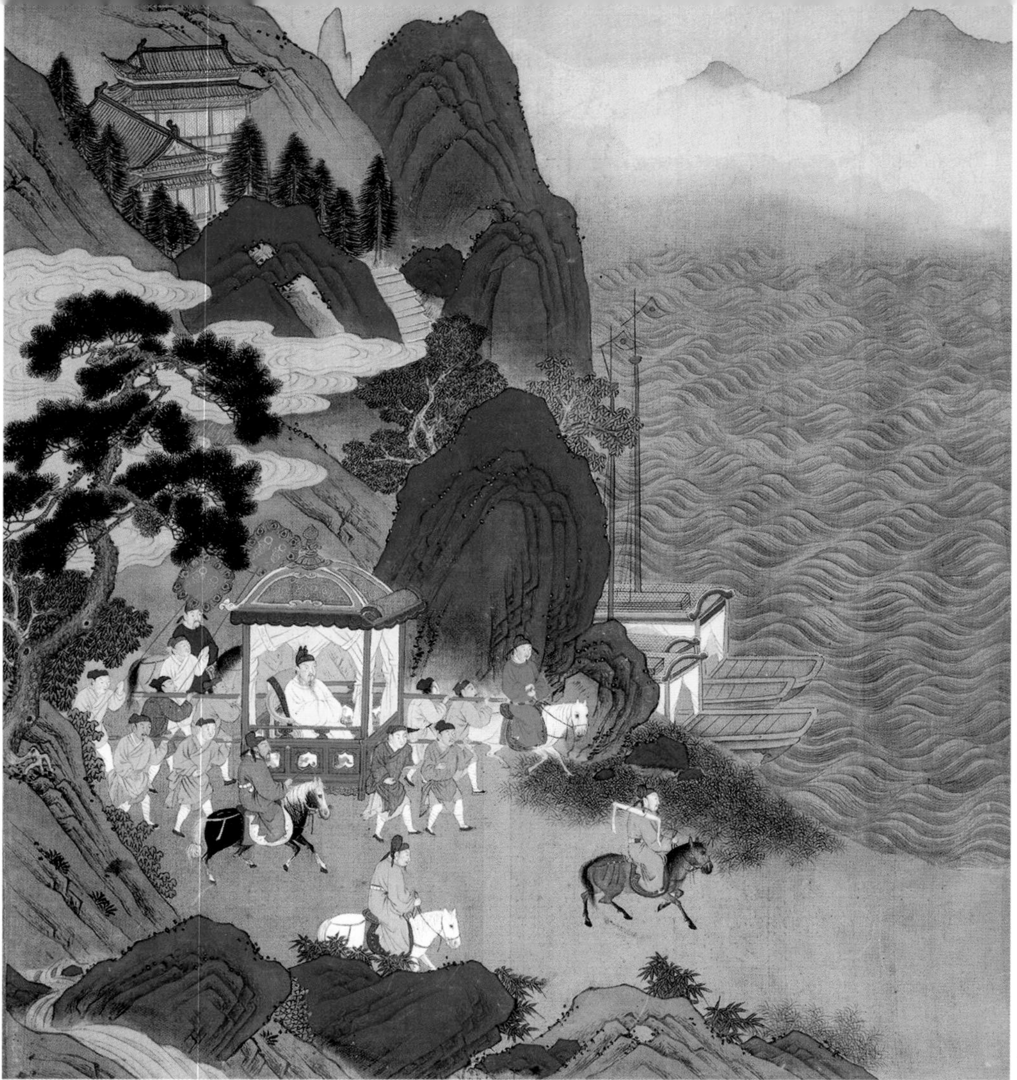

FIG. 117
This eighteenth-century album painting is a fanciful depiction of the First Emperor's imperial tours and is anachronistic in many ways. However, it shows the fascination that he held for later artists.

date no earlier than the fourth and third centuries BC, and most likely were edited by the classicists – including the *Documents* expert Fu Sheng (b. 260 BC) – at the Qin imperial court.[16] The exact model for the First Emperor's tours is the account of Shun's journey to the sacred mountains of the Chinese realm:

> In the second month of the year,[17] [Shun] went east to visit [for inspection] those under his protection and arrived at [Mt.] Venerable Tai.[18] He made a burnt offering [to heaven] and performed *wang* sacrifices in the correct sequence to the mountains and streams. Then he gave audience to the lords of the east, regulated the [calendar of the] seasons and months, rectified the [designations of the] days, and made uniform the pitchpipes and the measures of length, capacity, and weight.[19]

In the same year Shun performed the identical set of rites and regulations during subsequent tours to the south, the west and the north;[20] each time his destination proper was the main peak of the respective direction. Prominent features in this account are the recurring initial sacrifices to heaven and to the important mountains and streams, signalling the universal ruler's prerogative to order the world by performing the correct sequence of cosmic sacrifices. Thus, when the First Emperor embarked on his own tours and set up inscriptions that portrayed him as the new 'sage' who turned chaos into order and prosperity, he consciously placed himself into the purported tradition of the founding sages – a 'classical' tradition enshrined in the *Documents* that may, in fact, have only recently been invented.

As Shun's cosmos was defined by the sacred mountains of the four directions, the landscape through which the First Emperor conducted his tours was pregnant with religious meaning. In choosing the sites for his inscriptions, he claimed to revive the sacrifices of old and to attach himself to the culture heroes of antiquity. This was true for the *feng* and *shan* rituals addressed to heaven – something the emperor only partially accomplished at his visit to Mt. Tai[21] – as well as for the sacrifices at Mt. Zhifu and Mt. Langye, the next two localities favoured with stelae inscriptions: these sites belonged to eight peaks located in the former state of Qi where the ancient 'eight [cosmic] spirits' (*ba shen*) had once received their offerings. Purporting to revive lost tradition, the Qin emperor sacrificed to the spirit of the *yang* cosmic force at Mt. Zhifu and to the spirits of the four seasons at Mt. Langye. In addition, he performed a series of different sacrifices to the four mountains of Qi – Mt. Tai, Mt. Yi, Mt. Zhifu and Mt. Langye – and presented additional *wang* offerings to the other 'famous mountains and great streams' (*mingshan dachuan*) of the empire.[22] Available only to a universal ruler, these *wang* sacrifices to outlying regions served to express the spatial extension of sovereignty just like the emperor's own physical movements, the far-flung tours of inspection.[23] Accordingly, the First Emperor even honoured Shun himself – who had performed the ritual at Mt. Tai – with a *wang* sacrifice.

Through his cosmic sacrifices as much as through his inscriptions, the emperor incorporated the large polity of Qi – the final state conquered in 221 BC – into the empire, sealing his military conquest with the trappings of religious and political ritual. Moreover, through his offerings to Yu and Shun he fused cosmic with historical legitimacy, connecting himself to cosmic spirits who were also political ancestors and mapping his new empire onto their primordial geography, which transcended the political divisions of the recent past. As such, his inscriptions spoke back to the spirits of old, but they also created a prospective memory for all future. When the emperor had his merits recited and inscribed on mountain peaks, he commemorated his past achievements while simultaneously historicizing his own act of commemoration.

The text from Mt. Zhifu exemplifies a rhetorical gesture common to the inscriptions altogether: in its first nine lines it mentions the date, the designation of the emperor's tour, the gaze over his new territory and the officials' recollection of his feats. Following this self-referential recognition of the inscription's own situational context, the main portion of the text then relates the actual contents of the officials' historical narrative: the previous times of chaos and warfare, the First Emperor's resolute and just elimination of the six former states, the consolidation of the new empire, and the prospect of eternal peace. Then, with its final six lines, the text returns once again to a reflection on its own circumstances of composition: 'The multitude of officials recite His merits, / Ask to carve [the present text] into stone, / To express and transmit the constant model.' Together with the beginning lines, this closure frames the historical narrative with an account of its own ritualized performance and representation – an act of commemoration to be remembered forever. Thus the inscription became part of its own history, ready to be deciphered by the spirits and living humans of past and present, and remembered by the infinite posterity of those to come.

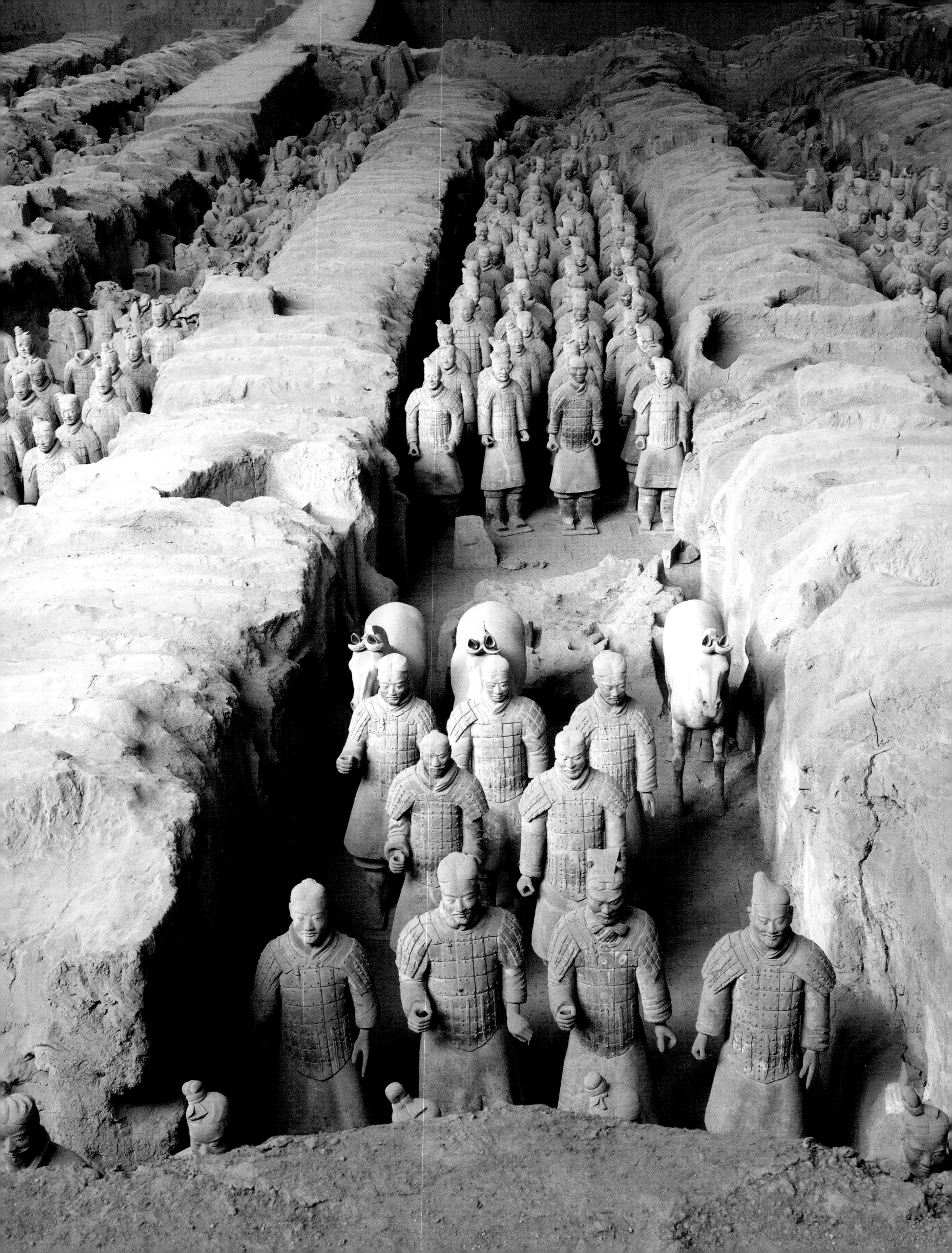

THE FIRST EMPEROR'S TOMB
THE AFTERLIFE UNIVERSE

JESSICA RAWSON

The First Emperor of China controlled a vast territory and wielded enormous power. He ordered 120,000 families to move to the new capital, Xianyang; he summoned 700,000 men to build his tomb and other structures; and he was self-consciously aware of his authority and of the new era that this marked.[1] Long inscriptions carved at his command on mountains in eastern China described his achievements and proclaimed his universal, indeed cosmic, rulership: 'The bright virtue of the August Emperor aligns and orders the whole universe.'[2]

Yet this powerful ruler was assailed at the same time by his human frailty: he feared conspiracy and death by human or by supernatural forces. He consulted occult specialists and insisted that his whereabouts be kept secret. In search of eternal life, the First Emperor urged his officials and associates to seek out herbs and plants that would enable him to evade death and live for ever. Several fruitless expeditions were sent out into the eastern sea to find the mythical islands of Penglai, Yingzhou and Fangzhang, where these plants were believed to flourish. None of these efforts succeeded.[3] How then did the emperor resolve his fears of death and make them compatible with his claims to be a universal and eternal ruler? His solution lay in preparing a great tomb for himself on the slopes of Mt. Li near present-day Lintong to ensure his power on the journey into and throughout eternity.

FIGS 118 & 119
(left and following pages)
Terracotta warriors lined up in Pit 1 with remains of a four-horse chariot. The warriors guarded the First Emperor's afterlife empire.

What the First Emperor created astonishes us today with its haunting lines of soldiers, officials, acrobats and servants to do his bidding, frozen for all time in clay; we are fascinated by the extraordinary technical feats of the exquisite bronze chariots and the intricate sets of stone armour. But it must have been all the more

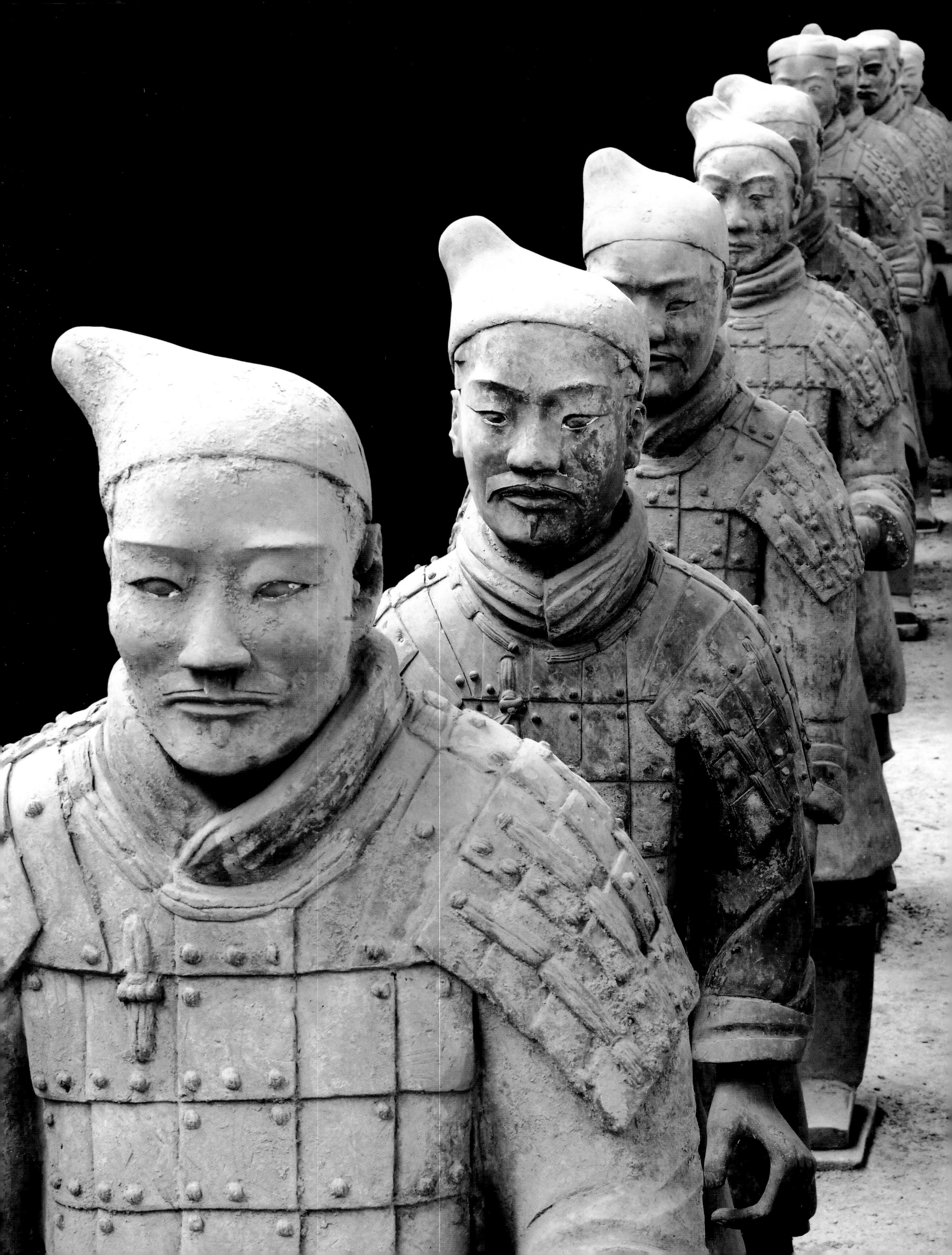

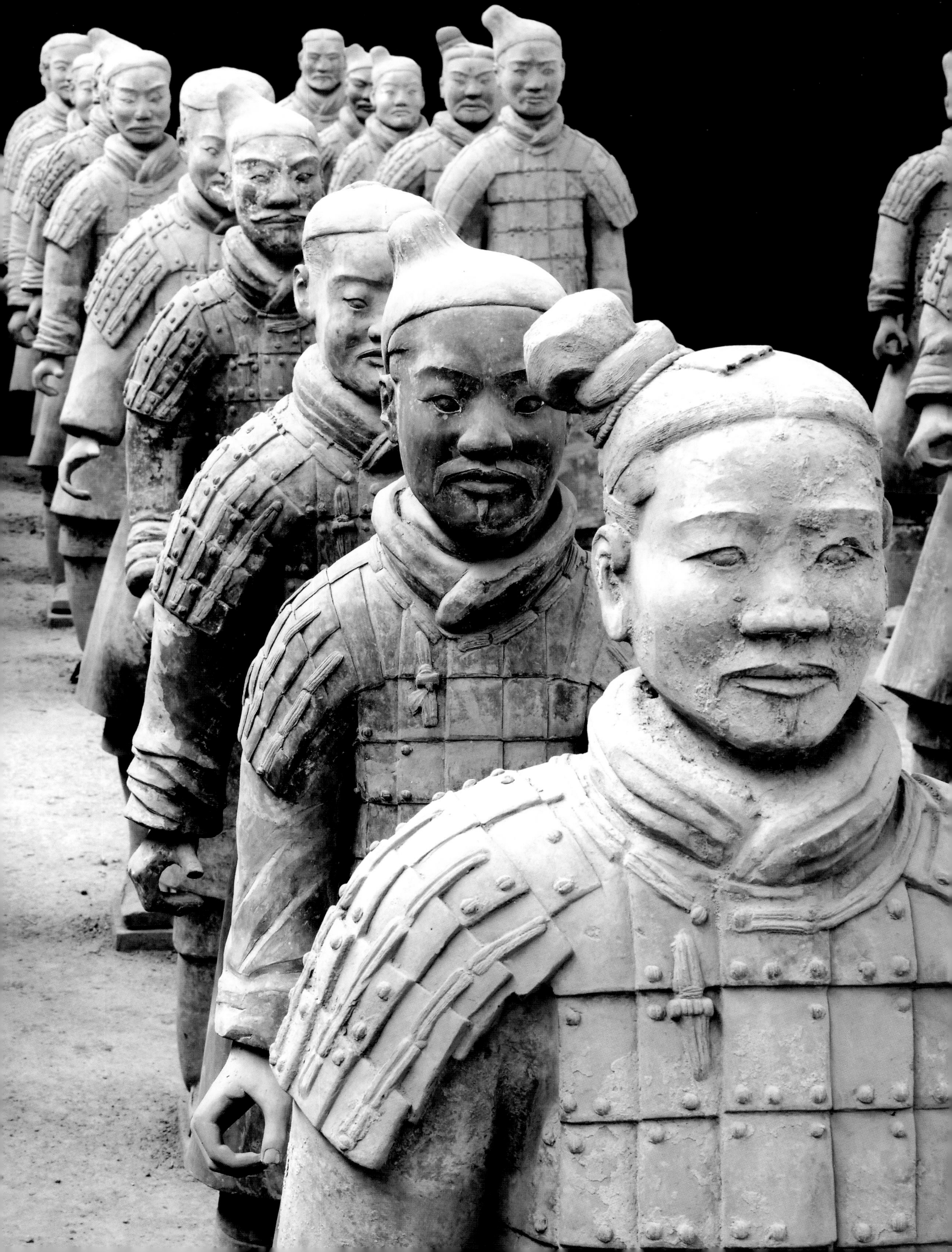

astonishing for his ministers and officials as they laboured at the immense task to bring into being this universe for the emperor. Nothing on such a scale had been attempted before. In death, as in life, the First Emperor was unique.

The cosmic ruler and ritual traditions

We are faced with several questions. What was the emperor trying to do and why did he do it? Was the tomb a record of his past powers, namely a monument, or was it a means to extend his rule into the future? What would a world combining buried humans and massed clay soldiers achieve? It is too easy for us, today, to see the clay figures as representations or symbols of a spirit army, or to contemplate concepts of immortality in our own terms as life in a remote paradise. Neither of these notions

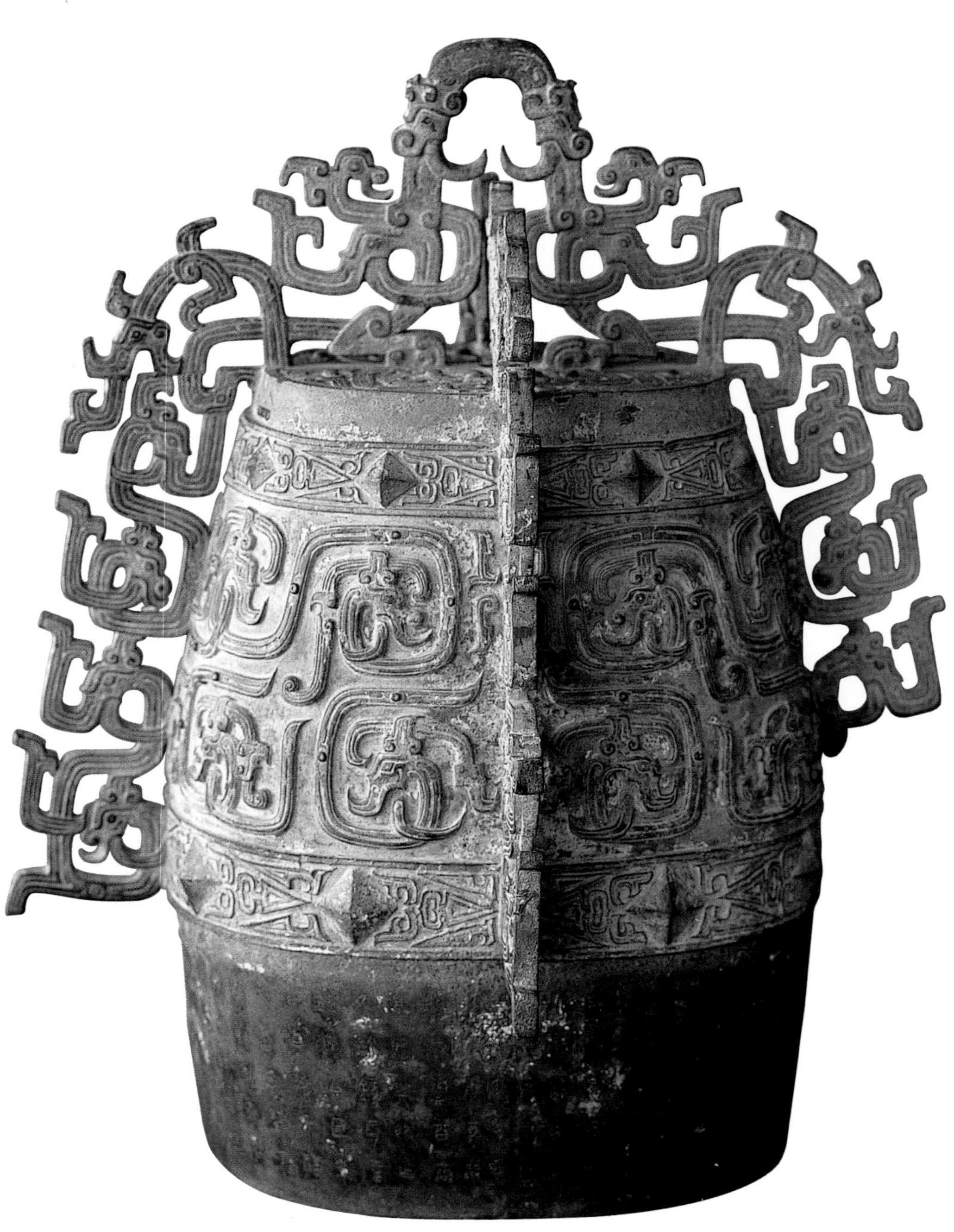

FIG. 120
The largest of a set of three *bo* bells excavated from Taigong Temple, Baoji, site of Pingyang, the old capital of the Qin state from 714 to 677 BC. The three *bo* bells were also found with a set of five *zhong* bells (see *fig. 48*). During the Zhou period, bell music would have accompanied the ritual offerings of food and wine to the ancestors in ceremonies designed to invoke the goodwill of ancestor spirits. The bells are an important discovery as they document the Qin lineage and their mandate to rule. This *bo* bell is inscribed with a 135-character text which begins: 'The Duke of Qin says: My foremost ancestor has received the heavenly mandate, was rewarded with a residence and received his state.' It is thought that Duke Wu (r. 697–678 BC) had the bells cast.
Cat. no. 93

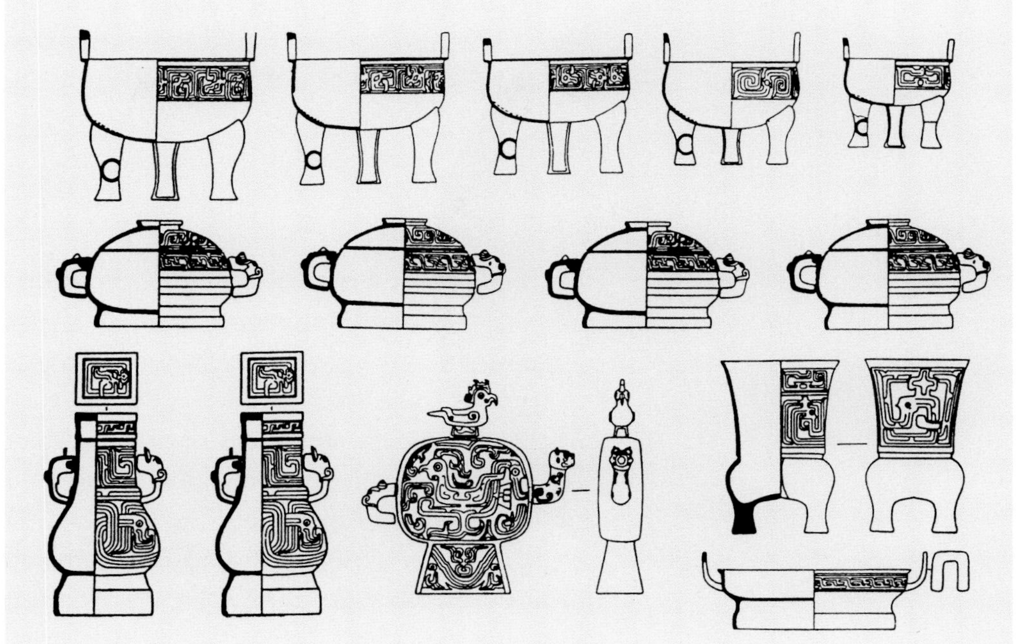

FIG. 121
Line drawing of ritual bronze vessels excavated from Tomb 5 at Bianjiazhuang, Longxian, Shaanxi province.

fits well with the emperor's ambitions. For the emperor saw himself not simply as a ruler of a vast geographic territory but also as a cosmic ruler – the 'First August Thearch', as explained in Martin Kern's article above (pp. 104–13). He had not only unified the states, he had also unified the universe of spirits, drawing them into his control through sacrifices at the northern and southern limits of his world and by inscribing, with records of his achievements, the mountains on the eastern sea coast at the frontier of human territory.[4] Moreover, the emperor, as his inscriptions stated, had set himself in the line of sage kings who, according to legend, had first paced out and ordered the world.

The emperor went even further in asserting his central position in the historical narrative and in the cosmos. As he built and named his palaces, he mapped them onto the stars, which were at that time understood as the dwellings of a supreme deity and his officials. He designated a palace built south of the Wei River as the *Jimiao*, or 'Polar Temple', as Kern notes (p. 105), 'to represent the celestial pole, the cosmic counterpart to his own position on earth'. The Wei River was seen as the Milky Way, with other buildings and palaces regarded as the equivalents of astral bodies.[5] If the structures in and around his capital at Xianyang could be envisaged as paralleling the stars – the dwellings and administrative offices of the spirits – then here, in the physical world, the power of the First Emperor would also replicate that of the spirits. In this same context the emperor must also have regarded his palace for the afterlife as the seat of his future power, equally aligned with the cosmos.

The First Emperor was the inheritor of a long tradition in which tombs were constructed as eternal dwellings. The First Emperor's ancestors, the lords of Qin, had not been modest in their burials. Their tombs were of amazing dimensions. In the Qin funerary park at Fengxiang, to the west of the First Emperor's capital, Tomb M1, prepared for one of the sixth-century rulers, is 40 metres wide, 60 metres long and 24 metres deep.[6] It is a vertical shaft tomb, in which the coffins, each nested in at least one outer coffin, are placed at the bottom of the pit reached by two access ramps. This basic form had survived from the ancient dynasties of the Shang (*c.*1500–*c.*1050 BC) and the early Zhou (*c.*1050–771 BC). With the sack of the capital (near the modern city of Xi'an) of the dynasty now described as the Western Zhou, several local lords came to power in states that acknowledged the nominal rule of the Zhou but were otherwise independent. These rulers followed ancient precedents in their burials and beliefs about the afterlife and contributed their own variations.[7]

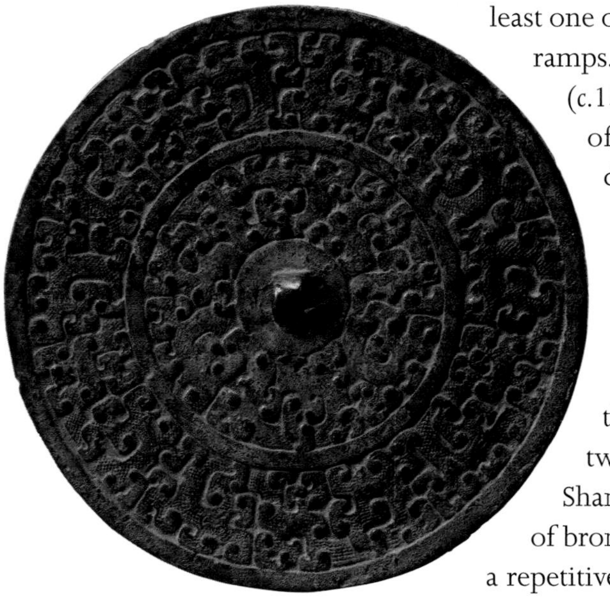

A widely held belief system was founded on the notion that the dead, as much as the living, were part of a single community. The two communities were joined by the major rituals established by the Shang and the Zhou, that is, by banquets performed with elaborate sets of bronze ritual vessels (*fig.* 121). In these ceremonies foods were offered on a repetitive cycle to the dead, often accompanied by music, of which bells are the most tangible remains (*figs* 48 & 120). The dead were deemed present as the offerings were made. Sets of bronze vessels and bells found in tombs seem to have been intended for the dead to use in the afterlife, as they continued to provide food and wine for their ancestors, whom they had now joined in cemeteries as their dwellings.[8]

In the centuries prior to the conquests by the First Emperor, the rituals had changed and the bronzes used were no longer as elaborate as those of the Shang and Zhou. Indeed, by the time of the First Emperor bronze was employed in other forms for communication with the spirits, as incense burners (*fig.* 124) and as mirrors (*fig.* 122).[9] In place of the large sets of ritual bronzes, more lacquers, ceramics and furnishings for daily life were included. A few bronzes imitated the shapes of every-day lacquer pieces. These changes were a product of new views about the relative powers of different spirits. The ancestors as part of the living community remained important. To these were added many local spirits, star deities and immortals, who might inhabit distant mountains.[10]

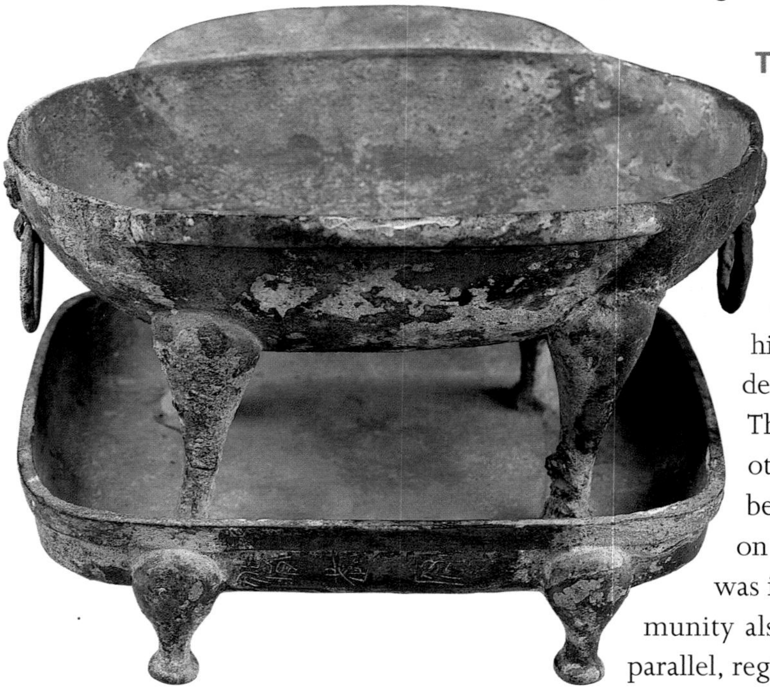

The parallel world of the afterlife

The concept of immortality was, however, different to that in the West. The word in Chinese (*bu si*) means 'non-death'. And this is the immortality that the First Emperor sought. For this reason he sent emissaries to the islands of the Eastern Sea to seek for herbs that would enable him to live for ever. Death was caused by an attack of malign demons and spirits, and these had to be avoided at all costs.[11] There is no evidence at this date that the First Emperor, or others of his time, thought that there was a spiritual land beyond the present world that was an alternative to the life on earth. If the correct herbs could not be obtained and it was impossible to live for ever, then the dead formed a community also in this world, but one that abided by a different, if parallel, regime.

FIG. 122
(opposite, above) **The interlocking design on the back of this mirror, also found on contemporary jade and gold objects, is characteristic of bronze design from the Houma foundry in Shanxi. Located in the capital of the state of Jin from 585 to 453 BC, the Houma foundry mass-produced bronzes in large scale not only for the Jin state but also for a wider market.**
Cat. no. 94

FIG. 123
(opposite, below) **An inscription on the bottom of the bronze cup and the side of the brazier stand indicates that it comes from the state of Wei, which was absorbed by Qin in 225 BC. This vessel along with a bronze *zhong* were excavated from Ta'erpo, Xianyang. The unusual shape of this oval cup – the projections or tabs on either side are often called 'ears' – was inspired by a lacquer prototype. The four legs elevate the cup allowing its contents, usually wine, to be gently heated by hot embers burning in the brazier.**
Cat. no. 95

FIG. 124
(right) **Incense would have been burnt at ritual ceremonies for the ancestors. This highly ornate incense burner was excavated from the old Qin capital at Yong.**
Cat. no. 96

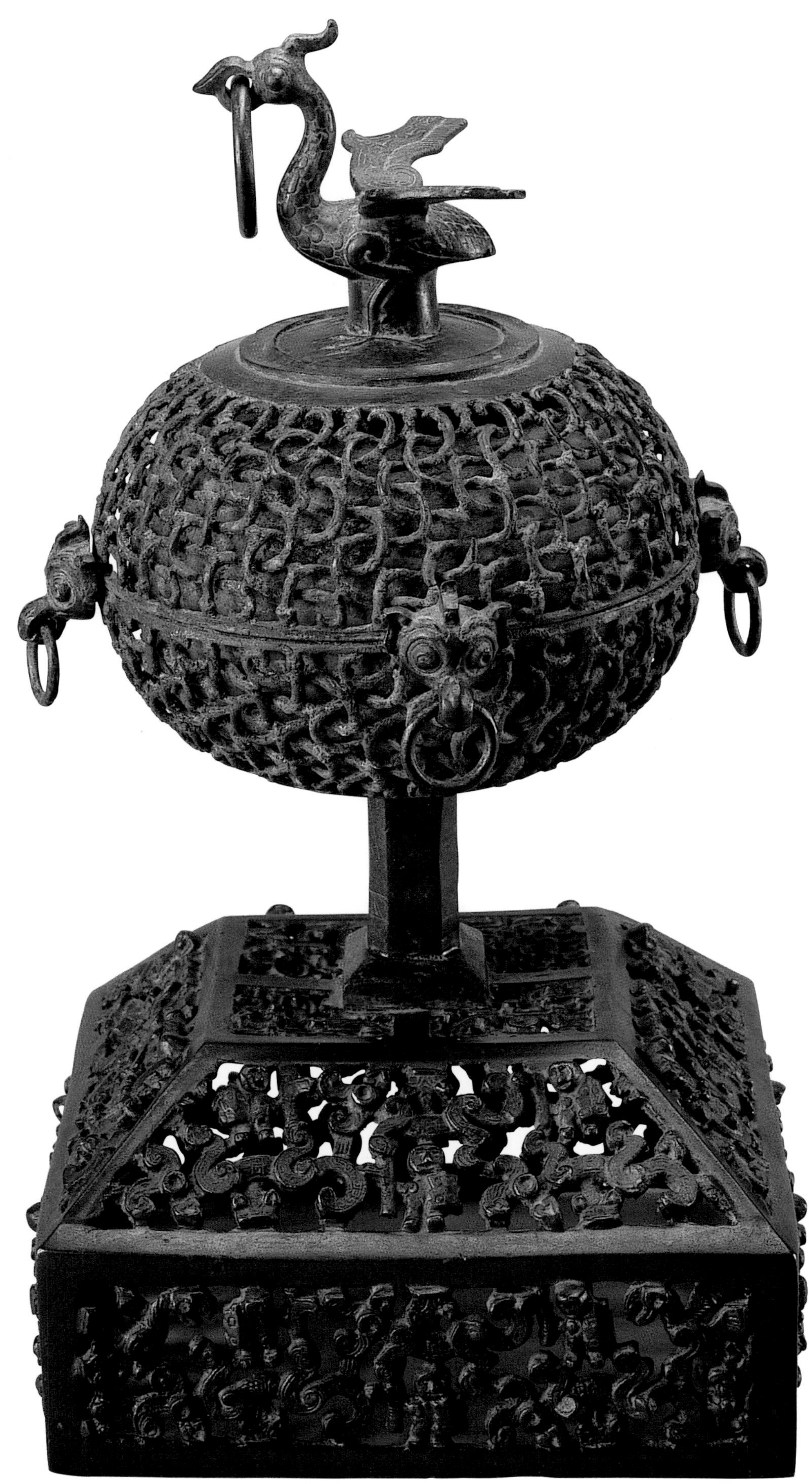

To ensure the posthumous existence of their occupants, all Chinese tombs were microcosms of the world known during life. Only those of the very highest elite could provide all the luxuries of life and all the servants needed to support such existences. Sumptuous vessels, bells and lacquers were placed inside the most lavish tombs; servants, warriors and female consorts were killed to accompany their lords in death; chariots, horses and charioteers were buried in separate pits (*fig. 126*) and were the forerunners of the terracotta warriors. The Zhou started to create subdivisions within the main part of the tomb.[12] The lords of the Qin state, and the rulers of the southern states of Chu and Zeng, carried this practice much further, creating rooms in the larger burials.[13] While the Qin continued to bury bronzes, horses and chariots in some tombs, pottery replicas were occasionally used.[14] Other rulers, notably those of the northern state of Zhongshan in the fourth century, created numerous separate deposits around major tombs, a procedure that the First Emperor followed.[15]

As his conquests of the six states brought all their ritual knowledge within his control, the First Emperor was able to draw on rich and diverse traditions when contemplating ways of extending his life beyond death. While it is tempting to describe such tombs as models, they were much more than that. Being an analogue of life, they were at the same time a realization of the buildings and social structures

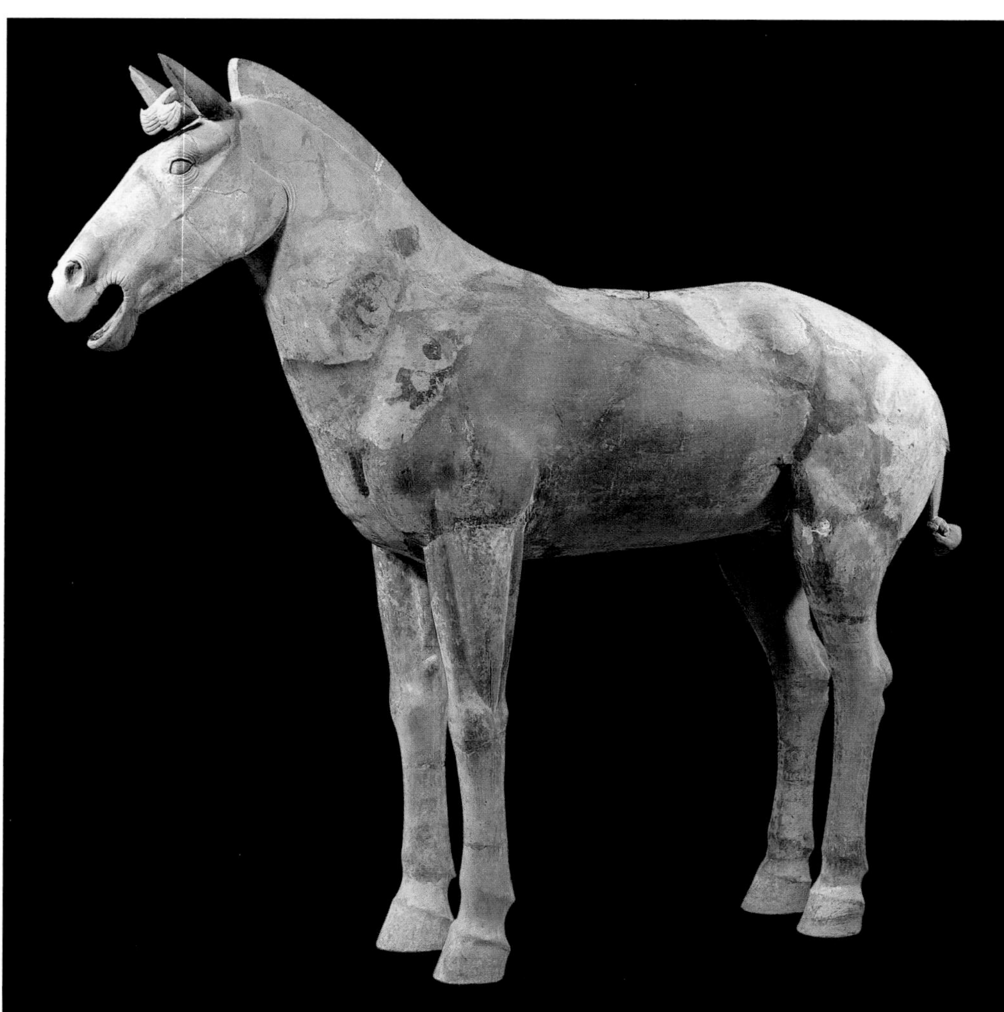

FIG. 125
Horses played an integral role in armed warfare of the imperial army as the discovery of the terracotta army pits have revealed. Over 30 chariots, each drawn by 4 horses, were found in Pit 1, while 64 chariots and 108 cavalrymen (364 horses) were arranged in battle formation in Pit 2.
Cat. no. 97

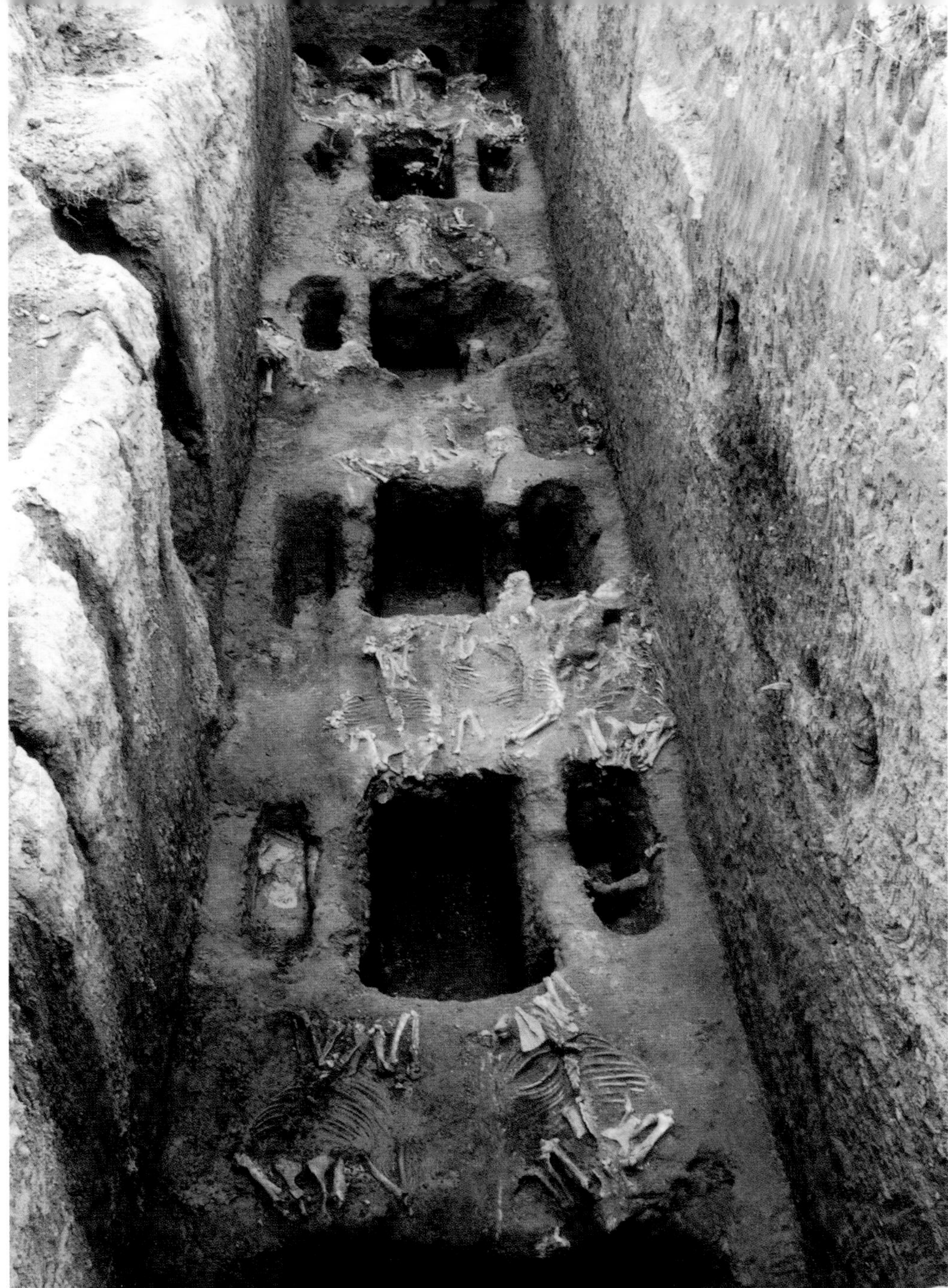

FIG. 126
Chariot burial of a Qin tomb excavated from Li county, Gansu province.

for a life after death. Texts demonstrate that these tombs were adjuncts to a whole, generally invisible, society peopled by officials and administrators, as well as by spirits and demons.

From the fifth century BC, if not earlier, we learn from documents buried in tombs that there was a growing sense of the complexities of the spirit world. Anxiety is evident in the spells and charms written on bamboo to defeat demons that might cause bodily decay (see pp. 188–9). And the organization of the afterlife becomes clearer in other documents. Inventories, which accompanied the goods buried, implied a system of checking the objects and were sometimes accompanied in the same document by letters addressed to afterlife officials; over time more almanacs, calendars, divination records and texts on medicine, some including titles of the afterlife officials, were interred. These suggest a hierarchy of bureaucrats in the parallel universe with powers over the dead.[16]

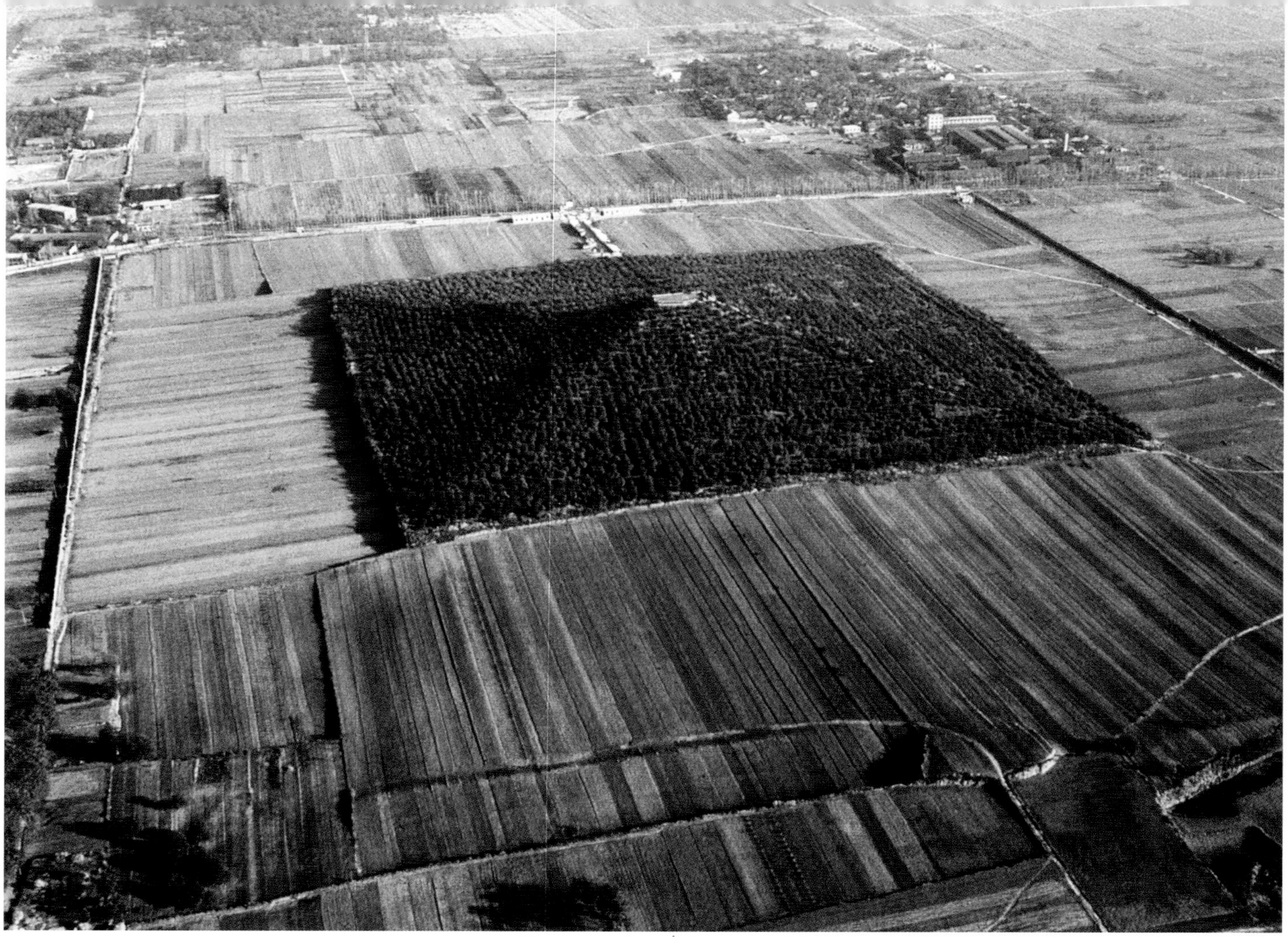

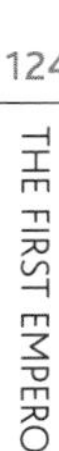

FIG. 127
Aerial view of the First Emperor's tomb mound. The First Emperor started building his tomb as soon as he ascended the throne of the Qin kingdom in 246 BC. The site was chosen for its ideal location: protected by mountains in the south (Mt. Li) and west (Qinling mountains) and water to the north (Wei River). The east led to the Great Central Plains, but was protected by the terracotta army. The mound has reduced in size over the years. Current data of its height varies from 55 to 87 metres. Its base measures 350 x 345 metres.

An account found in a tomb at Fangmatan in Gansu province and dated 297 BC describes the afterlife from the perspective of a man who claimed to have returned from death.[17] Here we have mention of officials whom he had encountered and of the notion of a 'life-mandate', a set period given to a person to live. While belief in an afterlife with recognizable officials and an organization may have seemed reassuring, the uncertainties presented by the unknown clearly generated fear, as petitions in later tombs make clear. And these fears were compounded by the recognition of the demons that caused sickness, death and decay. The inner coffin of the fifth-century-BC Marquis Yi of the state of Zeng bears pictures of armed spirits to ward off demons that might attack the tomb occupant (*fig.* 192). The First Emperor had a special reason to fear the spirit world; he had killed, indeed massacred, the armies of the six states. In a universe where the living continue after death in the roles that they occupied when alive, the First Emperor could imagine that rank upon rank of vengeful spirit soldiers waited for him.[18]

Significance of the tomb site and its occupants

In building his tomb, the First Emperor exploited traditions of the past, but at the same time, as in everything he did, he expanded and reinterpreted these legacies. For, while he shared commonly held beliefs, he had developed, as mentioned earlier, his own understanding of his role in the cosmos. In the first place the emperor chose a site separate from the cemeteries of his ancestors, to demonstrate that he was not dependent on them for his supremacy[19] The tomb was not simply a dwelling, it was his palace, his whole court, his army and an entire universe centred on himself.

Set on the slopes of Mt. Li near Lintong, east of Xi'an, the present-day capital of Shaanxi province, the carefully designed tomb complex added new features to the landscape, and this landscape survives today. The artificial hill above the tomb was enclosed by two sets of walls on a rectangular plan, which originally had towers at their gateways. The terracotta army, buried in pits to the east, defends this precinct, facing towards the pass in the mountains through which the enemies in the former states might have been expected to come. Other pits contained pottery figures of officials and acrobats, horses and miniature chariots in bronze, stone armour and bronze birds. But these simply completed a scheme in which human officials, members of the court, real horses and other animals, and the bodies of criminals were essential components of an afterlife existence for the emperor.[20] The physical mapping of the all required aspects of an eternal imperial life across a large area was one of the principal ways in which the tomb complex created a whole world. We have a further glimpse of the ways in which this was destined to create

FIG. 128
Plan of the First Emperor's tomb complex. The building of the tomb was recorded by the Han historian, Sima Qian, but the terracotta army pits, located 1.5 km east of the mound, were a surprise discovery when local villagers stumbled upon them whilst digging a well. The tomb and its accompanying burial pits (over 600 have thus far been excavated) cover an area of about 56 sq. km .

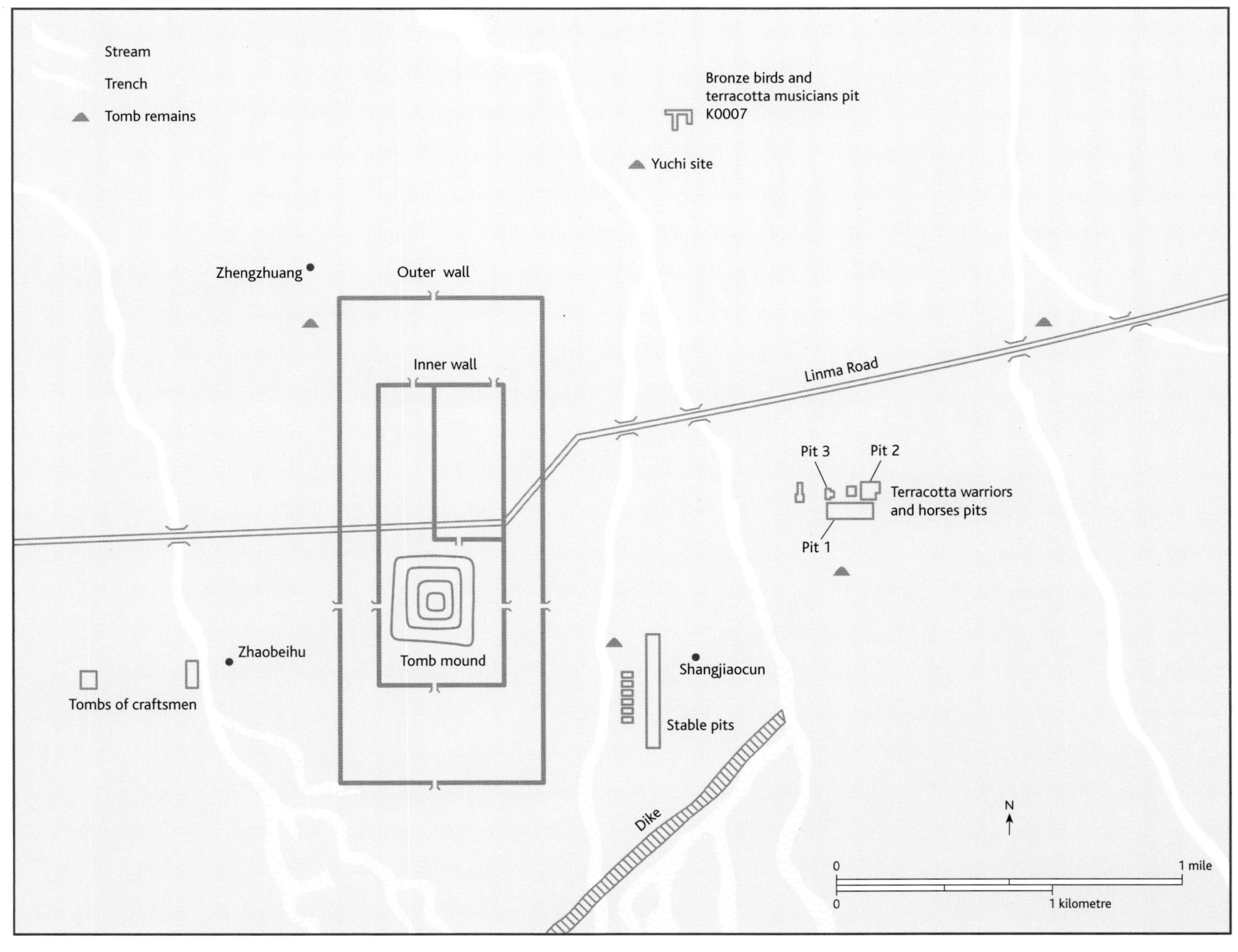

the afterlife from an account of the interior of the burial chamber itself by the renowned Han-dynasty historian, Sima Qian (c.145–c.87 BC):

> When the Emperor first came to the throne he began digging and shaping Mt. Li. Later, when he unified the empire, he had over 700,000 men from all over the empire transported to the spot. They dug down to the third layer of underground springs and poured in bronze to make the outer coffin. Palaces, scenic towers, and the hundred officials, as well as rare utensils and wonderful objects, were brought to fill up the tomb. Craftsmen were ordered to set up crossbows and arrows, rigged so that they would immediately shoot down anyone attempting to break in. Mercury was used to fashion the hundred rivers, the Yellow River and the Yangtze, and the seas in such a way that they flowed. Above were set the heavenly bodies were, below, the features of the earth. 'Man-fish' oil was used for lamps, which were calculated to burn for a long time without going out.[21]

FIG. 129
The First Emperor's tomb viewed from the west.

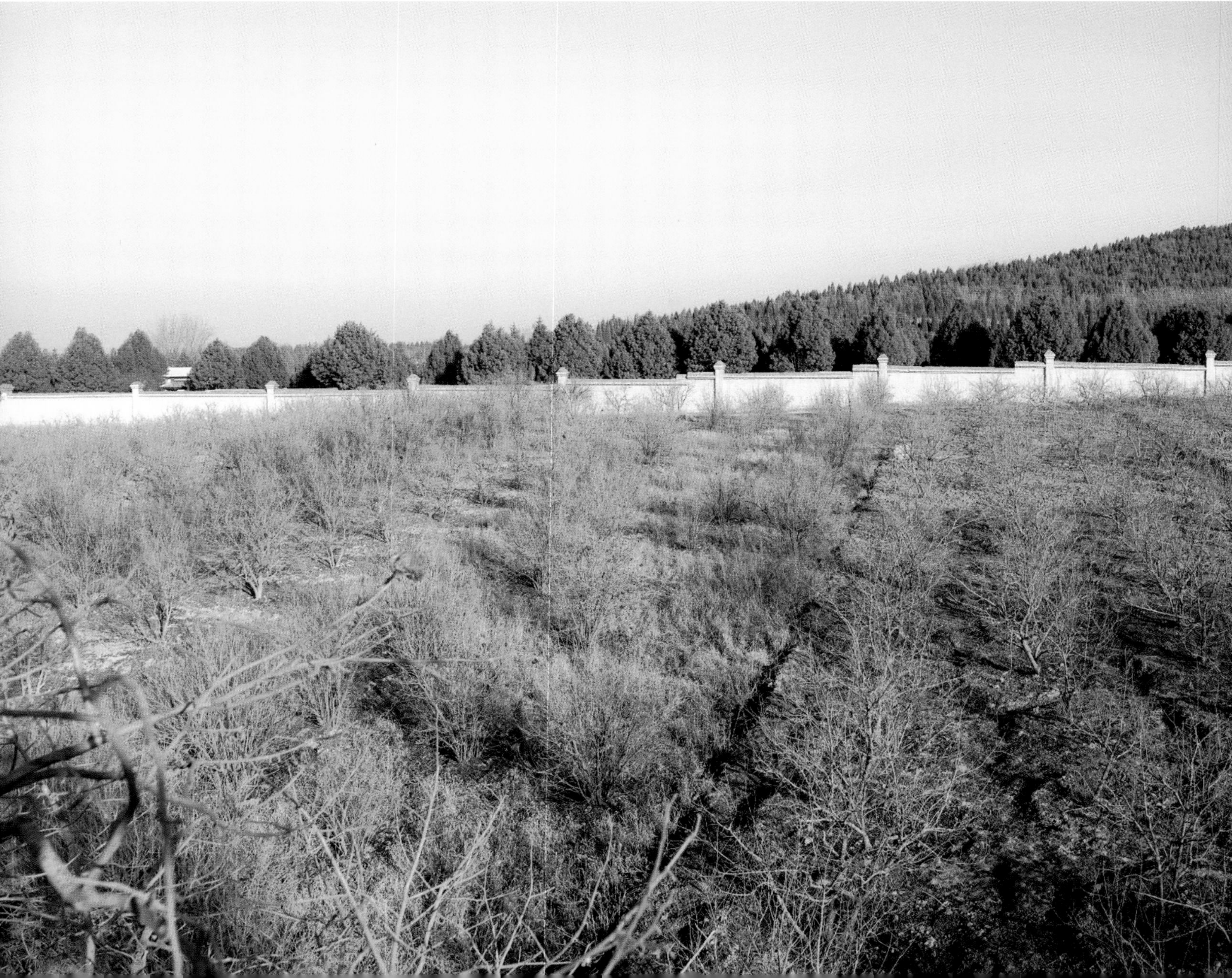

As Sima Qian was writing more than a hundred years after the death of the First Emperor, we do not know how accurate this account is. We should note, however, that Sima Qian does not use the words 'model' or 'imitation' in his writings, although some translations of this famous passage put in these words. Above I have used the word 'analogue' to describe the tomb as both a representation of life and as a functioning dwelling and even universe for the afterlife. Sima Qian also described the tomb mound, once it had been planted with trees, as an analogue of a mountain.[22] In the traditions of the day, gods, spirits and people who had evaded death, and thereby become immortal, lived in mountains. Thus this tomb mound was a mountain dwelling for a god-like ruler. By being made as analogues, the mound and the tomb assumed the roles that their creators sought. Further, by placing his eternal palace in a mountain, the First Emperor gave it a geographical position alongside and in parallel with the great mountains of his territory that marked out the directions and the borders of his lands.[23]

The emperor had in life already built a large series of life-size buildings at the capital, realizing in captivity, so to speak, the palaces of the states that he had conquered, as Sima Qian recounts:

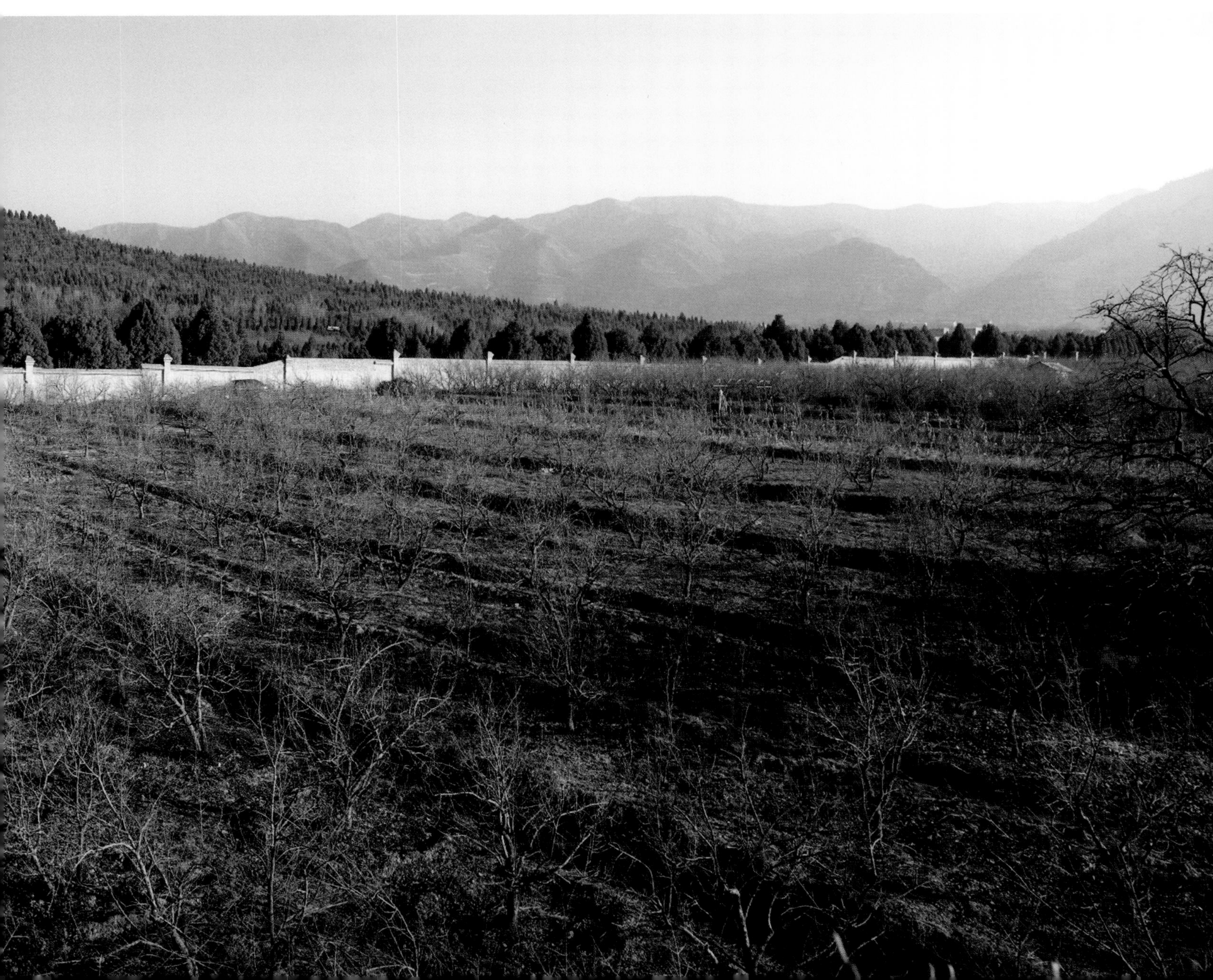

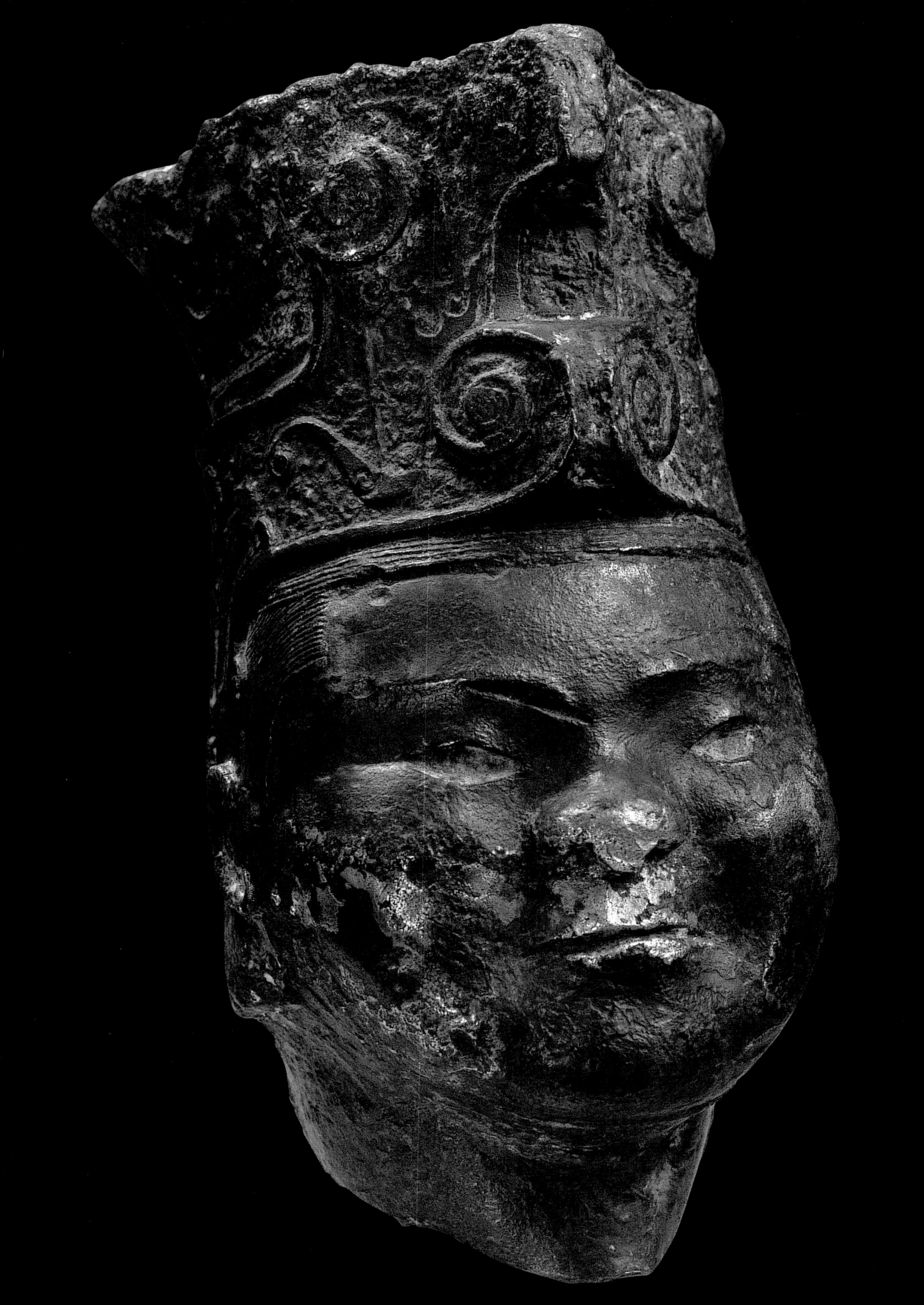

> And whenever Qin would wipe out one of the feudal states, it would recreate its halls and palaces and reconstruct them on the slope north of Xianyang, facing south over the Wei. From Yongmen east to the Jing and the Wei rivers, mansions, elevated walks, and fenced pavilions succeeded one another, all filled with beautiful women and bells and drums that Qin had taken from the feudal rulers.[24]

Here the full extent of the emperor's conquest was, like his eternal palace, mapped onto the landscape of the capital. Moreover, the whole enterprise was of such a scale that the emperor might, if he wished, walk among the buildings and contemplate his triumphs in terms of the looted bells and captured women. This full-size enclave was one of the parallels for the project at Mt. Li, sharing with it immense size and occupants who included many real people. The other occupants, the soldiers and acrobats in clay unknown to Sima Qian, have caused astonishment in the present day. How did the emperor come by the idea of filling some roles of his afterlife universe with figures of clay?[25] Sima Qian provides another account that may give a hint of what had provoked this new phenomenon. To commemorate his conquest, the First Emperor had twelve immense bronze figures cast:

> Weapons from all over the empire were confiscated, brought to Xianyang, and melted down to be used in casting bells, bell stands and twelve men made of metal. These last weighed 1,000 piculs each and were set up in the palace.[26]

These were immense sculptures and would have required great skill in modelling and in casting to realize them. The ancient techniques of bronze casting, which required complex ceramic moulds, were the technologies with which the emperor's officials created the great army in clay.[27] But life-like figures in bronze of any size were unprecedented in early Chinese culture. Could the emperor have heard, as if in a distant echo, news of the massive sculptures at the courts of the kings in the regions of present-day Iran or even in the Mediterranean area? There is much evidence of contact across central Asia during the preceding and following centuries.[28] It seems possible that such contact, and the resulting bronze figures, sowed the seeds of an idea in the minds of the emperor's court that blossomed in the extraordinary army of terracotta warriors.

Construction of the tomb complex

During the last thirty years test digging and excavations at the tomb site have been carried out over a vast area of several square kilometres and no doubt will continue long into the future. Figs 128 and 131 shows the First Emperor's tomb complex. But a single present-day plan of the site obscures the fact that we are looking at three very different landscapes. First in chronological time is the landscape across which workers moved building the tomb, and many of them are now buried south-west of the tomb. Succeeding that landscape in time, following the death and funeral of the First Emperor, there stood the completed mound over the tomb at the centre of

FIG. 130
The *Shiji* records that when the First Emperor created the Qin empire, weapons were collected and brought to the capital, melted down and cast as bells, bell stands and twelve men made of metal. This bronze head is one of the earliest naturalistic figural sculptures in bronze and may have been a decorative finial for a bell stand.
Cat. no. 98

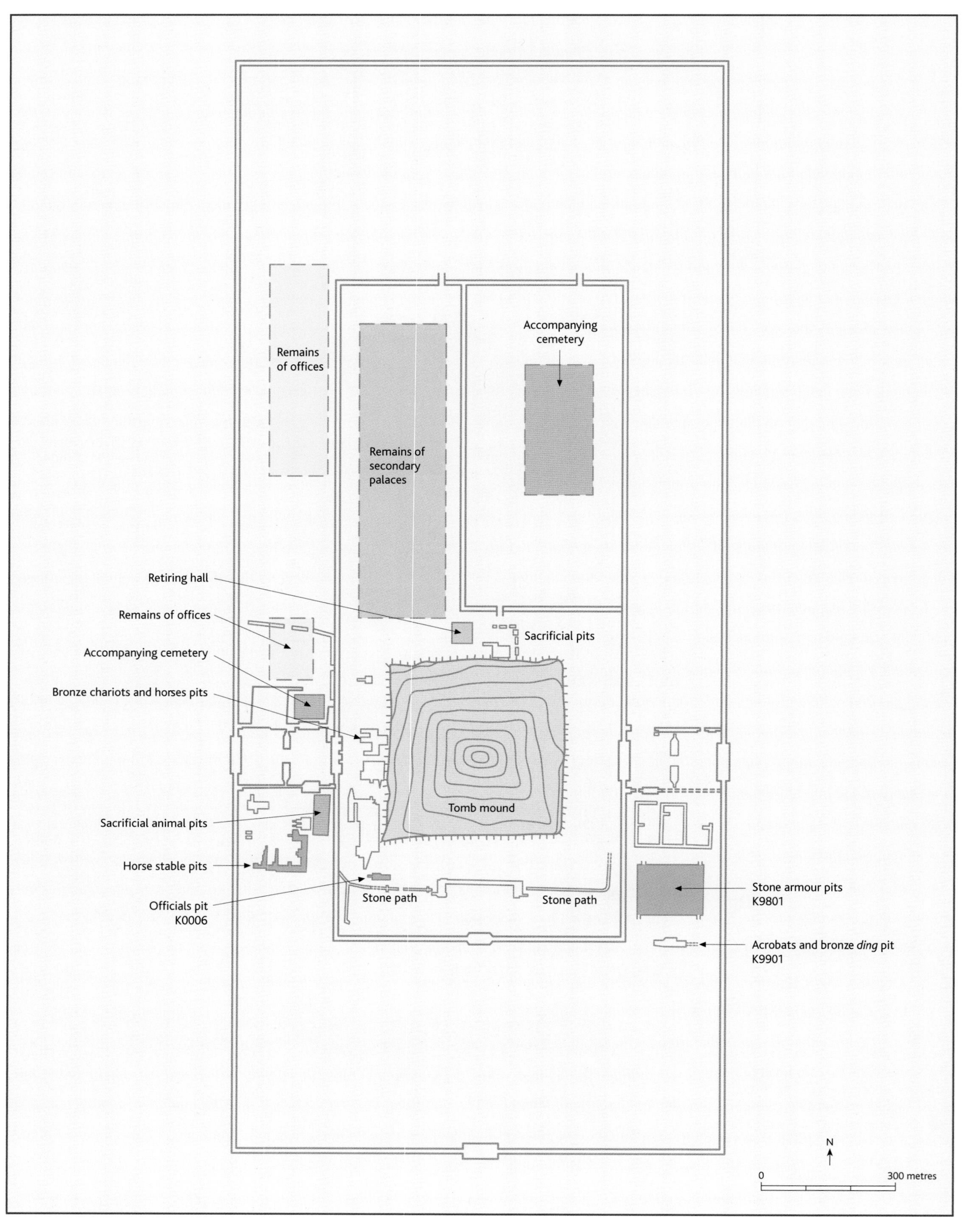
Accompanying cemetery
Remains of offices
Remains of secondary palaces
Retiring hall
Remains of offices
Sacrificial pits
Accompanying cemetery
Bronze chariots and horses pits
Tomb mound
Sacrificial animal pits
Horse stable pits
Officials pit K0006
Stone path
Stone path
Stone armour pits K9801
Acrobats and bronze *ding* pit K9901
N
0
300 metres

its high defensive walls and surrounded by buildings in which offerings were made by the living to the dead emperor; this was the ritual landscape above ground. Last, but most intriguing, is the landscape of the afterlife, invisible to the living, as its different aspects were buried in pits and underground structures.

We will look at these three landscapes in turn and then consider how that of the tomb provided for the emperor's eternal rule. The three landscapes give us three different perspectives on the ways in which the emperor and his needs were addressed. But we must never think of these landscapes as having been static. All three of them were peopled: the first with administrators, craftsmen and labourers; the second with ritual experts and servants to prepare the offerings for the dead emperor; and the third by the members of the court, the administration and the army in the realm of the afterlife.

Sima Qian (see pp. 24–5) tells us something about the work on the tomb and its final form . Although written at a later date by a strong critic of the First Emperor, his history has provided essential information about the life and ambitions of the First Emperor and is accepted as being a reasonably reliable account. Sima Qian claims that the First Emperor embarked on the construction of his tomb when he came to the throne as King of Qin in 246 BC. It is clear that work intensified a fter the emperor's triumphal unification in 221 BC, eleven years before he died in 210 BC. Some archaeologists believe that the work was undertaken in the latter, shorter period.

The burial chamber under the tomb mound, probably the largest single component, was a monumental enterprise that surely required diverse administrators,

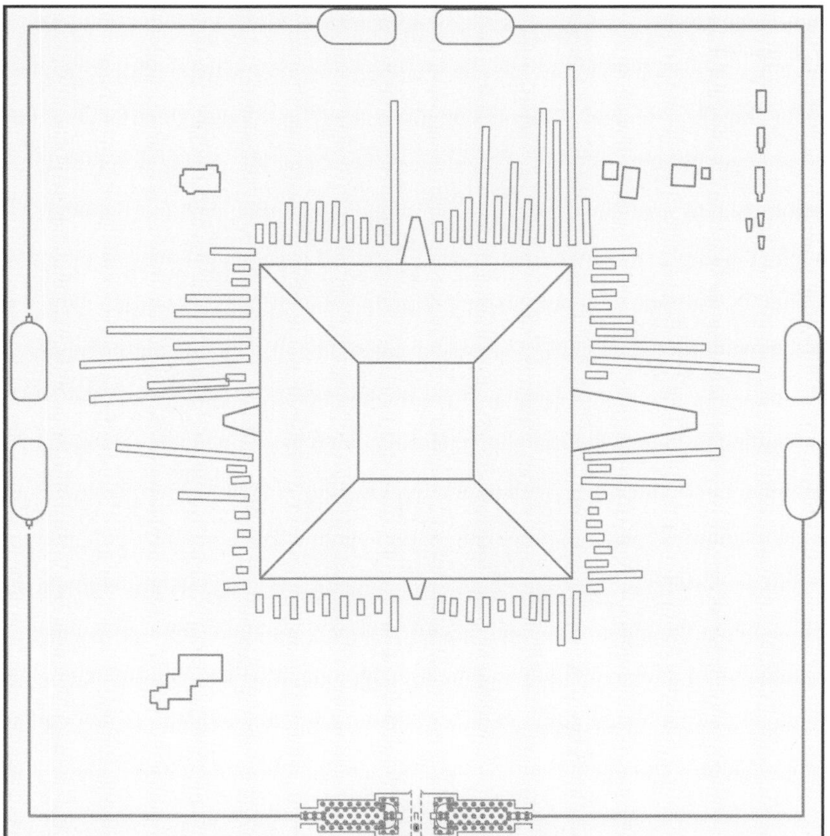

FIG. 131
(left) **Plan of the First Emperor's tomb.**

FIG. 132
(right) **Plan of Yangling, the tomb of Emperor Jingdi (r.156–141 BC) the fourth ruler of the Western Han dynasty. The tomb mound is in the centre with rectangular pits of varying lengths radiating out from all four sides. The pits contained pottery attendants and animals.**

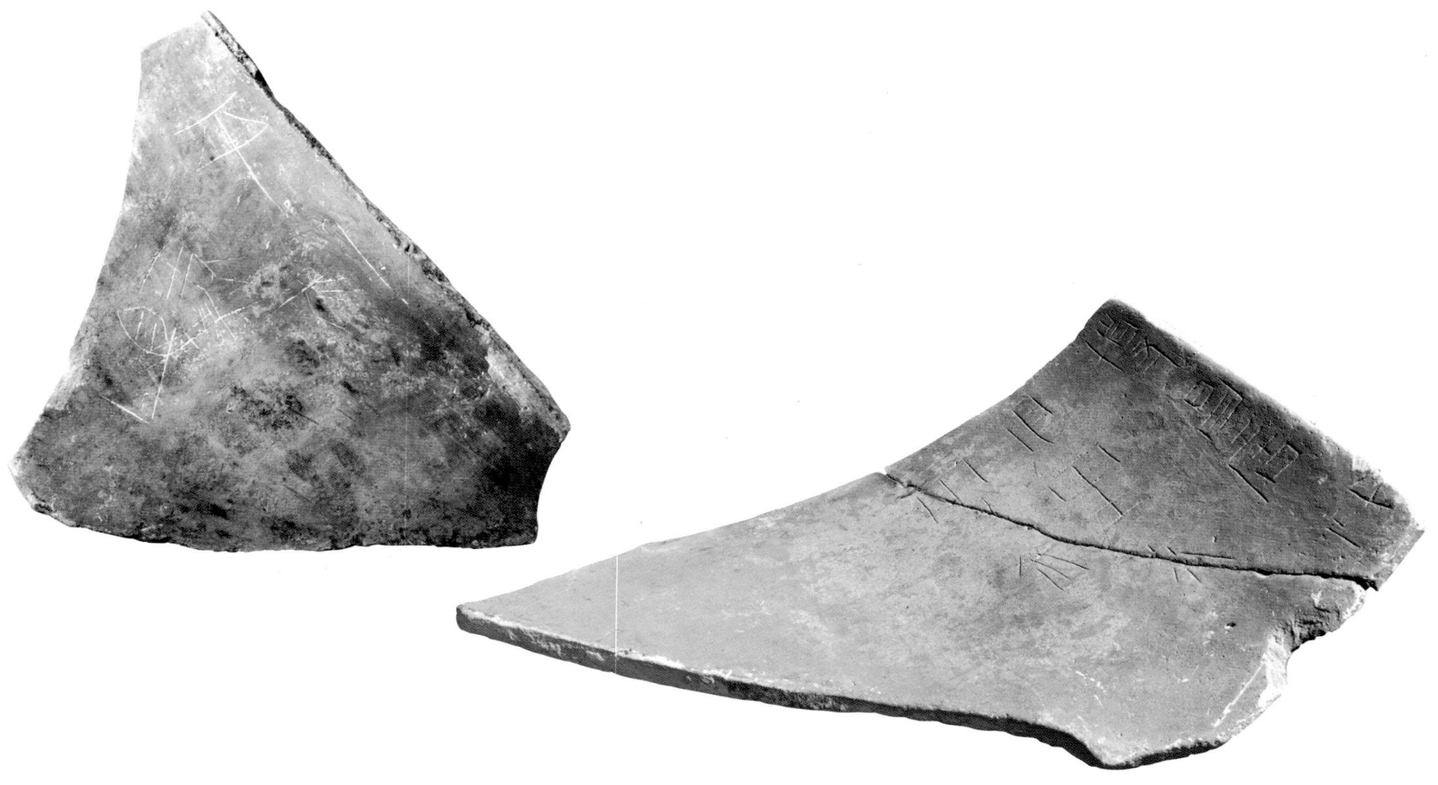

FIGS **133 & 134**
(above) **Pottery fragments, some with inscriptions, have been found west of the First Emperor's tomb in Zhaobeihu village, in the graves of labourers, often convicted criminals, who constructed the tomb of the First Emperor. Some inscriptions record the place of origin, the type of sentence, title and name of the person, and reveal how workers were mobilized from all over the country to work on the tomb. The fragement on the left is inscribed Pingyang station, the place where the deceased came from. The fragment on the right, inscribed with nine characters, describes the deceased, surname Yu and title *bugeng* (low-ranking civil servant) as coming from Bochang, a town located in the state of Qi during the Warring States period. He received a sentence to perform labour work in lieu of time in prison.**
Cat. nos 99 & 100

overseers and craftsmen. Archaeologists estimate that the burial chamber is at least 30 metres and perhaps 40 metres below the original ground surface. To excavate to that depth, a much larger area must have been opened up, with long access ramps allowing workmen to reach the deepest levels to install the outer and inner coffins and place the many grave goods. In addition, to protect the tomb from seasonal flooding, water courses had to be diverted around the southern side of the tomb, creating an artificial lake.

Each underground building would have required a plan, several overseers and many craftsmen. These buildings may have been developed in succession, one after another, rather than as part of a single scheme, as the individual pits are not placed in a symmetrical orderly arrangement, like those of the later tomb of the Han emperor, Jingdi (r. 156–141 BC), at the site of the Yangling (*fig.* 132). The diverse and elaborate archaeological discoveries make it evident to us today that there was overarching, immense and detailed bureaucratic organization that was responsible for the conception of the complex of different sites and for the detailed execution of them: the faithful arrangement of the different military groups and the several types of stone armour required a formidable understanding of the military arrangements of the day and of ways to map them onto the tomb area; and use of repetitive, even mass, production to create multiple versions of the individual terracotta warriors or the single stone plaques for the armour was a feat of management of a vast labour force. Without a series of plans in the form of some sort of 'blueprint' and strongly coordinated overseers who realized in physical form these conceptions, the end result could never have been achieved.

There are many physical traces of the organization of the thousands of workers. We know that labour was drawn from all over the empire from the inscriptions on pottery fragments carved with the names and places of origin of the conscripts. These were often criminals, recruited as forced labour, and, as mentioned already,

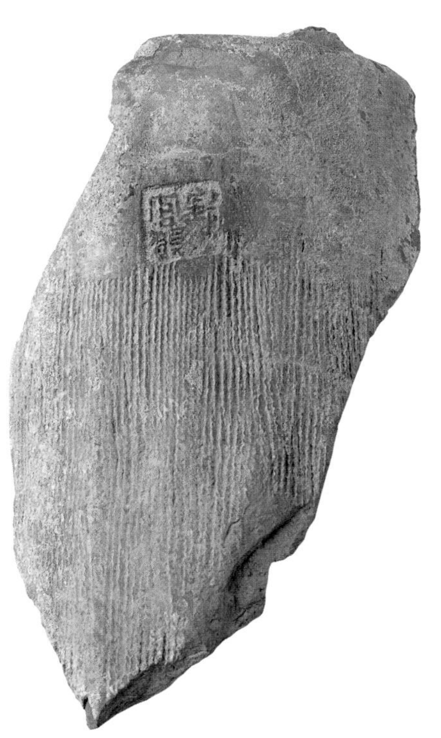

many are buried in one of the cemeteries to the west of the main complex (*fig.* 128).[29] They may even have been killed when the work was completed. The pottery fragment illustrated in *fig.* 133 gives the name of the person and his place of origin. Behind such a large labour force lay a large administration. At the tomb site the workforce had to be organized, fed and in due course buried. Their names and places of origin recorded on the pottery fragments demonstrate that the officials organizing them kept very careful records.

The building materials, especially the roof tiles, carry impressed seals of the workshops that made them (*figs* 135–8). From these we learn that many different sites were involved, indicating both the scale of the task and the speed with which it had to be undertaken.[30] Names of the overseeing craftsmen are also inscribed on the warriors themselves, as a form of accountability and hence of quality control. The foreman of groups of workers was probably responsible for the accomplishment of set tasks.[31] The same sort of recording may have been used for the stone armour.

We can, therefore, imagine a large body of actual workers and many layers of overseers and administrators at work day after day at the site – living, eating, sleeping

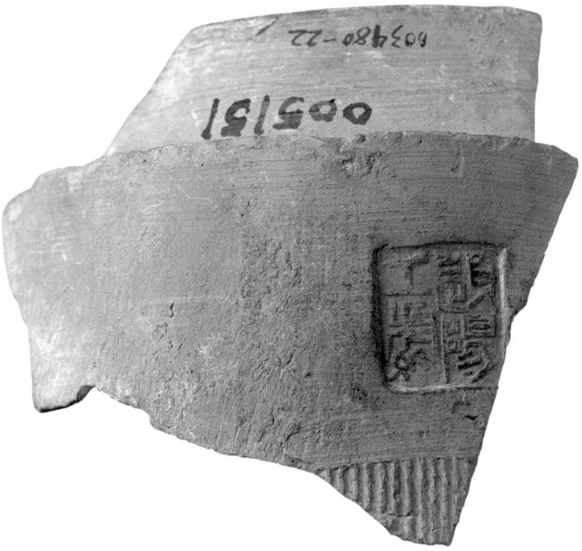

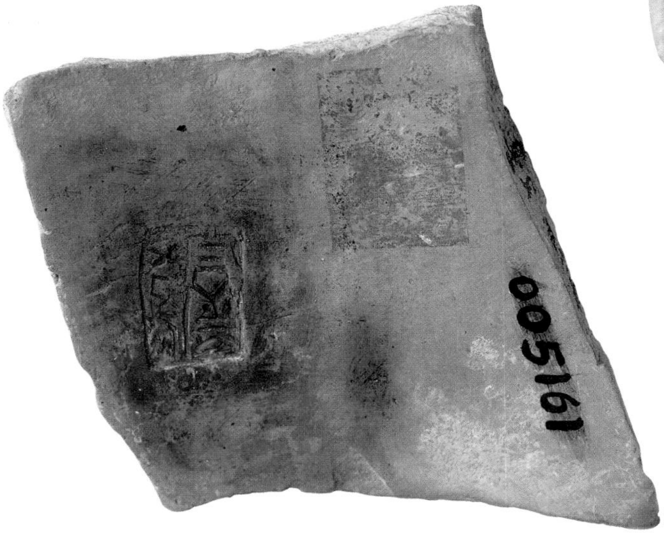

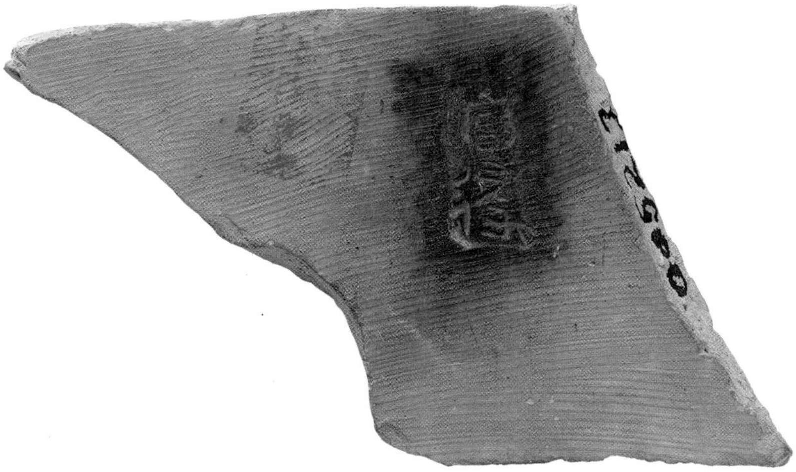

FIGS **135–8**
Fragments of building material impressed with marks identifying the various government workshops where they were made. These workshops not only produced architectural elements but also the terracotta figures. The armour piece from the right shoulder of an infantryman (*fig. 139*) was inscribed with Xianyang, the place of the work-shop, which also appears on the roof tile above.
Cat. nos 101–4

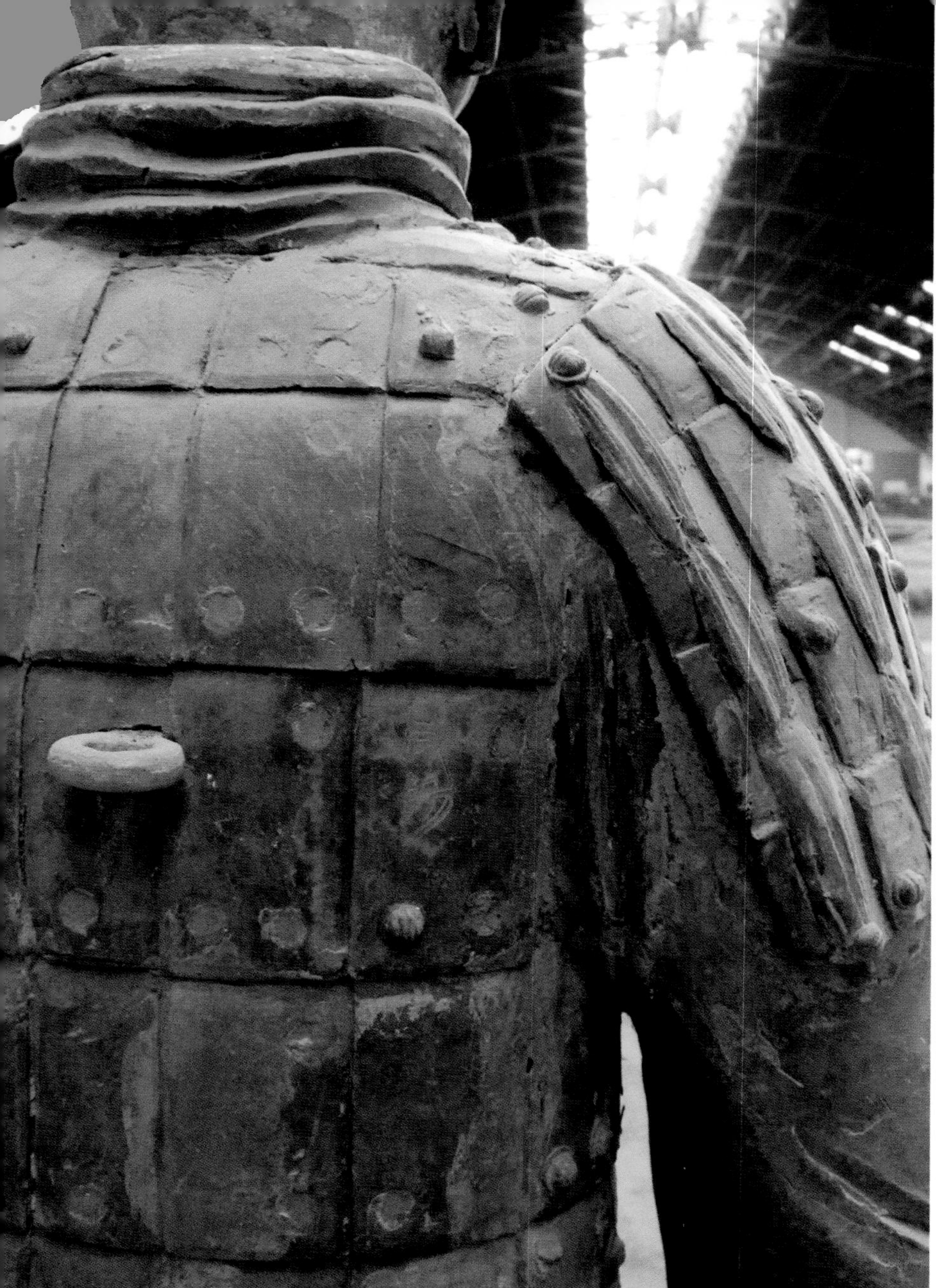

FIG. 139
The back shoulder of an armoured infantryman and the detail of it inscribed with the characters *Xianyang*.

and, in many cases, dying there. At the capital there are also likely to have been further administrators and planners. In addition, beyond the site itself, there would have been other groups of men ordered to obtain raw materials. These, too, must have been operations on a very large scale.

After the bustle of hundreds, or even thousands, of men, the upheaval of the earth and the creation of deep pits together with the diversion of rivers, the finished landscape following the First Emperor's death would have been much more tranquil. In place of a construction site, with vast pits open for all to see, the ground was restored and the only visible signs of the tomb were the tree-covered mound and its surrounding defensive walls. Within the inner and outer walls were structures for the daily rituals required to sustain the emperor in the afterlife. A small temple-like building was placed behind the mound to the north-west. This, the retiring, or *qin*, building housed imperial gowns, caps, armrests and staffs. Here the food and wine offerings to the dead emperor were made. A subordinate ritual building, the *bian dian*, seems to have been located to the north-west of the *qin*.[32] Large numbers

FIG. 140
(below) **This pottery lid of a vessel, found to the west of the tomb mound, is inscribed *Lishan shi guan*, 'Office of Food and Drink of Lishan'. Lishan is the name of the First Emperor's tomb. The inscription therefore indicates that there was a special department for providing food and drink not only for visitors to the tomb but also for ritual sacrifices to the deceased emperor.**
Cat. no. 105

FIG. 141
(below right) **This bell, decorated with gold and silver inlay, was cast with two seal-script characters, *yue fu*, on the side of its loop handle, identifying it as an instrument made for the emperor's music department.**
Cat. no. 106

of servants and ritual specialists were housed in the area to the west within the outer wall. They probably also occupied the buildings whose remains have been discovered in the northern sector. Within the west section of the outer wall was a building for the supply of food, the *shi guan*, or provisioning office. A number of whole ceramics and fragments have been found here.[33]

By contrast with the bustling activity at the construction site that must have preceded it, the ritual attention of the living was governed by a formidable ceremonial decorum. The actual funeral, with a spectacular ritual, was a major event, probably involving hundreds, maybe even thousands, in processions. Deposition of the emperor in his deep tomb must also have been a major feat. But once sealed, and the workmen disposed of, the activities at the tomb area were undoubtedly restricted to smaller groups of people than before. Thus, following the many years of activity, even turmoil, a period of measured organization would have been the main feature of the years after the emperor's death in 210 BC.

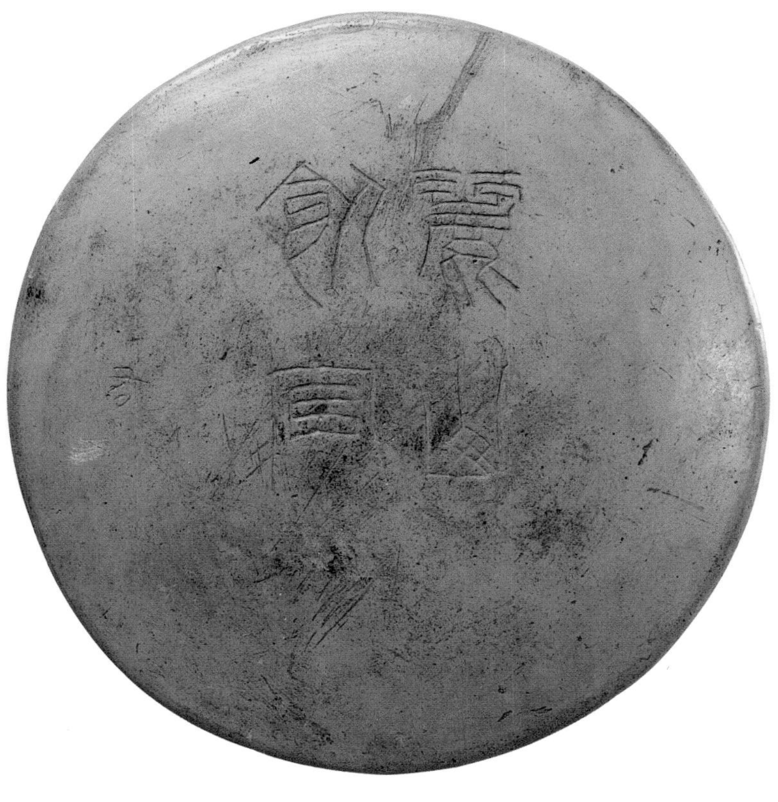

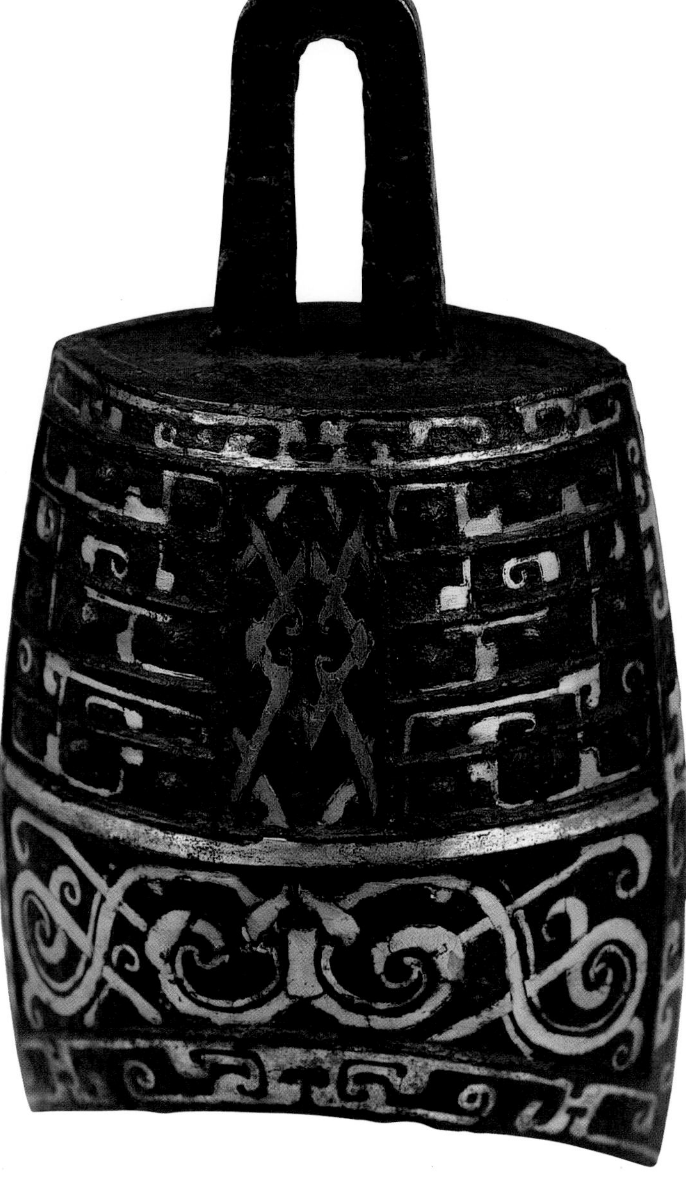

The palace underground

While all was regulated above ground, what was happening in the buildings installed below ground? As we have noted already, the Chinese of the day believed that the dead continued to be present among the living and to exert influence over the lives of their descendants. The world that the First Emperor realized for himself was on a scale beyond any of those of his predecessors. Like all afterlives, it was active, with the individuals in it having roles and indeed duties, all taking place within the landscape in and around the mound. The army, for example, was to defend the emperor from an attack or invasion of the spirits of the armies he had massacred.

While some have concentrated on and talked about the army alone, it is perhaps better simply to take the tomb and its surroundings as a totality, recognizing that everything that the emperor did had a universalizing purpose. The palaces of the living mirrored and thus incorporated the authority of the palaces and offices of the spirits of the cosmos. In such an intellectual environment the care with which the tomb was constructed suggests that the emperor once more projected from one context to another, this time from life to the afterlife. The tomb was not a monument but an analogue of life, through which this ruler perpetuated his authority over the known universe into the invisible one of life after death. The world embodied in the emperor's tomb complex was simultaneously a way of understanding the future, a way of determining it and a way of providing for it.

The subterranean burial chamber was the emperor's palace. While we do not know what the interior of the chamber looks like (see the Appendix, pp. 204–7, for details of scientific testing of the First Emperor's burial mound), it almost certainly consisted of several linked rooms, as had the tombs of his ancestors and of other kings of the states. As Sima Qian records that 'the hundred officials', an idiom referring to the officials of the state administration, were interred, this sentence may indicate that actual individuals were forced to accompany the emperor in death into the tomb itself. Servants and workers were certainly buried. Undoubtedly the vessels and furnishings must have been sumptuous. Archaeologists working at the site suggest that within the mound – above the actual burial chamber itself – may have

FIG. 142
(opposite) **Pottery figure of an official. Eleven other pottery figures were discovered in the same pit. Eight have been identified as officials by their writing 'tools' – a knife and stone sharpener – which hang from their belt. The other four are modelled with their arms outstretched. Various theories have been put forward as to what they may be doing – they may be charioteers or perhaps low-ranking officials working in the penal and legal department.**
Cat. no. 107

FIG. 143
(below) **Line drawing of the officials pit (K0006).**

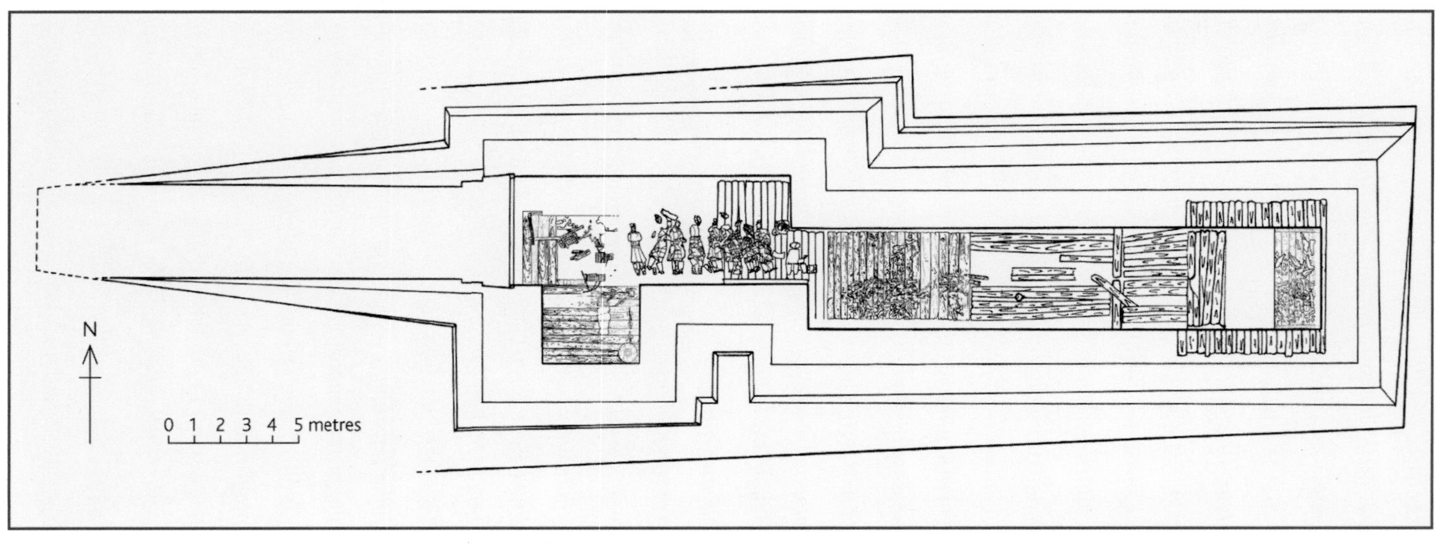

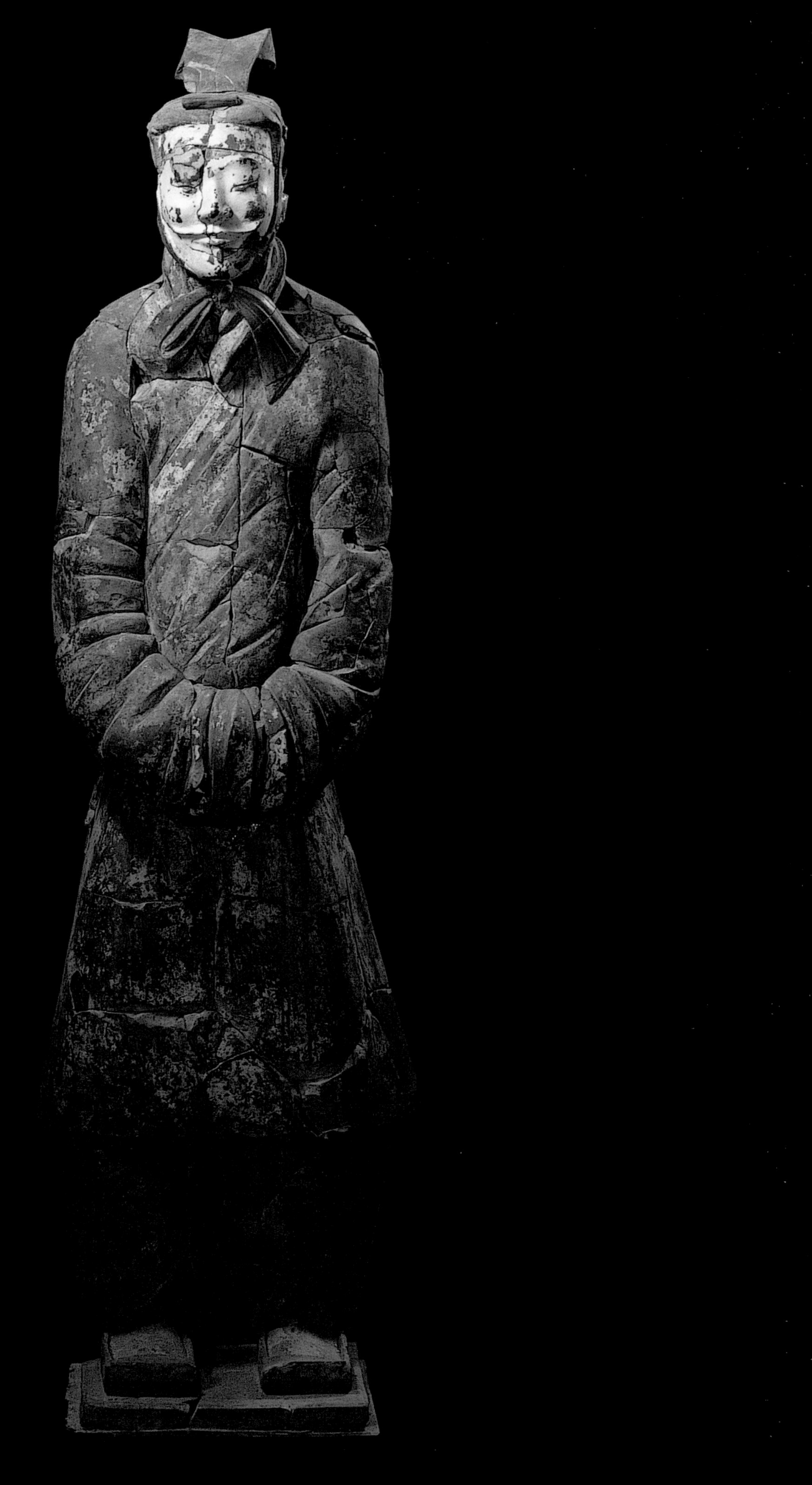

FIG. 144
(below) **Kneeling stable boy excavated from the stable pits at Shangjiaocun, east of the First Emperor's tomb. There are thought to be three to four hundred of these pits in total, each one holding a horse skeleton or kneeling stable boy or both. Inscriptions on pottery sherds verify that the horses came from palace stables. The line drawing shows a kneeling stable boy with a horse skeleton.**
Cat. no. 108

been terraced structures, with galleries and even towers, perhaps the towers mentioned by Sima Qian.[34] If these structures were built, then it is likely that they were intended for the emperor to ascend from his underground palace to view his precincts and the territories beyond. The two walls and their gates bounded the main palace grounds, mirroring the inner and outer court spaces of the palaces of the living.

Archaeologists have not only found the tombs of the convicts who worked at the site (who would have provided a labour force in the afterlife), they have uncovered graves of high-ranking people who accompanied the emperor. A row of tombs lies outside the outer east wall of the compound.[35] These held officials and some women. We know that there are further major figures of individuals to be discovered. A pit directly to the south of the emperor's tomb contained pottery figures of officials and charioteers in a wooden building as their office. Actual horses and a chariot were also buried. They seem to have been a part of the Qin central administration. Their building was constructed below ground, as many were, in wood, with several rooms.[36] The charioteers and their horses were intended to carry out the bidding of the officials, who in turn would have taken orders from a higher-ranked official who occupied a side room in the structure. It has been suggested that the official in charge was the *tingwei*, who organized prisons and legal affairs.[37] No figure of the *tingwei* is in the pit, and it is possible that the human *tingwei* was buried, either in one of the higher-ranking tombs alongside the outer wall or in some part of the main tomb itself. In Pit 3 of the army the central commanding general is also missing. The missing leader was either the First Emperor himself, living in his palace under the mound, or a high-ranking military official also buried in a large grave beside the army or in the actual tomb.

Other deposits in the inner tomb precinct were probably all important to the emperor's daily life – official and private. These included one or more ancillary burials, caches of grave goods for use in the afterlife, and two exquisitely made miniature chariots in bronze (*figs* 23–4). Their most conspicuous feature is the very faithful replication in bronze of every component of the chariots, piece by piece.[38] Here the superior value of the chariots seems to have been guaranteed by the use of metal, while at the same time they were made 'real' by the individual parts, which duplicated exactly the parts of full-size wooden chariots with their bronze fittings. Their miniature size made their exquisite character more pronounced, emphasizing their preciousness in the service of the emperor. It is sometimes suggested that these vehicles were to carry the emperor's soul to an immortal land. It is certainly likely that they were for the emperor's afterlife journeys. However, it seems more plausible that

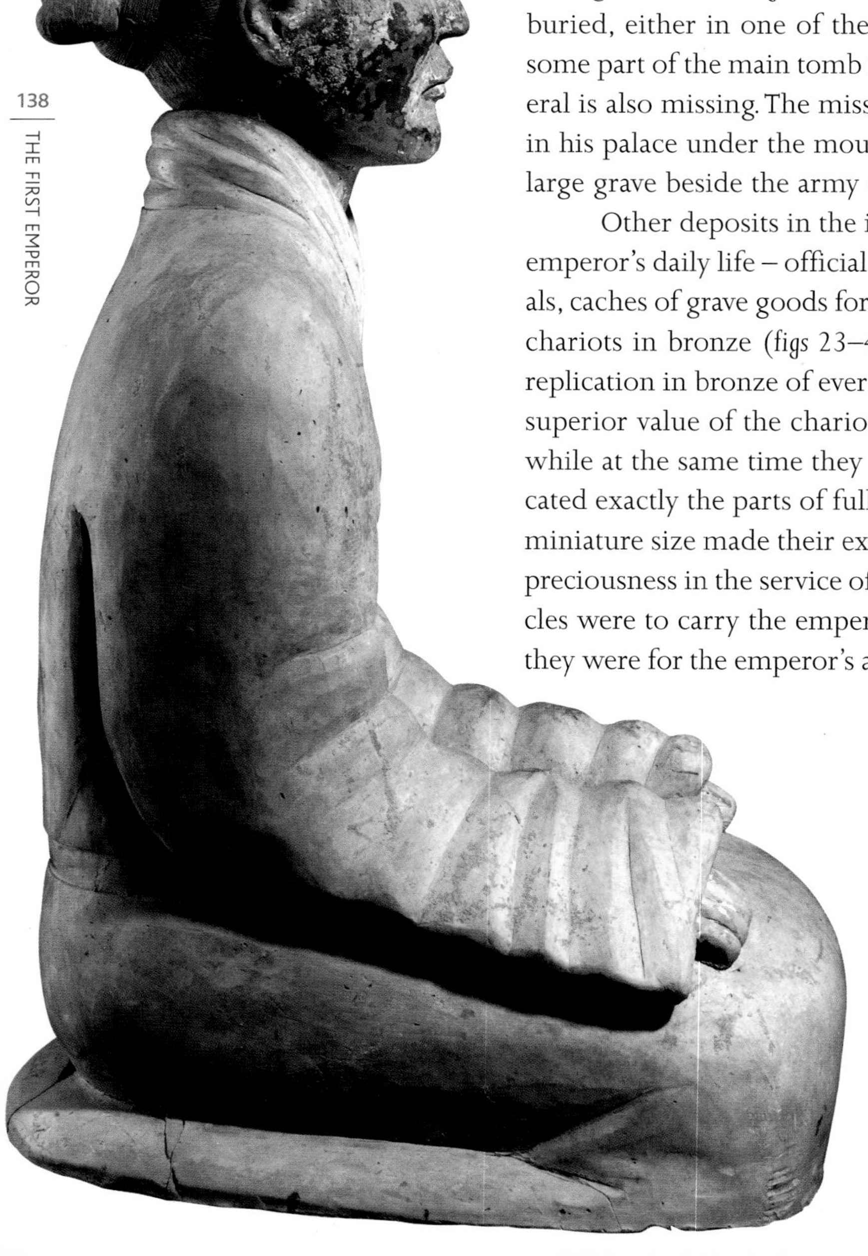

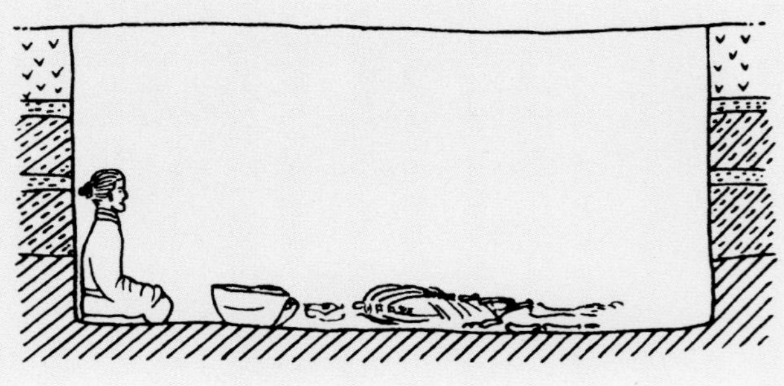

FIG. 145
(right) **Limestone armour pieces in the stone armour pit (K9801);** **see pp. 80–91.**

FIG. 146
(below) **Pottery coffins containing the bones of animals and birds, as well as clay dishes for food were found in a vertical line of pits to the west of the First Emperor's tomb. Either side of them were pits containing kneeling pottery figures, presumably keepers. The animals and birds may have been rare specimens acquired as gifts and kept in the imperial gardens or the vast imperial hunting park, Shanglin ('Supreme Forest').**
Cat. no. 109

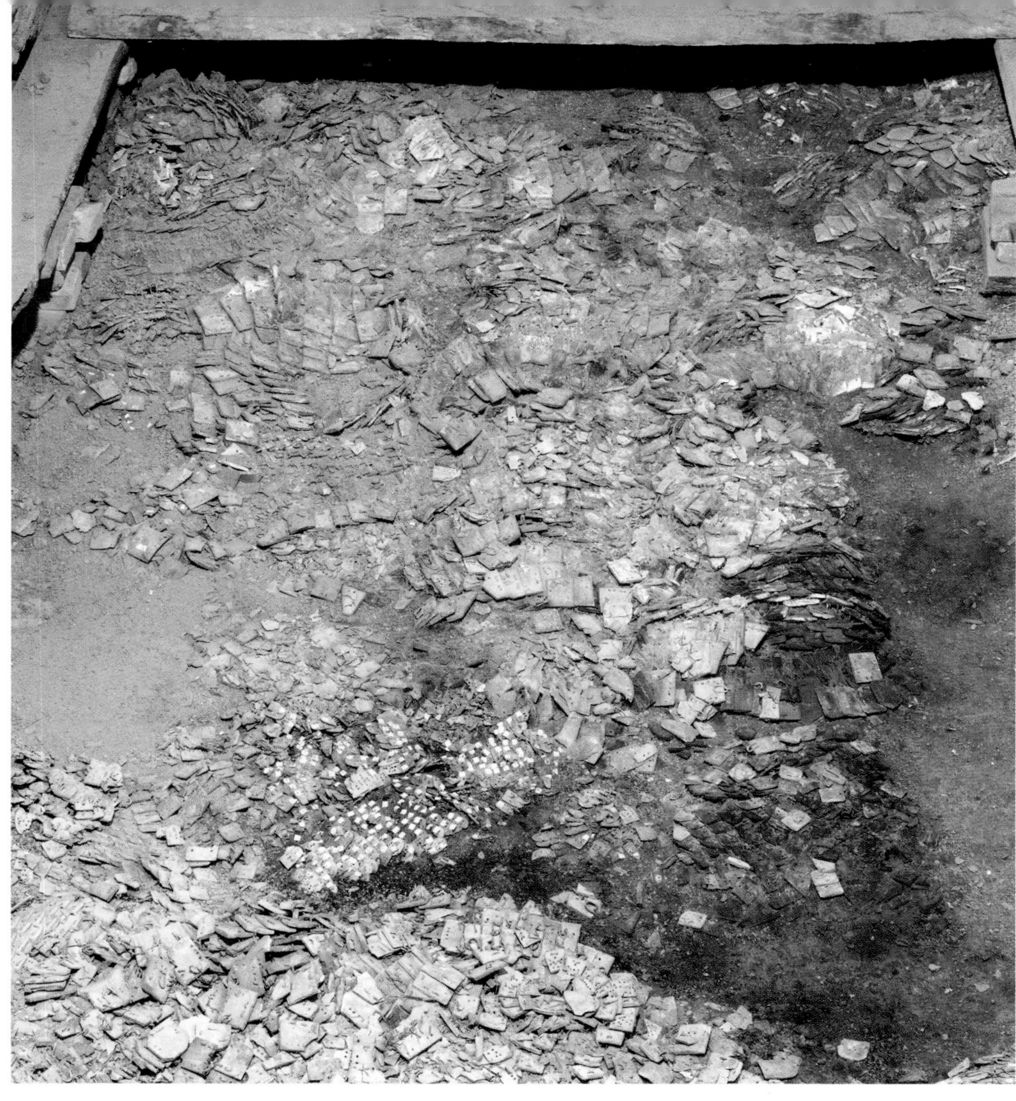

journeys to lands of the immortals would have been only some of many journeys that the emperor himself wished to make. The major excursions across his territories marking out the boundaries of his world, described by Kern above (pp. 104–13), were very likely the most essential routes he intended to revisit. Or he may simply have wished to enjoy his pleasure park to the north, where archaeologists have discovered a small artificial waterway with exquisite bronze birds and pottery figures of musicians (see pp. 192–202).[39]

The outer precinct deposits were less closely linked with the emperor's person. To the west were two groups of animals. A large stable-like structure housed horses, all of them the actual beasts; they were accompanied by miniature, kneeling pottery figures, often supplied with a dish or flask to indicate their roles as

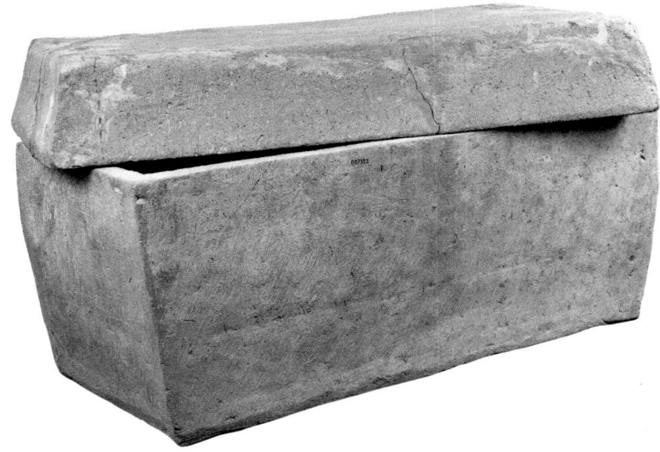

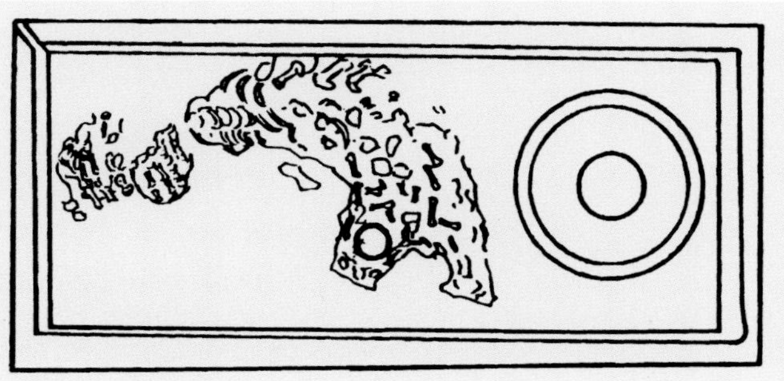

FIG. 147
(opposite, left) **The 'long cap', a flattened headdress set at an angle on the head and tied under the chin, identifies this figure as a military officer. The same headdress with a vertical line down the centre would indicate a higher rank.**
Cat. no. 110

FIG. 148
(opposite, right) **This pottery bare-chested animated figure is thought to be an acrobat by Chinese archaeologists. It was found in a pit near the First Emperor's tomb along with ten other figures modelled in equally animated poses. A massive bronze ritual food vessel (*fig. 37*) was found on top of the figures. The raised right index finger of this figure has a 12 cm deep hole suggesting that something was inserted into it.**
Cat. no. 111

guardians of esteemed creatures (*fig.* 144). Even more precious, probably, were the wild animals and birds, each buried in a coffin, belonging to the emperor's private menagerie or hunting park (*fig.* 146). At this period rulers hunted in large artificial parks, which we know from the next dynasty of the Han were configured to represent the entire world, with animals from the different regions placed in corresponding directions within the parks.[40] To provide the specific qualities, the fleetness of the horses, the ferocity of wild animals or the glorious plumage of exotic birds, the actual beasts had to be buried. In these instances the generic would not have sufficed, as it was specific individuals that were prized.

On the east were two extraordinary pits (*fig.* 131, K9801). One very large underground building, 100 x 130 metres in size, held many hundreds of sets of armour in stone, mounted on stands that have subsequently collapsed. In the very small sections excavated, eighty-nine sets of body armour, forty-three helmets and one set of horse armour were recovered. The sets were not uniform, but were varied according to rank and function of the soldiers for whom they were made. It would have been far easier and more economical to have buried hundreds of sets of lacquered leather or iron armour. The chief and most important factor must, therefore, have been the stone. It could not have protected against living enemies, as metal would have shattered it. This armour was an aspect of a new fashion for stone as protection against spirits.[41] The armour may even have been the precursor of the jade suits of the next century, as argued by James Lin (pp. 186–9). We should imagine that the armour would have been worn either by the individuals buried with the emperor or, as Lin suggests, by the many Qin soldiers who had been killed in the wars over previous decades who might have been thought to be waiting to join the emperor as an army in the afterlife.[42]

An adjacent pit contained a group of pottery figures of entertainers, wrestlers and acrobats (*fig.* 131, K9901). Their most striking feature is their realistic modelling. A massive figure stands with his hands held in front of him (*fig.* 160). Another much more slender entertainer has a hand raised (*fig.* 148). A major difference between these figures and those of the officials, mentioned above, and the warriors in the army is the sense conveyed that they are actually moving. Their lifelike gestures and diverse bodies, ranging from very slender to heavy and muscular, are very different from the impassive uniform stance of the officials and the immobility of most of the warriors, who were clearly forbidden to move unless directed to do so by superiors. The craftsmen of the day could readily achieve a sense of movement, but only occasionally was it appropriate. More important, only rarely was such individual realism required for functional purposes. It is evident that at each site different features were emphasized according to the functions required. Acrobats could move, officials were to be impassive, the army imposing.[43]

What indeed did the army itself provide? First of all, it was a perfectly organized fighting force. In Pit 1 stands the infantry of what is known as the Right Army, perhaps as many as 6,000 soldiers with 160 chariots, set out as thirty-eight columns of single-file warriors, reinforced by their chariots, some with drums and bells. In front were 200 archers with real crossbows. Indeed, the army was equipped throughout with real weapons. In Pit 2 were war chariots, sections of archers and a section of cavalry, all identified by present-day scholars as the Left Army. It included 939

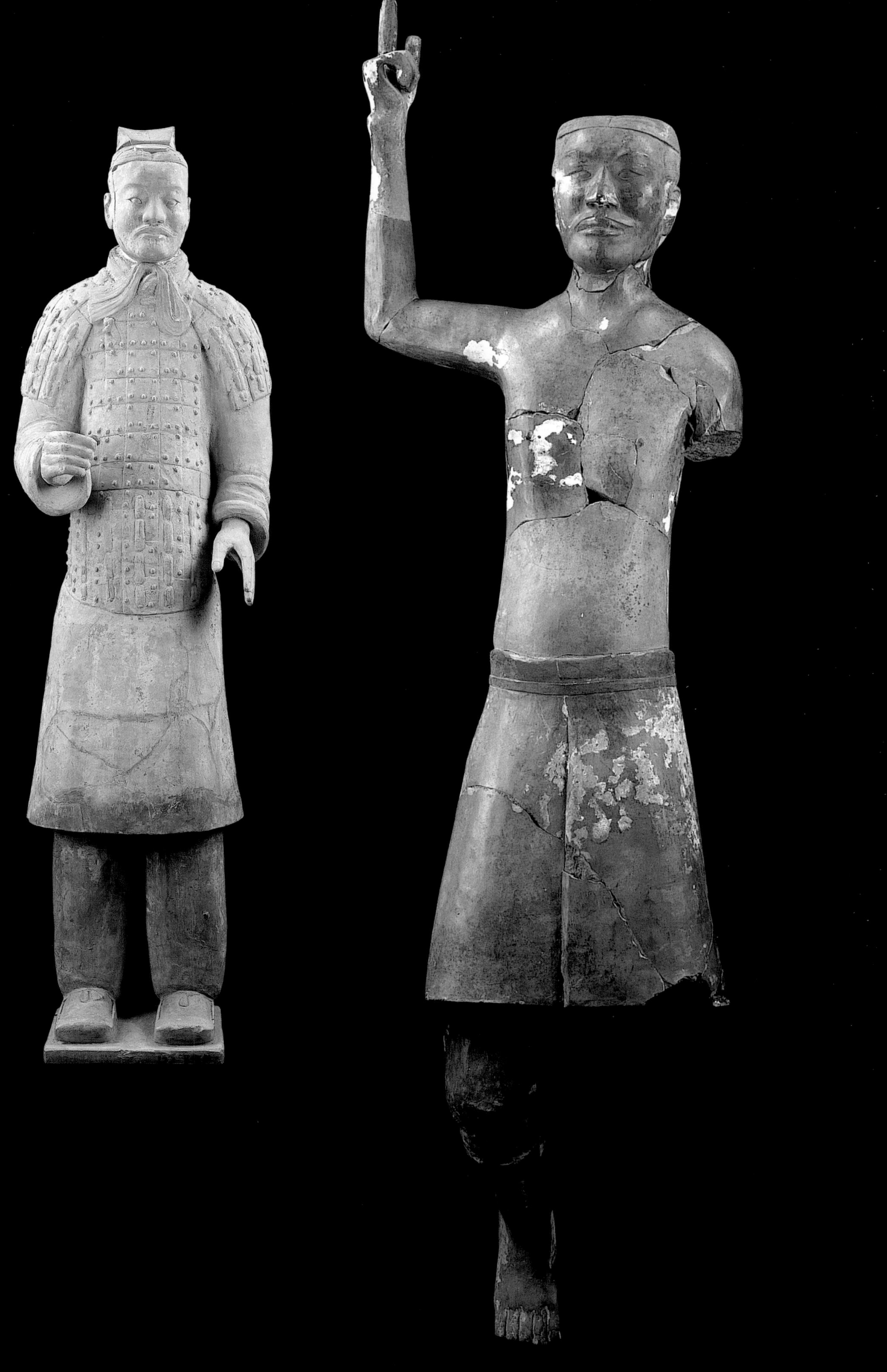

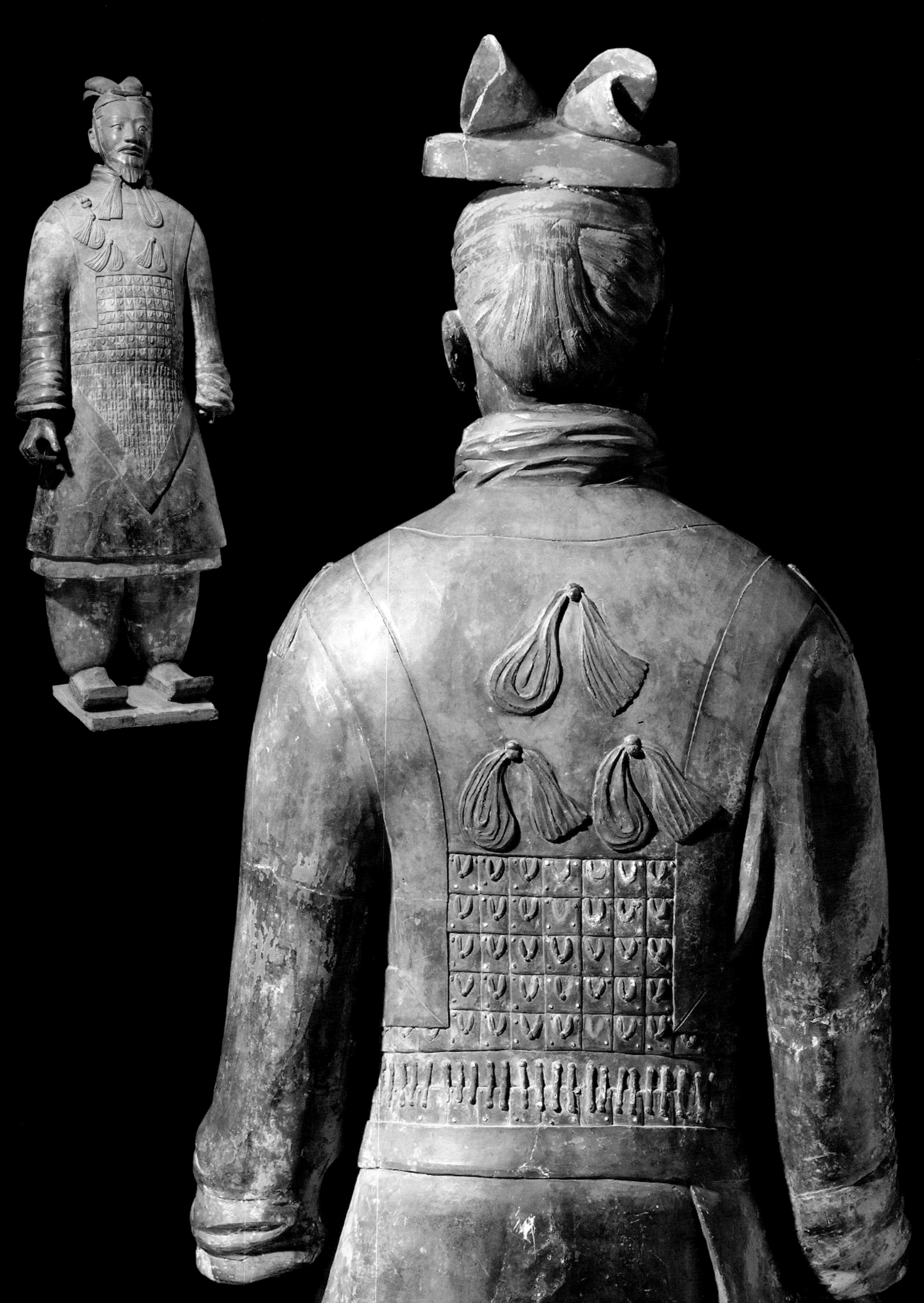

pottery warriors and 472 horses arranged in four groups: a square group of kneeling archers on the eastern side; a square group of war chariots on the southern side; a rectangular group of chariots and foot soldiers in the centre; and a rectangular group of mounted cavalry in the northern part. Here a formidable figure 196 cm high commanded a chariot in the rear. Pit 3 was a command post. The commander-in-chief is not present, but his decorated chariot and four supporters occupy the central position. It is likely that the commander is buried elsewhere, as already mentioned.[44]

Clay seems to have been chosen for the army for one outstanding reason. It made possible the creation of a perfect army. Had a large portion of the fighting force been slaughtered to follow the emperor, a much less complete army would probably have resulted. We can assess the kinds of completeness required from the many different caps, hair styles and beards found among the warriors – these indicate not only rank and function but probably also place of origin (see pp. 144–51). An army modelled in this way was an ideal fighting force. Exceptionally tall individuals could be chosen, each personalized, but without the burdens that come with organizing groups of armed warriors. This army was far easier to control in administrative and military terms than an army of men would have been. In clay, too, a full range of required officers and lower ranks could be mustered, as they could be designated with clearly modelled and painted armour, badges and headdress. The real weapons were equally essential to the functions of the soldiers. If the physical reality of the slaughtered and buried horses and the proper visual presentations of officials and acrobats were essential, then in a similar way we must argue that the clay figures of the army, in which rank and role were accurately achieved, gave them their credibility and functionality as a fighting force. Indeed, the different features emphasized in the various pits around the tomb make it clear that diverse functions were sought after. This was no model but an ordered world in which each part was designed for a special purpose.

Power of the emperor's tomb

The value of keeping tombs and their contents out of human view was well known. It had been and would continue to be the custom of a successful dynasty to destroy the tombs of a predecessor that it had defeated as part of their conquest strategy. The opening of the sealed tomb dwellings and the ransacking of the possessions of the dead seem to have been regarded as the best ways to destroy their universes and eliminate what power the dead might have over the living. Once revealed, the functions of the tomb were destroyed. It is in this context that we can view the destruction of the tomb complex by the rebel leader, Xiang Yu, in the bloody series of wars that followed the death of the First Emperor. The control of life was contested by two claimants, Liu Bang – the ultimate victor and founder of the Han dynasty – and Xiang Yu, in their rivalry for the empire. Xiang Yu did not leave anything to chance and he attempted to destroy the site that would have ensured immortal power for the First Emperor.

The tomb was a work of a supreme conqueror and administrator. The First Emperor claimed in life to have created order out of chaos. He then used the order

FIG. 149
Generals can be distinguished by their distinctive headdress, called a 'pheasant-tail' cap. Their armour extends down to a point at the front and ends at the waist at the back. Also distinctive are ribbons tied into bows, attached to the front, back and shoulders, which may be a sign of rank.
Cat. no. 112

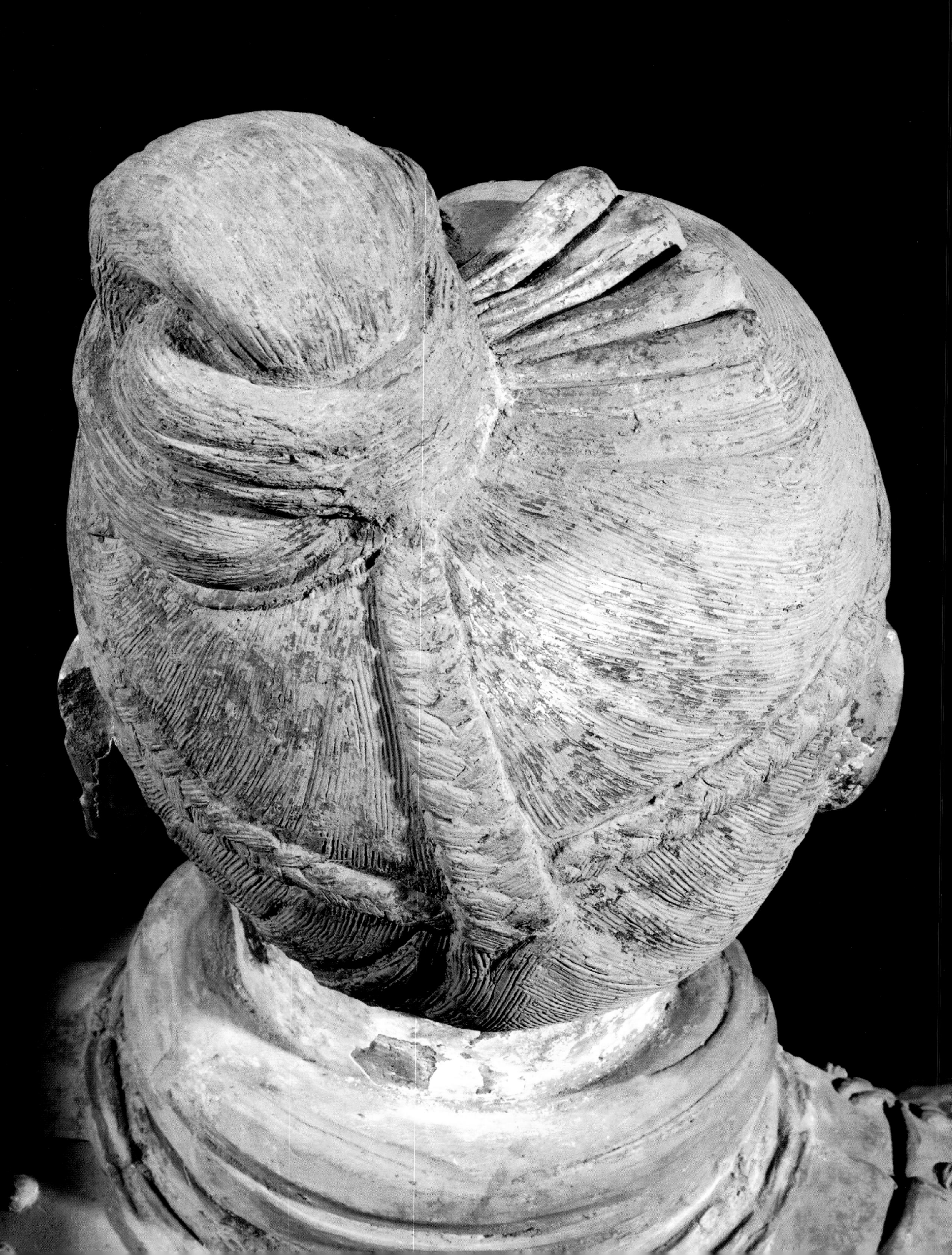

FIG. 150
(opposite) **Plaited and knotted hairstyle of a kneeling archer.**

FIG. 151
(right) **The sole of a kneeling archer. The shoes of warriors were mainly painted dark brown with the borders decorated in vermilion, violet or green with orange or violet laces.**

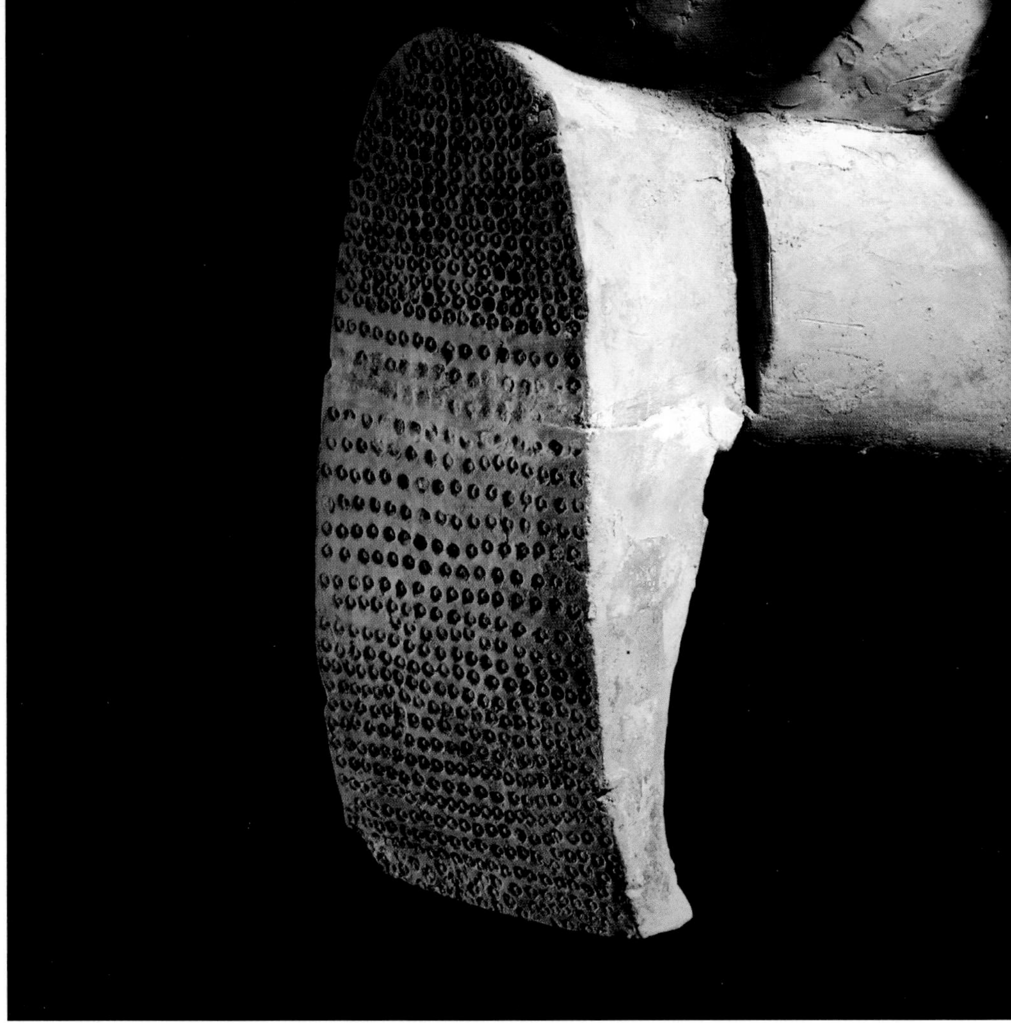

FIG. 152
(pages 146–7) **Details of terracotta figures showing various hairstyles and headdresses.**

On the left-hand page are different round hair-knot hairstyles. Strands of hair are taken from the sides and nape of the neck and plaited, whilst the main bulk of the hair is gathered into a topknot. The acrobat (top left) does not have any plaits but instead the hair is combed back and twisted into a knot.

On the right-hand page, the armoured infantryman and charioteer (top) wear soft caps over their plaited hairstyles. The general (below, left) is distinguished by his 'pheasant-tail' headdress. The stable boy (below, right) has a simple bun at the back of his head with no headdress.

FIGS 153 & 154
(pages 148–9) **The light infantryman on the left has a large nose and a beard, suggesting a Central Asian ancestry, while the general on the right has a more squat nose and Mongolian features.**
Cat. nos 26 & 35

FIGS 155 & 156
(pages 150–1) **The cavalryman on the left has a close-fitting riding cap tied under his chin, while the infantryman on the right has a soft hat tied at the back for easy adjustment.**
Cat. nos 17 & 113

generated by his powerful administration and army to replicate them both and perpetuate them into the future. So the realm of the future became peopled by officials, servants and armies, unlike the afterlife populated by gods and spirits described by so many of the world's religions. A new eternal order was thus brought into being by the organization that the emperor had wrought to rule his empire, which it then mirrored.

It is a human quality to pattern the unknown on the known and then to reverse the interpretation and read the known as a true exemplar of the unknown. No one was more adept at this than the First Emperor. In life he set himself in the lineage of the sage kings and took control over the spirits of the regions he dominated. He thereby gave his empire a supernatural dimension and achieved the role of a cosmic ruler. In life he claimed his power by analogy with the powers of the sage kings and of those of the supernatural forces. He gave his tomb the features of life and thus made it a complete analogue, with buried humans, a perfect clay army, hundreds of sets of stone armour and miniaturized bronze chariots. So the First Emperor contrived his power base for all eternity. Here the unknown was created out of the known. But, as in life the emperor claimed a role at the centre of the cosmos, in death he did not relinquish it. His tomb mound reminds us still today that, when buried there – in the embodiment of a mountain – the emperor has created a new space in the revered geography of China, which he had so carefully charted and ordered in his lifetime.[45] By residing in his tomb, he reconfigured his universe and even added to that of our own time. Few have achieved such power over the minds of those who followed them.

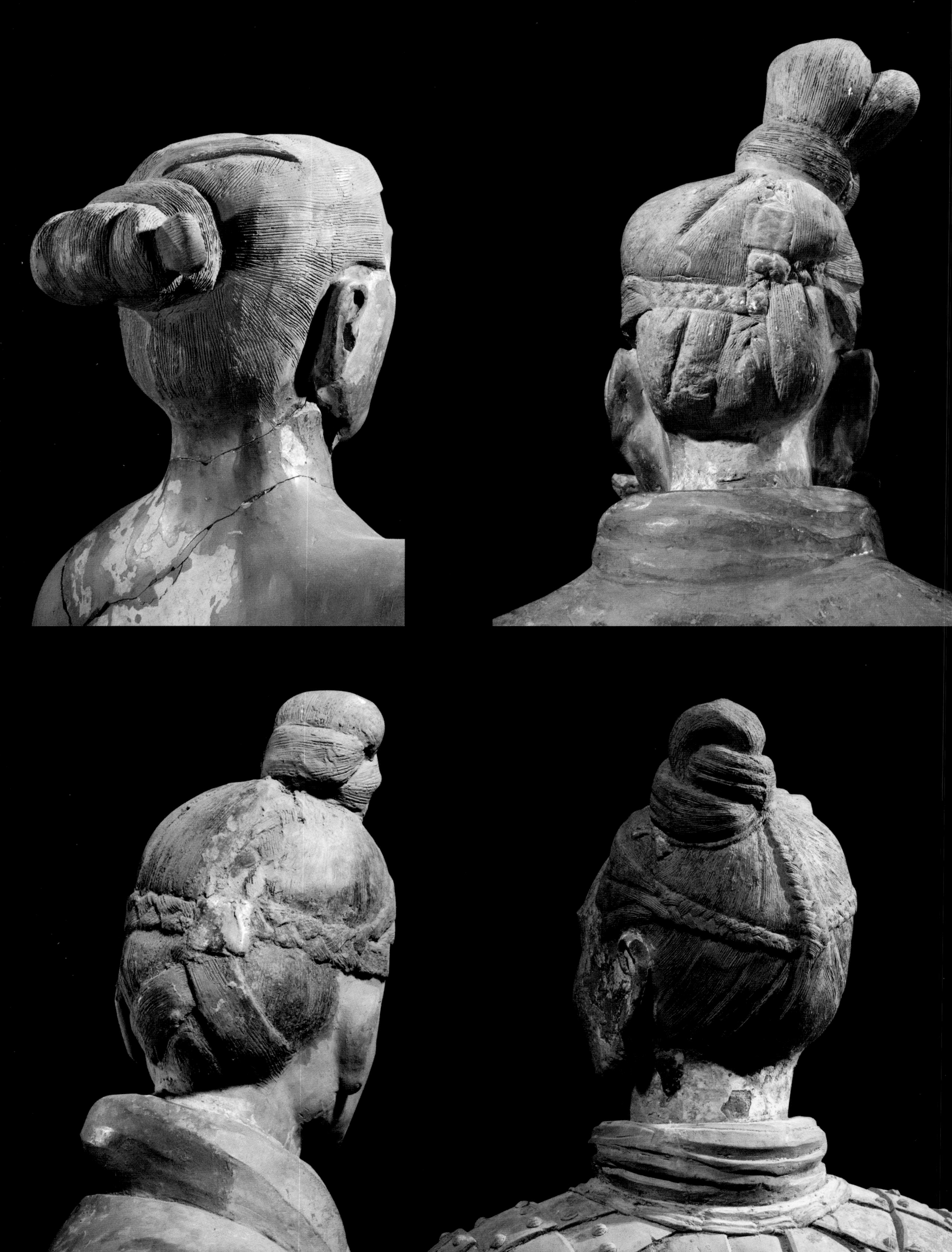

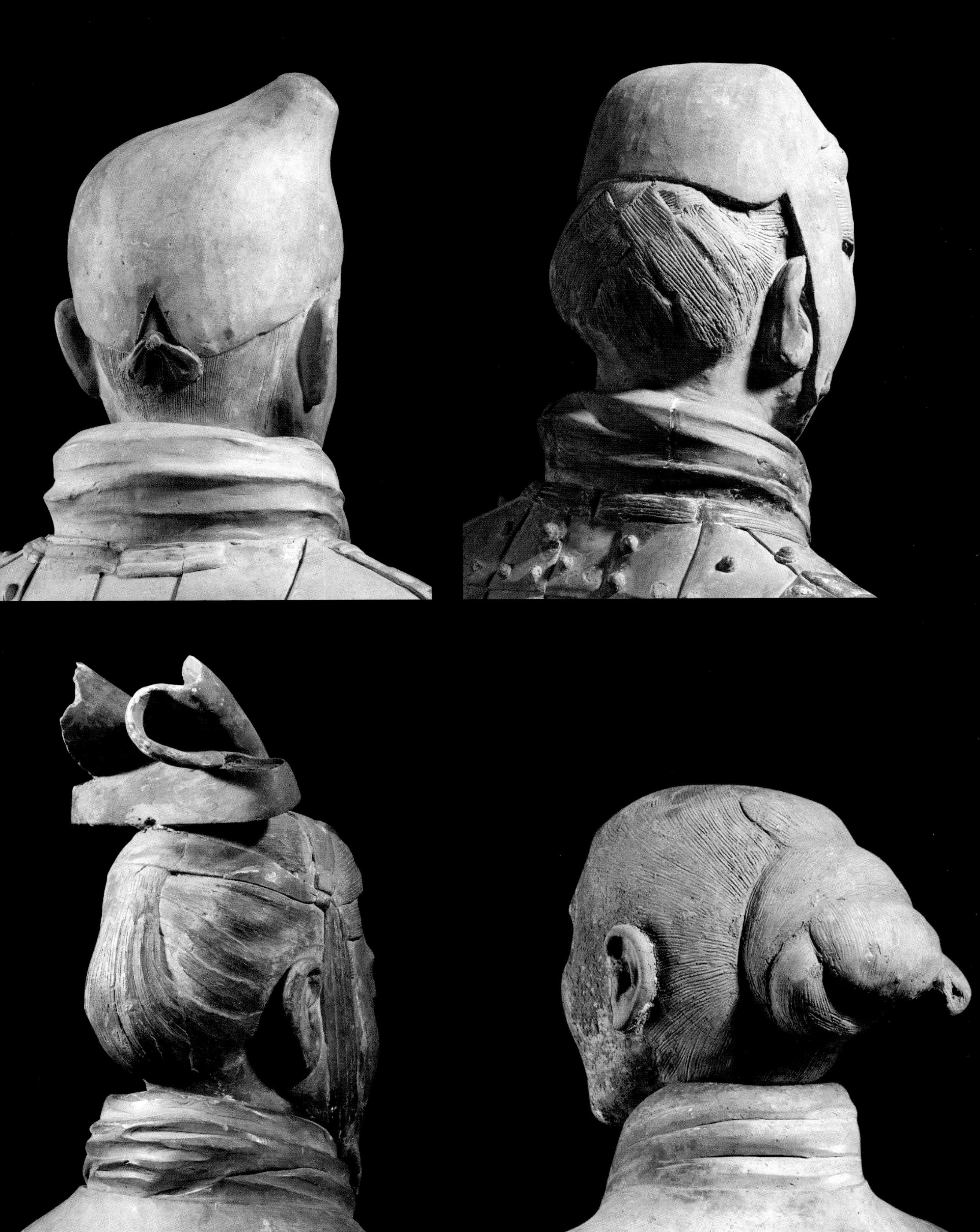

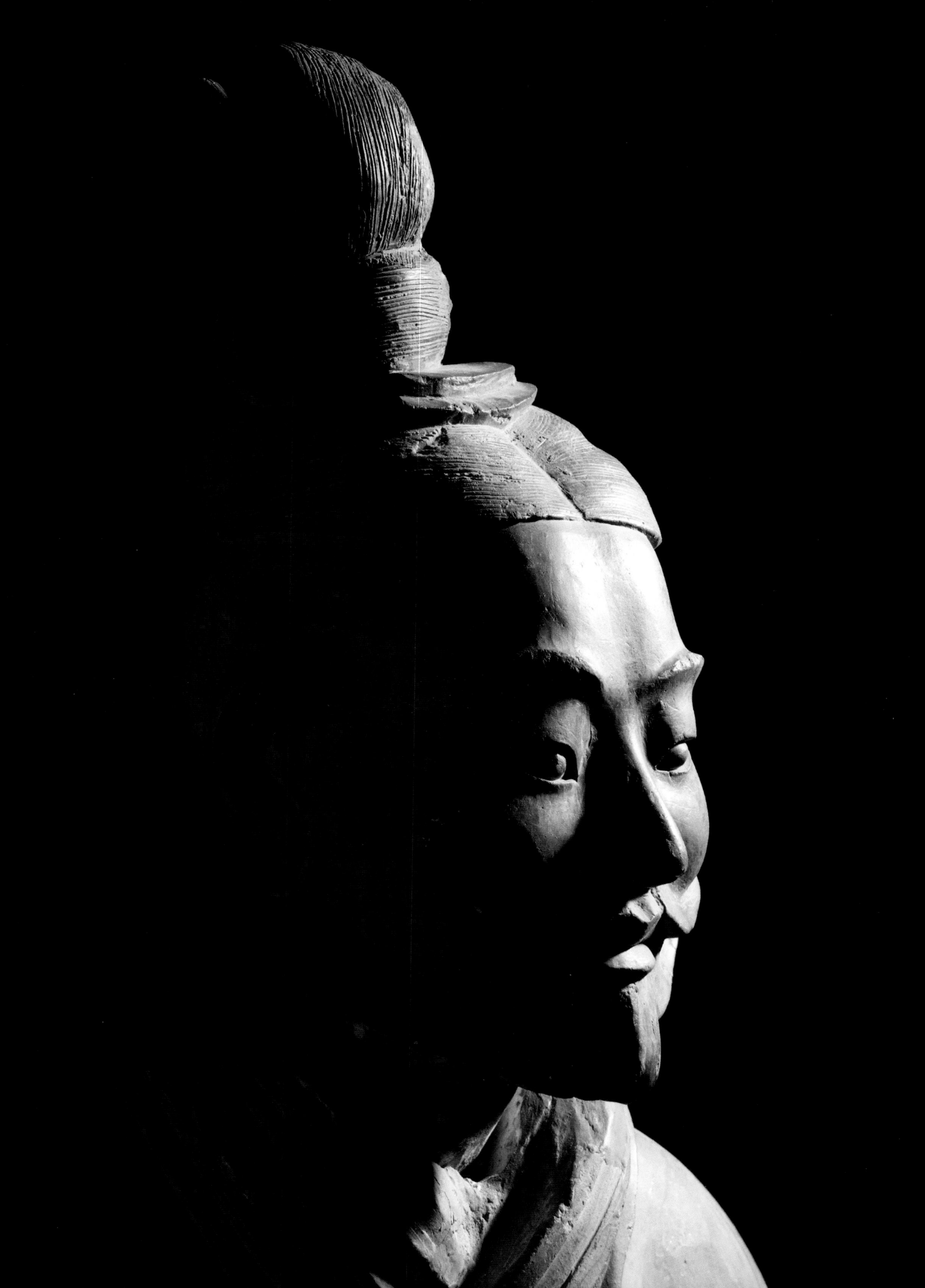

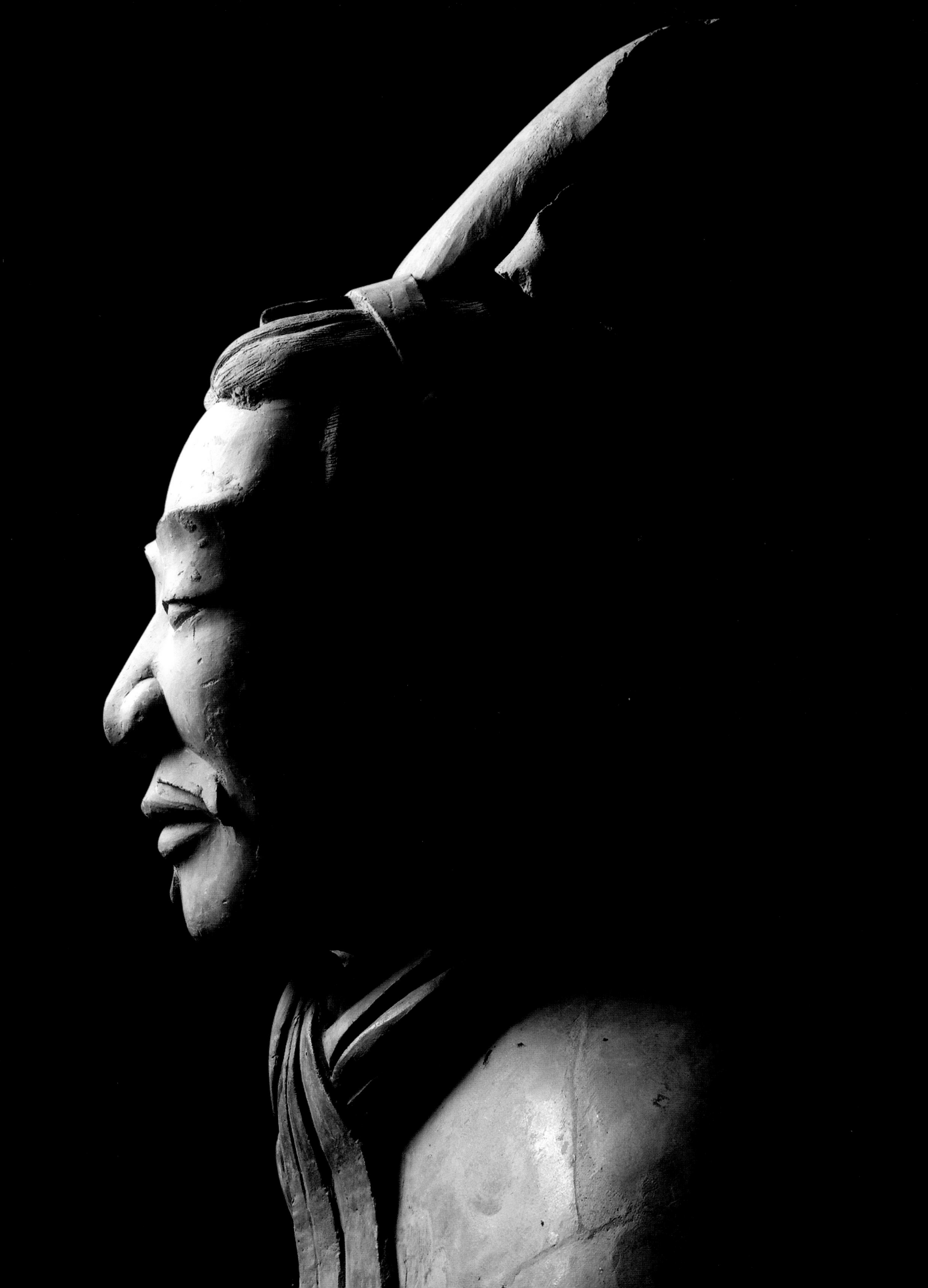

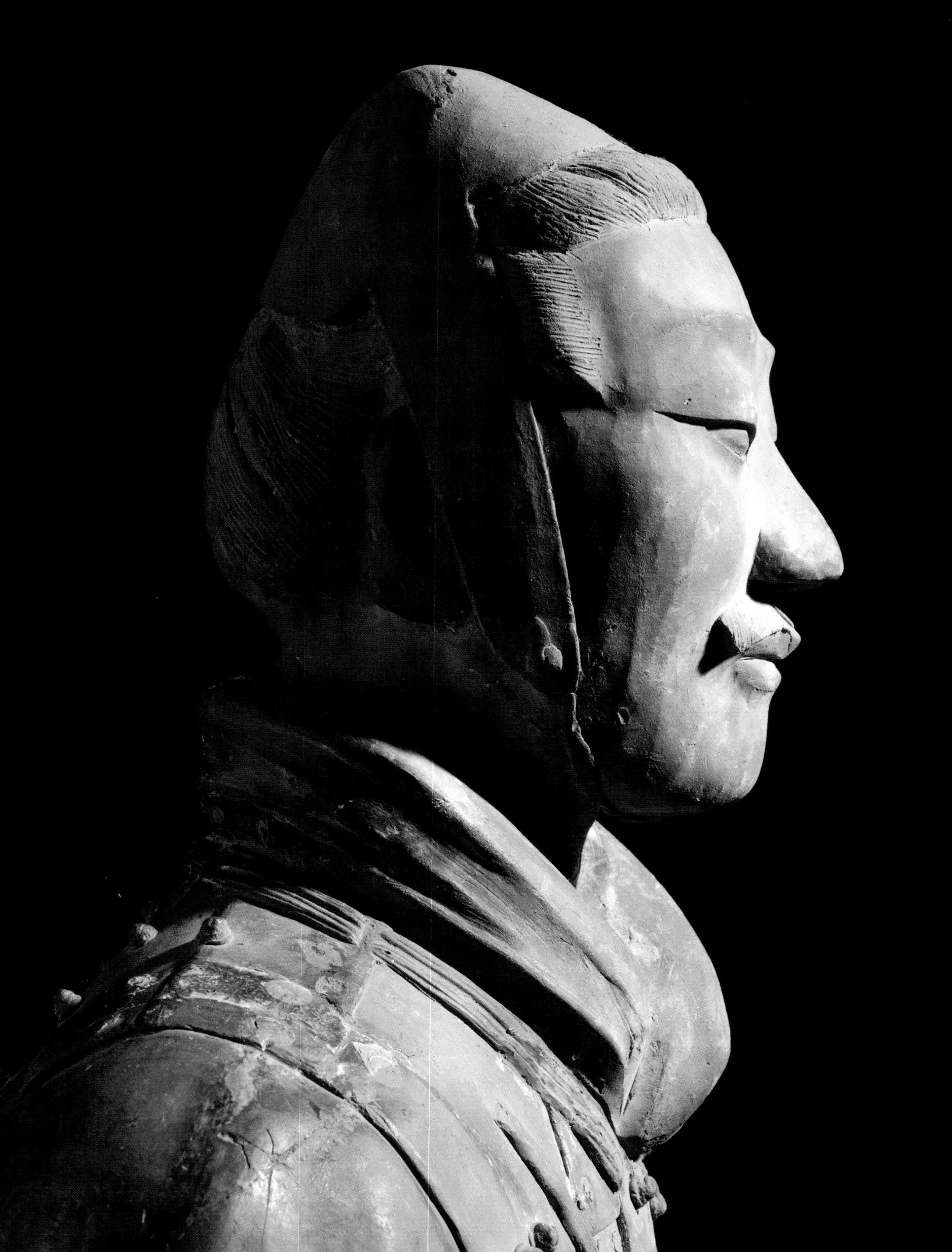

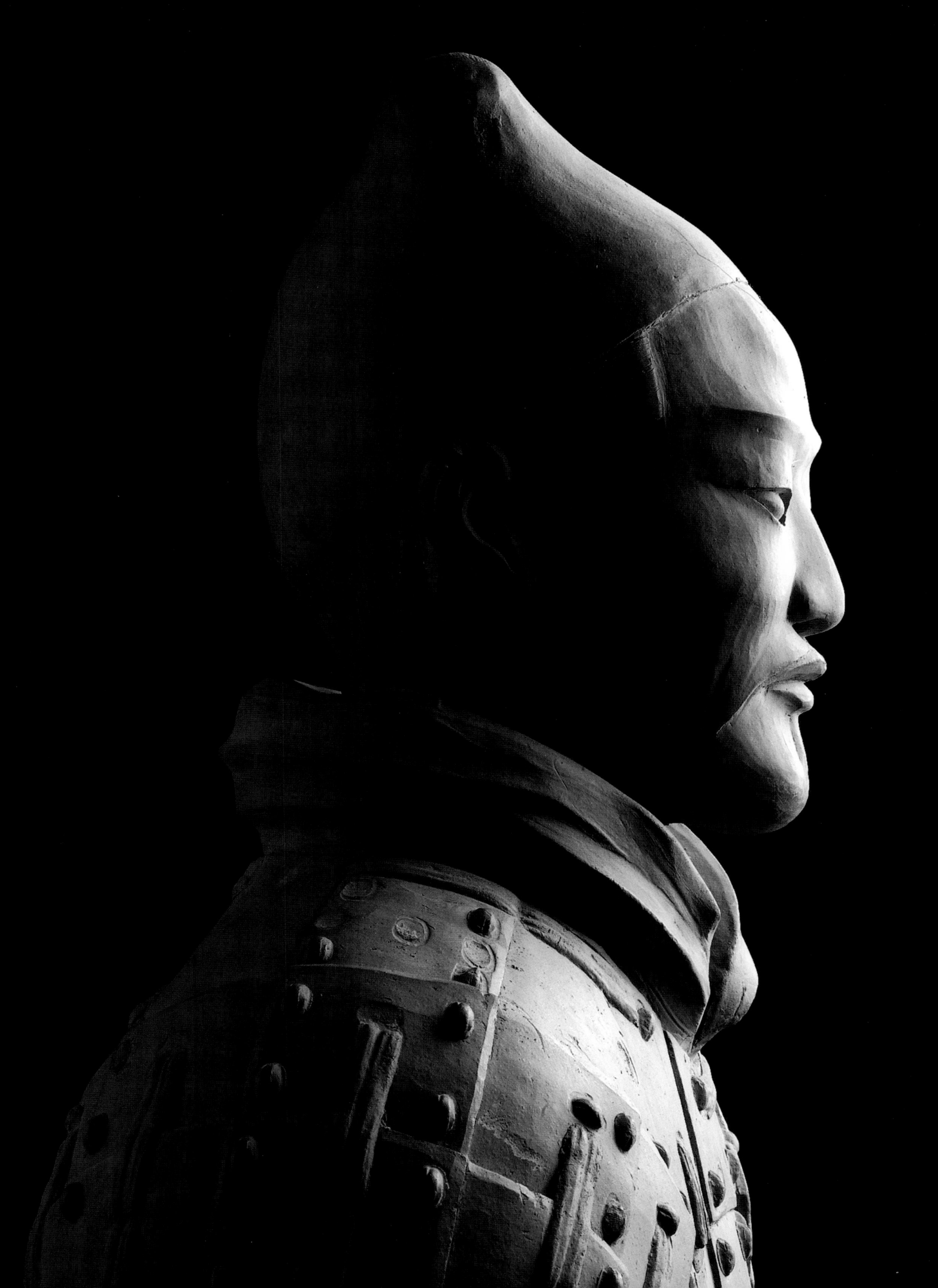

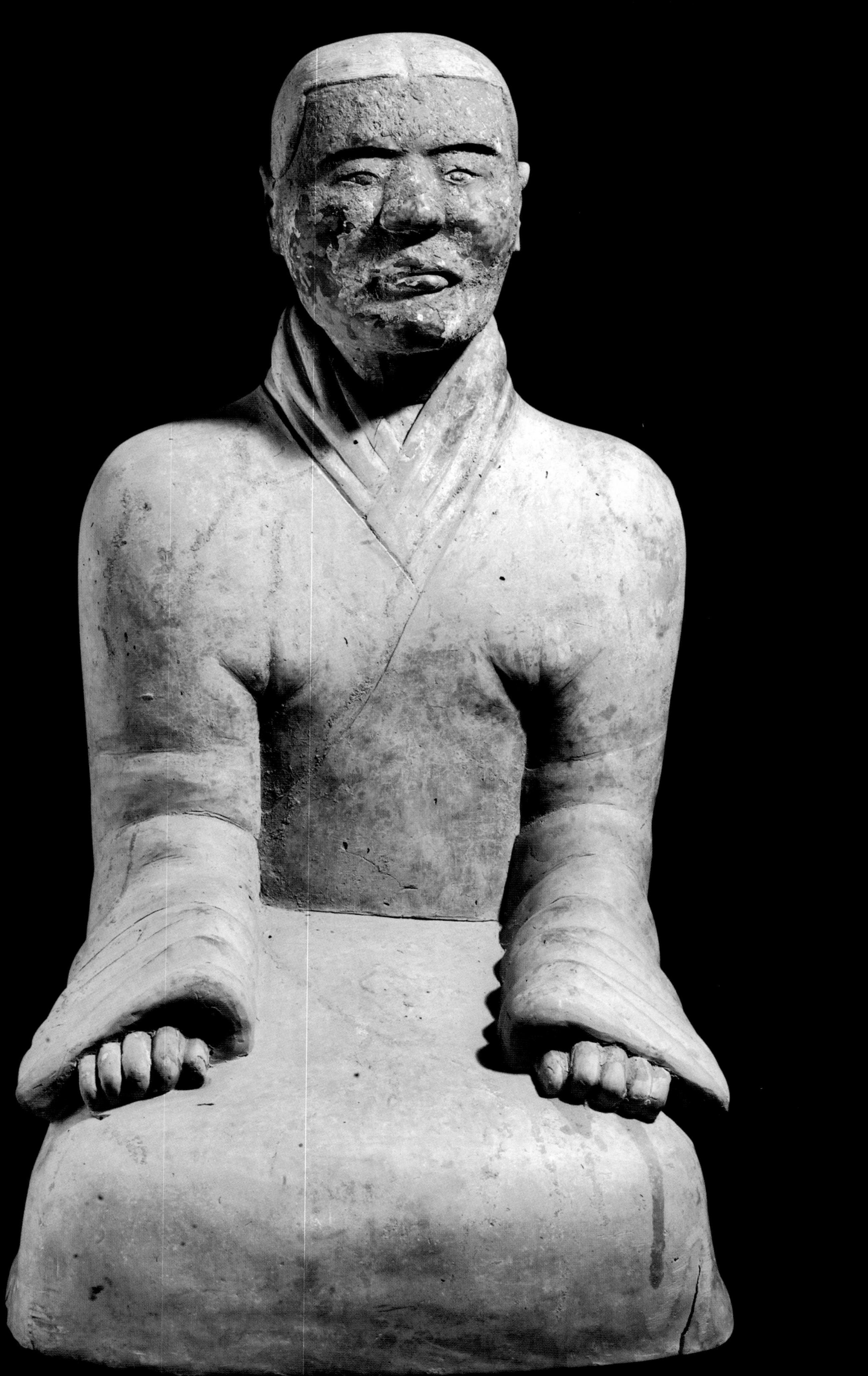

CHAPTER 5

A TWO-THOUSAND-YEAR-OLD UNDERGROUND EMPIRE

WU YONGQI

Construction of the grand imperial mausoleum near Lintong, Shaanxi province, the final resting place of the great First Emperor or Qin Shihuangdi, began in 246 BC and was unfinished when he died in 210 BC. The emperor, whose name was Ying Zheng, lived for only fifty years, but this splendid subterranean empire has existed for over two millennia.

It is said that Qin-dynasty bronze and pottery objects were frequently discovered in the vicinity of the Qin mausoleum from the 1930s onwards. Because the local villagers often made mistakes in recognizing valuable cultural relics around the mausoleum area, a phrase, 'mistaking a golden bell for a copper bell' (*cuo ba jinzhong dang tongling*), was coined to mock people's stupidity. Over the past fifty years archaeological investigations have gradually uncovered more relics and sites that are related to the Qin mausoleum. Among those are some half life-size kneeling terracotta figurines that were originally identified as women of the Qin period (*fig.* 157). It is only during the last twenty years, while restoration and conservation work was being carried out, that delicately carved beards were discovered on the faces of the pottery figures behind the colour painting and flakes of clay. Accompanying burial items, such as pottery lamps, basins, horse bones and other animal skeletons, have further confirmed that these kneeling pottery figurines are officials who reared horses and pets for the First Emperor (see also, pp. 138–9). Archaeological surveys and excavations of the Qin mausoleum were increased after the discovery of the terracotta army in 1974, as a result of which more objects and pits have been unearthed.

FIG. 157
(left) Kneeling stable boy or groom, one of a group of such figures found together with horse skeletons in several hundred pits to the east of the outer wall of the tomb complex. It is thought that these pits represent the imperial stables. At only 68 cm in height, these figures are smaller than the fully grown warriors.
Cat. no. 108

FIG. 158
(opposite) **Terracotta armoured infantryman excavated from Pit 1. The warriors found in Pit 1 are predominantly armoured infantrymen, arranged in a battle formation of rows of four behind chariots and originally armed with crossbows, halberds or swords. This standing warrior is wearing puttees, short trousers and a long tunic under his armour. His hair is in a topknot to one side of his head but he wears no helmet. His right hand is half closed around a weapon (now lost), probably a crossbow.**
Cat. no. 113

Mausoleum layout and contents

To the east of the mausoleum are pits containing terracotta warriors and horses, tombs of sacrificed aristocrats and a number of stables. Pits with bronze horses and chariots, and others with rare birds and animals are located in the western region. To the north are small palaces and halls that are believed to be the buildings used for rituals and their administration. A series of interconnected underground drainage pipes, both inside and outside the halls, have also been found there, as well as pits for rare animals and bronze water birds. In the southern part of the mausoleum are the stone armour and helmet pit, the terracotta acrobats pit and the pottery civil officials pit, as well as the overground anti-flood dam and the underground devices built to prevent water from infiltrating the tomb. Inner and outer walls were found to surround the subterranean palace (*digong*) where the emperor was buried. The entire complex, covering an area of 2.13 sq. km within the outer wall, consists of a variety of palace halls, secondary burial tombs and sacrificial pits. In the surviving walls the remains of entrance gateways can be identified facing east, west and south. If a line is drawn connecting all 600 satellite pits and tombs unearthed to date, the area totals over 50 sq. km – truly a huge underground empire.

One of the most spectacular finds from the Qin mausoleum is the pit with bronze chariots and horses excavated in 1980. The objects are half life-size, and each is made of 2.2 tonnes of bronze (figs 23–4). The horses and chariots alone are decorated with 15 kg of gold and silver ornaments. The two carriages are painted, and the scheme includes giant floating cloud motifs and stylized dragons (*kuiwen*) on a white background. Each chariot, composed of hundreds of individual pieces, is drawn by four white horses and driven by one officer, the charioteer. The relationship between horses and chariots in terms of the driving and controlling mechanisms can be so clearly identified that a vehicle similar to that used by the rulers of the Qin period could easily be reproduced today.

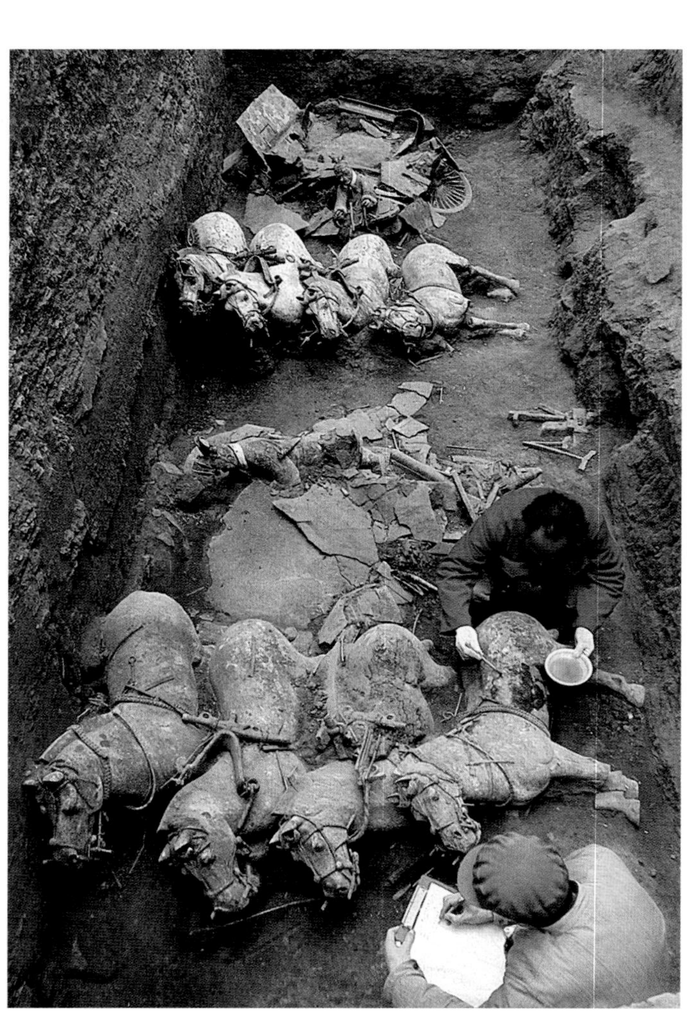

FIG. 159
(below) **View of the bronze chariots and horses pit situated due west of the tomb mound within the inner wall of the tomb complex. This pit, containing two half life-sized chariots each pulled by four horses, was excavated between 1980 and 1982.**

Among the largest funerary objects are the spectacular terracotta warriors and horses, discovered by local farmers drilling water wells (see pp. 158–79). The more archaeological research is done, the greater the admiration and awe this discovery inspires. The terracotta warriors and horses are an underground army guarding the deceased emperor. They are arranged in three separate pits containing officers, soldiers and horses. The army comprises infantry soldiers, charioteers and cavalry, as well as archers, spearmen and guards of honour. The clay soldiers and horses are richly decorated in colour. Each figure is armed with real bronze weapons and has unique facial features and body shape. They are a testimony to the immense commitment of the artisans who made the figures two thousand years ago. The three pits cover a total area of 19,000 sq. metres, and, based on

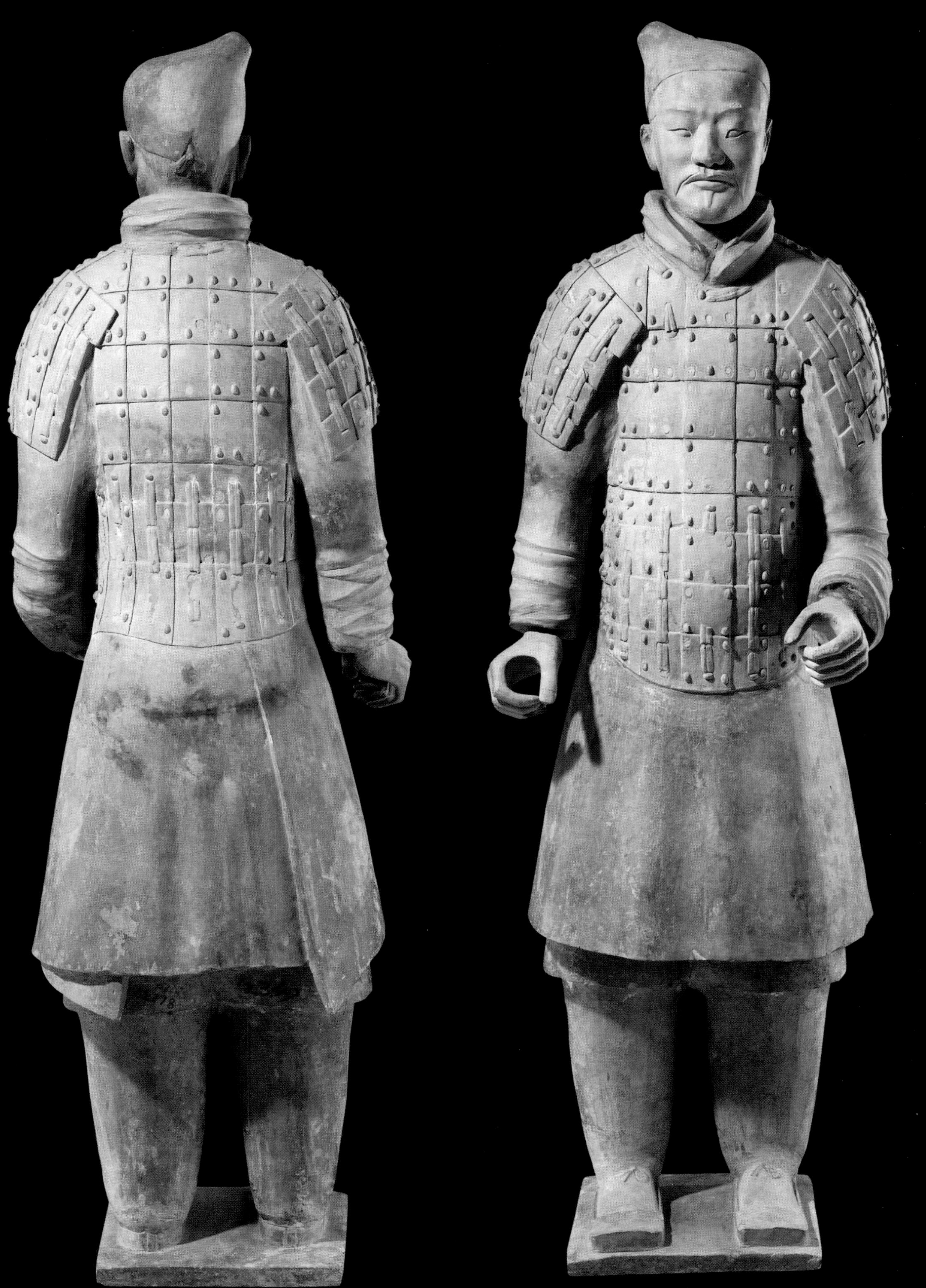

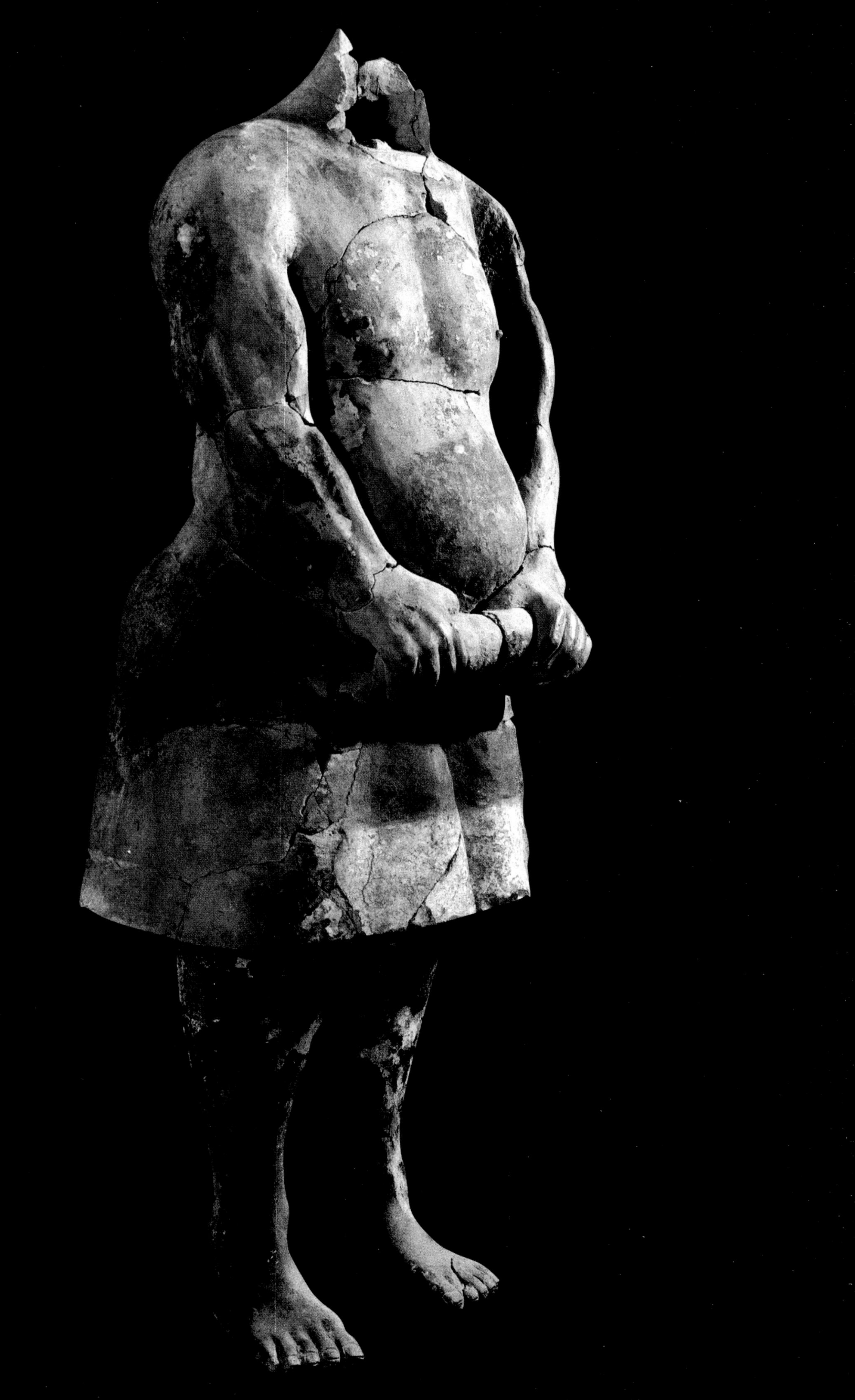

FIG. 160
(left) **Terracotta strongman, possibly a weightlifter, excavated in 1999 together with acrobats (*fig. 148*). Designed to entertain the First Emperor in the afterlife, this strongman's highly developed muscles can clearly be seen on his arms and shoulders, while his belt acts as a support for his large protruding stomach.**
Cat. no. 114

FIG. 161
(right) **View of pit containing eleven life-sized terracotta acrobats and strongmen, excavated in 1999 to the south-east of the tomb mound between the inner and outer walls of the tomb complex.**

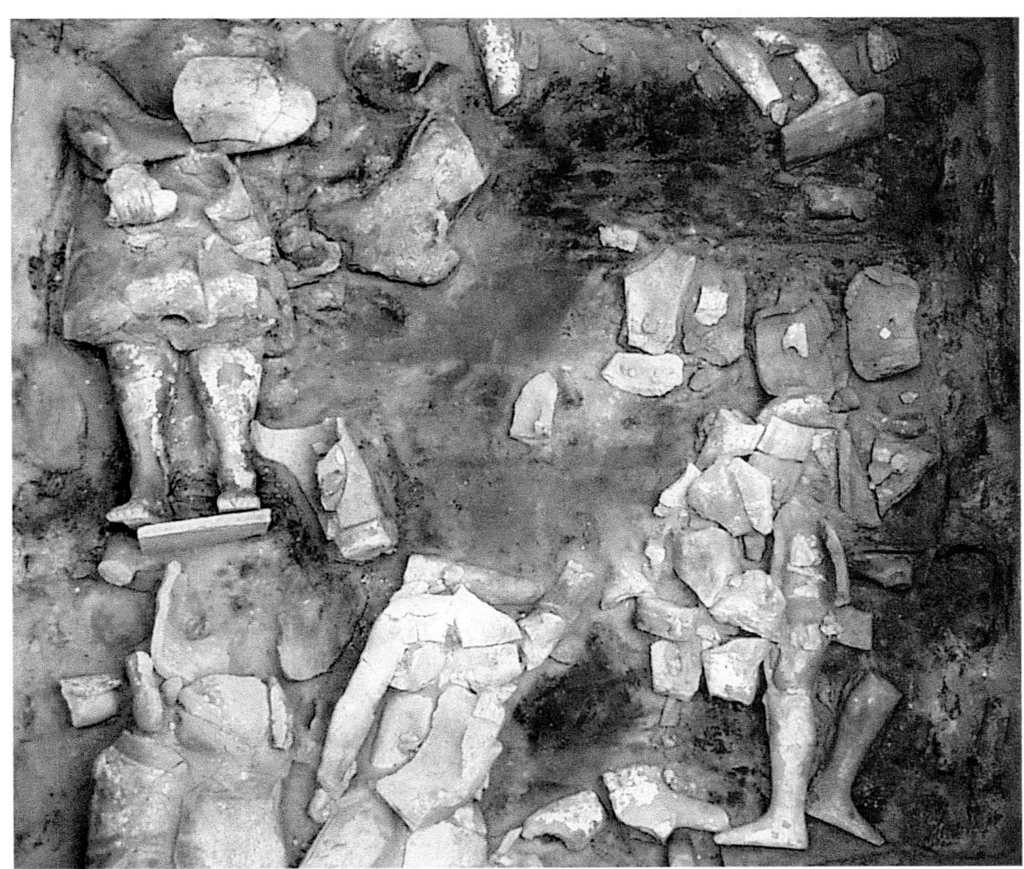

the density of the arrangement, it is estimated that they house some 7–8,000 life-size terracotta warriors and horses.

The ancient Chinese believed that the deceased would live in a different world, which has led to the idea of *shisi ru shishen*, 'the dead should be treated the same as the living'. This is referred to in the funerary rite with which the elderly and sage were interred. Showing the supreme power gained during his reign, Qin Shihuangdi constructed the massive imperial necropolis with its all-inclusive subterranean empire in order to continue his rule in the nether world. The construction lasted forty years, mobilizing state resources on a massive scale at that time. It is hard to imagine how spectacular it would have been in its entirety.

Although a growing number of mysteries of the Qin mausoleum have gradually been revealed after over half a century of archaeological investigations, our knowledge of it still remains superficial. We should not, however, excavate the mausoleum indiscriminately, especially the emperor's tomb. We should respect our ancestors and our cultural heritage, and any measures we take should not damage the physical remains of either relics or sites. We should aim to compile the historical facts gradually. The responsibility of Chinese archaeologists is to conduct research and analysis based on these criteria in order to preserve the entire subterranean city. I dream of a day when technology will shed light on all that is buried there and we will be able to unravel all the mysteries surrounding the Qin Shihuangdi mausoleum through processes of scientific conservation, without disturbing the sleeping emperor and his two-thousand-year-old underground empire.

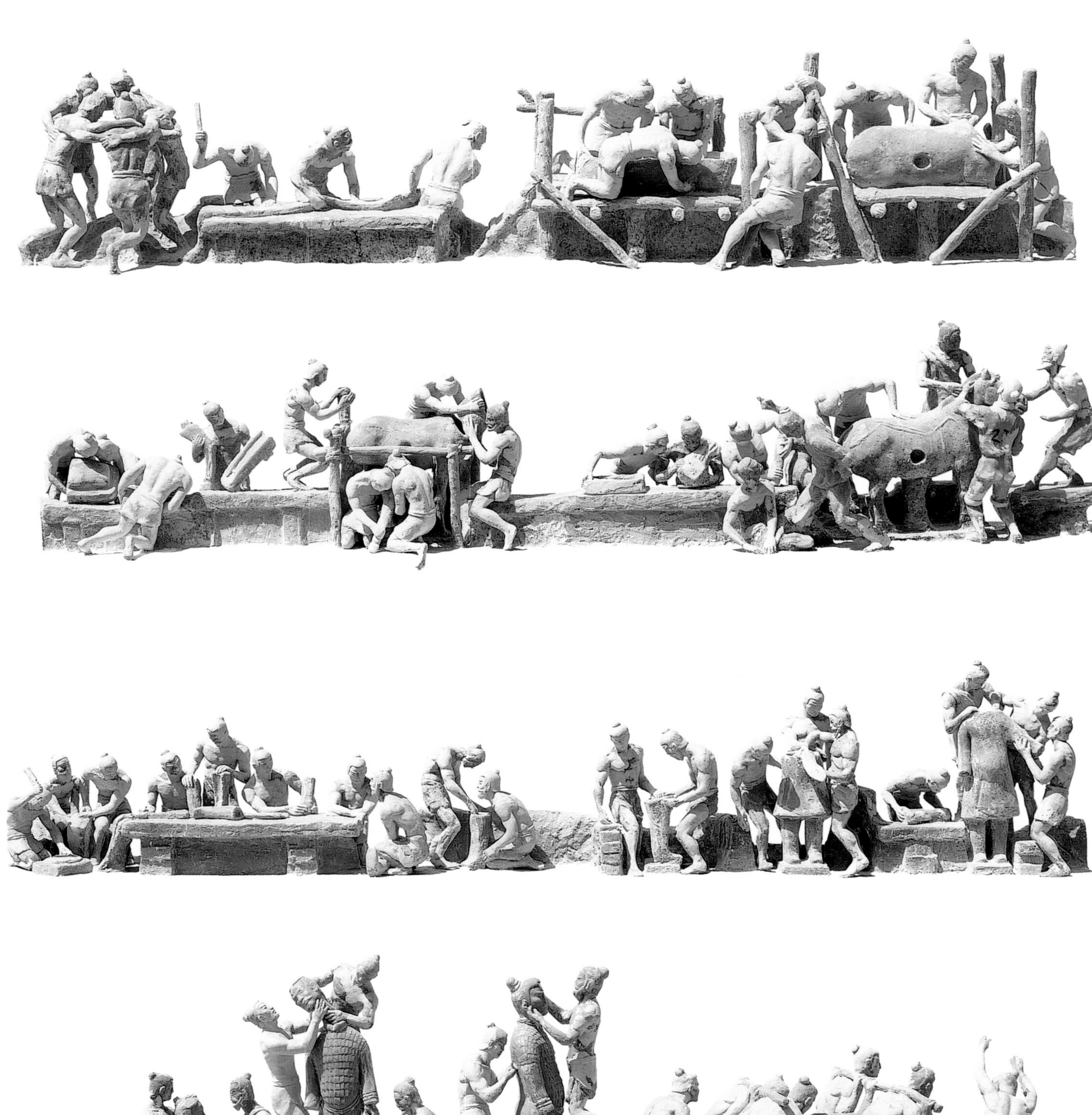

THE TERRACOTTA ARMY

LUKAS NICKEL

FIG. 162
(left) Contemporary model showing the production process of the c.7,000 figures comprising the terracotta army. Techniques included coiling, rolling, slab building and the use of moulds. Details were applied by hand and the figures were fired and then painted. There was division of labour, and groups of workers were supervised by foremen who signed or stamped their names on some of the figures to ensure quality control. The terracotta army is an impressive example of early mass production, involving over 1,000 men, many of whom were buried in mass graves to the west of the tomb mound.
Cat. no. 115

FIG. 163
(below) Qin-dynasty terracotta tubular drainpipe excavated from the First Emperor's tomb site, showing the same technique of manufacture as the legs of some of the terracotta army.
Cat. no. 116

The imperial ministers who received the command to install a complete, life-size army of terracotta sculptures in the tomb complex of their ruler Qin Shihuangdi, the First Emperor of China, faced an unprecedented challenge. No ruler on the Asian continent had ever demanded such an ostentatious display of funereal megalomania. Officials would have had records of burial pits next to princely tombs interred with corpses of horses and wooden carriages, but none of these burial sites had ever been constructed on a scale that could hold clay replicas of thousands of soldiers, much less a burial complex extending to the 26,000 sq. metres required to accommodate the imperial mandate. Even if they had opportunities to learn of clay sculptures depicting human figures, these would have been of a simpler and smaller scale. None of the wood or clay sculptures that had occasionally been buried in tombs of the nobility was life-size, and none had been designed to resemble actual persons with any degree of verisimilitude.[1] In any case surviving evidence suggests that they would have been extremely scarce.[2] By the time that work on the terracotta army of the First Emperor began, the art of figural sculpture in China was still at a nascent stage.

To carry out this extraordinary task, the officials in charge turned to well-established procedures and traditional technology. Without experienced sculptors at their disposal, they commissioned workshops that normally produced ceramic building materials to construct the burial pits and sculptures. They established a hierarchy of masters and craftsmen and set out a division of labour. As the main building material for the architecture of the pits and their contents, they employed clay, a resource easily available in the vicinity of the site. Finally, they divided the work on the sculptures into separate steps, some of which could then be simplified by the use of moulds and prefabricated modules.[3]

Underground architecture

Planning began, we may assume, with a detailed outline, a chart that probably did not look much different from the modern top view reconstructions archaeologists draw to visualize the army layout (fig. 162). That plans existed we know from a find in another large-scale tomb structure of northern China built during the Warring States period. In the 1970s a huge bronze plate was recovered from a site that is believed to have been the tomb of King Cuo (r. c.327– c.313) of Zhongshan state. Engraved in the plate was a detailed blueprint of the tomb. It was a line drawing with the complete compound seen from above. Inscriptions made it clear that the drawing was produced in two copies, one for use at the construction site, the other being kept at the king's palace, to make sure that the builders did not alter any detail of the pre-defined

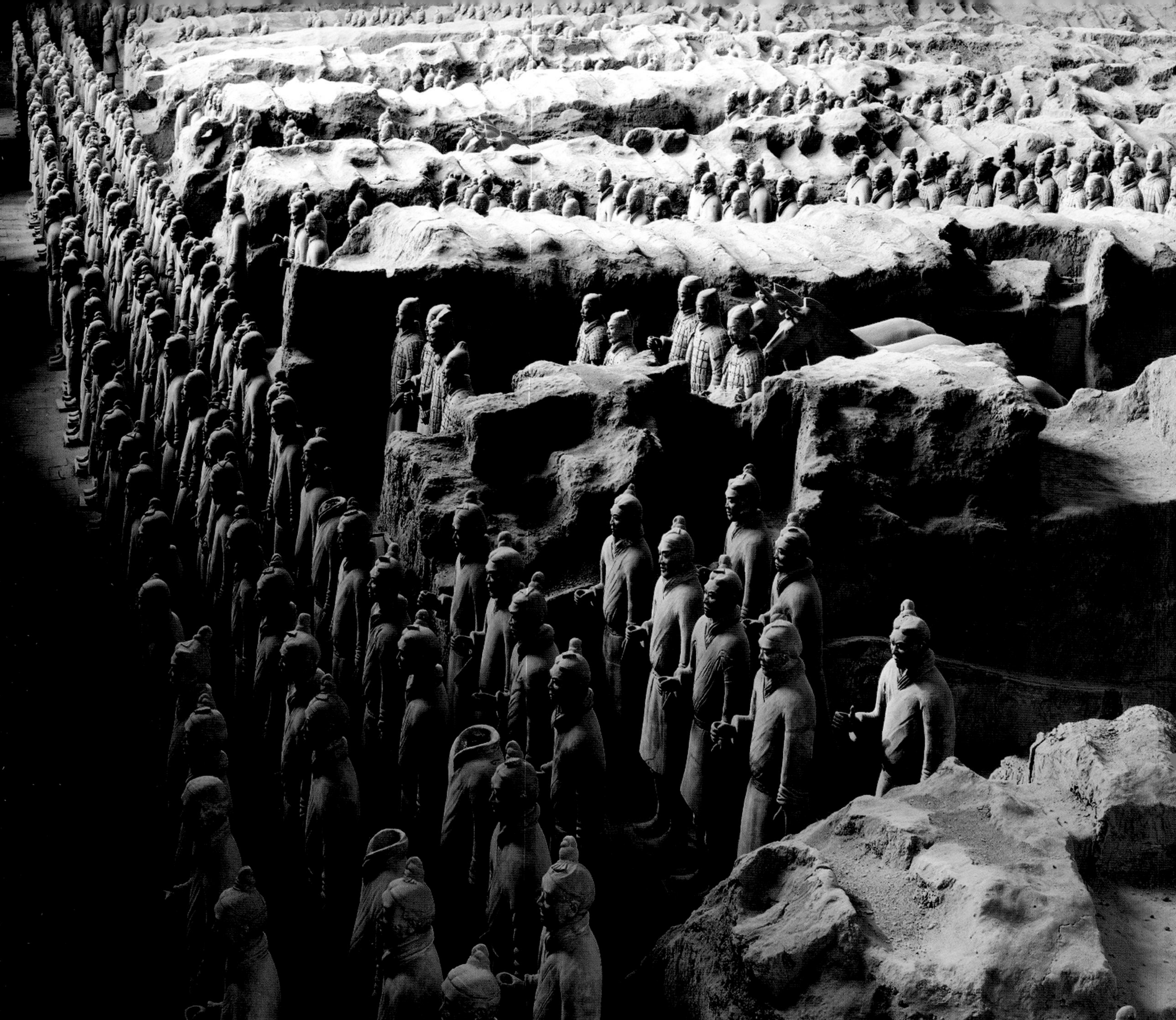

FIG. 164
View of Pit 1 showing the terracotta army lined up at attention facing east, with unarmoured infantry at the front and facing out to the sides.

design.[4] It was a master plan that the builder had to follow. Since the First Emperor's tomb, and especially the army pits, were more complex structures than the Zhongshan tombs, and since the construction was expected to go on for decades, we may be almost certain that such a blueprint existed.

Four large pits were designed to house the army of terracotta warriors. They were placed more than 1.5 km east of the burial mound (*fig.* 128). Pit 1, the largest of the compound, contained the main army, comprising foot soldiers, armoured officers and wooden carriages drawn by four horses each. All soldiers stood at attention facing eastwards, apart from the rows to the sides and the back of the army, which faced outwards, forming side and rear guards. Pit 2, 20 metres to the northeast of the main pit, housed the cavalry with armoured cavalrymen standing in front of their horses, war chariots drawn again by four horses each, and a group of archers

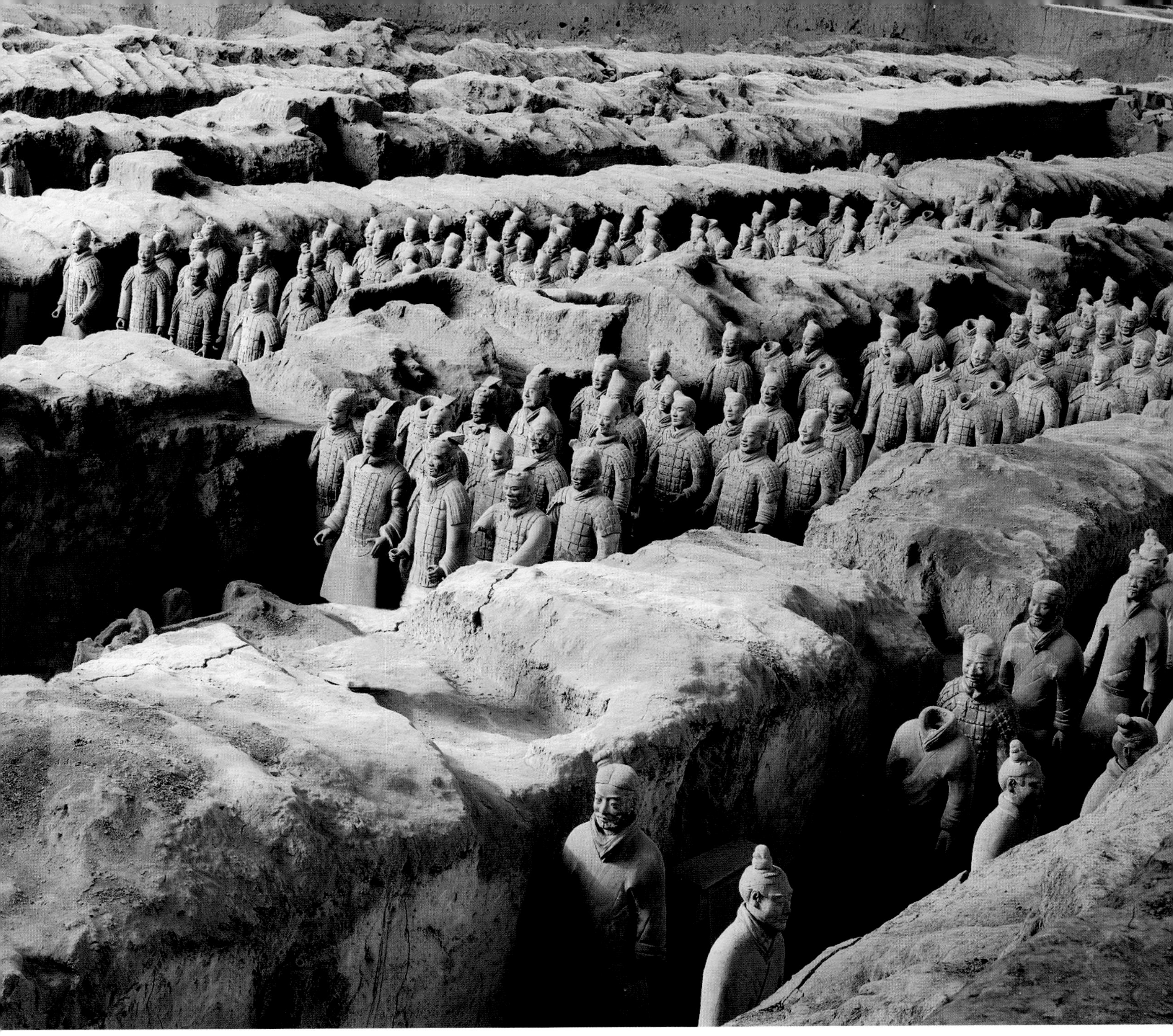

and foot soldiers. The much smaller Pit 3, positioned about 30 metres to the north-west of Pit 1, remains so far the only pit that has been excavated in its entirety. It contained only one chariot at its centre, and sixty-eight high-ranking officers and foot soldiers. A horseshoe-shaped structure, Pit 3 may very well have been designed as the headquarters of the army. A large fourth pit, placed between Pits 2 and 3, was found empty by the excavators. It is believed that the pit was left unfinished when the works on the tomb came to a halt during the uprisings following the death of the emperor in 210 BC.

How were the pits constructed? The architecture of all four pits is basically similar. Pit 1 has been studied most thoroughly and may serve as an example for the others. Measuring 230 by 62 metres, it was dug nearly 5 metres deep into the ground. That means that more than 70,000 cu. metres of earth had to be moved, which

FIG. 165
Plan and cross-section of Pit 1 showing the main army.

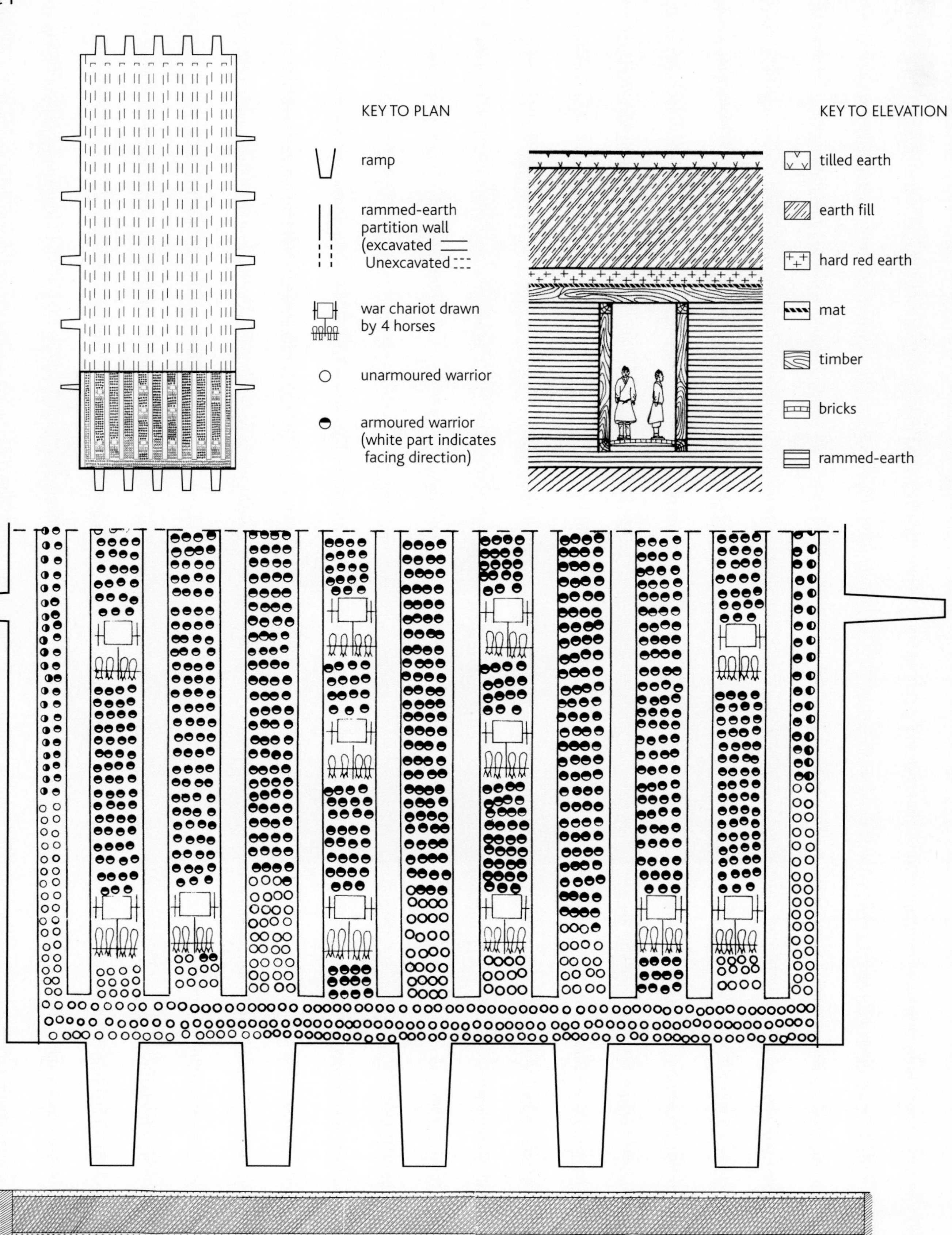

FIG. 166
Plan of Pit 2, including cavalry units, infantry units and war chariots.

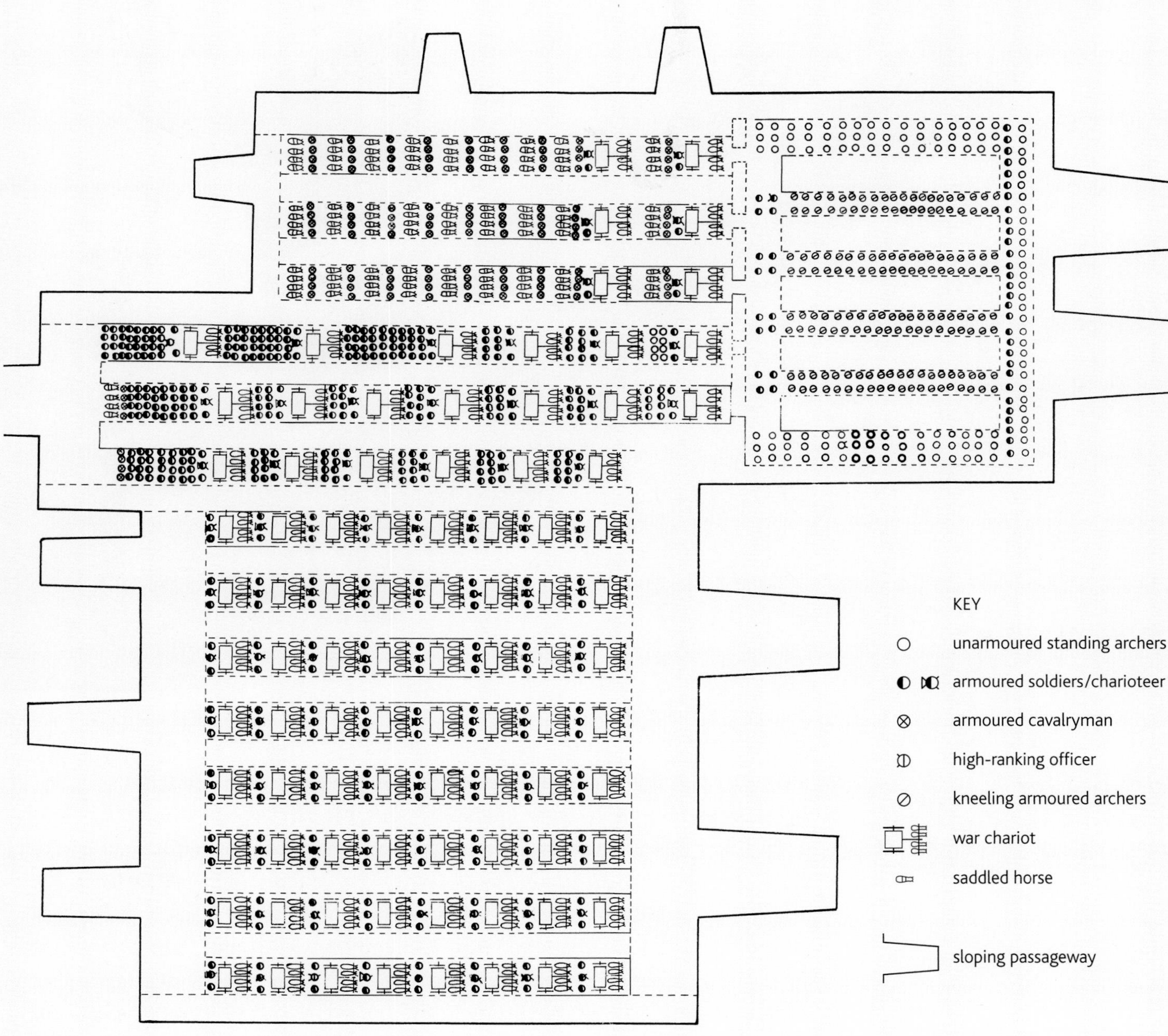

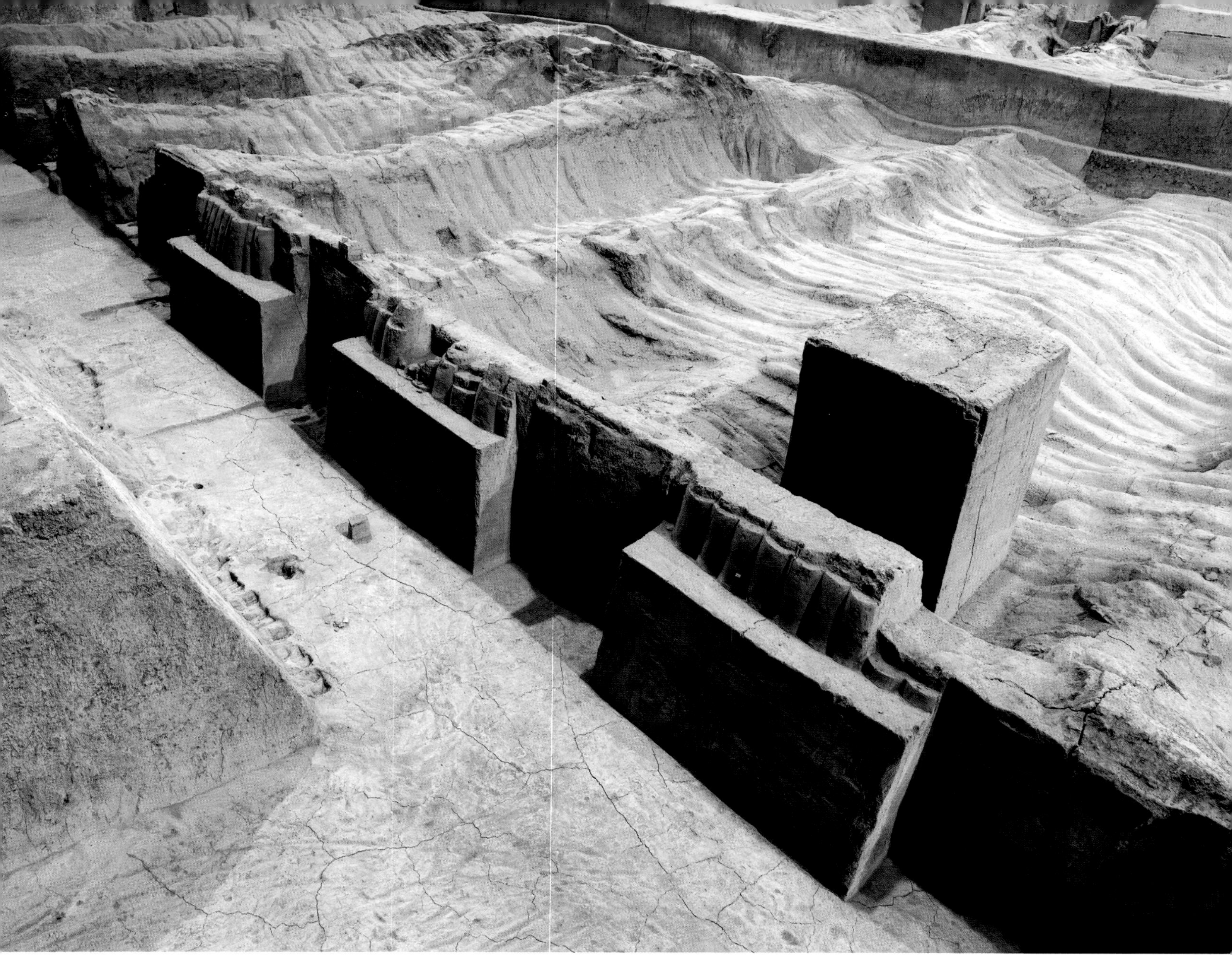

FIG. 167
(above) **View of Pit 2, which has been kept largely unexcavated to show the structure of the pit, with the remains of the roof planks still in place covering the army.**

would equal 5,500 loads of modern lorries. On each side of the rectangular pit five wide ramps were built, to let workers and transport carriages in and out.

But this was not simply an earth pit. Instead, enormous efforts were taken to make the structure as durable as possible. The ground and wall surfaces were reinforced with thick layers of rammed earth to make them as hard as concrete. Ten rammed-earth embankments, running lengthwise through the pit, converted the space into eleven corridors, nine of which were 3.2 metres wide. Narrow corridors on the long sides of the rectangle and transverse corridors on its small sides completed the structure. Originally, these hallways were more than 3 metres high (*fig.* 165).

The floors of the corridors were paved with small bricks. The walls were lined with wooden beams and posts. Embankments and posts held a massive wooden ceiling construction. On modern photographs of the excavation site, impressions of the huge, rounded beams can still be seen on top of the embankments (*fig.* 167). This combination of rammed earth and woodwork construction basically followed the architecture of noblemen's tombs and auxiliary pits of the time. The brick

FIG. 168
Plan and view of Pit 3, the command post, with high ranking officers and the command chariot drawn by four horses to the right.

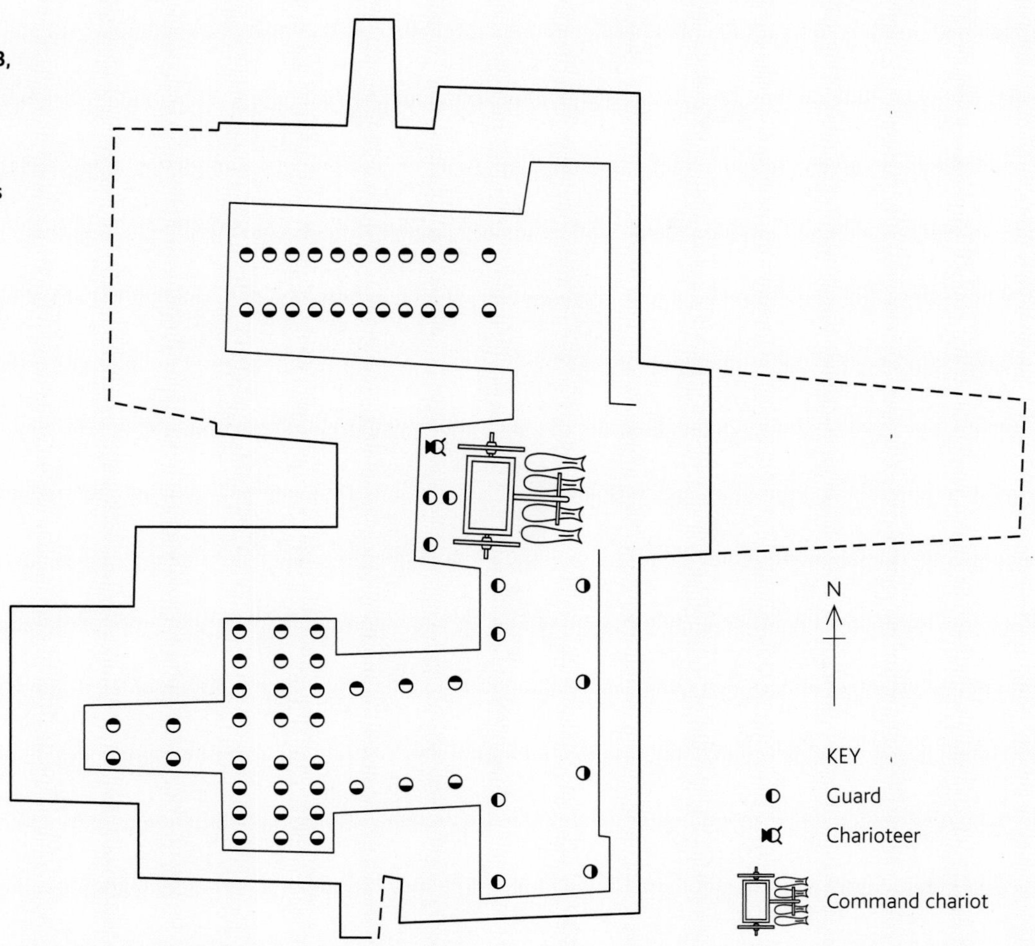

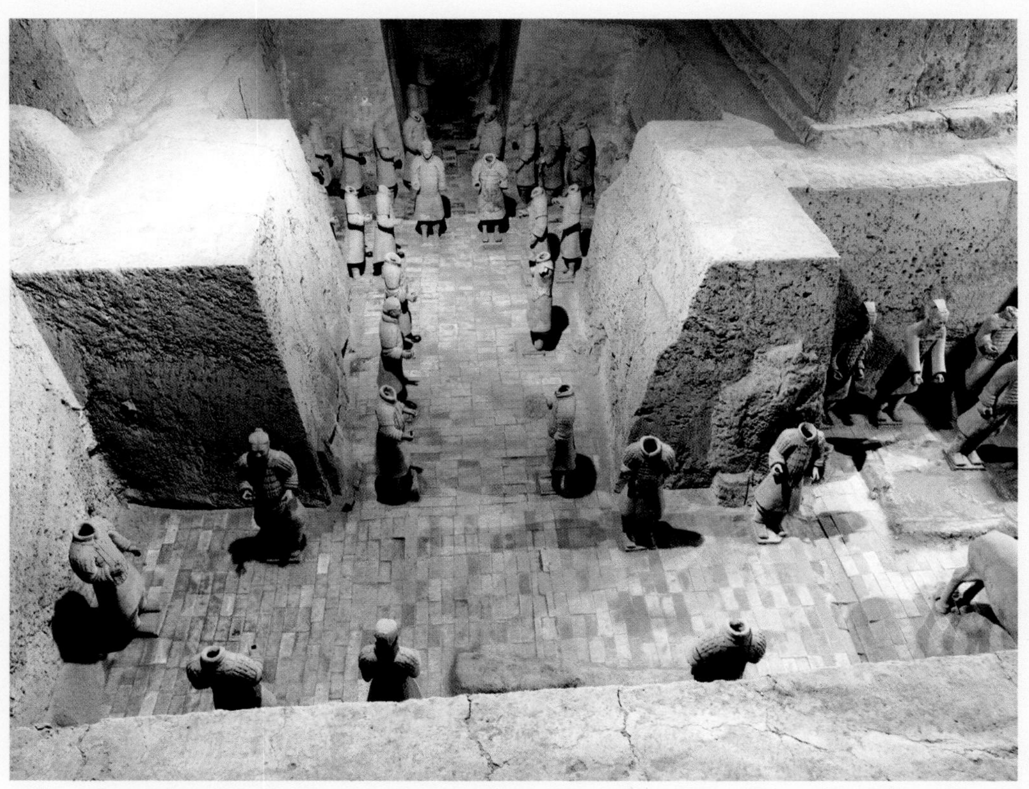

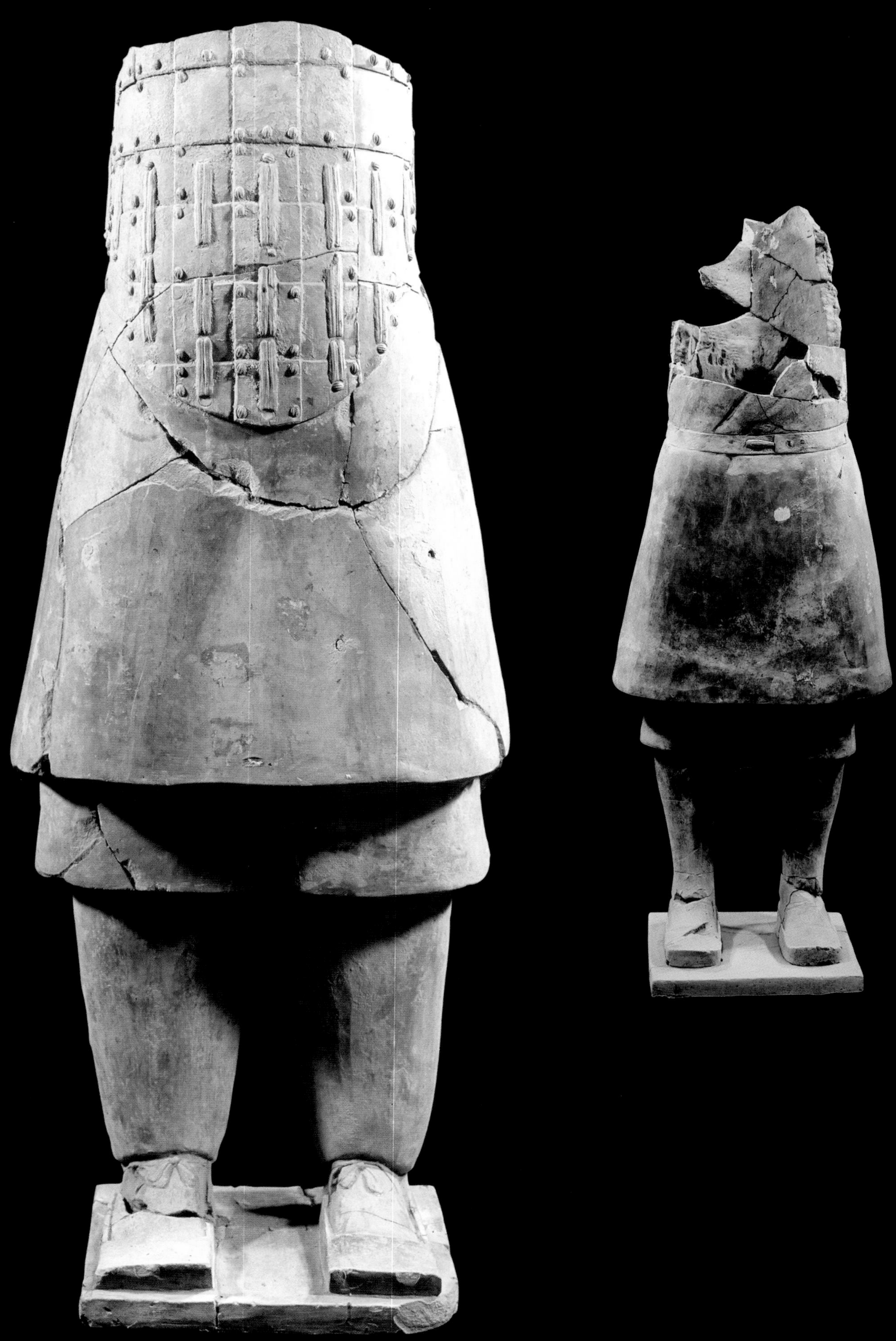

FIG. 169
(left) **Parts of standing warriors showing details of the belt and belt hook as well as the overlapping armour, based on real lacquered leather armour.**
Cat. no. 118

FIG. 170
(below) **Line drawing of a standing warrior showing the internal structure.**

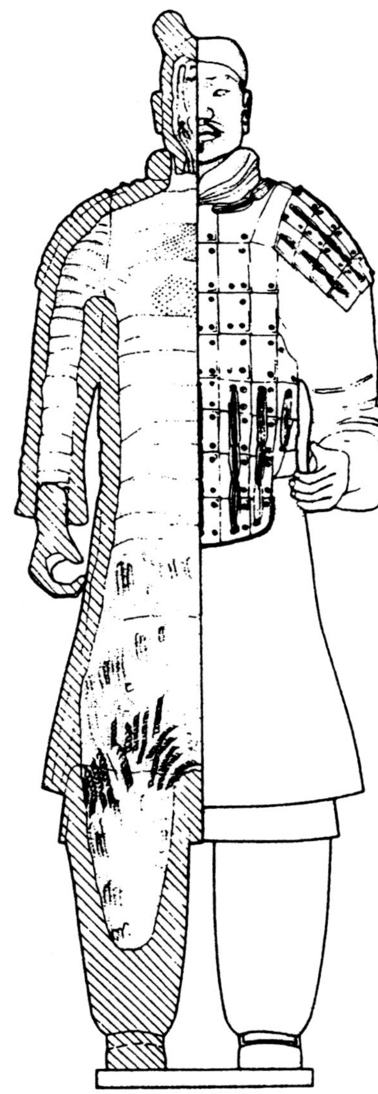

FIG. 171
(following pages) **View of Pit 2 showing warriors in disarray before excavation and parts of broken warriors (right). The warriors were looted of weapons and smashed and the pit was burned in the uprisings that followed the death of the First Emperor. The roof of the pit collapsed and the warriors fell down, losing their original formation.**
Cat. nos 119 & 120

pavement and the wood lining of the walls made the corridors resemble hallways of palaces.

On top of the ceiling beams, reed mats were spread out, followed by layers of clay, to prevent water penetration. Finally earth was filled in the remaining cavity in the ground and rammed, and further layers of soil were heaped over the structure. Two thousand years ago, the mounds or platforms on top of the pits were 2–3 metres higher than the surrounding ground and were widely visible. Since in the top layers no tiles have been found, one may assume that no buildings were erected above the pits.[5]

For the grey paving bricks craftsmen used the local clay, as is still done by hundreds of rural brick factories around modern Xi'an. The provenance of the woodwork is less clear. Beams and posts were of varied quality, wood types and sizes. In Pit 2 the ceiling beams were between 4 and 12 metres long and had varying diameters. Tests revealed that they were made using conifers like spruce and larch as well as members of the family of elm plants.[6] The wood may have come from a variety of places, especially if one takes into account that, at that time, forests were still abundant in the northern plains.

Figure construction

To date, more than 1,900 sculptures of foot soldiers have been unearthed from the pits. The majority of the figures are still underground and untouched. It is estimated that all three pits contain around 7,000 sculptures of soldiers, 130 chariots with 520 chariot horses, and 150 cavalry horses.[7]

The clay for the production of the terracotta warriors was taken from nearby Mt. Li. Tests on many figure fragments revealed a surprisingly consistent clay quality and structure. This indicates a high degree of organization. Clay may have been prepared centrally, before it was handed out to the workshops.[8] The sculptures known to date were produced following the same basic procedures. In some details like the fashioning of fingers and heads, each workshop seems to have had its own way to achieve the desired result. Some general features of the figure-making process will be described here.

The sculptures were mostly built up from foot to head (*fig. 170*). The base and feet were solidly constructed to provide the necessary strength to hold the body weight. The body was modelled over the lower legs or connected to them using a tenon and mortise system. The torso was then fashioned by coiling technique. Rolls of wet clay would be built up, shaping waist, breast and shoulders. Another method employed was slab building. For this, flat bands of leather-hard clay would be bent and joined to form arms and legs. Sometimes the torsos were made in one piece. In other cases bodies were made in two parts, which were then connected at the waist.

Arms, hands and heads were produced separately and later attached to the torso using clay slip. Hands and fingers were formed in bipartite moulds and then bent into the desired position. The heads were often pressed into two moulds, while sometimes only the face was made in a mould whereas the back of the head was done completely freehand. The use of moulds as a means to facilitate serial

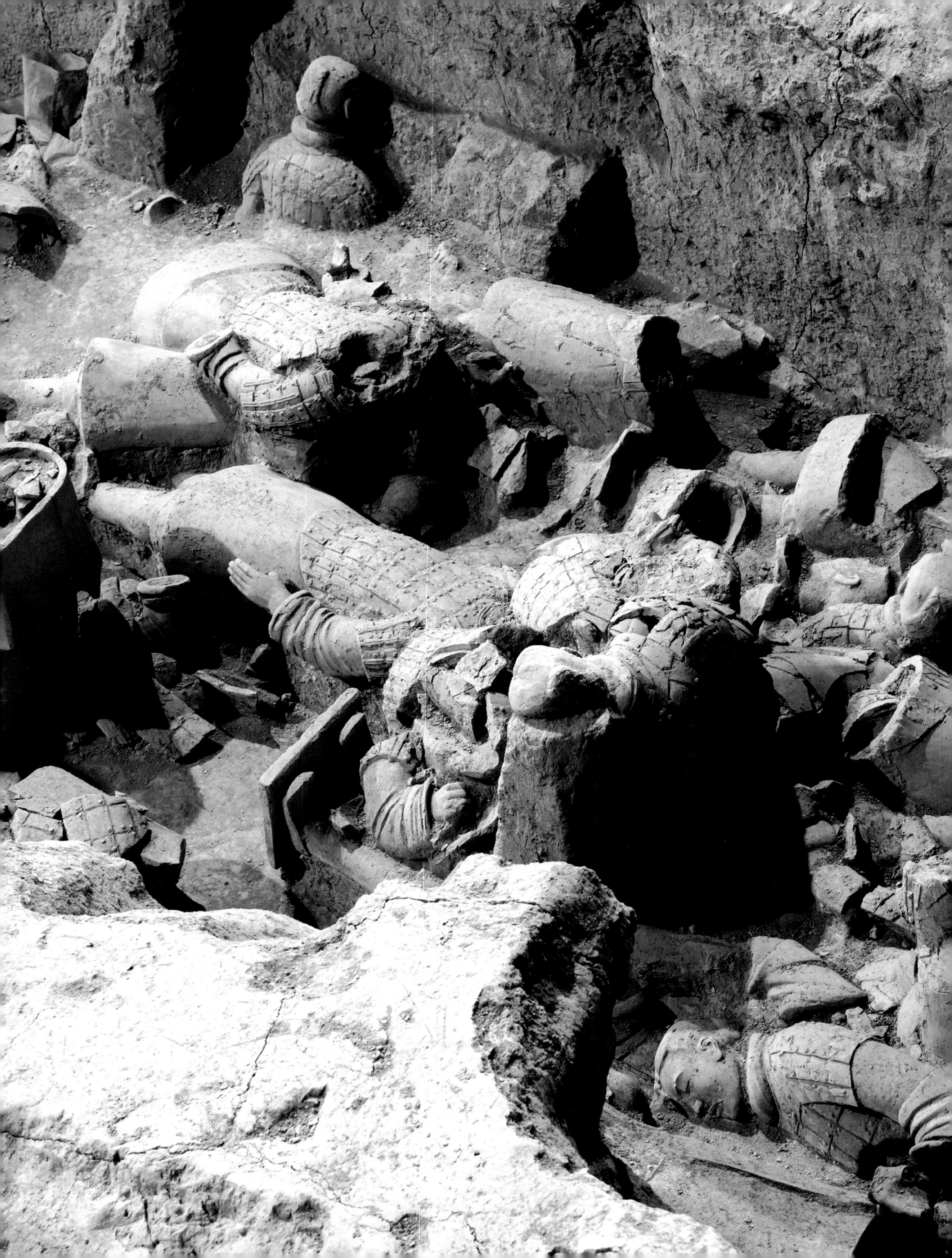

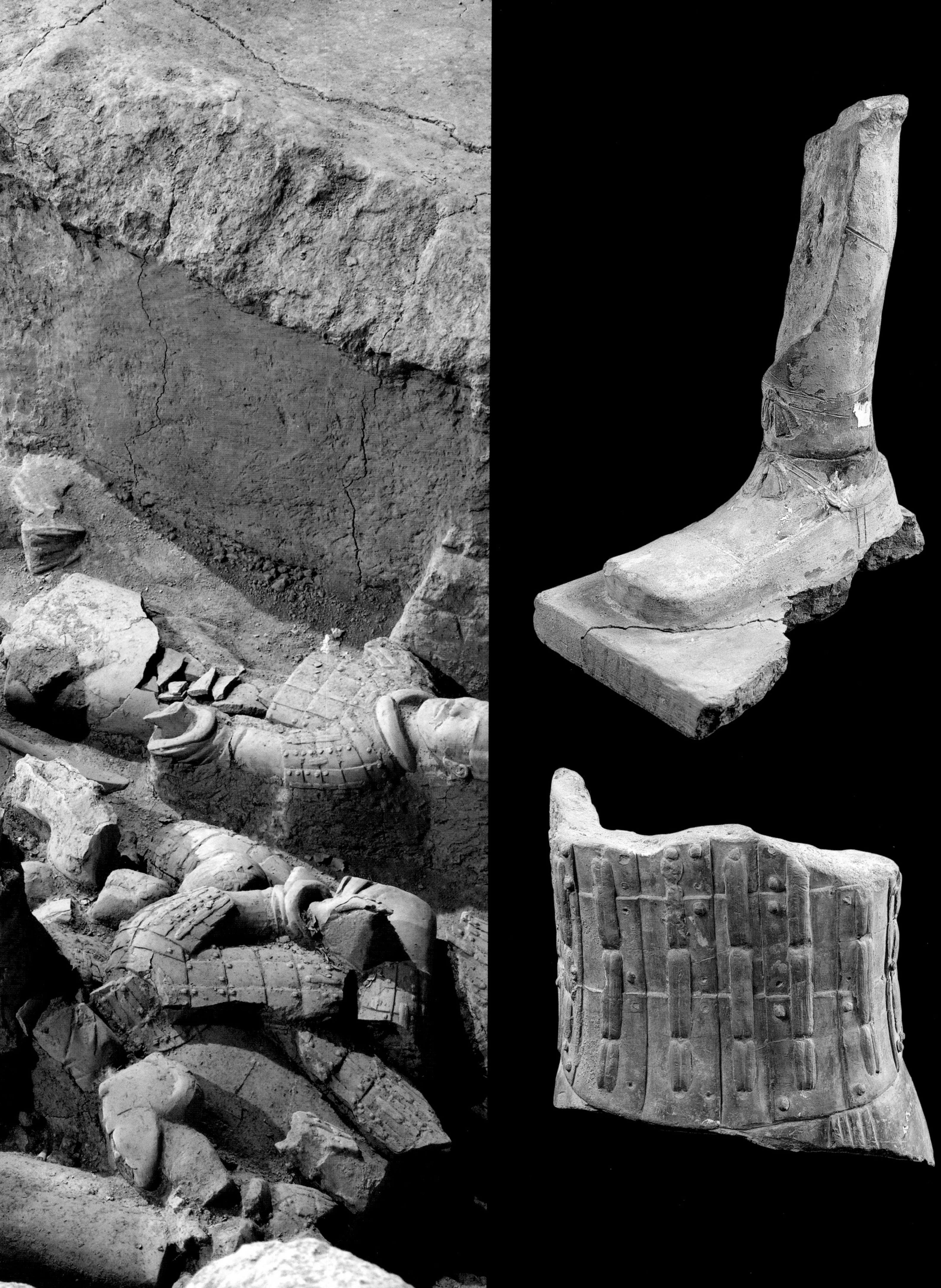

FIG. 172
(opposite) **These three figures show the differences in types of armour, which varied according to rank. The general (right) has longer beribboned armour with an extended flexible pointed flap at the front; the armed infantryman (centre) has armour covering his torso and shoulders; while the cavalryman (left) only has armour on the chest.**
Cat. nos 17, 113 & 112

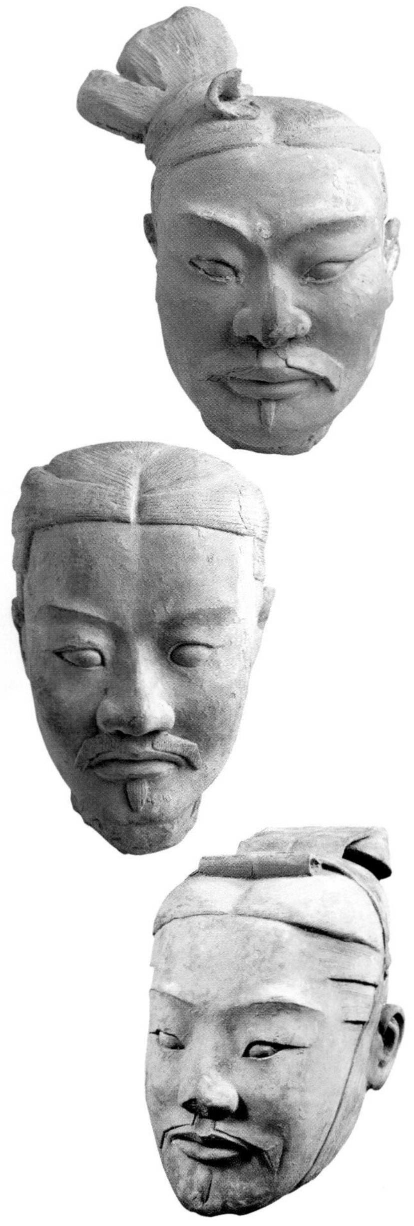

FIG. 173
(above) **Heads of three warriors showing the variety of facial types and hairstyles. Some had high cheekbones and others had thinner noses. The heads were formed in two-part moulds with the join down the sides behind the ears. Moustaches and beards as well as fine details of the hair were added by hand.**
Cat. nos 121–3

production was certainly familiar to the craftsmen. By the time the tomb of the First Emperor was built, moulds had been employed by Chinese artisans for more than a millennium.[9]

Scholars have differentiated eight basic face shapes, which would suggest that at least eight face moulds were being used.[10] When looking at the sculptures in the pits, however, the modern viewer perceives individual rather than mass-produced faces. This is because the Qin artisans tried to conceal the evidence of serial production. Layers of clay slip were added to the surface, and beards, eyebrows, hair and other individual facial features were modelled from them. Hair knots and caps were often prefabricated and applied to the head. All other body parts and clothes were carefully reworked as well. Every precaution was taken to make each figure look different. The sculptures were made to appear as as diverse as soldiers of a real army would be.

Armour

Many of the terracotta warriors were equipped with body armour. The armour covered the torso, the waist and sometimes the shoulders and arms. Six groups of armour have been identified corresponding to rank and military division. High-ranking officers wore waist-long armour with a triangular extension covering the abdomen. The armour suits consisted of up to 250 scales, which were attached to one-another by coloured ribbons, straps and buttons. The plates showed finely ornamented borders. Middle-ranking officers were dressed in shorter armour either covering the torso and waist or shielding the breast only, again equipped with colourful ribbons and straps and showing borders decorated with geometric ornaments (fig. 172). Armour of low-ranking officers consisted of large plates that lacked the ornamental ribbons and borders of the higher ranks. Different types of armour were used for charioteers, infantrymen and cavalrymen. Charioteers wore longer armour to allow for maximum protection, while cavalrymen had shorter and lighter armour than foot soldiers, which provided the mobility necessary for riding and shooting arrows. Ordinary soldiers wore no armour at all. These unprotected men were mainly placed in the vanguard of the army.[11]

One surprising aspect of the armour of the terracotta warriors is the fact that no soldiers with helmets or shields have been found to date. From the excavation of the stone armour pit south-east of the main burial mound of the First Emperor as well as from literary sources we know that helmets were standard equipment of armies of the time (see pp. 180–91). Moreover, officers, charioteers and cavalrymen in the pits were fashioned with flat hair knots on the back of the head, as opposed to the high rounded hair knots on top of the heads of common soldiers. This indicates that the artisans were aware that higher-ranking soldiers would have needed a hairstyle that would allow them to wear helmets. It has been argued that the absence of helmets and shields would have symbolized the valour and fearlessness of the emperor's guards.[12] Another explanation might be that what was placed in the pits was an army at attention rather than in battle formation. An army standing at attention, awaiting orders to march, to stand by or to prepare for battle, would not necessarily wear all heavy equipment.

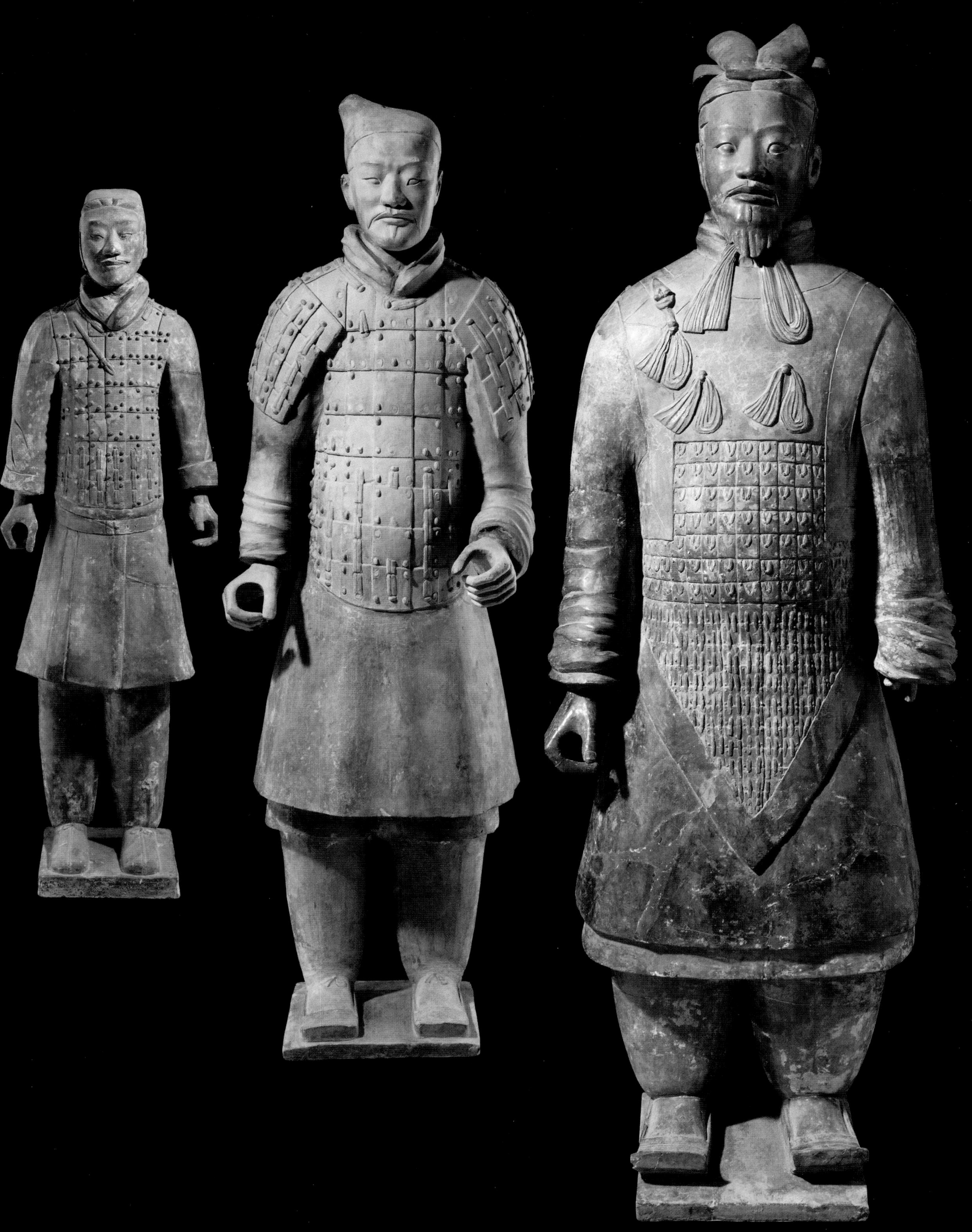

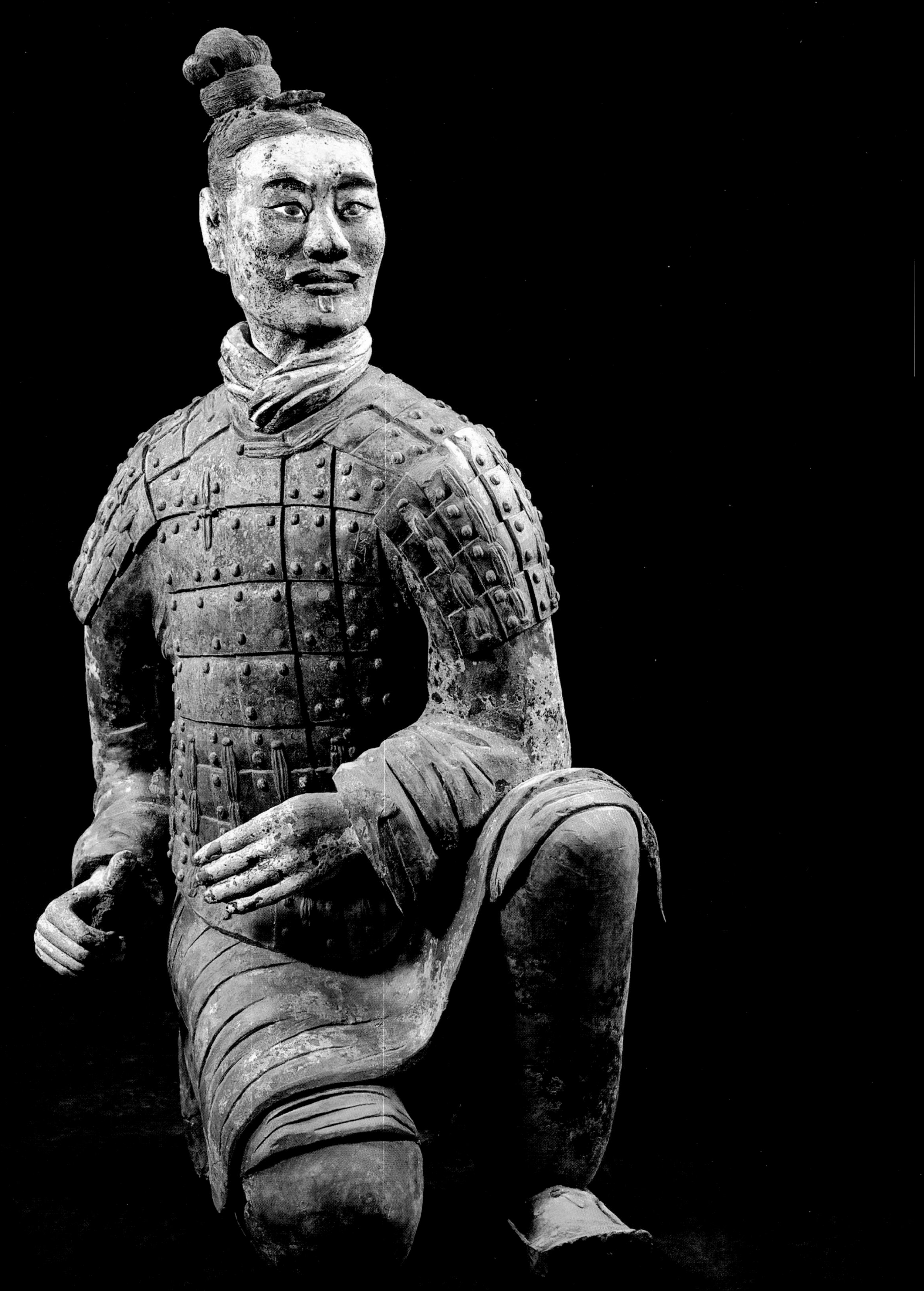

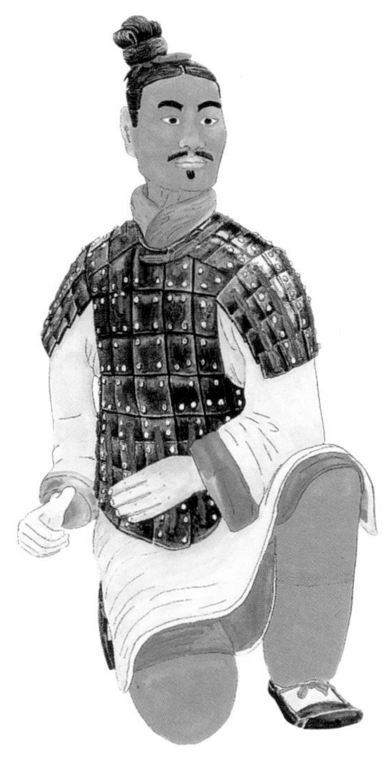

Firing of the terracotta figures

After the figures were assembled, refined, finished and dried, they were fired at the relatively low temperature of 950–1050°C. Most soldiers as well as the horses were fired in one single piece. The successful firing of objects of such size is problematic even for modern ceramicists. It would have required kilns with huge firing chambers and a most advanced technology.

To date, no pottery kiln large enough to fire soldiers and horses has been found in the vicinity of the army. However, in order to facilitate the transportation of the fragile sculptures and to reduce the risk of damage, the kilns were almost certainly placed near the warrior pits. One possible location may have been an area about 200 metres south-east of Pit 1. Local peasants reported that, prior to the discovery of the warriors, they noticed kiln remains and scattered sculpture fragments in this area when levelling the ground for construction work.[13]

Colours

FIGS **174 & 175**
(left and above) **Kneeling archer with pigment, excavated from Pit 2. Recent improvements in conservation techniques have resulted in some original pigment being preserved. This figure was excavated in a corridor with forty kneeling soldiers arranged in rows of two. Red pigment can be seen on parts of his armour. Faces, hands and feet are usually painted in a flesh colour, but one archer has been found with his face painted green.**

FIG. **176**
(right) **Two replicas made to show the original bright colour scheme of the warriors, as well as the geometric patterns on their armour. Mineral colours such as cinnabar, azurite and malachite were used on top of a lacquer ground. These replicas were coloured according to a chemical analysis of the pigments remaining on original warriors and in the ground surrounding them.**

One distinctive original characteristic of the sculptures that can no longer be immediately perceived by modern viewers is that all of the soldiers were entirely painted with bright and colourful pigments. The horses were painted in brown and black. The sculptures were first covered with a dark-brown lacquer ground and then painted with pigments in one or two layers, sometimes rather thick. The artisans used cinnabar, malachite and azurite, as well as bone white and 'Han purple', a rare pigment that was an artificially produced barium copper silicate.[14]

One kneeling archer (*fig.* 175) wears a pink long-sleeved robe with blue undergarment, green trousers and a blue scarf. The hair knot is tied with a red ribbon. The brownish armour plates are fastened with red laces and white rivets. Other figures demonstrate the same tendency towards strong contrasts in pigmentation. Often complementary colours like red and green are combined. This fact may reveal some idea about the aesthetics of Qin people rather than indicating rank or unit of the soldier. According to a recent study, there was no colour ruling prescribed for soldiers' clothes. The conscripts were not provided with uniforms. Instead, they were supposed to prepare their own robes, using the materials they could afford.[15]

The skin on the face of the kneeling archer is painted in a tint of green. Other sculptures have several shades of yellow or pink flesh colours. In the white eyeballs the iris and even the pupils were clearly marked, giving the sculpture a life-like expression. The hair and the leather armour reveal the dark lacquer ground.

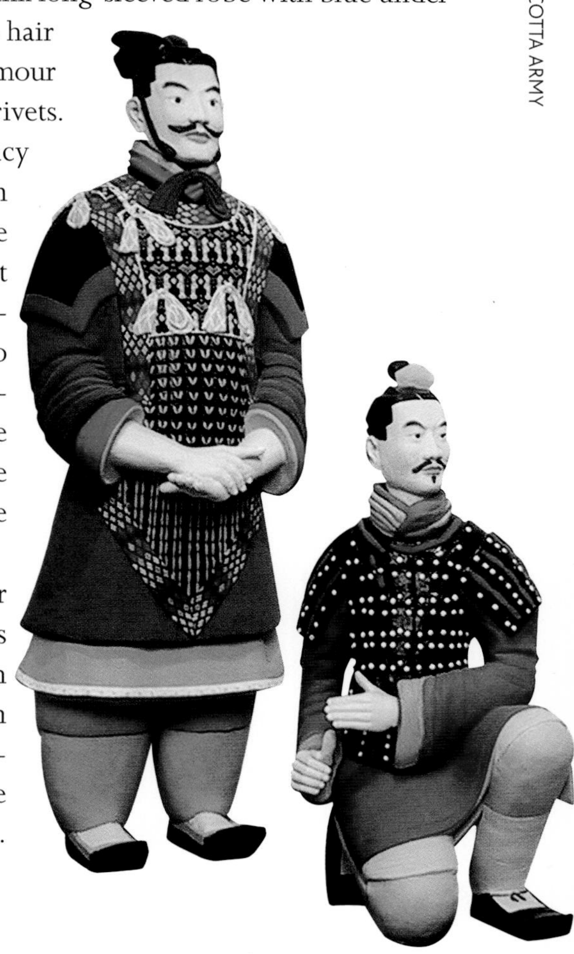

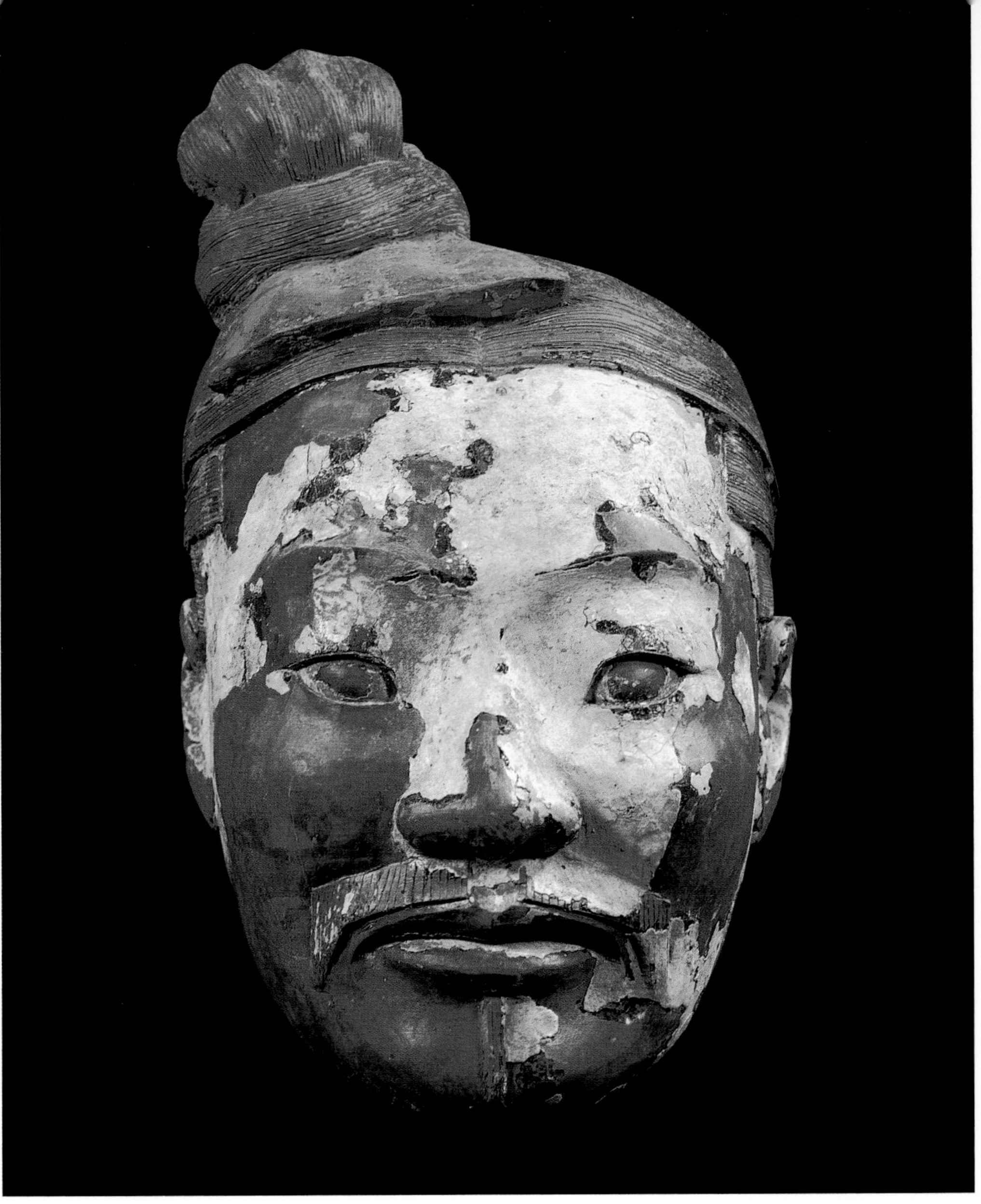

FIG. 177
Head of an infantryman excavated from Pit 1 showing the original pigment on the face. Bone white was used.
Cat. no. 125

Officers' armour bore intricate geometric ornamentation, which apparently followed embroidery patterns of the time. Microscopic analysis of the pigments allowed a precise reconstruction of some of the patterns (*figs* 178–9). The application of such painting must have been an extremely time-consuming process. However, preparing the colours may have been an even more difficult task. Colours would have to be collected or artificially produced, and then ground by hand into fine powder before painting. It has been estimated that – for the red pigment of the terracotta soldiers and horses alone – about 2 tonnes of cinnabar would have had to be ground and prepared.[16]

Weapons

The terracotta soldiers were equipped with real bronze swords, halberds, dagger axes, crossbows and bows. Up to now about 40,000 bronze weapons and arrowheads have come to light in Pit 1.[17] Many swords are still razor-sharp. Some weapons bear inscriptions, mentioning the name of the workshop, the manufacturer, his assistants, a production number and the date of production. The dates range from 245

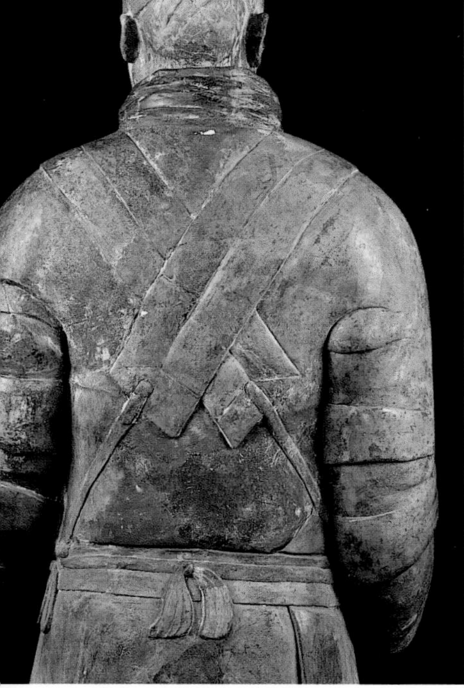

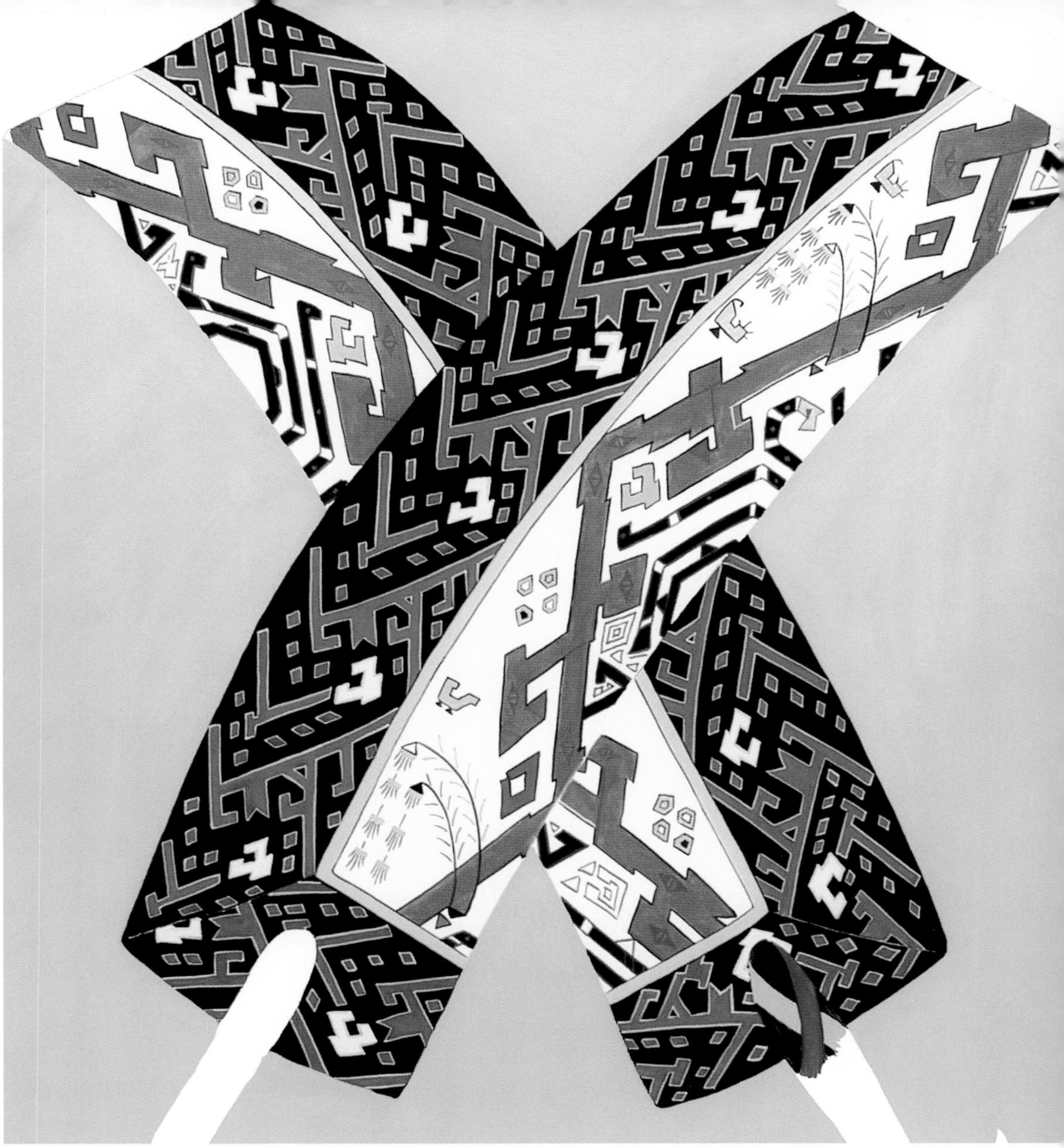

FIG. 178
(above) **Backview of a charioteer showing the crossed straps of his armour.**

FIG. 179
(right) **Reconstruction of the geometric pattern on the crossed straps of the charioteer.**

to 228 BC.[18] This indicates that the weapons placed in the hands of the sculptures may have been used before by real soldiers (see p. 43).

The emperor's chariot?

In addition to bronze weapons, the terracotta army was equipped with wooden chariots as used in real battle. So far the remains of 126 war chariots have been located. The two-wheeled vehicles were drawn by four horses each, and were provided with reins and bronze fittings. In most cases the crew consisted of three persons. One was the charioteer, holding both hands in front as if grasping reins. He was accompanied by two armoured soldiers, who possibly carried long weapons like spears or halberds.[19]

FIG. 180
(following pages) **View of Pit 3, showing the command chariot with the commanding officer missing. Some scholars think that the Emperor was the commanding officer, others that the commanding officer would have been buried nearby.**

The single chariot in Pit 3 differed from the common carriages in Pits 1 and 2. The beautifully painted vehicle body was crowned by a round ornamented canopy, indicating that this chariot had a special function. It may have been designed to carry the commander of the army. The chariot was manned by four soldiers – one charioteer and three armoured personnel. None of them, however, wore the armour and

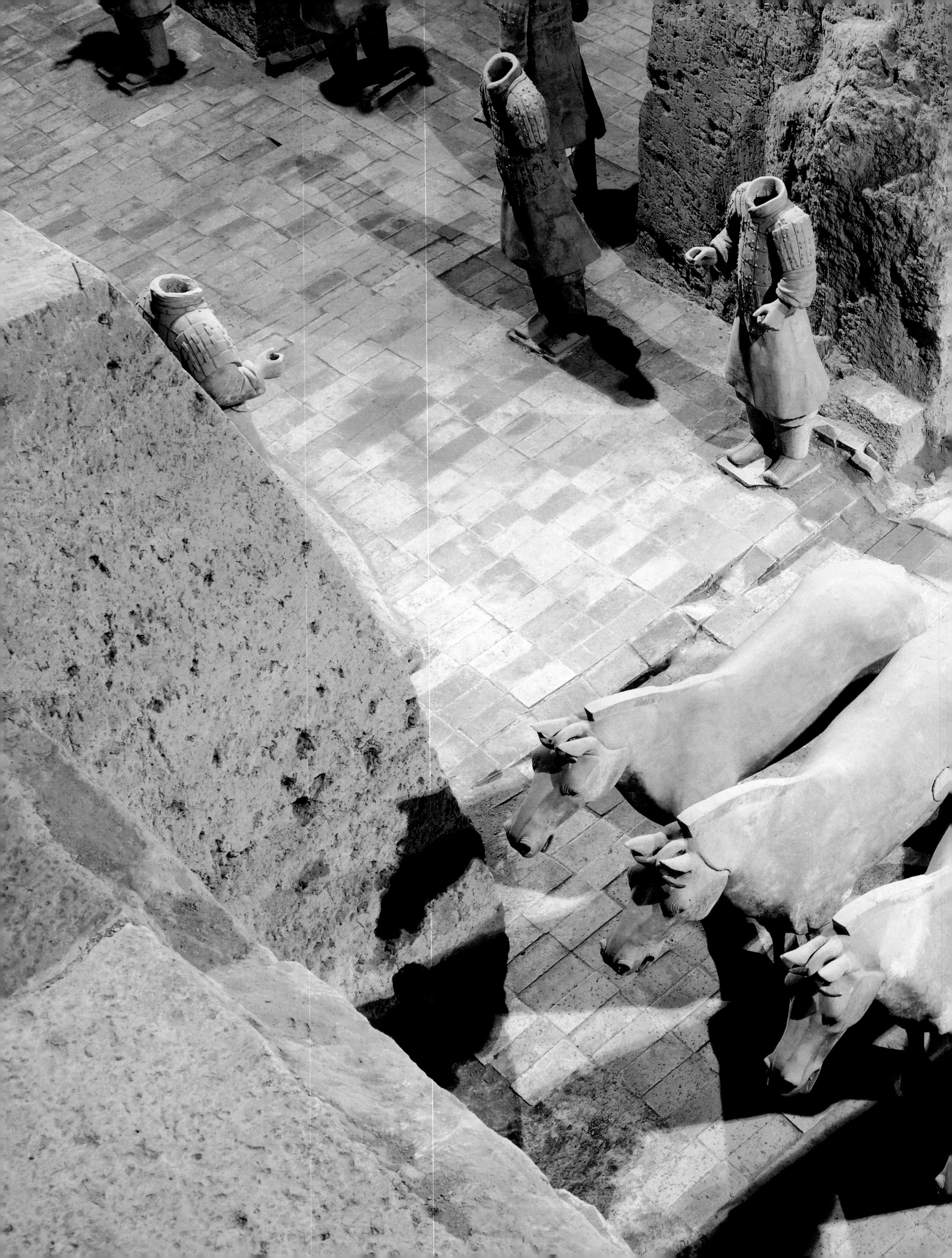

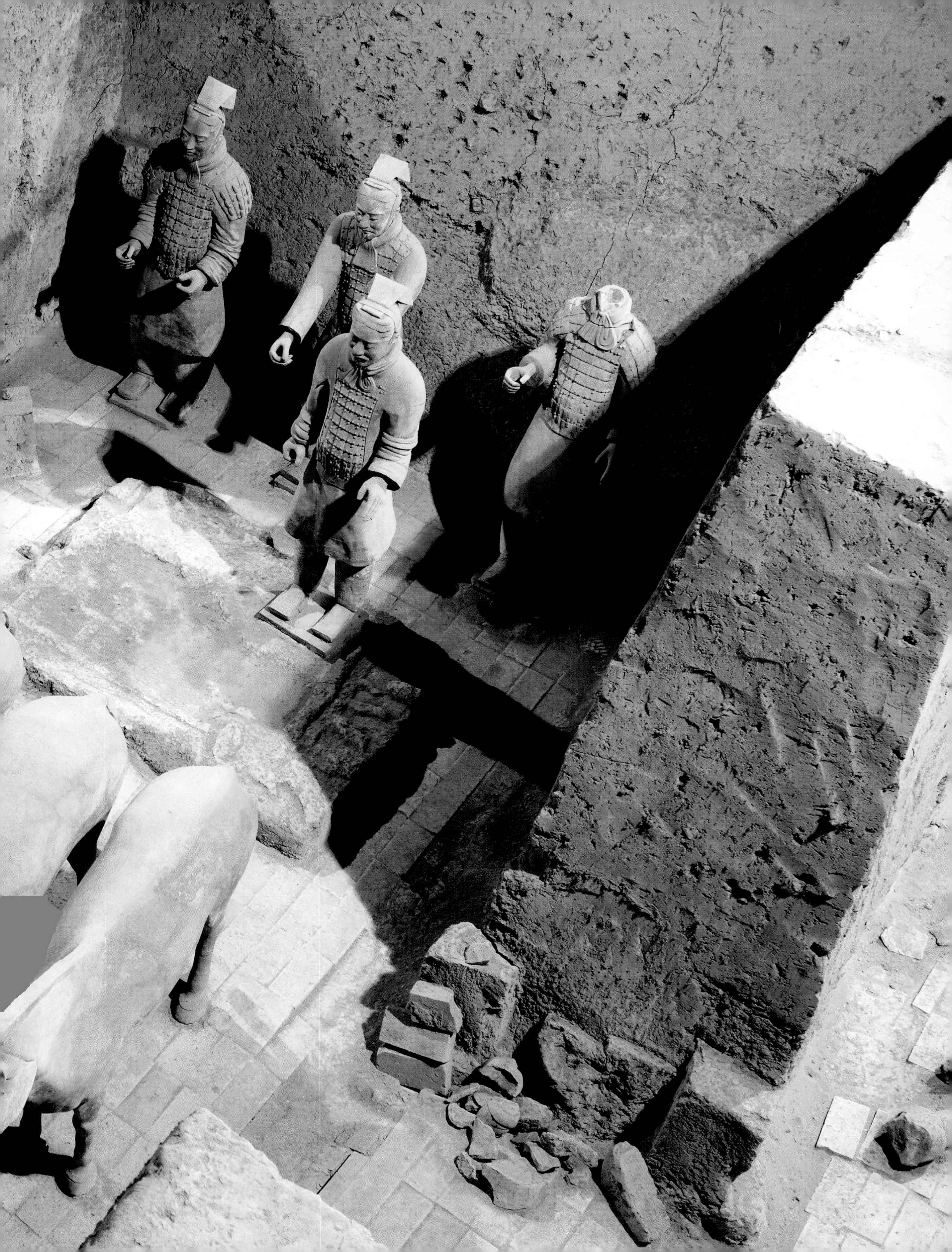

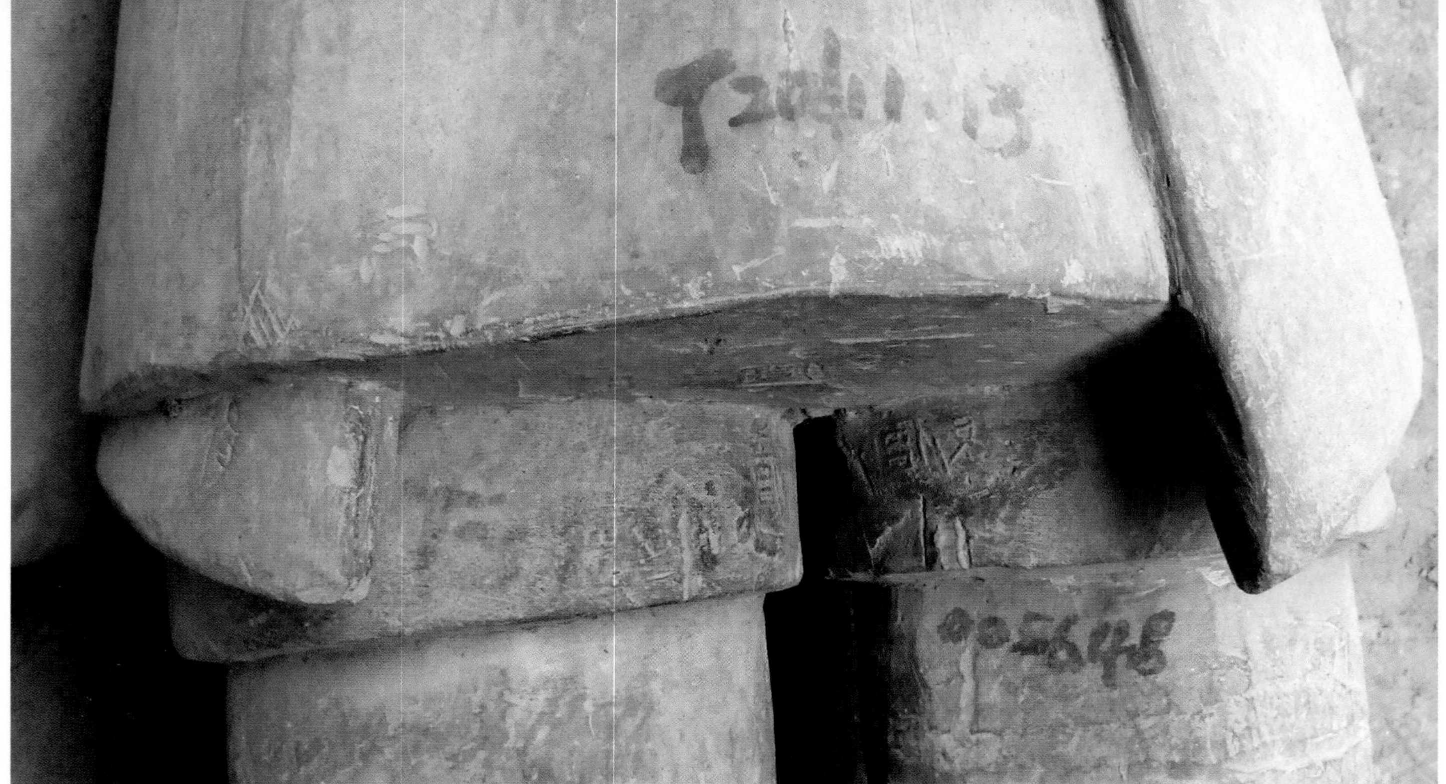

FIG. 181
Three different characters stamped on to the back of a warrior identifying the workshop which made the figure. This ensured quality control.

headdress of a high-ranking officer that would identify him as the commander himself. The main person of the terracotta army appears to be missing.

The arrangement of the sculptures in Pit 3 provides a clue for this problem. The soldiers are not facing eastwards as their counterparts in the other pits do. Instead, they are lined up along the walls, leaving a path in-between them that leads from the western ends of the pit towards the chariot in the centre (*fig.* 168). Quite clearly, the soldiers form a cordon or a guard of honour, respectfully awaiting the arrival of another person who was supposed to come from the direction of the main burial mound. This person may very well have been the commander-in-chief we are looking for. The identity of the commander remains unclear. Some scholars assume that it was a general who served the emperor in his lifetime and was buried in person in one of the tombs that have been located in-between the warrior pits and the emperor's tomb chamber. It is also possible that the emperor himself was expected to appear in this headquarters after his tomb was closed, enter the main chariot and take charge of the army prepared for his afterlife.[20] The two luxury bronze chariots found in a pit west of the tumulus may support this assumption. Both were driven by a bronze charioteer, but the passenger seats were found empty. Similar to the war chariot in Pit 3, these chariots were apparently waiting to be used by the deceased emperor (see pp. 37–41).

The date of construction

Sima Qian, the grand historian who lived about a century after the First Emperor and who provided us with the only literary information about the tomb and its contents, stated that the timber necessary for the tomb was shipped especially from the area of the southern states of Chu and Shu, a fact that led many scholars to believe that work on the warrior pits did not begin before 223 BC, the year when Qin finally conquered Chu and gained access to its vast resources.[21] The mixed quality of the

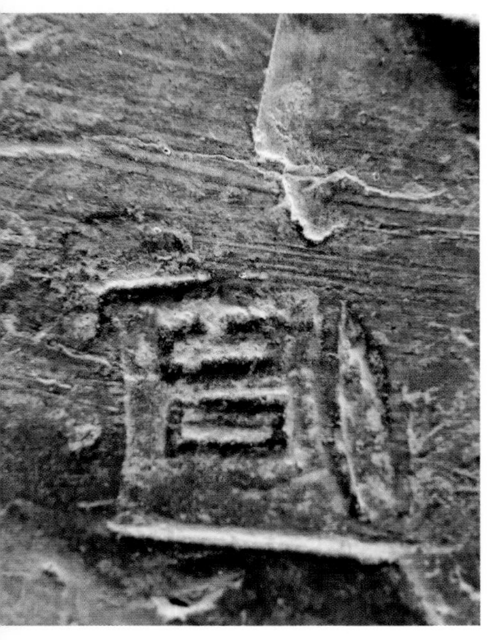

FIG. 182
Detail of the character '*gong*' meaning 'palace', referring to one of the workshops producing the figures.

beams and posts does not completely back the claim of the historian. Judging from the test results mentioned above, it appears rather that the material for the woodwork was collected from any available source. Other possible dates are indicated by the inscriptions on the bronze weapons mentioned above. It seems safer to assume that work started after 228 BC, the date when the last inscribed weapon was produced. This means that construction of the warrior pits probably began about two decades after that of the main burial mound had commenced, as a grand extension to an already huge project.

Labour organization

Following long-established practice in Qin society, a strict hierarchy of responsibilities was built up on the construction ground. Foremen were in charge of production of individual figures.[22] The foremen were controlled by supervisors, as can be deduced from short inscriptions in the clay on many sculptures. Foremen stated their name and office or place of provenance, making themselves accountable if the sculpture proved to be faulty.

Many sculptures were produced by eleven foremen from the imperial workshops, who identified themselves by using seals. Next to the name, the inscriptions displayed the character '*gong*' ('palace'; *fig.* 182). *Gong* might be the short form of *gongshui*, an office responsible for water works, or the abbreviation of *gongsikong*, which was an office in charge of building palaces and tombs during the Qin and Han periods. Impressions of *gong*-seals have also been found on many of the bricks used for paving the floor of the pits.[23] Twenty-three additional craftsmen were recruited from local workshops. Not being part of the bureaucracy, these people did not use stamps but inscribed their name and home town by hand. Forty-eight persons stated only their name, and no workshop or city. They may have been part of either group of foremen.[24]

The foremen in turn supervised subordinates. It is assumed that about a dozen workers served under one foreman. Since eighty-seven different names of foremen are known to date, it can be calculated that over a thousand people participated in the production.[25] If we assume that every team had the same workload, and further take into account that work on the army pits went on for at least twelve years, the production of the 7,000 soldiers breaks down to not more than seven completed sculptures per year and per team.

Many of the methods that the Qin ministers used for their enormous task are still not completely understood by modern archaeological research. What technology allowed the craftsmen to fire sculptures as large as the horses and soldiers from the warrior pits? How did they provide the vast amount of mineral colours necessary for the decoration? And, how were the craftsmen able to handle sculpture without developing this form of art step by step over centuries, as ancient Greek or Indian sculptors did? This study of the production methods and the above calculation, however, suggest that proper preparation, sufficient workforce and strict labour organization led to the creation of such a vast terracotta army being a manageable challenge.

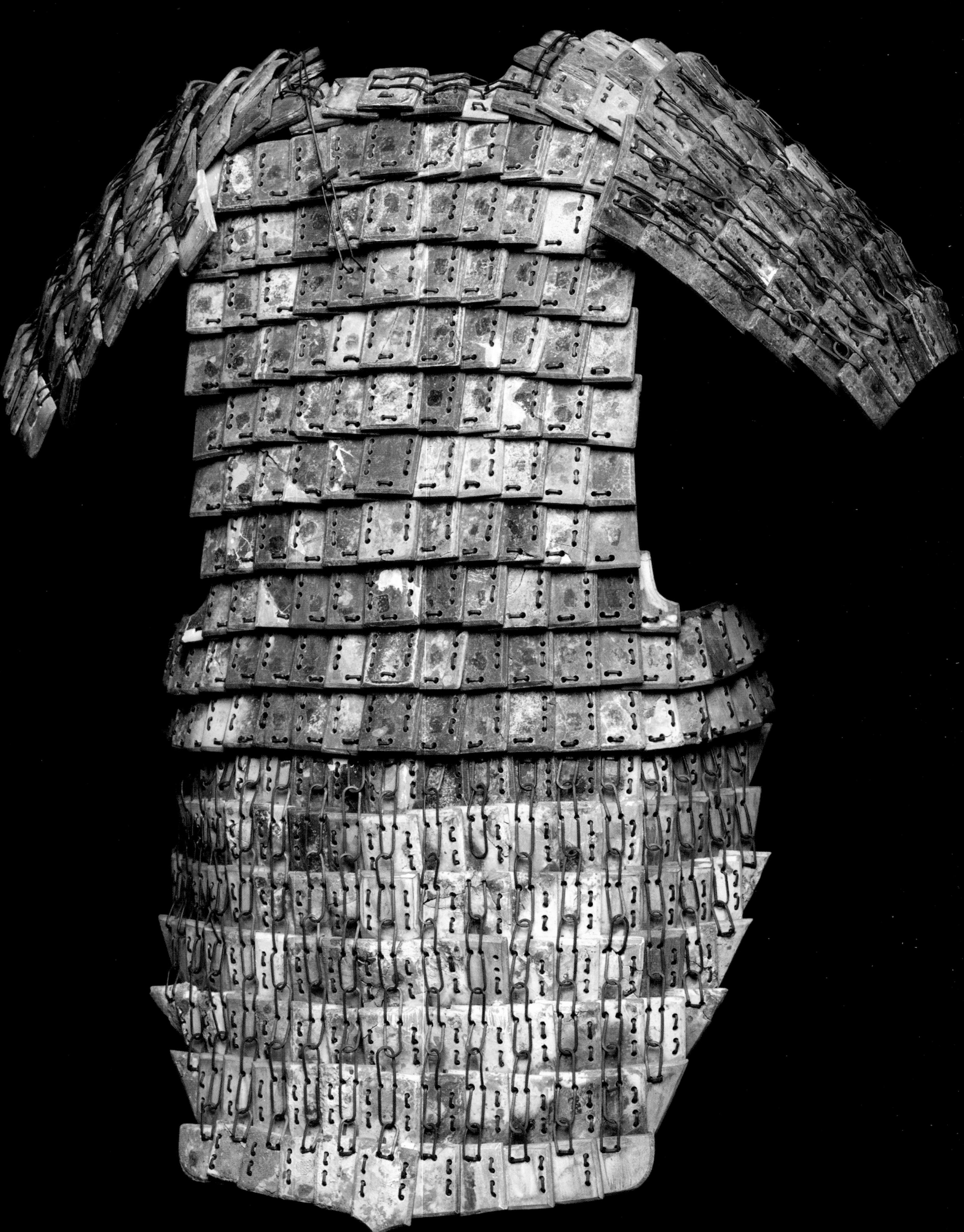

ARMOUR FOR THE AFTERLIFE

JAMES LIN

During a trial excavation in 1999 eighty-seven sets of stone armour and forty-three stone helmets were unearthed in the south-western Pit K9801, which is the biggest accessory burial pit to the south-east of Qin Shihuangdi's mausoleum at Lishan (*fig. 131*). The pit had suffered from fire after it was constructed and the buried items were burned to different degrees as a result of the combustion of wooden support structures inside. So far two sets of armour and a helmet have been restored.

FIG. 183
(left) **Reconstructed set of limestone armour excavated from Pit K9801 to the south-east of the Emperor's tomb mound (see tomb plan, *fig. 131*). This pit, which has been only partially excavated, is thought to represent an armoury for the afterlife.**
Cat. no. 126

A set of armour consisting of upper body, two arms and lower front and lower back parts has been reconstructed (*fig. 183*). Comprising 612 plates, it weighs 18 kg, is 74 cm in height and has a circumference at the waist of 128 cm. The stone plaques are rectangular, square, trapezoid, fish-scale shaped or irregular, depending on their position within the armour, and were laced together using flat copper strips. The reconstructed helmet is made from seventy-four stone laminae (thin plates or layers) laced together, weighs 3.168 kg and is 32 cm in height (*fig. 186*). The surface is slightly arched outward. A large round, flat disc with holes around its edge forms the top of the helmet. The plaques that radiate from the disc are round-cornered trapezoid or rectangular and are laced from top to bottom. The bottom row would have rested on the body and shoulders below the neck, thus providing more protection; it is the first example of such a design in Chinese archaeology. In most cases the edges of the stone plaques were carefully cut, smoothed and polished.

FIG. 184
(below) **Part of Pit K9801 showing the armour as it was found. Originally the sets of armour would have been supported from the ceiling or on wooden stands in rows. The entire pit is thought to cover 13,600 sq. metres.**

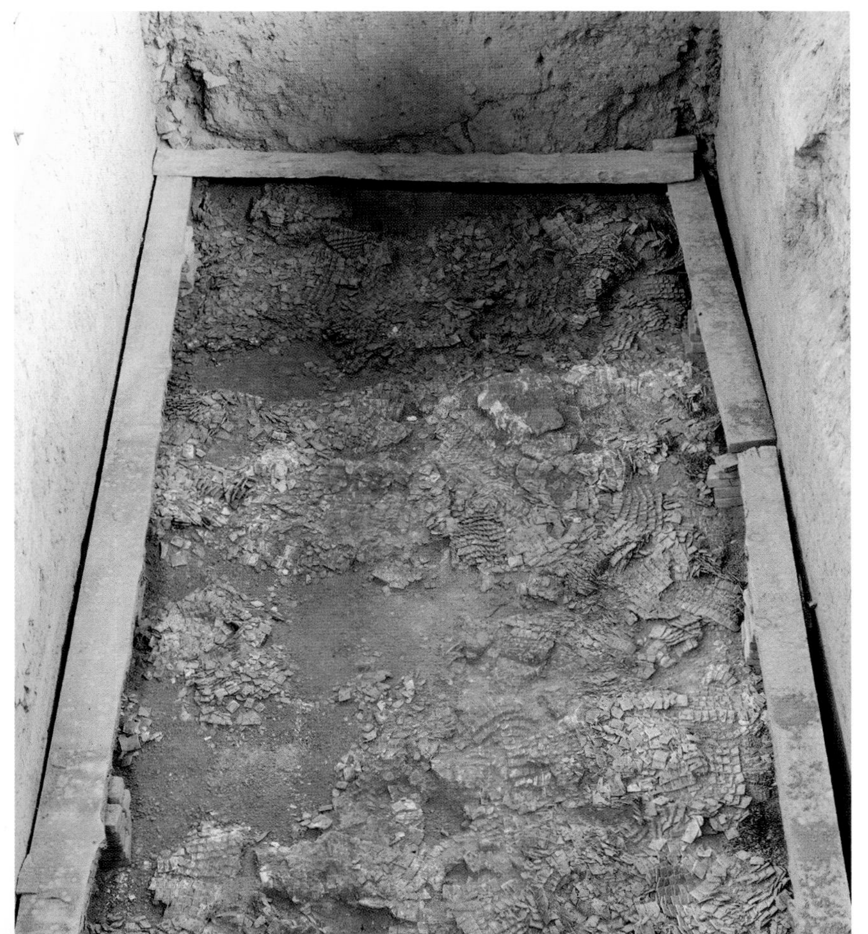

Judging from archaeological evidence, the stone armour was either supported by a wooden stand or suspended from the beams of the wooden support structure before it collapsed. The unequal number of stone armour suits and helmets suggests that only around half of the sets of armour would have included a helmet. The provision of a full or partial set may have been dependent on rank, as can be seen in the use of the armour on the terracotta warriors found nearby: high-ranking officers wore a double-layered tunic under a fish-scale armour apron, while middle-ranking officers wore armour of overlapping rectangular plaques, joined with cords and rivets. One set of stone armour for a horse has also been found nearby,

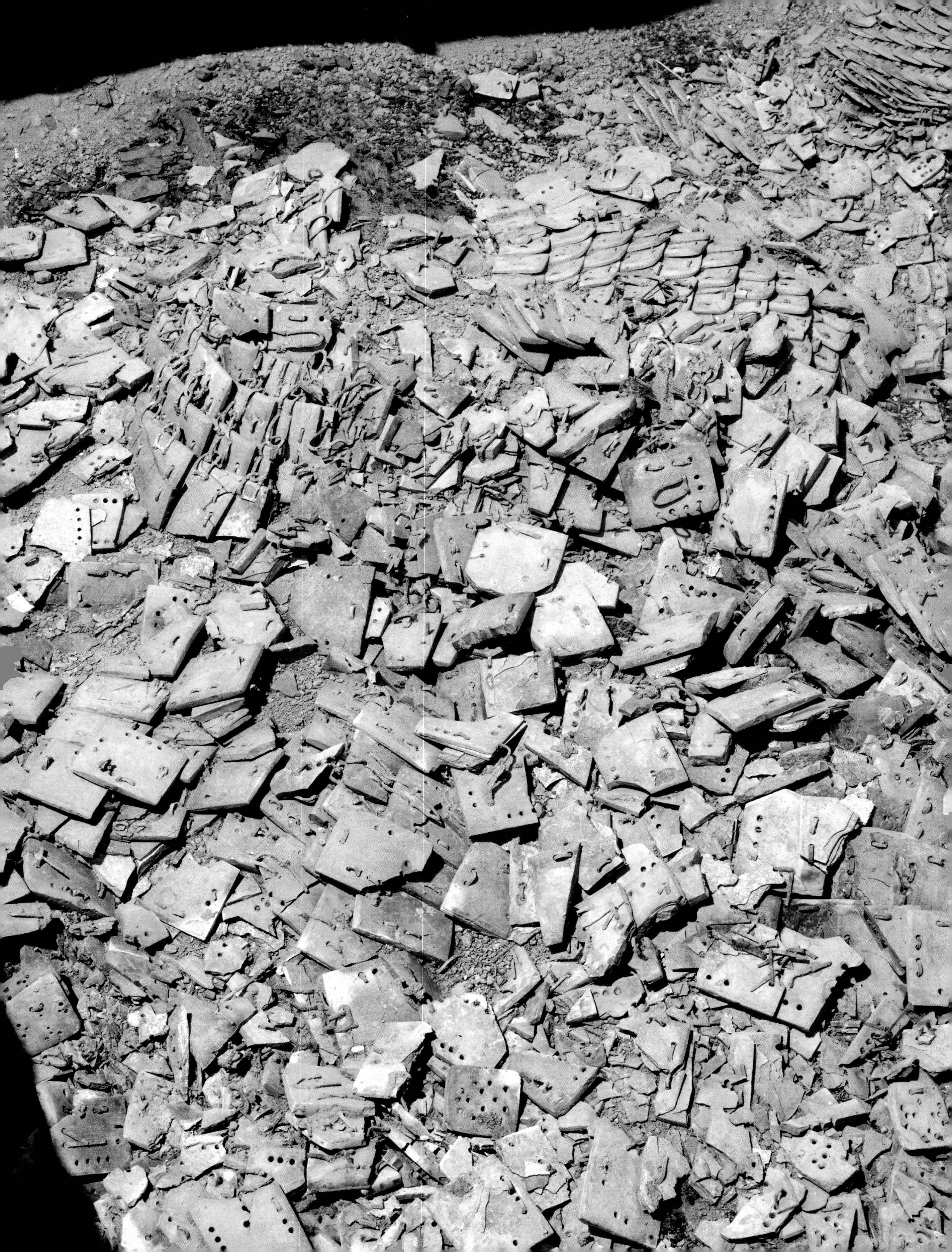

FIG. 185
(left) Detail of Pit K9801 showing the clusters of armour fragments belonging to a set, as well as the holes drilled in each piece and the different shaped pieces.

FIG. 186
(right) Reconstructed stone armour helmet. The stone helmets are particularly useful sources of information as the terracotta army had no helmets.
Cat. no. 127

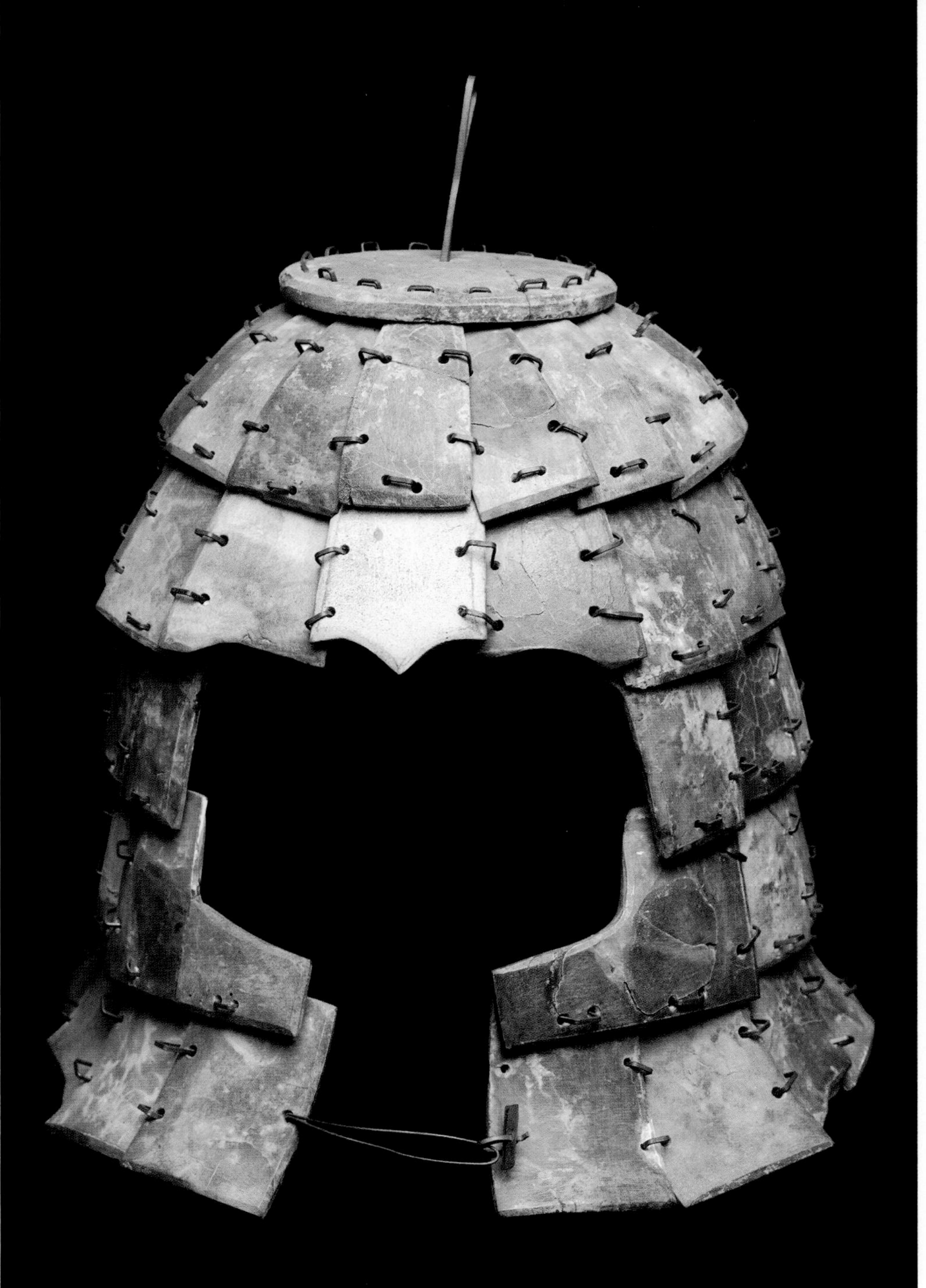

but unfortunately it was seriously damaged by fire and is impossible to reconstruct at this stage. It was designed to cover the whole body of the horse and comprises approximately 300 large stone plaques (*fig.* 180).

Production methods and markings

Like the terracotta warriors, the stone armour must have been prepared in a large workshop. However, the production of stone armour was much more complicated than the production of terracotta warriors, simply because of the method of construction and the material involved. First, a blueprint based on iron armour must have been sent to the workshop as a model. From this the number of stone plaques required could have been calculated. In order to complete the task in time for the

FIG. 187
Line drawing showing the possible arrangement of the stone horse armour, which has not yet been reconstructed but is thought to have consisted of approximately 300 pieces, larger than the human armour pieces.

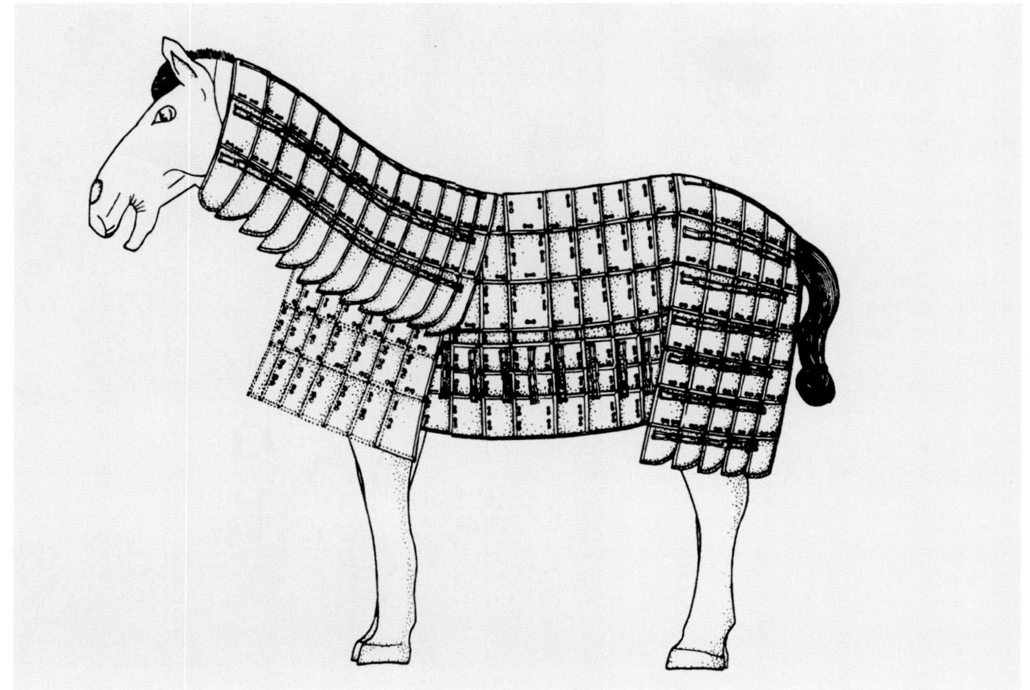

burial, work would have been divided between a team, whose roles would have included cutting the stone plaques, making them into the desired shapes, drilling the holes, edge-abrasion, grinding and polishing the surfaces, preparing the copper strips and lacing the plaques together.

The most difficult task would have been to cut the plaques to the required thickness of 0.5 cm. In order to make the best use of material, the maximum thickness of the plaques would be 1 cm. If the plaques were too thick then more labour would be needed to abrade them. The drilling of eight to twelve small holes within the 7 x 6 cm plaques also presented a challenge. The holes had to be small and drilled equally from both sides, otherwise the plaques would break during drilling.

Three types of mark are found incised on the back of some of the stone plaques. The first one consists of arrow-shaped characters. They were mostly found on the upper arms, shoulders, neck and lower skirt areas. It is not clear what they represented. The second type comprises numbers, seemingly random figures such as 5,

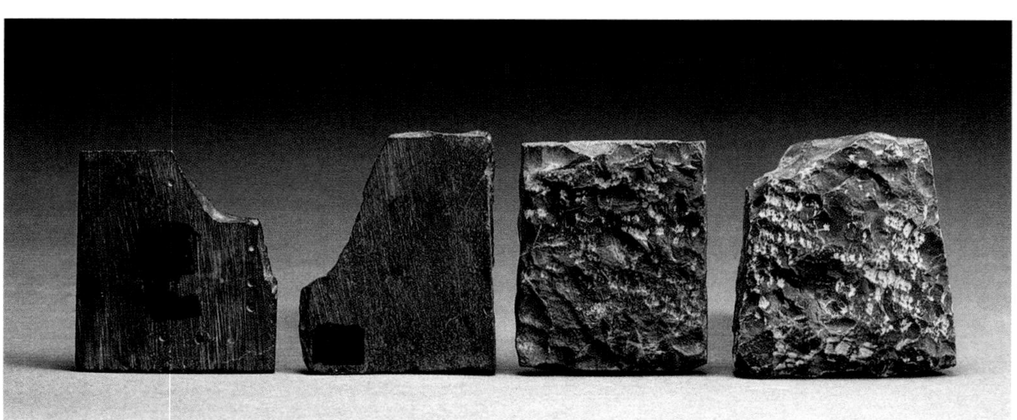

FIG. 188
Fragments of stone armour showing incised marks.
Cat. no. 128

18, 80 and 90. It is possible that these record the number of pieces an individual workman made. Alternatively, it may indicate the placing of individual pieces in the overall pattern. Some of the numbers were carefully carved, which made the archaeologists surmise that they were made by imperial or official workmen; others were roughly carved and might have been produced by local workmen. The last type of mark is the Chinese character *gong*, which caused the archaeologists to suggest that this was an abbreviation for *gongjiang* (artisan) or *kaogong* (official artisan). According to texts, a *kaogong* was a subordinate official under the *shao fu* (chamberlain for palace revenues) of the Qin dynasty, responsible for supervising the production of weapons and chariots. Since stone armour is a means of protection, its production should have been under the supervision of a *kaogong*. However, until more sets of stone armour and helmets have been reconstructed and more research done, it is not possible to determine what these marks really mean.

After analysing the stone plaques and the textual records from the *Records of the Historian* (*Shiji*), the archaeologists have suggested that the raw material for the stone armour may have been quarried at Fenghuangshan between Lei village and Gongli town in Fuping county, 55 km from Qin Shihuangdi's mausoleum. Metallographic analysis indicates that the strips were hammered after annealing and that they were made of copper with small amounts of lead, tin, zinc and iron. In the process of armour restoration, archaeologists estimated that it took 341–441 man-hours to make one set of armour composed of 600 plates. It takes only 146 man-hours when modern technology is utilized.

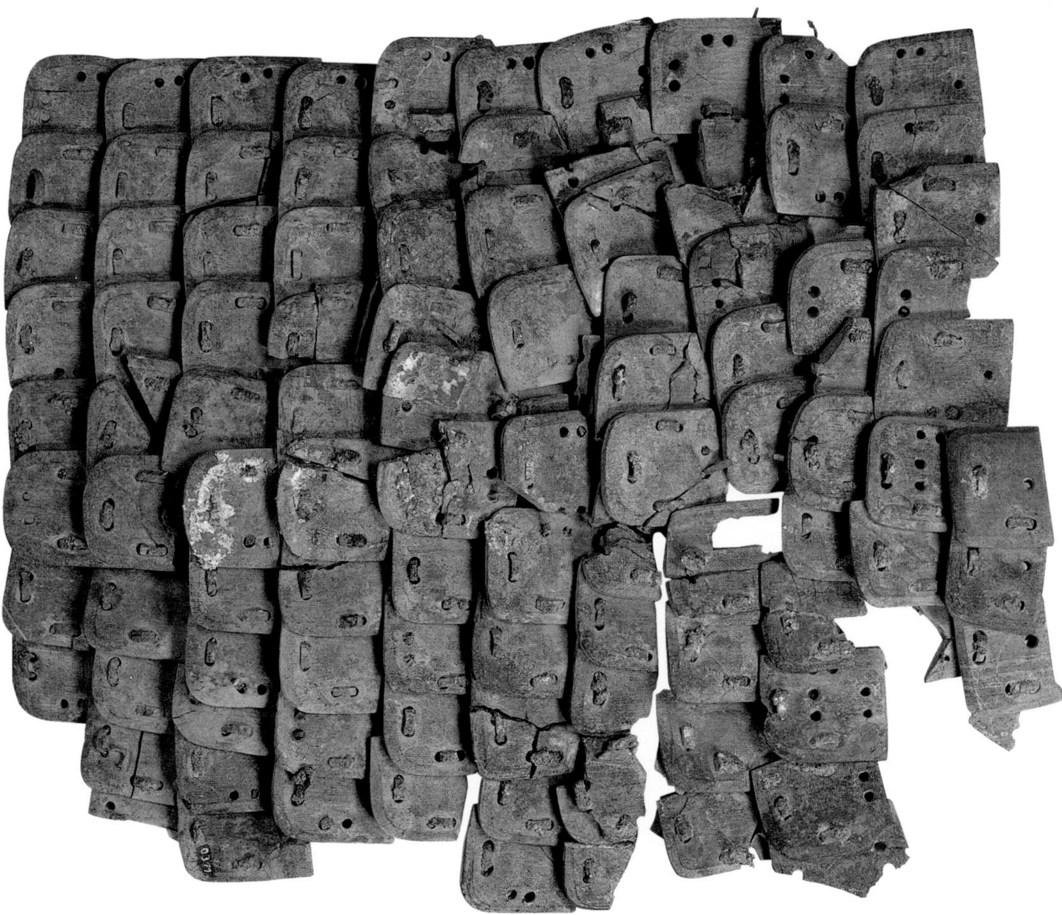

FIG. **189**
Group of stone armour pieces still joined together with their original hammered copper strips.
Cat.no. 129

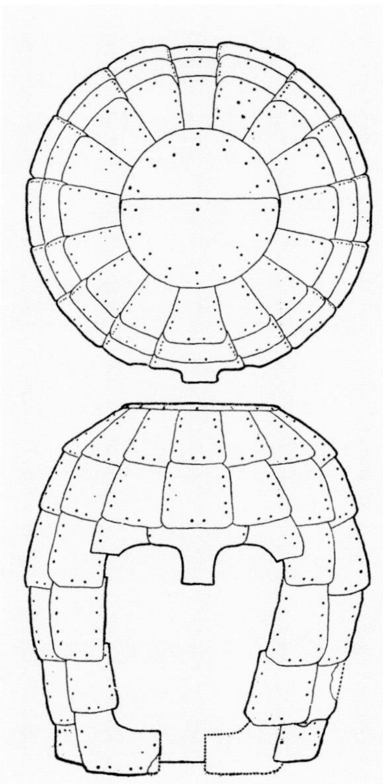

FIG. 190
(above) **Drawing of the iron helmet discovered in Tomb M44 at Yixian, the lower capital of the state of Yan, Hebei province. Late Warring States period, fourth–third century BC. This is very similar in design to the stone armour discovered in the First Emperor's tomb complex.**

FIG. 191
(opposite) **Top view of a Western Han-dynasty jade burial suit, showing the construction of the helmet, similar to the Warring States iron helmet and the Qin stone armour helmet.**

History and function of buried armour

Armour made of metal or leather appeared long before the unification of China. However, this is the first example in Chinese history of a burial accompanied by stone armour. Judging from its construction, the stone armour copied iron or leather armour and was expected to serve a similar function, i.e. protection. The most convincing evidence is the iron armour excavated from Tomb M44 at Yanxiadu, Yixian, Hebei province, which dates to the late Warring States period. Twenty-two skeletons and a large quantity of coins and weapons, including spears, swords, arrows, daggers, halberds, crossbows, helmets and knives, are buried in a rectangular vertical earthen pit. Judging from the scattered skeletons, damaged weapons and lack of furniture, archaeologists suggested that it was a burial pit for soldiers who had died in the war.[26] An armour workshop containing 261 iron laminae was found nearby. Among the 117 complete laminae, 55 were identified as belonging to helmets and the remaining 62 as body armour laminae.[27]

A helmet from Tomb M44 composed of eighty-nine iron pieces is especially relevant. These iron plaques have small holes at the edge and overlap each other. They were sewn together with silk thread or leather to form a helmet. On the top of the iron helmet there is a disc-shaped section, which was made of two iron pieces (*fig.* 190). The plaques adjacent to the circular section on the top of the helmet and head-cover, in the case of both armour and later Han-dynasty jade suits, are trapezoidal. Therefore, the iron helmet from the Warring States period is very likely to be the precursor of the stone helmet found at Qin Shihuangdi's burial site and the later, Han, jade head-covers from the tombs of imperial Liu family members, particularly Liu Xiu (*fig.* 191).

Stone armour and helmets could not be used in life as they are too heavy to wear and would be easily damaged by weapons. Therefore, they seem more likely to have been prepared for the emperor's guards in the afterlife. It has been suggested that Qin Shihuangdi's burial of a large, life-sized terracotta army facing east in front of his mausoleum was in order to protect him in the spirit world against a possible attack by the people he had killed during his conquest of China (see pp. 124–5).[28i] Another theory is that the stone armour was prepared as a form of appeasement for those Qin soldiers who had died during the conquest of China. As they had died in an unnatural way and without a proper burial, their spirits might become evil and turn against the First Emperor in the afterlife.

Large numbers of terracotta warriors and the decayed weapons that they were holding indicated the tomb owner's desire for protection in the afterlife. These well-designed defence systems recall the description of the First Qin Emperor's mausoleum in Sima Qian's *Shiji* (see also p. 126): 'Replicas of palaces, scenic towers, and the hundred officials, as well as rare utensils and wonderful objects, were brought to fill up the tomb. Craftsmen were ordered to set up crossbows and arrows, rigged so they would immediately shoot down anyone attempting to break in.'[29] However, neither the terracotta warriors nor the stone armour were mentioned in this text.

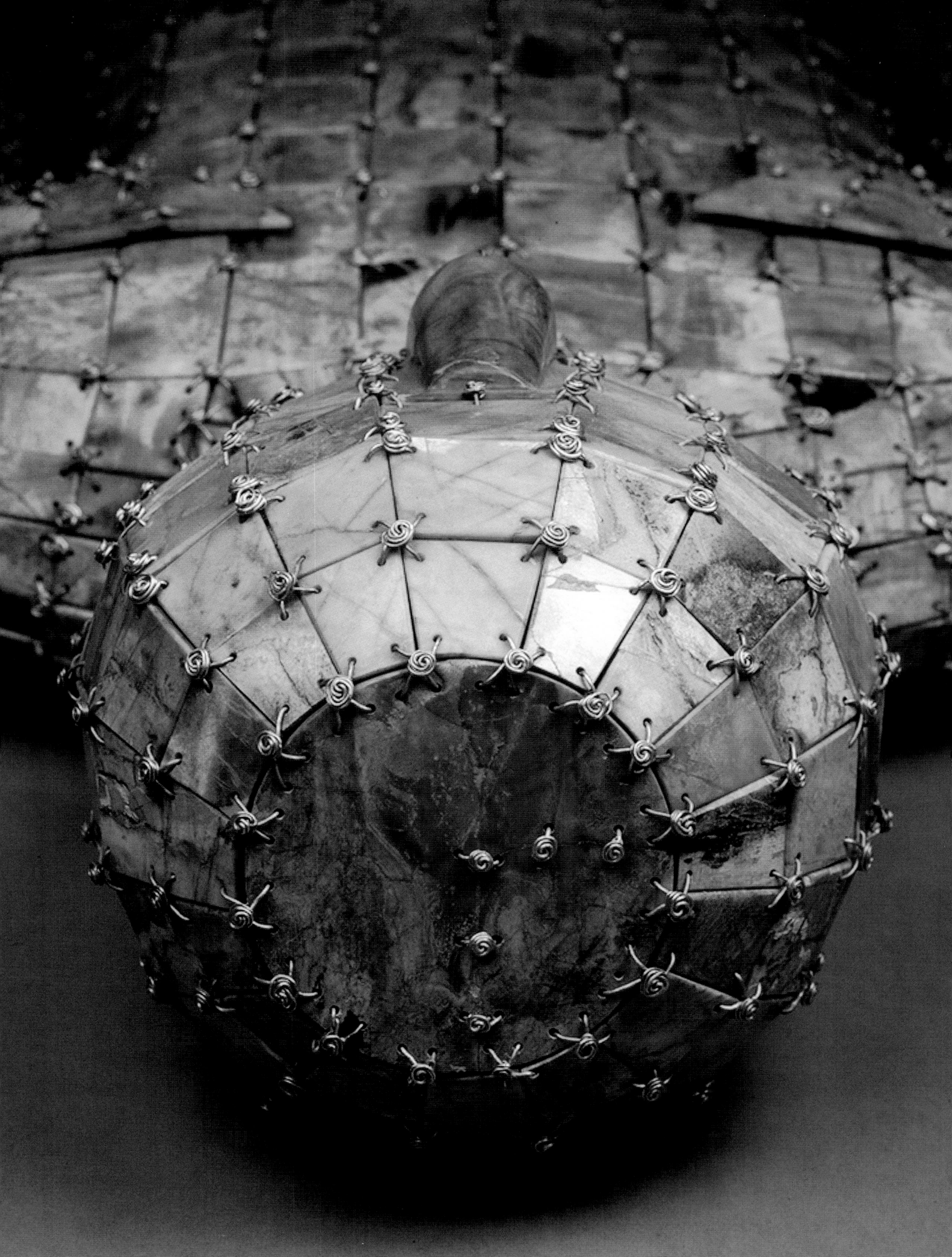

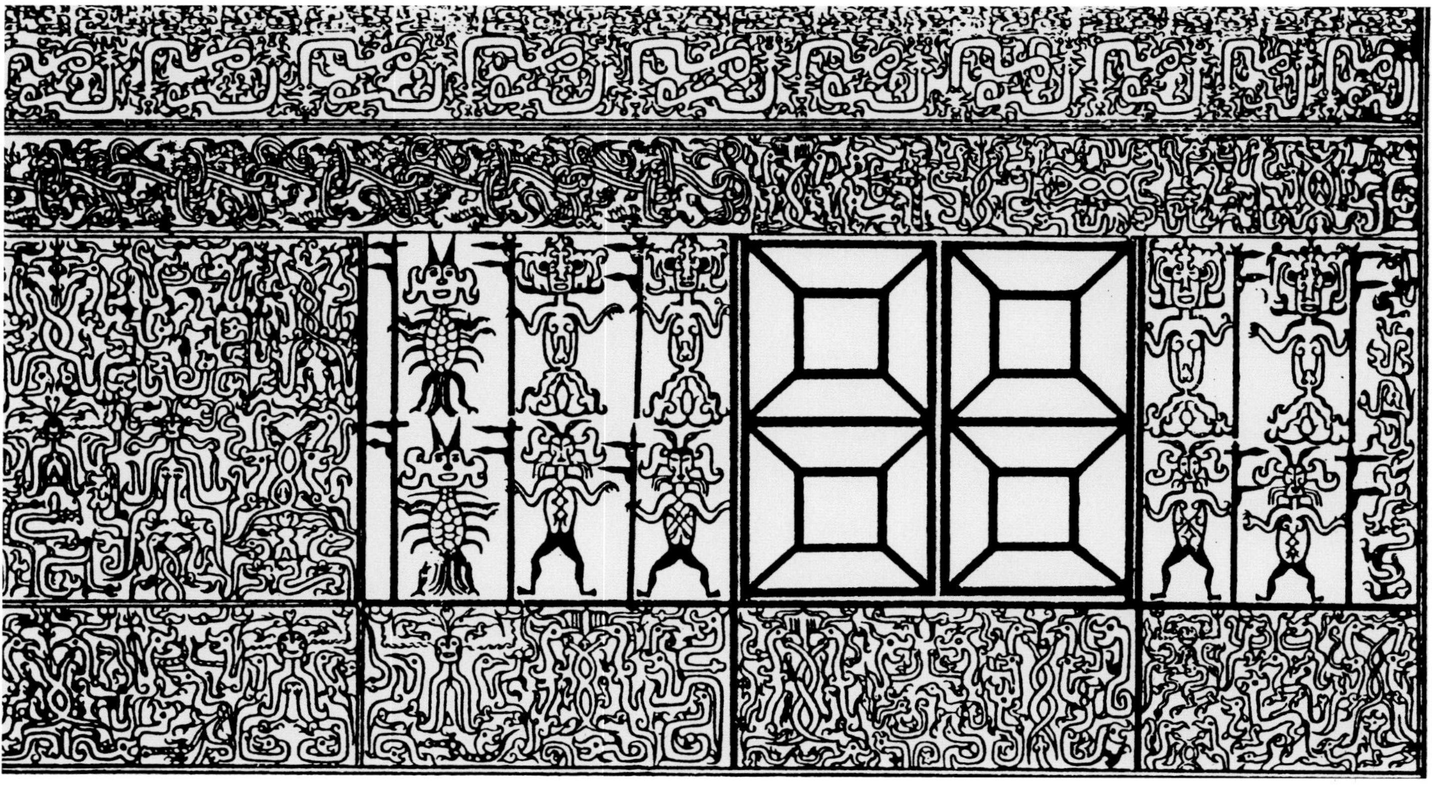

FIG. 192
Line drawing of the design painted on the inner coffin of Marquis Yi of the state of Zeng, Suizhou, Hubei province, showing guardian creatures holding halberds in their hands, warding off attacking spirits. Early Warring States period, *c*.433 BC.

Protection against evil spirits

Large numbers of bamboo slips recovered from a Qin tomb at Shuihudi, Hubei (*fig.* 63), dating to 217 BC, four years before the unification of China, provide us with substantial and much more reliable evidence of the daily life and religious beliefs during that time.[30] Most of the contents of 'daybooks', chapters of bamboo slips, from Shuihudi were also found in different sections of bamboo slips from the Western Han (206 BC–AD 6) Mawangdui tomb. Donald Harper has pointed out that the bamboo slip manuscripts from Shuihudi and Mawangdui are clearly writings that circulated among the literate elite of the period, and that they may be treated as exemplars of books used in life. He suggests that these burial items were in general use at that time and that the manuscripts were not a special category of tomb literature but were themselves aids in life, which therefore made them appropriate items to be included among the burial goods. After comparing the entries and format from the Shuihudi bamboo slips and a Six Dynasties (AD 265–589) text *Bai ze tu* (*Diagrams of the White Marsh*), Donald Harper further pointed out that 'the particular significance of archery in the Shui-hu-ti [Shuihudi] demonography lies in the fact that it shows the demonifugal bow and arrow already in use as popular devices for countering spectral attacks'.[31] This may reflect the fears of the tomb owner and it seems that the tomb was guarded as much against spirits as against mortal robbers.

The most prominent example of this idea is the decoration on coffins from the fifth-century-BC tomb of Marquis Yi of Zeng. The inner coffin was painted with doors and windows. Each of the painted creatures on the inner coffin holds a halberd in its claws, with the points of the halberd directed away from the openings.

They were obviously intended to be in charge of the doors and should be seen as guardians.[32] Apart from these images on the inner coffin, more than 4,500 bronze weapons were also found in the tomb.[33]

It is almost certain that the use of stone rather than iron armour in Qin Shihuangdi's mausoleum suggests that the enemy was perceived to be a supernatural force. Stone would not have been much protection against a human enemy with an iron or steel weapon, for one blow would have shattered it. But it would seem that the burial officials of the Qin emperor thought that the armour would be useful in the afterlife, presumably against spirits or demons.[34] This hypothesis was confirmed by the *Jie* (Spells) section of the daybooks from Shuihudi, which instructs people on how to protect themselves from demons. On the reverse of slip 868, third register, from the *Jie* section it records: 'The ghosts often call people out of their homes, and toward where the ghosts reside. Ignore the ghost's entreaty, throw a white stone at it, and it will stop.'[35] The magical power of white stones and their use as a defence were recorded once again in an early fourth-century-BC Daoist work *Baopuzi* (*c*.320 BC): 'If you encounter an official in the mountains, but only hear his voice without seeing any shape as it keeps shouting to you, throw a white stone at it, and it will stop.'[36] Later, in the Han period, *Huainan wanbishu* by Liu An (*c*.180–122 BC) mentioned that burying stones at the four corners of the house would prevent it from being disturbed by ghosts.[37]

As Donald Harper has shown, bamboo slips reveal that during those centuries peoples in the south, and probably elsewhere, believed that demonic intrusion was a significant cause of illness. Indeed, special recipes (including magical, exorcistic methods of making up drugs and therapeutic treatments) were devised to cure the disease.[38] It is therefore quite possible that, instead of believing that decomposition was a natural process, the Han people may have thought that it was caused by an attack of evil spirits. In a discussion of the transition from Zhou to Han religion and Daoism Anna Seidel has pointed out that there was a progression from exorcistic to physiological and therapeutic attitudes: 'Re-examined in this context, the term *shi jie*, or decomposition of the body, might have originated as the name of an exorcistic rite intended to safe-guard the corpse from demon attack.' She further explains that the exorcist officiating at the burial was believed to prevent a particular type of ghoul, Wang-hsiang ghouls, from eating the liver and brain of the corpse.[39]

From the daybooks we know that these demons could be expelled or even killed. Many of the preparations of the tomb may have been intended to prevent demons from attacking the dead person's body and causing it to decompose. In order to prevent such an attack, they needed weapons such as bows, arrows, swords, armour, white stones, peachwood and even tomb guardians to protect them.[40] The stone armour and helmets found near Qin Shihuangdi's mausoleum, which were too heavy to wear in life, were therefore prepared for the terracotta army and other guards in the afterlife. As Pascal Boyer has discussed, notions concerned with religion or the supernatural often combine the real with the counterintuitive, thereby suggesting their powers.[41] The stone armour used by the terracotta army, as well as the jade suits worn by the following Han-dynasty imperial family members, were analogous to real armour and would be expected to have protective powers in the afterlife.

FIG. 193
(following pages) **Jade burial suit belonging to Prince Liu Sheng, dating to the Western Han dynasty, second century BC, from Mancheng, Hebei. The stone armour from the First Emperor's tomb complex may be a precursor of the jade burial suits of the following Han dynasty, both designed for protection in the afterlife.**

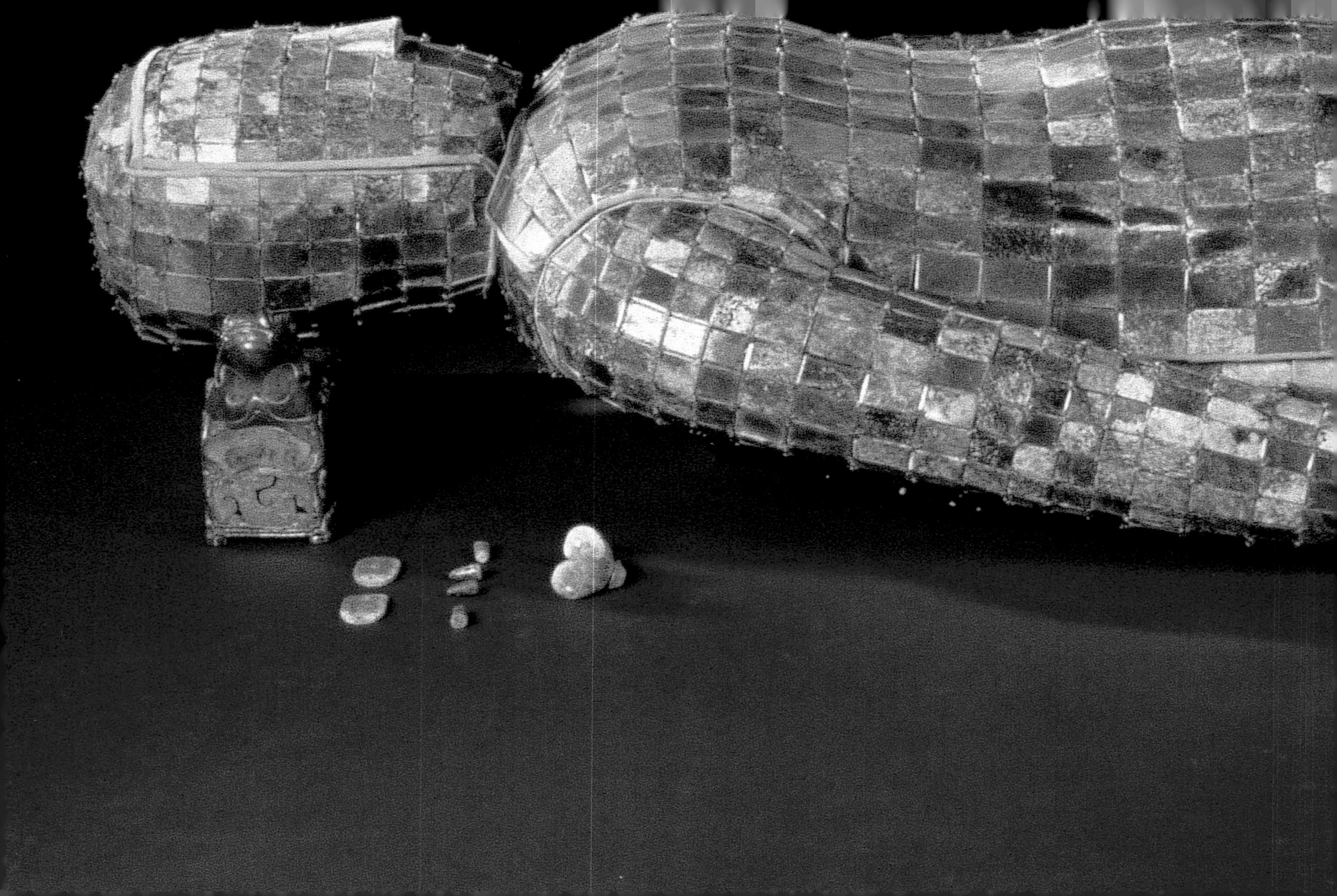

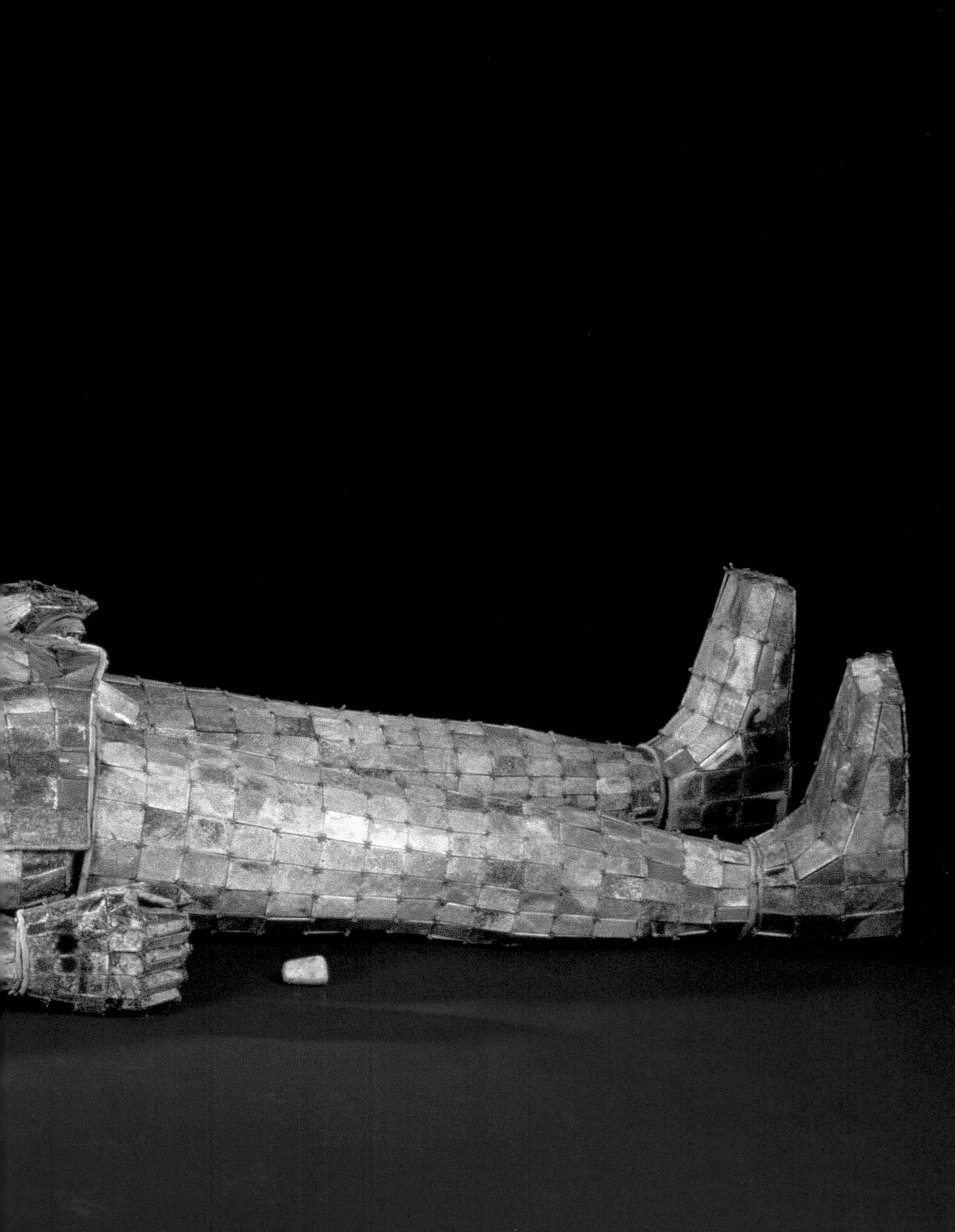

ENTERTAINMENT FOR THE AFTERLIFE

DUAN QINGBO

The sky is a clear blue and a small palace orchestra is about to demonstrate its exquisite skill by playing some pieces of music. In front of the banquet mat, different groups of birds, including charming swans, elegant cranes and well-disciplined wild geese, are ready to dance to the music. Their delightful steps and elegant movements will soon be reflected in the waves of a clear pond. This is exactly the scene displayed in the sacrificial Pit K0007, located 3 km to the north-east of the earthen mound of the First Emperor's tomb. No one can help but be surprised by this impressive picture. It must be a scene found in heaven – what a rare chance to discover it in this world!

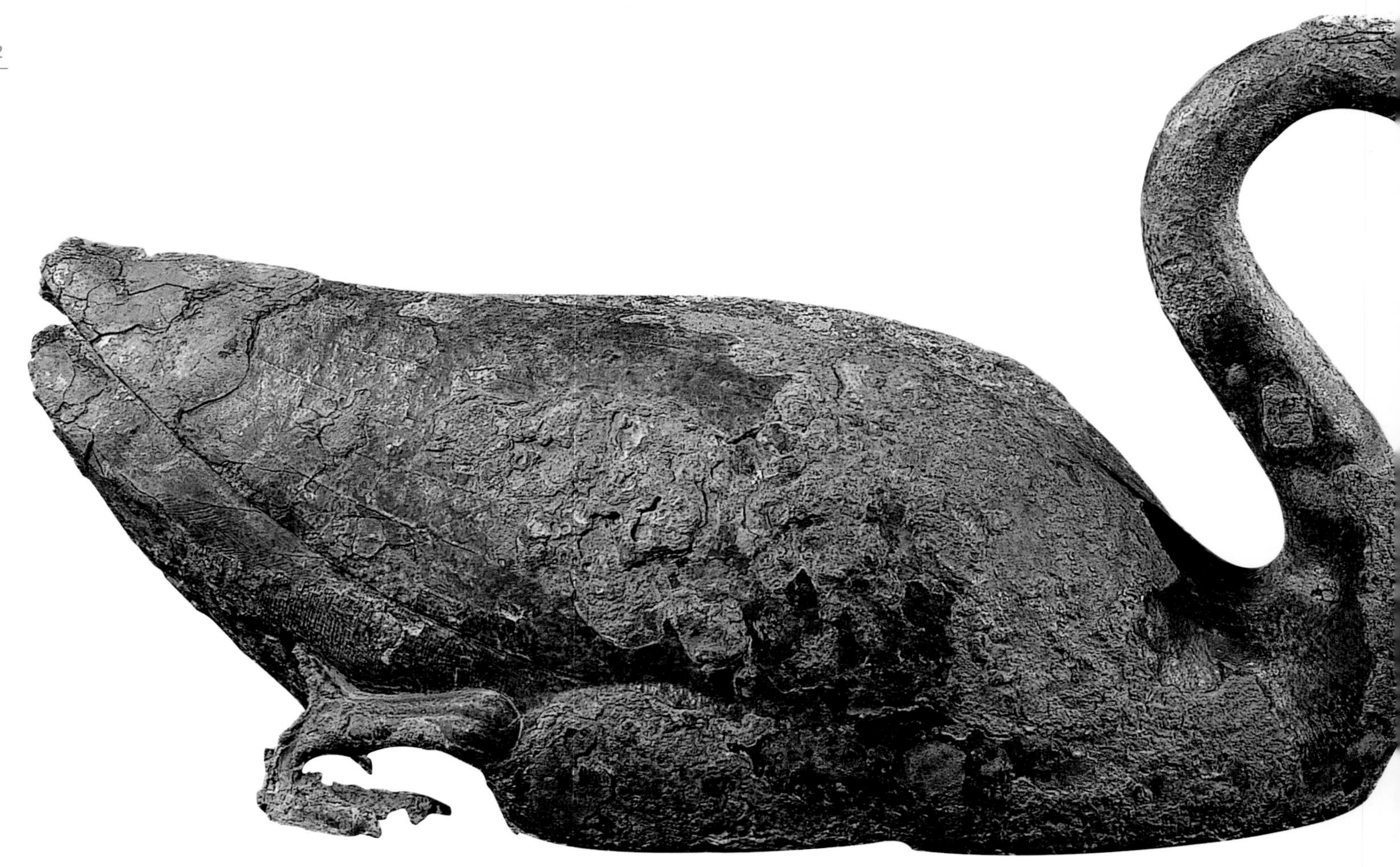

FIG. **194**
(right) **Bronze goose excavated from Pit K0007. This goose has been tentatively identified as *Anser cygnoides*, the swan goose, a large brown and white goose from Mongolia that spends the winter in southern China.**
Cat. no. 131

FIG. **195**
(below) **Bronze swan, with painted feathers, excavated from Pit K0007, to the north-east of the First Emperor's tomb mound (see tomb plan, *fig. 131*).**
Cat. no. 130

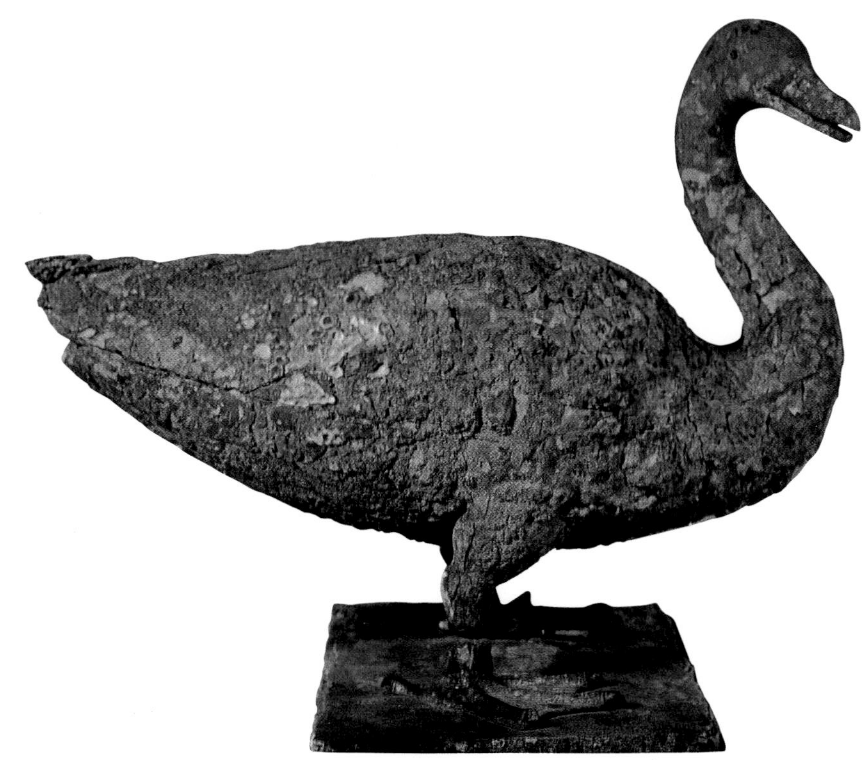

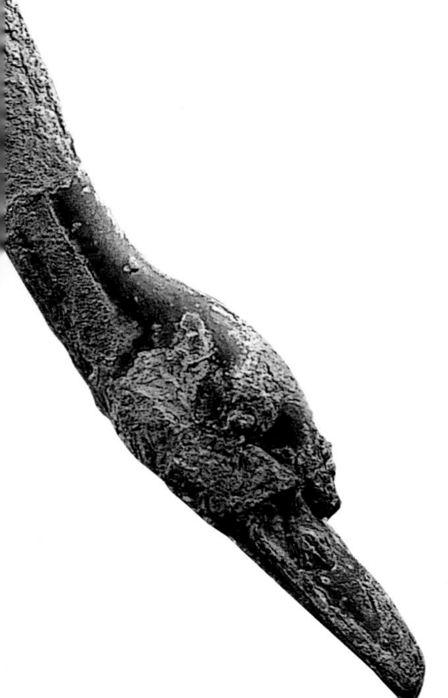

Structure and design of the pit

The sacrificial pit is F-shaped in plan. The underground structure of the pit is lined with planks of wood and measures 925 sq. metres in size. It consists of a sloping passageway and two narrow tunnels running north to south, with a longer one running east to west. The pit was constructed beside a lake, and its location and structure, as well as the artefacts found inside clearly show its relationship with the surrounding water, the waves in the pond encouraging endless poetic images. Situated at the southern bank of a fish pond, the east–west tunnel in the pit and the north–south one on its eastern side parallel the river system above. The structure at the sides of the pit, consisting of pounded earth and wooden planks, is in fact the underground version of the riverbanks above, and the bronze swans, cranes and wild geese are neatly distributed along this riverside. Moreover, an elongated trench representing the riverbed can be found between the two underground riverbanks. Terracotta figures of musicians are placed in niches in the other tunnel of the pit. They are sitting on a mat holding different types of musical instruments in their hands.

The construction of the niches and the whole architectural design imitating the physical form of a river show the creativity of the designers of this pit. The designers also made use of the natural water in the area when the water level of the lake was high. This generated a harmonious atmosphere and perfect interaction between human beings, the water and the birds. Through this can be seen the designers' plan to demonstrate the mutual relationship between humans and nature, and between culture and environment.

FIG. 196
Line drawing of Pit K0007. The water birds were found in the top 'horizontal' area and the musicians in the central 'vertical' area in niches. Forty-six life-size bronze water birds (twenty swans, six cranes and twenty geese) were found along an artificial watercourse about 60 metres long and 1 metre wide.

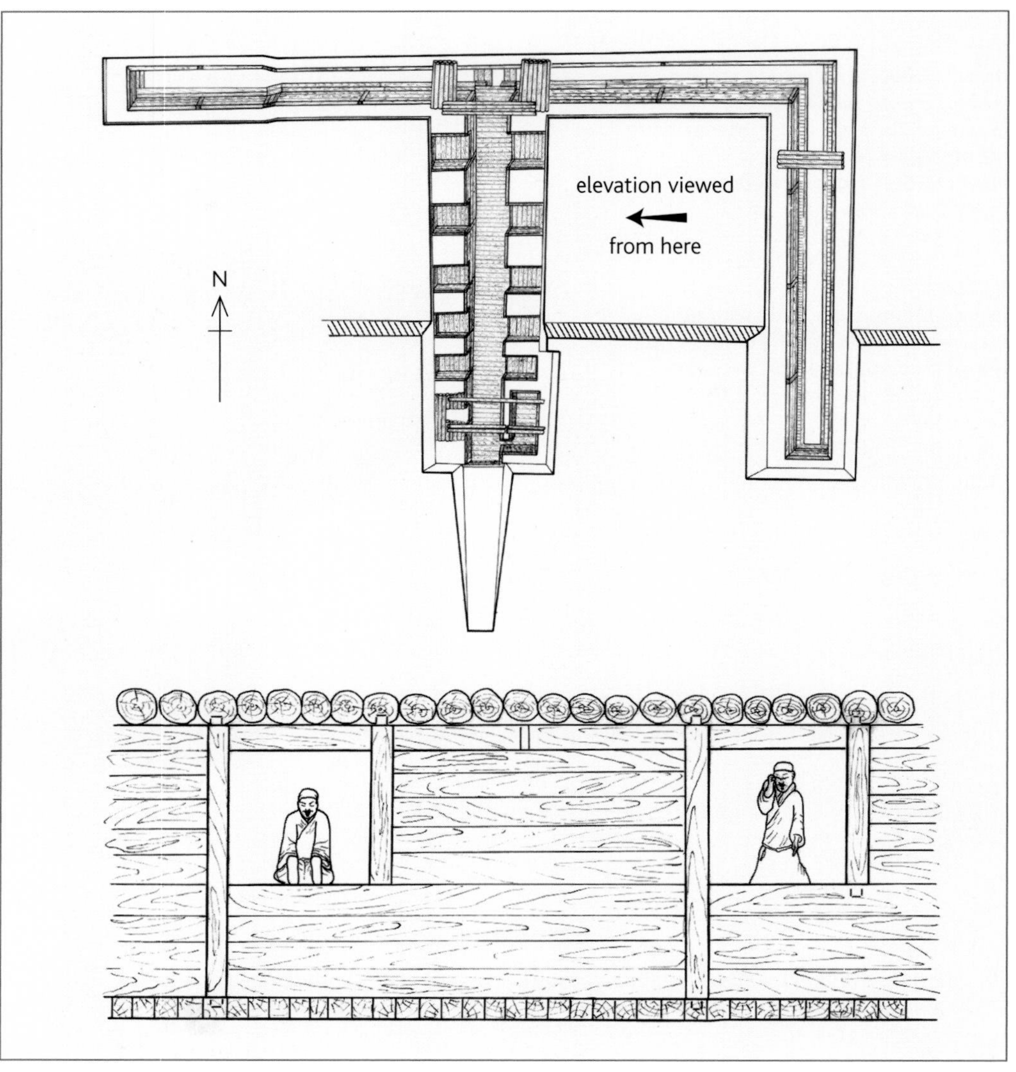

Production and design of the figures

The figures of the fifteen terracotta musicians are as full of charm as real imperial musicians. They were made with very similar techniques to those of the terracotta warriors, acrobats and officials discovered before them. Their production largely followed three steps, namely, shaping the clay sculptures, firing and painting. In the first step different parts of the figures, such as heads, hands and torsos, were made out of clay using the techniques of pressing, moulding and coiling. Next they were covered with a second layer of clay on which the details were carved out, and then the different parts were assembled together. After drying at room temperature, the figure was put into a kiln for firing. The next step was to paint them. Different colours were applied to different parts of the sculptures.

Dressed in painted clothes, with wrinkled foreheads, these figures look fairly old, and they are either indoors or sitting on a mat. Despite the difference in posture, as some of them are kneeling while others are sitting, they are all invariably dressed in the same costume: a soft cloth cap; a long gown with the front closing from the right, which is tucked and tied with a leather waist strap; a hanging

FIG. 197
(opposite) **View of the watercourse inside Pit K0007, showing the swans as they were found.**

FIG. 198
(following pages) **View of Pit K0007 showing the area where the terracotta musicians were found.**

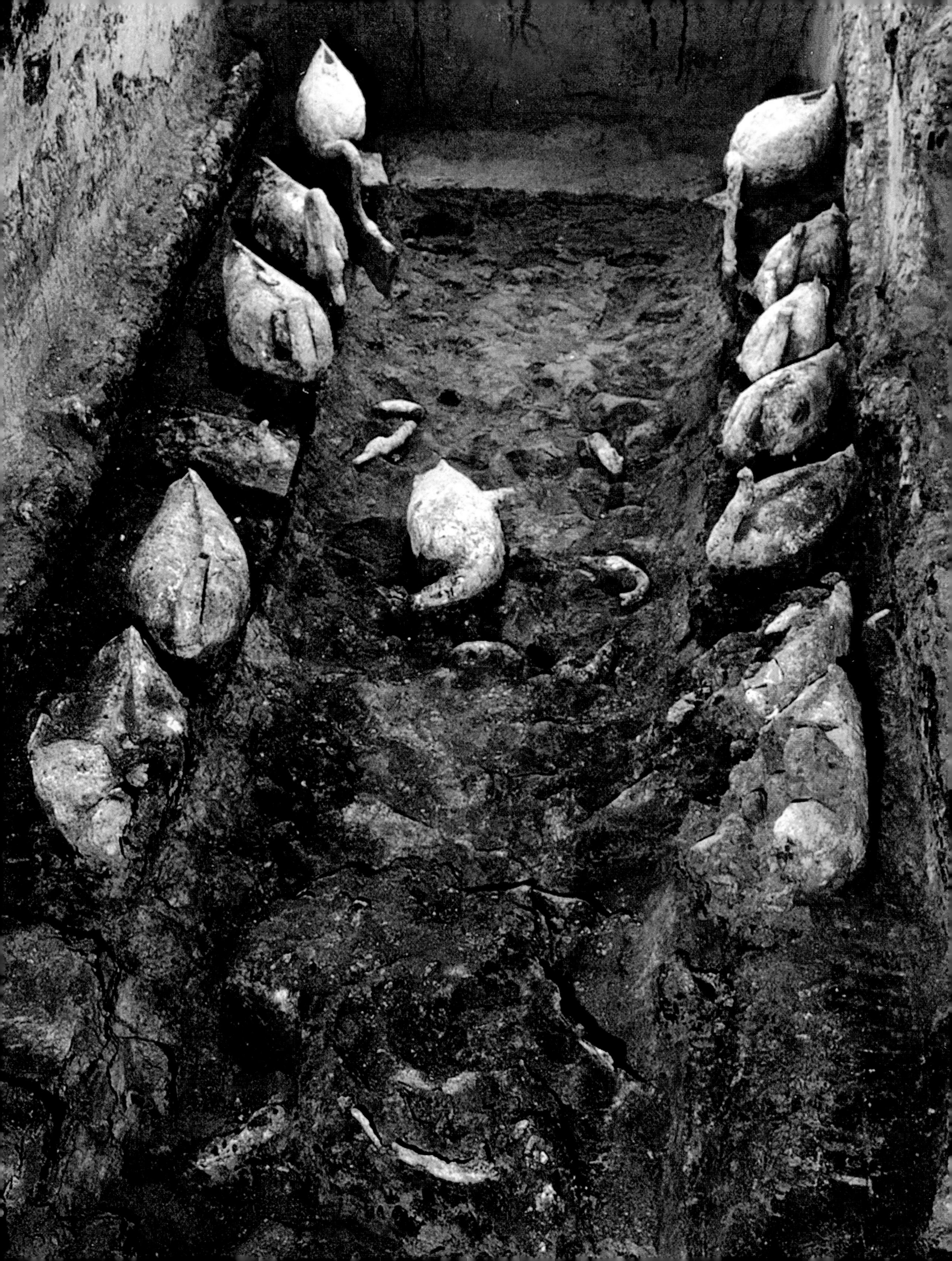

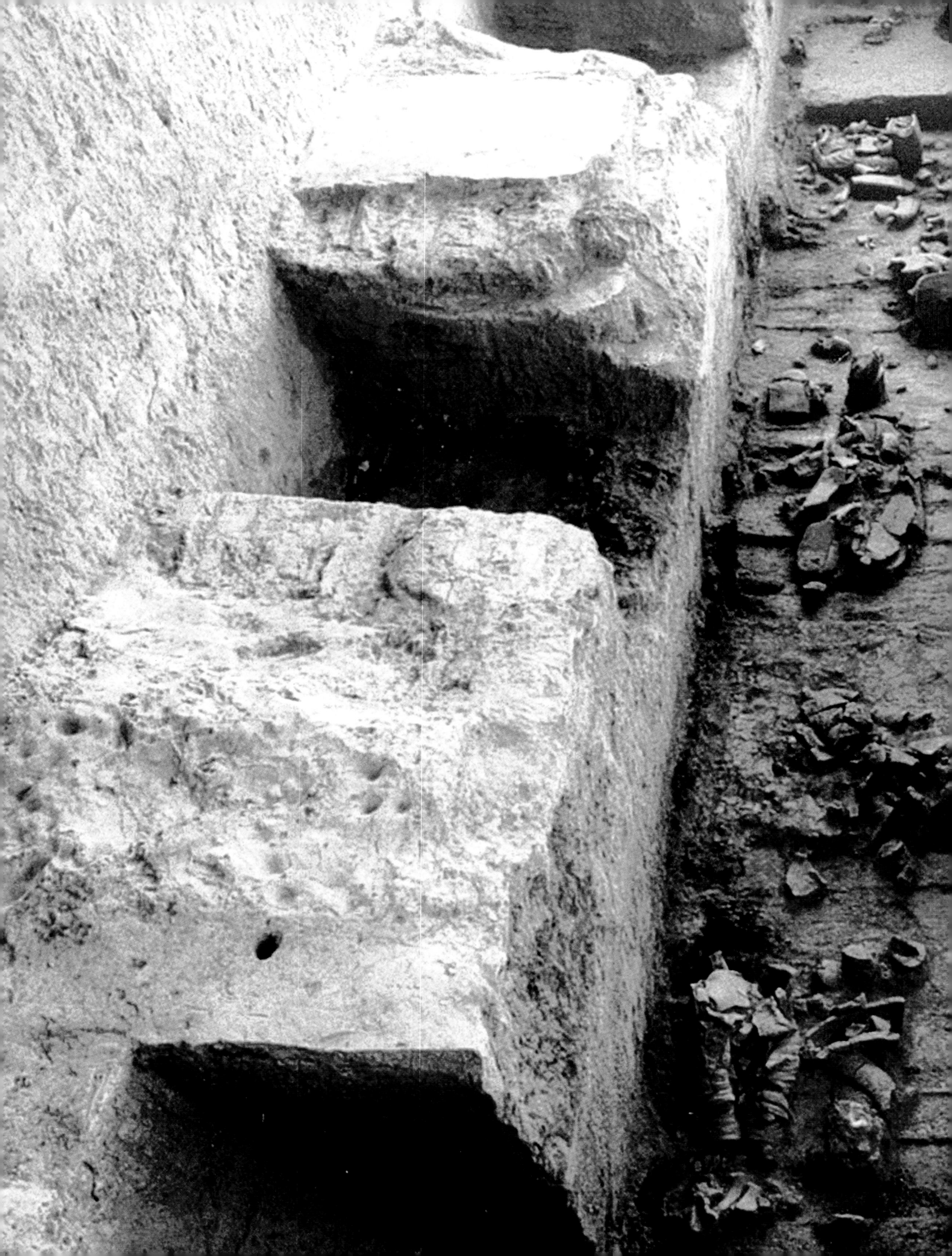

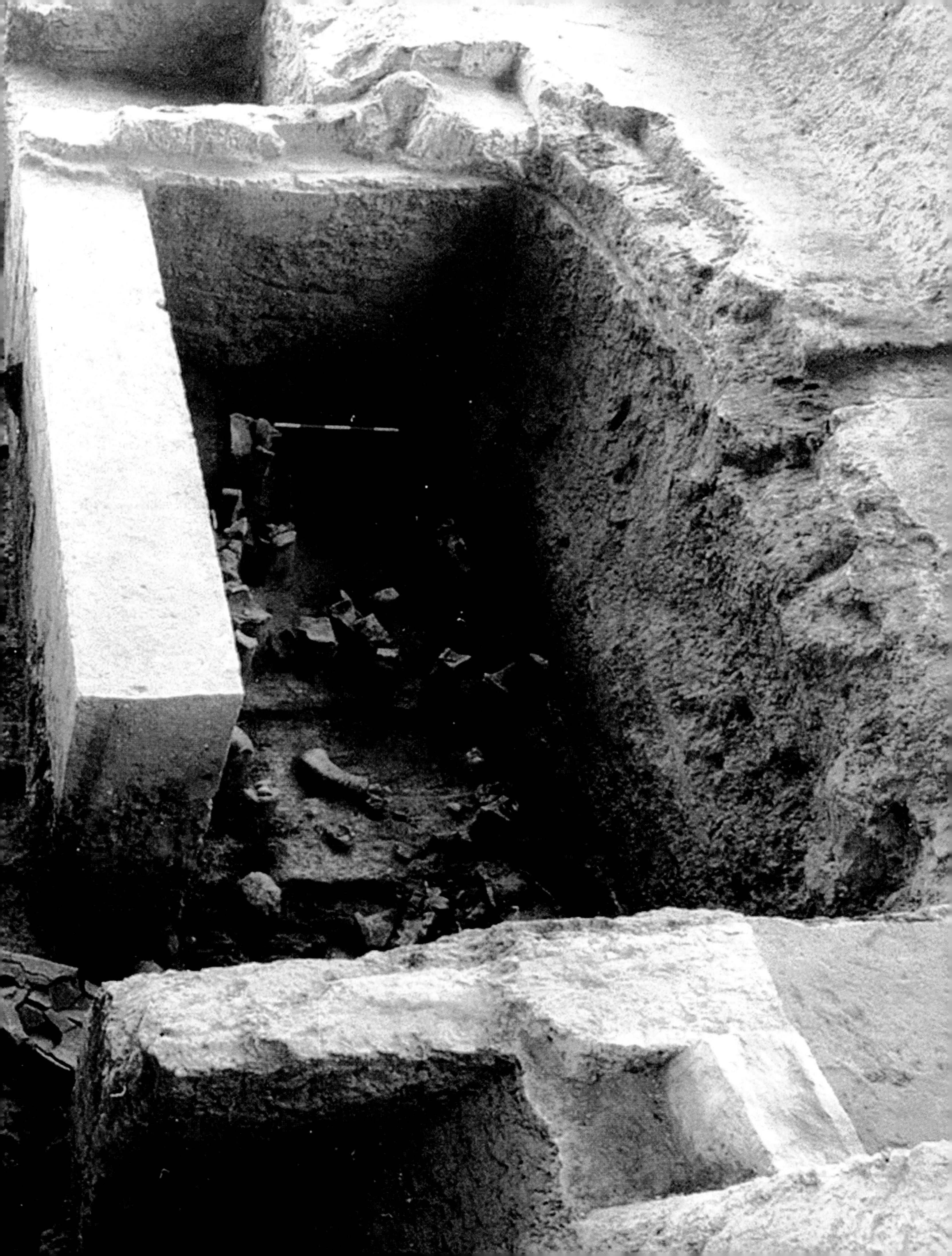

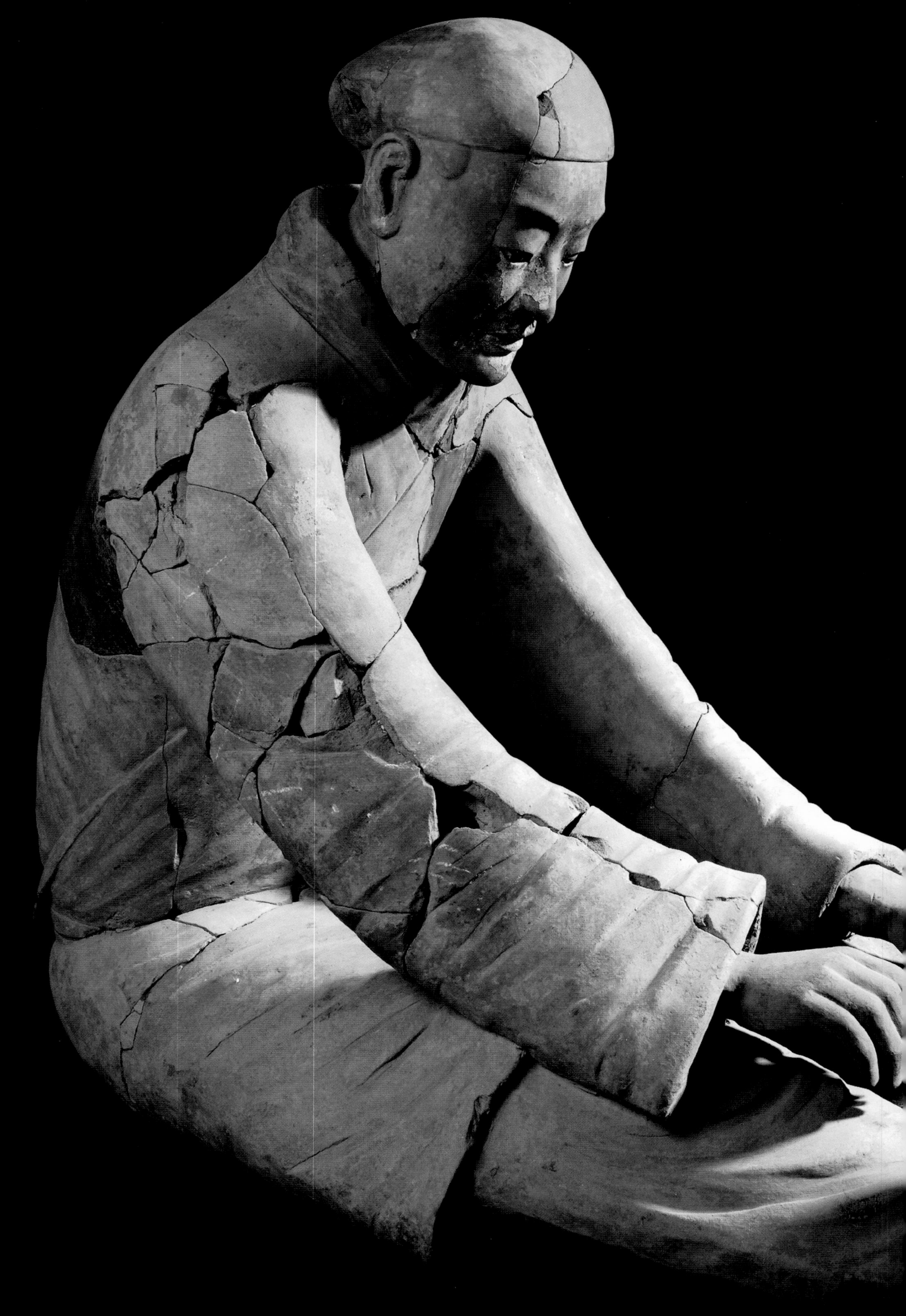

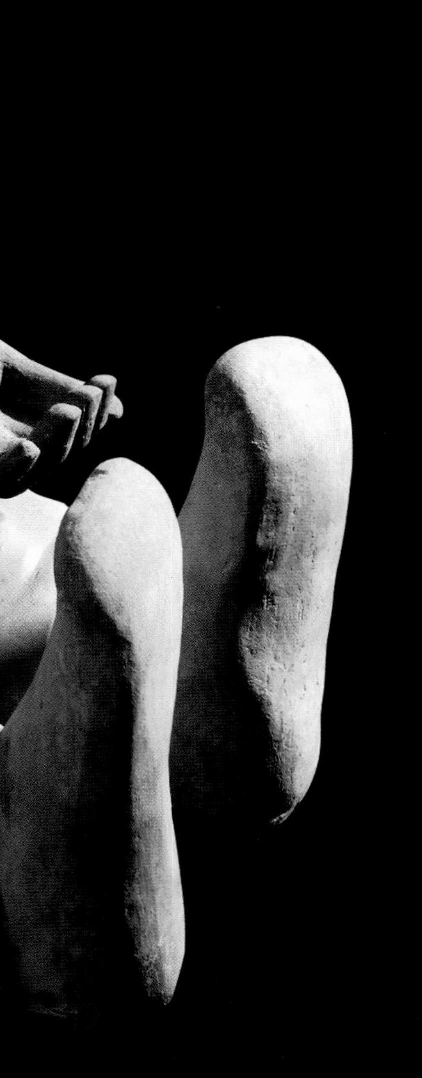

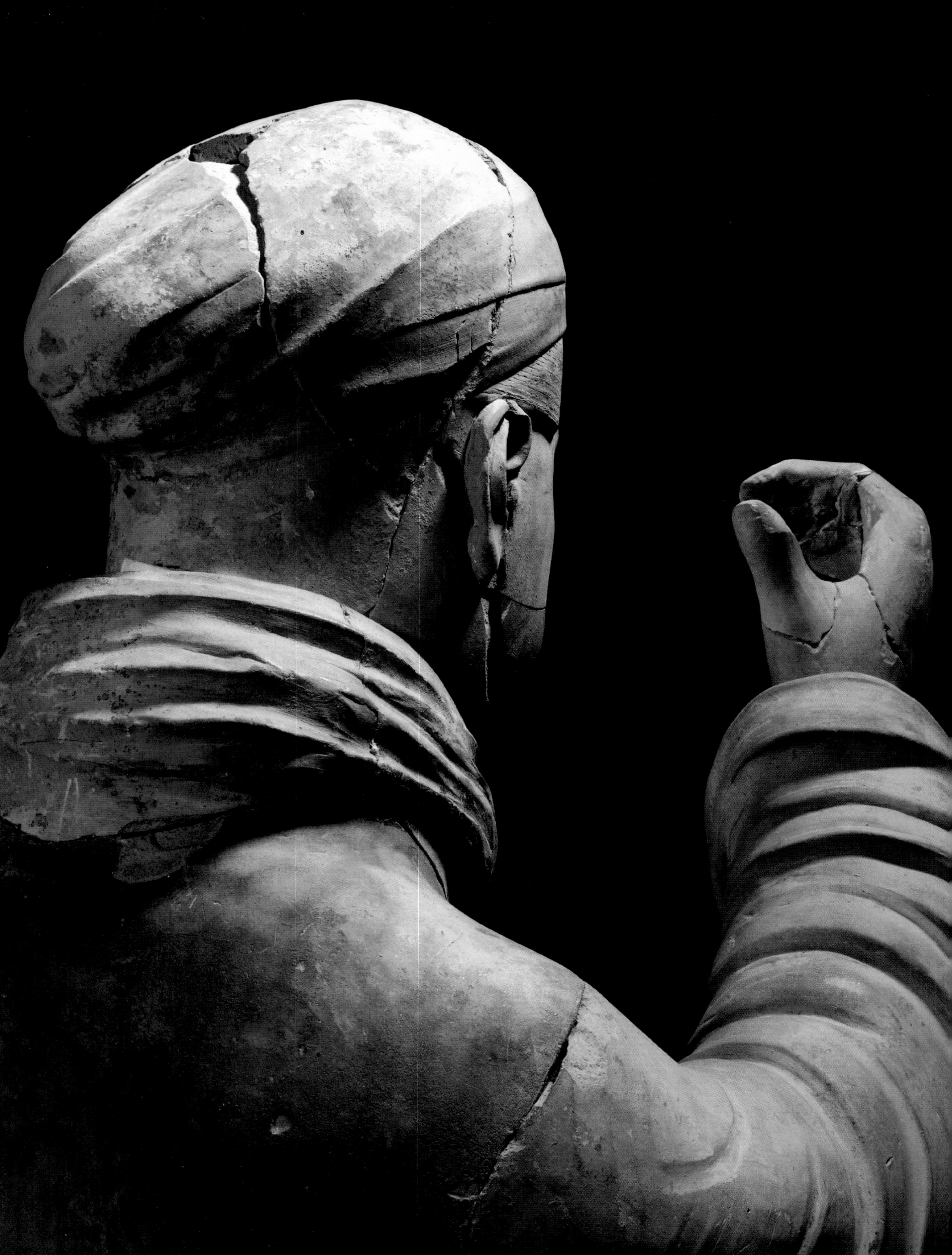

FIG. 199
(preceding pages) **Seated terracotta musician excavated from Pit K0007. It is thought that he played a stringed musical instrument called a *yijia*, similar to a zither. The musicians played to the bronze birds, who danced to the music.**
Cat. no. 132

FIG. 200
(left) **Detail of the back of a kneeling musician excavated from Pit K0007, who seems to be holding a hammer or mallet, perhaps striking a percussion instrument such as a bell or drum. All the musicians were dressed in cloth caps and plain indoor clothes.**
Cat. no. 3

FIG. 201
(following pages) **Bronze crane with painted feathers, excavated from Pit K 0007. This realistic crane with a small fish in its beak was found in the artificial stream.**
Cat. no. 133

rectangular bag; long trousers; and plain socks. This costume suggests that the figures are performing music indoors. The kneeling figures (height 112 cm) hold a mallet in their right hand, which is raised high in the air as though striking a bell or a drum, while their left hand rests on their left thigh (*figs 12 and 200*). The sitting figures (height 86 cm) play the musical instrument called a *yijia*, with their legs lying flat on the floor, arms outstretched above their legs (*fig. 199*). One hand is half closed with the palm upwards, as if holding something with which to strike the instrument, and the other is half closed with the palm downwards, as if plucking the strings or holding a long thin stick with which to strike the strings.

Arrangement of the birds

The forty-six bronze birds are lined up in order. As the pit gets narrower towards the east, the size of the birds gets smaller. Twenty large fat bronze swans with long necks are placed in the west end of the pit (*fig. 195*). The standing ones are 57.5 cm tall, while the lying ones measure 39.5 cm. To their east are six bronze cranes, all 77.5 cm tall and 126 cm long. East of these are twenty bronze wild geese at the point where the tunnel starts to get narrower (*fig. 194*). The standing ones are 40 cm tall and 48 cm long, while the lying ones are 15.2 cm tall and 53 cm long. The swans at the far western end of the pit are the largest in size. The swans are the best preserved, while the cranes are quite seriously damaged, with only a few found intact. The wild geese are basically intact, and the problem of oxidation is not so apparent.

The bronze birds are laid in neat order along the riverbanks with each type displaying different characteristics and positions. In fact, each bird is unique: even birds of the same species are slightly different to each other. Their necks are particularly noteworthy because they show the different gestures of the birds more clearly: some are bent and scavenging in water, others are lying or crouching. Interestingly, one of the bronze cranes is holding a little worm in its beak (*fig. 201*). This creature is frozen at the moment when the crane plucked it from the water, presenting a vivid picture of a bird eating and resting by a river. The bronze birds were made in moulds. When they were unearthed, the pinkish white paint on many of them had survived to differing degrees. On a closer look, one can even observe the careful carving of the feathers of the birds.

Like the other sacrificial pits found within the tomb complex of the First Emperor, Pit K0007 represents one of the offices of the imperial central government. This one provided tame birds for musical performances for the emperor.

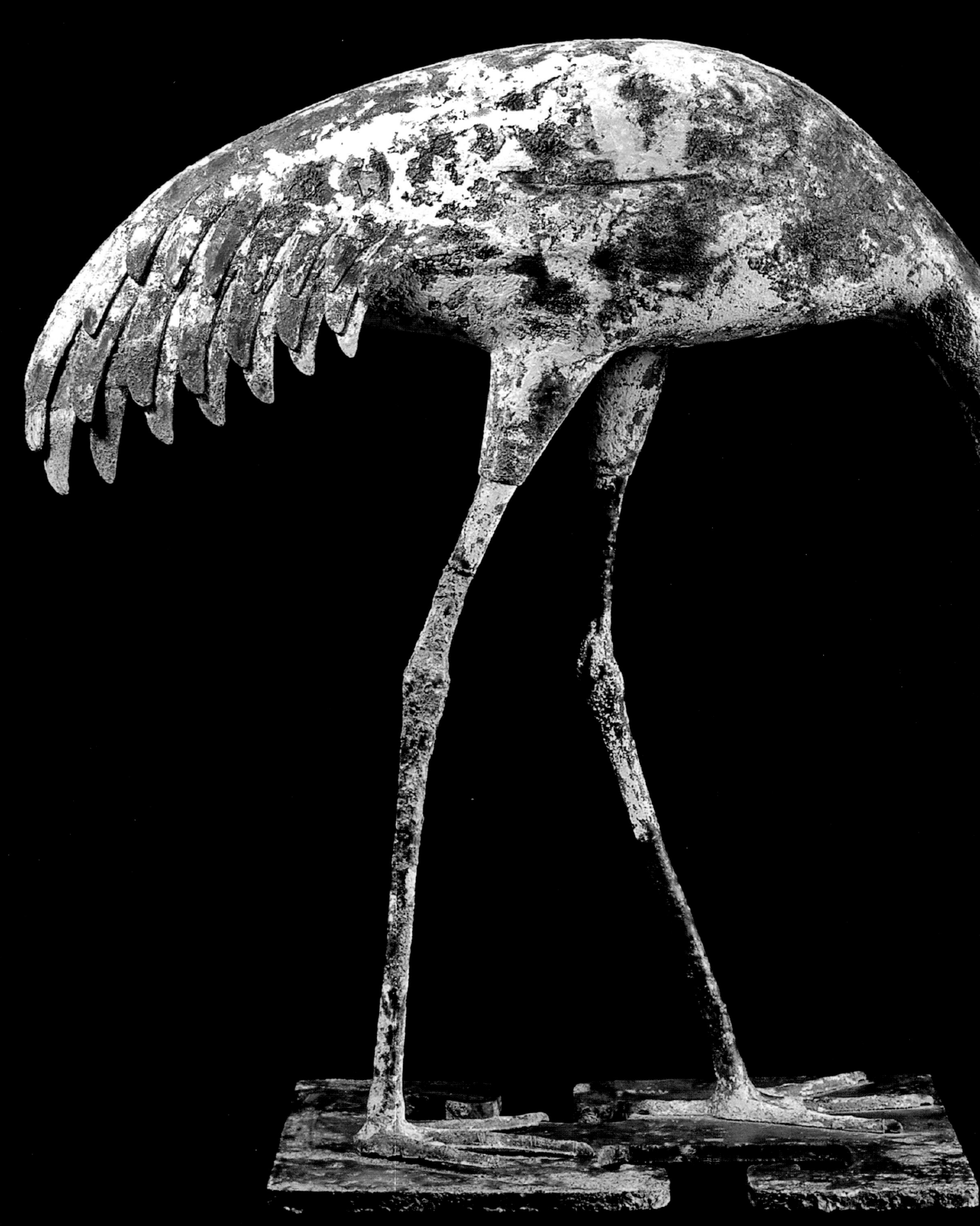

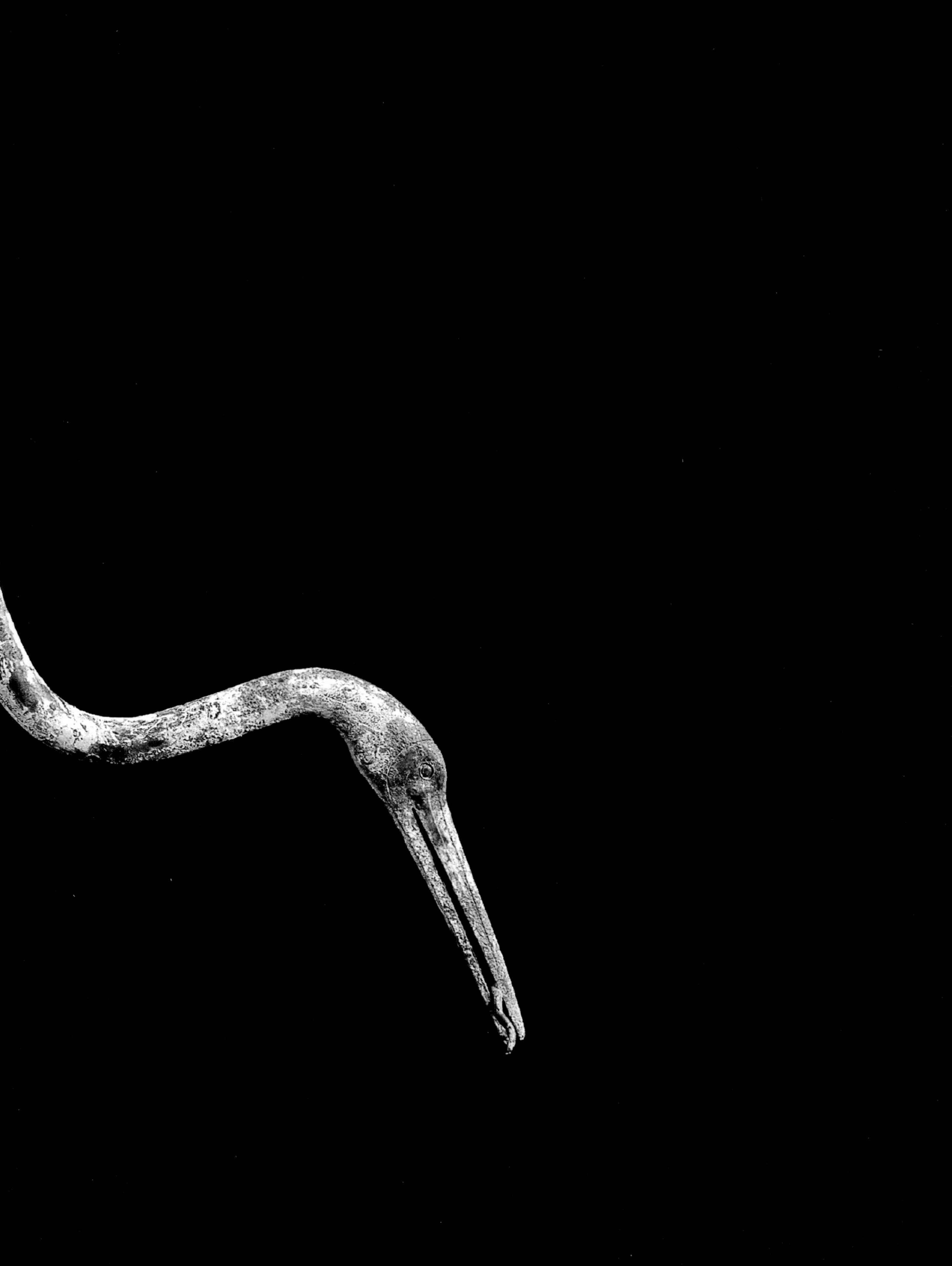

APPENDIX

SCIENTIFIC STUDIES OF THE HIGH LEVEL OF MERCURY IN QIN SHIHUANGDI'S TOMB

DUAN QINGBO

The historian Sima Qian described in his book *Records of the Historian (Shiji)* that the First Emperor's tomb contained a mercury map of his territory. While this has been unchallenged for over two millennia, recent scientific studies have been carried out to investigate the question. The results, in fact, verified Sima's description.

The first scientific study on the tomb mound's mercury level was carried out in the 1980s by the Institute of Geophysical and Geochemical Exploration from the China Institute of Geo-Environment Monitoring. It discovered an area of approximately 12,000 sq. metres in the centre of the mound that had an unusually high level of mercury. In this area the mercury concentration varied between 70 and 1,500 ppb, averaging 250 ppb. In the rest of the tomb mound mercury concentration was less than 70 ppb. Outside the mound mercury concentration varied between 5 and 65 ppb, averaging 30 ppb. These numbers show that the high level of mercury found in the centre of the tomb mound is not natural.[1]

In 2003 two geophysical surveys were again performed. Project 863 measured the level of mercury in the soil as well as the amount of mercury vapour in the gases found in the soil. The former measurement shows the cumulative amount of mercury absorbed by the soil since the tomb was built, while the latter reflects the current amount of mercury in the soil gases. The results affirmed that there is an unusually high level of mercury around the centre of the mound, and that high mercury levels are restricted to the tomb mound area. Once again, these surveys confirmed that there is a large amount of mercury to be found inside the tomb.[2] Moreover, the distribution of mercury level corresponds to the location of waterways in the Qin empire – there is no unusual amount of mercury in the north-west corner of the tomb, while the mercury level is highest in the north-east and second highest in the south.

The use of mercury to show the empire's territory is unique to the tomb of Qin Shihuangdi, and is the biggest difference between this tomb and all the other royal tombs in China. Mercury has been found in royal tombs before Qin Shihuangdi's time, either to act as a preservative for the bodies or as a deterrent to would-be tomb raiders. There had also been a long history of cinnabar and cinnabar-derived mercury usage in ancient China. However, the amount of mercury stored in the First Emperor's tomb is unmatched by any other.

Distribution of mercury concentration in the soil of the tomb mound in 1981.

SUMMARY OF SCIENTIFIC TESTING CARRIED OUT ON THE FIRST EMPEROR'S TOMB TO ADDRESS VARIOUS QUESTIONS

ABOUT THE STRUCTURE OF THE TOMB

Gravity anomaly arises when there is a change in density of the measured medium. Due to the difference in density between compacted earth and natural earth, gravitational-force surveys taken at the centre of the tomb mound confirm the initial excavated area of the First Emperor's underground palace.[3] Furthermore, by using the negative resistivity-survey technique, TEM technique and symmetrical four-pole resistivity-survey technique one can also confirm that the underground palace is located at the centre of the mound.[4] The mound was originally square at the base and is thought to have measured 515 metres north to south and 485 metres east to west. Present measurements are 350 metres north to south and 345 metres east to west.[5]

The plan of the underground palace can be deduced from the signals of the magnetic anomaly. Results show that the shape of the magnetic anomaly is rectangular, so it is believed that the plan view of the underground palace's main area is rectangular in shape. Using the gravity-inversion method, results show that the cross-section shape of the underground palace's excavated area is like an inverted truncated pyramid. These two features are both found in excavated tombs of the First Emperor's ancestors.[6] Results of a field archaeological survey also conclude that there is a multiple-step soil structure underneath the tomb mound.[7] Thus the structure of the underground palace should be similar to large-scale tomb structures of the Spring and Autumn, Warring States, Qin and Han periods, in that the soil vault has multiple steps and is rectangular in shape.

The results of the magnetic anomaly and the archaeological field surveys show that a perimeter wall, which served as the underground palace's wall, was built with bricks around the inner face of the soil vault. This wall measures 460 metres north to south, 390 metres east to west, and is 4 metres high. On top of the wall there is a 30–40-metre-high enclosing wall made of tamped earth. About half of these walls reach the original ground surface.[8] From known archaeological information, there are

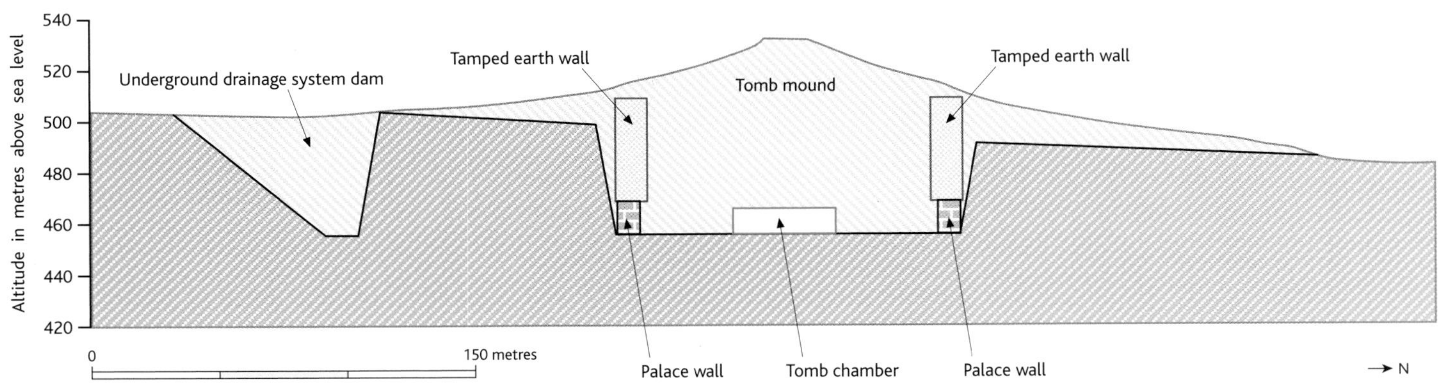

Cross-section of the tomb mound viewed westwards showing the underground palace and tomb chamber.

sloping tomb passageways leading to the four walls of the soil vault; five are on the east side, one on the west side, one on the north side and it is unclear how many are on the south side. Geophysical surveys including resistivity and gravity have confirmed the existence of tomb passages in the east and west. Also it has been found that the east and west sides of the tamped-earth wall were broken off where they were connected to the tomb passages.[9] The main passage is located in the middle of the east side. The tomb is sitting with its back to the west. The west tomb passage is rather special as it is connected to a large E-shaped accompanying pit (*fig. 131*) which contained the half-size bronze chariots and horses. The sloping passageway of this pit leads to the surface.[10]

The dimensions and the depth of the underground palace can be deduced by combining different types of physical tests and analyses:

- The tomb chamber (including any stone tomb passageways) is 80 metres long east to west, and 50 metres wide north to south. It is about 15 metres high.
- The compacted soil wall measures 145 metres east to west, and 125 metres north to south. At its highest point, the wall is 15 metres wide. Overall the wall is just over 30 metres high.

The underground palace excavated area is about 170 metres long from east to west, 145 metres wide north to south and about 30 metres deep. Due to magnetic interference, the above readings may have errors of up to 10%.[11]

MAKING THE UNDERGROUND PALACE WATERPROOF

In the *Records of the Historian* (*Shiji*), Sima Qian mentioned that the underground palace 'passes through three-springs'. In ancient times 'three-springs' referred to groundwater. This means that during construction the tomb had reached the water table. Modern-day scientific measurements suggest that the water table is at a depth of 30 metres. So, how did the palace prevent water from leaking in? Many ancient texts record methods of sealing the underground palace.

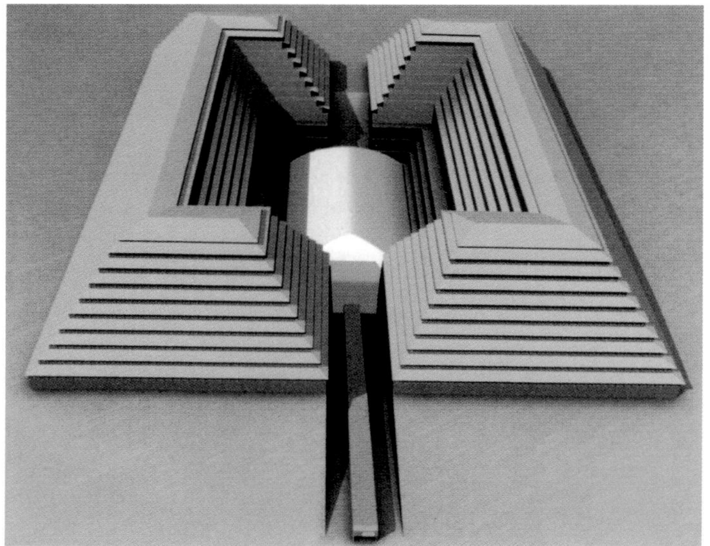

3-D reconstruction of the underground palace.

For example, one text *Shuijing* mentions laying stones or stone slabs and painting their surfaces with red lacquer in order to make them watertight and moisture-proof.[12]

In 2000 a team of archaeologists discovered an underground dam and drainage system in the tomb complex area. The system consists of an eastern and western part. The channel in the east measures 778 metres in length. It is U-shaped and encloses the southern part of the mound. The channel in the west is 186 metres long and its eastern end is joined to the eastern channel.[13] The main function of this drainage system was to prevent surface and ground water from penetrating the underground palace when it was being constructed. After the underground palace was built, the U-shaped channel was refilled with grey mud and tamped earth. This formed an underground dam to stop the underground water flowing back to the palace.[14]

The inversion results of Surface Nuclear Magnetic Resonance (SNMR) show that within the tomb chamber and the underground palace area, no water was detected at the depth of the palace, but the southern side of the drainage system has water. Therefore according to these measurements, the archaeological team deduces that the tomb chamber has not been flooded, and that the drainage system still functions properly. Natural Electric Field technique was used to measure the groundwater flow rate and direction. The results illustrate that the drainage system is still sealing water today.[15]

HAS THE TOMB CHAMBER COLLAPSED?

The resistivities of air and wood are much higher than soil, so this parameter can be used to determine whether the tomb chamber has collapsed. The resistivity survey suggests that a void or wooden structure exists underneath the tomb mound. In addition, as underground radon gas escapes through cracks, low detection levels of radon gas indicate areas with inactive development of cracks. A low level was recorded above the tomb chamber, so it is reasonable to conclude that cracks have not advanced above the tomb chamber and that the main body of the tomb chamber has not collapsed.[16]

IS THERE METAL IN THE UNDERGROUND PALACE?

When the resistivity measurement technique was applied to locate the tomb chamber and measure its depth, a weak phase anomaly was detected. Phase anomaly is usually caused by electrical conductors such as metals, metal-sulphide ore and graphite. So, it is possible that the phase anomaly in the underground palace could indicate the existence of mercury or metal or both. At present, we cannot differentiate between them.[17]

HAS THE UNDERGROUND PALACE BEEN LOOTED?

At present, tomb robbing on a small scale has been discovered around the perimeter of the mound and the outer surface of the underground palace. However, the damage done by robbing cannot be judged precisely. Because the First Emperor's underground palace is large and is buried deep into the ground, and the mound is very thick, it would be difficult for tomb robbers to reach the area where the coffin was placed. Since the mound is still well preserved, it cannot be proved that Xiang Yu robbed the imperial mausoleum after the death of the First Emperor. Also, the underground palace still has stronger than normal mercury levels. The high level of mercury is concentrated and follows a regular pattern. These facts suggest that the mercury in the underground palace has not been subjected to large scale disturbance and burning. However, scattered ashes, fired earth, broken bricks, and tile fragments were found within the tomb complex area, suggesting that the above-ground buildings in the tomb complex area were burned at the end of Qin dynasty.[18]

GLOSSARY OF CHINESE CHARACTERS

Anyi 安邑

Ba 巴
Bai Qi 白起
Bai ze tu 白澤圖
banliang 半兩
Baoji 寶鷄
Baopuzi 抱樸子
ba shen 八神
Bayi 八一
Beidi 北地
Beijing 北京
ben 畚
bi 璧
bian dian 便殿
bian fa 變法
Bianjiazhuang 邊家莊
bo 鎛
Bochang 博昌
boshi 博士
bu (unit) 布
bu (pace) 步
bugeng 不更
bu si 不死

Chahai 查海
Chang'an 長安
Changling 長陵
Changping 長平
Chencang 陳倉
Chezhang 車張
chi 尺
Chiang Kaishek 蔣介石
Chu 楚
Chunqiu 春秋
chunyu 錞於
Chuxueji 初學記
cong 琮
Congshu jicheng chubain 叢書集成初編
Cuo (king)
cun 寸
cuo ba jinzhong dang tongling 錯把金鐘當銅鈴

Dai 軑
Daimiao 岱廟
dan 石
digong 地宮
ding 鼎
Dongting 洞庭
dou 鬥
dou (unit) 斗
Du Mu 杜牧
dun 鐓
Dunhuang 敦煌

Ebang 阿房
Ebang gong fu 阿房宮賦
Erlitou 二里头
Ershi 二世

fa 法
Fangmatan 放馬灘
Fangzhang 方丈
feng 封
Feng 豐
fengchang 奉常
Fenggeling 鳳閣嶺
Fenghuang shan 鳳凰山
Fengxiang 鳳翔
Fuping 富平
Fu Sheng 伏勝
Fu Su 扶蘇

Ganquan 甘泉
Ganquan gong 甘泉宮
Gansu 甘肅
Gaonu 高奴
Gaoyao 高窯
Gaozhuang 高莊
Ge 個
ge 戈
geng fa 更法
gong 工
gong (palace) 宮
gongcheng 公乘
gongjiang 工匠
Gongli 宮裏
gongshui 宮水
gongsikong 宮司空
Gongsun Yang 公孫鞅
Guangdong 廣東
Guanghan 廣漢
Guangzhou 廣州
Guo Moruo 郭沫若
Guoyu 國語
Guyang 固陽

Han (dynasty) 漢
Handan 邯鄲
Han Fei 韓非
Hanfeizi 韓非子
Han (state) 韓
Han Wudi 漢武帝
Hao 鎬
Hebei 河北
Henan 河南
heng 珩
Hohhot 呼和浩特
Hongshan 紅山
Hong Shidi 洪世滌
Houma 侯馬
Hsiao I-shan 蕭一山
Huai 淮
Huainan wanbishu 淮南萬畢術
Huangdi (Yellow Emperor) 黃帝
huangdi 皇帝
Huangshan Palace 黃山宮
Hubei 湖北
Hui (duke) 蕙
Huiwen Wang 惠文王

ji 戟
Jian (duke) 簡公
Jiangsu 江蘇
Jia Yi 賈誼
Jiayuguan 嘉峪關
Jie 詰
Jie 介
Jieshi 碣石
Jieshi *men* 碣石門
Jimiao 極廟
jin 斤
Jin 晉
Jing 荊
Jing (River) 涇
Jing (duke) 景
Jingdi 景帝
Jing Ke 荊軻
Jinyu 晉語
Jiuyi 九疑
jue 爵
jun 郡

kaogong 考工
Kongzi (Confucius) 孔子
Kuaiji 會稽
kui 葵
kuiwen 夔紋

Langye 琅邪
Laozi 老子
Lei 雷
Liangzhu 良渚
Lian Po 廉頗
Liaoning 遼寧
Lidai diwang xiang 歷代帝王像
Li Kui 李悝
Lintong 臨潼
Liquan 禮泉
Lishan 驪山
Li Si 李斯
Liu An 劉安
Liu Bang 劉邦
Liujiagou 劉家溝
Liu Lexian 劉樂賢
Liu Xiu 劉修
Liu Sheng 劉勝
Liu Zongyuan 柳宗元
Longxi 隴西
Longxian 隴縣
Lu 魯
Lü Buwei 呂不韋
Luoyang 洛陽

Mancheng 曼成
mao 矛
Mao Zedong 毛澤東
Mawangdui 馬王堆
mazhu 麻洙
Meng Tian 蒙恬
Mengzi (Mencius) 孟子
Ming 明
mingshan dachuan 名山大川

Nantou 南頭
Nanyue 南越
Nanzhihuicun 南指揮村

pei 珮
Penglai 蓬萊
pi 鈹
Ping 平
Pingyang 平陽

Qi 齊
qi 氣
qian 錢
qian (neck iron) 鉗
qianshou 黔首
Qijia 齊家
Qin 秦

qin 寢
Qing 清
Qin Gong 秦公
Qinjing 秦井
Qin Shihuangdi 秦始皇帝
Qin Shihuang benji 秦史皇本紀
Qiyuan 漆垣
Qu 詘
quan 權

Rong 戎
ru 儒

San 傘
Sancai tuhui 三才圖會
Sanqiao 三橋
Sanxingdui 三星堆
Shaanxi 陝西
shan 禪
Shandong 山東
Shang 商
Shangguodian 上郭店
Shangjiaocun 上焦村
Shang jun shu 商君書
Shanglin 上林
Shangquan 上泉
Shang Yang 商鞅
Shanxi 山西
shaofu 少府
Shen Buhai 申不害
sheng 升
Shi 詩
shi (authority) 勢
shi (arrow) 矢
Shibeidi 石碑地
shi guan 食官
Shihuangdi 始皇帝
Shiji 史記
Shijiaying xiang 石家營鄉
shi jie 屍解
Shu 蜀
Shu 書
shu (govt) 術
shu (macehead) 殳
shuide 水德
Shuihudi 睡虎地
Shuijing 水經
Shun 舜
Shundian 舜典
Sichuan 四川
Sima Qian 司馬遷
Sima Tan 司馬談
Sofugawa Hiroshi 曾布川寬
Song 宋
Sui 隋
Suizhou 隨州
Sun Bin 孫臏
Sunjia 孫家
Sunzi 孫子

Ta'erpo 塔兒坡
Tai 泰
Tai'an 泰安
Taigong 太公
Taiping yulan 太平禦覽
taishanghuang 太上皇
taishi ling 太史令
Tan Dun 譚盾
Tang 唐
taotie 饕餮
tingwei 廷尉
Toufu village 豆腐村

wang 望
wang (king) 王
Wang Mang 王莽
Wang-hsiang 魍象
Wayaotou 瓦窯頭
Wei (river) 渭水
Wei 魏
wei 尉
Weijiaya 魏家崖
Wei Yang 衛鞅
wen 文
Wey 衛
Wolong 臥龍
wu (military) 武
Wu (duke) 武
Wu 吳
wu 伍
wu daifu 五大夫
wu de 五德
Wuhan 武漢
Wuling 武靈

Xi
xi 觿
Xia 夏
Xi'an 西安
xian 縣
Xian (duke) 獻
xiang 象
Xiang Yu 項羽
Xianyang 鹹陽
Xiao (duke) 孝
Xin 新
Xinfengzhen 新豐鎮
Xingping 興平
Xingyuan 杏園
Xiongnu 匈奴
Xun Qing 荀卿
xunshou 巡守
Xunzi 荀子

Yan 燕
Yanchuan 延川
yang 陽
Yannan 晏南
Yangling 楊陵
Yanxiadu 燕下都
Yanzhaicun 宴寨村
Yaodian 堯典
Yaowangdong 藥王洞
Yi (Marquis) 乙
Yi (Mt.) 嶧
yijia 義甲
Yimen 益門
Yin 殷
Ying Fusu 嬴扶蘇
Ying Huhai 嬴胡亥
Ying Zheng 嬴正
Yingzhou 瀛洲
Yiwen leiju 藝文類聚
Yixian 易縣
yong (bell) 甬
Yong 雍
Yongmen 雍門
Youjiazhuang 尤家莊
Yu 禹
Yu (surname) 餘
Yuchi 魚池
Yugong 禹貢
Yuan 元
Yuan Jiang 袁江
Yuan Yao 袁耀
Yuchi 魚池
Yue 越
yue fu 樂府
Yueyang 櫟陽
Yulin 榆林
Yunmeng 雲夢
Yunyang 雲陽
Zeng 曾
zhang 丈
Zhangjiapo 張家坡
Zhanguo 戰國
Zhang Yimou 張藝謀
Zhao 趙
Zhaobeihu 趙背戶
Zhao Gao 趙高
Zhao Kuo 趙括
Zhang Shoujie 張守節
Zhanguoce 戰國策
Zhaoxiang (king) 昭襄
Zhejiang 浙江
Zheng 政
Zheng Wang 正王
Zhengzhuang 鄭莊
Zhifu 之罘
Zhifu *dongguan* 之罘東觀
Zhihui 指揮
zhong 鍾
zhong pian 中篇
Zhongshan (state) 中山
Zhou 周
Zhouzhi 周至
Zhuangxiang (king) 莊襄
Zhuanxu 顓頊
Zhuangzi 莊子

LIST OF EXHIBITS

1
Kneeling archer
Qin dynasty (221–206 BC)
Terracotta with pigment
h 125 cm, w 74 cm
Excavated in 2001 from Pit No.2
Museum of the Terracotta Warriors and Horses of Emperor Qin Shihuang, Lintong, inv. no. 005506
References: Lanciotti and Scarpari 2006, no. 83; Museum of Qin Shihuang Terracotta Army 1999, nos 114–22; Ledderose and Schlombs 1990, no. 68

2
Inscribed weight (*quan*)
Qin dynasty (221–206 BC)
Bronze
Inscribed with a 40-character imperial edict by the First Emperor, dated 221 BC, and a 60-character imperial edict by the Second Emperor, dated 210 BC
h 9.2cm, d 12.9 cm
Excavated in 1975 from Yanzhaicun just inside the west outer wall of the First Emperor's tomb complex
Museum of the Terracotta Warriors and Horses of Emperor Qin Shihuang, Lintong, inv. no. 002838
References: Yuan Zhongyi 2002, pp. 509–10; Qiu Guangming 1992, pp. 350–2

3
Kneeling musician
Qin dynasty (221–206 BC)
Terracotta
h 112 cm, w 58 cm, d 86cm
Excavated in 2001 from Pit K0007
Shaanxi Provincial Archaeological Institute, Xi'an, inv. no. 006481
References: Bonn 2006, no. 77; Ciarla 2005, pp. 182–3; Shaanxi Institute of Archaeology and Museum of Qin Shihuang Terracotta Army 2005, p. 33

4
Finial (*dun*)
Qin state, 343 BC
Bronze
h 5.25 cm, d 2.3 cm
Inscribed: 十九年大良造庶長鞅之造殳犛鄭 (In the 19th year [343 BC], Shang Yang supervised the making of this *dun*)
Excavated in 1995 from a Qin tomb at Ta'erpo, Xianyang city
Xianyang Institute of Cultural Relics and Archaeology, inv. no. 27063:15
References: Xianyang Cultural Relics Bureau 2002, p. 43; Wang Xueli 1999, pp. 264–7

5
Crossbow trigger mechanism
Qin dynasty (221–206 BC)
Bronze
l 16.3 cm
Excavated in 1975 from Pit 1
Museum of the Terracotta Warriors and Horses of Emperor Qin Shihuang, Lintong, inv. no. 000945
References: Ledderose and Schlombs 1990, no. 86, pp. 314–15; Museum of Qinshihuang Terracotta Army 1999, no. 220; Wang Xueli 1994b, pp. 319–24; Hebei Institute of Cultural Relics 1995, vol. 1, p.105

6
Chariot no. 2
Modern replica
Bronze
l 317cm, h 106.2cm, w 176cm
Museum of the Terracotta Warriors and Horses of Emperor Qin Shihuang, Lintong
References: Ciarla 2005, pp. 144–59; Museum of Qin Shihuang Terracotta Army and Shaanxi Institute of Archaeology 1998; Ledderose and Schlombs 1990, no. 58; Yuan Zhongyi 2002, pp. 119–29

7
Chariot driver
Qin dynasty (221–206 BC)
Terracotta
h 195cm, w 93cm, wt 180 kg
Excavated in 1977 from Pit No.2
Museum of the Terracotta Warriors and Horses of Emperor Qin Shihuang, Lintong, inv. no. 001
References: Ledderose and Schlombs 1990, no. 76; Bonn 2006, no. 34; Museum of Qinshihuang Terracotta Army 1999, no. 105–6

8
War chariot
Modern replica
Wood
l 300 cm, w 200 cm, h 170 cm
Museum of the Terracotta Warriors and Horses of Emperor Qin Shihuang, Lintong
References: Shaanxi Institute of Archaeology and Excavation Team of the Terracotta Army 1988, pp. 208–29

9
Chariot horse
Qin dynasty (221–206 BC)
Terracotta
h 166 cm, l 206 cm, w 51 cm
Excavated in 1977 from Pit 1
Museum of the Terracotta Warriors and Horses of Emperor Qin Shihuang, Lintong, inv. no. 000845
References: Ledderose and Schlombs 1990, nos 70–3; Shaanxi Institute of Archaeology and Excavation Team of the Terracotta Army 1988, pp. 183–92

10
Standing archer
Qin dynasty (221–206 BC)
Terracotta
h 186 cm, w across arms 97 cm, wt 180 kg
Excavated in 1980 from Pit 2
Museum of the Terracotta Warriors and Horses of Emperor Qin Shihuang, Lintong, inv. no. 002817
References: Bonn 2006, no. 28; Ledderose and Schlombs 1990, no. 69

11
Reconstructed crossbow
Wood
l 105 cm, w 72 cm
Museum of the Terracotta Warriors and Horses of Emperor Qin Shihuang, Lintong
References: Ledderose and Schlombs 1990, no. 87; Wang Xueli 1994b, pp. 319–24

12
Dagger-axe (*ge*)
Qin state, 221 BC
Bronze
L. 27.1 cm
Inscribed: 二十六年_ _ 守 _ _ 造， 西工室閹，工_ (26th year of the reign of Ying Zheng, King of Qin [221 BC])
Excavated in 1978 from Fenggeling, Baoji County
Baoji Municipal Bronze Ware Museum, inv. no. IAB–121
References: Museum of Qin Shihuang Terracotta Army 1999, no. 217; Wang Xueli 1994b, pp. 279–95

13
Ten arrowheads
Qin dynasty (221–206 BC)
Bronze
l 16.5–20 cm
Excavated in 1976 from Pit 1
Museum of the Terracotta Warriors and Horses of Emperor Qin Shihuang, Lintong, inv. no. 002565
References: Yuan Zhongyi 1990, pp. 177–84; Wang Xueli 1994b, pp. 313–19

14
Spearhead (*mao*)
Qin dynasty (221–206 BC)
Bronze
l 19.3 cm
Excavated in 1977 from Pit No.1
Museum of the Terracotta Warriors and Horses of Emperor Qin Shihuang, Lintong, inv. no. 004554
References: Yuan Zhongyi 1999, nos 218 & 219; Yuan Zhongyi 1990, p. 171; Wang Xueli 1994b, pp. 273–8, 285–95

15
Sword (*jian*)
Qin dynasty (221–206 BC)
Bronze
l (overall) 92.9 cm, blade 75 cm
Excavated in 1976 from Pit 1
Museum of the Terracotta Warriors and Horses of Emperor Qin Shihuang, Lintong, inv. no. 00865
References: Museum of Qin Shihuang Terracotta Army 1999, no. 213; Wang Xueli 1994b, pp. 325–42

16
Lance head (*pi*)
Qin state, 232 BC
Bronze
l (overall) 35.4 cm, blade 24.2 cm
Inscribed on the blade: 十九年寺工邦工目 (19th year [232 BC]. Government Workshops, produced by Master Bang, worker Mu)
Excavated in 1976 from Pit 1
Museum of the Terracotta Warriors and Horses of Emperor Qin Shihuang, Lintong, inv. no. 00856
References: Yuan Zhongyi 1990, p. 197, fig. 108.3; Ledderose 2000, p. 60–1; Wang Xueli 1994b, pp. 296–311

17
Cavalryman
Qin dynasty (221–206 BC)
Terracotta
h 184 cm, wt 180 kg
Excavated in 1977 from Pit 2
Museum of the Terracotta Warriors and Horses of Emperor Qin Shihuang, Lintong, inv. no. 002763
References: Ledderose and Schlombs 1990, no. 66; Wang Xueli 1994b, 143–66

18
Tiger-shaped tally
Warring States period (475–221 BC)
Bronze inlaid with gold
l 9 cm
Inscribed: 甲兵之符，左在皇帝，右在東郡 (Fu of the armoured forces; the left half to the emperor, the right half with the eastern commandery)
Excavated in 1953 from Zhouzhi county, Xi'an city
Zhouzhi County Administration of Cultural Heritage, inv no. ZXL0430
References: Wu Yongqi et al. 2004, p. 79; Ledderose and Schlombs 1990, no. 83

19
Massive tripod food vessel (*ding*)
Warring States period, 5th century BC, Jin state
Bronze
h 61 cm, d (mouth) 71 cm
Excavated in 1998 from Pit K9901
Museum of the Terracotta Warriors and Horses of Emperor Qin Shihuang, Lintong, inv. no. DM: 009
References: Ciarla 2005, p. 171; Excavation Team of the First Emperor's Tomb 2001a, pp. 65–7, pl. 8.3; Yuan Zhongyi 2002, pp. 501–4

20
Ritual mace heads (*shu*)
Qin dynasty (221–206 BC)
Bronze
h 10.7 cm, d 2.5 cm
Excavated in 1977 from Pit 3
Museum of the Terracotta Warriors and Horses of Emperor Qin Shihuang, Lintong, inv. no. 001923, 001924
References: Yuan Zhongyi 1990, p. 172; Ledderose and Schlombs 1990, no. 91

21
Percussion instrument (*chunyu*)
Late Warring States period, 3rd century BC
Bronze
h 69.6cm, circumference at waist 88 cm and base 118 cm
Excavated in 1979 from Ta'erpo, Xianyang
Xianyang Municipal Museum, inv. no. 5–1487
References: Wang Xueli 1994b, p. 74; Chang Tao 1996, p. 146; Li Xixing 1994, no. 239

22
Battle bell (*yong*)
Qin dynasty (221–206 BC)
Bronze
h 26.3 cm, w 12.8cm, thickness 10.4 cm
Excavated in 1997 from Pit 1
Museum of the Terracotta Warriors and Horses of Emperor Qin Shihuang, Lintong, inv. no. 002811
References: Ledderose and Schlombs 1990, no. 84; Museum of Qin Shihuang Terracotta

Army 1999, no. 224; Bonn 2006, no. 35; Shaanxi Institute of Archaeology and Excavation Team of the Terracotta Army 1988, vol. 1, p. 229

23
Cavalry horse
Qin dynasty (221–206 BC)
Terracotta
h 174 cm, l 240 cm (including tail), w 45 cm, wt 340 kg
Excavated in 1977 from Pit 2
Museum of the Terracotta Warriors and Horses of Emperor Qin Shihuang, Lintong, inv. no. 003160
References: Lanciotti and Scarpari 2006, no. 81; Ledderose and Schlombs 1990, no. 67; Wang Xueli 1994b, 143–66

24
Official
Qin dynasty (221–206 BC)
Terracotta
h 185 cm
Excavated in 2000 from pit K0006
Shaanxi Provincial Archaeological Institute, Xi'an, inv. no. 001172
References: Ciarla 2005, pp. 162–4; Shaanxi Institute of Archaeology and Museum of Qin Shihuang Terracotta Army 2006, pp. 65–95; Excavation Team of the First Emperor's Tomb 2002

25
Bells (*zhong*)
Spring and Autumn period (697–678 BC)
Bronze
h 48 cm, w 27 cm, depth 18 cm
h 45.7 cm, w 25.4 cm, thickness 16 cm
h 27.6 cm, w 15.2 cm, thickness 10.2 cm
Each inscribed with part of a 135-character text
Excavated in 1978 from Taigong temple, Chencang, Baoji county
Baoji Municipal Bronze Ware Museum, inv. no. IA5.6, IA5.8, IA5.10
References: Kern 2000, pp. 65, 85–6; Chang and Xu et al. 2005, pp. 250–1; Chang Tao 1996, p. 144

26
Light infantryman
Qin dynasty (221–206 BC)
Terracotta
h 193 cm
Excavated in 1980 from Pit 1
Museum of the Terracotta Warriors and Horses of Emperor Qin Shihuang, Lintong, inv. no. 000850
References: Museum of Qin Shihuang Terracotta Army 1999, no. 134; Bonn 2006, no. 31.

27
Garlic-headed vessel (*hu*)
Warring States, 5th–3rd century BC, Qin state
Bronze
h 34.7 cm, d 32.5 cm
Excavated in 1988 from a Qin tomb at Gaozhuang, Fengxiang
Shaanxi Provincial Archaeological Institute, Xi'an, inv. no. 01158
References: Ledderose and Schlombs 1990, no. 18; Wang Xueli et al. 1994, pp. 243–4, 246; Li County Museum 2004, p. 129; Zhongguo Qingtongqi Quanji 1998, nos. 6–7

28
Vessel (*gui*)
Qin state, 222 BC
Bronze
h 15 cm, d of mouth 20 cm, d of base 12.5 cm
Inscribed on the base: 一斗八升, 廿五年造 __ ([capacity of] one *dou* eight *sheng*, made in the 25th year [222 BC])
Found in 1959
Shaanxi Provincial History Museum, inv. no. 56.256
References: Qiu Guangming 1992, pp. 142–3; Lanciotti and Scarpari 2006, no. 44

29
Vessel (*zhong*)
Warring States period (475–221 BC)
Wei state
Bronze
h 56cm, waist circumference 116 cm, d of mouth 19 cm, wt 19.7 kg
Inscribed: 容十三斗一升 (capacity 13 dou 1 sheng); another 27-character inscription describes its capacity and that it was made in Anyi, in the state of Wei.
Excavated in 1966 from Ta'erpo, Xianyang
Xianyang Municipal Museum, inv. no. 5–1073
References: Xianyang Cultural Relics Bureau 2002, p. 45; Qiu Guangming 1992, pp. 146–7

30
Knife
Spring and Autumn period (770–475 BC)
Bronze
l 19 cm, w 2 cm
Excavated in 1977 from Gaozhuang M18, Fengxiang
Shaanxi Provincial Archaeological Institute, Xi'an, inv. no. 004322
References: Bonn 2006, p. 140, nos 2 and 3; Shaanxi Institute of Archaeology 2004, pp. 656–7; Wang Xueli et al. 1994, pp. 245, 247

31
Grindstone
Spring and Autumn period (770–475 BC)
Stone
l 9cm, w 3.5 cm
Excavated in 1986 from Nanzhihuicun, Fengxiang
Shaanxi Provincial Archaeological Institute, Xi'an, inv. no. 000576
References: Bonn 2006, p. 140, no. 4

32
Restraining iron (*qian*)
Qin dynasty (221–206 BC)
Iron
l 17 cm, w 16.5 cm, thickness 2 cm
Excavated from tomb complex
Museum of the Terracotta Warriors and Horses of Emperor Qin Shihuang, Lintong, inv. no. 004564
References: Yuan Zhongyi 2002, p. 544; Ledderose and Schlombs 1990, no. 44

33
Dagger-axe (*ge*)
Qin state, 238 BC
Bronze
Length 26.1cm
Inscribed: Made in the 8th year [238 BC] at orders of Chancellor Lü Buwei)
Found in 1978, Baoji city
Baoji Municipal Bronze Ware Museum, inv. no. IAB–120
References: Li Zhongcao 1979; Wang Xueli 1994b, pp. 279–95; Museum of Qin Shihuang Terracotta Army 1999, no. 217

34
Model of Xianyang Palace No. 1
Modern replica
Wood
l 196 cm, w 116 cm, Height 40 cm
Xianyang Municipal Museum

35
Unarmoured general
Qin dynasty (221–206 BC)
Terracotta
h 197 cm
Excavated in 1988 from Pit 1
Museum of the Terracotta Warriors and Horses of Emperor Qin Shihuang, Lintong, inv. no. 002747 (T1G3.112)
References: Museum of Qin Shihuang Terracotta Army 1999, no. 87

36
Model of granary
Warring States period, Qin state
Pottery
h 20.3 cm, d 10.4 cm
Excavated in 1981 from tomb M7 at Yong city, Fengxiang county
Museum of the Terracotta Warriors and Horses of Emperor Qin Shihuang, Lintong, inv. no. 003113
References: Ciarla 2005, p. 271; Ledderose and Schlombs 1995, no. 25; Wang Xueli et al. 1994, pp. 16–18

37
Seal
Qin dynasty (221–206 BC)
Bronze
Inscribed: __ 遽
l 1.9 cm
Found in 1998 in Xianyang
Museum of the Terracotta Warriors and Horses of Emperor Qin Shihuang, Lintong, inv. no. 005523

38
'Gaonu' weight
Qin state, 244 BC
Bronze
h 17.2 cm, d 23.6 cm, wt 30.75 kg
Cast in relief (pictured): 三年，漆工配，丞誳造，工隸臣平。禾石，高奴。(3rd year [244 BC] managed by Xi of Qi [Qiyuan county], supervised by Qu and made by worker Ping. [wt] 1 *dan* [1 *dan* = 120 *jin* (1 *jin* = 256 g) or 30.75 kg]. [Made in] Gaonu [present-day Yanchuan county, north-east Shaanxi province]. Inscribed on the other side with two imperial edicts of the First Emperor (dated 221 BC), and Second Emperor (dated 210 BC) decreeing the standardization of weights and measures.
Excavated in 1964 from the Ebang Palace site, Gaoyao village, Sanqiao
Shaanxi Provincial History Museum, inv. no. 65
References: Ledderose and Schlombs 1990, no. 55; Shaanxi Provincial Museum 1964; Qiu Guangming 1992, p. 336–7; Wang Xueli 1999, p. 455

39
Plaque with edict
Qin dynasty (221–206 BC)
Bronze
l 12cm, w 6.6 cm, thickness 0.15 cm
Inscribed with an imperial edict, dated 221 BC, decreeing the standardization of weights and measures by the First Emperor
Found in 1957
Shaanxi Provincial History Museum, inv. 176
References: Ciarla 2005, p. 116; Wang Renbo 2001b, p. 12; *note that the provenance in these references is incorrect

40
Bronze vessel (*zhong*)
Qin dynasty (221–206 BC)
Bronze
h 44 cm, d 19 cm
Inscribed on the base:
麗山園，容十二斗三升，重二鈞十三斤八兩 (Lishan Garden [tomb complex of First Emperor], contains 12 *dou* 3 *sheng* [24570 ml], weighs 2 *jun* 3 *jin* 8 *liang* [19.75 kg]
Excavated in 1958 from Angoucun, east of the tomb mound
Lintong County Museum, inv. no. 01966
References: Yuan Zhongyi 2002, pp. 18–19, 504, 507; Wang Xueli 1999, p. 235

41
Half *dou* measure
Qin dynasty (221–206 BC)
Bronze
h 7 cm, l (of mouth) 20.8 cm, w 12.5 cm
Inscribed on its handle with 'Half *dou*' and 北私府, a department in the Qin imperial palace. Its sides are inscribed with the First Emperor's edict of 221 BC and its base with the Second Emperor's edict of 210 BC.
Excavated in 1982 from Yaowangdong, Liquan county
Shaanxi Provincal History Museum, inv. no. 87.1
References: Bonn 2006, no. 6; Wang Renbo 2001, p. 16; Qiu Guangming 1992, pp. 196–7; Li Xixing 1994, no. 209

42
Spade money
Chu state, 4th–3rd century BC
Bronze
l 10.65 cm, w 4 cm; wt 35.71 g
Inscribed on obverse: 柣錢當斤 (spade for circulation, value 1 jin); the reverse with 十貨 (ten *huo*)
British Museum, reg. no. 1913,1011.17
References: Wang Qingzheng 1988, pp. 1048–53, nos 4176–93; Thierry 1997, pp. 245–7, no. 376

43
Spade money
Zhao state, 4th–3rd century BC
Bronze
l 7.4 cm, w 3.6 cm, wt 17.21 g
Inscribed on obverse: 閔(Lin, a place name); the reverse with 五 (five)
British Museum, reg. no. 1996, 0612.22
References: Wang Qingzheng 1988, pp. 563–75, nos 2346–421; Thierry 1997, pp. 208–10, nos 131–8

44
Spade money
Zhao state, 4th–3rd century BC
Bronze
l 5.5 cm, w 3.1 cm, wt 6.01 g
Inscribed on obverse: 兹氏半 (Ci clan, half)
British Museum, reg. no. 1996,0217.18
References: Wang Qingzheng 1988, pp. 286–96, nos 741–99; Thierry 1997, pp. 206–7, nos 112–19

45
Spade money
Wei state, 4th–3rd Century BC
Bronze
l 6.3 cm, w 4 cm, wt 28.24 g
Inscribed: 梁新金斤五十當 (new jin of Liang [a place name], with 50 making 1 lie)
British Museum, reg. no. 1996,0217.32
References: Wang Qingzheng 1988, pp. 394–5, nos 1334–42; Thierry 1997, p. 215, nos 163–4

46
Spade money
Han state, 4th–3rd century BC
Bronze
l 4.9 cm, w 2.8 cm, wt 6.23 g
Inscribed on obverse: 公 (Gong, a place name)
British Museum, reg. no. 1996,0612.21
References: Wang Qingzheng 1988, p. 377, nos 1232–6; Thierry 1997, p. 228, no. 223

47
Spade money
Zhao (?) state, 4th–3rd century BC
Bronze
Inscribed on obverse: 安陽 (Anyang, a place name)
l 4.7 cm, w 3 cm, wt 5.74 g
British Museum, reg. no. 1983.1018.10
References: Wang Qingzheng 1988, pp. 519–30, nos 2083–149; Thierry 1997, pp. 207–8, nos 119–27

48
Knife money
Qi state, 4th–3rd century BC
Bronze
l 18.6 cm, w 2.8 cm, wt 48.39 g
Inscribed: 齊法化 (legal money of Qi)
British Museum, reg. no. 1883,0802.15
References: Wang Qingzheng 1988, pp. 636–72, nos 2589–661; Thierry 1997, pp. 239–40, nos 339–42

49
Knife money
Zhao state, 4th–3rd century BC
Bronze
Inscribed: 柏化 (Bai hua, money of Bairen, a place name)
l 14.4 cm, w 1.8 cm, wt 11.07 g
British Museum, reg. no. 1996,0612.82
References: Wang Qingzheng 1988, pp. 981–2, nos 3888–93; Thierry 1997, p. 203, nos 94–8

50
Knife money
Yan state, 4th–3rd century BC
Bronze
l 13.8 cm, w 1.8 cm
Inscribed: 易刀 (knife of Yi, a place name)
British Museum, reg. no. GC.20
References: Wang Qingzheng 1988, pp. 727–954, nos 2874–3783; Thierry 1997, pp. 229–36, nos 225–315

51
Ant-nose money
Chu state, 4th–3rd century BC
Bronze
l 1.8 cm, w 1.2 cm, wt 2.84 g
Inscribed on obverse: 貝 (cowry)
British Museum, reg. no. 1979,0228.27
References: Wang Qingzheng 1988, pp. 1042–3, nos 4134–50; Thierry 1997, pp. 243–4, nos 346–65

52
Round coin with round hole
Wei state, 4th–3rd century BC
Bronze
D 4.1 cm, wt 9.8 g
Inscribed: 垣 (Yuan, a city name)
British Museum, reg. no. 1883,0802.86
References: Wang Qingzheng 1988, pp. 1026–7, nos 4026–35; Thierry 1997, p. 220, nos 181–2; Wang et al. 2005, p. 11, no. 1

53
Round coin with square hole
Qi state, 4th–3rd century BC
Bronze
D 3.6 cm, wt 7.47 g
Inscribed: 賹六化 (six *hua* money)
British Museum, reg. no. 1885,0304.18
References: Wang Qingzheng 1988, p. 1036, nos 4108–13; Thierry 1997, pp. 240–2, nos 343–4

54
Round coin with square hole
Qin state or Qin dynasty, 4th–3rd century BC
Bronze
d 3.1cm, wt 6.6 g
Inscribed: 半兩 (*banliang*, half ounce)
British Museum, reg. no. 1981,1216,48
References: Wang Qingzheng 1988, pp. 1062–66, nos 4282–320; Thierry 1997, pp. 247–60, nos 377–538

55
Mould for half–ounce coins
Qin state, 255–206 BC
Bronze
l 29.9 cm, w. 10.9 cm, thickness 2 cm
Excavated in 1983 from Lintong county
Shaanxi Provincial Archaeological Institute, Xi'an, inv. no. 000223
References: Bonn 2006, no. 14; Yuan Zhongyi 2002, p. 519–20

56
Rectangular paving tile with 'sun' design
Qin dynasty (221–206 BC)
Pottery
l 47 cm, w 38 cm, thickness 3.5 cm
Excavated in 1974 from the Qin Palace site, Xianyang
Xianyang Municipal Museum, inv. no. 14–1039
References: Shaanxi Institute of Archaeology 2004, p. 380

57
Hollow brick with geometric design
Qin state, 4th–3rd century BC
l 118 cm, w 39 cm, h 16.3 cm
Excavated in 1974 from the Qin Palace site, Xianyang
Xianyang Municipal Museum, inv. no. 14–758
References: Shaanxi Institute of Archaeology 2004, pp. 311–12; Ledderose and Schlombs 1990, no. 37; Wang Renbo 2001, p. 155, VII 4

58
Hollow brick with dragon and *bi* disc design
Qin dynasty (221–206 BC)
Pottery
l 117 cm, w 39 cm, h 16.3 cm
Excavated in 1982 from the Qin Palace no. 2 site, Xianyang
Xianyang Municipal Museum, inv. no. 005444
References: Shaanxi Institute of Archaeology 2004, pp. 384–12; Ledderose and Schlombs 1990, no. 34; Chang Tao 1996, p. 146

59
Pentagonal-shaped drain pipe
Qin dynasty (221–206 BC)
Pottery
l 68 cm, w 44 cm
Excavated from Changling site, Xianyang city
Xianyang Municipal Museum, Xianyang, inv no. 14–750
References: Bonn 2006, no. 22; Ledderose and Schlombs 1990, no. 62; Yuan Zhongyi 2002, p. 474

60
Architectural fittings
Spring and Autumn period, 6th–5th century BC
Bronze
l 43 cm, w 16.5 cm
l 65 cm, w 16.2 cm
l 46.5 cm, w 16.5 cm
Excavated in 1973 from Yong city site, Fengxiang county
Fengxiang County Museum, inv. no. *zong* 0049, 0050, 0051
References: Ledderose and Schlombs 1990, no. 19; Lanciotti and Scarpari 2006,
p. 34; Wang Xueli et al. 1994, pp. 370, 373–6

61
Roof tile
Qin dynasty (221–206 BC)
Pottery
Ll 38.6 cm
Excavated in 1997 from Zhengzhuang, First Emperor tomb complex
Museum of the Terracotta Warriors and Horses of Emperor Qin Shihuang, Lintong, inv. no. 003465
References: Shaanxi Institute of Archaeology and Museum of Qin Shihuang Terracotta Army 2006, pp. 45, 46, fig. 26.1; Wang Renbo 2001, p. 156, VII 7

62
Roof tile end with phoenix motif
Qin dynasty (221–206 BC)
Pottery
d 10.5cm, l 33cm
Excavated in 1985 from Yong city site, Fengxiang county
Museum of the Terracotta Warriors and Horses of Emperor Qin Shihuang, Lintong, inv. no. 002974

63
Mould for a roof tile end with 'sunflower' (*kui*) motif
Warring States period, 5th–4th century BC
Pottery
d 15 cm, thickness 2 cm
Excavated in 2006 from workshop in Toufu village, south Fengxiang city
Shaanxi Provincial Archaeological Institute, Xi'an, inv. no. BT5H6: 24
References: Tian Yaqi et al. 2006

64
Pigeon-shaped pottery roof ridge decoration
Warring States period, 5th–4th century BC
Pottery
l 15 cm, w 16.5 cm, h 10 cm
Excavated in 2006 from workshop in Toufu village, south Fengxiang city
Shaanxi Provincial Archaeological Institute, Xi'an, inv. no. 06 *feng dou* TG1: H1:12
References: Tian Yaqi et al. 2006

65
Roof tile end with phoenix motif
Early–mid Warring States period, 5th–4th century BC
Pottery
d 15 cm, l 8 cm
Excavated in 2005 from workshop in Toufu village, south Fengxiang city
Shaanxi Provincial Archaeological Institute, Xi'an, inv. no. 05 *feng dou* T1202: 89
References: Tian Yaqi et al. 2006

66
Mould for a decorative plaque with phoenix motif
Warring States period, 5th–4th century BC
Pottery
l 15.5 cm, thickness 2 cm
Excavated in 2005 from workshop in Toufu village, south Fengxiang city
Shaanxi Provincial Archaeological Institute, Xi'an, inv. no. 05 *feng dou* T1202: 66
References: Tian Yaqi et al. 2006

67
Ornamental plaque with phoenix motif
Warring States period, 5th–4th century BC
Pottery
l 21 cm, w 11.5 cm, thickness 1.5 cm
Excavated in 2005 from workshop in Toufu village, south Fengxiang city
Shaanxi Provincial Archaeological Institute, Xi'an, inv. no. 05 *feng dou* T1102: 187
References: Tian Yaqi et al. 2006

68
Mould for an ornamental plaque with tiger-attacking-deer motif
Warring States period, 5th–4th century BC
Pottery
l 15.5 cm, thickness 2 cm
Excavated in 2005 from workshop in Toufu village, south Fengxiang city
Shaanxi Provincial Archaeological Institute, Xi'an, inv. no. 05 *feng dou* T1202:190
References: Tian Yaqi et al. 2006

69 (not illustrated)
Roof tile kiln waster
Warring States period, 5th–4th century BC
Pottery
l 70 cm, w 50 cm, h 28 cm
Excavated in 2006 from workshop in south Toufu village, Fengxiang city
Shaanxi Provincial Archaeological Institute, Xi'an, inv. no. *feng dou* T1202: 106
References: Tian Yaqi et al. 2006

70
Roof tile end of Qinian Palace
Warring States period, Qin state
Pottery
Four characters moulded in relief: 蕲年宫當 (Tile end of Qinian Palace)
diameter 16.5 cm, thickness 2.2–6 cm
Excavated in 1996 from Nantou, Sunjia, Fengxiang county
Shaanxi Provincial Archaeological Institute, Xi'an, inv. no. 004440
References: Ciarla 2005, p. 63; Wang Xueli et al. 1994, pp. 75–7

71
Roof tile end of Tuoquan Palace
Warring States period, Qin state
Pottery
Four character moulded in relief: 橐泉宫當 (Tile end of Tuoquan Palace)
d 16.7 cm, thickness 2–3.3 cm
Excavated in 1997 from Nantou, Sunjia, Fengxiang county
Shaanxi Provincial Archaeological Institute, Xi'an, inv. no. 004439
References: Wang Xueli et al. 1994, pp. 75–7

72
Large roof tile end with *kui* design
Qin dynasty (221–206 BC)
Pottery
l 51.5 cm, h 38.5 cm, thickness 26.5 cm
Excavated in 1993 from Huangshan Palace, Xingping, Xianyang
Shaanxi Provincial Archaeological Institute, Xi'an, inv. no. 003001
References: Chang and Xu et al. 2005, p. 263, fig. 8.19; Shaanxi Institute of Archaeology and Museum of Qin Shihuang Terracotta Army 2002b, p. 23, fig.16; Yuan Zhongyi 2002, p. 420–3; Shaanxi Institute of Archaeology and Museum of Qin Shihuang Terracotta Army 2006, pp. 48–9; Wang Renbo 2001, p. 164, VII 13

73
Roof tile end with deer motif
Warring States period, Qin state, 4th–3rd century BC
Pottery
d 14.5 cm, thickness 2.6 cm
Excavated in 1982 from Yong city site, Fengxiang county
Museum of the Terracotta Warriors and Horses of Emperor Qin Shihuang, Lintong, inv. no. 002966
References: Ciarla 2005, p. 61

74
Roof tile end with frog motif
Warring States period, Qin state, 4th–3rd century BC
Pottery
d 15.5 cm
Excavated in 1984 from Toufu village, Shijiaying xiang, Fengxiang county
Fengxiang County Museum, inv. no. *zong* 0519
References: Ledderose and Schlombs 1990, no. 23

75
Roof tile end with dragon motif
Qin dynasty (221–206 BC)
Pottery
d 13.9 cm, thickness 4 cm
Excavated in 1998 from First Emperor tomb site
Museum of the Terracotta Warriors and Horses of Emperor Qin Shihuang, Lintong, inv. no. 002973
References: Wang Renbo 2001, p. 156, VII 9; Chang Tao 1996, p. 139; Ciarla 2005, p. 63

76
Inlaid vessel (*hu*) with chain handle
Warring States period, 3rd century BC
Bronze inlaid with gold and silver
h 21.5 cm, d (mouth) 8.5 cm, d (base) 10.2 cm
Excavated in 1974 from Chencang district, Baoji city
Chencang District Museum of Baoji City, inv. no. 015
References: Lanciotti and Scarpari 2006, no. 45; Wu Yongqi et al. 2004, p. 51

77
Inlaid tripod food vessel (*ding*)
Warring States period, 4th–3rd century BC
Bronze inlaid with gold and silver
h 13.7 cm, d 16.8 cm
Excavated in 1971 from Zhengyang, Xianyang city
Xianyang Municipal Museum, inv. no. 5–0062
References: Lanciotti and Scarpari 2006, no. 43; Xianyang Cultural Relics Bureau 2002, p. 44; Wu Yongqi et al. 2004, p. 49; Li Xixing 1994, no. 37

78
Inlaid washer (*yi*)
Warring States period, 3rd century BC
Bronze inlaid with silver and gold
h 9.9 cm, l 27.4 cm, w 24 cm, wt 1.76 kg
Excavated in 1957 from Liujiagou, Wolong temple, Baoji
Shaanxi Provincial History Museum, inv. no. 60.225
References: Zhongguo Qingtongqi Quanji 1998, no. 15; Hebei Institute of Cultural Relics 1995, vol. 1, pp. 128–9

79
Tiger fitting
Warring States period (475–221 BC)
Gold
l 5.5 cm, h 3.4 cm
Excavated in 1972 from Weijiaya, Chencang district, Baoji city
Chencang District Museum of Baoji City, inv. no. 363
References: Wu Yongqi et al. 2004, p. 27.

80
Miniature washer
Middle–late Spring and Autumn period, 6th–5th century BC
Gold inlaid with turquoise
d 7.8 cm, h 2.6 cm
Excavated in 2001 from Shangguodian village, Fengxiang county
Fengxiang County Museum, inv. no. *zong* 1008
References: Wu Yongqi et al. 2004, p. 31

81
Inlaid belt hook
Warring States period (475–221 BC)
Gilt bronze with shell inlay
l 23 cm
Excavated from a Warring States period graveyard in the northern suburbs of Youjiazhuang, Xi'an city
Xi'an Municipal Institute for Cultural Property, inv. no. M20: 5
References: *Wenwu* 1994.1, pp. 6–11

82
Belt hook with dragons
Late Spring and Autumn period, 6th–5th century BC, Qin state
Gold
l 5 cm, w 2.6 cm
Excavated in 2001 from Shangguodian village, Fengxiang county
Fengxiang County Museum, inv. no. *feng zong* 1014
References: Wu Yongqi et al. 2004, p. 3

83
Duck-shaped belt hook
Spring and Autumn period (770–475 BC), Qin state
Gold inlaid with turquoise
h 1.9 cm, l 4.5 cm, w 3 cm
Excavated in 1992 from Yimen tomb no. 2, Baoji city
Baoji Municipal Archaeological Work Team, inv. no. M2: 24
References: Liu Junkang 2006, p.15; Liu Yunhui 2006, p. 172; Wu Yongqi et al. 2004, p. 13

84
Arc-shaped dragon-headed pendant (*xi*)
Late Spring and Autumn period, 6th–5th century BC, Qin style
l 10.1 cm, w (of head) 2.2 cm, thickness 0.4 cm
Excavated in 1974 from Bayi village, south Zhihuixiang, Fengxiang county
Fengxiang County Museum, inv. no. *zong* 0311
References: Liu Yunhui 2006, p. 63

85
Arc-shaped pendant (*heng*)
Late Spring and Autumn period, 6th–5th century BC, Qin style
Jade
l 12.1 cm, w 4.9 cm, thickness 0.6 cm
Excavated in 1974 from Bayi village, south Zhihuixiang, Fengxiang county
Fengxiang County Museum, inv. no. *zong* 0310
References: Liu Yunhui 2006, p. 61

86
Tube-shaped pendant (*pei*)
Late Spring and Autumn period, 6th–5th century BC, Chu style
Jade
l 12.7 cm, w 1.65 cm, thickness 0.4–0.65 cm
Excavated in 1992 from Yimen tomb no. 2, Baoji city
Baoji Municipal Archaeological Work Team, inv. no. M2: 168
References: Liu Junkang 2006, p. 40; Liu Yunhui 2006, p. 157; Baoji 1993, p. 13

87
***Taotie* mask and ring ornament**
Warring States period (475–221 BC), Qin state
Gold and jade
l 2.8 cm, thickness 1.5 cm
Excavated in 1992 from Weijiaya, Chencang district, Baoji county
Baoji city Chencang District Museum, inv. no. 364
References: Liu Yunhui 2006, p. 174; Wu Yongqi et al. 2004, p. 25

88
Circular pendant (*pei*)
Late Spring and Autumn period, 6th–5th century BC, Qin style
Jade
d 4.89 cm, h 5.14 cm, thickness 0.3 cm
Excavated in 1986 from Yong city site, south M1, Fengxiang county
Museum of the Terracotta Warriors and Horses of Emperor Qin Shihuang, Lintong, inv. no. 002889
References: Liu Yunhui 2006, pp. 85–7

89
Rectangular pendant
Late Spring and Autumn period, 6th–5th century BC, Qin style
Jade
l 10 cm, w 6 cm, thickness 0.74 cm
Excavated in 1986 from Yong city site, south M1, Fengxiang county
Museum of the Terracotta Warriors and Horses of Emperor Qin Shihuang, Lintong, inv. no. 002888
References: Liu Yunhui 2006, pp. 82–3

90
Ritual disc (*bi*)
Late Spring and Autumn period, 6th–5th century BC, Qin style
Jade
d 16.8 cm, d (of hole) 4.2 cm, thickness 0.5 cm
Excavated in 1972 from south Zhihui, Fengxiang county
Fengxiang County Museum, inv. no. *zong* 0126
References: Liu Yunhui 2006, pp. 56–9

91
Ritual object (*cong*)
Late Neolithic to early Dynastic period (c.2000–1200 BC)
Jade
h 12.6 cm, w 6.5 cm
Excavated in 1975 from Wayaotou village, Fengxiang county
Fengxiang County Museum, inv. no. *zong* 0133
References: Liu Yunhui 2006, p. 62; Lanciotti and Scarpari 2006, no. 36

92
Beaker
Warring States to Qin period, 5th–3rd century BC
Jade
h 14.5 cm, d (mouth) 6.2 cm
Excavated in 1976 from Chezhang village, Chang'an district
Xi'an Institute of Archaeology and Cultural Relics Conservation inv. no. g14
References: Liu Yunhui 2006, pp. 220–2; Wang Renbo 2001, p. 198, VIII 40; Guangzhou et al. 1991, vol. 1, pp. 202–3

93
Bell (*Bo*)
Spring and Autumn period, 7th century BC
Bronze
Inscribed with a 135-character text
h 74 cm, w 65 cm, depth 66 cm
Excavated in 1978 from Taigong temple, Chencang, Baoji county
Baoji Municipal Bronze Ware Museum, inv. no. IA5.3
References: Kern 2000, pp 65, 85–6; Chang and Xu et al. 2005, p. 250–1; Lanciotti and Scarpari 2006, p. 258, no. 33

94
Mirror
Warring States period, 5th–6th century BC
Bronze
d 10 cm, thickness 0.2 cm
Found in 1974
Fengxiang County Museum, inv. no. *zong* 0032
References: Lanciotti and Scarpari 2006, no. 40; Wang Xueli 1999, p. 499; Wang Xueli et al. 1994, p. 360–2

95
Wine warmer and stand
Warring States period, Wei state
Ear cup: l 12.9 cm, w 15 cm
Wine warmer: l 15 cm, w 11.5 cm, h 11 cm
Excavated in 1966 from Ta'erpo, Xianyang city
Xianyang Municipal Museum, inv. no. 5–1321
References: Zhongguo Qingtongqi Quanji 1998, no. 14; Li Xixing 1994, no. 30

96
Incense burner with phoenix–shaped finial
Warring States period, 5th–4th century BC
Bronze
h 35.5 cm
Excavated in 1995 from the site of Yongcheng, Fengxiang county
Fengxiang County Museum, inv. no. *zong* 0838
References: Lanciotti and Scarpari 2006, no. 41; Chang Tao 1996, p. 142

97
Chariot horse
Qin dynasty (221–206 BC)
Terracotta
h 173 cm, l 218 cm, width 50 cm
Excavated in 1977 from Pit 2
Museum of the Terracotta Warriors and Horses of Emperor Qin Shihuang, Lintong, inv. no. 002767
References: Lanciotti and Scarpari 2006, no. 78; Ledderose and Schlombs 1990, nos 70–3; Shaanxi Institute of Archaeology and Excavation Team of the Terracotta Army 1988, pp. 183–92

98
Head
Qin dynasty (221–206 BC)
Bronze with traces of gilding
h 10.2 cm, w 7.5 cm
Excavated in 1982 from the eastern suburbs of Xianyang city
Xianyang Municipal Museum, inv. no. 5–1166
References: Shaanxi Institute of Archaeology 2004, p. 198

99
Inscribed fragment or epitaph
Qin dynasty (221–206 BC)
Pottery
l 36.7 cm, w 30 cm
Inscribed: 平陽驛 (Pingyang station)
Excavated from convicts graves at Zhaobeihu, west of tomb
Museum of the Terracotta Warriors and Horses of Emperor Qin Shihuang, Lintong, inv. no. 003428
References: Ciarla 2005, p. 269; Yuan Zhongyi 2002, p. 342–9

100
Inscribed fragment or epitaph
Qin dynasty (221–206 BC)
Pottery
Length 32cm, Width 35cm
Inscribed: 博昌居貲用里不更余 ([From] Bochang, received a sentence to perform labour work in lieu of prison-time, a low-ranking civil servant, surname Yu)
Excavated from convicts graves at Zhaobeihu, west of tomb
Museum of the Terracotta Warriors and Horses of Emperor Qin Shihuang, Lintong, inv. no. 003427
References: Ciarla 2005, p. 269; Yuan Zhongyi 2002, p. 343–9; Museum of Qinshihuang Terracotta Army 1999, no. 298

101
Roof tile fragment
Qin dynasty (221–206 BC)
Pottery
l 26 cm, w 16 cm
Stamped with 宫得 (Palace [workshop] De [name])
Excavated in 1987 from Yuchi site, north-east of tomb mound
Museum of the Terracotta Warriors and Horses of Emperor Qin Shihuang, Lintong, inv. no. 5206
References: Shaanxi Institute of Archaeology and Museum of Qin Shihuang Terracotta Army 2000; Yuan Zhongyi 2002, p. 563

102
Fragment
Qin dynasty (221–206 BC)
Pottery
l 12 cm, w 11 cm
Stamped with 咸陽 _ _ (Xianyang [workshop] – –)
Excavated in 1987 from Yuchi site, north-east of tomb mound
Museum of the Terracotta Warriors and Horses of Emperor Qin Shihuang, Lintong, inv. no. 5161
References: Shaanxi Institute of Archaeology and Museum of Qin Shihuang Terracotta Army 2000; Yuan Zhongyi 2002, p. 578

103
Roof tile fragment
Qin dynasty (221–206 BC)
Pottery
l 13 cm, w 12 cm
Stamped with 瀕陽工處 (Binyang [workshop])
Excavated in 1987 from Yuchi site, north-east of tomb mound
Museum of the Terracotta Warriors and Horses of Emperor Qin Shihuang, Lintong, inv. no. 5151
References: Shaanxi Institute of Archaeology and Museum of Qin Shihuang Terracotta Army 2000; Yuan Zhongyi 2002, p. 575

104
Fragment
Qin dynasty (221–206 BC)
Pottery
l 20 cm, w 11 cm
Stamped with _ 右 _ 宫 _
Excavated in 1997 from Yannan
Museum of the Terracotta Warriors and Horses of Emperor Qin Shihuang, Lintong, inv. no. 5213
References: Shaanxi Institute of Archaeology and Museum of Qin Shihuang Terracotta Army 2000; Yuan Zhongyi 2002, pp. 562–3

105
Inscribed vessel cover
Qin dynasty (221–206 BC)
Pottery
Inscribed: 麗山食官 (Department of food and drink at Lishan)
d 8.7 cm, thickness 1.7 cm
Excavated in 1984 from the tomb site
Shaanxi Provincial Archaeological Institute, Xi'an, inv. no. 000668
References: Ledderose and Schlombs 1990, no. 60; Bonn 2006, no. 26; Yuan Zhongyi 2002

106
Inlaid bell (*zhong*)
Qin dynasty (221–206 BC)
Bronze with gold and silver inlay
h 13.14 cm
Inscribed originally on side of handle: *Yuefu* 樂府 (Department of Music)
Excavated in 1976 from the tomb site
Museum of the Terracotta Warriors and Horses of Emperor Qin Shihuang, Lintong, inv. no. 002823
References: Ciarla 2005, p. 139; Wang Renbo 2001b, p. 120; Yuan Zhongyi 2002, p. 504–6

107
Official
Qin dynasty (221–206 BC)
Terracotta
h 183 cm
Excavated in 2000 from Pit K0006
Shaanxi Provincial Archaeological Institute, Xi'an, inv. no. 006479
References: Ciarla 2005, pp. 162–4; Shaanxi Institute of Archaeology and Museum of Qin Shihuang Terracotta Army 2006, pp. 65–95; Excavation Team of the First Emperor's Tomb 2002

108
Kneeling stable boy
Qin dynasty (221–206 BC)
Terracotta
h 68 cm
Excavated in 1972 from stable pit at Shangjiaocun, east of tomb
Museum of the Terracotta Warriors and Horses of Emperor Qin Shihuang, Lintong, inv. no. 002541
References: Ciarla 2005, p. 184; Ledderose and Schlombs 1990, no. 59; Yuan Zhongyi 2002, pp. 200–13

109
Coffin
Qin dynasty (221–206 BC)
Pottery
h 57 cm, l 101 cm, w 45 cm
Excavated in 1997 from Xingyuan, Shangjiaocun, east of tomb
Museum of the Terracotta Warriors and Horses of Emperor Qin Shihuang, Lintong, inv. no. 03352
References: Yuan Zhongyi 2002, p. 145–8

110
Armoured officer
Qin dynasty (221–206 BC)
Terracotta
Height 187cm
Excavated in 1976 from Pit 1
Museum of the Terracotta Warriors and Horses of Emperor Qin Shihuang, Lintong, inv. no. T22G9.11
References: Ledderose and Schlombs 1990, no. 79

111
Acrobat
Qin dynasty (221–206 BC)
Terracotta
h 178 cm, w 51 cm, depth 50 cm
Excavated in 1999 from Pit K9901
Museum of the Terracotta Warriors and Horses of Emperor Qin Shihuang, Lintong, inv. no. DM:002
References: Ciarla 2005, pp. 170–7; Yuan Zhongyi 2002, pp. 179–84; Institute of Archaeology of Shaanxi Province and the Museum of the Terracotta Warriors of the First Emperor 2000, pp. 179–80; Excavation Team of the First Emperor's Tomb 2001a, p. 67, pl. 5

112
Armoured general
Qin dynasty (221–206 BC)
Terracotta
h 195 cm, w 186 kg
Excavated in 1976 from Pit 1
Museum of the Terracotta Warriors and Horses of Emperor Qin Shihuang, Lintong, inv. no. 002830
References: Yuan Zhongyi 2002, p. 242; Ledderose and Schlombs 1990, no. 75; Bonn 2006, no. 29

113
Armoured infantryman
Qin dynasty (221–207 BC)
Terracotta
h 187 cm
Excavated in 1976 from Pit 1
Museum of the Terracotta Warriors and Horses of Emperor Qin Shihuang, Lintong, inv. no. 02778
References: Museum of Qin Shihuang Terracotta Army 1999, no. 130

114
Strongman
Qin dynasty (221–206 BC)
Terracotta
h 171 cm
Excavated in 1999 from Pit K9901
Museum of the Terracotta Warriors and Horses of Emperor Qin Shihuang, Lintong, inv. no. DM:005 (K9901T1G3–5)
References: Ciarla 2005, pp. 171–3; Yuan Zhongyi 2002, pp. 187–9; Excavation Team of the First Emperor's Tomb 2001a, p. 69, pl. 7

115
Production model
Modern replica
Fibreglass
l 534 cm, w 28 cm, h 34–8 cm
Museum of the Terracotta Warriors and Horses of Emperor Qin Shihuang, Lintong
References: Ledderose and Schlombs 1990

116
Drainpipe
Qin dynasty (221–206 BC)
Pottery
l 59 cm, d 25–30 cm
Excavated in 1987 from Yuchi site, north-east of tomb mound
Museum of the Terracotta Warriors and Horses of Emperor Qin Shihuang, Lintong, inv. no. 003174
References: Yuan Zhongyi 2002, pp. 474–6; Museum of Qin Shihuang Terracotta Army 1999, no. 292

117 (not illustrated)
Paving brick
Qin dynasty (221–206 BC)
Pottery
l 25.9 cm, w 13.4 cm, thickness 7.5 cm
Excavated in 1976 from Pit. 1
Museum of the Terracotta Warriors and Horses of Emperor Qin Shihuang, Lintong, inv. no. 02677
References: Ledderose and Schlombs 1990, no. 82

118
Broken figures
Qin dynasty (221–206 BC)
Terracotta
h 131 cm and h 145 cm, w 50 cm, depth 45cm
Excavated in 1974 from Pit 2 and in 1999 from Pit 1
Museum of the Terracotta Warriors and Horses of Emperor Qin Shihuang, Lintong, inv. no. 2820 and *lin* 2005–3 (005713)
References: Bonn 2006, no. 36

119
Leg fragment
Qin dynasty (221–206 BC)
Terracotta
h 46.5 cm, w 36 cm
Excavated in 1976 from Pit 1
Museum of the Terracotta Warriors and Horses of Emperor Qin Shihuang, Lintong
References: Shaanxi Institute of Archaeology and Excavation Team of the Terracotta Army 1988, pp. 164–70

120
Torso fragment
Qin dynasty (221–206 BC)
Terracotta
h 32.5 cm, w 40 cm
Excavated in 1976 from Pit 1
Museum of the Terracotta Warriors and Horses of Emperor Qin Shihuang, Lintong
References: Shaanxi Institute of Archaeology and Excavation Team of the Terracotta Army 1988, pp. 170–2

121
Head of infantryman
Qin dynasty (221–206 BC)
Terracotta
h 32 cm, w 18 cm, depth 23 cm
Excavated in 1980 from Pit 1
Museum of the Terracotta Warriors and Horses of Emperor Qin Shihuang, Lintong, inv. no. T2: 2: 50 (02536)
References: Shaanxi Institute of Archaeology and Excavation Team of the Terracotta Army 1988, pp. 176–81

122
Head of infantryman
Qin dynasty (221–206 BC)
Terracotta
h 29 cm, w 16.5 cm, depth 23 cm
Excavated in 1976 from Pit 2
Museum of the Terracotta Warriors and Horses of Emperor Qin Shihuang, Lintong, inv. no. 02826
References: Shaanxi Institute of Archaeology and Excavation Team of the Terracotta Army 1988, pp. 176–81

123
Head of an officer
Qin dynasty (221–206 BC)
Terracotta
h 30cm, w 25 cm, depth 24 cm
Excavated in 1980 from Pit 1
Museum of the Terracotta Warriors and Horses of Emperor Qin Shihuang, Lintong, inv. no. T19:9
References: Bonn 2006, no. 38; Shaanxi Institute of Archaeology and Excavation Team of the Terracotta Army 1988, pp. 176–81

124
Kneeling archer (not illustrated)
Qin dynasty (221–206 BC)
Terracotta with pigment
h 120 cm
Excavated in 1999 from Pit 2
Museum of the Terracotta Warriors and Horses of Emperor Qin Shihuang, Lintong, inv. no. 002812
References: Museum of Qin Shihuang Terracotta Army 1999, nos 114–22; Ledderose and Schlombs 1990, no. 68

125
Head of infantryman
Qin dynasty (221–206 BC)
Terracotta with pigment
h 26 cm, w 19 cm, depth 26 cm
Excavated in 1994 from Pit 1
Museum of the Terracotta Warriors and Horses of Emperor Qin Shihuang, Lintong, inv. no. T20G1–003 (*lin* 2005–4)
References: Bonn 2006, no. 37

126
Suit of armour
Qin dynasty (221–206 BC)
Limestone
h 74 cm., w 31 cm
Excavated in 1998 from Pit K9801
Shaanxi Provincial Archaeological Institute, Xi'an, inv. no. 006484
References: Lanciotti and Scarpari 2006, no. 87; Ciarla 2005, pp. 178–81; Bonn 2006, no. 58; Yuan Zhongyi 2002, pp. 157–63; Shaanxi Institute of Archaeology and Museum of Qin Shihuang Terracotta Army 2000

127
Helmet
Qin dynasty (221–206 BC)
Limestone
h 38 cm, w 21 cm
Excavated in 1998 from Pit K9801
Shaanxi Provincial Archaeological Institute, Xi'an, inv. no. 006483
References: Ciarla 2005, pp. 178–81; Yuan Zhongyi 2002, pp. 163–4; Shaanxi Institute of Archaeology and Museum of Qin Shihuang Terracotta Army 2000

128
Four unfinished armour plaques
Qin dynasty (221–206 BC)
Limestone
l 5.4 cm, w 4.4cm, thickness. 0.5–1cm
Excavated in 2001 from Qinjing site, Xinfengzhen
Shaanxi Provincial Archaeological Institute, Xi'an, inv. nos 40/46/64/86
References: Bonn 2006, nos 66–9; Shaanxi Institute of Archaeology and Museum of Qin Shihuang Terracotta Army 2000

129
Armour fragment
Qin dynasty (221–206 BC)
Limestone
l 35 cm, w 30 cm
Excavated in 1998 from Pit K9801
Shaanxi Provincial Archaeological Institute, Xi'an, inv. no. BML 001
References: Bonn 2006, no. 71; Shaanxi Institute of Archaeology and Museum of Qin Shihuang Terracotta Army 2000

130
Swan
Qin dynasty (221–206 BC)
Bronze
h 60 cm, l 110 cm, w 50 cm
Excavated in 2000 from Pit K0007
Shaanxi Provincial Archaeological Institute, Xi'an, inv. no. K0007T3:27
References: Ciarla 2005, p. 183; Shaanxi Institute of Archaeology and Museum of Qin Shihuang Terracotta Army 2005

131
Goose
Qin dynasty (221–206 BC)
Bronze
h 40 cm, l 50 cm, w 33.5 cm
Excavated in 2001 from Pit K0007
Shaanxi Provincial Archaeological Institute, Xi'an, inv. no. K0007T3:34
References: Ciarla 2005, p. 183; Shaanxi Institute of Archaeology and Museum of Qin Shihuang Terracotta Army 2005

132
Seated musician
Qin dynasty (221–206 BC)
Terracotta
h 90 cm
Excavated in 2001 from Pit K0007
Shaanxi Provincial Archaeological Institute, Xi'an, inv. no. 006482
References: Ciarla 2005, p. 183; Shaanxi Institute of Archaeology and Museum of Qin Shihuang Terracotta Army 2005

133
Crane with fish in beak
Qin dynasty (221–206 BC)
Bronze with pigments
h 75 cm, l 115 cm
Excavated in 2001 from Pit K0007
Museum of the Terracotta Warriors and Horses of Emperor Qin Shihuang, Lintong, inv. no. DM: 012
References: Ciarla 2005, p. 183; Shaanxi Institute of Archaeology and Museum of Qin Shihuang Terracotta Army 2005

134
Rubbing
Modern
Paper and ink
h 154.5 cm, l 145.5 cm
From a later carving (AD 993) of the inscription that the First Emperor erected on Mt. Yi in 219 BC.
British Museum, reg. no. 2007, 3002.1
References: Kern 2000, pp. 10–15

NOTES

INTRODUCTION

1 See Shaanxi Institute of Archaeology and Excavation Team of the Terracotta Army 1988.
2 Watson 1993, p. 63.
3 Ledderose 2000, pp. 51–73.
4 Bodde 1986, p. 20. Bodde refers to the words 'Thinai' and Sinai' appearing in Greek and Roman writings of the first and second centuries AD.
5 Bodde 1938 (reprinted 1967) is the classic work on this subject.
6 Bodde 1986, pp. 78–81.
7 Ledderose 2000, pp. 69–70.
8 Bodde 1986, pp. 95–8.
9 See Li Yu-ning 1975, pp. xv–xviii.
10 Li Yu-ning 1975, pp. xlix–li.
11 Li Yu-ning 1975, p. liii.
12 Bodde 1986, p. 90.

CHAPTER 1

1 Zhu Zhongxi 2004, pp. 2–12.
2 Watson 1993, p. 1; Nienhauser 1994, vol. I, p. 87; Bodde 1986, pp. 30–1.
3 Pines forthcoming.
4 Shelach and Pines 2006, p. 208.
5 Teng Mingyu 2002, pp. 80–4; Falkenhausen 2004, pp. 124–5, 135–8.
6 Falkenhausen 2004, pp. 117–20; Pines forthcoming.
7 Wang Xueli has suggested that the rank of all terracotta warriors in the First Emperor's pits can be identified by the type of headgear they wear. He believes that only the first nine ranks are represented (Wang Xueli 1994a, pp. 173–205). If he is correct, this means that a general of an entire Qin army is not represented among the figurines, neither are ordinary members of the rank and file, commoners without degrees of rank, nor surrendered enemy soldiers, who according to newly discovered laws could be enrolled in the Qin army with the status of 'bondservant', the name of a three-year hard-labour punishment. Indeed, since none of the figurines shows any signs of wounds from combat, the pottery army cannot have been modelled on real live Qin soldiers and the figurines cannot have been portraits of actual individuals. Rather, they represent an ideal army to protect the First Emperor and his possessions in his grave. The Qin authorities obviously had a complex system of reporting back to local authorities the promotions in rank achieved by soldiers in the field.
8 Hulsewé 1985, pp. 21–5, 30–46; Huo Yinzhang 1998, pp. 100–3.
9 1 'pace' was approximately 1.38 metres long.
10 Sage 1992, pp. 83–156.
11 Some Chinese archaeologists believe that Pit 4, which was entirely empty when it was discovered, was intended to represent a supply column, but others, like Yuan Zhongyi, believe that it was intended for the figures representing the central army (Yuan Zhongyi 1990, pp. 164–5). Since the pits were abandoned and burned before they could be completed, we do not know what Qin baggage carts and handlers looked like or whether Yuan's suggestion is closer to the truth.
12 Needham 1994, pp. 188–93.
13 Lau and Ames 1996, pp. 195–200.
14 Watson 1993, pp. 122–4; Chen Ping 2005, pp. 652–5. Some of the pits into which Bai threw the executed Zhao soldiers have been excavated by archaeologists (Shanxi Institute of Archaeology et al. 1996).
15 Museum of Qin Shihuang Terracotta Army and Shaanxi Institute of Archaeology 1998. For the account of the First Emperor's death and secret transportation of his corpse back to Xianyang in a closed carriage and packed with salted fish to hide the smell of his decomposing body, see Watson 1993, pp. 62–3; Nienhauser 1994, vol. I, pp. 154–5.
16 Some of the drivers in Pit 1 stood on the left.
17 Wang Xueli 1994a, pp. 134–9.
18 Sun Ji 2001, p. 13; see also Yang Hong 1992, pp.127–38.
19 There were a number of different styles of armour, depending on the soldier's function and rank, and the size and shape of the individual plates, and where the holes for the strings were located, depended on the position of the piece in the suit. A single suit could be made up of a hundred or more carefully crafted pieces. The suits were designed for maximum protection and flexibility, depending on the function of the soldier wearing it. Some officers were armoured, others not. Although helmets made of stone plates were found in Pit K9801, none of the soldiers in Pits 1–3 so far discovered has been equipped with such a helmet. A detailed analysis of Qin armour can be found in Zhang and Ma 2004.
20 Chen Ping 2005, p. 697.
21 Wang and Liang 2001, p. 251.
22 Trousdale 1975.
23 A few single-bladed short sabres have also been discovered in Qin sites, but none has been found as yet in the First Emperor's pits. The sabre became the standard weapon in the following Han period as iron and steel technology developed and as cavalry became the main force in the army. Such steel sabres are more effective than the double-edged straight swords when being brandished from the back of a horse. In addition, a rare weapon in the shape of a curved sword approximately

71 cm long was also found in the pottery warrior pits (see Shaanxi Institute of Archaeology and Excavation Team of the Terracotta Army 1988, p. 252, fig. 149.5). This seems to have been a Qin version of a weapon that was invented in the south-eastern state of Wu, near modern Shanghai, and was known as the 'Wu Hook'. Its exact function is unknown.

24 Di Cosmo 2002, pp. 93–126.
25 Yates 2002, pp. 36–40; Di Cosmo 2002, pp. 134–8; Yuan Zhongyi 1990, pp. 132–4; Wang Xueli 1994a, pp. 152–5.
26 Goodrich 1984.
27 Yates 2002, pp. 37–9; Lau and Ames 1996, pp. 258–9.
28 Hulsewé 1985, p. 102.
29 Wang Xueli 1994a, pp. 48–50.
30 For example, yellow would be worn by the men in the middle of a formation; red in the south.
31 Wang Xueli et al. 1994, pp. 27–59; Wang Xueli 1999, p. 197.
32 Hulsewé 1985, p. 53.
33 Institute of Archaeology, Chinese Academy of Social Sciences 2005.
34 Shaanxi Institute of Archaeology 2000, pp. 48–166.
35 Sun Jinming 2002, pp. 131–7.
36 Wu Jiulong 1985, slip 0585, 0766, 1332, 1486.
37 Harper suggests that the incantation verbalizes the act of a man stopping the bleeding and a woman pouring vinegar on the wound, while the drawing of the five lines 'creates a magical diagram' intended 'to create a magical space that protects the wounded person from further harm' (Harper 1998, p. 225, notes 2 and 3). This interpretation is certainly correct for the establishment of a ritual space for safe healing, but I have some doubts about the interpretation of the incantation.
38 Liu Lexian 1994, p. 231.
39 Harper 1998, pp. 228–9.
40 The Qin, like the Romans, paid particular attention to the development of transportation networks, developing an empire-wide road network and digging a canal in modern Guangdong province, the 'Spirit Canal', which linked the north and south watersheds, allowing for the movement of barges from the southern ocean all the way into north China (Huo Yinzhang 1998, pp. 91–9).
41 Huang Linshu 1992; Xu Pingfang 2001, pp. 260–70; Chang and Xu et al. 2005, pp. 268–70.
42 Di Cosmo 2002, pp. 161–252.

CHAPTER 2

1 The term *Chunqiu* derives from a chronicle of the period arranged chronologically under the major headings of Spring and Autumn for each year.
2 E.G. Jin, AD 265–419; Wei, AD 220–64 and 386–533; Zhou, AD 557–80; Song, AD 420–78 and 960–1279; Qi, AD 479–501.
3 The accuracy of the vivid descriptions of some buildings around the ancient capital is questioned by scholars today.
4 *Shiji* 6, p. 256 and translated in Watson 1993, p. 56.
5 Yang Xiaoneng 2004, pp. 222–4.
6 Yang Xiaoneng 2004, p. 223.
7 Qin Xianyang 1976, p. 14.
8 Qin Xianyang 1976, p. 19.
9 See Shaanxi Institute of Archaeology 2004, pp. 535–65.
10 Two rooms in Palace 1 were found with pentagonal-shaped stoves in the corner of the room, and it is thought that food was stored in the wells in baskets that were hoisted and lowered by rope (Wang Xueli 1999, p. 312). See Shaanxi Institute of Archaeology 2004, pp. 535–65.
11 See Wang Zhongshu 1982.
12 Tian Yaqi et al. 2006.
13 See Nickel, this volume (pp. 158–79) and Ledderose 2000, pp. 52–73 for a description of the production of the terracotta figures. Architectural elements of similar shape have been excavated from both the Epang Palace site and the First Emperor's tomb (Yang and Duan 2006, p. 53).
14 See Shang Zhiru 1990 for line drawings of the various methods of making roof tiles.
15 Watson 1993, p. 56.
16 Although popularly known as Ebang Palace, the sound gloss given in Zhang Shoujie's (fl. AD 725) commentary of the *Shiji* suggests that the pronunciation should be Ebang (see Knechtges 1982, p. 174, L.334 note). The editors are grateful to Freda Murck and Bob Thorp for pointing this out and Stephen Allee for confirming this.
17 King Wen of Western Zhou had his capital at Feng and King Wu had his at Hao (*Shiji* 6, p. 256 and translated in Watson 1993, p. 56).
18 1 *bu* (pace) was approximately 1.38 metres and 1 *zhang* was about 2.3 metres long. Excavated examples of Warring States period linear measurements made of bone, bronze and wood have *chi* marking ranging from 22 to 24 cm (Qiu Guangming 1992, pp. 6–11). The validity of such enormous proportions is discussed in Bodde 1986, p. 102.
19 Yang and Duan 2006, p. 54.
20 Hubei Provincial Museum 1989, vol. 2, pls 13 and 15 (lacquers), pl. 17 (gold vessel). See also Yang Xiaoneng 1999, pp. 275–307.
21 For a comprehensive history of the place of jade in Chinese culture, see Rawson 1995a.
22 For the history of this interaction, see Di Cosmo 2002.
23 Rawson 1995b, pp. 26–37, and 1995a, pp. 60–75.

24 The *Zhanguoce*, whose present form dates from c.10 BC, includes anecdotes concerning the major kingdoms of the Warring States period.
25 See Rawson 1995a, pp. 290–4.
26 Michaelson 1999, pp. 47–8.
27 Zavitukhina and Barkova 1978.
28 Cooke 2000, pp. 36–8; *Shiji* 43, p. 1811 and, in translation, Chavannes 1895–1905, vol. 5, p. 84.
29 Lawton 1982, pp. 89–126. See also Wang 1996, Bunker et al. 2002.
30 Cooke 2000, p. 63.
31 Cook and Major 1999, in particular, the essay by Jenny F. So, 'Chu Art: Link between the Old and New', pp. 33–47.
32 Rawson 1975, pp. 36–55.
33 Rawson 1995a, p. 150.
34 Rawson 1995a, p. 256.
35 Personal communication with Yang Meili.
36 Rawson 1995a, pp. 259–62.
37 James Watt suggests this in a private note.
38 Guangzhou et al. 1991; see vol. 2, pl. 17, for jade beaker on bronze stand, pl. 25 for rhyton and pl. 4 for pendant set.

CHAPTER 3

1 See *Shiji* 6; for translations of the chapter, see Watson 1993, Nienhauser 1994, vol. I, Yang and Yang 1979, Chavannes 1895–1905, Dawson 1994.
2 For this reading, see e.g. Lewis 1999b, pp. 308–17, with further references.
3 For an annotated translation and discussion of the seven texts, see Kern 2000, pp. 10–49; for further references, including previous translations into English and French, see Kern 2000, p. 7.
4 *Shiji* 6, p. 260; *Shiji* 28, p. 1370; *Hanshu* 25A.1205.
5 *Shangshu* 6, p. 35a, *Shiji* 2, pp. 52, 67. For the dense web of other references to Yu and his relation to Kuaiji (as well as to Jieshi), see Kern 2000, p. 117.
6 See Shi Zhecun 1987, pp. 267–74; Yuan Weichun 1990, pp. 42–9; Rong Geng 1935, pp. 164–7; Kern 2000, p. 117.
7 *Shiji* 6, p. 267.
8 The Mt. Langye stele survived until 1900 when it finally fell into the sea. Fragments have been re-assembled and are now on display in the Museum of Chinese History in Beijing; see Rong Geng 1935, pp. 128–9, 140–1. The two fragments purportedly from the Mt. Tai stele are kept in the Temple of Mt. Tai (Daimiao) in Tai'an, Shandong province.
9 *Shiji* 6, p. 242, *Shiji* 28, p. 1366, *Hanshu* 25A, p. 1201.
10 *Shiji* 28, p. 1366, *Hanshu* 25A, p. 1201.
11 The text is in *Shiji* 6, p. 249; for full annotation, see Kern 2000, pp. 35–7.
12 For a detailed analysis of the language and structure of the inscriptions, see Kern 2000, pp. 119–47.
13 For discussions of Qin classical scholarship, see Wang Guowei 1961, 1, pp. 174–6; Ma Feibai 1982, 1, pp. 337–41, 2, pp. 893–901; Kanaya 1992, pp. 230–57; Kern 2000, pp. 183–96.
14 *Shiji* 6, p. 255, *Shiji* 87, p. 2546–7. See also Petersen 1995; Kern 2000, pp. 188–94.
15 On the political implications of the imperial tour of inspection, see Wechsler 1985, pp. 161–9.
16 See Chen Mengjia 1985, pp. 135–46; Jiang Shanguo 1988, pp. 140–68. The *Documents* chapters in question (in the received 'ancient text' version) are *Yaodian*, *Shundian* and *Yugong*; for a translation, see Legge 1985, pp. 15–51, 92–152.
17 Compare line two of the Mt. Zhifu inscription: 'the season of mid-spring'.
18 Another name for Mt. Tai. 'To visit [for inspection] those under his protection' reflects a traditional understanding of the term *xunshou*, usually translated as 'tour of inspection'.
19 *Shangshu* 3, pp. 126b–27c; Legge 1985, pp. 35–6. The passage is also cited in *Shiji* 28, pp. 1355–56 and *Hanshu* 25A, p. 1191, which further testifies to its importance in the early empire.
20 Following the sequence of seasons and directions in the Five Phases cosmology of late Warring States and early imperial times, Shun made his four tours of inspection all in the second month of the respective season: in spring to the east, in summer to the south, in autumn to the west and in winter to the north.
21 See *Shiji* 28, pp. 1366–67; *Hanshu* 25A, pp. 1201–2.
22 *Shiji* 28, p. 1367–68; *Hanshu* 25A, p. 1202.
23 On the *wang* sacrifice, see Bilsky 1975, vol. 1, pp. 143–5 and vol. 2, p. 248; Zhang Hequan 1989, pp. 40–2.

CHAPTER 4

1 The history of the period of the First Emperor is described by Sima Qian in *Shiji* 6, pp. 223–94; Watson 1993, pp. 35–83.
2 Kern 2000 and this volume (pp. 104–12).
3 *Shiji* 6, p. 247; Watson 1993, p. 49.
4 Kern 2000. See also the chapter on the *feng* and *shan* sacrifices, *Shiji* 28, pp. 1355–404; Watson 1961, pp. 13–69.
5 *Shiji* 6, p. 256; Watson 1993, p. 56.
6 Yongcheng Archaeological Team 1987 gives a report on the excavation of major tombs at the Qin funerary park at Fengxiang in Shaanxi province.
7 For an account of the variety of tombs, see Thote 2004.
8 For a general overview of burial practices and offerings to

the ancestors, see Loewe and Shaughnessy 1999, chs 3, 5, 8 and 10.

9 Rawson 2002b considers the changes in the range of utensils employed in offerings to the dead.

10 See Poo 1998 for an account of some of the spirits and deities whose worship became popular over several centuries.

11 Discussed by James Lin in this volume (pp. 186–9); see also Harper 1985.

12 Institute of Archaeology, Chinese Academy of Social Sciences 1999 describes tombs excavated at Zhangjiapo, Xi'an, in Shaanxi province. Two of these, M152 and M170, have separate 'head sections'; see figs 18 and 21.

13 Falkenhausen 2004 has attributed this development to the Qin state based on the rather brief reports in Han Wei 1983 and Yongcheng Archaeological Team 1987. See especially the tomb of the Marquis Yi of Zeng: Wu Hung 1999, pp. 721–6; Hubei Provincial Museum 1989; Thote 1991 and 2004.

14 Falkenhausen 1999, p. 495, fig. 7.16.

15 For the Zhongshan tombs see Wu Hung 1999, pp. 711–12; Hebei Institute of Cultural Relics 1995; Hebei Institute of Cultural Relics 2005.

16 For an overview of the beliefs in the period up to the unification by the First Emperor, see Harper 1999. See also Seidel 1987 and Brashier 1996.

17 Harper 1994 gives an account of this find.

18 Sofukawa 1989.

19 Zhao Huacheng 2006.

20 Wide-ranging accounts of the excavations are given in Wang Xueli 1994b and Yuan Zhongyi 2002.

21 *Shiji* 6, p. 265; Watson 1993, p. 63, amended by the author to remove references to models and imitations.

22 In choosing the word 'analogue', I follow Schafer 1977, pp. 55–6. This is a translation of the Chinese term *xiang*, used by Sima Qian when describing the effect of the tress on the tomb mound that made it an analogue of a mountain. This topic is discussed in greater detail in Rawson 2002a. See Peterson 1982 for further discussion of the word *xiang*.

23 The Emperor's concern with mountains in the geography of his realm is evident in both Sima Qian's account of his reign (*Shiji* 6, Watson 1993, pp. 35–83) and in his chapter on the *feng* and *shan* sacrifice (*Shiji* 28, Watson 1961, pp. 13–61).

24 *Shiji* 6, p. 239; Watson 1993, p. 45.

25 Falkenhausen has suggested that the earlier pottery figures found in lesser Qin tombs may have been one of the stimuli for the manufacture of the terracotta soldiers: Falkenhausen 1999, p. 495, fig. 7.16.

26 *Shiji* 6, p. 239; Watson 1993, p. 45.

27 For the application of moulding technologies in the creation of the terracotta figures, see Ledderose 2000, pp. 51–73, and Nickel in this volume, pp. 167–70.

28 For discussion of the evidence of such contacts across Central Asia, see Rawson 1999.

29 Yuan Zhongyi 2002, p. 327.

30 Yuan Zhongyi 2002, pp. 571–9.

31 For a discussion of the organization of the manufacture of the terracotta warriors, see Nickel in this volume (p. 179) and Ledderose 2000, pp. 51–73.

32 For an outline plan of the position of these buildings, see Yuan Zhongyi 2002, p. 55.

33 For finds from the *shi guan*, see Yuan Zhongyi 2002, pp. 97–106.

34 Personal communication from the archaeologists working at the site.

35 Yuan Zhongyi 2002, p. 314, fig. 116.

36 Shaanxi Institute of Archaeology and Museum of Qin Shihuang Terracotta Army 2006 gives a full account of the excavation of this site.

37 Loewe 2006, p. 28.

38 Described in Museum of Qin Shihuang Terracotta Army and Shaanxi Institute of Archaeology 1998.

39 For the excavation of the water course with birds, see Shaanxi Institute of Archaeology and Museum of Qin Shihuang Terracotta Army 2005.

40 Yuan Zhongyi 2002, pp. 136–48; Ledderose 1983.

41 Paludan 2006, pp. 101–3, describes some other instances in the Warring States, Qin and Han periods in which stone was clearly of great importance in the function of sculptures to affect spirits.

42 Shaanxi Institute of Archaeology and Museum of Qin Shihuang Terracotta Army 2000, pp. 33–166.

43 Shaanxi Institute of Archaeology and Museum of Qin Shihuang Terracotta Army 2000, pp. 166–99.

44 For a description of the army in English with plans of the pits, see Wu Hung 2006, pp. 59–67.

45 I am indebted to the article by Martin Kern in this volume (pp. 104–13) and to private communications from him for these comments.

CHAPTER 5

1 For a survey of Eastern Zhou burials, see Thote 2004, pp. 65–107. Pre-unification sculpture was recently discussed in Wu Hung 2005, pp. 13–47.

2 Among the 317 Qin tombs excavated recently near Xi'an, and built between the sixth and the third century BC, only one contained a few clay figurines. See Xi'an 2004a, pp. 322–5 and col. pl. 3:4.

3 This aspect has been discussed in Ledderose 2000, pp. 51–73.
4 For the Zhongshan tomb plan, see Wang Tao 2003, pp. 17–24.
5 Information on the architecture of the pits can be found in Shaanxi Institute of Archaeology and Excavation Team of the Terracotta Army 1988, pp. 13–45; Yuan Zhongyi 1990, pp. 67–70; Ledderose and Schlombs 1990, pp. 272–6.
6 Simon et al. 2001, pp. 677–81, and Yuan Zhongyi 2003, p. 21.
7 Yuan Zhongyi 2003, p. 45. Since the exploration is an ongoing project, the published figures vary. Another source mentions that about 2,000 sculptures have been unearthed from Pit 1 alone: Shaanxi Institute of Archaeology and Museum of Qin Shihuang Terracotta Army 2000, pp. 21–2.
8 Yuan and Snethlage 2005.
9 Moulds were widely used in bronze production from the middle of the second millennium BC. For a brief introduction, see Bagley 1980.
10 Shaanxi Institute of Archaeology and Excavation Team of the Terracotta Army 1988, pp. 144–50. See also Erdberg 1990, pp. 225–9.
11 For discussion of the armour, see Yuan Zhongyi 1990, pp. 241–54; and the translation in Yuan Zhongyi 2001a.
12 Yuan Zhongyi 2001a, pp. 188–91.
13 Yuan Zhongyi 1990, p. 352.
14 Thieme 2001; Blänsdorf and Xia 2005.
15 Yuan Zhongyi 2001b.
16 Estimates have been done on the basis of replication experiments by the Bayerische Landesamt für Denkmalpflege. I am grateful to Catharina Blänsdorf for this information.
17 Shaanxi Institute of Archaeology and Museum of Qin Shihuang Terracotta Army 2000, pp. 21–2.
18 Shaanxi Institute of Archaeology and Excavation Team of the Terracotta Army 1988, vol. 1, p. 249; Yun-Kremer 1990, pp. 306–9; Ledderose 2000, pp. 60–1.
19 Some chariot remains discovered in Pit 1 are described in detail in the excavation report, Shaanxi Institute of Archaeology and Excavation Team of the Terracotta Army 1988, pp. 208–43. See also Yuan Zhonghyi 2003, pp. 105–23. For a discussion of late Zhou and Qin period chariots and their security equipment, see Dewall 1990, pp. 49–57.
20 The two explanations are discussed in Yuan Zhongyi 2003, pp. 122–3. See also Wu Hung 2005, pp. 13–47 (esp. pp. 44–5).
21 *Shiji* 6, p. 256; Yang and Yang 1979, p. 179.
22 Yuan Zhongyi 2003, p. 169; Schlombs 1990.
23 Schlombs 1990, p. 94, and Yuan Zhongyi 2003, p. 169.
24 For a discussion of the inscriptions, see Ledderose 2000, pp. 69–70.
25 Yuan Zhongyi 2003, p. 169.
26 Coins help to date the tomb to the late Warring States period. See Hebei Cultural Relics Administrative Office 1975.
27 Hebei Cultural Relics Administrative Office 1982.
28 Sofukawa 1989; Rawson 1998.
29 Watson 1993, p. 63.
30 The bamboo slips were recovered from Tomb M11 at Shuihudi between December 1975 and January 1976. See Ji Xun 1976; also Beijing 1977.
31 Harper 1985, pp. 492–3.
32 Thote 1991, pp. 37–8.
33 Hubei Provincial Museum 1989; also Keightley 1987, p. 19.
34 Rawson 1998; Rawson 1999.
35 Beijing 1981, pl. 132.
36 *Baopuzi* 17.278; Ware 1966, p. 288.
37 See *Huainan wanbishu*.
38 Harper 1999.
39 Seidel 1987, pp. 21–57; particularly n. 88.
40 Liu Lexian 1994, pp. 225–68.
41 Boyer 1994; Rawson 1999, p. 50.

APPENDIX

1 Chang and Li 1983.
2 Liu Shiyi et al. 2005, pp. 26–9.
3 Liu Shiyi et al. 2005, p. 17.
4 Liu Shiyi et al. 2005, p. 21.
5 Yuan Zhongyi 2002, pp. 20–4.
6 Liu Shiyi et al. 2005, p. 35.
7 Yuan Zhongyi 2002, p. 40.
8 Yuan Zhongyi 2002, p. 33; Liu Shhiyi et al. 2005, p. 29.
9 Liu Shiyi et al. 2005, pp. 29–30.
10 Yuan Zhongyi 2002, pp. 33, 40.
11 Liu Shiyi et al. 2002, p. 35.
12 Yuan Zhongyi 2002, pp. 35–8.
13 Shaanxi Institute of Archaeology and Museum of Qin Shihuang Terracotta Army 2002a; Yuan Zhongyi 2002, p. 36.
14 Yuan Zhongyi 2002, p. 38.
15 Liu Shiyi et al. 2005, p. 24–6.
16 There are differing views as to the structural material of the coffin chamber. From the results of scientific surveys and analyses, some scholars conclude that the coffin chamber is made of stone (Liu Shiyi et al. 2005, p. 23, 40). The archaeologist Yuan Zhongyi, however, believes it to be a wood structure (Yuan Zhongyi 2002, pp. 39–40).
17 Liu Shiyi et al. 2005, p. 35.
18 Yuan Zhongyi 2002, p. 51.

FURTHER READING

The following list is intended as a guide for those interested in pursuing the subject further using Western languages, with an emphasis on books which are still available in bookshops or libraries. Books in Chinese are not included, neither are articles in specialist academic journals – these are listed below under Works Cited.

Blänsdorf, Catharina, Erwin Emmerling, Michael Petzet (eds). *Die Terracottaarmee des Ersten Chinesischen Kaisers Qin Shihuang*. Munich, 2001.

Bodde, Derk. *China's First Unifier*. Leiden, 1938.

Bodde, Derk. 'The State and Empire of Ch'in' in Denis Twitchett and Michael Loewe (eds), *The Cambridge History of China*, Volume 1, 'The Ch'in and Han Empires, 221 B.C. A.D. 220'. Cambridge, 1986.

Ciarla, Roberto (ed.). *The Eternal Army: The Terracotta Soldiers of the First Chinese Emperor*. Vercelli, 2005.

Chang, Kwang-chih and Xu Pingfang et al. *The Formation of Chinese Civilization: An Archaeological Perspective*. Sarah Allan (ed.). New Haven, 2002.

Clements, Jonathan. *The First Emperor of China*. 2006.

Dawson, Raymond (trans.). *The First Emperor: Selections from the Historical Records*. Oxford, 2007.

Hearn, Maxwell. 'The Terracotta Army of the First Emperor of Qin (221–206 BC)' in *The Great Bronze Age of China*. Wen Fong (ed.). New York, 1981.

Hulsewé, A.F.P. *Remnants of Ch'in Law: An annotated translation of the Ch'in legal and administrative rules of the 3rd century B.C. discovered in Yün-meng Prefecture, Hu-pei Province, in 1975*. Leiden, 1985.

Kern, Martin. *The Stele Inscriptions of Ch'in Shih-huang: Text and Ritual in Early Chinese Imperial Representation*. New Haven, 2000.

Kunst- und Ausstellungshalle der Bundesrepublik Deutschland, Bonn. *Xi'an, Kaiserliche Macht im Jenseits: Grabfunde und Tempelschätze aus Chinas alter Haupstadt*. Mainz, 2006.

Lanciotti, Lionello and Maurizio Scarpari. *Cina: Nascita di un Impero*. Rome and Milan, 2006.

Ledderose, Lothar. 'A Magic Army for the Emperor' in *Ten Thousand Things – Module and Mass Production in Chinese Art*. Princeton, 2000, pp. 51–73.

Ledderose, Lothar and Adele Schlombs. *Jenseits der grossen Mauer – der Erste Kaiser und seine Terracotta-Armee*. Munich, 1990.

Lewis, Mark Edward. *The Early Chinese Empires: Qin and Han*. Cambridge, Mass., 2007.

Li Yu-ning. *The First Emperor of China*. White Plains, 1975.

Loewe, Michael and Edward Shaughnessy (eds). *The Cambridge History of Ancient China. From the Origins to 221 B.C.* Cambridge, 1999.

Michaelson, Carol. *Gilded Dragons*. London, 1999.

Paludan, Ann. *Chinese Sculpture: a great tradition*. Chicago, 2006.

Rawson, Jessica (ed.). *The British Museum Book of Chinese Art*. London, 1992.

Watson, Burton (trans.). *Records of the Grand Historian: Qin Dynasty*. Hong Kong and New York, 1993.

Wood, Frances. *The First Emperor of China*. London, 2007.

Zhang Wenli. *The Qin Terracotta Army: Treasures of Lintong*. London, 1996.

WORKS CITED

Bagley 1980

Bagley, Robert W. 'The Beginnings of the Bronze Age: The Erlitou Culture Period' in Wen Fong (ed.), *The Great Bronze Age of China*. New York, 1980, pp. 69–73.

Baoji 1993

Baoji Archaeological Work Team 寶鷄市考古工作隊. 'Baoji shi Yimencun er hao Chunqiu mu fajue jianbao' 寶鷄市益門村二號春秋墓發掘簡報, *Wenwu* 文物 1993.10, pp. 1–14.

Baopuzi

Ge Hong (葛洪283–343). *Baopuzi neipian jiaoshi*. 抱朴子內篇校釋, Wang Ming 王明 (ed.). Beijing, 1980.

Beijing 1977

Shuihudi Qin mu zhujian 睡虎地秦墓竹簡. Beijing, 1977.

Beijing 1981

Yunmeng Shuihudi Qin mu 雲夢睡虎地秦墓. Beijing, 1981.

Bilsky 1975

Bilsky, Lester James. *The State Religion of Ancient China*, 2 vols. Taipei, 1975.

Blänsdorf et al. 2001

Blänsdorf, Catharina, Erwin Emmerling, Michael Petzet (eds). *Die Terracottaarmee des Ersten Chinesischen Kaisers Qin Shihuang*. Munich, 2001.

Blänsdorf 2005

Blänsdorf, Catharina. 'Neue Untersuchungen zur Farbigkeit der Terrakottaarmee – Kniende Bogenschützen und Musterborten der Offiziere' in *Jahresbericht 2004, Erprobung und Optimierung von Konservierungstechnologien für Kunst- und Kulturgüter der Provinz Shaanxi, VR China*. Munich, 2005, pp. 8–19.

Blänsdorf and Xia 2005

Blänsdorf, Catharina and Xia Yin. 'Die Terrakottaarmee – Befunde und Analysen für eine originalgetreue Rekonstruktion der Farbigkeit' in Bonn 2006, pp. 169–71.

Blänsdorf and Xia 2006

Catharina Blänsdorf and Xia Yin. 'A Colourful world for the Emperor's soul: the polychromy of the terracotta sculptures at Qin Shihuang's burial complex' in Saunders et al. 2006, pp. 177–83.

Bodde 1938

Bodde, Derk. *China's First Unifier: a Study of the Ch'in Dynasty as seen in the life of Li Ssu 289?208 B.C.* Leiden, repr. Hong Kong, 1967.

Bodde 1986

Bodde, Derk. 'The State and Empire of Ch'in' in Denis Twitchett and Michael Loewe (eds), *The Cambridge History of China*, Vol. 1, *The Ch'in and Han Empires, 221 B.C.–A.D. 220*. Cambridge, 1986.

Bonn 2006

Kunst- und Ausstellungshalle der Bundesrepublik Deutschland, Bonn. *Xi'an, Kaiserliche Macht im Jenseits: Grabfunde und Tempelschätze aus Chinas alter Haupstadt*. Mainz, 2006.

Boyer 1994

Boyer, Pascal. *The Naturalness of Religious Ideas: A Cognitive Theory of Religion*. Berkeley, 1994.

Brashier 1996

Brashier, K.E. 'Han thanatology and the division of souls', *Early China* 21 (1996), pp. 1–35.

Bunker et al. 2002

Bunker, Emma, James Watt and Sun Zhixin. *Nomadic Art of the Eastern Eurasian Steppes: The Eugene V Thaw and other New York Collections*. New York and New Haven, 2002.

Chang Tao 1996

Chang Tao張濤. *Qin Shihuang bingmayong* 秦始皇兵馬俑. Taipei, 1996.

Chang and Xu et al. 2005

Chang, Kwang-chih, Xu Pingfang et al. *The Formation of Chinese Civilization: An Archaeological Perspective*, Sarah Allan (ed.). New Haven, 2005.

Chang and Li 1983

Chang Yong 常勇 and Li Tong 李同, 'Qin shihuang lingzhong maicang gong de chubu yanjiu' 秦始皇陵中埋藏汞的初步研究, *Kaogu* 考古 1983.7, pp. 659–63, 671.

Chavannes 1895–1905

Chavannes, Édouard (1895–1905 and 1969). *Les Mémoires historiques de Se-Ma Ts'ien* vols 1–5. Paris, 1895–1905; vol. 6 repr. Paris, 1969.

Chen Mengjia 1985

Chen Mengjia 陳夢家. *Shangshu tonglun* 尚書通論. Beijing, 1985.

Chen Ping 2005

Chen Ping 陳平. *Guan Long wenhua yu Ying Qin wenming* 關隴文化與嬴秦文明. Nanjing, 2005.

Ciarla 2005

Ciarla, Roberto (ed.). *The Eternal Army: The Terracotta Soldiers of the First Chinese Emperor*. Vercelli, 2005.

Committee for the Publication of Zhongguo Qingtongqi Quanji 1998

Committee for the Publication of Zhongguo Qingtongqi Quanji (ed.) 中國青銅器全集編輯委員會 (編). *Zhongguo Qingtongqi Quanji, 12: Qin-Han* 中國青銅器全集, 12: 秦漢. Beijing, 1998.

Cook and Major 1999

Cook, Constance A. and John S. Major (eds). *Defining Chu: Image and Reality in Ancient China*. Honolulu, 1999.

Cooke 2000

Cooke, Bill (ed.). *Imperial China: The Art of the Horse in Chinese History*. Lexington, KY, 2000.

Creel 1974

Creel, Herrlee G. *Shen Pu-hai: A Chinese Political Philosopher of the Fourth Century B.C.* Chicago and London, 1974.

Dawson 1994

Dawson, Raymond. *Sima Qian: Historical Records*. Oxford, 1994.

de Bary et al. 1960

de Bary, Wm. Theodore et al. *Sources of Chinese Tradition*, 2 vols. New York and London, 1960.

Dewall 1990

Dewall, Magdalene von. 'Wagen und Gespanne in Qin' in Ledderose and Schlombs 1990, pp. 49–57.

Di Cosmo 2002

Di Cosmo, Nicola. *Ancient China and its Enemies: The Rise of Nomadic Power in East Asian History*. Cambridge, 2002.

Dien 1981–2

Dien, Albert E. 'A Study of Early Chinese Armor', *Artibus Asiae* 43 (1981–2), pp. 5–66.

Dien 1990

Dien, Albert E. (ed.). *State and Society in Early Medieval China*. Stanford, 1990.

Duyvendak 1928

Duyvendak, Jan Julius Lodewijk. *The Book of Lord Shang: A Classic of the Chinese School of Law*. London, 1928; repr. London, 1963.

Erdberg 1990

Erdberg, Eleanor von. 'Die Soldaten Shih Huang Tis – Porträts?' in Dietrich Seckel et al. (eds), *Das Bildnis in der Kunst des Orients*. Stuttgart, 1990, pp. 225–9.

Excavation Team of the Terracotta Army of the First Emperor 1982

Excavation Team of the Terracotta Army Pits of the First Emperor 始皇陵秦俑抗考古發掘隊. 'Qin Shihuang ling xizhe Zhaobeihucun Qin xingtu mu' 秦始皇陵西側趙背戶村秦刑徒墓. *Wenwu* 文物1982.3, pp. 1–11.

Excavation Team of the Terracotta Army of the First Emperor 1983

Excavation Team of the Terracotta Army Pits of the First Emperor 陝西始皇陵秦俑坑考古發掘隊 and the Museum of the Terracotta Army of the First Emperor 秦始皇兵馬俑博物館. *Qin Shihuang ling bingmayong* 秦始皇兵馬俑. Beijing, 1983.

Excavation Team of the First Emperor's Tomb 2001a

Excavation Team of the First Emperor's Mausoleum 秦陵考古隊. 'Qin Shihuang lingyuan K9901 shijue jianbao' 秦始皇陵園K9901試掘簡報, *Kaogu* 考古 2001.1, pp. 59–73.

Excavation Team of the First Emperor's Tomb 2001b

Excavation Team of the First Emperor's Mausoleum 始皇陵考古隊. 'Qin Shihuang lingyuan K9801 peizangkeng diyici shijue jianbao' 秦始皇陵園K9801陪葬坑第一次試掘簡報, *Kaogu yu wenwu* 考古與文物 2001.1, pp. 3–34.

Excavation Team of the First Emperor's Tomb 2002

Excavation Team of the First Emperor's Mausoleum 秦陵考古隊. 'Qin Shihuang lingyuan K0006 peizangkeng diyici fajue baogao' 秦始皇陵園K0006陪葬坑第一次發掘簡報, *Wenwu* 文物 2002.3, pp. 4–31.

Falkenhausen 1999

Falkenhausen, Lothar von. 'The Waning of the Bronze Age' in Loewe and Shaughnessy 1999, pp. 450–544.

Falkenhausen 2004

Falkenhausen, Lothar von. 'Mortuary behaviour in Pre-Imperial Qin: a religious interpretation' in Lagerwey 2004, pp. 109–72.

Falkenhausen 2006
Falkenhausen, Lothar von. *Confucian Society in the Age of Confucious (1000–250 BC), The Archaeological Evidence*. Los Angeles, 2006.
Fiuza, Duan and Wang
Fiuza, Sandra Bucher, Duan Qingbo and Wang Dongfeng. 'Stone armor 2200 years ago; early mass production methods in China' in Saunders et al. 2006, pp. 170–6.
Fong 1980
Fong, Wen (ed.). *The Great Bronze Age of China*. London, 1980.
Goodrich 1984
Goodrich, Chauncey S. 'Riding Astride and the Saddle in Ancient China', *Harvard Journal of Asiatic Studies* 44.2 (1984), pp. 279–305.
Guo Zhikun 1989
Guo Zhikun 郭志坤. *Qin Shihuang dazhuan* 秦始皇大傳. Shanghai, 1989.
Guangzhou et al. 1991
Guangzhou City Cultural Relics Management Committee 廣州市文物管理委員會, Institute of Archaeology, Chinese Academy of Social Sciences 中國社會科學院考古研究所 and Guangdong Provincial Museum 廣東省博物館 (eds). *Xi Han Nanyue wang mu* 西漢南越王墓, 2 vols. Beijing, 1991.
Hanshu
Hanshu 漢書. Comp. Ban Gu 班固. Beijing, 1987.
Han Wei 1983
Han Wei 韓偉 and Yongcheng Archaeological Team of Shaanxi Province 陝西省雍城考古隊. 'Fengxiang Qin gong lingyuan zuantan yu shijue jianbao' 鳳翔秦公陵園鑽探與試掘簡報, *Wenwu* 文物 1983.7, pp. 30–7.
Han Yangling 2004
Han Yangling Archaeological Museum (ed.) 漢陽陵考古陳列館 (編). *Han Yangling chenlieguan* 漢陽陵考古陳列館. Beijing, 2004.
Harper 1985
Harper, Donald. 'A Chinese Demonography of the Third Century B.C.', *Harvard Journal of Asiatic Studies* 45.2 (1985), pp. 459–98.
Harper 1994
Harper, Donald. 'Resurrection in Warring States popular religion', *Taoist Resources* 5, 2 (1994), pp. 13–28.
Harper 1998
Harper, Donald. *Early Chinese Medical Literature: The Mawangdui Medical Manuscripts*. London and New York, 1998.
Harper 1999
Harper, Donald. 'Warring States Natural Philosophy and Occult Thought' in Loewe and Shaughnessy 1999, pp. 813–84.
He Han 1986
He Han 何漢. *Qin shi shuping* 秦史述評. Hefei, 1986.
Hebei Cultural Relics Administrative Office 1975
Hebei Provincial Cultural Relics Administrative Office 河北省文物管理處. 'Hebei Yixian Yanxiadu 44 hao mu fajue baogao' 河北易縣燕下都44號墓發掘報告, *Kaogu* 考古 1975.4, pp. 228–40, 243.
Hebei Cultural Relics Administrative Office 1982
Hebei Provincial Cultural Relics Administrative Office 河北省文物管理處. 'Hebei Yixian Yangxiadu 21 hao yizhi fajue baogao' 河北易縣燕下都21號遺址發掘報告, *Kaoguexue jikan* 考古學輯刊 2, p. 27.
Hebei Institute of Cultural Relics 1995
Hebei Provincial Institute of Cultural Relics 河北省文物研究所. *Cuo mu, Zhanguo Zhongshanguo guowang zhi mu* 譽墓——戰國中山國國王之墓, 2 vols. Beijing, 1995.
Hebei Institute of Cultural Relics 2005
Hebei Province Institute of Cultural Relics 河北省文物研究所. *Zhanguo Zhongshanguo Lingshoucheng* 戰國中山國靈壽城. Beijing, 2005.
Hsu 1965
Hsu, Cho-yun. *Ancient China in Transition: an Analysis of Social Mobility, 722–222 B.C.*. Stanford, 1965.
Hsu 1999
Hsu, Cho-yun. 'The Spring and Autumn Period' in Loewe and Shaughnessy 1999, pp. 545–86.
Huang Linshu 1992
Huang Linshu 黃麟書. *Qin huang changcheng kao* 秦皇長城考. Taipei, 1992.
Huainan wanbishu
Huainan wanbishu 淮南萬畢術, attributed to Liu An 劉安 (c.180–122 BC). See *Congshu jicheng chubian* 叢書集成初編. Hunan, 1939, preface.
Hubei Provincial Museum 1989
Hubei Provincial Museum 湖北省博物館. *Zeng Hou Yi mu* 曾侯乙墓, 2 vols. Beijing, 1989.
Hulsewé 1985
Hulsewé, A.F.P. *Remnants of Ch'in Law: An annotated translation of the Ch'in legal and administrative rules of the 3rd century B.C. discovered in Yün-meng Prefecture, Hu-pei Province, in 1975*. Leiden, 1985.
Huo Yinzhang 1998
Huo Yinzhang 霍印章. *Zhongguo junshi tongshi* 中國軍事通史, Vol. 4, Qin Dai Junshi Shi 秦代軍事史. Beijing, 1998.
Institute of Archaeology, Chinese Academy of Social Sciences 1999
Institute of Archaeology, Chinese Academy of Social Sciences 中國社會科學院考古研究所. *Zhangjiapo Xi Zhou mudi* 張家坡西周墓地. Beijing, 1999.
Institute of Archaeology, Chinese Academy of Social Sciences 2005
Institute of Archaeology, Chinese Academy of Social Sciences 中國社會科學院考古研究所. *Han Chang'an cheng wuku* 漢長安城武庫. Beijing, 2005.
Jiang Shanguo 1988
Jiang Shanguo 蔣善國. *Shangshu zongshu* 尚書綜述. Shanghai, 1988.
Ji Xun 1976
Ji Xun 季勛. 'Yunmeng Shuihudi qinjian gaishu' 雲夢睡虎地秦簡概述, *Wenwu* 文物 1976.5, pp. 1–6.
Kanaya 1992
Kanaya Osamu 金谷治. *Shin Kan shisôshi kenkyû* 秦漢思想史研究. 2nd rev. edn. Kyoto, 1992.
Keightley 1987
Keightley, David N. 'The Quest for Eternity in Ancient China: The

Dead, their Gifts, their Names' in George Kuwayama (ed.), *Ancient Mortuary Traditions of China; papers on Chinese ceramic funerary sculpture*, Los Angeles, 1987, pp.12–24.

Kern 2000

Kern, Martin. *The Stele Inscriptions of Ch'in Shih-huang: Text and Ritual in Early Chinese Imperial Representation*. New Haven, 2000.

Kesner 1995

Kesner, Ladislav. 'Likeness of no one: (re)presenting the First Emperor's army', *Art Bulletin*, vol. 77, no. 1, March 1995, pp. 115–32.

Klose 1985

Klose, Petra. 'Das Grab des Königs Cuo von Zhongshan (gest. 308 v. Chr.)', *Beiträge zur allgemeinen und vergleichenden Archäologie* 7, Mainz, 1985, pp. 1–93.

Knechtges 1982

Knechtges, David R (trans.). *Wen xuan, or, Selections of Refined Literature. Vol. 1: Rhapsodies on Metropolises and Capitals, Xiao Tong* (501–531). Princeton, 1982.

Knoblock 1988–94

Knoblock, John. *Xunzi: a Translation and Study of the Complete Works*, 3 vols. Stanford, 1988–94.

Lagerwey 2004

Lagerwey, John (ed.). *Religion and Chinese Society, vol. 1: Ancient and Medieval China*. Hong Kong and Paris, 2004.

Lanciotti and Scarpari 2006

Lanciotti, Lionello and Maurizio Scarpari. *Cina: Nascita di un Impero*. Rome and Milan, 2006.

Lau and Ames 1996

Lau, D.C. and Roger T. Ames (trans.). *Sun Bin: The Art of Warfare*. New York, 1996.

Lawton 1982

Lawton, T. *Chinese Art of the Warring States period: Change and Continuity 480–222* BC. Washington DC, 1982.

Ledderose 1983

Ledderose, Lothar. 'The Earthly Paradise: Religious Elements in Chinese Landscape Art' in Susan Bush and Christian Murck (eds), *Theories of the Arts in China*, Princeton, 1983, pp. 165–83.

Ledderose 2000

Ledderose, Lothar. *Ten Thousand Things – Module and Mass Production in Chinese Art*. Princeton, 2000.

Ledderose and Schlombs 1990

Ledderose, Lothar and Adele Schlombs. *Jenseits der grossen Mauer – der Erste Kaiser und seine Terracotta-Armee*. Munich, 1990.

Legge 1985

Legge, James. *The Chinese Classics. Vol. 3: The Shoo King*. Taipei, 1985.

Lewis 1999a

Lewis, Mark Edward. 'Warring States: Political History' in Loewe and Shaughnessy 1999, pp. 587–650.

Lewis 1999b

Lewis, Mark Edward. *Writing and Authority in Early China*. Albany, 1999.

Li County Museum 2004

Li County Museum 禮縣博物関 and Li County Institute for the Study of Qin culture at Xichui 禮縣秦西垂文化研究所會. *Qin Xichui ling qu* 秦西垂陵區. Beijing, 2004.

Li County Museum 2005

Li County Museum 禮縣博物関 and the Li County Institute for the Study of Qin culture at Xichui 禮縣秦西垂文化研究所會. *Qin Xichui wenhua lunji* 秦西垂文化論集. Beijing, 2005.

Li Jian 1998

Li Jian (ed.). *Eternal China: Splendors from the First Dynasties*. Ohio, 1998.

Lin 2004

Lin, James. 'Jade suits and iron armour', *East Asia Journal*, London, 2004, pp. 20–43.

Li Tang 1992

Li Tang 李唐. *Qin bing Liuguo yu Chu Han xiangzheng* 秦併六國與楚漢相爭. Taipei, 1992.

Li Xixing 1994

Li Xixing (ed.) 李西興 (編). *Shaanxi qingtongqi* 陝西青銅器. Shaanxi, 1994.

Li Yu-ning 1975

Li Yu-ning. *The First Emperor of China*. White Plains, 1975.

Li Zhongcao 1979

Li Zhongcao 李仲操. *Ba nian Lü Buwei ge kao* 八年呂不韋戈考. *Wenwu* 文物 1979.12. p. 17

Lin Jianming 1981a

Lin Jianming 林劍鳴. *Qin shigao* 秦史稿. Shanghai, 1981.

Lin Jianming 1981b

Lin Jianming 林劍鳴. *Qin guo fazhan shi* 秦國發展史. Xi'an, 1981.

Liu Junkang 2006

Liu Junkang 劉俊康. *Diguo baocang:Yimen 2 hao Chunqiu mu tanyi* 帝國寶藏一益門2號春秋墓探疑. Xi'an, 2006.

Liu Lexian 1994

Liu Lexian 劉樂賢. *Shuihudi Qin jian rishu yanjiu* 睡虎地秦簡日書研究. Taipei, 1994.

Liu Shiyi et al. 2005

Liu Shiyi et al 劉士毅等. *Qinshihuang ling digong diqiu wuli tance chengguo yu jishu* 秦始皇陵地宮地球物理探測成果與技術. Beijing, 2005.

Liu Tingfeng et al. 2006

Liu Tingfeng 劉庭風, Liu Qinghui 劉慶惠, Chen Yijia 陳毅家, 'Qin Han yuanlinshi nianbiao' 秦漢園林史年表, *Zhongguo yuanlin* 中國園林, 2006, pp. 87–91.

Liu Yunhui 2006

Liu Yunhui 劉雲煇. *Shaanxi chutu Dong Zhou yuqi* 陝西出土東周玉器. Beijing and Taipei, 2006.

Loewe 2006

Loewe, Michael. *The Government of the Qin and Han Empires 221* BCE*–* 220 CE. Indianapolis and Cambridge, 2006.

Loewe and Shaughnessy 1999

Micahel Loewe and Edward Shaughnessy (eds). *The Cambridge History of Ancient China: From the Origins to 221* B.C. Cambridge, 1999.

Ma Feibai 1982

Ma Feibai 馬非百. *Qin jishi* 秦集史. Beijing, 1982.

Michaelson 1999

Michaelson, Carol. *Gilded Dragons*. London, 1999.

Museum of Qin Shihuang Terracotta Army 1996

Museum of Qin Shihuang Terracotta Army 秦始皇兵馬俑博物館. *Qin yong xue yanjiu* 秦俑學研究. Xi'an, 1996.

Museum of Qin Shihuang Terracotta Army and Shaanxi Institute of Archaeology 1998

Museum of Qin Shihuang Terracotta Army 秦始皇兵馬俑博物館, and Shaanxi Institute of Archaeology 陝西省考古研究所. *Qin Shihuang ling tongchema fajue baogao*. 秦始皇陵銅車馬發掘報告, 2 vols. Beijing, 1998.

Museum of Qin Shihuang Terracotta Army 1999

Museum of Qin Shihuang Terracotta Army 秦始皇兵馬俑博物館. *Qin Shihuang bingmayong bowuguan* 秦始皇兵馬俑博物館, Yuan Zhongyi (ed.) 袁仲一 (主編). Beijing, 1999.

Needham 1994

Needham, Joseph and Robin D.S. Yates et al. *Science and Civilisation in China*. Vol. 5, part 6: 'Military Technology: Missiles and Sieges'. Cambridge, 1994.

Nienhauser 1994

Nienhauser, William H., Jr. (ed.). *The Grand Scribe's Records*, Vols. I and VII. Trans. by Tsai-fa Cheng, Zongli Lu, William H. Nienhauser, Jr., and Robert Reynolds. Bloomington and Indianapolis, 1994.

Paludan 2006

Paludan, Ann. *Chinese Sculpture: a great tradition*. Chicago, 2006.

Peterson 1982

Peterson, Willard. 'Making connections: "Commentary on the Attached Verbalizations" of the *Book of Changes*', *Harvard Journal of Asiatic Studies* 42 (1982), pp. 67–116.

Petersen 1995

Petersen, Jens Østergård. 'Which Books Did the First Emperor of Ch'in Burn? On the Meaning of *Pai Chia* in Early Chinese Sources', *Monumenta Serica* 43 (1995), pp. 1–52.

Pines 2004

Pines, Yuri. 'The Question of Interpretation: Qin History in the Light of New Epigraphic Evidence', *Early China* 29 (2004), pp. 1–44.

Pines forthcoming

Pines, Yuri. 'Biases and their Sources: Qin History in the Shiji', *Oriens Extremus* 45, forthcoming.

Poo 1998

Poo, Mu-chou. *In Search of Personal Welfare, A View of Personal Religion*. Albany, 1998.

Qin Xianyang 1976

Qin capital Xianyang Archaeological Work Station 秦都咸陽考古工作站. 'Qindu Xianyang diyihao gongdian jianzhu yizhi jianbao 秦都咸陽第一號宮殿建築遺址簡報', *Wenwu* 文物 1976.11, pp. 12–30.

Qiu Guangming 1992

Qiu Guangming 丘光明. *Zhongguo lidai duliangheng kao* 中國歷代度量衡考. Beijing, 1992.

Rawson 1975

Rawson, Jessica. 'The surface decoration of jades of the Zhou and Han dynasties', *Oriental Art* 21, Spring no. 1 (1975), pp. 36–55.

Rawson 1995a

Rawson, Jessica. *Chinese Jade from the Neolithic to the Qing*, London, 1995; repr. 2002.

Rawson 1995b

Rawson, Jessica. 'Jade and Gold: Some sources of Ancient Chinese Jade Design', *Orientations*, June 1995, pp. 26–37.

Rawson 1998

Rawson, Jessica. 'Transformed into Jade: Changes in Material in the Warring States, Qin and Han Periods', *East Asian Jade: Symbol of Excellence*, Hong Kong, 1998, vol. 2, pp. 125–36.

Rawson 1999

Rawson, Jessica. 'The Eternal Palaces of the Western Han: A New View of the Universe', *Artibus Asiae* vol. LIX (1999), pp. 5–58.

Rawson 2002a

Rawson, Jessica. 'The power of images: the model universe of the First Emperor and its legacy', *Historical Research* 75, no. 188, May 2002, pp. 123–54.

Rawson 2002b

Rawson, Jessica. 'Ritual vessel changes in the Warring States, Qin and Han periods' in Hsing I-tien (ed.), *Regional Culture, Religion, and Arts before the Seventh Century*, Papers from the Third International Conference on Sinology, History Section. Taipei, 2002, pp. 1–57.

Rong Geng 1935

Rong Geng 容庚. 'Qin Shihuang keshi kao' 秦始皇刻石考. *Yanjing xuebao* 燕京學報 17 (1935), pp. 125–71.

Sage 1992

Sage, Steven F. *Ancient Sichuan and the Unification of China*. Albany, 1992.

Saunders et al. 2006

Saunders, David, Joyce H. Townsend and Sally Woodcock (eds). *The Object in Context: Crossing Conservation Boundaries*, Contributions to the Munich Congress, 28 August – 1 September 2006. London, 2006.

Schafer 1977

Schafer, Edward. *Pacing the Void, T'ang Approaches to the Stars*. Berkeley, 1977.

Schlombs 1990

Adele Schlombs. 'Die Herstellung der Terrakotta-Armee' in Lothar Ledderose and Adele Schlombs, *Jenseits der grossen Mauer – der Erste Kaiser und seine Terrakotta-Armee*, Munich, 1990, pp. 88–97.

Seidel 1987

Seidel, Anna. 'Traces of Han Religion in Funerary Texts Found in Tombs' in Akizuki Kan'ei (ed.) 秋月觀暎 (編). *Dokyo to shokyo bunka*, 道教と宗教文化 Tokyo, 1987, pp. 678–714 (also numbered counting from the end, pp. 21–57).

Shaanxi Bureau of Cultural Relics 2004

Shaanxi Bureau of Cultural Relics 陝西省文物館 and Shanghai Museum 上海博物館. *The Civilization of Zhou, Qin, Han and Tang Dynasties* 周秦漢唐文明. Shanghai, 2004.

Shaanxi Institute of Archaeology 2001

Shaanxi Province Institute of Archaeology 陝西省考古研究所. Han Yangling 漢陽陵. Chongqing, 2001.

Shaanxi Institute of Archaeology 2004

Shaanxi Province Institute of Archaeology 陝西省考古研究所.

Qin du Xianyang kaogu baogao 秦都咸陽考古報告. Beijing, 2004.
Shaanxi Institute of Archaeology and Excavation Team of the Terracotta Army 1988
Shaanxi Province Institute of Archaeology 陝西省考古研究所 and Archaeological Excavation Team of the Qin Shihuang Terracotta Army Pits 始皇陵秦俑坑考古發掘隊. *Qin Shihuang ling bingmayong keng, yihao keng fajue baogao 1974–1984* 秦始皇陵兵馬俑坑一號坑發掘報告 1974–1984. Beijing, 1988.
Shaanxi Institute of Archaeology and Museum of Qin Shihuang Terracotta Army 2000
Shaanxi Province Institute of Archaeology 陝西省考古研究所 and Museum of Qin Shihuang Terracotta Army 秦始皇兵馬俑博物館. *Qinshihuang lingyuan kaogu baogao (1999)* 秦始皇陵園考古報告. Beijing, 2000.
Shaanxi Institute of Archaeology and Museum of Qin Shihuang Terracotta Army 2002a
Shaanxi Province Institute of Archaeology 陝西省考古研究所 and Museum of Qin Shihuang Terracotta Army 秦始皇兵馬俑博物館. 'Qin Shihuang lingyuan 2000 niandu kantan jianbao' 秦始皇陵園2000年度勘探簡報 *Kaogu yu wenwu* 考古與文物 2002.2, pp. 3–15.
Shaanxi Institute of Archaeology and Museum of Qin Shihuang Terracotta Army 2002b
Shaanxi Province Institute of Archaeology 陝西省考古研究所 and Museum of Qin Shihuang Terracotta Army 秦始皇兵馬俑博物館. 'Qin Shihuang lingyuan neicheng nan qiang shijue jianbao' 秦始皇陵园内城南墙試掘簡報, *Kaogu yu wenwu* 考古與文物 2002.2, pp. 16–27.
Shaanxi Institute of Archaeology and Museum of Qin Shihuang Terracotta Army 2005
Shaanxi Province Institute of Archaeology 陝西省考古研究所 and Museum of Qin Shihuang Terracotta Army 秦始皇兵馬俑博物館. 'Qin Shihuang lingyuan K0007 peizangkeng fajue jianbao' 秦始皇陵園K0007陪葬坑發掘簡報, *Wenwu* 文物 2005.6, pp. 16–38.
Shaanxi Institute of Archaeology and Museum of Qin Shihuang Terracotta Army 2006
Shaanxi Province Institute of Archaeology 陝西省考古研究所 and Museum of Qin Shihuang Terracotta Army 秦始皇兵馬俑博物館. *Qin Shihuangdi lingyuan kaogu baogao (2000)* 秦始皇帝陵園考古報告 (2000). Beijing, 2006.
Shaanxi Provincial Museum 1964
Shaanxi Provincial Museum 陝西省博物館. Xi'an shi xijiao Gaoyaocun chutu Qin Gaonu shi quan 西安市西郊高窯村出土秦高奴銅權, *Wenwu* 文物 1964.9, pp. 42–3.
Shanxi Institute of Archaeology et al. 1996
Shanxi Province Institute of Archaeology 山西省考古研究所, Cultural Bureau of Jincheng City 晉城市文化局, and Gaoping City Museum 高平市博物館. 'Changping zhi zhan yizhi yonglu yihao shigukeng fajue jianbao' 長平之戰遺址永錄1號尸骨坑發掘簡報, *Wenwu* 文物 1996.6, pp. 33–40.
Shangshu
Shangshu 尚書. *Shisan jing zhushu* 十三經注疏. Ed. Beijing, 1987.
Shang Zhiru 1990
Shang Zhiru 尚志儒. 'Qin wa yanjiu' 秦瓦研究, *Wenbo* 文博1990.5, pp. 252–60.
Shelach and Pines 2006
Shelach, Gideon and Yuri Pines. 'Secondary State Formation and the Development of Local Identity: Change and Continuity in the State of Qin (770–221 B.C.)' in Miriam T. Stark (ed.), *Archaeology of Asia*. Malden, MA and Oxford, 2006.
Shi Zhecun 1987
Shi Zhecun 施蟄存. *Shuijing zhu beilu* 水經注碑錄. Tianjin, 1987.
Shiji
Shiji 史記. Comp. Sima Qian 司馬遷, Beijing, 1959.
Simon et al. 2001
Stefan Simon, Zhang Zhijun and Zhou Tie. 'Analyses of Soil and Wood' in Blänsdorf et al. 2001, pp. 677–81.
Sofukawa 1989
Sofukawa, Hiroshi 曾布川寬. 'Lingmu zhidu he linghun guan' 陵墓制度和靈魂觀, *Wenbo* 文博1989.2, pp. 34–38.
State Administration of Cultural Heritage 1994
State Administration of Cultural Heritage 國家文物局 (ed.). *Zhongguo wenwu jinghua daquan—Qingtong juan* 中國文物精華大全—青銅卷. Hong Kong, 1994.
State Administration of Cultural Heritage 2001
State Administration of Cultural Heritage 國家文物局 (ed.). *Major Archaeological Discoveries in China: 1999* 中國重要考古發現: 1999. Beijing, 2001.
State Administration of Cultural Heritage 2002
State Administration of Cultural Heritage 國家文物局 (ed.). *Major Archaeological Discoveries in China: 2001*中國重要考古發現: 2001. Beijing, 2002.
State Administration of Cultural Heritage 2004
State Administration of Cultural Heritage 國家文物局 (ed.). *Major Archaeological Discoveries in China: 2003*中國重要考古發現: 2003. Beijing, 2004.
Sun Ji 2001
Sun Ji 孫機. *Zhongguo gu yufu luncong* 中國古輿服論叢, Beijing, 2001.
Sun Jingming 2002
Sun Jingming 孫敬明. 'Qi Bing Xinkao' 齊兵新考 in Xie Zhixiu 謝治秀 (ed.), *Qi Lu wenbo: Shandong sheng shoujie wenwu kexue baogao yue wenji* 齊魯文博: 山東省首屆文物科學報告月文集. Ji'nan, 2002, pp. 120–39.
Tao Fu 1976
Tao Fu 陶复. 'Qin Xianyang gong diyihao yizhi fuyuan wenti de chubu tantao' 秦咸陽宮第一號遺址復原問題的初步探討, *Wenwu* 文物 1976.11, pp. 31–41.
Teng Mingyu 2002
Teng Mingyu 滕銘予. *Qin wenhua: Cong fengguo dao diguo de kaoguxue guancha* 秦文化: 從封國到帝國的考古學觀察. Beijing, 2002.
Thieme 2001
Thieme, Christian. 'Paint Layers and Pigments on the Terracotta Army: A Comparison with Other Cultures of Antiquity' in Wu Yongqi et al. 2001, pp. 52–7.
Thierry 1997
Thierry, François. *Monnaies chinoises. I: L'antiquité préimpériale*. Paris, 1997.

Thorp 1983
Thorp, Robert. 'An Archaeological Reconstruction of the Lishan Necropolis' in George Kuwayama (ed.), *The Great Bronze Age of China: A Symposium*. Los Angeles, 1983, pp. 72–83.
Thote 1991
Thote, Alain. 'The Double Coffin of Leigudun Tomb No.1: Iconographic Sources and Related Problems' in Thomas Lawton (ed.), *New Perspectives on Chu Culture during the Eastern Zhou period*. Princeton, 1991, pp. 23–46.
Thote 2004
Thote, Alain. 'Burial Practices as Seen in Rulers' Tombs of the Eastern Zhou Period: Patterns and Regional Traditions' in Lagerwey 2004, pp. 65–107.
Tian Yaqi et al. 2006
Tian Yaqi et al 田亞岐等. 'Shaanxi Fengxiang faxian Zhanguo zaoqi Qin Yongcheng zhitao zuofang yizhi' 陝西鳳翔發現戰國早期秦雍城制陶作坊遺址 in *Zhongguo wenwu bao* 中國文物報, 11 August 2006. Also published in State Administration of Cultural Relics Heritage (ed.) 國家文物局 (主編), Zhongguo zhongyao kaogu faxian 2006 中國重要考古發現 2006. Beijing, 2007, pp. 82–6.
Trousdale 1975
Trousdale, William. *The Long Sword and Scabbard Slide in Asia*, Smithsonian Contributions to Anthropology 17. Washington DC, 1975.
Wang 1996
Wang, Wellington. *Belt Ornaments through the Ages, The Wellington Wang collection*. Taipei, 1996.
Wang et al. 2005
Wang, Helen et al. (eds). *Metallurgical analysis of Chinese coins at the British Museum*. London, 2005.
Wang Guowei 1961
Wang Guowei 王國維. *Guantang jilin* 觀堂集林. Beijing, 1961.
Wang Qingzheng 1988
Wang Qingzheng 王慶正 (ed.). *Zhongguo lidai huobi daxi. (I) Xian Qin huobi* 中國歷代貨幣大希 (1) 先秦貨幣. Shanghai, 1988.
Wang Renbo 2001
Wang Renbo 王仁波 (ed.). *Qin Han wenhua* 秦漢文化. Shanghai, 2001.
Wang Tao 2003
Wang Tao. 'The Blueprint for the Zhongshan king's Graveyard', *East Asia Journal* 2003 (1), pp. 17–24.
Wang Wang-sheng 1999
Wang Wang-sheng 王望生. 'Qing Shihuang lingyuan qingshi kaijiakeng de kaogu shijue' 秦始皇陵園青石铠甲坑的考古試掘, *Wenbo* 文博 1999.6, pp.12–17.
Wang Xueli 1994a
Wang Xueli 王學理. *Qin yong zhuanti yanjiu* 秦俑專題研究. Xi'an, 1994.
Wang Xueli 1994b
Wang Xueli 王學理. *Qin Shihuang ling yanjiu* 秦始皇陵研究. Shanghai, 1994.
Wang Xueli et al. 1994
Wang Xueli 王學理, Shang Zhiru 尚志儒, and Hu Lingui 呼林貴 (eds). *Qin wuzhi wenhua shi* 秦物質文化史. Xi'an, 1994.
Wang Xueli 1999
Wang Xueli 王學理, *Xianyang didu ji* 咸陽帝都記. Xi'an 1999.
Wang Zhongshu 1982
Wang Zhongshu 王仲殊. 'Zhongguo gudai ducheng gaishuo' 中國古代都城概說, *Kaogu* 考古1982.5, pp. 505–15.
Wang and Liang 2001
Wang Xueli 王學理 and Liang Yun 梁云. *Qin wenhua* 秦文化. Beijing, 2001.
Ware 1966
Ware, James R. *Alchemy, Medicine and Religion in the China of* A.D.320: *The Nei P'ien of Ko Hung (pao-p'u-tzu)*. Cambridge, 1966.
Watson 1961
Watson, Burton (trans.). *Records of the Grand Historian of China*, translated from Shih Chi of Ssu-ma Chien. Vol. 2: *The Age of Emperor Wu, 140–c.100* BC. New York and London, 1961
Watson 1964
Watson, Burton. *Han Fei Tzu: Basic Writings*. New York and London, 1964.
Watson 1993
Watson, Burton (trans). *Records of the Grand Historian: Qin Dynasty*. Hong Kong and New York, 1993.
Wechsler 1985
Wechsler, Howard J. *Offerings of Jade and Silk: Ritual and Symbol in the Legitimation of the T'ang Dynasty*. New Haven, 1985.
Wu Hung 1999
Wu Hung. 'Art and architecture of the Warring States period' in Loewe and Shaughnessy 1999, pp. 651–744.
Wu Hung 2005
Wu Hung. 'On Tomb Figurines – the Beginning of a Visual Tradition' in Wu Hung and Katherine R. Tsiang (eds), *Body and Face in Chinese Visual Culture*. Harvard East Asian Monographs 239, 2005, pp. 13–47.
Wu Hung 2006
Wu Hung. 'From the Neolithic to the Han' in Angela Falco Howard, Li Song, Wu Hung, Yang Hong (eds), *Chinese Sculpture*. New Haven and Beijing, 2006, pp. 17–103.
Wu Jiulong 1985
Wu Jiulong 吳九龍. *Yinqueshan Han jian shiwen* 銀雀山漢簡釋文. Beijing, 1985.
Wu Rusong 1998
Wu Rusong 吳如嵩, Huang Pumin 黃朴民, Ren Li 任力, Liu Ling 柳玲. *Zhongguo Junshi Tongshi* 中國軍事通史. Vol. 3: *Zhanguo junshi shi* 戰國軍事史. Beijing, 1998.
Wu Yongqi et al. 2004
Wu Yongqi et al 吳永琪等. *Shaanxi chutu jin yin qi* 陝西出土秦金銀器. Xi'an, 2004.
Wu Yongqi et al. 2001
Wu Yongqi, Zhang Tinghao, Michel Petzet, Erwin Emmerline, Catharina Blänsdorf. *The Polychromy of Antique Sculptures and the Terracotta Army of the First Chinese Emperor*, Monuments and Sites 3. Munich, 2001.

Xi'an 2004a
Xi'an Municipal Institute for Cultural Property (ed.) 西安市文物保護考古所 (編). *Xi'an nanjiao Qin mu* 西安南郊秦墓. Xi'an, 2004.
Xi'an 2004b
Xi'an Municipal Institute for Cultural Property (ed.) 西安市文物保護考古所 (編). *Xi'an wenwu jinghua:Yuqi* 西安文物精華：玉器. Xi'an, 2004.
Xianyang Institute of Archaeology 1998
Xianyang City Institute of Archaeology (ed.) 咸陽市考古研究所 (編). *Ta'erpo Qin Mu* 塔兒坡秦墓. Xi'an, 1998.
Xianyang Cultural Relics Bureau 2002
Xianyang Cultural Relics Bureau 陝西省咸陽市文物局. *Xianyang wenwu jinghua* 咸陽文物精華. Beijing, 2002.
Xu Pingfang 2001
Xu Pingfang. 'The Archaeology of the Great Wall of the Qin and Han Dynasties', *Journal of East Asian Archaeology* 3.1–2 (2001), pp. 259–81.
Yang Hong 1992
Yang Hong. *Weapons in Ancient China*. New York and Beijing, 1992.
Yang Xiaoneng 1999
Yang Xiaoneng (ed.). The *Golden Age of Chinese Archaeology, Celebrated Discoveries from the People's Republic of China*. Washington DC, Kansas City and New Haven, 1999.
Yang Xiaoneng 2004
Yang Xiaoneng. *New Perspectives on China's Past: Chinese Archaeology in the 20th century*. New Haven, 2004.
Yang and Yang 1979
Yang Hsien-yi and Gladys Yang (trans.), *Selections from Records of the Historian by Szuma Chien*. Peking, 1979.
Yang and Duan 2006
Yang Dongyu 杨东宇 and Duan Qingbo 段清波. 'Ebang gong gainian yu Ebang gong kaogu' 阿房宫概念与阿房宫考古, *Kaogu yu wenwu* 考古與文物 2006.2, pp. 51–6.
Yates 2002
Yates, Robin D.S. 'The Horse in Early Chinese Military History' in Huang Ko-Wu 黃克武 (ed.), *Junshi zuzhi yu zhanzheng* 軍事組織與戰爭. Taipei, 2002, pp. 1–78.
Yates forthcoming
Yates, Robin D.S. 'Law and the Military in Early China' in Nicola Di Cosmo (ed.), *Culture and War in Chinese History*. Cambridge, forthcoming.
Yongcheng Archaeological Team 1987
Yongcheng Archaeological Team of Shaanxi Province 陝西省雍城考古隊. 'Fengxiang Qin gong lingyuan dierci zuantan jianbao' 鳳翔秦公陵園第二次鑽探簡報, *Wenwu* 文物1987.5, pp. 55–65.
Yuan Weichun 1990
Yuan Weichun 袁維春. *Qin Han bei shu* 秦漢碑述. Beijing, 1990.
Yuan Zhongyi 1988
Yuan Zhongyi 袁仲一. *Qin Shihuang ling bingmayong* 秦始皇陵兵馬俑. Taipei, 1988.
Yuan Zhongyi 1990
Yuan Zhongyi 袁仲一. *Qin Shihuang ling bingmayong yanjiu* 秦始皇陵兵馬俑研究. Beijing, 1990.
Yuan Zhongyi 1994
Yuan Zhongyi (ed.) 袁仲一 (編). *Qin Shihuangdi ling bingmayong cidian* 秦始皇帝陵兵馬俑辭典. Shanghai, 1994.
Yuan Zhongyi 2001a
Yuan Zhongyi 袁仲一. 'Frisuren, Panzer und Kleidung der Terracottaarmee' (trans. Shing Soong-Müller) in Blänsdorf et al. 2001, pp. 169–91.
Yuan Zhongyi 2001b
Yuan Zhongyi 袁仲一. 'The Costume colors of Qin Terracotta Warriors' in Wu Yongqi et al. 2001, pp. 13–15.
Yuan Zhongyi 2002
Yuan Zhongyi 袁仲一. *Qin Shihuang ling kaogu faxian yu yanjiu* 秦始皇陵考古發現與研究. Xi'an, 2002.
Yuan Zhongyi 2003
Yuan Zhongyi 袁仲一. *Qin bingmayong keng* 秦兵馬俑坑. Beijing, 2003.
Yuan and Snethlage 2005
Yuan Zhongyi and Rolf Snethlage, 'Die Herstellung und die Zerstörung der Tonkrieger des Ersten Kaisers Qin Shihuangdi' in Bonn 2006, pp. 165–8.
Yuan and Zhang 1990b
Yuan Zhongyi 袁仲一 and Zhang Zhanmin 張占民 (eds). *Qin yong yanjiu wenji* 秦俑研究文集. Xi'an, 1990.
Yun-Kremer 1990
Yun-Kremer, Myong-ok. 'Waffen' in Ledderose and Schlombs 1990, pp. 306–9.
Zavitukhina and Barkova 1978
Zavitukhina MP and L.L. Barkova. *Frozen Tombs: The Culture and Art of the Ancient Tribes of Siberi*. London, 1978.
Zhang Hequan 1989
Zhang Hequan 張鶴泉. *Zhoudai jisi yanjiu* 周代祭祀研究. Taipei, 1989.
Zhang Jinguang 2004
Zhang Jinguang 張金光. *Qin zhi yanjiu* 秦制研究. Shanghai, 2004.
Zhang Wenli 1996
Zhang Wenli. *The Qin Terracotta Army: Treasures of Lintong*. London, 1996.
Zhang Wenli 1999
Zhang Wenli 張文立. *Qin yong xue* 秦俑學. Xi'an, 1999.
Zhang and Ma 2004
Zhang Weixing 張衛星 and Ma Yu 馬宇. *Qin jiazhou yanjiu* 秦甲胄研究. Xi'an, 2004.
Zhao Huacheng 2006
Zhao Huacheng 趙化成. 'Cong Shang Zhou 'jizhong gongmu zhi' dao Qin Han 'duli lingyuan zhi' de yanhua guiji' 從商周 '集中公墓制' 到秦漢 '獨立陵園制' 的演化軌跡, *Wenwu* 文物 2006.7, pp. 41–8.
Zhongguo Qingtongqi Quanji 1998
Zhongguo Qingtongqi Quanji Bianji Weiyuanhui (ed.) 中國青銅器全集編輯委員會 (编). *Zhongguo Qingtongqi Quanji* 中國青銅器全集. Vol. 12: *Qin, Han*. Beijing, 1998
Zhu Zhongxi 2004
Zhu Zhongxi 祝中熹. *Zaoqi Qin shi* 早期秦史. Lanzhou, 2004.

ILLUSTRATION ACKNOWLEDGEMENTS

John Williams and Saul Peckham/© The Trustees of the British Museum with the kind permission of the Shaanxi Cultural Heritage Promotion Center Figs 1, 2, 7, 12, 17, 22 left, 24, 27, 28, 35, 36, 46, 49, 53 right, 61, 62, 77, 81, 85, 88 top, 118, 119, 134, 144, 145, 149, 150–8, 164, 167, 171, 172, 180, 183–6, 199, 200

Fang Guowei/The Museum of Terracotta Warriors and Horses of Emperor Qin Shihuang Figs 6, 20, 23, 26, 29, 30, 31, 32, 37, 41, 42, 50, 52, 56, 57, 60, 64, 66, 67, 78, 79, 80 top, 84, 88 bottom, 102, 103, 123, 133, 135–8, 141, 146–8, 162, 163, 169 right, 171 right, 173 top & middle

Yan Yu/ Baoji Municipal Bronze Ware Museum Figs. 48, 86, 87 top & middle, 88 right, 93, 94, 97–99, 100, 104, 120

Zhang Minghui/Shaanxi Provincial Archaeological Institute Figs. 53 left, 54, 55, 87 bottom, 189

Shaanxi Cultural Heritage Promotion Center Figs 25, 33, 34, 38, 39, 40, 51, 65, 68, 75, 80 bottom, 83, 90, 91, 92, 95, 96, 101, 105, 108, 122, 124, 125, 130, 132, 140, 142, 159, 161, 169 left, 173 bottom, 174, 175, 177, 188, 194, 195, 201

INTRODUCTION

Fig. 3 Victor Segalen, *Mission Archéologique en Chine* (1914 et 1917), *La Sculpture et les Monuments Funérarires, Paris*, 1923, plate 1. Permission of S.N. Librairie Orientaliste Paul Geuthner, Paris
Fig. 4 After from Bonn 2006, p. 26. Paul Goodhead/© The Trustees of the British Museum
Fig. 5 John Williams and Saul Peckham/© The Trustees of the British Museum
Fig. 8 John Hadley Cox Archaeological Study Collection, Freer Gallery of Art and Arthur M. Sackler Gallery Archives. 11.1. Photographer: John Hadley Cox
Fig. 9 Jessica Rawson (ed.), *Mysteries of Ancient China*, London, 1996, no. 22
Figs 10–11 By permission of The British Library, 15024.a.1; 15286.a.3
Fig. 13 Bibliothèque nationale de France, Paris
Figs 14–6 By permission of The British Library, Or. 2331; Chin. F 633–8 Box 2, Vol. 3, p. 46; Or. 11515

CHAPTER 1

Fig. 18 After Kern 2000, p. 60. Paul Goodhead/© The Trustees of the British Museum
Fig. 19 Photographer: Wang Baoping
Fig. 21 After Xu Pingfang 2001, pp. 262–3. Paul Goodhead/© The Trustees of the British Museum
Fig. 22 right Ann Searight/© The Trustees of the British Museum
Fig. 33 bottom Ann Searight/© The Trustees of the British Museum
Fig. 43 Wang Renbo 2001, p. 14
Figs 44–5 National Museum of China, Beijing

CHAPTER 2

Fig. 47 After Bodde 1986, p. 41. Paul Goodhead/© The Trustees of the British Museum
Fig. 58 Princeton University Art Museum. Far Eastern Seminar Collection, 2002–307.22 (74 x 64 cm)
Fig. 59 Yuan Yao, *Penglai*, hanging scroll, ink and colours on silk, 266.2 x 163cm, Palace Museum, Beijing
Fig. 63 Chang Kwang-chih et al. 2002, p. 273
Figs 69–74 Stephen Dodd/© The Trustees of the British Museum
Fig. 76 After Michaelson 1999, p. 32. Paul Goodhead/© The Trustees of the British Museum
Fig. 82 Photographer: Hiromi Kinoshita
Fig. 83 left After Ledderose and Schlombs 1990, p. 156. Ann Searight/© The Trustees of the British Museum
Fig. 89 Yuan Jiang, *Ebang Palace*, 12 hanging scrolls, ink and colours on silk, 193.5 x 658cm, Palace Museum, Beijing
Figs 106–7 Hotung Collection. Photographer: John Williams

CHAPTER 3

Fig. 110 After Kern 2000, p. 108. Paul Goodhead/© The Trustees of the British Museum
Figs 109, 113 John Williams/© The Trustees of the British Museum
Fig. 111 Photographer: Spike Geilinger
Fig. 112 Wang Renbo 2001, p. 39
Fig. 114 © Lowell Georgia/CORBIS
Figs 115–16 National Library of China, Beijing
Fig. 117 Bibliothèque nationale de France, Paris

CHAPTER 4

Fig. 121 Falkenhausen 2004, p. 140, fig. 18
Fig. 126 Li County Museum 2004, p.22
Fig. 127 Chang Kwang-chih 2004, p. 263
Fig. 128 Paul Goodhead/© The Trustees of the British Museum
Fig. 131 Paul Goodhead/© The Trustees of the British Museum
Fig. 132 After Shaanxi Institute of Archaeology 2001, fig. 12. David Hoxley/© The Trustees of the British Museum
Fig. 139 Photographer: Hiromi Kinoshita
Fig. 143 After Excavation Team of the First Emperor's Tomb 2002, p. 5. David Hoxley/© The Trustees of the British Museum
Fig. 144 right Yuan Zhongyi 2002, p. 206
Fig. 146 right Yuan Zhongyi 2002, p. 148

CHAPTER 5

Fig. 160 Photographers: Xia Juxian and Guo Yan
Figs 165–6 After Museum of Qin Shihuang Terracotta Army 1999, pp. 228–33. David Hoxley/© The Trustees of the British Museum
Fig. 168 After Museum of Qin Shihuang Terracotta Army 1999, pp. 234. David Hoxley/© The Trustees of the British Museum
Fig. 170 Bonn 2006, p. 168
Fig. 175 Catharina Blänsdorf
Fig. 176 Photographer: Hiromi Kinoshita
Fig. 178 The Museum of Terracotta Warriors and Horses of Emperor Qin Shihuang
Fig. 179 Catharina Blänsdorf
Figs 181–2 Photographer: Hiromi Kinoshita
Fig. 187 Yuan Zhongyi 2002, p. 167
Fig. 190 *Kaogu* 1975.4, p. 231
Fig. 191 National Museum of China, Beijing
Fig. 192 Hubei Province Museum 1989, p. 39
Fig. 193 Jessica Rawson (ed.), *Mysteries of Ancient China*, London, 1996, no. 81
Fig. 196 After drawings provided by Duan Qingbo. David Hoxley/© The Trustees of the British Museum
Figs 197–8 Provided by Duan Qingbo

APPENDIX

pp. 204–5 Adapted from Liu Shiyi et al. 2005, pp. 26 & 32. Paul Goodhead/© The Trustees of the British Museum
Fig. 206 Bonn 2006, p. 132

INDEX

Page numbers in *italic* type refer to illustrations or their captions.

Zhou state 13, 19, 100
Zhuangxiang, King of Qin 13
Zhuangzi 18
Zhuanxu, Emperor 32

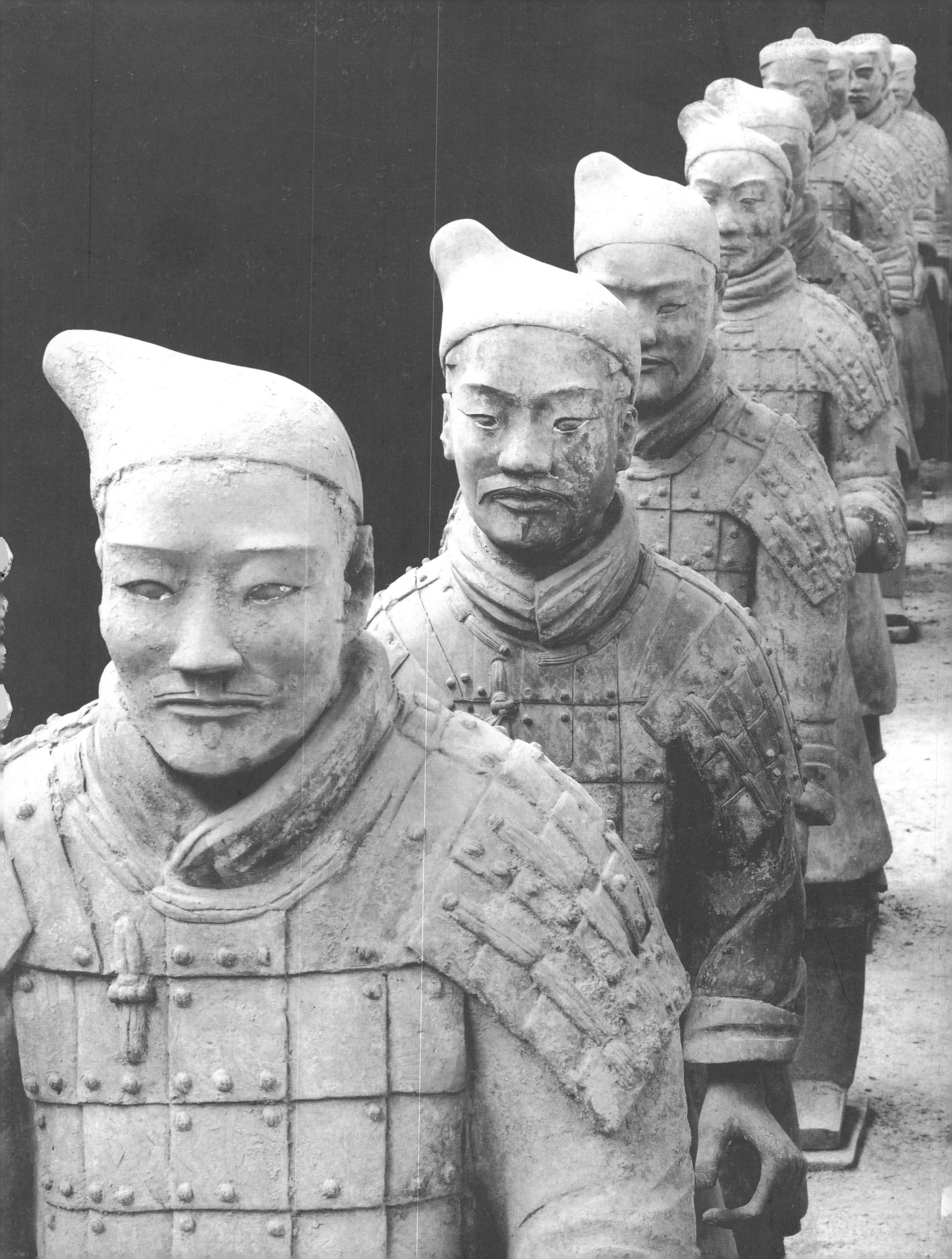